A Companion to
ARTHURIAN
and CELTIC
Myths and Legends

MIKE DIXON-KENNEDY

SUTTON PUBLISHING

50,1263311

First published in 2004 by
Sutton Publishing Limited · Phoenix Mill · Thrupp · Stroud · Gloucestershire · GL5 2BU

Copyright © Mike Dixon-Kennedy, 2004

All rights reserved. No part of this publication may be reproduced, stored in a retrieval system, or transmitted, in any form, or by any means, electronic, mechanical, photocopying, recording or otherwise, without the prior permission of the publisher and copyright holder.

Mike Dixon-Kennedy has asserted the moral right to be identified as the author of this work.

British Library Cataloguing in Publication Data
A catalogue record for this book is available from the British Library.

ISBN 0-7509-3310-0

R 398.22 DIXO

Typeset in 9/11pt Times.
Typesetting and origination by
Sutton Publishing Limited.
Printed and bound in England by
J.H. Haynes & Co. Ltd, Sparkford.

For Christopher, Charlotte, Thomas and Rebecca

Queen Boudicca, the scourge of the invading Romans. (Mary Evans Picture Library/Edwin Wallace)

PREFACE

When one considers the sheer weight of material that has been published on the subjects of King Arthur and the Celtic peoples one is, perhaps, almost spoilt for choice. Yet, many of the volumes that a reader is presented with convey more of the personal opinions of the author than they do the true fact, if indeed mythology and legend can ever be called fact. The purpose of this book, therefore, is not to convey to you my personal ideas and opinions, of which I have many, but simply to present you with a simple to use, ready reference work to the myriad of people, places and events that colour the Arthurian and Celtic world.

The one question I have been asked is why have I bundled Arthurian and Celtic myth and legend into a simple volume? The answer is surprisingly simple, and I hope logical. You cannot study Arthurian myth and legend without encompassing the Celtic world, and vice versa. The two are intertwined and can only truly be studied as a single entity. Sure, you could simply study one or the other, but when you sat down and considered just what you were studying you would find your research had covered both anyway.

This book represents over twenty years of passionate research into the subjects of King Arthur and the Celts, though my passion for mythology and legend stretches far beyond these two fields of study and now encompasses every corner of the globe. My passion for the subject stretches way back to my childhood when my late father used to tell me the stories of ancient Greece and Rome. It is these stories that sparked my interest in mythology, and as a result led me to many, many years of research and study, this book being just one product of that research.

In this book I hope you will find something that will fascinate you, something that makes you think 'Now that I did not know', something that will spark your imagination and even something that might make you go off and undertake your own research. I have tried to make this book as complete and authoritative as I can. However, I will undoubtedly have omitted something, or made some false assumption – after all, to err is human. Should you wish to bring anything to my attention, then please address your comments to the publisher and they will make sure that your letters reach me.

No such book as this could ever be completed without the help of a great many people, but to list every single person who has ever helped me would require a book all of its own. Suffice it to say that I offer a great big thank you to them all: they will all know who they are. There are, however, several people whom I cannot neglect. Firstly, I should like to thank Christopher Feeney at Sutton Publishing for commissioning this book,

Irish gold torc. (© Werner Forman/Corbis)

and to his staff for taking the raw manuscript and turning it into the volume you now hold, in particular Mary Worthington for her tireless editing, spotting the multitude of errors that had slipped through. Without her you might have been as confused as I am sure she was at times. The other person I have to offer my greatest thanks to is my son Christopher, who has endured the countless questions I have thrown at him, and the hours when my 'Do not disturb' sign has held him at bay. I thank him for his tolerance and patience while I have been locked away in my own world preparing the text, and then for having the considerable patience to sit down and read the whole thing from cover to cover, and for bringing some glaring errors to my attention.

Mike Dixon-Kennedy
Lincolnshire, 2004

The sword Excalibur is returned to the Lady of the Lake. (Aubrey Beardsley, 1893–4/Mary Evans Picture Library)

How to Use this Book

Even though this book is basically arranged as a simple, straightforward dictionary, several conventions have been adopted to make cross-referencing much easier, and thus the text more decipherable.

(i) Where headwords have alternative spellings that consist solely of the omission or addition of letters, those letters so affected within the headword are enclosed in brackets. For example, **Dag(h)d(h)a** would lead to *Daghdha*, *Dagda*, *Daghda* or *Dagdha*, all being acceptable variants. Where variants are created by different spellings, the entry is given under the most correct form of the word, the variant endings being given in the form of, for example, **Bor-mo, -vo** which gives alternative spellings of *Bormo* and *Borvo*. This is also sometimes used for complete words that might vary; e.g. **Gronw-Bebyr, -Pebyr**. Where names have a part of their full form normally omitted, that part is enclosed in brackets, e.g. **Conchobar (mac Nessa)**.

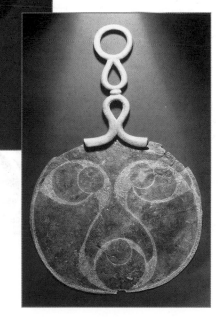

(ii) Words that appear in CAPITALS indicate that there is a separate entry for the word or words in question. Where the word(s) appear in *ITALICISED CAPITALS,* the reference is to an entry concerning a text.

(iii) When a country is indicated under a headword, that country does not imply that the character, myth or legend concerned was solely restricted to that country. Rather it indicates the country of origin, and it may well be that the character, myth or legend was known much further afield. Characters or legends from the Arthurian cycle are simply indicated as *Arthurian* irrespective of country of origin.

Top: *Bronze enamelled brooch.* (© Werner Forman/Corbis) Bottom: *Celtic mirror.* (© Werner Forman/Corbis)

SPELLING AND PRONUNCIATION GUIDE

When the legends of King Arthur and of the Celts were being recorded, standardised spelling was not common. As a result there are a great many variations within the many works that have been consulted during the preparation of this book. I have tried – and I must stress tried – to adopt the most common or correct form of each word. I apologise if you consider I have made mistakes in my choices. This system does, however, lead to one small problem, that being multiple entries under variant spellings.

As far as is humanly possible I have tried to weed out these entries, but some are sure to have slipped through my net. Again, I apologise. The main problem here is one of association, for how does one recognise a true variant, if the stories related under the variants differ? Here I make no apologies, for the fault here is not mine, but that of those who first put pen to paper to preserve these stories for our enjoyment. The translators of the nineteenth century did little to improve the situation, for these show amazing variations, even within the same work!

Although many of the names within this volume may look peculiar to modern readers, they are not difficult to pronounce. A little effort and the following guide will help you to ensure that these names are pronounced correctly. Please bear in mind, however, that the same word can be pronounced differently depending on regional accents.

Consonants: as in English, but with a few exceptions:

- c: hard, as in *c*-at (never soft as in *c*-entury)
- ch: Gaelic –v, as in *v*-an
- ch: Welsh – hard, as in Scottish Lo-*ch* (never soft as in *ch*-ur-*ch*)
- dd: *th* as in *th*-en (never as in *th*-istle)
- f: v, as in o*f*
- ff: f, as in o*ff*
- g: hard, as in *g*-irl (never soft as in *g*-em)
- gh: silent, as in English
- ll: a Welsh distinctive, sounded as 'tl' or 'hl' on the sides of the tongue
- r: trilled lightly
- rh: as in *hr*, heavy on the 'h' sound
- s: always as in *s*-ir (never as in hi-*s*)
- th: as in *th*-istle (never as in *th*-en)

Vowels: as in English, but with the general lightness of short vowel sounds:

- a: as in f-*a*-ther
- e: as in m-*e*-t or sometimes long, as in l-*a*-te
- i: as in p-*i*-n or sometimes long, as in *e*-at
- o: as in n-*o*-t
- u: as in p-*i*-n or sometimes long, as in *e*-at
- w: a 'double-u', as in vac-*uu*-m, or t-*oo*-l; but becomes a consonant before vowels, such as in the name Gwen
- y: as in p-*i*-n or as in *e*-at, but sometimes as 'u' in b-*u*-t

Accent

Welsh: normally on the next to last syllable

Gaelic: as indicated. A circumflex (^) indicates length, thus dûn is pronounced *doon* not *dewn*

Diphthongs: none in Welsh, each vowel being pronounced individually

THE CELTS

Although a true history of the Celts would require a volume of its own, the following is intended to give a very brief insight into these people.

THE PEOPLE

The Celts originated, so it is widely accepted today, in central Europe *c.* 1200 BC in the basin of the Upper Danube, the Alps, and parts of France and south Germany. Classical legend accounts for the naming of the people through the story of Celtina, daughter of Britannus, who had a son by Hercules named Celtus who became the progenitor of the Celtic people.

The Celts developed a transitional culture between the Bronze and Iron Ages, the ninth to fifth centuries BC, a culture know as the Halstatt culture from the excavations carried out at Halstatt, south-west of Salzburg. They farmed and raised cattle, and were pioneers of iron working, reaching their peak in the period from the fifth century BC to the Roman conquest, this latter culture being known as the La Tène culture from the archaeological site in Switzerland.

In the sixth century BC they spread into Spain and Portugal and were known as Celtiberi ('Iberian Celts'). Over the next three hundred years they also spread into the British Isles, northern Italy (sacking Rome in 390 BC), Greece and the Balkans, although they never established a united empire, probably because they were divided into numerous tribes. Their various conquests were made by emigrant bands, which made permanent settlements in these areas, as well as in that part of Asia Minor that was later to be known as Gallatia. In the first century BC the Celts were defeated by the Roman Empire, and by Germanic tribes, and confined to Western Europe, especially England, Wales and Ireland. Even here they were not safe, for the Romans invaded Britain in AD 43 and sought to annihilate Celtic beliefs. This they failed to do, and it was not until the arrival of the Anglo-Saxons in the fifth century AD that the Celts were pushed into the furthest corners of Britain. By the time the continental Celts had all but disappeared, those left as true Celts were confined to the south-west of England, parts of Wales and almost all Ireland. The advent of Christianity was the final nail in the Celtic coffin, although Ireland has managed to retain most of its Celtic beliefs, customs and traditions right up to modern times.

Top: *Bronze handle of short sword, c. first century AD.* (© Werner Forman/Corbis)
Bottom: *Celtic spoon.* (© Werner Forman/Corbis)

ART

Celtic art originated as a style *c.* 500 BC, possibly on the Rhine, and spread westwards to Gaul and the British Isles, and southwards to Turkey and Italy. Metalwork using curving incised lines and inlays of coloured enamel and coral survived at La Tène, Switzerland. The most remarkable example of Celtic art has to be the Gündestrup Cauldron, which was discovered in a peat bog in Vesthimmerland, Denmark in 1891. Dating possibly from the first or second century BC, this remarkable vessel clearly demonstrates the advances the Celts made in their artistic style from the primitive origins as demonstrated by the finds at Halstatt.

Celtic bronze openwork ornament, c. *first century AD.* (© Werner Forman/Corbis)

LANGUAGES

Celtic languages are a branch of the Indo-European family and are divided into two groups: the Brythonic or P-Celtic, which covers Welsh, Cornish, Breton and Gaulish; and the Goidelic or Q-Celtic, which covers the Gaelic languages of Irish, Scottish and Manx. Celtic languages once stretched from the Black Sea to Britain, but have been in decline for centuries, limited to small areas of Western Europe, the so-called Celtic Fringe.

As their names suggest, a major distinction between the two groups is that, while Brythonic has 'p' (as in Old Welsh *map*), Goidelic has a 'q' sound (as in Gaelic *mac*). Gaulish is the long-extinct language of Gaul, while Cornish died out as a natural language in the late eighteenth century, and Manx in 1974, though Cornish is now undergoing a serious local revival. All surviving Celtic languages have experienced official neglect in recent centuries, and have suffered from emigration.

Celtic bronze shield, c. *second–first century BC.* (© Werner Forman/Corbis)

A

AALARDIN
Arthurian
A knight possessing magical knowledge. Married to GUIGENOR, the grandniece of King ARTHUR; Aalardin supplied GUIGNIER, the wife of CARADOC BRIEFBRAS, whom he had once loved, with an enchanted shield boss, thus providing her with a golden breast to replace that which she had lost whilst helping her husband.

ABANDINUS
British
A local deity of unknown attributes and characteristics, whose name occurs only at Godmanchester in Cambridgeshire.

ABARTACH
Irish
The son of ALCHAD, a magician who mysteriously made a number of the FIAN disappear. GOLL and OSCAR rescued them, and a levy, which was to include his wife, was imposed on him for his trickery. Abartach, however, simply used his magic to disappear and thus escape the fine.

ABCAN MAC BICELMOIS
Irish
When LUGH arrived at TARA, Abcan mac Bicelmois was the harper of the TUATHA DÉ DANANN.

ABELLEUS
Arthurian
A knight, he is simply described as having been slain by TOR.

ABLAMOR OF THE MARSH
Arthurian
By killing two of the greyhounds that belonged to GAWAIN and GAHERIS, retaliation for their having killed the white hart he owned, Ablamor was challenged to do combat with Gawain. Just as Gawain was about to kill Ablamor, his lady, who remains unnamed, threw herself between them, and it was she that the hapless knight killed. Gawain was so horror-stricken that he could not continue the fight, so Ablamor was spared.

ACALLAMH NA SENORÁCH
Irish
Colloquy with the Ancients, one of the most attractive and interesting pieces of Irish mythological literature. A long narrative, dating from about the thirteenth century, the *Colloquy* is a collection of stories set against a mythological framework, and thus contains much primitive material.

ACCOLON
Arthurian
A Gallic knight with whom MORGAN Le Fay had become enamoured. While out hunting, Accolon with URIEN and ARTHUR, became separated from their companions, and, coming upon a vessel, they settled down for the night. To his astonishment Accolon awoke in a field, where he was given the sword EXCALIBUR, being told that he would have to use it in a fight. When that time came, his opponent turned out to be none other than Arthur himself, but neither recognised the other. It seemed that Accolon might be victorious, as Arthur had been given a fake copy of Excalibur, but in the nick of time the LADY OF THE LAKE appeared and caused the true Excalibur to fall to the ground. Arthur immediately seized it and promptly defeated Accolon, inflicting a mortal wound upon him. However, it was then discovered that Morgan Le Fay had organised the whole affair, and Arthur assured Accolon that he would not be punished for his actions. Accolon died a short while later from his injuries.

ACHEFLOUR
Arthurian
In the English romance *SIR PERCEVAL OF GALLES*, Acheflour is named as the sister of ARTHUR, and the mother of PERCEVAL. Believing her son to be dead, Acheflour went mad and took to living like a wild animal in the woods where Perceval later found her. The knowledge that her son still lived once more restored her sanity and she went to live with her son and his lover, LUFAMOUR.

ACHTLAND

Irish

According to the *LONGES MAC NDUIL DERMAIT*, one of the daughters of DOEL. She is the wife of CONNLA, a giant who allegedly sleeps with his head on a rock in the west of his island home and his feet in the east. When CÚ CHULAINN came to this island, Achtland kindly agreed to help him locate her brothers, who had mysteriously disappeared. She led Cú Chulainn to another island, where he successfully released her brothers from the enchantment they had been placed under by EOCHO ROND.

ACORN

General

The Celtic symbol of life, fecundity and immortality. The acorn is to be found widely portrayed in Celtic works of art, and may have been used as a votive offering.

ADAM

Arthurian

According to the *Sone de Nausay*, Adam was the son of JOSEPH OF ARIMATHEA, and thus the brother of JOSEPHE.

ADDANC

Welsh

Also AFANC

A legendary Welsh monster whose name, in modern Welsh, means 'beaver'. This would appear to be consistent with the watery connections usually applied to this mythical creature. The word *addanc*, when employed as a noun rather than a proper noun, has also been used simply to refer to a spirit that dwells in a watery location, and not an actual creature. In this case the spirit is not an animal, but has a more human appearance. There is, however, no description of the Addanc in either form.

Welsh legend says that PEREDUR overcame one example of an Addanc that appears to have had manipulative skills, for it hurled spears and other missiles at that knight. However, Peredur prevailed, as he had been rendered invisible to the monster by means of a magical stone given to him by the EMPRESS OF CONSTANTINOPLE. The later Arthurian romances attributed this episode to PERCEVAL. King ARTHUR is also said to have killed a similar beast at LLYN BARFOG, while HU GADARN is also said to have slain one. This last appearance of an Addanc may well be a late concoction, as it would seem that Hu Gadarn himself is nothing more than the invention of Iolo MORGANNWG.

ADDANZ

Arthurian

A character about whom nothing is known, other than that he is referred to as an ancestor of PERCEVAL.

ADDAON

Welsh

The son of TALIESIN. Noted for his wisdom, he was killed by LLONGAD GRWRM FARGOD EIDYN. Sources do not make it clear whether or not Addaon was the only son of Taliesin, nor do they mention the name of his mother.

ADELUF

Arthurian

In Rauf de BOUN's romance *PETIT BRUT* several characters are given this name. Two of them were kings before the time of King ARTHUR, but the third is named as one of the sons of Arthur.

ADRAGAIN

Arthurian

One of the KNIGHTS OF THE ROUND TABLE who, after the death of King ARTHUR, eventually became a hermit.

ADVENTUROUS BED

Arthurian

A bed to be found in Castle CARBONEK in which GALAHAD slept, and where a fiery lance wounded him. Some dubious sources say that it was Galahad's father, LANCELOT, who slept in this bed, having previously lain with ELAINE, a coupling that led to the birth of Galahad.

AED

Irish

1 The son of the King of CONNACHT and husband of the beautiful IBHELL.
2 The son of the DAGHDHA who was killed by CONCHEANN for seducing his wife. The Daghdha punished Concheann by making him carry Aed's corpse until he found a stone long enough to cover his grave. Some sources make this Aed an alternative name for the Daghdha himself, which would, in this case, mean 'fire'.
3 The husband of AIDE. His wife and family were killed when DUB sank the boat they were travelling in, thus drowning them.

AED ABRAT

Irish

The father of LI BAN, FAND and OENGHUS. Nothing more is known about this character.

AED FINN
Irish

Possibly a historical character who is thought to have been responsible for the writing-down of the famous *IMMRAM CURAIG MAÍLE DÚIN*. The final passage of this text describes Aed Finn as the chief sage of Ireland, but he remains unknown from any other source.

AED RUADH
Irish

A tyrannical king whose own champion invoked the powers of the sea, sun, wind and firmament against him. The sun grew so hot that Aed Ruadh was forced to bathe in the sea. A great wind blew up that whipped the sea into a frenzy, and Aed Ruadh drowned.

AEDA
Irish

(1) A dwarf, the FILI of FERGUS MAC LEDA. He accompanied EISIRT to FAYLINN, the realm of IUBDAN, a land inhabited by an elfin race. There, even though he was smaller than the average four-year-old child, Aeda caused panic, for to the inhabitants of Faylinn he appeared to be a veritable giant.

(2) A prince to whom the giantess BEBHIONN had been betrothed by her father TREON against her wishes. In an attempt to escape her forthcoming wedding, Bebhionn sought the protection of FIONN MAC CUMHAILL. No sooner had Fionn mac Cumhaill pledged to protect her, however, than a male giant appeared and ran her through with a spear before Fionn mac Cumhaill could respond.

This giant was Aeda, who had heard of Bebhionn's flight from her commitment and swore that he would avenge the dishonour she had brought on him. Even though Fionn mac Cumhaill and his men chased Aeda, they could not catch him as he strode out to sea, climbed into a huge ship, and sailed away.

AEDÁN MAC GABRÁIN
Irish

A King of DÁL RIADA and father of the appropriately named ARTHUR OF DÁL RIADA. He was helped in his fight against the SAXONS by his ally FIACHNA LURGAN, King of DÁL NARAIDI, and the magical intervention of MANANNÁN MAC LIR. Aedán mac Gabráin has been widely associated with the Arthurian legends, but this appears to be simply based on the name of his son.

AEDD
Welsh

Sometimes given the epithet 'the Great', Aedd was the father of PRYDEIN, the eponym of BRITAIN in Welsh tradition. Aedd also appears in Irish mythology, but with the same connotation as he does within the Welsh traditions.

AEDH
Irish

The son of the King of LEINSTER, Aedh was enticed into a SÍDH by the daughters of BODB. For three years Aedh was cared for by the inhabitants of the sídh, but eventually he and fifty other youths managed to escape, whereupon they met Saint PATRICK, who had just arrived in IRELAND. He told his story to the saint, who must have converted him to Christianity on the spot, for Aedh is reputed to have told the saint that he would eventually die as God willed, the TUATHA DÉ DANANN having no further power over him.

AEGIDIUS
General

Historical Roman count who ruled GAUL between AD 461 and 464. The fourteenth-century writer Jacques de Guise claimed that King ARTHUR flourished during this time, whilst the sixteenth-century Philippe de Vignelles intimated that Aegidius was actually in frequent contact with Arthur.

AEIFE
Irish

Appearing in the *ACALLAMH NA SENÓRACH*, Aeife and her sisters, CLIODNA and EDAEIN, eloped from TÍR TAIRNGIRI with CIABHAN, LODAN and EOLUS. When they reached IRELAND a huge wave rolled in from the sea and engulfed the boat they had been travelling in.

AELENS
Arthurian

The King of ICELAND and father of ESCOL, who later became one of ARTHUR's followers.

AELLE
British and Arthurian

A SAXON King of Sussex who, along with his sons CISSA, CYMEN and WLENCING, defeated the Britons at Cymenes ora in AD 477, once again fighting against them at Mearc raedesburna in AD 485, and capturing Anderida (modern Pevensey, Sussex) in *c.* AD 491. According to BEDE, he held

Aeneas and Anchises, *Giovanni Lorenzo Bernini (1598–1680). Aeneas was the legendary founder of the Roman and British peoples.* (Rome, Galleria Borghese © 1990, Photo Scala, Florence – courtesy of the Ministero Beni e Att. Culturali)

the archaic title Bretwalda (Britain-Ruler), perhaps suggesting a primacy amongst the Saxon kings. It has also been suggested that he led the Saxons at BADON, thus seeming to indicate that he may well have been a leading adversary of the historical ARTHUR.

AEN-EAS, -EUS
Graeco-Romano-British
In classical Graeco-Roman mythology, Aeneas was the son of Anchises by the goddess Aphrodite (Roman Venus). According to Virgil (70–19 BC), Aeneas, a member of the Trojan royal family, was reported to have survived the sack of Troy and to have made his way to Italy with a group of Trojan refugees. There, again according to Virgil, Aeneas became the legendary founder of the Roman people and a direct ancestor of the Emperor Augustus.

His great-grandson BRUTUS brought a group of Trojan descendants to ENGLAND. Landing at TOTNES in Devon, Brutus and his followers overcame a race of giants to found their capital city of TROIA NOVA, or TROYNOVANT (New Troy), which is today known as LONDON. Through this relationship Aeneas is regarded as the legendary founder not only of the Roman people but also of the British people, and the supposed ancestor of King LEIR. GEOFFREY OF MONMOUTH categorically states that Aeneas was the ancestor of the ancient British kings, while John Dryden (1631–1700) specifically names Aeneas as a direct ancestor of King ARTHUR. Both associations may have some historical background, but it has never been conclusively proven that Brutus ever came to England, and thus the connection with Aeneas seems suspect.

AENGABA
Irish
One of the TUATHA DÉ DANANN, he fought against the FIR BHOLG at the first Battle of MAGH TUIREDH. Curiously, Aengaba is usually referred to as 'Aengaba of Norway', but no explanation for this association can be found in the ancient texts. It may well be that Aengaba is actually a foreign interloper into the Irish myths, and has no real role to play.

AENGHUS
Irish
1 A variant of OENGHUS, and one from which the anglicised version of Oenghus – Angus – may be seen to be derived.
2 The name of an ULSTER warrior who challenged CET in the SCÉLA MUCCE MAIC DÁ THÓ.

AERACURA
Gaulish
The name given to an ancient earth goddess whose image is known only from an altar stone found at Oberseebach in Switzerland. It appears that she was later displaced in her role by 'DIS PATER', although this is by no means certain and the goddess known as Aeracura may have been a tutelary goddess.

AES SÍD(H)
Irish
Meaning 'hill folk', Aes sídh was the collective name for the TUATHA DÉ DANANN.

AESC
British
The traditional founder of the AESCING tribe, Aesc reigned, in KENT, between AD 488 and 512. He was possibly the son of HENGIST, and his story may be related to that of Askr, one of the first two people of Norse-Teutonic mythology, the other being Embla. This association seems to be further supported by the fact that Hengist, his father, claimed descent from WODEN, the ANGLO-SAXON variant of the Norse god Odínn.

AESCING
British
Kentish ANGLO-SAXON tribe that was, according to tradition, founded by AESC.

AESUS
Romano-Gaulish
One of a triad of deities recorded by Lucan (AD 39–65), the other two members being TARANIS and TEUTATES. Aesus appears to be a Latinised form of ESUS, the normal spelling of the deity usually included in this triad.

AETURNUS
British
The son of PATERNUS and father of CUNEDDA, according to the latter's traditional pedigree.

AFAGDDU
Welsh
Also AVAGDDU
The son of TEGID VOEL and his goddess wife CERRIDWEN, brother of MORFRAN AB TEGID and CREIRWY. He is described as the most ill-favoured man in the world, dark and ugly, in contrast to his sister Creirwy, who was the fairest maiden in the entire world, light and beautiful. Some sources, however, indicate that, rather than a personal name,

Afagddu was a nickname applied to Morfran ab Tegid, and in this case Afagddu and Morfran ab Tegid would be one and the same. Cerridwen attempted to brew her son a divine potion of inspiration, but the three essential drops derived from the cauldron fell on GWION BACH. Cerridwen chased and caught Gwion Bach, who was later reborn as TALIESIN, but whether or not she brewed Afagddu a fresh potion is not recorded in ancient texts.

AFANC
Welsh

Variant of ADDANC that comes about from the pronunciation of the Welsh 'double-d' sound, though more directly this might be thought to give rise to a variant Athanc.

AFOLLONAU
Welsh

A Welsh MYRDDIN (MERLIN) poem that names the little known CHWIMLEIAN as a flower-maiden. This characterisation has let to the later association of Chwimleian with both BLODEUWEDD and GUENDOLOENA.

AGANIPPUS
British

A King of the FRANKS. According to GEOFFREY OF MONMOUTH he was the husband of CORDELIA, the youngest daughter of the then King of BRITAIN, the semi-mythical King LEIR who came to live with them after REGAN and GONERIL, Leir's two eldest daughters, along with Regan's husbands HENWINUS and MAGLAURUS, had seized Leir's throne and kingdom. Aganippus raised an army, routed Leir's two sons-in-law and reinstated Leir as king for the last three years of his life.

AGLOVALE
Arthurian

A brother of PERCEVAL and the father of MORIAEN. He was killed on the occasion that LANCELOT carried off Queen GUINEVERE.

AGNED, MOUNT
Arthurian

The site of the eleventh of ARTHUR'S BATTLES as listed in the writings of NENNIUS, though one tenth-century manuscript gives the name BREGUOIN. It later became known as the CASTLE OF MAIDENS, and has had High ROCHESTER suggested as its actual location.

AGNOMAN
Irish

1 A son of SERA, the brother of STARN and PARTHOLÁN and the father of NEMHEDH.
2 The father of CRUNDCHU.

AGRAVADAIN
Arthurian

The husband of the mother of ECTOR DE MARIS, the child being born after his wife's adulterous affair with King BAN.

AGRAVAIN
Arthurian

The son of LOT and MORGAUSE, the brother of GAWAIN, and one of the KNIGHTS OF THE ROUND TABLE. He married LAUREL, the niece of LIONORS and LYNETTE. Knowing of the affair between LANCELOT and GUINEVERE, he, accompanied by MORDRED and twelve other knights, succeeded in trapping the lovers together in the queen's bedchamber. Though unarmed, Lancelot managed to fight his way free, killing Agravain and the other twelve knights in the process, leaving only Mordred alive to report Guinevere's infidelity to ARTHUR. Other sources say that Agravain survived Lancelot's escape, only to be killed by him when the latter rescued Guinevere after her condemnation to death for adultery.

AGRESTES
Arthurian

During the time of JOSEPH OF ARIMATHEA, Agrestes is said to have been the ruler of CAMELOT.

AGRESTIZIA
Arthurian

Otherwise known as DINDRANE, Agrestizia is the name applied to the sister of PERCEVAL in the Italian romance *TAVOLA RITONDA*.

AGRICOLA
Welsh

Called a good king by GILDAS, Agricola was the ruler (*c.* AD 500) of DEMETIA, the ancient name for the Welsh kingdom of DYFED. Some sources claim that he liberated Demetia from the UÍ LIATHÁIN, the Irish dynasty that had ruled the kingdom before his reign. Later sources connect him with King ARTHUR, as his reign was certainly well within the traditional period ascribed to the historical Arthur, saying that he may well have been one of Arthur's commanders or that he and Arthur were in frequent contact.

AGUISANT

Arthurian

The son of KARADAN and an unnamed sister of King ARTHUR, thus making him Arthur's nephew.

AGUYSANS

Arthurian

One of the eleven rulers who rebelled against King ARTHUR at the onset of the young monarch's reign. He is given various names, although he is most commonly simply referred to as the KING WITH A HUNDRED KNIGHTS.

AHES

Gaulish and Arthurian

A MARI-MORGAN, a class of supernatural beings peculiar to BRITTANY, where she was held responsible for the destruction of the legendary city of YS. Later tradition connects her with MORGAN Le Fay, the connection simply stemming from the classification of being Mari-Morgan, of which Ahes was but one.

See also DAHUT

AI

Irish

A FILI of the TUATHA DÉ DANANN.

AIDE

Irish

The wife of AED. She and her children were drowned by DUB, who caused the seas to swell and engulf her boat.

AIDED CHLAINNE LIR

Irish

The Children of Lir, an ancient text that tells the story of the children of LIR. Lir was disgusted at the choice of BODB DEARG as King of the TUATHA DÉ DANANN, and he would have been punished had Bodb not intervened and given Lir his own daughter, AOBH, as his wife. Before she died, Aobh bore Lir four children, two boys and two girls, although some sources vary the numbers of both sexes. Bodb compensated Lir for her death by giving him his other daughter AOIFE, but she was jealous of her stepchildren and transformed them into swans, a shape they kept for 900 years, even though they retained the powers of speech and reason and were blessed with the most exquisite song. Bodb punished Aoife by changing her into a demoness. The children of Lir resumed their human form during the time of Saint PATRICK, accepted the Christian faith and died.

AIDED CHLAINNE TUIRENN

Irish

The Children of Tuirenn, a text that gives one version of the story of LUGH at TARA, although this is not the usual story of that god's appearance at the court of the TUATHA DÉ DANANN. This version says that Lugh arrived riding AONBARR, the horse of MANANNÁN MAC LIR, his countenance being so bright that none could look upon him. He killed many of the FOMHOIRÉ when they came to claim their tribute, an act that led BALAR's wife CÉTHLIONN to acknowledge that it had been prophesied that, after the arrival of Lugh, the power of the Fomhoiré would be no more. BRES saw Lugh riding towards the Fomhoiré as the 'sun rising in the west'. He begged for his life in return for delivering the Fomhoiré into the hands of the Tuatha Dé Danann.

This account is contrary to the normally accepted story of the arrival of Lugh at Tara and the subsequent Second Battle of MAGH TUIREDH, which this story simply seems to replace with the meeting between Lugh and Bres.

AIDEEN

Irish

The wife of OSCAR, she died of grief after the death of her husband at the Battle of GABHRA and was buried on BED EDAR by OISÍN, Oscar's father, who built the great dolmen that still stands over her grave.

AÍF-E, -A

Irish

The rival of SCÁTHACH, Aífe is described as the fiercest and strongest woman warrior in the world. She was fought and conquered by CÚ CHULAINN, although at one stage in the fight she shattered his sword and appeared to have the upper hand. Cú Chulainn then took Aífe as his concubine, and after he had returned to IRELAND she bore him a son, CONALL or CONLAÍ.

AIGE

Irish

An unfortunate maiden who was transformed into a fawn by the SIABHRA and forced to wander around IRELAND. Later she was killed, and all that remained of her was a bag of water, which was thrown into a river that carried her name from that time onwards.

AIL-ILL, -ELL

Irish

The consort of MEDHBHA, Queen of CONNACHT, and the father of ÉDÁIN ECHRAIDHE, who was considered the most beautiful woman in all IRELAND. Ailill and Medhbha were the great legendary enemies of CONCHOBAR MAC NESSA, against whom they bid for ownership of MAC DÁ THÓ's dog and boar, and against whom they fought in Medhbha's attempt to obtain the DONN CUAILNGÈ.

AILILL
Irish

The father of MAÍL DÚIN. Having been killed and buried under the rubble of a ruined church, Maíl Dúin set off on a long voyage to avenge the death of his father, a voyage that is recounted in the *IMMRAM CURAIG MAÍLE DÚIN*.

AILILL AINE
Irish

A King of LEINSTER. The son of LOEGHAIRE LORC, King of IRELAND, Ailill Aine was killed by his uncle COBTHACH COEL, the brother of Loeghaire Lorc, when the former usurped the throne of the latter. Ailill Aine's son, LABHRAIDH LOINGSECH, was driven into exile but used this time to gather together an army with which he later returned, killed his usurping uncle and his supporters and so regained the kingdom of Leinster that was rightfully his.

AILILL ANGLONNACH
Irish

The brother of EOCHAIDH AIREMH, he fell in love with ÉDÁIN ECHRAIDHE, the wife of his brother. They arranged a tryst on three occasions, but on each occasion Ailill Anglonnach was given a sleeping potion by MIDHIR, who was seeking to reclaim Édáin for himself. Édáin refused to leave her husband for Midhir, and, when she recounted what had happened to Ailill Anglonnach, he was cured of his illicit love.

AILILL OLUM
Irish

A King of MUNSTER who ravished AINÉ and was subsequently killed by her magic.

AILLEAN(N)
Irish and Arthurian

An OTHERWORLD woman who had a tendency to turn herself into a deer, and who appears in the Irish romance *VISIT OF GREY HAM*. Said to be descended from the King of ICELAND through his granddaughter RATHLEAN, she led ARTHUR and his men away to marry otherworldly women, reserving King Arthur for herself.

AILLÉN MAC MIDHNA
Irish

A terrible being of whom there is no complete description. He came to TARA every year at SAMHAIN and, having first bewitched all the warriors with enchanting music, burned down the court. When the eight-year-old FIONN MAC CUMHAILL came to Tara, he pressed the point of his spear into his forehead and thus remained immune when Aillén mac Midhna started his enchantment. Then, when Aillén mac Midhna advanced, breathing fire, Fionn mac Cumhaill calmly stepped out and beheaded him.

AINÉ
Irish

(1) A variant of ANA, which is itself a variant of DANU.

(2) A daughter of EOGABAL, Ainé dwelt on CNOC AINÉ in MUNSTER. Originally a fertility deity, she was ravished by AILILL OLUM, whom she killed by use of magic. Ainé persisted well into the Christian era, when she was said to have been captured by Lord Desmond, whom she married and subsequently bore a son. Soon afterwards she and her son disappeared, but they made many visits, until Lord Desmond died and the son, Gerald, became the 4th Earl of Desmond. He disappeared, so it is said, in 1398, but legend says that he may still be seen once every seven years riding around the banks of Loch Gur, beneath whose waters he lives.

Although the Lord Desmond legend is fairly recent, Ainé is obviously a very early figure, for her father Eogabal is a member of the TUATHA DÉ DANANN. He was killed by FERCHESS while he was leading his cattle to pasture outside his SÍDH. Ainé, who was accompanying him, was outraged or raped by OILILL, whom she struck so hard that there was no flesh left on his right ear, which earned him the epithet 'Bare Ear'.

Ainé swore vengeance against Ferchess and Oilill. Some years later LUGIAD EOGHAN, the son of Oilill, and LUGAID MAC CON heard sweet music drifting from a yew tree. When they went to investigate, they found a small harper inside the tree, whom they took to Oilill. However, as both Eoghan and Lugaid mac Con claimed the harper as their own, Oilill was forced to choose who might be a rightful owner. He naturally favoured his son, a choice that led to the Battle of MAGH MUCRIME, in which all seven of Oilill's sons were killed.

(3) A daughter of CULANN and sister to MILUCHRADH. Both she and her sister fell in love with FIONN MAC CUMHAILL, but Ainé let it slip

that she would never marry a man with grey hair. On hearing this, Miluchradh caused a lake to appear, the waters of which would turn anyone who bathed in them grey in an instant. Miluchradh then turned herself into a hind and allowed herself to be hunted by Fionn mac Cumhaill, drawing him inexorably towards the lake into which she leapt. Fionn mac Cumhaill followed her into the water, whereupon Miluchradh disappeared. When Fionn mac Cumhaill emerged from the lake as a grey-haired man, Ainé lost her love for him, but Miluchradh got her just reward when Fionn mac Cumhaill subsequently shunned her.

AINGE
Irish

A daughter of the DAGHDHA, Ainge features in a short parable about the magical creation of woodland. She had gathered together a bundle of twigs to build herself a tub to bathe in. However, these twigs were stolen by GAIBLE, son of NUADHA, who threw them to the wind. When they landed, they immediately became trees, thus betraying Ainge's identity as a fertility deity.

AINNLE
Irish

A son of UISNECH and one of the two brothers of NAOISE, the other being ARDÁN. Both brothers accompanied Naoise and DERDRIU when they fled to ALBA (or SCOTLAND). They were killed on their return from exile by CONCHOBAR MAC NESSA even though they had been promised safe passage.

AIREM
Irish

One of the three leaders of the Sons of MÍL ÉSPÁINE who killed the three kings of the TUATHA DÉ DANANN. Airem killed MAC CÉCHT, EBER killed MAC CUILL and AMHAIRGHIN killed MAC GRÉINE.

AIRMED
Irish

A daughter of DIAN CÉCHT and sister of MIDACH. After the death of Midach, Airmed sorted the medicinal herbs that had been collected by her brother, but Dian Cécht muddled them up again as he feared that their potency might diminish his position as a divine healer.

AISLINGE OENGHUS
Irish

The Dream of Oenghus, one of the earliest sections of the *BOOK OF LEINSTER*, having been written some time before 1160.

ALAISIAGAE
British

A generic name given to four war goddesses who were originally worshipped in the Teutonic heartland, and whose worship was brought to BRITAIN by the Romans. Named as BEDE, FINNILENE, BAUDIHILLIE and FRIAGABI, they had similar characteristics to the Norse-Teutonic Valkyrie. Their worship in Britain appears to have been localised to that area immediately south of Hadrian's Wall, and they were possibly invoked as protection against the marauding PICTS. Their names have been found, along with that of the Roman god of war Mars, on a stone at Housesteads on Hadrian's Wall.

ALAN
Arthurian

The son of BRONS and ENYGEUS, though some sources make him the son of King PELLINORE. Remaining unmarried, he was made ruler over his brothers and sisters, although, in the *DIDOT PERCEVAL* he is said to have been the father of PERCEVAL, having been told by the Holy Spirit that he was destined to become the father of the GRAIL KING.

ALANS
Arthurian

A tribe of the barbarian SARMATIAN peoples who inhabited RUSSIA in Roman times. Their bloodline still survives today in the OSSETES, who inhabit the Caucasus. These descendants tell a very similar story to that concerning the passing of King ARTHUR, which appears to date from when the historical Arthur is traditionally said to have lived.

ALARON
British

The consort of BLADUD, whom she assisted in the building of the therapeutic baths at KAERBADUS, or BATH.

ALAW
Welsh

A river on the island of ANGLESEY, on whose banks BRANWEN, the sister of BENDIGEID VRAN, was alleged to have died from a broken heart. Close to the river lies BEDD BRANWEN, the traditional site of her burial.

ALBA
Irish

An archaic, originally Irish term that was used to refer to SCOTLAND, and is still sometimes used in a poetic sense today. In the post-ANGLO-SAXON period the name developed into the better-known and more widely used form of ALBANY.

ALBANACT(US)
Arthurian

Named by GEOFFREY OF MONMOUTH as a son of BRUTUS, and thus a great-great-grandson of the Trojan AENEAS, Albanact had two brothers, LOCRINUS and KAMBER. After Brutus had died, the three brothers shared the country between themselves, Locrinus becoming the King of ENGLAND, Kamber the King of WALES, and Albanact taking the kingdom of SCOTLAND. Geoffrey of Monmouth says that this is how each of these countries derived their early names: LOCRIS for England, CAMBRIA for Wales and ALBANY for Scotland. This is, however, false etymology, for Locris comes from the Welsh LLOEGR, Cambria from Cymry (meaning 'fellow countrymen'), and Albany from ALBA or ALBION. According to Geoffrey of Monmouth, invading Huns killed Albanact, but this is just one more example of the fictitious nature of the work of Geoffrey of Monmouth, as the Huns never invaded BRITAIN.

The name Albanactus later surfaces as the name given to the captain of ARTHUR's guard by DRYDEN in his opera *KING ARTHUR*.

ALBANIO
Arthurian

The hero of a poem written by one Jegon, whose works form a continuation to SPENSER's *FAERIE QUEENE*. In this work King ARTHUR knighted Albanio.

ALBAN(Y)
General

An archaic, post-ANGLO-SAXON term, traditionally Irish in origin and derived from ALBA, which is used to refer to SCOTLAND, although it might equally well have derived from ALBION.

ALBINE
British

According to the fifteenth-century *Chronicles of Great Britain* by John de Wavrin, Lady Albine and her three, some say fifty, sisters came to the island that was to be named ALBION in her honour, having been banished from their own country for killing their husbands. This story has a direct parallel in the classical Greek myth of the fifty Danaides, the daughters of Danaus, who killed their husbands, the fifty sons of Aegyptus, on their wedding night. John de Wavrin places the time of their arrival as

coinciding with the rule of Jahir, the third judge of Israel after Joshua. A demon who took the form of a man came to live with the women, and as a result their offspring were giants who continued to multiply until the arrival of BRUTUS. It is quite possible that one of these giants was none other than Albion himself.

ALBION
British

A legendary giant who was said by GEOFFREY OF MONMOUTH to have been the eponymous first ruler of BRITAIN, the island itself being referred to as Albion before the arrival of BRUTUS. Some accounts say that he was the son of an unnamed sea god, while others say that he might have been one of the giant offspring of ALBINE and her sisters, however many that might have been. Later Romano-Celtic tradition states that Albion travelled south to help his brothers fight Hercules during that hero's tenth labour and was killed in the resulting battle. The career of this giant ruler was outlined in Holinshed's *Chronicles* of 1577, and his name is still used to refer poetically to Britain, or, more correctly, ENGLAND, in much the same way as ALBA or ALBANY is still sometimes used to refer to SCOTLAND.

ALCARDO
Arthurian

The brother of ISEULT and companion of TRISTAN, possibly acting as the latter's squire. Later he became known as LANTRIS, in which persona he was definitely referred to as a squire, being killed in his attempt to rescue his sister Iseult from King MARK.

ALCHAD
Irish

A King of TÍR TAIRNGIRI and father of ABARTACH.

ALCHENDIC
Arthurian

A giant who ruled the ancient city of SARRAS, according to the *PROPHÉCIES DE MERLIN*, having gained the throne by murdering the previous ruler. Even though he became king in this manner, the people of the city were loyal to him and would not desert him, even when Crusaders led by King Richard of Jerusalem placed the city under siege. Alchendric was successful in defeating four Crusader champions, and a truce was finally negotiated. A month later the barbarian Alchendic was converted to Christianity and baptised.

ALCINA

Arthurian

In the Italian romances of Ludovico ARIOSTO and Matteo Maria BOIARDO, Alcina appears as one of the enchantress sisters of MORGAN Le Fay.

ALCLUD

Arthurian

The Roman name for DUMBARTON. It was here that King ARTHUR's ally HOEL, King of BRITTANY, was besieged by PICTS and Scots until Arthur came to relieve him.

ALDAN

Welsh

A historical daughter of a South WALES nobleman and, in Welsh tradition, the mother of MYRDDIN (MERLIN).

ALDERLEY EDGE

Arthurian

A ridge in Cheshire, England, where, according to local legend, a farmer living at Mobberley had his horse purchased by a wizard for the use of a king and his knights, who were slumbering beneath the ridge. At the time when this legend first appeared, apparently towards the end of the seventeenth century, the identity of the slumbering king was not given. However, a later rhyming version (by J. Roscoe) specifically identifies that king as King ARTHUR.

ALDROENUS

Arthurian and Gaulish

Also AUDRIEN

A King of BRITTANY, also known as AUDRIEN, and the brother of CONSTANTINE, ARTHUR's grandfather. He sent his brother to rule the Britons at their own request after he had himself declined their offer to become the King of BRITAIN.

ALEMAIGNE

Arthurian

The realm of NUC, which has been identified with either ALBANY (SCOTLAND) or GERMANY, the latter obviously being derived from the French for that country, a word that has its origins in the fourth-century Alemanni people of Germany.

ALEMANDINE

Arthurian

The queen of a kingdom that was plagued by a wild beast until it was defeated by FLORIANT, who then refused the offer of her hand as a reward.

Alderley Edge, Cheshire, where local legend says King Arthur and his knights sleep beneath the ridge. (© Mick Sharp)

ALEXANDER

Arthurian

1 Emperor of CONSTANTINOPLE, husband of TANTALIS and thus the father of ALIS and ALEXANDER.

2 Son of ALEXANDER and TANTALIS, husband of SOREDAMOR and father of CLIGÉS.

3 Son of the King of India who was changed, along with his brothers, into a variety of 'canine creature' by his stepmother. Alexander himself was turned into a creature known as the CROP-EARED DOG.

ALEXANDER THE GREAT

Arthurian

Historical ruler of Macedonia (365–323 BC) who, at the age of nineteen, succeeded his father, Philip II, as the King of Macedon and Olympias. Alexander's historical career is of little relevance to Arthurian studies. His appearance in the Arthurian legends is totally fictitious, for in *PERCEFOREST* he is said to have led an invasion of BRITAIN, which he never did, making BETIS the King of ENGLAND and GADDIFER the King of SCOTLAND.

ALEXIUS
Arthurian

The variant of ALIS that is usually regarded as the root from which Alis is derived. Five historical emperors of CONSTANTINOPLE have had this name, the first being made emperor in 1081.

ALFASEIN
Arthurian

After the conversion of KALAFES to Christianity, this name was given to him at his subsequent baptism.

ALICE
Arthurian

The wife of ALISANDER THE ORPHAN, she became known as the BEAUTIFUL PILGRIM.

ALIFATIMA
Arthurian

King of SPAIN and follower of the Roman Emperor LUCIUS HIBERIUS. He was killed while fighting ARTHUR's forces during the latter's campaign against Rome and the Romans. It seems likely that his name has a Moorish root following their influence in Spain during the Middle Ages.

ALIS
Arthurian

The son of ALEXANDER and TANTALIS, and brother to ALEXANDER. He became the Byzantine Emperor and married FENICE, with whom CLIGÉS, his nephew, was also in love. Alis is a form of ALEXIUS, a name, or title, borne by a number of Byzantine emperors.

ALISANDER THE ORPHAN
Arthurian

The son of BALDWIN and ANGLIDES. Following the murder of his father by King MARK, his uncle, he was imprisoned by MORGAN Le Fay, but was helped to regain his freedom by ALICE, the BEAUTIFUL PILGRIM. Subsequently he married Alice and was later welcomed at King ARTHUR's court.

ALISANOS
Gaulish

A generic name applied to deities of rocks and rock formations.

ALLITERATIVE MORTE ARTHURE
Arthurian

A Middle English poem dating from *c.*1400 and consisting of 4,346 lines concerning King ARTHUR's war against Rome and the Romans, MORDRED's rebellion and Arthur's final battle.

ALLOIT
Irish

A mysterious deity who is sometimes named as the father of MANANNÁN MAC LIR, although presumably without his usual epithet. This association would seem to suggest that Alloit was a sea deity who was later replaced by LIR.

ALOIS
Arthurian

The King of NORTHGALIS who went to war with AMOROLDO, the King of IRELAND. In this war, Alois was supported by TRISTAN, and Amoroldo by LANCELOT. In the end peace was brought about between the two warring leaders by the intervention of both ISEULT, Tristan's lover, and GUINEVERE, Lancelot's lover.

ALON
Arthurian

A grandnephew of King ARTHUR who became one of the KNIGHTS OF THE ROUND TABLE.

ALSPRADOC
British

The legendary enemy of the equally legendary COEL. Unlike Coel, however, nothing further is known of Alspradoc.

ALVREZ
Arthurian

An Irish king and the father of MIROET and KAMELIN, both of whom went on to become KNIGHTS OF THE ROUND TABLE.

AMAETHON
Welsh

A son of DÔN and brother to the likes of GWYDION FAB DÔN, GILFAETHWY, GOFANNON and ARIANRHOD. Amaethon seems to have been an agricultural deity, for his name appears to be derived from the Welsh *amaeth*, 'ploughman'. Amaethon brought OTHERWORLDLY animals to earth from ANNWFN, which led to the mythical Battle of CATH GODEU at which he defeated ARAWN with the help of his brother Gwydion fab Dôn.

AMA(I)RG-EN, -IN
Irish
See AMHAIRGHIN.

AMAITE AIDGILL

Irish

'Hags of Doom'. During the First Battle of MAGH TUIREDH, the voices of Amaite Aidgill, along with those of the BADBHA and BLEDLOCHTANA, were raised on the command of the DAGHDHA against the FIR BHOLG.

AMANGONS

Arthurian

The ruler of GRANLAND, according to the Old French *Le Chevalier as deus espées.*

AMANT

Arthurian

A knight who, having accused his master, King MARK, of treachery, was challenged to trial by combat, and duly defeated by Mark.

AMAZON(S)

Arthurian

Medieval legend claimed that the female Amazon warriors of classical Greek mythology were, in fact, originally Goths who, under MARPESIA, formed an army of women and journeyed, by way of the Caucasus, to Africa. By simple association, the medieval writers included this wonderful mythical race in the Arthurian legends. TRISTAN THE YOUNGER was supposed to have saved their Queen from the King of the IDUMEANS, and they fought with GAWAIN, their Queen being killed by the CROP-EARED DOG.

In the *ALLITERATIVE MORTE ARTHURE* they were said to have been the subjects of LUCIUS HIBERIUS, ARTHUR's bitter foe, while in SPENSER's *FAERIE QUEENE*, their Queen, RADIGUND, was killed by BRITOMART.

AMBROSIUS AURELI(AN)US

Arthurian

Also AURELIUS AMBROSIUS

An undoubted historical character who live in the fifth century and whose career is chronicled by GEOFFREY OF MONMOUTH. The brother of UTHER and King CONSTANS of BRITAIN, he was smuggled to BRITTANY following the murder of his brother Constans by the usurping VORTIGERN. It was from Brittany that he later returned with his brother Uther, intent on taking back the throne that was rightfully his. Landing at TOTNES in Devon, Ambrosius Aurelius was proclaimed king there. He laid siege to Vortigern's tower and succeeded in burning it down whilst Vortigern was still inside, thus killing the usurper. He went on to defeat the

SAXONS and had their leader, HENGIST, executed, commissioning MERLIN to build a monument on SALISBURY PLAIN to commemorate the British leaders Hengist had massacred there. Finally, PASCHENT, Vortigern's son, made war against him and succeeded in having him poisoned by a Saxon named EOPA. He was allegedly buried within the GIANTS' RING he had commissioned Merlin to build, a stone circle better known today as STONEHENGE.

These meagre facts are all that can be said about the historical life of Ambrosius Aurelius. The remaining 'facts' are pure fabrication. Legend has it that, when Ambrosius Aurelius commissioned Merlin to build his monument on Salisbury Plain, the wily old magician simply brought it over from IRELAND, though modern science tells us that by that time the stone circle had been standing for 3,000 years or more.

GILDAS, who used perhaps the most correct form of his name, Ambrosius Aurelianus, supports Geoffrey of Monmouth in his claim that it was he who instituted the fighting that finally put a halt to the Saxon attacks, saying that he was the 'last of the Romans', a reference to his ability to halt the advance of the Saxons where others had failed. NENNIUS, however, says that this Ambrosius was the fatherless child whom Vortigern intended to sacrifice when his tower kept falling down, but then contradicts himself by saying that Ambrosius Aurelius was the son of a Roman consul. Geoffrey of Monmouth maintains that it was Merlin whom Vortigern intended to sacrifice, and that Ambrosius Aurelius was ARTHUR's nephew. Other writers have even suggested that he is the original Arthur, while the fifteenth-century poet Rhys Goch Eryri said that, following his death at the hands of Eopa, his head was taken and buried beneath DINAS EMRYS, but this is simply poetic licence.

AMBROY OYSELET

Arthurian

This knight, who appears in *Merlin* by Lovelich, owes his existence, so it would appear, to the author's misunderstanding of the French phrase *oiseau au brai*, thinking it to be a personal name.

AMENE

Arthurian

The Queen of a kingdom that had been almost entirely conquered by the evil knight ROAZ when King ARTHUR sent WIGALOIS to her aid. *En route* Wigalois was guided by LAR, the dead husband of Queen Amene, and, having routed Roaz, Wigalois married her daughter LARIE as a reward.

AMERGIN
Irish
See AMHAIRGHIN

AMESBURY
Arthurian
Situated in a bend in the River Avon, north of Salisbury, Wiltshire, Amesbury is a small and pleasant market town. Sir Thomas MALORY asserts that Queen GUINEVERE came to Amesbury Abbey when she heard of King ARTHUR's death. In AD 979 the abbey was succeeded by a nunnery that eventually became one of the richest in ENGLAND, achieving fame as the retreat of Mary, daughter of King Edward I, and her grandmother, Queen Eleanor, King Henry III's widow.

AMFORTAS
Arthurian
Also ANFORTAS
The GRAIL KING or the FISHER KING according to WOLFRAM VON ESCHENBACH. The son of FRIMUTEL, also a Grail King, he was wounded in the scrotum by a poisoned lance while jousting and, carried into the presence of the GRAIL, he awaited the coming of the questioner, PERCEVAL, who would ask the GRAIL QUESTION and thus restore him to health. He appears in Wagner's *PARSIFAL*. Some think that his name may be a derivation of the Latin word *infirmitas*, though this is by no means certain.

AMHAIRGHIN
Irish
A son of MÍL, a FILI who was one of the leaders of the Sons of MÍL ÉSPÁINE, or GAELS, who came from Spain to IRELAND, landing on 1 May, the feast of BELTANE. *En route* his wife SKENA fell overboard and was drowned. Defeating an army of the TUATHA DÉ DANANN, the invaders set out for the capital TARA and met the three goddesses BANBHA, FÓDLA and ÉRIU, the three wives respectively of the three Tuatha Dé Danann kings: MAC CUILL, MAC CÉCHT and MAC GRÉINE. The invaders promised each goddess in turn that the land should bear their name if she would favour them. Finally Ériu told Amhairghin that the Sons of Míl Éspáine would conquer all of Ireland and rule there forever. However, she warned DÔNN, their discourteous king, that neither he nor his heirs would ever enjoy the land. Soon afterwards Dônn was drowned and buried on the island of TECH DUINN, to which he still welcomes the spirits of dead warriors.

When they reached Tara, the three kings of the Tuatha Dé Danann disputed the right of the Sons of Míl Éspáine to Ireland. As a compromise they asked Amhairghin to judge their claims, and he ruled that the invading Sons of Míl Éspáine should put out to sea again to beyond a magical boundary referred to as the ninth wave. They did so, but when they turned and attempted to return to the land, the Tuatha Dé Danann sent an enchanted wind against them. Amhairghin called upon the SPIRIT OF IRELAND to help them and the wind dropped, allowing the Sons of Míl Éspáine to land. They then defeated the Tuatha Dé Danann at the Battle of TAILTIU, all three kings being killed in the battle: Mac Cuill by EBER, Mac Cécht by AIREM and Mac Gréine by Amhairghin himself.

The Tuatha Dé Danann were still determined not to be exiled, however, and they used their magical powers to deprive the conquerors of both milk and grain. Eventually the Sons of Míl Éspáine agreed to divide the land with them, the Tuatha Dé Danann receiving the underground half. Their leader, the DAGHDHA, gave each of their chiefs a SÍDH for his dwelling place. There the Tuatha Dé Danann continue to live.

AMHAR
Arthurian
According to the *MABINOGION*, Amhar was a son of King ARTHUR who appears to be identical with AMR.

AMINABAD
Arthurian
According to the pedigree of JOHN OF GLASTONBURY, Aminabad was the son of JOSHUA, father of CASTELLORS, and an ancestor of King ARTHUR.

AMINADUC
Arthurian
According to the *LIVRE D'ARTUS*, Aminaduc was a SAXON who was the ruler of DENMARK.

AMITE
Arthurian
In French romance, Amite was the mother of GALAHAD.

AMLAWDD (WLEDIG)
Welsh and Arthurian
Also ANLAWDD
According to Welsh sources, the husband of GWENN, and the father of IGRAINE (EIGYR).

Sir Galahad and the dying Grail King, Amfortas. (Edwin Austin Abbey, 1895. © Burstein Collection/Corbis)

He is also credited with being the father of GOLEUDDYDD and RIEINGULID, who were, respectively, the mothers of CULHWCH and ILLTYD, ARTHUR's cousins. 'Wledig' is a title that, roughly translated, means 'chief', and would appear to indicate Amlawdd's position within the community.

AMORG(H)IN
Irish
The father of CONALL CERNACH.

AMOROLDO
Arthurian
Appearing in the Italian romance *TAVOLA RITONDA*, Amoroldo was the son of MARHAUS, who was made a knight by TRISTAN. Later, he ascended to the Irish throne and became embroiled in a war against King ALOIS of NORTHGALIS, during which time he was supported by Tristan, his enemy being supported by LANCELOT. ISEULT and GUINEVERE, the lovers of the respective supporters, brought about the reconciliation between the warring leaders, though Amoroldo was later killed by Lancelot. Amoroldo is the Italian equivalent of the name Marhaus, and here the name is used for both father and son.

AMR
Arthurian
The son of ARTHUR, according to NENNIUS and probably identical with AMHAR, the son of Arthur who is mentioned in the *MABINOGION*. Nennius states that he was buried under a mound named LICAT ANIR after he had been killed by his father at ARCHENFIELD, this burial-mound giving rise to his alternative name of ANIR.

AMREN
Welsh and Arthurian
Simply mentioned as the son of BEDWYR. Amren's name later passed into the Arthurian cycle as the son of BEDIVERE.

AMURFINE
Arthurian
One of the ladies who is described in various sources as having been the wife of GAWAIN.

AMUSTANT
Arthurian
The chaplain to GUINEVERE who had previously been the chaplain to her father. Eventually he became an anchorite, or religious hermit.

AMYTANS
Arthurian
In the anonymous Scottish poem *LANCELOT OF THE LAIK*, which dates from the fifteenth century, Amytans appears as a wise man who scolded King ARTHUR. This poem is derived from an earlier French one, but in that the wise man remains unnamed.

AN GLAS GHAIBHLEANN
Irish
The wondrous milk-bearing cow of GOIBHNIU. When she was stolen by BALAR she simply magically disappeared and returned to her master.

ANA
Irish
See DANU

ANDARTA
Gaulish
A bear goddess who, along with her counterpart ARTIO, had a classical parallel in the Greek goddess Artemis. Like the Greek goddess, Andarta could assume the form of a bear, her totem animal, at will.

ANDATE
British
A deity of unknown characteristics and attributes. It has been suggested that Andate may simply be an alternative spelling for ANDRASTE or a British adoption and adaptation of the Gaulish bear goddess ANDARTA.

A(N)DRASTE
British
A fierce goddess of victory to whom her opponents were sacrificed in a sacred grove. Described in Dio Cassius' *Annals XIV*, Andraste was said to be both mysterious and terrible. At one stage she was reputed to have been invoked by Queen BOUDICCA when she revolted against Roman tyranny during the first century AD. She is of the same type as the Irish goddess the MÓRRÍGHAN, and it is possible that she may also have been known as ANDATE. This leads to a further assumption that she may have originated in the Gaulish bear goddess ANDARTA, since Andate has also been mooted as a British variant of that goddess.

ANDRED
Arthurian
Originally hailing from LINCOLN, Andred was a cousin of TRISTAN, who was resident at the court of King MARK. He spied on his cousin and

eventually betrayed the affair between Tristan and ISEULT to Mark.

ANDRIVETE
Welsh and Arthurian

The daughter of King CADOR of NORTH-UMBERLAND. Following her father's death, her uncle, AYGLIN, having usurped her rightful inheritance, tried to marry Andrivete off to an unnamed man of his choosing, but she managed to evade his plans by escaping and marrying CEI, who later became better known as the Arthurian knight Sir KAY. She prepared to overthrow her uncle, supported by her husband, and in later accounts with the support of King ARTHUR, but before any fighting could break out the people of Northumberland forced Ayglin to surrender, and Andrivete regained her kingdom. Originally a story with only local Northumbrian significance, this story later passed into the Arthurian cycle because of the presence of Cei, or Sir Kay, in the story.

ANDROGEUS
British

The son of LUD and brother of TENUANTIUS. When Lud died, neither of his sons was old enough to become king, so CASSIVELAUNUS, Lud's brother, assumed the crown, making Androgeus Duke of KENT and Tenuantius Duke of CORNWALL in an attempt to forestall potential trouble. During JULIUS CAESAR's first foray into BRITAIN, Cassivelaunus, Androgeus and Tenuantius fought together and forced the Romans to withdraw, NENNIUS, Cassivelaunus's brother, managing to take the sword from Julius Caesar himself but dying shortly afterwards from the wounds he received.

Two years later Julius Caesar tried to invade Britain again, and was once more repulsed. During the victory celebrations, however, an argument arose over a fatal blow that had been foully struck in a boxing match by a nephew of Androgeus. So severe was the disagreement that civil war broke out. Androgeus betrayed his uncle and brother to Caesar, whom he arranged to help when he landed for the third time. Led by Androgeus, the Romans besieged Cassivelaunus at CANTERBURY. Androgeus now changed colours again and mediated a peace between the two sides before leaving with Caesar to live, and later die, in ROME.

ANFERE
Arthurian

The realm of Queen LAUDAME, who married GAREL.

ANFORTAS
Arthurian

A variant of AMFORTAS that was used by WOLFRAM VON ESCHENBACH in his work *PARSIFAL*.

ANGELICA
Arthurian

The mother of TOM A'LINCOLN by King ARTHUR.

ANGHARAD (GOLDEN-HAND)
Welsh and Arthurian

A maiden who appears in the *MABINOGION* as the lover of PEREDUR (PERCEVAL). At first she refused to become Peredur's lover, so he refused to speak to any Christian until she changed her mind, which she eventually did. It has been suggested that her epithet 'Golden-hand' is indicative of her generous nature.

ANGIS
Arthurian

Simply named as a squire to Sir LANCELOT.

ANGLES
General

A Germanic tribe, originating in the Schleswig-Holstein region of northern Europe, which, along with its neighbours, the SAXONS, invaded BRITAIN during the fifth century AD and settled in East Anglia (hence its name), MERCIA and NORTHUMBRIA.

ANGLESEY
General

A large island situated off the north-west coast of WALES, separated from the mainland by the Menai Straits. The island has a long Celtic history, and is reputed to be the last resting place of BRANWEN, who died there of a broken heart after being brought back from IRELAND, her alleged grave being BEDD BRANWEN close to the banks of the River ALAW.

ANGLIDES
Arthurian

The wife of BALDWIN and mother of ALISANDER THE ORPHAN. Following the murder of Baldwin by his brother King MARK, she raised her son in secret.

ANGLITORA
Arthurian

The daughter of PRESTER JOHN. She eloped with TOM A'LINCOLN, King ARTHUR's son by

ANGELICA, and bore him the BLACK KNIGHT. However, she later abandoned and then subsequently murdered Tom a'Lincoln, his death being avenged by their son, the Black Knight.

ANGLO-SAXON
General

Collective name for the ANGLES and SAXONS, who, along with the JUTES, conquered much of BRITAIN between the fifth and seventh centuries AD. The Angles settled in East Anglia, MERCIA and NORTHUMBRIA; the Saxons in Essex, Sussex and WESSEX; and the Jutes in KENT and southern Hampshire, most notably on the Isle of Wight. The Angles and Saxons came from the Schleswig-Holstein area, and may have united before the invasion, while the Jutes are usually said to have originated in Jutland. There was probably considerable inter-marriage with Romanised Celts, although the latter's language and civilisation almost disappeared.

Following the invasion and conquest, a number of kingdoms were set up, commonly referred to as the Heptarchy ('seven kingdoms'), which survived until the early ninth century, when they were united under the overlordship of Wessex.

ANGLO-SAXON CHRONICLE, THE
British

A history of England from the time of the Roman invasion to the eleventh century. Begun in the ninth century, during the reign of King Alfred, and written as a series of chronicles in Old English, the work was still being executed in the twelfth century.

The *Chronicle*, which is made up from a total of seven different manuscripts, forms a unique record of early English history, and of the development of Old English prose up to its final stages in the year 1154, by which time it had been superseded by Middle English.

ANGUIS-H, -EL
Irish and Arthurian

King of IRELAND and father of ISEULT. His name, a form of OENGHUS, appears to be genuinely Irish, and at the time in question a King Oenghus was believed to have reigned in southern Ireland at Cashel. It appears that his name may be a translational error from the original Gaelic into Old English. The variant form of his name, Anguisel, leads to confusion with the Scottish King AUGUSELUS in the works GEOFFREY OF MONMOUTH.

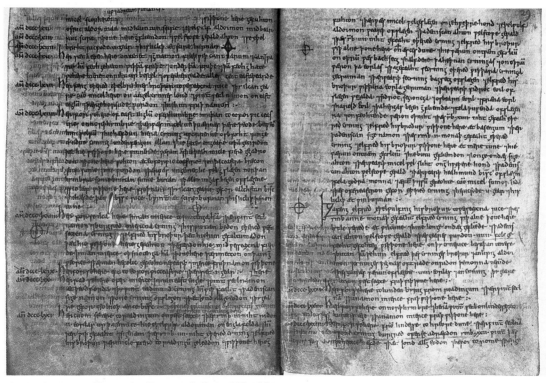

The Anglo-Saxon Chronicle. (By permission of The Master and Fellows of Corpus Christi College, Cambridge)

ANIR

Arthurian

The name applied by NENNIUS to AMR, a son of King ARTHUR, who was killed by his father at ARCHENFIELD and buried under a mound known as LICAT ANIR.

ANJOU

General and Arthurian

An old count-ship and former province in FRANCE that was conquered by VORTIGERN and given to HENGIST. Its first count was KAY, King ARTHUR's seneschal (steward), while in WOLFRAM VON ESCHENBACH its queen was HERZELOYDE. Historically, in 1154, the Count of Anjou became King of ENGLAND as Henry II, but King John lost the territory in 1204. In 1480 the count-ship was annexed to the French crown.

ANKEU

Gaulish

An obscure god of death in BRITTANY. He is described as the 'master of the world', and is sometimes known as the harbinger of death. Ankeu usually appears as a skeleton in a white shroud, driving a cart with squeaky wheels.

ANLAWDD

Arthurian

A variant of AMLAWDD that is found only in the family tree for King ARTHUR put forward by T.W. Rolleston. It appears to be a simple transcriptive error. Rolleston, however, also alters the normal relationships within the genealogy, and makes Anlawdd the father of YSPADDADDEN, CUSTENNIN and GOLEUDDYDD.

ANLUAN

Irish

The son of MAGA and brother of CET, Anluan is sometimes known as HANLON. With his brother he appears in the *SCÉLA MUCCE MAIC DÁ THÓ*, when they are invited by MEDHBHA and AILILL to participate in the hunt for the DONN CUAILNGÈ (brown bull), the story of MAC DÁ THÓ and his boar forming one of the perambulatory stories to this much longer work. At the feast where the honour of carving the boar had been taken by Cet, none dared to challenge him for that privilege. When CONALL CERNACII arrived, however, Cet yielded the honour to him but taunted him by saying that his brother, Anluan, would challenge him. Thereupon Conall Cernach threw the bloody severed head of Anluan onto the table.

ANNA

Arthurian

The sister of King ARTHUR who, according to GEOFFREY OF MONMOUTH, married either LOT of LODONESIA or BUDIC, King of BRITTANY. Other sources say that she was also known as ERMINE and married Budic, while it was her sister who married Lot. It has also been suggested that she may be identified with MORGAN Le Fay, and could possibly have derived from the Celtic goddess ANU, the earth mother.

Margaret of Anjou. (V&A Images/Victoria and Albert Museum)

ANNALES CAMBRIAE

Arthurian

A set of Welsh annals dating from the tenth century that mention the battles of BADON and CAMLANN, stating that both MORDRED and King ARTHUR fell in the latter.

ANNALES TOLEDANOS

Arthurian

Spanish annals that state that the Battle of CAMLANN took place in AD 580, the latest recorded date for this, the final battle fought by King ARTHUR.

ANNALS OF TIGERNACH

Arthurian

Irish annals that state that the Battle of CAMLANN, King ARTHUR's final battle, was fought in AD 541.

ANNOWRE

Arthurian

A sorceress who wanted King ARTHUR to be her lover, but, even though she brought him under her spell, he still refused to comply. Tipped off by NIMUE, LANCELOT rescued Arthur just as Annowre was about to have him killed, and instead it was she who was killed by Lancelot.

ANNW(F)N

Welsh and Arthurian

The name given to the Welsh OTHERWORLD that was ruled over by ARAWN. PWYLL, Lord of DYFED, agreed to spend a year in Annwfn after he had insulted Arawn by driving his hounds away from a stag. During his time in Annwfn, Pwyll disposed of HAFGAN, Arawn's sworn enemy. For the year that Pwyll was to spend in the Otherworld, he and Arawn assumed each other's appearance and each ruled the other's domain. Arawn later sent PRYDERI, Pwyll's son, a herd of swine, animals that had never been heard of, let alone seen before on the earth.

Although usually considered as the Welsh underworld, the domain of the dead and a dark shadowy realm, Annwfn is described in the *MABINOGION* as a recognisable kingdom that appears to have had various regions along the same lines as Hades, the underworld of classical Greek mythology.

The early Welsh poem *PREIDDEU ANNWFN* (*Spoils of Annwfn*) gives perhaps the best description of the realm, although this poem embroiders the traditional view by weaving its story around King ARTHUR's expedition to this Otherworld to capture a magic cauldron. The narrator of this poem is the famous Welsh bard TALIESIN, a member of the group that took part in the expedition.

Sailing overseas in the ship PRYDWEN to reach their goal, the group first came to CAER WYDYR, a glass fort, but could not induce its watchman to talk to them, thus suggesting a land of the silent dead, which is also referred to in the *HISTORIA BRITONUM* of NENNIUS. Arthur and his men next came to CAER FEDDWIDD (the Fort of CAROUSAL) or CAER RIGOR. Here the fountain ran with wine and no one ever knew old age or suffered from any form of illness, thus suggesting an idyll to which most men would hope to pass after their life on earth had come to an end. This land is also sometimes referred to as CAER SIDDI, in which case it is said to be ruled over by ARIANRHOD. From this expedition, which would later seem to have evolved into the Quest for the Holy GRAIL, only seven returned. This final factor would seem to indicate that this story owes its origins to the story concerning the expedition of BENDIGEID VRAN to IRELAND. Taliesin is also named among the survivors of that expedition, which again numbered just seven.

ANSWERER, THE

Irish

A translation of FRAGARACH, the name given to the divine sword owned by LUGH.

ANTHEMIUS

Arthurian

A historical Roman Emperor who ruled between AD 467 and 472. During his battle against EURIC the Visigoth, a large army brought across from ENGLAND by King RIOTHAMUS assisted him.

ANTIKONIE

Arthurian

According to WOLFRAM VON ESCHENBACH, Antikonie was the sister of King VERGULAHT of ASCALUN and the lover of GAWAIN.

ANTONY

Arthurian

In continental romance Antony was an Irish bishop and secretary to MERLIN.

ANTOR

Arthurian

Appearing in French sources as the fosterfather of King ARTHUR, Antor would seem to be simply a variant of ECTOR.

ANU

Irish and Arthurian

The earth mother of Irish mythology who is better known as DANA or DANU, though in this form she would appear to be the origin of ANNA, the sister of King ARTHUR. Many sources dispute the true name of this deity, some saying that Anu was the original name, and Danu the corruption, whilst an equal number argue the opposite. An argument that Anu may be the correct form of the Irish MOTHER GODDESS comes from the fact that the myths tell us that Danu was the daughter of DELBAETH, who was in turn the brother of the DAGHDHA, but, as is usual with matters of this nature, the argument will remain open to conjecture.

ANU, PAPS OF

Irish

A pair of hills in Kerry, southern IRELAND, that resemble a woman's breasts. They derive their name from ANU and are said to be one of the homes of the TUATHA DÉ DANANN.

See also DA CHICH NANANN

AOBH

Irish

A daughter of BODB. She became the wife of LIR in an attempt to resolve Lir's differences with the TUATHA DÉ DANANN after he had been overlooked for the kingship. She bore Lir four children, two sons and two daughters, before she died. Her sister AOIFE became Lir's next wife, but she grew jealous of her stepchildren and changed them into swans.

AODH

Irish

1 According to quite a late tradition, Aodh is mentioned in the genealogy of Saint BRIDE. He is said to be the son of ART and the father of DUGAL the Brown, who was better know as the DAGHDHA.

2 The son of MORNA. He lost an eye in a battle during which he killed CUMHAILL and was thenceforth known as GOLL ('One-Eyed'), the name by which he is usually known.

3 A member of the TUATHA DÉ DANANN whose unnamed wife fell in love with DONN and turned him into a stag when he did not respond to her advances.

AOIFE

Irish

A daughter of BODB and the second wife of LIR. She grew jealous of Lir's four children by his first wife,

her sister AOBH, and during a trip to visit Bodb she turned them into four swans. They were fated to remain in that form for 900 years, after which they would revert to their human form. Bodb turned Aoife into a raven, or 'demon of the air', as a reward for her evil. Later tradition said that she had been turned into a crane, which was killed by MANANNÁN MAC LIR, who then used the skin of the bird to make a bag in which he kept all his treasures.

AONBARR

Irish

Also ENBARR

The horse of MANANNÁN MAC LIR, which was said to be able to travel, like the wind, over both land and sea, while no rider on his back could be killed. Some accounts say that LUGH rode Aonbarr when he came to TARA.

See also AIDED CHLAINNE TUIRENN.

APOLLO

Arthurian

The son of LUCIUS, according to the *PROSE TRISTAN*, which gives the early history of LIONES. Unwittingly he married his own mother, but later married GLORIANDE, by whom he became the father of CANDACES.

APOLLO CUNOMAGLUS

Romano-British

Although this deity, whose name is found only at Nettleton, is a derivation of the classical Roman god Apollo, his epithet, or surname, is Celtic, meaning 'Horned Lord'. This would appear to be an attempt by the Romans to combine the attributes of their own deity with those of the Celtic CERNUNNOS.

APPLES, ISLE OF

Arthurian

The name used by GEOFFREY OF MONMOUTH in his *VITA MERLINI* to refer to AVALON, the paradisiacal land of the dead. The use of this name possibly derives from the Irish EMHAIN ABHLACH, an island that is associated with the Irish god of the sea MANANNÁN MAC LIR and whose name means 'Emhain of the Apple Trees'. Irish tradition makes this island the Isle of ARRAN.

AQUAE SULIS

Romano-British

The Roman name for the city of BATH, whose temples were dedicated to the Romano-Celtic goddess SULIS MINERVA, an amalgam of the Roman Goddess Minerva and the local British deity SULIS.

AQUITAIN(E)
Arthurian
According to GOTTFRIED VON STRASSBURG, the region of south-west FRANCE in which the dwarf MELOT, who spied on TRISTAN and ISEULT for King MARK, lived. However, EILHART VON OBERGE called the dwarf Aquitain rather than the region.

ARANRHOD
Welsh
A variant of ARIANRHOD.

ARAV-IA, -IUS
Welsh and Arthurian
The mountain home of the giant RIENCE (RHITTA), which is better known today as Mount SNOWDON.

ARAWN
Welsh and Arthurian
The King of ANNWFN, the Welsh OTHERWORLD, and thus, by the association of his realm with the land of the dead, god of the dead. PWYLL and Arawn agreed to change places for a year after Pwyll had offended Arawn by driving his hounds away from a stag, the exchange being Pwyll's apology for this insult. During his year in Annwfn, Pwyll killed HAFGAN, the sworn enemy of Arawn, and behaved honourably towards Arawn's wife, for, although he resembled Arawn, Pwyll refused to lie with Arawn's wife even though they shared a bed and she assumed him to be her husband. When Pwyll returned home at the end of the year, he found that Arawn had ruled his realm of DYFED with unprecedented wisdom. Contact between Arawn and Pwyll continued for many years. After Pwyll's death Arawn sent a gift of a herd of swine to PRYDERI, the son of Pwyll, animals that had never even been heard of on earth before, let alone seen. Arawn was alleged to have been defeated by AMAETHON at the mythical Battle of CATH GODEU, although whether he was actually killed – if indeed it is possible to kill the lord of Annwfn – is not made clear.

Later tradition says that King ARTHUR and a band of followers travelled to Arawn's kingdom of Annwfn to capture a magical cauldron. In a Welsh version of GEOFFREY OF MONMOUTH, the name Arawn is used to translate AUGUSELUS, the brother of URIEN, while the *TRIADS (TRIOEDD YNYS PRYDEIN)* also mention an Arawn, this time making him the son of KYNVARCH. In both instances it is the lord of the dead, the ruler of Annwfn, who is the undoubted original.

ARCHENFIELD
Arthurian
The place where AMR, son of King ARTHUR, was killed by his father, and where he was buried under a mound known as LICAT ANIR.

ARCHIER
Arthurian
The name taken by the cannibal King GURGURANT following his conversion to Christianity.

ARCILE
Arthurian
A variant of ARSILE.

ARD-MHAC-LÉINN
Irish
The name used by CÚ CHULAINN, in the cycle of tales that surround that hero, to refer to the UNDER-WORLD, the world to which he will travel after death.

ARD-RIESHIP
Irish
'High Kingship', the position that a King of all IRELAND would assume, his title being ARDRÍ, or 'High King'.

ARD RIGH
Irish
A simple variant of ARDRÍ.

ARDÁN
Arthurian
An uncle of King ARTHUR according to French romance.

ARDÁN
Irish
A son of UISNECH and one of the two brothers of NAOISE, the other being AINNLE, who fled with him and DERDRIU to ALBA. He and his brothers, all of whom had once held positions of importance and favour at the court of CONCHOBAR MAC NESSA, were killed by that King upon their return from exile, even though they had all been promised safe passage by the three emissaries sent by the King to ask them to come back.

ARDRÍ
Irish
'High King', the title assumed by one becoming the King of all IRELAND, and thus attaining the ARD-RIESHIP. This title is, however, sometimes recorded as ARD RIGH.

ARDUINNA

Gaulish

A goddess, possibly of the hunt, or a protectress of wild animals, who is depicted seated on a wild boar.

ARES

Arthurian

The father of DO and grandfather of LORETE and GRIFLET.

AR(F)DERYDD

Welsh and Arthurian

A battle fought *c.* AD 575 for a 'lark's nest' (*sic*) between the British Prince GWENDDOLEU and his cousins GWRGI and PEREDUR. RHYDDERCH HAEL killed Gwenddoleu and MYRDDIN, having fought in the battle, winning a golden torc (a necklace or armband made of twisted metal), lost his reason and became a hermit in the Scottish forest of CELYDDON (SILVA CALEDONIAE or CAT COIT CELIDON). The fact that the battle was for a 'lark's nest' appears to indicate that the fight was actually for ownership of the important harbour of CAERLAVERLOCK, which translates as Fort Lark.

ARGAN

Arthurian

Forced to build a castle for UTHER after the latter, who was in love with his wife, had defeated him.

ARGANTE

Arthurian

An elf and the Queen of AVALON, who, according to LAYAMON, received King ARTHUR after his final battle. Her name, it has been suggested, is a form of the goddess ARIANRHOD.

ARGISTES

Arthurian

According to Italian romance, MERLIN, while still a boy, foretold that Argistes would be hanged, drowned and burned. Later Argistes set fire to Merlin's house, but the flames spread to his own. As he rushed to the well to fetch water to douse the fire, the chain wrapped around his neck and he fell down the well into which people threw burning rafters. Thus Argistes was hanged, drowned and burned, fulfilling Merlin's prophecy.

ARGUS

Arthurian

In the *Y SAINT GRAAL*, the Welsh version of the GRAIL story, Argus is another son of ELAINE, and thus a brother of GALAHAD.

ARGUTH

Arthurian

Simply mentioned as being an ancestor of LOT.

AR(I)ANRHOD

Welsh and Arthurian

An important Celtic goddess who appears as one of the main characters in the *MABINOGION* story of *MATH FAB MATHONWY* (Math, Son of Mathonwy). Arianrhod clearly belongs to a pre-Christian tradition. She is not simply a local or national deity who has been preserved in myth and legend, but is also a stellar figure, a goddess of time, space and energy associated with the observation of a particular group of star. Her stellar role is supported by the fact that in Welsh the constellation of corona borealis is known as CAER ARIANRHOD, 'Arianrhod's Castle', although this name is also applied to the aurora borealis, the northern lights. Her name means 'queen of the wheel', 'silver wheel' or 'high fruitful mother', which has led to her being referred to as the goddess of the starry wheel.

The sister of GWYDION FAB DÔN, she was put forward by her brother for the position of foot-holder (a court post held by a virgin) to King MATH FAB MATHONWY. She failed the rite of stepping over the wand to confirm her virginity when two bundles fell from her. One contained a golden-haired baby who was christened DYLAN and who immediately set forth for the sea, whose nature he assumed, thenceforth being known as DYLAN EIL TON.

The second bundle was also a baby boy. Gwydion fab Dôn quickly concealed him in a chest and later adopted him. Four years passed before Gwydion fab Dôn showed the boy to her mother, but, embarrassed by the reminder of her shame, Arianrhod cursed the boy, saying that he should have no name until she herself gave him one, something she had no intention of doing. Gwydion fab Dôn evaded this curse by disguising both himself and the boy and tricking his sister into naming her son LLEU LLAW GYFFES. Furious at the trick, for Gwydion fab Dôn could not resist taunting his sister with the fact that she had indeed named her son, Arianrhod again cursed the boy, saying that he would never bear arms until she herself bestowed them upon him. Again her brother found a way around this curse, this time by magically laying siege to her castle, Caer Arianrhod, on ANGLESEY. In her horror at being attacked she hurriedly gave weapons to her son and begged him to protect her, although, as he was once more in disguise, there was no way she could know his true identity. As soon as she gave the weapons to her son, the forces attacking her castle disappeared.

Once more Gwydion fab Dôn could not resist taunting his sister, so Arianrhod cursed the unfortunate Lleu Llaw Gyffes for a third time, this time saying that he should never marry a mortal woman. This final curse was again overcome by Gwydion fab Dôn, although this time he needed the help of the magician Math fab Mathonwy. Together they manufactured Lleu Llaw Gyffes a wife from the flowers of oak, broom and meadowsweet and called her BLODEUWEDD ('Flower Face').

Even though the rationalisation and extension of the mythology of Arianrhod is confused, it cannot disguise her true nature as a goddess. The theme of twin brothers magically borne by a virgin, or, in the case of Arianrhod, one who claimed to be a virgin, is repeated in various forms throughout Celtic mythology and folklore. It also resonates throughout world mythology and into Christianity. Arianrhod is the ruler of CAER SIDDI, a magical realm in the north, although later poetic works, such as the *PREIDDEU ANNWFN*, place this realm within the OTHERWORLD, ANNWFN.

Her association with Arthurian legend is confined to the fact that she is described as the ruler of CAER SIDDI, an idyllic realm, to which King ARTHUR and his party were said to have travelled during their expedition to the OTHERWORLD to capture a magical cauldron. It has also been suggested that her name gave rise to ARGANTE, the elfin Queen of AVALON.

The medieval MYRDDIN texts use the Greek goddess Ariadne to suggest a connection with Arianrhod. This is no mere coincidence, for their names, and even their attributes, are remarkably similar, for Ariadne is an earth goddess who also has stellar significance.

ARIES
Arthurian
According to Sir Thomas MALORY, Aries was a cowherd who raised TOR, the illegitimate son of King PELLINORE and his wife, believing him to be his own son. However, French romance makes Aries a king and the real father of Tor.

ARIMATHEA, JOSEPH OF
See JOSEPH OF ARIMATHEA

ARIOSTO, LUDOVICO
Arthurian
Italian poet (1474–1533), born in Reggio Emilia. Originally intending to be a lawyer, he abandoned that in favour of poetry. In 1503 he entered the court of the Cardinal Ippolito d'ESTE at Ferrara, and during the next ten years produced his *ORLANDO FURIOSO* (1516), the ROLAND epic that forms a continuation of BOIARDO's *ORLANDO INNAMORATO*. Over the next sixteen years Ariosto expanded his *Orlando Furioso*, until, in 1532, it was published in the form in which it still exists today. He died the following year and was buried in the church of San Benedetto, at Ferrara, where a magnificent monument marks his last resting place.

ARLECCHINO
Arthurian
The Italian name under which HELLEKIN appeared as the HARLEQUIN of the *Commedia dell'arte*.

ARMENIA
Arthurian
During the traditional Arthurian period, either Persian representatives or leaders in revolt against Persia ruled this country. However, the thirteenth-century French romance *FLORIANT ET FLORETE* makes King TURCANS the ruler of Armenia during King ARTHUR's time.

ARMES PRYDEIN
Welsh and Arthurian
The Prophecy of Britain, a heroic tenth-century Welsh poem that was probably written between AD 900 and 930. Unique in being the first work to refer to the magician MYRDDIN (MERLIN), the *Armes Prydein* can be regarded as a work of propaganda, for it calls upon the British to unite against the SAXON invaders. It foretells that the last British King, CADWALLADER, son of CADWALLON, will rise to lead a great army, including the Men of Dublin, the Irish Gaels and the Men of CORNWALL and STRATHCLYDE, and drive the Saxons back into the sea from whence they came.

ARMORICA
Gaulish
An ancient name for the region of GAUL that is today known as BRITTANY.

ARNIVE
Arthurian
According to WOLFRAM VON ESCHENBACH, Arnive was the mother of King ARTHUR, who was rescued from KLINGSOR by GAWAIN.

ARON
Arthurian
Simply named as one of the TWENTY-FOUR KNIGHTS of King ARTHUR's court.

ARONDIEL

Arthurian

The horse of the ploughboy FERGUS, who aspired to become a knight and married GALIENE, the Lady of LOTHIAN, thus fulfilling his ambition.

ARRAN, ISLE OF

Irish and Arthurian

In Irish mythology, the Isle of Arran, situated in the Firth of Forth, SCOTLAND, is usually identified with the paradisiacal island of EMHAIN ABHLACH ('Emhain of the Apple Trees'), an island associated with the Irish Sea god MANANNÁN MAN LIR. In his *VITA MERLINI*, GEOFFREY OF MONMOUTH refers to AVALON as the Isle of APPLES, and this would seem to suggest that his naming of the idyllic land was taken from earlier Celtic tradition.

ARSILE

Arthurian

Also ARCILE

One of the companions of MORGAN Le Fay, along with MAGLORE, according to the thirteenth-century French romance *li jus Aden*.

ART (AOINFHEAR)

Irish and Arthurian

The son of CONN CÉTCHATHLACH, a legendary king who was thought to have reigned in prehistoric times and might have his origins in a forgotten deity. A late genealogy of Saint BRIDE supports this relationship, saying that Art (here without his epithet) was the son of CONN and the father of AODH, which in turn would make him the grandfather of the DAGHDHA, who is called DUGAL the Brown in the genealogy. A later Irish romance, the *CAITHRÉIM CONGHAIL CLÁIRINGNIGH*, develops the character of Art Aoinfhear and makes him son of King ARTHUR.

ARTAI-OS, -US

Romano-British

A deity of unknown characteristics and attributes who, some suggest, was the original of King ARTHUR, although this would appear to be based on etymology alone. In GAUL Artaios was equated with Mercury, which has led some to speculate that Artaios is simply a derivation of ARTIO.

ARTEGALL

Arthurian

Also ARTGUALCHAR

Described as an Earl or Count of Guarensis (Warwick), Artegall appears in GEOFFREY OF MONMOUTH as ARTGUALCHAR. Other sources make him a KNIGHT OF THE ROUND TABLE and the 1st Earl of Warwick, while SPENSER says that he was the son of King CADOR of CORNWALL, married BRITOMART, the daughter of King RIENCE, and bore the arms of Achilles.

ARTGUALCHAR

Arthurian

The name under which ARTEGALL appears in GEOFFREY OF MONMOUTH.

ARTHGEN

Gaulish

Also ARTOGENUS

A name known from the Roman period that simply means 'son of the bear', or perhaps 'son of the bear god'.

ARTHOUR AND MERLIN

Arthurian

An obscure fourteenth-century English poem whose author remains unknown.

ARTHUR

Arthurian

Semi-legendary, mythologised King of BRITAIN whose name is perhaps a form of *Artorius*, a Roman *gens* name, though it might also be Celtic in origin, coming from *artos viros* (bear man). Historically he was perhaps a fifth- or sixth-century chieftain or general, though he is not mentioned by any contemporary historian. One argument says that he is to be identified with the Celtic king RIOTHAMUS, but legend would seem to suggest that he is, rather, a composite figure, combining the attributes and achievements of more than one person. In Europe he has connections with the Serbian Prince Marco and the Russian Ilya Musomyets.

The sixth-century monk GILDAS records a great British victory over the pagan SAXONS at Mount BADON (possibly BADBURY HILL in Devon, BADBURY RINGS in Dorset, somewhere on the north Wiltshire Downs, or a hill near BATH), a battle that later came to be associated with the name of King Arthur, and his most important victory. There are six possible sites for this battle based on place-names alone. Most people, however, think of Arthur as the idealised chivalrous knight described by Sir Thomas MALORY in *LE MORTE D'ARTHUR* (1470). By the ninth century the inflation of Arthur into a superhuman being was well under way, for a description by NENNIUS says of

King Arthur and the strange mantle that is sometimes erroneously cited as one of the Thirteen Treasures of Britain. (Aubrey Beardsley, 1893–4/Mary Evans Picture Library)

the Battle of Mount BADON that '960 of the enemy fell in a single attack by Arthur', whom he calls *dux bellorum* (leader of troops). Records kept in a Welsh monastery from about the same period refer to the victory at Mount Badon (now thought to have been fought *c.* AD 490, though the *Easter Annals*, a fifth-century tract, record it as having occurred *c.* AD 516), and to Arthur's death along with MORDRED at the Battle of CAMLANN. These would seem to establish Arthur as the 'leader of battles' for the British kings, a statement that is likely to have been factual. Early records serve to tell us very little extra, except that many of these sources are now considered suspect, and a more contemporary view is that Arthur was a professional soldier in service to the British kings after the Roman occupation had come to an end.

Where he actually functioned is also subject to much controversy. Different opinions place him as a leader in the south-west, the north, in WALES, or throughout Britain. The truth of the matter is that, as the evidence stands, we cannot be certain. Even the battles attributed to him do not help in deciding this matter, for many of those are suspect as well.

His family tree is just as dubious as both his role and his area of operation. Early Celtic writings make him the cousin of CULHWCH, whom he helped to win the hand of OLWEN, the daughter of the chief giant YSPADDADDEN. However, the first complete, coherent narrative of the life of King Arthur appears in the fanciful eleventh-century *HISTORIA REGUM BRITANNIAE* (*History of the Kings of Britain*) by the historian GEOFFREY OF MONMOUTH. This work combined the works of Nennius and Welsh folklore to give the Arthurian legends known today, along with many of the major characters and events.

Arthur's story is as follows.

King UTHER Pendragon became infatuated with IGRAINE, the wife of Duke GORLOIS of CORNWALL, who had been waging a long war against the King. While Gorlois was besieged by Uther in Castle TERRABIL, Igraine was in the castle at TINTAGEL, but Uther could take no part in the fighting because he was sick with love for Igraine. One of his men sought out the renowned wizard MERLIN, who said he would help if the King would reward him with whatever he desired. Merlin required that any child born from their magical union be delivered to him to raise, though Sir Thomas Malory, in the fifteenth century, says the requirement was that the child should be delivered to ECTOR. Most commentators agree that Ector fostered the child.

Merlin rode to Uther's pavilion, where the King agreed to his terms, and with the aid of his magic Merlin so altered the King's appearance that, when Uther came to her in the castle at Tintagel, Igraine believed him to be her husband. That very night, while the disguised King lay with Igraine, Gorlois was killed in battle with Uther's troops. When she heard of her husband's death, Igraine wondered who the knight who had lain with her might have been. Even when she assented to marriage with Uther, to unite their two houses, he did not tell her. Their son, conceived on that night, was Arthur, brother to MORGAN Le Fay, and, as Uther had agreed, Merlin came to take the baby away, reassuring the father that he would be well cared for.

Uther was unable to spend a long and happy life with Igraine, for within two years he had fallen sick and died, to the great sorrow of Igraine, who had learned to love him. The rule of the kingdom fell into jeopardy, for there was no known heir. Many lords laid claim to the throne, and fought bitterly for the right to reign, but none could take the kingdom by just cause.

When Arthur was fifteen he was chosen as king. The more romantic legends say the choice was made by his drawing the magical sword EXCALIBUR from a stone, something that no other had been able to achieve, and on this sword were engraved the words 'Whosoever shall draw this sword from the stone is the true-born king of all England'. Many maintain that this sword had been placed in the stone by Merlin, who 'arranged' that Arthur should be the only person capable of drawing it out, and that the sword was not Excalibur, but a sword that received no special name. Others say Merlin or Ector brought him to London, where he won the kingship in a tournament. Still others combine both events, saying that Arthur drew the sword from the stone *en route* to the tournament.

The crowning of King Arthur resulted in a rebellion by eleven rulers that Arthur successfully put down. He then led an army against the Saxons, defeating their leader COLGRIN and a mixed force of Saxons, Scots and PICTS at the River DOUGLAS. Colgrin took refuge in YORK and Arthur laid siege, but he was obliged to abandon that siege and return to London. Now he sought the aid of HOEL, King of BRITTANY, his cousin (or possibly his nephew), who duly landed at SOUTHAMPTON with a great army. Together they defeated the Saxons at LINCOLN, at CELIDON WOOD and at BATH. They put down the Scots, Picts and Irish in Moray, and toured Loch Lomond. Next they raised the siege of York, and Arthur restored that city to its former glory, returning their lands to the three dispossessed Yorkist princes, LOT, URIAN and AUGUSELUS.

Having now restored the entire kingdom, Arthur took as his wife the most beautiful woman in all Britain, GUINEVERE, the daughter of King LEODEGRANCE or the ward of Duke CADOR, and a lady of noble Roman descent. Having married, Arthur sailed to IRELAND, defeated its King, GILMAURIUS, and conquered the whole island. Hearing of his great might and prowess in battle, DOLDAVIUS and GUNPHAR, the Kings of Gotland and the ORKNEYS respectively, came to pay him homage. Now Arthur began to invite the most distinguished men of other lands to join his court, and the fame of his knights spread to the ends of the earth.

The romances placed his court at CAMELOT, which has been variously identified, but the name is simply the invention of twelfth-century poets. Since at least 1540, Camelot has been identified with CADBURY CASTLE in Somerset. Archaeological excavation, however, shows that Cadbury Castle might instead have been the strong post or fortified rallying point that the historical Arthur needed to defend Britain against the Saxons. The hill-fort had been first built *c.* 500 BC, but was refortified with a stone and timber rampart and gates that can be dated between AD 460 and 540, the years during which Arthur is now thought to have flourished. Foundations of a large hall have been discovered, and the site, some eighteen acres in area, would have been large enough to accommodate an army of 1,000 men. Early Welsh traditions named Arthur's court as CELLIWIG, and this is probably to be identified with KILLIBURY, or with CAERLEON-ON-USK. Another tradition associated Arthur with CASTLE-AN-DINAS near Saint Columb, the largest Celtic hill-fort in Cornwall, which was also known as the seat of Cornish kings after Arthur's time.

His next expedition was to conquer Europe, beginning with NORWAY, which he duly vanquished and then gave to Lot. Sailing then to GAUL, he defeated and killed the Tribune FROLLO and took Paris. Within nine years and with the aid of HOEL, Arthur had conquered all of Gaul and, holding court in Paris, he established the government of that kingdom on a legal footing.

Returning to Britain, Arthur decided to hold a plenary court at Whitsun at the CITY OF THE LEGIONS (Caerleon-on-Usk or CHESTER), and to this court came representatives from all of Europe.

Now Arthur was summoned to Rome by LUCIUS HIBERIUS to answer the charge of having attacked the empire, and, with 183,000 men, Arthur crossed to FRANCE and marched southwards. *En route* he had a vision of a dragon fighting and conquering a bear, and decided that this represented his coming conflict with the Emperor, though some of his company interpreted it as meaning he would fight and overcome a giant. Indeed, at the Mont SAINT MICHEL, Arthur did defeat and kill a giant. He also routed the imperial Roman troops at Saussy, and was about to march on Rome when he received news that his nephew Mordred, son of Lot, whom he had left as his regent in Britain, had usurped the throne and taken Queen Guinevere as his mistress. Some accounts, however, say that Arthur successfully defeated Lucius Hiberius and became emperor himself.

The later romances treat this period in a different manner, and include the most romantic knight of them all, Sir LANCELOT, his adultery with QUEEN GUINEVERE, and the quest for the HOLY GRAIL.

Having achieved the quest for the Holy GRAIL, those knights who survived returned to Arthur's court and to the company of the ROUND TABLE. For a while it seemed as if the kingdom would be restored to its former glory, but Lancelot soon forgot the repentance and vows made on the holy quest, and began to resort to Queen Guinevere again. Arthur was told of the affair, but refused to believe it unless Lancelot and his Queen could be caught together.

AGRAVAIN and Mordred lay in wait with twelve other knights and succeeded in trapping Lancelot in the Queen's chamber. Even though Lancelot was unarmed, he managed to fight his way free, killing all who had sought to trap him, except Mordred, who fled to the King. Guinevere was sentenced to be burned at the stake, but Lancelot rescued her, and the pair left LOGRES for Lancelot's home in France. There is now some inconsistency in the romances, for even though Guinevere was now supposed to be in France the next part of the romances puts her back in Logres, or England. In these cases, Guinevere was said to have been taken to JOYOUS GARD, Lancelot's castle, which has been identified with BAMBURGH Castle in NORTHUMBERLAND.

Arthur, who had earlier loved Lancelot, wished to go to France and compel him to return in peace, but, upon taking the counsel of GAWAIN, who desired revenge, for Lancelot had slain his brethren in his escape, was persuaded that this would be folly, and so Arthur left for France, taking a vast army with him.

Leaving Sir Mordred as his regent, to rule in his absence, for Mordred was his son (the result of an unwitting incestuous affair between Arthur and his sister MORGAUSE, thus making Mordred his nephew as well), and placing Queen Guinevere under Mordred's governance, Arthur set sail for France. While he was waging war there, Mordred made mischief by forging letters that he said had been sent from France. They told of Arthur's death in battle, and as a result he had himself crowned king at CANTERBURY.

Next Mordred announced that he was to marry Guinevere, and, though the Queen still mourned Arthur, she consented. Trusting her, Mordred gave Guinevere permission to travel to London to buy what she would need for their wedding. Arriving in London, she went straight to the Tower of London, which she stocked for a long siege. News of these events reached Arthur, and he recalled his troops.

Hurrying back, Arthur landed at RICH-BOROUGH, where he fought and defeated Mordred. At the Battle of WINCHESTER he defeated him again (the romances make this the site of GAWAIN's death), and then pursued him to the River Camlann in Cornwall, though the romances make this SALISBURY PLAIN, the final battle to be fought on the day after the Trinity Sunday. Cornish legend associates the Battle of Camlann with SLAUGHTERBRIDGE, where the river ran crimson with the blood of slain warriors.

In a dream, the spirit of Gawain appeared to Arthur and told him that, if he were to fight the following day, both he and Mordred would be slain. However, if he waited, Sir Lancelot and all his noble knights would come to his aid within the month. Waking, Arthur called his two most trusted knights, Sir BEDIVERE, and Sir LUCAN, and charged them with making a truce with Mordred. All was agreed, and each side, with just fourteen knights each present, met on the field of combat to sign the treaty.

Just then an adder slithered from a bush and bit one of the knights in the foot. As he drew his sword to kill the snake, the opposing armies saw the sword, glinting in the sunlight, and, amidst shouts of treachery, the battle began.

Mordred was slain by Arthur, but the King was also mortally wounded before the battle came to an end. Calling Sir Bedivere, he told that knight to take his enchanted sword, Excalibur, and throw it into a nearby lake. Bedivere took the sword, but hid it behind a tree before returning to Arthur to tell him that his command had been carried out. However, when Arthur asked Bedivere what he had seen, Bedivere answered that he had seen nothing but waves and wind on the water. Immediately Arthur knew he was lying, and charged Bedivere to return to the lake and carry out his command. This time Bedivere hurled the sword out over the lake, and as it fell towards the water a hand rose and caught the sword. Returning to the King, he told them what he had seen. Cornish legend says that Sir Bedivere was sent to DOZMARY POOL on Dartmoor, some six miles from Slaughterbridge, the traditional Cornish location for Camlann, but this is just one of the many locations associated with the returning of Excalibur to the LADY OF THE LAKE.

Arthur, finally satisfied that his orders had been carried out, told Bedivere to take him down to the lake, where a barge drew alongside. In the barge were a number of fair ladies, all with black hoods, who wept as they saw Arthur. Bedivere laid the weak King in the barge, which then sailed away from the site of the battle to the Isle of AVALON, AVALLACH or the vale of AVILION, so that his wounds might heal. In the imagination of Alfred, Lord Tennyson, the dying Arthur was carried down to the narrow harbour of BOSCASTLE to be borne away on the funeral barge to Avalon. Before leaving, the King gave the crown to his cousin CONSTANTINE, son of Cador, Duke of Cornwall. This was reputed to be in the year AD 542.

According to Geoffrey of Monmouth, Guinevere, following Arthur's death, fled to the abbey at AMESBURY, where she took the veil and finally became the abbess. After her death, her body was taken to GLASTONBURY by Sir Lancelot to be buried beside that of her husband.

The belief that Arthur would return in the hour of Britain's greatest need and inaugurate a golden age was well established in both England and France by the early part of the twelfth century, and persisted until the latter part of the nineteenth century, although accounts of how and where the King would reappear varied considerably. In his *VITA MERLINI*, Geoffrey of Monmouth had called Avalon the Isle of APPLES, thus suggesting an otherworldly realm, but some fifty years later, in 1190 or 1191, Avalon had become identified with Glastonbury, where Arthur's body, and that of Guinevere, were said to have been exhumed, the inscription *Hic jacet Arthurus, rex quondam, rex futurus* (Here lies Arthur, king that was, king that shall be) summing up the flavour of his legendary life and death. All trace of the tombs mysteriously disappeared straight afterwards, but the claim attracted widespread interest at the time when the stories of King Arthur were beginning to spread beyond purely Welsh legend. Elsewhere he is said to lie sleeping at Cadbury Castle in Somerset, in a cave on CRAIG-Y-DINAS near SNOWDON in WALES, or even in a cave on Mount ETNA, this last one probably deriving from the Norman occupation of Sicily.

The Passing of Arthur *by Julia Margaret Cameron.* (© Hulton-Deutsch Collection/Corbis)

So tenacious were the Cornish in their belief that Arthur would one day come again to rescue them from bondage that in 1177 there was a riot in Bodmin church between local men and some visiting French monks, one of whom had scoffed at such an article of faith. His spirit was believed to fly over the Cornish cliffs in the form of the Cornish CHOUGH – a bird now extinct in the country except for one or two pairs held in captivity.

The stories of King Arthur and his gallant knights have become some of the most potent of all European myths and legends, forming the basis of innumerable stories, poems, plays and operas, not only in Britain and France, but also particularly in GERMANY, as well as occurring in most other Western European countries. The early development of these tales resulted from the cross-fertilization of Celtic and Christian material in which the King's company of knights becomes the Christian order of the Round Table, which is dedicated to chivalry and the quest for the Holy Grail.

The early twelfth-century writer WACE first refers to the famous Round Table in the *ROMAN DE BRUT*. This work was written in French, but was quickly translated and expanded by LAYAMON in his *BRUT*, written between 1189 and 1199.

According to Wace, the barons quarrelled over precedence, so King Arthur made the Round Table. Layamon develops this theme by saying that the quarrel arose during a Christmas feast, and resulted in the death of several men. He goes on to tell that Arthur visited Cornwall a short while afterwards, and there he met a foreign carpenter who had heard of the disagreement, and offered to make Arthur a portable table at which 1,600 could sit without any one having precedence over another. Arthur immediately commissioned the piece, which was finished in just six weeks.

Later versions of the story credit Merlin with the invention and building of the Round Table, while some Anglo-French romances make the table, which now seats just 150, the gift of Arthur's father-in-law, King Leodegrance. One seat at this table, the SIEGE PERILOUS, or Seat of Danger, was reserved for the knight who was to seek and achieve the Holy Grail, the dish from which Jesus was said to have eaten lamb at the Last Supper, and which had then been used to catch drops of Christ's blood as he hung, dying, on the Cross.

The legend held that the Holy Grail had been brought to England by Jesus' uncle, JOSEPH OF ARIMATHEA, who had established a church at Glastonbury. His descendants, the FISHER KINGS, guarded the Holy Grail within the confines of their castle CARBONEK, where it was hidden away from prying eyes. Associated with the Holy Grail was a bleeding lance that was sometimes identified with the LANCE OF LONGINUS. This was the lance said to have been used by the centurion to pierce Jesus' side as he hung on the Cross (John 19:34).

Later versions of the story of the Holy Grail make it the cup from which Jesus and his disciples drank at the Last Supper (Matthew 26:27–28), though the association of the bleeding lance remains unaltered. This cup brought about many miracles when it was carried to Britain by Joseph of Arimathea, and was said to have fed the saint and his followers when they were imprisoned. Subsequently the Holy Grail disappeared, thenceforth to be seen only by those few who were 'pure in heart' – a condition medieval Christian writers define as 'celibate'. Thus the magical dish of Celtic tradition becomes the symbolic cup of the Eucharist, and paganism becomes Christianity.

In CHRÉTIEN DE TROYES's early version of the myth of the Holy Grail, the mysterious holy vessel is housed in the GRAIL CASTLE, where a GRAIL KEEPER guards it. The wounded Fisher King of the castle has been maimed by a wound through his thighs (*sic*), and is sustained only by a magical dish. As a result the land has become infertile and will revive only if the King can be healed, but this will happen only if there is a knight brave enough to face and conquer all the dangers of the perilous journey to the Grail Castle, and then still be wise enough to ask a certain question that will immediately break the spell under which the Fisher King and the land are held. Some commentators omit the Fisher King and rather connect the story with Arthur himself. In these instances it is the King who has lost the will to survive, following the discovery of Guinevere's adultery with Lancelot, and, as the King and the land are inexorably connected, the land becomes infertile. Only the discovery of the Holy Grail can restore health and prosperity to both King and country.

This curious tale appears to derive from an ancient fertility rite, and although one early writer derives the Fisher King's name from the fish symbol or Christ, it also has connections with the god of the sea, who in Celtic myth is a king of the mysterious OTHERWORLD to which selected heroes journey. The Welsh *PREIDDEU ANNWFN* describes one such journey, in which King Arthur travels to this mysterious land in search of a magical cauldron.

In the later medieval legends of King Arthur, the quest for the Holy Grail is undertaken by Sir Lancelot of the Lake, Sir GALAHAD, Sir PERCEVAL and Sir BORS.

Possibly the most mysterious aspect of Arthur's reign is his relationship with Morgan Le Fay. In Malory she is made his sister, but Geoffrey of Monmouth seems to know nothing of their kinship, nor does he, interestingly, mention any enmity between them. This would therefore appear to be a later development of the romances. One possible explanation is that Morgan Le Fay was originally Arthur's lover, later being represented as his sister. It is, however, generally accepted that her enmity towards Arthur springs from the fact he killed her father, Gorlois, which would of course make it impossible for her to have been his sister. Arthur was also said by the different sources to have had many children, including the sons LOHOLT, LLACHEU, BORRE, ARTHUR THE LITTLE, MORDRED, ROWLAND, GWYDRE, AMR, ADELUF, MORGAN THE RED, ILINOT and PATRICK THE RED and the daughters MELORA, ELLEN and GYNETH.

Places linked with both the historical and the legendary Arthur are widespread throughout Britain, though most of the names connected with Arthur, King MARK and TRISTAN have no genuine historical significance. All they do is show a popular habit of naming ancient ruins after long-dead heroes. However, Cadbury Castle and MOTE OF MARK have both produced pottery that dates from the correct period, c. AD 500, thus indicating that they may have some connections with the historical chieftain who became the most potent of all British, and indeed European, legendary figures. However, Arthur remains an enigmatic figure whose story is shrouded in such a tangle of history, myth and folklore that the truth will probably never be known.

ARTHUR AND GORLAGON

Arthurian

A thirteenth-century Latin work that notably features a werewolf.

ARTHUR OF BRITTANY

Arthurian

A descendant of LANCELOT and the hero of a romance in which he seeks the hand of FLORENCE, the daughter of the King of SORLOIS, a place now to be found in modern Iraq.

ARTHUR OF DÁL RIADA

Irish and Arthurian

The son of AEDÁN MAC GABRÁIN, the King of DÁL RIADA. Although he lived somewhat later than the traditional dates ascribed to ARTHUR, it has been argued that he is the historical character around whom the myths and romances have been woven. This Arthur is said to have fallen in a battle against the forces of Aethelfrith, his death allegedly being foretold to his father by Saint COLUMBA.

ARTHUR THE LITTLE

Arthurian

According to the *PROSE TRISTAN*, the illegitimate son of ARTHUR following the rape of his mother by Arthur. He was said to have been a supporter of Arthur against both his SAXON and his Cornish foes, and to have been a quester in the search for the Holy GRAIL.

ARTHUR'S BATTLES

Arthurian

NENNIUS presents us with a list of twelve battles in which ARTHUR was said to have led the British forces against the SAXONS. There is no certainty that any of the battles was actually associated with Arthur, but Nennius lists them as follows.

1 At the mouth of the River GLEIN. There are two English rivers having this name and either might be considered as the site.

2–5 The River DOUGLAS in LINNIUS.

6 On the River BASSUS.

7 At CAT COIT CELIDON, or CELYDDON, in the north, the region being known in Latin as *Silva Caledonia* (Wood of Scotland). Some sources, however, locate this particular battle at CELIDON WOOD, which, though sometimes still located in SCOTLAND, is usually identified with a wood to the north of LINCOLN.

8 At GUINNION.

9 At the CITY OF THE LEGIONS, identified as either CHESTER (called *Urbs Legionis* in Latin) or CAERLEON-ON-USK.

10 At the River Tribuit.

11 At Mount AGNED, for which High ROCHESTER has been suggested. One tenth-century manuscript calls this place BREGUOIN, but there seems to be confusion here with a victory elsewhere ascribed to URIEN of RHEGED.

12 BADON.

ARTHUR'S CAVE

Arthurian

There are a number of caves associated with King ARTHUR. One is located on the Isle of Anglesey, where Arthur was said to have sheltered during his battles with the Irish. His treasure was believed to have been hidden in a cromlech, surrounded by stones, that once stood there, and was supposedly guarded by supernatural creatures. Another is located at CRAIG-Y-DINAS and yet another at ALDERLEY EDGE.

ARTHUR'S INSIGNIA
Arthurian
Nennius says that ARTHUR carried an image of the Virgin Mary on his shoulders during the Battle of GUINNION. The Church of Saint Mary at Wedale at Stow in SCOTLAND once held what were believed to have been fragments of the image of Saint Mary that Arthur wore. The *ANNALES CAMBRIAE* claim that Arthur instead carried the Cross on his shoulders at BADON.

ARTHUR'S O'ON
Arthurian
A Roman temple near FALKIRK, SCOTLAND, that dated from the second century AD. It was destroyed in 1743, but the dovecote at nearby Penicuick House was built as a replica of it. It has been argued that the temple was used by ARTHUR and was the original of the ROUND TABLE.

ARTHUR'S OVEN
Arthurian
Although its location cannot be identified with certainty, this feature undoubtedly lay to the west of Exeter, King Oven on Dartmoor being suggested as a possible site. In 1113 some French priests were reported to have been shown it.

ARTHUR'S QUOIT
Arthurian
ARTHUR was alleged to have thrown a great number of quoits in different parts of the country. Two notable examples are CARREG COETAN ARTHUR, a cromlech near Newport, GWENT, and the LLIGWY CROMLECH near Moelfre on the east side of Anglesey, GWYNEDD.

ARTHUR'S SEAT
Arthurian
A volcanic plug 823 feet high, in east EDINBURGH, SCOTLAND, that was, according to legend, the place where ARTHUR watched his army defeat the PICTS. Another such rock exists in WALES.

ARTHUR'S STONE
Arthurian
There are six features known throughout BRITAIN and WALES as Arthur's Stone. The two best known are given below. The others have been omitted as there seems to be little or no legend attached to them, and they would appear to have been named Arthur's Stone for no particular reason relevant to King ARTHUR.

(1) A stone at CEFN-Y-BRYN, Gower, WALES. On the way to his final battle at CAMLANN, Arthur felt a pebble in his boot. Taking it out he flung it into the distance, and it landed seven miles away at Cefn-y-Bryn. In fact this relic is an ancient burial chamber with four stones supporting a millstone-grit capstone, making it a prominent feature on the ridge. The huge capstone is thought to weigh about 25 tons, and has been partly split, either by King Arthur with EXCALIBUR or by Saint DAVID, who wished to prove that it was not a sacred stone.

At midnight on nights of the full moon, maidens from the Swansea area used to place cakes made of barley meal and honey, wetted with milk and well kneaded, on the stone. Then, on hands and knees, the maidens would crawl three times around the stone, this ritual being carried out to test the fidelity of their lovers. If the young men were faithful, they would come to the stone. If they did not arrive, the girls regarded this as a sign of their fickleness, or their intention never to marry.

Below the stone lies a spring called FYFNNON FAWR that is supposed to run according to the ebb and flow of the tide. The water used to be drunk from the palm of one hand while a wish was made. On nights with a full moon a ghostly figure wearing shining armour emerges from under the stone and proceeds to Llanrhidian. Those who have seen this mysterious spectral figure claim that it is King Arthur.

(2) A stone at Dorstone, Herefordshire, from which Arthur was alleged to have drawn EXCALIBUR. The flaw in this legend is that it was not Excalibur that Arthur drew from the stone, but some other unnamed sword. The stone is also said to cover the burial place of King Arthur, or to mark the burial place of a king defeated by Arthur.

ARTHUR'S TABLE
Arthurian
The name given to two prominent features in Clwyd, WALES. One is a circle of twenty-four indentations in a rock that is said to represent ARTHUR's knights at a table (cf. TWENTY-FOUR KNIGHTS), and the other is a barrow at Llanfair Dyffyn Ceiriog.

ARTHUR'S TOR
Arthurian
An earthwork in Country Durham that is said to contain treasures that are guarded by the ghosts of ARTHUR's warriors.

ARTHURET, BATTLE OF
Welsh and Arthurian
The Latinised form of the Welsh word ARFDERYDD.

ARTHURS, SUCCESSION OF
Arthurian

In the book *Men among Mankind* by B. Le Poer Trench (1962), an argument is put forward that there was a series of Arthurs, hereditary priests of the GREAT GODDESS, and that the last of these was identical with the ARTHUR of legend, accepting the identification of Arthur with ARVIRAGUS as proposed by J. Whitehead.

ARTIO
Gaulish

The goddess of the bear cult who was worshipped by the continental Celts in the area of present-day Berne, Switzerland. A figurine of a goddess feeding a bear was found at Berne ('bear-city'), the inscription on the box reading *Deai Artioni Licinia Sabinilla* (Licinia Sabinilla [dedicated this] to the goddess Artio). The box pedestal has a slit in it through which coins could be dropped in offering. She appears to bear a striking resemblance to the classical Greek goddess Artemis with whom she shares the ability to change into a bear at will, and has a counterpart in ANDARTA.

ARTOGENUS
Gaulish
See ARTHGEN

ARVIRAGUS
British and Arthurian

An historical King of BRITAIN who, according to GEOFFREY OF MONMOUTH, succeeded his brother GUIDERIUS, who had been killed during the Roman invasion led by CLAUDIUS in AD 43. Peace was established between Claudius and Arviragus when the latter married GENVISSA, Claudius's daughter, on the banks of the River SEVERN where Arviragus and Claudius jointly founded the city of Gloucester. Arviragus later revolted against the Roman oppression, but peace was once more restored through the offices of Genvissa.

Other sources name Arviragus as having given JOSEPH OF ARIMATHEA the twelve hides of land at GLASTONBURY on which he founded the abbey. Others identify Arviragus with CARATACUS, while others further argue that Arviragus, Caratacus and ARTHUR were different names for the same person. The most likely supposition is that Arviragus was a local Somerset prince who managed to maintain his independence after the Roman invasion of Claudius, possibly through marriage but more likely by capitulation in return for keeping his kingdom.

ASAL
Irish

The original owner of the seven magical swine of LUGH. The swine could be killed and eaten one day, and yet be alive, ready and willing to be eaten again the following day. Asal is simply described as the King of the Golden Pillars, an obviously OTHERWORLDLY kingdom, as the seven magical swine would indicate, for swine originated in the Otherworld. Asal may, therefore, be seen as the Irish counterpart of ARAWN, the ruler of ANNWFN in Welsh tradition, for he too owned a herd of magical swine which he gave to PRYDERI.

ASCALUN
Arthurian

According to WOLFRAM VON ESCHENBACH, VERGULAHT was the King of this domain.

ASCAPART
British

A giant, possibly one of the companions, or even brothers, of ALBION. He was killed by BEVIS and buried under Bevis Mound near Southampton, Hampshire.

ASCHIL
Arthurian

The King of DENMARK, according to GEOFFREY OF MONMOUTH, who makes him an ally of ARTHUR at the Battle of CAMLANN.

ASCLEPIODOTUS
British

According to GEOFFREY OF MONMOUTH, a King of BRITAIN during the time of Diocletian (AD 245–313). Maintaining his autonomy against Rome cost him the crown, for he was so preoccupied with staving off the attentions of the Roman Empire that COEL easily deposed him. History records an Asclepiodotus, but he was a Roman, as his name would seem to suggest, and Geoffrey of Monmouth's assertion that he was a British King is a pure flight of fancy.

ASCLUT
Arthurian

An intermediate form of ALCLUD, the old name for DUMBARTON, that is thought by some to have given rise to ASTOLAT.

ASSURNE
Arthurian

A river that marked the boundary between the kingdoms of SURLUSE and LOGRES.

ASSYSLA

Arthurian

According to the *BRETA SOGUR*, a Scandinavian version of the works of GEOFFREY OF MONMOUTH, Assysla was the name of the island on which ARTHUR died, this making it cognate with AVALON.

ASTLABOR

Arthurian

A variant of ESCLABOR.

ASTOLAT

Arthurian

Also SHALLOT

The name of ELAINE the White, who died for the love of LANCELOT. It is thought that the name may come from ALCLUD, the old name for DUMBARTON, through the intermediate form of ASCLUT, though Sir Thomas MALORY places Astolat at Guildford in Surrey.

ATEPOMAROS

Gaulish

A deity whose name means 'possessing great horses' and who possibly dates from the Roman period. This connection leads to the supposition that he was originally a native horse or solar deity who became assimilated with the classical Apollo along with his chariot and horses, which daily traversed the sky, bearing with them the light of the sun, though apparently without Apollo's other atributes.

ATHRWYS

Welsh and Arthurian

The son of MEURIG, King of GLENVISSIG, he may have been the King of GWENT, although, dealing in the shady areas of early Welsh history, this cannot be said for certain. He has been identified with ARTHUR, but, as he probably lived in the seventh century, he comes 200 years too late.

ATLANTIS

Arthurian

The legendary lost continent of classical Greek mythology that was, according to some occultists, the original home of both MERLIN and IGRAINE.

AUDRIEN

Gaulish and Arthurian

Also ALDROENUS

The King of BRITTANY and brother of CONSTANTINE, Arthur's chosen successor.

AUGUSELUS

British and Arthurian

Designated as the King of SCOTLAND in the writings of GEOFFREY OF MONMOUTH. The brother of URIEN, and sometimes also of LOT, he is possibly identifiable with ARAWN, the ruler of ANNWFN. An ally of King ARTHUR, he supported the latter in his campaign against the ROMAN EMPIRE, but on his return he was killed at RICHBOROUGH by MORDRED.

AURELIUS AMBROSIUS

Arthurian

A variant of AMBROSIUS AURELI(AN)US.

AURELIUS CANINUS

British and Arthurian

The name given by GILDAS to AURELIUS CONAN.

AURELIUS CONAN

British and Arthurian

According to GEOFFREY OF MONMOUTH, the second successor to ARTHUR following CONSTAN-TINE, though GILDAS, a contemporary, makes both Constantine and Aurelius Conan local kings, and calls him AURELIUS CANINUS, saying that he enjoyed making war and plundering the spoils.

AVAGDDU

Welsh

A variant of AFAGDDU.

AVALLACH

Welsh and Arthurian

The name sometimes used to refer to AVALLOCH, the son of BELI MAWR and father of MODRON. Within the Arthurian cycle Avallach became a variant for the Isle of AVALON.

AVALLO

Arthurian

A variant of AVALON used by GEOFFREY OF MONMOUTH in his *HISTORIA REGUM BRITANNIAE*.

AVALLO(C(H))

Arthurian

Also AVALLACH

Evidently originally a god of obscure origins and attributes. William of MALMESBURY maintained that he lived on the island of AVALON with his daughters. His origin is to be found in Welsh legend, where he is named as the son of BELI MAWR, and father of the goddess MODRON, while in the Arthurian romances he appears under the name of EVELAKE. His variant name of AVALLACH is sometimes used to refer to the Isle of Avalon itself.

AVALON

British and Arthurian

A mythical paradise, 'The Fortunate Island', that magical realm to which the mortally wounded ARTHUR was taken by MERLIN and TALIESIN after his final battle with MORDRED so that his wounds might be healed by the goddess MORGAN Le Fay, the shape-changing mistress of therapy, music and the arts, co-ruling the realm with her NINE SISTERS. Significantly, the ferryman for Arthur's final journey was BARINTHUS, a mysterious character who echoes the role of the ancient sea gods. It is from Avalon that Arthur will one day return in the time of BRITAIN'S greatest need, to inaugurate a new golden age. GEOFFREY OF MONMOUTH refers to Avalon as the Isle of APPLES, or *Insula Pomorum*, in his *VITA MERLINI*, while in his *HISTORIA REGUM BRITANNIAE* he

gives it the name AVALLO, which appears to be a corruption of AVALLOCH, the son of BELI MAWR, who was said to live on the island with his daughter.

William of MALMESBURY maintained that AVALLOC lived on Avalon with his daughters, thus mirroring the sentiments of Geoffrey of Monmouth, and it is widely thought that this association, or the Burgundian place-name of Avallon, may have influenced the present form of the name. The name appears in Welsh legend, around which most of the Arthurian stories have been wound, where it is a kingdom of the dead (ANNWFN), though an alternative school of thought says the word, and thus the place, is Irish in origin.

It was said to have been ruled over by Morgan Le Fay and her Nine Sisters, or her lover GUINGAMUER, or by a mysterious king named BANGON. In *PERLESVAUS*, both GUINEVERE and LOHOLT died before Arthur, and were buried there. Still, the exact location of this wonderful realm remained a mystery. In the reign of King Henry II it came to be recognised as GLASTONBURY, as the tombs of King Arthur and

Glastonbury Tor, Somerset, as seen from Glastonbury Abbey. (© Jean Williamson/Mick Sharp)

Guinevere were reported to have been found there. Subsequently the tombs vanished, never to be seen again, thus adding more to the mystery. Some having identified Glastonbury with CAER WYDYR, the Fort of Glass, and, as Caer Wydyr is traditionally located in the Welsh OTHERWORLD realm of Annwfn, Avalon has become connected with this realm, such is the confusion that clouds the Arthurian legends.

The realm has much older origins than the fifth century from which Arthur dates and has, since early times, been regarded as a place for only the bravest and the most virtuous of mortal beings. Early Celtic legends say that the island could be reached only on a boat guided by the sea god Barinthus, a point that was later to resurface within the Arthurian cycle. The island was said to be co-ruled by ten maidens, one of whom, MORGEN, is undoubtedly the origin of Morgan Le Fay, for like her Morgen is referred to as the shape-changing mistress of therapy, music and the arts. Other sources say that the island was ruled over by Bangon, a mysterious being about whom nothing more is known.

Avalon is a confused realm, not so much by the fact that it is nothing more than the paradise to which the fortunate are received after their time on earth is at an end, but because of the myriad of variations to both its name and its possible origins. Further confusion may be added when it is considered that some sources state the name has a biblical origin stemming from the place Ajolon, where the sun was made to remain in the sky to enable the Israelites to win a great battle (Joshua 10:12). As with so much that is Celtic, the origins of the name have long disappeared and all that is left is speculation, usually based on etymology.

AVENABLE

Arthurian

A damsel who went to the court of JULIUS CAESAR disguised as a page, calling herself GRISANDOLE. Eventually marrying Julius Caesar, she was said to have introduced MERLIN to the court.

AVILION

Arthurian

A variant name for AVALON that has been used by Sir Thomas MALORY and, in more modern times, by Alfred, Lord Tennyson.

AYGLIN

Welsh and Arthurian

The usurping uncle of ANDRIVETE. When he usurped the throne of NORTHUMBRIA he wanted Andrivete to marry someone of his own choosing so that he might keep her in check. She flouted his wishes, escaped and married CEI, who helped her regain her realm. Later tradition renamed Cei as the Arthurian knight Sir KAY, and because of this Ayglin has a tenuous link with the Arthurian cycle.

B

BABYLON
Arthurian

Lying on the east bank of the River Euphrates and situated in modern Iraq, Babylon was the capital of the ancient Mesopotamian kingdom of Babylonia. In the Arthurian legends this city was the realm of THOLOMER, who was drawn into a war against EVELAKE when the latter became the King of SARRAS.

BACH BYCHAN
Arthurian

'Little small one', the page of TRISTAN in the Welsh romance *TRYSTAN*.

BADBA
Irish

'Furies', supernatural spirits who were said to have been employed by the DAGHDHA during the first Battle of MAGH TUIREDH. They were invoked on the fourth day of the battle along with the BLEDLOCHTANA and AMAITE AIDGILL.

BADBURY HILL
Arthurian

A hill in Devon that is considered one of the many possible sites for the Battle of BADON.

BADBURY RINGS
Arthurian

A place in Dorset that is numbered among the possible locations for the Battle of BADON.

BAD(H)B(H)
Irish

The goddess of war whose name appears to mean 'scald-crow'. She is depicted as a raven or hooded crow. Bird-shaped, red-mouthed, with a sharp countenance, the Badhbh was one aspect of the triad goddess the MÓRRÍGHAN, her other aspects being MACHA and NEMHAIN. There are countless triple goddesses in Celtic and other pagan systems. Some authorities consider them as three aspects of the

same thing, such as the waxing, fullness and waning of the moon; or as youth, maturity and old age; but more commonly they are seen as agricultural deities whose aspects reflect the sowing, ripening and harvesting of crops.

In common with her sisters, the other aspects of the Mórríghan, the Badhbh sometimes appeared as a foul hag, sometimes as an alluring maiden, but most commonly as a bird. She was often to be seen on the battlefield near those she had selected to die, for it was her duty to preside over the field of battle. Before a battle the Badhbh would usually be encountered beside a stream in which she was washing the armour and weapons of those who were about to die.

The Badhbh not only selected those to die in battle, but could also, by the use of powerful magic, alter the course of a battle to suit her own ends. This is a trait she shared with her sisters. Other shared traits were an affinity with water, an ability to alter her form at will and an insatiable lust for both men and gods.

CÚ CHULAINN once encountered the Badhbh as a red woman wrapped in a red cloak driving a chariot drawn by a one-legged red horse. The pole connecting the horse to the chariot passed through the animal and emerged from its forehead, where it was fixed with a wooden peg. The Badhbh was accompanied by a man who drove a cow using a forked hazel switch. Cú Chulainn asked their names, a question the Badhbh answered in a series of riddles. Infuriated by this, Cú Chulainn leapt onto the chariot, which immediately disappeared, leaving the hero sprawling on the ground. Above him the Badhbh circled in the form of a carrion crow.

In combination with her sisters, the Badhbh became one of the most fearsome of all Celtic deities. There was no known protection against her charms, and, once selected, all that the chosen one could hope for was a quick and painless death.

BADON
Arthurian

There are six possible sites for this mount, the scene of the battle in which ARTHUR totally defeated the SAXONS. GILDAS makes the first reference to the battle in his *DE EXCIDIO ET CONQUESTU BRITANNIAE*, but does not mention Arthur by name. Arthur is named as the leader (though not a king) by NENNIUS, who describes the battle 'in which 960

Badbury Rings, Dorset, one of the many sites connected with the Battle of Badon. (© Mick Sharp)

enemy fell in a single attack by Arthur'. He is also named in the *ANNALES CAMBRIAE* and by GEOFFREY OF MONMOUTH, who regards Badon as identical with BATH. It was described as a siege, but it remains uncertain as to who was besieged by whom. The date is also unfixed, and is usually regarded as falling somewhere between AD 490 and 516. Various suggestions have been put forward for the location of the battle, including Bath, BADBURY HILL, BADBURY RINGS and LIDDINGTON CASTLE near Swindon, Wiltshire, though there is also a Badbury Castle on the Marlborough Downs, just to the south of Swindon, that might also be considered.

BAGDEMAGUS
Arthurian
A cousin of ARTHUR, the King of GORE and one of the KNIGHTS OF THE ROUND TABLE. He appears to have been a benign character, but when TOR was made a Knight of the Round Table before him, he took umbrage. He was the father of MELEAGAUNCE, whom he prevented from raping

GUINEVERE when his son had carried her off. During the Quest for the Holy GRAIL he carried a special shield with a red cross on it that was intended for GALAHAD. For this he was wounded by a white knight, and was eventually killed by GAWAIN.

BAGOTA
Arthurian
The giantess mother of GALEHAUT by BRUNOR.

BALAN
Arthurian
The younger brother of BALIN. He had to assume the role of a knight he had slain, fighting all-comers in his place. In this capacity he was forced to fight his brother, though neither recognised the other, and during the combat each inflicted a mortal wound on the other.

BAL-AR, -OR
Irish and Arthurian
Known as Balar of the Dreadful, Baleful or Evil Eye, this hero, god and monster, a one-eyed giant,

was the King of the FOMHOIRÉ. His power lay, not in his size, but in his single eye. Even though it took four men to lift his eyelid, once his eye was exposed, a single glance could unman a host.

A supposed direct ancestor of LUGH, whom some name as Balar's grandson by his daughter ETHLINN, Balar was killed by that very god as the final conflict of the Second Battle of MAGH TUIREDH. Lugh dispatched a slingshot with such accuracy and force that not only did it penetrate Balar's eye but continued through the giant's head to wreak havoc amongst the Fomhoiré hordes assembled behind their King. Some sources say that the slingshot killed twenty-seven of the Fomhoiré who had been too slow in taking cover, although the actual number killed is open to speculation, many going so far as to say only a few of the Fomhoiré escaped to flee the country. Balar's corpse was hung on a sacred hazel, which dripped poison and split asunder.

In some respects, Balar is similar to the giant of Welsh mythology YSPADDADEN, the giant father of the maiden OLWEN in the *MABINOGION* story of *CULHWCH AND OLWEN*, although it is unclear whether there is any direct connection between the two giants.

See also AIDED CHLAINNE TUIRENN

BALBHUAIDH
Arthurian
The name under which GAWAIN appears in Irish romances.

BALDUDUS
British
See BLADUD

BALDULF
Arthurian
The brother of the SAXON leader COLGRIN. On his way to aid his brother during the siege of YORK, he was attacked and defeated by CADOR, but managed to sneak into York disguised as a minstrel. He was eventually killed at BADON.

BALDWIN
Arthurian
A variation of BEDWIN who appears in *SIR GAWAIN AND THE CARL OF CARLISLE*.

BALIN
Arthurian
The KNIGHT OF THE TWO SWORDS and brother of BALAN. Originating from NORTHUMBER-LAND, he incurred ARTHUR's displeasure by

killing a LADY OF THE LAKE, but he and his brother still became supporters of Arthur following their capture of RIENCE. He killed GARLON, the brother of PELLAM, who then tried to avenge his brother. Balin struck Pellam with the LANCE OF LONGINUS, a wound that was known as the DOLOROUS STROKE. Unwittingly he was challenged to combat by his brother, neither recognizing the other, and each received a mortal wound. Balin's name is thought to be a variant of BRULAN, who was, elsewhere, thought to have inflicted the Dolorous Stroke long before the traditional time ascribed to King Arthur.

BALL-SEIRC
Irish
The beauty spot said to have been placed on the forehead of DIARMAID UA DUIBHNE by the young maiden who revealed herself to him as the personification of youth.

BAMBURGH
Arthurian
Situated on the NORTHUMBERLAND coast, this small town boasts a castle standing on a crag above the North Sea that was once the seat of the kings of Northumbria. It has been suggested that Bamburgh Castle is JOYOUS GARD, the castle of Sir LANCELOT that was originally known as DOLOROUS GARD, and later reverted back to its former name. If Bamburgh Castle is Joyous Gard, then it was to this imposing structure that Lancelot brought GUINEVERE after he had rescued her from being burnt for adultery.

BAN
Arthurian
The King of GOMERET or BENWICK, but possibly best known simply as Ban of BRITTANY, the father of Sir LANCELOT, brother of King BORS of GAUL, and owner of the sword COURECIIOUSE. He supported ARTHUR against the eleven rebellious leaders at the outset of the young King's reign, and in return Arthur aided him against his enemy, King CLAUDAS. When Claudas succeeded in destroying Ban's castle at TREBES, the King died of a broken heart. ELAINE is usually named as Ban's wife, but the medieval French romance *ROMAN DES FILS DU ROI CONSTANT* names her as SABE, and gives him a daughter named LIBAN. He is most famous through his legitimate offspring, Lancelot, but he also had an illegitimate son named ECTOR DE MARIS, whose mother was the wife of AGRAVADAIN.

In origin it has been suggested that he was the god BRÂN, and that the name Ban de Benoic (Ban of Benwick) was simply a corruption of Brân le Benoit (Brân the Blessed). His name has also been connected with the Irish word for 'white', *ban*.

BANÁNACHS

Irish

Spirits of an unknown nature, who were reputed to have shrieked in the air around CÚ CHULAINN while the hero fought with FERDIA, their cries being joined by those of the BOCÁNACHS and the GENITI GLINNE. They would seem to be a representation of the battle fury of Cú Chulainn and may be a partial origin of the BANSHEE.

BANB(H)A

Irish

One of the triad of goddesses known collectively as the SPIRIT OF IRELAND or the SOVEREIGNTY OF IRELAND, her other aspects being FÓDLA and ÉRIU. Like that other Irish triad goddess, the MÓRRÍGHAN, she and her sisters have bird characteristics. Early myth says that she was the leader of a company that came to IRELAND in a time before the biblical Flood, although this company is also said to have been led by CESAIR. Of these people, all but one, FINTAN, drowned in the Flood, and Banbha passed into the realms of deification.

She later reappears as the wife of MAC CUILL. Now she is an eponymous goddess and primal figure of sovereignty, and is combined in trio with Fódla and Ériu, whom some call her sisters. They, with their three husbands, opposed the invasion of Ireland by the Sons of MÍL ÉSPÁINE with magic. After the invaders had landed and defeated a TUATHA DÉ DANANN army, they marched towards TARA. *En route* they encountered and wooed Banbha and her sisters, each promising victory to the invaders if the bribe they offered them was sufficient. That offered to Ériu was best, for that promised the naming of the country in her honour. Since that time Ireland has been known as EIRE.

BANBLAI

Irish

The father of BUIC.

BANGON

British and Arthurian

A mysterious character who is named in a few sources as the ruler of AVALON. However, nothing more is known about this deity, and it remains questionable whether he is Celtic or simply a later invention.

BANIN

Arthurian

One of the KNIGHTS OF THE ROUND TABLE and the godson of King BAN.

BANSHEE

Irish

A fairy being in Irish folklore whose wailing lament is supposed to warn of an impending death. The origin of the banshees may lie with the BANÁNACHS, BOCÁNACHS and GENITI GLINNE, supernatural beings who were reported to have filled the air with their screams during the battle between CÚ CHULAINN and FERDIA.

BARATON

Arthurian

In Arthurian romance Baraton is named as the King of RUSSIA.

BARDSEY

Welsh and Arthurian

Known as YNYS ENLLI in Welsh, the small island of Bardsey lies just off the tip of the beautiful Lleyn Peninsula in GWYNEDD, at the northern entrance of Cardigan Bay. Now a bird sanctuary and observatory, the island was an important holy site to the Celts, who built a monastery there, now ruined, in the sixth century. The island later became known as the Island of Twenty Thousand Saints, the reputed last resting place of PADARN, who lies there in the company of 20,000 saints. Later still it became one of the alleged resting places of MERLIN, along with the golden throne of BRITAIN, as he awaits the return of King ARTHUR.

BARINTHUS

Welsh and Arthurian

A mysterious OTHERWORLDLY sea deity about whom very little is known. He does, however, make an appearance in the later Arthurian legends as the boatman who ferried the mortally wounded King ARTHUR, in the company of MERLIN and TALIESIN, on his final journey to AVALON, to be cured of his deadly wound by the goddess MORGAN Le Fay.

The character of Barinthus remains shrouded in mystery. Why he should appear only in late legends is a mystery, as he is clearly a very early deity. One possible explanation for the existence of Barinthus is the widespread belief that the land of the dead, the OTHERWORLD, lay across a vast sea, and Barinthus was duly accorded the honour of ferrying the dead to the eternal land.

See also MANANNÁN MAC LIR

Bardsey Island, one of the many alleged resting places of Merlin. (© Mick Sharp)

BARUC
Arthurian

In the *LIVRE D'ARTUS*, Baruc is simply named as a knight, while WOLFRAM VON ESCHENBACH, in *PARZIVAL*, names Baruc as the CALIPH OF BAGHDAD with whom GAHMURET took service. The title appears to come from the Hebrew personal name Baruch. The reference to the Caliph of Baghdad is an anachronism, since the traditional Arthurian period pre-dates Muhammad and the foundation of the Caliphate.

BARUCH
Irish

One of the RED BRANCH and a close ally of CONCHOBAR MAC NESSA. When FERGUS MAC ROICH arrived back in IRELAND with NAOISE, DERDRIU, ARDÁN and AINNLE, Baruch placed Fergus mac Roich under an obligation to spend the night with him, thus keeping him away from EMHAIN MHACHA, where Conchobar mac Nessa intended to kill the three sons of UISNECH.

See also GESSA

BASCNA
Irish

The leader of one of the two clans that made up the FIAN, the other being Clan MORNA. Both Bascna and Morna fought alongside their chief FIONN MAC CUMHAILL.

BASSUS, RIVER
Arthurian

According to the list given by NENNIUS, the unidentified site of one of ARTHUR'S BATTLES.

BATAILLE LOQUIFER
Arthurian

Obscure medieval romance that contains a number of Arthurian references. In this work CORBON is named as the son of RENOART and MORGAN Le Fay, the latter being said to have a servant named KAPALU, whose name no doubt derives from CAPALU, the continental version of CATH PALUG.

BATH
British and Arthurian

City in the county of Avon, England. Legend says that the city was founded on the site of the healing waters that cured BLADUD, the magical son of King HUDIBRAS. The Roman name for the city was AQUAE SULIS, so named after the goddess SULIS, to whom the hot springs found in the city were dedicated. The Romans obviously thought it politically prudent to incorporate the local deity into their name for the city, as the site was quite obviously one of great religious significance to the indigenous population. The city has also been put forward as one of the many suggested sites of the decisive Battle of BADON, in which ARTHUR, assisted by his cousin HOEL, King of BRITTANY, finally defeated the pagan SAXONS.

BATRADZ
Arthurian

The hero of the OSSETES, a SARMATIAN people who still inhabit the Caucasus today. The story of his death is remarkably similar to that of ARTHUR. Having received a mortal wound, Batradz instructed two of his companions to throw his sword into the water. Twice they pretended to have carried out the orders, but when they finally complied the waters turned blood-red and became very stormy. It has been suggested that this may have been the origin for the story of the returning of EXCALIBUR to the LADY OF THE LAKE. Sarmatian soldiers were known to have served in the Roman army in BRITAIN under Lucius Artorius Castus, so this is not wholly impossible.

BAUDEC
Arthurian

The realm of a king who was besieging Jerusalem, so the POPE sent RICHARD, son of the besieged king, to ARTHUR to ask for help.

BAUDIHILLIE
British

The name of one of the ALAISIAGAE, the others being BEDE, FINNILENE and FRIAGABI, to whom an altar was dedicated at Housesteads on Hadrian's Wall. It is thought that her name means 'Ruler of Battle'. Her worship, which appears to have been brought to BRITAIN during the Roman period, seemingly continues well after the withdrawal of the Roman armies, although whether it was the Celts or the PICTS who continued this worship remains uncertain.

BAUDWIN
Arthurian

The knight whom ARTHUR made a constable of his realm at the time of his accession. During Arthur's war with the ROMAN EMPIRE he was one of the governors of BRITAIN, later becoming a hermit and physician.

BAV
Irish
See MÓRRÍGHAN

BAVE

Irish

The shape-shifting daughter of CALATIN. Having assumed the shape of NIAMH, she coaxed CÚ CHULAINN to leave his place of safety, thus instigating the series of events that were to lead to his death. Some think that Bave is a simple variant of BAV, an alternative name given to the MÓRRÍGHAN. This may indeed be the case, for it was Cú Chulainn's ignorant behaviour towards the Mórríghan that ultimately caused his death.

BAYEUX

Arthurian

Town in Normandy that is famous for the Bayeux tapestry, depicting the Norman Conquest of BRITAIN. Arthurian sources name its founder as BEDIVERE, the father of PEDRAWD and grand-father of the second Bedivere, the companion of ARTHUR.

BÉ FIND

Irish

The generic name given to water-sprites, semi-divine women who live by, or in, streams, lakes and fountains, or in forests and woods. Later tradition included mermaids under this name.

BEÄLCU

Irish

The warrior from CONNACHT who found CONALL CERNACH hideously wounded and dying after he had killed CET. Conall Cernach pleaded with him to kill him, but Beälcu would not kill a man so close to death. Instead he carried the dying warrior home and cured him of his wounds, fully intending to kill Conall Cernach in single combat. However, fully recovered, Conall Cernach was set upon by the three sons of Beälcu, but by some unrecorded ploy Conall Cernach managed to have them kill their own father before he killed and beheaded them and carried their heads back to ULSTER in triumph.

BEANN GHULBAN

Irish

Also BEN BULBEN

The owner of a magical boar with no ears or tail that was the foster brother of DIARMAID UA DUIBHNE.

Opposite: *The Roman Baths at Aquae Sulis or, as it is known today, Bath.* (© Mick Sharp)

The boar itself is usually referred to as Beann Ghulban, although it was actually unnamed. Even though it had been prophesied that Diarmaid ua Duibhne would be killed by the boar, he still went ahead and hunted it. During the hunt Diarmaid ua Duibhne was mortally gored, seconds before he managed to dispatch the beast with his broken sword.

BEAROSCHE

Arthurian

In WOLFRAM VON ESCHENBACH's *PARZIVAL*, the scene of a siege where its lord, Duke LYPPAUT, defended it against his sovereign, King MELJANZ of LIZ, who had declared war when the Duke's daughter, OBIE, had rejected him. GAWAIN fought on the side of Duke Lyppaut while PERCEVAL fought on the side of King Meljanz. Peace was at last restored through the offices of OBILOT, the younger sister of Obie.

BEATRICE

Arthurian

The wife of CARDUINO, who rescued her from an enchantment.

BEAUMAINS

Arthurian

'Fair Hands', the impertinent nickname of GARETH, son of LOT and MORGAUSE, given to him by Sir KAY.

BEAUTE

Arthurian

The maid of GUINEVERE who fell in love with GLIGLOIS, Sir GAWAIN's squire.

BEAUTIFUL PILGRIM

Arthurian

The name by which ALICE, the wife of ALISANDER THE ORPHAN, became known.

BEBHIONN

Irish

Also VIVIONN

A giantess, the daughter of TREON from TÍR INNA MBAN, who sought the protection of FIONN MAC CUMHAILL after her father had betrothed her to AEDA against her will. While she was sitting with Fionn mac Cumhaill, Bebhionn's intended strode ashore, killed her with a single cast of his huge lance and then strode back out to a huge waiting boat before Fionn mac Cumhaill or his men could respond.

BÉBIND

Irish

The sister of BOANN and the mother of FRAOCH.

BEBO

Irish

The Queen of FAYLINN and wife of IUBDAN, whom she accompanied to ULSTER to visit the giant humans who lived there, for she and her husband are commonly referred to as 'Wee Folk' or fairies. She and her husband were held captive for a short while until, after a series of plagues imposed by Iubdan's subjects, they were released for a ransom of magical items.

BÉCHUILLE

Irish

A member of the TUATHA DÉ DANANN. She is described as a witch and is also sometimes described as a foster mother to the gods, although this role is not developed in the legends.

BÉCUMA

Irish

The enchantress who was banished by the TUATHA DÉ DANANN for seducing the son of MANANNÁN MAC LIR. She later returned and caused CONN CÉTCHATHLACH to exile his son ART, and then lived with the King for a year, during which time no corn grew and no cows gave milk. Conn Cétchathlach's advisers told him that the sacrifice of the son of a 'sinless couple' would be needed to break the enchantment of Bécuma. Just such a child was found, but his mother arrived with a wondrous cow, which was accepted in the child's place. Bécuma now turned her attentions to Art, but left the Tuatha Dé Danann forever after Art had succeeded in returning from the land of the dead with DELBCHAEM.

Some authorities have sought to connect Bécuma with the similarly named BÉCHUILLE, but, although both are enchantresses, there is nothing further to support this assimilation.

BEDD ARTHUR

Arthurian

'Arthur's Grave' in the PRESELI HILLS, DYFED. Yet another of the many places where King ARTHUR is supposed to be buried, Bedd Arthur consists of twelve stones placed at regular intervals. However, there are references to an Arthur Petr who ruled Dyfed in the seventh century, so perhaps it was his grave. The Preseli Hills can boast more Arthurian objects than any other region in BRITAIN for such a small area. Below Bedd Arthur is CARN ARTHUR, with a stone perched precariously on its top. It was allegedly thrown by Arthur from Dyffryn, a farm of that name being near the Gots Fawr circle. Alternatively, it is claimed that he threw it from Henry's Moat, about five miles away.

BEDD BRANWEN

Welsh

The alleged burial place of BRANWEN, situated on the banks of the River ALAW one mile north-east of the church in Treffynnon on ANGLESEY. The burial chamber beneath this cromlech was excavated in 1813 and an urn containing the cremated bones of a woman discovered.

BEDD TALIESIN

Welsh and Arthurian

North-east of Talybont, on the slopes of Moel-y-Garn, DYFED, is a CAER reputed to contain the remains of TALIESIN. Many of the legends associated with this ancient poet are to be found in the *MABINOGION*. The barrow consists of a large stone slab and cairn, the other stones having been removed over the years as building materials.

In the nineteenth century an attempt was made to discover the bones of Taliesin, and to remove them for burial in a Christian rather than pagan site. During the excavation a sudden terrible thunderstorm arose. Lightning struck the ground nearby, and, fleeing for their lives, the men abandoned their tools, never returning to collect them or try again.

BEDE

(1) (*British*) The name of one of the four ALAISIAGAE, Teutonic war goddesses whose worship was brought to BRITAIN, most probably by the Romans. An altar to these four goddesses, the other three being FINNILENE, BAUDIHILLI and FRIAGABI, was dedicated at Housesteads on Hadrian's Wall.

(2) (*General*) ANGLO-SAXON scholar, theologian and historian (*c.* 673–735), who is usually referred to as the Venerable Bede. He was born near the town of Monkwearmouth, County Durham, and at the age of seven was placed in the care of Benedict Biscop within the monastery of Wearmouth, and in 682 moved to the new monastery of Jarrow, Northumberland. He was ordained a priest there in 703 and remained a monk for the rest of his life. A prolific writer, he produced homilies, lives of saints and of abbots, hymns, epigrams, works on chronology, grammar and physical science, as well

as commentaries on the Old and New Testaments. His greatest work was his Latin *Gesta ecclesiastica gentis anglorum* (Ecclesiastical History of the English People), which he completed in 731. It remains the single most valuable source for early English history.

BEDEGRAINE
Arthurian

A forest that was the site of a major battle between ARTHUR and the rebel forces of the eleven revolting leaders at the start of his reign. Sir Thomas MALORY identifies it with SHERWOOD FOREST, or a part of it. Within the forest lay the Castle of Bedegraine, which was loyal to ARTHUR, and to which the rebel forces had laid siege. One of the knights mentioned as having taken part in the battle was BRASTIAS.

BEDEVERE
Arthurian

A variant of BEDIVERE.

BEDIVERE
Arthurian

Also BEDEVERE, BEDWYR

(1) The father of PEDRAWD, grandfather of the second Bedivere, and the founder of BAYEUX.

(2) An important companion of ARTHUR, the grandson of BEDIVERE, founder of BAYEUX, and son of PEDRAWD. His son's name was AMREN and his daughter's ENEUAVC. He is mentioned in the earliest Welsh traditions as being one of Arthur's followers, and, even though he is described as having only one hand, he helped Arthur to fight the giant of Mont SAINT MICHEL. GEOFFREY OF MONMOUTH makes him the Duke of NEUSTRIA, who perished during Arthur's campaign against the ROMAN EMPIRE. Sir Thomas MALORY, however, says he was present at Arthur's last battle at CAMLANN. He and Arthur alone survived the fight and he was charged with returning EXCALIBUR to the LADY OF THE LAKE.

BEDWIN
Arthurian

Also BALDWIN

A bishop who appears under this name in the Welsh *TRIADS* as the chief Bishop of KELLIWIG, while in *SIR GAWAIN AND THE CARL OF CARLISLE* he is named Baldwin, and made a companion of GAWAIN, also being mentioned by this name in the famous, anonymous poem *SIR GAWAIN AND THE GREEN KNIGHT*. Other sources name him as the father of ALISANDER THE ORPHAN by ANGLIDES, and state that he was murdered by King MARK.

BED-WYR, -VYR
Welsh

(1) The father of PEDRAWD and thus grandfather of BEDWYR. Like his namesake, he appeared in the later Arthurian legends with the name BEDIVERE.

(2) A member of the party formed to help CULHWCH in his quest to locate and secure the maiden OLWEN. The other members of the party were CEI, CYNDDYLIG the Guide, GWRHYR the Interpreter, GWALCHMAI FAB GWYAR and MENW FAB TEIRGWAEDD. Each was chosen for his specialist skills. Bedwyr was picked because, even though he had only one hand, he was still faster with his sword than three others who fought together.

Bedwyr's father was named as PEDRAWD, whose own father was known as BEDWYR. He had two children by an unnamed wife, a son AMREN and a daughter ENEUAVC. Bedwyr re-emerged in the later Arthurian cycle as BEDIVERE.

BEFORET
Arthurian

According to WOLFRAM VON ESCHENBACH, the name of the domain over which IWERET was lord.

BEK, ANTHONY
Arthurian

It was said, according to the historian G.M. Cowling, that in 1282 Anthony Bek, at that time Bishop-elect of Durham, met MERLIN while out hunting in the forest.

BEL(EN-OS, -US)
Gaulish, British and Arthurian

One of the most widespread of all Celtic gods, whose variant name, Belenos, was most widely used in Alpine regions, particularly NORICUM, of which Belenos was the tutelary deity. The representation of the power of light, the word *bel* meaning 'bright' or 'brilliant', Bel has many solar attributes. It was these that led him to be identified, on both sides of the English Channel, with the Roman god Apollo during the time of the Roman occupation.

The patron of the festival of BELTANE, Bel was said to have been the son of Light rather than being the solar deity himself. He was also known as the Lord of Therapy, a distinction that again directly links Bel with the Roman god Apollo, although it is quite possible that this is a later idea, and was simply added to Bel's solar attributes to make him even more comparable to Apollo. It is quite probable that Bel was later personified in the legendary early Briton BELI MAWR.

BEL INCONNU, LE
Arthurian
'The Fair Unknown', the name by which GUINGLAIN was known at ARTHUR's court, for he had arrived there ignorant of his own name. He was told of his parentage, GAWAIN and RAGNELL, only when he went to the aid of BLONDE ESMERÉE.

BELAGOG
Arthurian
According to one tradition, Belagog was a giant who guarded ARTHUR's castle, even though that castle was nothing more than a simple grotto (cf. GOGMAGOG).

BELATUCADROS
British
'Fair shining one', a horned Celtic god of war, whose cult was active in Cumbria and who has often been equated with the Roman god of war, Mars. A number of stones dedicated to Mars Belatucadros have, in fact, been found in Cumbria. Belatucadros was obviously a popular deity among the northern Celts because he was worshipped by both soldiers and civilians, a trait not often found in the worship of warlike deities.

BELAYE
Arthurian
A princess of LIZABORYE who became LOHEN-GRIN's second wife.

BELCANE
Arthurian
The Queen of ZAZAMANC and mother of FEIREFIZ by GAHMURET.

BELI (MAWR)
British, Welsh and Arthurian
A legendary early Briton who is thought to have originated in the god BEL, although this connection is by no means certain. His two famous sons were LLUDD and LLEFELYS, while his daughter, or possibly sister, was PENARDUN, who, by LLYR, was the mother of BENDIGEID VRAN. According to Henry of Huntingdon (*c.* 1084–1155), Beli Mawr was the brother of the first-century British King CUNOBELINUS or CYMBELINE. Welsh legend makes him the father of AVALLOC, grandfather of MODRON, and Lord of the OTHERWORLD.

Bendigeid Vran was thought to be an ancestor of ARTHUR in both his paternal and his maternal pedigrees. His name is also thought to have given rise to BELINANT, who features in the Arthurian legends as the father of DODINEL, as well as possibly being considered the etymological original of PELLINORE (Beli Mawr to Pellinore does not need too much imagination).

BELIDE
Arthurian
The daughter of King PHARAMOND of FRANCE, who died of a broken heart when TRISTAN did not requite her love for him (cf. BELLICIES).

BELINANT
Arthurian
The father of DODINEL whose name is thought to have derived from BELI.

BELINUS
Arthurian
According to GEOFFREY OF MONMOUTH, the CITY OF THE LEGIONS, which in this case is taken to mean CAERLEON-ON-USK, was founded by a king named Belinus. His name perhaps derives from BEL or BELI.

BELISENT
Arthurian
A sister to ARTHUR who, in the thirteenth-century English poem *ARTHOUR AND MERLIN*, married LOT. She may be cognate with both BLASINE and HERMESENT.

BELISIMA
Irish
A late title afforded to BRIGHID. It seems quite possible that the word is of Italian derivation, for in Italian the word *bellissima* means 'beautiful', an apt description for Brighid.

BELLANGERE
Arthurian
The son of ALISANDER THE ORPHAN. He was the Earl of LAUNDES and the killer of King MARK of CORNWALL.

BELLEUS
Arthurian
LANCELOT made Belleus a KNIGHT OF THE ROUND TABLE following an unfortunate incident in which Lancelot came across Belleus's pavilion and went to bed there. When Belleus later entered

the tent and climbed into the bed, he mistook the sleeping Lancelot for his lover and embraced him. In surprise and shock (and some would believe horror), Lancelot arose and wounded Belleus. When the circumstances had become apparent, Lancelot made Belleus a Knight of the Round Table to atone for the harm he had done.

BELLICIES
Arthurian
The daughter of King PHARAMOND of GAUL who, in Italian romance, fell in love with TRISTAN. When her love went unrequited, she killed herself (cf. BELIDE).

BEL(L)INUS
British
A son of MOLMUTIUS and TONWENNA, the brother of BRENNIUS and, according to GEOFFREY OF MONMOUTH, the legendary founder of CAERLEON-ON-USK. His name is possibly a derivation of BEL or BELI MAWR. Belinus traditionally succeeded his father after a blood feud between him and his brother was settled by arbitration. Five years later Brennius broke the peace and sailed to Norway, where he married the King's daughter and raised an army. However, Belinus routed them on their return to ENGLAND. Brennius fled to GAUL, and Belinus became the undisputed sovereign. Some time later Brennius returned with a Gaulish army, but Tonwenna interceded, and the two brothers were reconciled. The two brothers now invaded Gaul, which they subdued before pressing on into Italy. Following their successful sacking of Rome, Brennius decided to remain in Italy while Belinus returned to England and ruled in peace for the rest of his life, adding greatly to the fortifications surrounding TROIA NOVA (LONDON) and founding several new cities.

The sacking of Rome, which appears in Geoffrey of Monmouth, took place in 390 BC. However, the leader of the Celtic army was a Gaul by the name of BRENNOS. It would seem that Geoffrey of Monmouth simply altered the name and gave him a semi-divine brother to claim the sacking of Rome for the British.

BELT-ANE, -ENE, -INE
General
A Celtic festival held on 1 May, which marked the beginning of the Celtic summer, It was presided over by, and named after, BEL. Fires lit on the night preceding the festival were held to purify the land after the ravages of winter and to herald a time of regeneration and regrowth. Formerly one of the Scottish quarter days, Beltane was said to have been the date on which the first of the human race, the Sons of MÍL ÉSPÁINE, landed on Irish soil. To this day, the rites of purification with spring water and the lighting of purifying bonfires are connected with the ancient festival of Beltane.

BELTENÉ
Irish
One of the many names applied to the god of death. However, even though an etymological connection to the feast of BELTANE is obvious, there is no connection, for that festival was one of rebirth and not, therefore, something in which a god of death would be involved.

BEN BULBEN
Irish
See BEANN GHULBAN

BEN EDAR
Irish
The burial place of AIDEEN, the wife of OSCAR. She died of a broken heart when her husband was killed and was buried by OISÍN, who built a huge dolmen over her grave.

BENDIGEID VRAN
Welsh and Arthurian
The giant son of LLYR and PENARDUN and brother of BRANWEN and MANAWYDAN FAB LLYR. Some sources, however, make Bendigeid Vran and Branwen the children of Llyr by IWERIADD, while Manawydan fab Llyr was the son of Llyr by Penardun. He is more commonly referred to as BRÂN THE BLESSED, and his story is told in the *MABINOGION*. He is the god of fertility and patron of craftsmen, warrior, harpist and poet; his name can sometimes mean 'raven'. His ranking among the gods was downgraded after the advent of Christianity, but early stories clearly illustrate his great importance.

Bendigeid Vran, whose court was alleged to be at Harlech, had a son named CARATACUS, who has been identified with the British leader of that name who opposed the Romans in AD 43 when CLAUDIUS landed with his invasion forces. It has been mooted, in direct contradiction of his own godly status, that Bendigeid Vran introduced Christianity to BRITAIN. The *Mabinogion* says that Bendigeid Vran gave his sister Branwen to MATHOLWCH, King of IRELAND, together with a magic cauldron. However, while Matholwch was in Britain, he was insulted by EFNISIEN, Bendigeid Vran's half-brother, and on his return to Ireland he exacted his revenge on Branwen. Learning of the suffering of his sister, Bendigeid Vran crossed from WALES to Ireland by walking on the seabed, and, once he was there, a mighty battle ensued. At first the forces of Matholwch held the upper hand, for every night they took their dead and wounded and placed them in the magic cauldron that Bendigeid Vran had given to Matholwch, an act that restored them to full health and vigour. However, after Efnisien had succeeded in destroying the cauldron, Bendigeid Vran and his men quickly exterminated the entire Irish population, save for five pregnant women, who hid in a cave, their resulting children becoming the forefathers of the new Irish race.

So fierce was the fighting that only seven of his men survived to return to Wales, and Bendigeid Vran himself was mortally wounded in the foot by a poisoned dart. During his absence, CASWAL-LAWN, the son of BELI, disinherited Manawydan fab Llyr, the brother and heir of Bendigeid Vran. The seven survivors of the expedition were PRYDERI, Manawydan fab Llyr, GLIFIEU, TALIESIN, YNAWAG, GRUDDIEU and HEILYN. Bendigeid Vran ordered these seven to cut off his head and carry it to the WHITE MOUNT in LONDON, there to bury it with the face towards FRANCE as a magical guardian over Britain. Bendigeid Vran also told the seven that they would be a long time travelling to their goal, adding that his head would be pleasant company for them during their long journey. For seven years, he told them, they would remain in Harlech, where they would feast in splendour while being detained by the magical singing of the birds of RHIANNON. He told them that they would live in PENVRO for eighty years, only leaving after they had opened a door that looked towards CORNWALL. Everything passed exactly as Bendigeid Vran had foretold, until finally the seven carried out his last wish and buried his head as ordered. Later stories say that King ARTHUR dug up the head, for he alone wanted to be the sole guardian of Britain. Popular belief still holds that the head of Bendigeid Vran is buried within the boundaries of the Tower of London, possibly beneath the White Tower.

Branwen, whom the seven brought back home with them, looked back towards Ireland and, thinking about the death and destruction that had been brought about for her sake, died of a broken heart. She was buried near the River ALAW on ANGLESEY, her grave being known as BEDD BRANWEN.

Bendigeid Vran has undoubtedly given much to the later Arthurian legends. His magical cauldron was, so it has been suggested, refined to reappear as none other than the Holy GRAIL, and his mortal wound has also been likened to the wound inflicted on the FISHER KING.

The translation of Bendigeid Vran's name as 'raven', although this is normally the translation of Brân, is particularly significant when the presence of ravens at the Tower of London is considered. These ravens, sacred birds to the Celts, are never permitted to leave the confines of the Tower of London, for, if they do, so it is said, the White Tower will fall into ruin and Britain will fall to invaders. It is perhaps just as well that today the birds have their wings clipped and that Bendigeid Vran's head remains just where he ordered it to be buried.

Bendigeid Vran should not be confused with the Irish hero BRÂN, who is an entirely different character, a hero rather than a god.

BENWICK
Arthurian
Literally the 'Kingdom of Ben' (BAN). The *LESTOIRE DE MERLIN* (a part of the mighty *VULGATE VERSION*) states that Benwick was to be identified with the town of Bourges. Sir Thomas MALORY states that Benwick should rather be identified with Bayonne or Beaune, while an association with Saumur has also been suggested.

BERCILAK DE HAUTDESERT
Arthurian
Alternative form of BERTILAK, the GREEN KNIGHT.

BERNARD OF ASTOLAT
Arthurian
Father of the LADY OF SHALOTT, ELAINE the White, and of LEVAINE.

BÉROUL
Arthurian
A twelfth-century French writer who was the author of an Anglo-Norman TRISTAN romance. Very little can be said for certain about his life.

BERRANT LES APRES
Arthurian
One of the names suggested, along with AGUYSANS and MALEGINIS, for the KING WITH A HUNDRED KNIGHTS.

BERSA
Irish
The husband of MAIR.

BERTHOLAI

Arthurian

The champion of the False GUINEVERE and her partner in the deception that caused the real Guinevere, her half-sister, to go into hiding.

BERTILAK

Also BERCILAK DE HAUTDESERT

The true name of the famous GREEN KNIGHT.

BETHIDES

Arthurian

The son of PERCEFOREST, who made an unfortunate marriage to the sorceress CIRCE.

BETIS

Arthurian

According to the French romance *PERCEFOREST*, ALEXANDER THE GREAT made Betis the King of England following the former's fictional conquest of BRITAIN. His brother, GADDIFER, was likewise made the King of SCOTLAND. Betis was quickly accepted by the populace, being renamed PERCE-FOREST after he had killed the magician DURMART.

BEUND, SAINT

Arthurian

A noteworthy saint in North WALES whose popularity survived the Reformation. Beund was said to be the grandson of King ARTHUR's sister ANNA through PERFERREN, her daughter.

BEUNO

Arthurian

According to Welsh tradition, the offspring of BUGI and PERFERREN, and thus the grandson of LOT. It would seem that this name is a simple derivation from, or a transcriptive error for, BEUND.

BEVIS

British

The traditional killer of the giant ASCAPART, whom he buried under a mound near Southampton, Hampshire, which is, appropriately, known as Bevis Mound.

BIAUSDOUS

Arthurian

The son of GAWAIN who managed to unsheath the sword HONOREE and by so doing win the hand of BIAUTEI, the daughter of the KING OF THE ISLES.

BIAUTEI

Arthurian

The daughter of the KING OF THE ISLES whom BIAUSDOUS won the right to marry by drawing the sword HONOREE.

BILÉ

Irish

According to some sources, the son of BREGON or ITH, and father of MÍL, though in these instances Míl is usually referred to as MÍLE.

BIRÔG

Irish

The Druidess who accompanied CIAN to TORY Island and enabled him to avenge himself on BALAR by seducing Balar's daughter ETHLINN, who was kept locked away in a solitary tower after it had been prophesied that her child would kill Balar. Ethlinn subsequently gave birth to three boys. Two were killed by Balar, but the third, LUGH, survived and later fulfilled the prophecy at the Second Battle of MAGH TUIREDH.

BIRTH OF ARTHUR

Arthurian

A fourteenth-century Welsh work that gives unusual details about ARTHUR's lineage.

BISHOP OF THE BUTTERFLY

Arthurian

The name by which the historical Bishop of WINCHESTER, PETER DES ROCHES (1204–38), became known after he was given by ARTHUR the power of closing his hand and opening it again to reveal a butterfly. This gift was bestowed on him so people would believe that he had come across a house in which he found Arthur still alive.

BITH

Irish

The son of NOAH and father of CESAIR. He was said to have been one of the possible leaders of the fifty-three people who came to IRELAND in a time before the Flood. Of these fifty-three, only three were men: Bith himself, FINTAN and the pilot LADRA. Alternatively, these invaders were led by BANBHA, who later became one of the triad of goddesses collectively known as the SPIRIT OF IRELAND.

BLACK ARCAN

Irish

According to Irish folk tradition the killer of FIONN MAC CUMHAILL, although the mythological cycles name this person as FINNÉCES, a character who was at one time his mentor.

BLACK BOOK OF CARMARTHEN, THE

Welsh and Arthurian

LLYFR DU CAERTYDDIN, an important source of Welsh mythological and legendary belief. Dating from *c.* 1105, although possibly copied from much earlier works, *The Black Book of Carmarthen* is so called as it was written by the black-robed monks of Carmarthen. The original manuscript is today housed in the National Library of Wales at Aberystwyth, along with the manuscripts for the WHITE BOOK OF RHYDDERCH and the *Book of Taliesin*.

BLACK KNIGHT

Arthurian

Common throughout Arthurian and medieval romance, the Black Knight was not always the villain of popular conception. Five main Black Knights occur in the Arthurian legends, being:

1 The son of TOM A'LINCOLN and ANGLI-TORA, and thus ARTHUR's grandson.
2 Sir PERCARD, who was killed by GARETH.
3 A knight (true name unknown) with whose wife PERCEVAL had innocently exchanged a ring. Furious, the Black Knight tied her to a tree, but Perceval overcame him and explained the situation. The Black Knight was then reconciled with his wife.
4 The son of the King of the CARLACHS and one of ARTHUR's knights, he was defeated by the KNIGHT OF THE LANTERN.
5 A warrior who guarded a wimple and a horn on an ivory lion. He was slain by FERGUS.

BLACKBIRD OF CILGWRI

Welsh and Arthurian

An ancient bird with whom GWRHYR the interpreter communicated during the expedition mounted to help CULHWCH locate the maiden OLWEN. The bird directed them to the STAG OF RHEDYNFRC, which in turn sent them to the OWL OF CWN CAWLWYD, which took them to the EAGLE OF GWERNABWY, which guided them to the SALMON OF LLYN LLW.

BLADUD

British and Arthurian

Also BALDUDUS

The magical son of HUDIBRAS, the founder of the hot springs and temples at BATH and a great master of the Druidic arts, including necromancy and magical flight. According to GEOFFREY OF MONMOUTH, he was directly ascended from AENEAS and BRUTUS. Geoffrey of Monmouth develops what was obviously an early belief by adding that Bladud was an ancestor of King ARTHUR. The association between Bladud and the Druidic arts possibly draws on Welsh or Breton bardic tradition. He is again mentioned in the *VITA MERLINI* as a guardian of therapeutic springs and wells. His story clearly derives from a local Somerset folk tradition, although it is the version given by Geoffrey of Monmouth that gives us the most commonly told version of the life of this King.

This story says that Bladud was sent by Hudibras to study philosophy at Athens, but, while he was there, his father died. Bladud returned home, sources say in the year 873 BC, to claim his throne, bringing with him some of the learned Greeks he had met in Athens. Together they founded a university at Stamford in Lincolnshire, which flourished until the coming of Saint Augustine, when Celtic learning was suppressed in favour of Catholicism. Skilled in magic, Bladud conjured up the hot springs at Bath and built a temple to Minerva over them, and in this he laced devices of his own invention to provide a perpetual flame. He also famously invented a means of flying with artificial wings. He flew on these to LONDON but crashed onto the temple of Apollo, which stood where SAINT PAUL'S CATHEDRAL stands today, and was killed. He had reigned for twenty years, and during that time is credited with founding not only the springs at Bath, but also the city, which he named KAERBADUS. That other famous mythical king, King LEIR, succeeded him.

However, a legend that was extant in the Somerset and Bath area from early times tells a slightly different version, although the similarities between the two are evident, and it is obvious that Geoffrey of Monmouth drew on and refined this version for his own. This early story says that, during the reign of Hudibras, Bladud contracted leprosy and was banished from the royal court. Before his departure his mother gave him a ring so that he would be instantly recognisable to her again. Bladud travelled to Greece and, following receipt of the news of his father's death, returned to ENGLAND, where he took up a lowly job tending a herd of swine, for no blemished king could ascend the throne, and his leprosy thus ruled him out. This job is traditionally said to have been at Swainswick near Bath. While he was tending the herd, he noticed that there was a favourite place in which they liked to wallow, and he noticed especially that those that had blemished skin were restored to full health by the mud. He tried the same treatment and was immediately cured, thus enabling him to claim his rightful throne. Over the spot where he was miraculously cured he and his consort ALARON built a temple that was the foundation of the city of Bath.

A less well-known story concerning the therapeutic waters at Bath and their connection with Bladud claims that they are the result of Bladud's experiments. During his time in Greece Bladud acquired advanced scientific knowledge. Using this skill he buried two tuns (a tun being a barrel with a capacity of 252 gallons) containing burning brass, and two more, this time of glass, containing seven types of salts, brimstone and wild fire. All four tuns were said to be the source of heat within the waters of Bath, their contents spilling over into the water itself. Consequently the waters were regarded as being poisonous and were not to be drunk under any circumstances. The habit of 'taking the waters' did not, apparently, begin until the reign of Charles II in the seventeenth century.

Some commentators, using the information concerning Bladud's skill in the Druidic arts, have connected the King with the OTHERWORLD. Indeed, in the cosmology of the *VITA MERLINI*, Bath is placed in the centre of BRITAIN, which is, in turn, placed in the centre of the world, thus providing a portal to the Otherworld, of which the swine is a native animal, and over which Bladud presides. This connection appears only in later works, and is a simple decoration of the earlier sources that give no reference to the Otherworld at all.

BLAES
Arthurian
Appearing in the *TRIADS* and possibly identical with BLAISE, the master of MERLIN, Blaes was the son of the Earl of LLYCHLYN and one of the TWENTY-FOUR KNIGHTS of ARTHUR's court.

BLAI
Irish
1 One of the five people responsible for raising CÚ CHULAINN. The other four were FINDCHÓEM, his aunt; SENCHA, described as the 'pacifist'; FERGHUS MAC ROICH; and AMHAIRGHIN. Blai is reputed to have defended the honour of the men of IRELAND, even during their pillaging.
2 An alternative name sometimes given to SAAR, the wife of FIONN MAC CUMHAILL and mother of OISÎN.

BLAISE
Arthurian
Hailing originally from Vercelli in Italy, Blaise was a hermit to whom MERLIN's mother was sent while she was pregnant. When the infant Merlin was just two years old he dedicated the story of the GRAIL to Blaise, who also wrote an account of ARTHUR's battles. It appears that he may be identical with the Welsh BLAES.

BLAMORE DE GANIS
Arthurian
The son of LANCELOT, brother of BLEOBERIS and a KNIGHT OF THE ROUND TABLE, who on one occasion accused King ANGUISH of murder, only to be defeated in trial by combat by TRISTAN, after which they became firm friends. When Lancelot quarrelled with ARTHUR, he and his brother supported their father, Blamore de Ganis being made the Duke of LIMOUSIN. Following Arthur's death he became a hermit.

BLANCHARD
Arthurian
The fairy horse that was given to LANVAL by his lover, TRYAMOUR.

BLANCHEFLEUR
Arthurian
1 The mistress of PERCEVAL who was besieged by King CLAMADEUS, who desired her for himself. She would have killed herself had not Perceval defeated Clamadeus in single combat.
2 According to GOTTFRIED VON STRASSBURG, the sister of King MARK. She eloped with RIVALIN of PARMENIE, and their son was TRISTAN. Hearing of her husband's death, she died of a broken heart.

BLASINE
Arthurian
A sister to ARTHUR who married NENTRES of GARLOT and became the mother, by him, of GALESCHIN, Duke of CLARENCE. It appears that she may be cognate with both BELISENT and HERMESENT.

BLÁTHNA-D, -T
Irish
A beautiful OTHERWORLDLY maiden. On the occasion when CÚ CHULAINN and his men were raiding the Otherworld, here depicted as SCOTLAND, CÚ ROÍ MAC DÁIRI appeared to the great hero in disguise and offered to help him. Thanks to his intervention, Cú Chulainn and his men captured a magical cauldron – a familiar icon in tales of the Otherworld – three magic crows and the beautiful Bláthnad. Cú Chulainn and his men broke their promise

Blanchefleur, the mistress of Perceval, though here depicted with Sir Galahad. (Edwin Austin Abbey, 1895. © Burstein Collection/Corbis)

to share the spoils, however, and the enraged Cú Roí mac Dáiri seized the lot and married the maiden.

Cú Chulainn planned his revenge and conspired with Bláthnad on the feast of SAMHAIN. Cú Roí mac Dáiri was murdered, and possession of Bláthnad passed to Cú Chulainn. Cú Roí mac Dáiri was avenged by FERCHERDNE his FILI, who, noticing Bláthnad standing close to the edge of the cliff, ran at the girl, caught her around the waist, and threw them both to their deaths on the rocks below.

BLEDDYN
Welsh

The name given by MATH FAB MATHONWY to the boy born as a wolf cub to GILFAETHWY and GWYDION FAB DÔN during the third year of their punishment for the rape of GOEWIN. The first year they had spent as a stag and hind, and had borne a fawn that Math fab Mathonwy had turned into a boy to whom he gave the name HYDWN. The second year was spent as a boar and a sow, in which guise they bore a wild piglet, who was likewise transformed and named HWYCHDWN. At the end of the third year, Gilfaethwy and Gwydion fab Dôn were returned to their human form, and found themselves the parents of three boys.

BLEDLOCHTANA
Irish

Monsters or supernatural beings who were invoked on the fourth day of the First Battle of MAGH TUIREDH by the DAGHDHA. They were accompanied on this occasion by the BADBA and AMAITE AIDGILL, also supernatural beings.

BLEEDING LANCE
Arthurian

Another way of referring to the LANCE OF LONGINUS.

BLENZIBLY
Arthurian

In the Icelandic *SAGA OF TRISTAN AND ISODD*, Blenzibly is named as the mother of TRISTAN. Her lover, PLEGRUS, was killed while jousting with KALEGRAS, who afterwards became her paramour and the father of Tristan.

BLEOBERIS
Arthurian

The son of LANCELOT (though some sources simply say that Lancelot was a relation), brother to BLAMORE DE GANIS, and a KNIGHT OF THE ROUND TABLE. When Lancelot quarrelled with ARTHUR, he and his brother supported their father. Bleoberis was made Duke of POITIERS and went on to join the Holy Crusades.

BLIOCADRAN
Arthurian

The father of PERCEVAL, according to French romance.

BLODEU(W)EDD
Welsh and Arthurian

A flower-maiden whose name means 'Flower Face'. She was created from the flowers of oak, broom and meadowsweet by MATH FAB MATHONWY and GWYDION FAB DÔN as a wife for LLEU LLAW GYFFES to circumvent the third curse put on him by his mother ARIANRHOD, that curse being that he would never have a mortal wife until she herself gave him one, a thing she, naturally enough, never intended to do. Regrettably, Blodeuwedd was unfaithful to Lleu Llaw Gyffes with the hunter GRONW BEBYR. She and her lover contrived to kill Lleu Llaw Gyffes, who could be killed only by a spear that had been worked for a year at Mass time on Sundays, and then only if he was standing with one foot on the back of a billygoat and the other in a bathtub.

Blodeuwedd persuaded her husband to demonstrate this curious position to her while Gronw Bebyr hid in the bushes armed with the appropriate spear. As Lleu Llaw Gyffes adopted the required stance, Gronw Bebyr cast the spear, but only managed to wound Lleu Llaw Gyffes. Lleu Llaw Gyffes immediately changed into an eagle and flew away. Blodeuwedd was changed into an owl by Gwydion fab Dôn for her infidelity, and Gronw Bebyr was killed by the cheated husband after he had been found and healed by Gwydion fab Dôn. Some authorities consider that Blodeuwedd was the original of GUENDOLOENA, who is, in turn, considered by some as the forerunner of the Arthurian GUINEVERE.

BLOIE
Arthurian

The true name of the Lady of MALEHAUT.

BLONDE ESMERÉE
Arthurian

The daughter of the King of WALES. She was turned into a serpent by the magicians MABON and EVRAIN, being freed from the enchantment only when GUINGLAIN kissed her.

BLUNDERBOAR
British and Arthurian

A giant who once managed to capture JACK THE GIANT-KILLER, but was killed, along with his brothers, when Jack managed to escape.

BOADICEA
British

Popular version of BOUDICCA.

BOANN(A(N))
Irish
Also BÓINN

The sister of BÉBIND, goddess of the river BOYNE, wife of NECHTAN and mother of OENGHUS MAC IN OG, the result of a secret union with the DAGHDHA. The story of their illicit union is told by the tenth-century poet Cináed uá hArtacáin. Boann travelled to stay with her brother ELCMAR, a vassal of the Daghdha, with whom she sought an affair, but Elcmar discovered this and swore never to stay away long enough to give them time to consummate their lust for each other. The Daghdha easily circumvented this by causing the sun to stay still for nine months, so Elcmar did not know he had been away that long. On his return he realised that something had been going on because of the changes he saw in the flowers and the trees. Shortly before Elcmar's return, Boann had given birth to a boy, whom she left outside the SÍDH of MIDHIR, who took the infant in and raised him as his own, although later he told the boy of his parentage.

BOCÁNACHS
Irish

Spirits of an unknown nature who were reputed to have shrieked in the air around CÚ CHULAINN, while the hero fought FERDIA, their cries being joined by those of the BANNACHS and the GENITI GLINNE. They seem to be a representation of the battle fury of the hero, and may be a partial origin of the BANSHEE.

BODB
Irish

The goddess of battle. Following the Second Battle of MAGH TUIREDH, Bodb gave a prophecy of doom after recounting the heroic struggle.

BODB (DEARG)
Irish
A King of MUNSTER, sometimes known as BÔV, who was employed by the DAGHDHA to seek out the dream woman with whom OENGHUS MAC IN OG had fallen in love. After a year he reported that he had found the maiden at a lake. Bodb and Oenghus mac in Og travelled to the lake, where they saw the maiden with her 149 sisters. Bodb informed Oenghus mac in Og that her name was CAER, the daughter of ETHAL ANUBAL, a prince of CONNACHT, and he told Oenghus mac in Og that he must enlist the help of AILILL and MEDHBHA if he wished to meet the maiden. This he did, and, after following their magical instructions, was united with Caer as a swan, and together they flew back to Oenghus mac in Og's home at BRUGH NA BÓINNE.

Bodb Dearg was chosen to be the King of the TUATHA DÉ DANANN after the death of the Daghdha, although this choice upset LIR, who had been neither consulted nor considered. To compensate Lir, Bodb Dearg gave Lir one of his daughters, AOBH, to be his wife. She bore him four children, two boys and two girls, before dying. Bodb Dearg then gave Lir his other daughter AOIFE, but she grew jealous of her stepchildren and changed them into swans, a form they would have to remain in for 900 years. Bodb Dearg cursed Aoife and turned her into a raven or, as some say, a 'demon of the air'. Some sources name a third daughter of Bodb Dearg as SAAR and make her the wife of FIONN MAC CUMHAILL and the mother of OISÎN.

BODHMHALL
Irish
The daughter of TADHG and sister of MUIRNE. According to the *LEABHAR NA HUIDHRE*, FIONN MAC CUMHAILL was born at her home. She subsequently became the guardian of the young Fionn mac Cumhaill and raised the boy, at that time called DEIMNE, in seclusion for the child's own safety.

BOECE, HECTOR
Arthurian
Scottish historian (*c.* 1465–1536), born in Dundee. He studied at Montaigu College, Paris, where *c.*1492–98 he was regent, or professor of philosophy. Invited to preside over the new university of Aberdeen, Boece accepted the office and was at the same time made a canon of the cathedral. In 1522 he published, in Latin, his lives of the bishops of Mortlach and Aberdeen. His Latin *SCOTORUM HISTORIA* (*History of Scotland*) contains Arthurian information written from an anti-ARTHUR viewpoint. Published in 1527, it was deemed distinctly scholarly at the time, though it proved to contain a large amount of fiction.

BOIARDO, MATTEO MARIA
Arthurian
Italian poet (1434–94), born in Scandiano, a village at the foot of the Lombard Apennines. He studied at Ferrara, and in 1462 married the daughter of the Count of Norellara. He lived at the court of Ferrara and was appointed governor of Modena in 1481, and of Reggio in 1487. His fame rests on his unfinished *ORLANDO INNAMORATO* (1486), a long narrative poem in which the Charlemagne romances are recast into *ottava rima* (Italian stanzas of eight eleven-syllabled lines, ten-syllabled in English, the first six lines rhyming alternately, the last two forming a couplet). This poem was to inspire Ludovico ARIOSTO's *ORLANDO FURIOSO*, the ROLAND epic that forms a continuation to Boiardo's unfinished work.

BÓINN
Irish
See BOANN

BONEDD YR ARWR
Arthurian
A Welsh manuscript that contains fascinating Arthurian genealogical material, making BENDIGEID VRAN an ancestor of ARTHUR in both the paternal and the maternal pedigrees.

BOOK OF LEINSTER, THE
Irish
An important source text, dating from the twelfth century. It contains one version of the *TAÍN BÓ CUAILNGÈ*, which possibly dates from the eighth century. It also contains the *DINNSHENCHAS*, an early Christian tract.

BOR-MO, -VO
Gaulish
A deity who is associated with seething or boiling waters and who is yet another god of the Apollo type. He is usually paired with the goddess DAMONA or 'Divine Cow'.

BORRE
Arthurian
The illegitimate son of ARTHUR by LIONORS who is usually identified with LOHOLT. When he came of age, he was made a KNIGHT OF THE ROUND TABLE.

BORS

Arthurian

(1) The elder Bors, the king of GAUL or GANNES and an ally of ARTHUR in the battle against the eleven rebellious leaders at BEDEGRAINE. He married EVAINE and, by her, became the father of the younger Bors. It is possible that this Bors should be identified with BAN.

(2) The younger Bors, the son of EVAINE and the elder Bors, whom he succeeded as King of GANNES. A KNIGHT OF THE ROUND TABLE, he was chaste, but the daughter of King BRANDEGORIS fell in love with him. Her nurse, with the aid of an enchanted ring, forced Bors to make love to her. As a result he became the father of ELYAN THE WHITE, who later became Emperor of CONSTANTINOPLE. During the Quest for the Holy GRAIL, Bors was one of the three knights who succeeded in their task. Unlike GALAHAD and PERCEVAL, he returned to ARTHUR's court, eventually dying on a Crusade. In origin Bors might be cognate with the legendary Welsh character GWRI (cf. TWENTY-FOUR KNIGHTS).

BOSCASTLE

Arthurian

Small Cornish village set in a glen whose narrow harbour is protected by cliffs on either side and was, in the imagination of Alfred, Lord Tennyson, the place from where the dying ARTHUR was borne away on the funeral barge to the mystical island of AVALON.

BOSCAWEN-UN

British

A stone circle in a particularly remote location approximately four miles west of Penzance, CORNWALL. A rocky outcrop nearby displays an impression said to be the footprint of one of the old Cornish giants, possibly CORMORAN himself. Boscawen-un stone circle is mentioned in the Welsh *TRIOEDD YNYS PRYDEIN* as one of the three main GORSEDDS (assembly places for bards and augurs) in BRITAIN. Although it certainly pre-dates the Celtic era by some considerable time, this stone circle was, like many other similar structures across the country, used by the DRUIDS for their worship.

Boscastle, Cornwall, from where Alfred, Lord Tennyson said Arthur was carried away to Avalon.
(© Jean Williamson/Mick Sharp)

BOSHERTON POOLS

Arthurian

Bosherton is a small village some six miles south of Pembroke in DYFED. Its beautiful freshwater lake is said to be one of the many reputed lakes from which ARTHUR obtained his sword, EXCALIBUR. Folklore also says that it was from this inlet that Arthur was carried away on his final journey to AVALON.

BOSO

Arthurian

The ruler of Oxford and one of the vassals who accompanied ARTHUR on his campaign against the ROMAN EMPIRE.

BOUDICCA

British

The first-century Queen of the ICENI in Norfolk, ENGLAND. Her husband PRASUTAGUS had tried to retain some independence from the invading Romans by remaining on good terms with ROME as a client king. After he had died, however, the Romans took charge and plundered the royal household. Boudicca was flogged and her daughters raped. Boudicca then roused her people and the people of the neighbouring TRI-NOVANTES, invoked the goddess ANDRASTE, and led a campaign against the Romans. At first successful, she razed *Camulodnum* (Colchester) late in AD 60, and then LONDON and finally the new city of *Verulamium* (Saint Albans) in AD 61. Finally, the Romans recovered from the surprise of Boudicca's attack and defeated her army, whereupon Boudicca took poison.

The location of Boudicca's grave remains one of the many unsolved mysteries of the era. For a while STONEHENGE was considered her monument. Others say that she lies under platform 10 at King's Cross station, or is buried under a mound in Parliament Hill Fields, Hampstead. Her ghost, however, appears to be able to move freely around, for it is often sighted near the earthworks of Amesbury Banks in Epping Forest, and in 1950 she was sighted driving her war chariot out of the mist at Cammeringham, Lincolnshire.

Boudicca's name may be an assumed one, for it appears to mean 'Victory', a name she may have adopted after her invocation of Andraste. She is generally portrayed as tall, fierce-looking and harsh-voiced, with a mass of flaming red hair that hung down to her waist.

BOUDIN

Arthurian

The brother of King MARK of CORNWALL and father of ALISANDER THE ORPHAN, his son gaining his epithet after Mark had murdered him.

BOUN, RAUF DE

Arthurian

French chronicler and author of the *PETIT BRUT*.

BOURGET, LAKE

Arthurian

A lake in the French Alps near which ARTHUR was said to have killed a giant cat, a fact that is commemorated in local names such as MONT DU CHAT (Mountain of the Cat), DENT DU CHAT (Cat's Tooth) and COL DU CHAT (Cat's Neck). It is possible that this animal was a CAPALU, the continental name for the CATH PALUG.

BÔV

Irish

See BODB DEARG

BOYNE

Irish

The Irish river of which BOANN was the patron goddess. The river rises in Westmeath and spills into the Irish Sea at Drogheda on the east coast of IRELAND to the north of Dublin. One of the most important and richly decorated of all the European monuments is to be found on the northern banks of the river at NEW GRANGE. This tumulus has an important role in the Irish mythological cycles. Known as BRUGH NA BÓINNE, it is the home of OENGHUS MAC IN OG, the son of the DAGHDHA, whom some hold responsible for its construction.

BRABANT

Arthurian

Former duchy of Western Europe, comprising the Dutch province of North Brabant and the Belgian provinces of Brabant and Antwerp. They were divided when Belgium became independent in 1830. It was within this realm that ELSA of Brabant was besieged by Frederick de TELRAMUND and subsequently rescued by LOHENGRIN.

BRACIACA

Gaulish

The goddess of ale, although to the Celts this was not the brew known today, but rather a divine drink consumed only by the gods.

BRADMANTE

Arthurian

A female warrior of the Carolingian era (AD

751–987) who was told, according to ARIOSTO, that the House of ESTE would descend from her.

BRÂN
Irish

(1) Not to be confused with BRÂN THE BLESSED, or more correctly BENDIGEID VRAN, this Brân is a hero of an OTHERWORLDLY adventure that is typically Irish in flavour and content. The son of FEBAL, Brân was lured away by a beautiful spirit to TÍR INNA MBAN, an Otherworldly realm, which the spirit described as a paradisal land. Brân set sail with twenty-seven companions and, *en route*, encountered the sea god MANANNÁN MAC LIR driving a chariot. As they came together, Manannán mac Lir changed the sea into a flowery plain, the fishes into flocks of sheep and the leaping salmon into frisking calves, before driving away over the now solid surface of the sea. As he disappeared the sea returned to normal.

Sailing on, Brân and his companions reached the magical island, but were afraid to land. However, the leader of the women on that island threw a ball of string out to him that adhered to his hand, and by this method their ship was hauled ashore. As soon as they had landed, a strange euphoria spread across the adventurers, who were led through Tír inna mBan to a great hall, where they were told there was a bed and a wife for every man, along with an unlimited supply of food and drink. Beautiful women inhabited the entire island, and soon Brân and his companions had settled into a life of comfort and happiness. After what seemed like just a year, Brân and his men returned to Ireland. As their ship appeared near the shore, a crowd of people gathered and called out to the ship asking his name. Brân replied, telling them both his name and that of his father. After a while they shouted back to him that the only Brân they knew of was from one of their ancient stories know as 'The Voyage of Brân'.

A strange apprehension gripped the adventurers, the truth of their absence becoming clear when one of them, eager for home, leapt ashore. The instant his foot touched the beach his body collapsed in a heap of dust. They had been absent not for just a year, but for many hundreds of years, and Brân and his companions were as dead men, alive only aboard their ship thanks to the enchantment of Tír inna mBan. Brân called out the details of their adventure to the people on the shore, then turned the ship back out to sea and sailed away, never to be heard of again.

(2) One of the hounds of FIONN MAC CUMHAILL, the other being called SGEOLAN. These dogs were the nephews of Fionn mac Cumhaill, for they had been born to TUIREANN, his sister, who had married ILLAN and had been transformed into a wolfhound by her husband's supernatural mistress, a form she retained until Illan renounced her.

As a boast, OENGHUS MAC IN OG stated that neither of these hounds would be capable of killing a single swine in his herd but, rather, that the black boar would kill them. A year later Fionn mac Cumhaill released his hounds against a herd of a hundred swine that had appeared outside Oenghus mac in Og's home and killed them all, Brân killing the prized black boar. Oenghus mac in Og complained that the swine had in fact been his children in disguise. A quarrel followed during which Fionn mac Cumhaill readied himself to attack Oenghus mac in Og, but he sued for peace.

BRÂN (THE BLESSED)
Welsh and Arthurian
The literal translation of BENDIGEID VRAN.

BRANDEGORIS
Arthurian
The King of STRANGGORE and one of the eleven kings or leaders who rebelled against the young ARTHUR at the start of his reign. His unnamed daughter became the mother of ELYAN THE WHITE by BORS. Some commentators have argued that he originated from the god BRÂN, and that his name means Brân of Gore.

BRANDILES
Arthurian
The son of Sir GILBERT and a KNIGHT OF THE ROUND TABLE, he is to be found in the Second *CONTINUATION* to CHRÉTIEN DE TROYES's *PERCEVAL* and the *GEST OF SIR GAUVAIN*, in which he did combat with GAWAIN, who had defeated his father and his two brothers, as well as seducing his sister. The fight, however, was stopped, to be resumed later, but the two never crossed paths again. In the Second *Continuation*, the two did re-meet, and during their second fight the ghostly image of Brandiles's sister was present, along with GUINGLAIN, her son by Gawain. It has been suggested that he is, at least in origin, identical with BRIAN DES ILES.

BRANGALED
Welsh and Arthurian
The owner of a horn, CORN BRANGALED, that was said to have been capable of providing any drink desired and to number amongst the THIRTEEN TREASURES OF BRITAIN.

BRANGIEN

Arthurian

According to GOTTFRIED VON STRASSBURG, Brangien was the exceptionally beautiful maid-servant of ISEULT who was given a love potion to administer to King MARK and ISEULT. Unfortunately, TRISTAN and Iseult drank the potion, thus expediting their famous affair. On her wedding night Iseult substituted Brangien for herself so that Mark would not guess that she had already lain with TRISTAN, and subsequently she tried to have Brangien murdered to ensure her silence. The attempt was unsuccessful, and Iseult later repented of it. Brangien had an affair with KAHEDRIN, the son of King HOEL of BRITTANY.

BRANWEN

Welsh and Arthurian

The daughter of LLYR, brother to BENDIGEID VRAN, and half-sister to EFNISIEN and NISIEN. Branwen was given to MATHOLWCH, the King of IRELAND, by her giant brother Bendigeid Vran, along with a magical cauldron. However, during the wedding celebrations in WALES, Efnisien insulted Matholwch so badly that, once they had returned to Ireland, he vented his anger on his new bride. Learning of this ill-treatment, Bendigeid Vran led an army to Ireland and, having first been on the losing side thanks to the healing properties of the very cauldron he had given to Matholwch, he finally laid Ireland to waste after Efnisien had succeeded in destroying the cauldron. However, so great was the destruction that only seven of the Welsh party survived, and only five pregnant Irish women lived on, for they had taken refuge in a cave. Bendigeid Vran himself was mortally wounded and, before he died, ordered the seven survivors to remove his head and bury it under the WHITE MOUNT in LONDON, face towards FRANCE, there to serve as a guardian to the island.

The seven survivors – TALIESIN, PRYDERI, MANAWYDAN FAB LLYR, GLIFIEU, YNAWAG, GRUDDIEU and HEILYN – brought Branwen back to Wales, but on their arrival in ANGLESEY she sat down and looked back towards Ireland. Thinking of the destruction that had been brought about on her behalf, she died of a broken heart and was buried at BEDD BRANWEN on the banks of the River ALAW, a site that was excavated in 1813, when the cremated remains of a woman was discovered in a contemporary urn.

The five Irish survivors all gave birth to sons. When they were of age, each of the five women took one of them for a husband, founded the five provinces of Ireland, and set about repopulating the decimated island.

BRANWEN FERCH LLYR

Welsh

Branwen, Daughter of Llyr, one of the four main stories of the *MABINOGION*, concerning the fate of BRANWEN and the destructive expedition mounted by BENDIGEID VRAN to IRELAND.

BRAS-DE-FER

Arthurian

In his work *LE TORNOIMENT DE L'ANTICHRIST*, the French poet Huon de Mery tells how he went to an enchanted spring in BROCELIANDE and Bras-de-Fer, the chamberlain of the Antichrist, rode up. In his company they rode to the scene of a battle where the forces of Heaven, including ARTHUR and his knights, fought against the forces of Hell.

BRASTIAS

Arthurian

Originally in the service of the Duke of TINTAGEL (possibly GORLOIS), Brastias became one of ARTHUR's knights, fought against the rebellious leaders at BEDEGRAINE and was made a warden in the north of England.

BREA

Irish

A contemporary of PARTHOLÁN, who is named as the first man ever to build a house or make a cauldron.

BREDBEDDLE

Arthurian

In the story of *KING ARTHUR AND THE KING OF CORNWALL*, Bredbeddle was a knight who accompanied ARTHUR, TRISTAN and GAWAIN to the King of Cornwall's residence. There, with the aid of a holy book, Bredbeddle controlled a fiend that the King of Cornwall had sent to spy on them.

BREGIA

Irish

A giant whose three herdsmen attempted to attack CÚ CHULAINN but were killed.

BREGON

Irish

The descendant of a Scythian noble expelled from Egypt who settled in Spain. Bregon built a high tower from which his son, ITH, sighted the far-off land of IRELAND. This sighting led to the invasion of Ireland by the Sons of MÍL ÉSPÁINE, although not directly, for the story that tells of this sighting says that Ith was the first to land in Ireland, having travelled there with ninety followers. At first he was warmly received by the TUATHA DÉ DANANN, but, after he had so richly praised the fertility of the land, the Tuatha Dé Danann suspected him of having designs on their realm and killed him. His body was taken back to Spain by his grieving companions, and it was this event that led to the subsequent invasion.

BREGUOIN
Arthurian
The name given to Mount AGNED, according to one tenth-century manuscript.

BRENG
Irish
'Lie', one of the three names of the wife of the DAGHDHA. Her other names were MENG and MEABEL.

BRENNIUS
British
A son of MOLMUTIUS and TONWENNA and the brother of BELINUS. After their father's death the two brothers quarrelled over who should reign in his place. The quarrel was settled by arbitration, and Belinus became King with Brennius subject to him as the overlord of the region to the north of the HUMBER. After five years of peace, Brennius was persuaded to rebel and travelled to Norway, where he married the King's daughter and sailed back with a large army. Belinus, who had received intelligence of the impending attack, was ready to meet his brother as he attempted to land in NORTHUMBRIA. Belinus routed the Norwegians and Brennius was forced to flee to GAUL. There he married for a second time and again raised an army against his brother. He crossed the English Channel at the head of a Gaulish army, but Tonwenna intervened and the two brothers were reconciled, the Gaulish army staying in BRITAIN. Sometime later the two brothers crossed the English Channel, the Gaulish army with them, subdued the Gauls and marched on Italy, where they sacked ROME. Brennius stayed in Rome, while Belinus came home and ruled in peace for the rest of his life.

Brennius appears to have been a figment of GEOFFREY OF MONMOUTH's fevered imagination, for the Celtic sack of Rome, which occurred in 390 BC, was led by a Gaul by the name of BRENNOS. The slight change in name and definite change in nationality seems to have been Geoffrey of Monmouth's way of claiming the sack of Rome for the British.

BRENN-OS, -US
Gaulish
1 An ancient god to whom the Celts attributed their success in the battles of Allia and Delphi, and who was mistaken by Roman and Greek chroniclers for a human leader.
2 The Gaulish leader of the Celtic forces that successfully sacked ROME in 390 BC. He is usually confused with the first Brennos.

BRENT KNOLL
Arthurian
A hill in Somerset, between Bridgwater and Weston-super-Mare, that was the site of a battle between YDER and three giants who lived there. Accompanying ARTHUR, Yder was sent on ahead and encountered the giants alone. By the time Arthur and his retinue arrived, Yder had dispatched the giants but had lost his own life in the fray.

BRES
Irish
(1) During the First Battle of MAGH TUIREDH, NUADHA, the King of the TUATHA DÉ DANANN, lost an arm, and, because the King had to be physically unblemished, could no longer reign and abdicated in favour of Bres who had been raised among the Tuatha Dé Danann, his mother's people, even though his father, ELATHA, was a FOMIIOIRÉ leader.

Bres was not a good ruler, even though his alternative name of GORMAC means 'dutiful son', being both tyrannical and mean, offering no form of entertainment to his followers and making even the greatest of them toil like common slaves. He married BRIGHID, the daughter of the DAGHDHA, but compelled her father to build him a fort. He treated OGHMA with contempt and made him collect firewood. Unable to stand the tyranny any longer, COIRBRE, the FILI of the Tuatha Dé Danann, cursed Bres in a magical satire that made his face erupt in boils. Forced to abdicate, he defected to the Fomhoiré and mustered an army against his former people.

During the Second Battle of Magh Tuiredh, Bres was captured and pleaded for his life, promising in return four harvests a year and continual supplies of milk from the Tuatha Dé Danann's cows. These offers were rejected, but his life was spared in return for essential advice on the best times to plough, sow and reap.

(2) The brother of MEDBHA, CLOTHRU, EITHNE, LOTHAR and NÁR.

(3) The emissary of the TUATHA DÉ DANANN who met with the emissary of the FIR BHOLG before the First Battle of MAGH TUIREDH.

Brent Knoll, Somerset, the site of the battle between Yder and three local giants.
(© Jean Williamson/Mick Sharp)

He proposed that the two factions should divide the land equally, but this was not to be and he was killed in the resulting battle.

See also SRENG

BRESAL ECHARLAM MAC ECHACH BAETHLAIM
Irish

A hero at TARA whose name was given by the doorkeeper to LUGH when that god was attempting to gain entry to the royal court. How he became a hero or why he was regarded as one is not recorded.

BRETA SOGUR
Arthurian

A Scandinavian version of the works of GEOFFREY OF MONMOUTH that names ASSYSLA as the island on which ARTHUR died, thus making that island cognate with AVALON. This work is also unique in asserting that Arthur was buried at CANTERBURY.

BREUNIS SAUNCE PYTÉ
Arthurian

Originally knighted by ARTHUR, he seems to have had the ability to be in more than one place at a time. He turned against his original ally, and was eventually slain by GARETH.

BREUNOR
Arthurian

The brother of DINADAN, and generally known as Breunor the Black, he arrived at ARTHUR's court with such a badly tailored coat that the ever impertinent KAY gave him the nickname LE COTE MALE TAILÉE – 'the badly cut coat'. He refused to remove his coat until he had avenged his father. He helped the damsel MALEDISANT, who at first hurled abuse at him (presumably because of his coat), but eventually married him, after which he became the Lord of PENDRAGON CASTLE.

BRÍ
Irish

The daughter of MIDHIR who was loved by LIATH. When Liath attempted to meet with Brí, her father's attendants kept him at bay with a barrage of slingshots. Liath was forced to retreat after his servant had been killed, and Brí subsequently died of a broken heart.

BRÍ LEITH
Irish

The SÍDH in County Longford, IRELAND, that was the home of MIDHIR, a god of TÍR TAIRNGIRI.

Although the sídh was an OTHERWORLDLY home, a home of the dead, Midhir had, like MANNANÁN MAC LIR, associations with rebirth.

BRIAN
Irish

A son of TUIRENN and brother of IUCHAR and IUCHARBA. Some name his mother as DANU, and it is thought that the three brothers are, in true Celtic style, really three aspects of the same person, Brian being a form of the Gaulish BRENNOS, the god to whom the GAULS attributed their success at the battles of Allia and Delphi.

For a long time the three brothers had been involved in a blood feud with CIAN, the father of LUGH. While Cian was travelling to ULSTER to muster an army, he was intercepted and killed by the three brothers. Lugh discovered this and punished them by setting increasingly difficult tasks that would arm him for the forthcoming Second Battle of MAGH TUIREDH. The first consisted of collecting three apples that were as large as a baby's head and could cure all wounds and ailments. The second was to obtain a magical pigskin that had the same properties. The third was to collect a spear whose point was so hot that it had to be housed in a block of ice. The fourth was to procure a chariot and horses that could outrun the wind over both land and water. The fifth was to collect the seven magical swine of King ASAL, which could be eaten one day but reappear again the next, ready and willing to be eaten again. The sixth was to obtain a young dog that was so awful it terrified every other beast in the world. The seventh was to collect a cooking spit from the sunken island of FINCHORY. The eighth and final task was to shout three times from the top of a hill owned by MIODCHAOIN, a king who was a close friend of Cian, and who was, with his sons, under a bond never to allow any man to raise his voice on the hill.

The three brothers completed the first seven tasks with relative ease, but were almost killed as they attempted to carry out the final task. Finally, they feebly gave the three required shouts, but lay mortally wounded. Lugh refused to use the pigskin they had obtained for him, and thus they died.

BRIAN DES ILES
Arthurian

Perhaps identical with BRANDILES in origin, and conceivably based on the historical Brian de Insula, the illegitimate son of Alan Fergeant (eleventh century). In *PERLESVAUS*, Brian des Iles, aided by KAY, who had killed ARTHUR's son LOHOLT, attacked Arthur's kingdom, laying siege to

CARDUEIL but eventually being driven off by LANCELOT. Subsequently he was defeated by Arthur, after which he became his seneschal (steward).

BRIANT OF THE RED ISLE
Arthurian
The King who was the father of TRISTOUSE.

BRICKUS
Arthurian
According to WOLFRAM VON ESCHENBACH, the son of MAZADAN and thus grandfather of ARTHUR.

BRICRENE
Irish
The name of the monk who advised MAÍL DÚIN of the identity of the murderers of his father.

BRICRIU
Irish
'Poisoned Tongue', a malicious hero who built a wonderful hall and gave a feast for all the men of ULSTER and CONNACHT, threatening untold strife if either party refused to attend. As it was customary for the most notable warrior present to carve the roast, there was much competition for this honour. Bricriu secretly persuaded three heroes, LOEGHAIRE BUADHACH, CONALL CERNACH and CÚ CHULAINN, all to claim this honour. A brawl ensued, which resulted in the three being sent to Connacht to seek the judgement of MEDHBHA. She awarded the victor's palm to Cú Chulainn. However, when the three returned, Loeghaire Buadhach and Conall Cernach refused to acknowledge the verdict, saying Cú Chulainn had undoubtedly bribed the queen. Bricriu then sent the three to the King of MUNSTER, CÚ ROÍ MAC DÁIRI, who also awarded the honour to Cú Chulainn. Again the other two refused to accept this verdict, but Cú Roí mac Dáiri proved his verdict to be correct, and finally the right of Cú Chulainn was accepted. Following this debacle, however, nobody would have anything further to do with Bricriu and he remained a social outcast for the remainder of his life.

BRID(E)
Irish
A virgin deity who later became known as BRIGHID, or Bride, and then Saint Bride. Her attributes were light, inspiration and the skills associated with fire, such as metalworking and purification. As for Vesta of classical Roman mythology, a perpetual flame was kept burning in her honour. A genealogy, of sort, for Saint Bride exists in a chanted protective prayer.

Church dedicated to Saint Bride. (© Macduff Everton/Corbis)

Modern sculpture of Saint Bride.
(By permission of artist Paul Borda/© Dryad Designs, www.dryaddesign.com)

BRIDEI

Welsh

The son of MAELGWYN who became King of the PICTS after he had been invited to assume the crown. A formidable figure, he conquered most of the western Highlands. Saint COLUMBA was reported to have visited him, travelling to him along the valley that is today filled with the waters of Loch Ness. Within this great valley there was a well that never dried up and whose waters had to be contained by a heavy lid. One day a woman left the cap off and the valley filled with water, to which the people cried '*Tha loch nis ann!*' ('There is a lake there now!'), which is why the lake is called Loch Ness. This event was supposed to have happened while Columba was on his way to visit Bridei and then Inverness.

BRIGANTES

British and Arthurian

An ancient and powerful Celtic people of northern England whose tutelary goddess was BRIGANTIA, hence their name. CARATACUS, a King of the CATUVELLAUNI, was traditionally handed over to the Romans, with whom he was at war by CARTI-MANDUA, Queen of the Brigantes.

BRIGANTI(A)

British

Almost certainly to be identified with the Irish BRIGHID, Brigantia was the tutelary goddess of the BRIGANTES. A pastoral and river goddess whose name means 'High One', Brigantia was inextricably connected to flocks and cattle, for she was said to have been reared on the milk of a white, red-eared cow, a beast that came from the OTHERWORLD.

The powerful Queen CARTIMANDUA worshipped Brigantia almost exclusively over other Celtic deities. Brigantia, the highest goddess of English Celtic belief, was depicted in several ways, although all seem to have some aspect of the warrior within them. She was crowned on top of a globe, a symbol of victory; armed and wearing a breastplate; or bare-breasted in the company of the war god and a ram-headed serpent. Her therapeutic aspects came through her association with water, both the Rivers Briant and Brent being named after her. A third-century inscription on Hadrian's Wall identifies Brigantia with DEA CAELISTIS.

BRIGGIDDA

Irish and British

An early form of BRIDE/BRIGHID, but, so it would appear, slightly later in date than the earliest form of all, BRID.

BRIG(H)ID

Gaulish, Irish and British

(1) Goddess of poetry, handicrafts and learning. The daughter of the DAGHDHA, she had two sisters, both called Brighid. She was especially worshipped by the FILIDH, who were under her direct inspiration. Brighid was Christianised as Saint Brighid or BRIDE, her popularity in both pagan and Christian times being attested to by the many sites that bear her name. The worship of Brighid survived well into the Christian era in both IRELAND and SCOTLAND, where pagan–Christian prayers and ceremonies in her honour were carried out until at least as recently as the nineteenth and early twentieth centuries. She is sometimes equated with BRIGANTIA, which is possibly an early form of her name. It was reported by the medieval chronicler GIRALDUS CAMBRENSIS that an eternal sacred flame was kept burning at her shrine at Kildare, southern Ireland.

It is not unusual for Brighid, whose name means 'exalted one', to be amalgamated with her two sisters into a single goddess, who was said to be the goddess of smiths and metalworking, poetry, inspiration, healing and fertility, the name Brighid being used as a generic name for the goddess.

Her primal function, as the burning of an eternal flame would suggest, was that of fire and illumination. In many Romano-Celtic temples she was frequently amalgamated with the goddess Minerva. As the patroness of the *filidhecht*, or poetry, she was of great importance to the DRUIDIC tradition, which also made her the goddess of divination.

(2) Sister of the other two Brighids listed here, hence a daughter of the DAGHDHA, this Brighid was the goddess of smiths and metalworking.

(3) Sister to the other two Brighids listed here, hence a daughter of the DAGHDHA, this Brighid was the goddess of healing and fertility.

As is common throughout Celtic tradition, the three Brighids form a triad goddess, each sister in fact being an aspect of the combined deity.

BRIGHID, SAINT

Irish

The Christianised version of the old Celtic goddess BRIGHID, although her attributes seem to suggest that she is in fact an amalgamation of all three of the Brighids who were the daughters of the DAGHDHA. Legend says that she was born at sunrise on the threshold of the house, being fed on the milk of a supernatural cow. This would appear to incorporate the nourishment of the goddess BRIGANTIA, herself thought to be an early version of Brighid, into the Christian saint. Christian folk tradition says that she was the midwife and foster mother of the baby Jesus.

It was said that any house in which she stayed was filled with light. She was attended by nineteen nuns, who helped her to guard a perpetual fire in a grotto surrounded by a hedge, a precinct into which no man was permitted to enter. Her feast day was 1 February, the old Celtic feast of IMBOLC, and her primal function was that of fire and illumination.

BRIGINDO

Gaulish

A variant of BRIGHID that is found on a few inscriptions in GAUL.

BRIGIT

British

A variant of BRIGHID. It is also possible that Brigit was the origin of the goddess BRIGANTIA, the tutelary deity of the powerful BRIGANTES.

BRIMESENT

Arthurian

The wife of URIEN, according to the *VULGATE Merlin Continuation*.

BRISEN

Arthurian

The maidservant of ELAINE who administered an enchanted potion to LANCELOT on the instructions of King PELLES. The effect of this potion, which Brisen managed to administer twice, was to cause Lancelot to think that Elaine was GUINEVERE. As a result he slept with Elaine and became the father, by her, of Sir GALAHAD.

BRITAIN

(1) (*General*) An island in north-west Europe that is thought to derive its name from *Priteni*, the name the PICTS used for themselves, and that consists of the countries of ENGLAND, SCOTLAND and WALES. The country has had a long and chequered history of invasion and conquest, a history that has all but destroyed the Celtic tradition in England, though it remains in fragmentary form in the West Country, especially CORNWALL, and in Wales. Scotland was never a true Celtic domain, although a number of Celtic stories involve that country.

In legend the island was first ruled over by a giant named ALBION, whose name was subsequently poetically applied to the island and whose career was outlined in Holinshed's *Chronicles* of 1577. Surprisingly, GEOFFREY OF MONMOUTH does not mention Albion, instead simply saying that giants pre-dated men in Britain. He continues to say that Britain was colonised by BRUTUS, a descendant of the Graeco-Roman AENEAS, and that the island then maintained its independence until the Roman invasion.

The *WHITE BOOK OF RHYDDERCH*, which dates from the fourteenth century, gives an entirely different – and decidedly Welsh – early history, saying that the country was first called Myrddin's Precinct, MYRDDIN being Latinised to the more famous variant of MERLIN in the text. It was then known as the Isle of Honey before becoming Britain, the country allegedly being named after PRYDEIN, son of AEDD (who may be cognate with the Irish sun god AEDH), had conquered it. Unsurprisingly Geoffrey of Monmouth makes no mention of this concept.

Other traditions say that Prydein came from Cornwall and conquered Britain after the death of PORREX, the latter appearing as one of the successors of Brutus in Geoffrey of Monmouth. Irish tradition says that the country was named after BRITAIN, the son of NEMEDIUS, who settled on the island. Still others say that Britain simply derives from the Latin name for the island – *Britannia*.

Histories of Britain before the Roman invasion and occupation tell us little more than the legendary concepts. Prior to 2800 BC the inhabitants were Neolithic hill farmers. These were followed by a people who worked both copper and gold, and who were, in all probability, true Celts. At some stage Celts who were able to work iron became the dominant people, but even archaeologists find it difficult to put a date to the start of that pre-eminence. JULIUS CAESAR made exploratory expeditions to Britain, but it was not until the reign of CLAUDIUS that the Roman occupation began. Eventually ROME abandoned Britain and left it to fend for itself against the Picts from the north, the Irish from the west, and the ANGLES, SAXONS and JUTES from the east.

(2) (*Irish*) The son of NEMEDIUS who is considered by some as the eponym of BRITAIN, the country in which he settled. His name is sometimes spelt BRITAN.

BRITAN

Irish

See BRITAIN (2)

BRITOMART

Arthurian

A warrior maiden, the daughter of RIENCE, who appears in SPENSER's *FAERIE QUEENE* and married ARTEGALL. She takes her name from the Cretan goddess Britomartis, and was said to have killed RADIGUND, Queen of the AMAZONS.

BRITTANY

General

A province of north-western FRANCE that, following the Roman occupation of BRITAIN, and thus during the traditional Arthurian period, was largely inhabited by an immigrant British population. GEOFFREY OF MONMOUTH says that the Breton royal family was closely related to the British one, and that the kingdom was formed when the Roman Emperor MAXIMIANUS (reigned 383–388, and properly called MAXIMUS) bestowed the crown on CONAN MERIADOC, a nephew of Octavius who is elsewhere called EUDAF, King of Britain. When the British needed, and indeed wanted, a king, ALDROENUS, the successor of Conan Meriadoc, gave the Britons his brother CONSTANTINE, his brother and ARTHUR's grandfather. In the Arthurian legends, HOEL was the King of Brittany and was Arthur's ally as well as a relation. This Hoel traditionally reigned from AD 510 to 545. Other sources name SOLOMON as the King of Brittany and make him the great-grandfather of Arthur.

BRITTO
British
A variant of BRUTUS, found in the writings of NENNIUS.

BRITU
British
The son of VORTIGERN by SEVIRA.

BROADB
Irish
The brother of OENGHUS MAC IN OG.

BROBARZ
Arthurian
According to WOLFRAM VON ESCHENBACH, the realm of Queen CONDWIRAMURS, who became the wife of PERCEVAL.

BROCELIANDE
Arthurian
Situated in BRITTANY, and now called the Forest of Paimpont, this forest was the setting for a number of Arthurian adventures. One of the most potent stories concerning this forest is told by the French poet Huon de Mery in his work *LE TORNOIMENT DE L'ANTICHRIST*. In this he explains how he travelled to an enchanted spring in the forest, and BRAS-DE-FER, the chamberlain of the Antichrist, rode up. In his company, Huon de Mery said, he rode to the scene of a battle where the forces of Heaven, including ARTHUR and his knights, were doing battle with the forces of Hell. The enchanted spring mentioned by Huon de Mery seems to bear close resemblance to the wondrous fountain within the forest that was said to have been guarded by ESCLADOS.

BROCHMAIL
Welsh
A legendary King of the Welsh kingdom of POWYS, who is said to have reigned some time during the fifth or sixth centuries, the traditional Arthurian period. His name appears on a pillar near the ruins of Valle Crucis Abbey in CLYWD. This pillar was erected by CYNGEN FAB CADELL, the last King of Powys, who died in ROME in 854. The pillar, which is today known as the Pillar of ELISEG, contains an inscription that appears to give the descent of the kings of Powys. The inscription makes Brochmail the son of Eliseg and the father of CADELL.

BROGAN
Irish
The scribe to Saint PATRICK, by whom he was employed to write down the legends surrounding FIONN MAC CUMHAILL and the FIAN.

BRONLLAVYN SHORT BROAD
Arthurian
The knife owned by OSLA BIG-KNIFE that was said to be capable of being used as a bridge. Its scabbard, however, proved the downfall of Osla Big-knife, for during the hunt for the boar TWRCH TRWYTH, it filled with water and dragged him under.

BRON(S)
Arthurian
Also HEBRON
The father of twelve sons by his wife ENYGEUS, the sister of JOSEPH OF ARIMATHEA, who gave him the Holy GRAIL. The *DIDOT PERCEVAL* says that Brons was the grandfather of PERCEVAL and became the RICH FISHER, being carried off by angels when he had been cured of his affliction. In origin it is thought that he might have been the god BRÂN. ROBERT DE BORON specifically names Brons as the FISHER KING, and says that he gained this title as a result of supplying fish for Joseph of Arimathea.

BRUGH NA -BÓINNE, -BOYNA
Irish
The home of OENGHUS MAC IN OG, the son of the DAGHDHA. It is located in an area formed by a twist in the River BOYNE between the present-day towns of Slane and Oldbridge. This mound is, after TARA, the most important Bronze Age relic in IRELAND.

Brugh na Bóinne, or NEW GRANGE, is an earth mound some 36 feet high and shaped like an inverted saucer. An entrance hall, lined with slabs of stone, runs 60 feet into the mound before opening out into a spacious chamber approximately 20 feet high. The roof of this chamber is corbelled – that is, it is made of overlapping stones with a circular stone to finish it off at its centre. It is so well constructed that the interior was bone dry when Edward Lhwyd discovered it in 1699.

Excavations at Brugh na Bóinne have revealed an unusual opening above the entrance that allows the morning sun on the winter solstice to penetrate and thus illuminate the central chamber, shining directly onto three linked spirals carved into the wall. By itself this is not particularly remarkable, but the entrance hall is slightly curved, and yet the sun manages to slice through at a precise angle and light up the design. This feat of engineering, coupled with the excellence of the construction and ornamentation, indicates that Brugh na Bóinne was constructed by a highly refined and skilled people.

The entrance stone to the tumulus is perhaps the finest example of megalithic art in Western Europe. It is finely carved with a complex pattern of arcs, spirals and diamonds, the entire surface being finely textured with dots, which gives it a rich green colour.

The date of the construction of Brugh na Bóinne is still open to question. Radiocarbon dating places this at about 2500 BC, but current thinking makes the tumulus at least 500 years earlier, thus making it contemporary with the construction of the pyramids in Egypt. Regrettably the exact purpose of Brugh na Bóinne, other than its legendary connection with Oenghus mac in Og, will never be known, as the Danes plundered the site in the ninth century.

BRUIGHEAN CAORTHUINN
Irish
The Fairy Palace of the Quicken-trees, an ancient text that tells the story of FIONN MAC CUMHAILL when he defeated and killed the king of LOCHLANN but spared his son MIDAC, whom he brought up in his own household. Later Midac had his revenge by inviting the FIAN to visit him at his palace, a magically created place known as the Palace of the Quicken-trees. Once inside, the fian found themselves fastened to their seats and unable to move. DIARMAID UA DUIBHNE arrived and fought the army of Midac and, entering the palace, released the trapped member of the fian, using the blood of three kings. A later addition to the story recounts how the blood ran out before Diarmaid ua Duibhne got to CONAN MAC MORNA. Conan mac Morna chided Diarmaid ua Duibhne for leaving him to last, whereupon Diarmaid ua Duibhne took a firm hold of Conan mac Morna and wrenched him free of the seat, leaving a large patch of skin behind.

BRULAN
Arthurian
A variant of VARLAN, a King of GALES.

BRUMART
Arthurian
A nephew of King CLAUDAS. He sat on the SIEGE PERILOUS but was destroyed for his boldness.

BRUNISSEN
Arthurian
The wife of JAUFRÉ.

BRUNOR
Arthurian
Described as being one of the best knights of the OLD TABLE.

BRUT
Arthurian
Usually said to have been written between 1189 and 1199, this ANGLO-SAXON alliterative-verse chronicle – a history of England that contains a great deal of Arthurian material – is a translation from French and amplification by LAYAMON of the slightly earlier *ROMAN DE BRUT* by the twelfth-century writer WACE. It is important in the history of English versification as the first poem written in Middle English.

BRUT, ROMAN DE
Arthurian
See ROMAN DE BRUT

BRUT D'ANGLETERRE
Arthurian
Alternative title for the work by WACE that is more commonly known as the *ROMAN DE BRUT*.

BRUTO
Arthurian
Appearing as the hero of the Italian romance *BRUTO DI BRETTAGNE*, Bruto obtained a hawk, two small hounds or brachets and a scroll at ARTHUR's court to give to his lover.

BRUTO DI BRETTAGNE
Arthurian
An Italian romance concerning BRUTO, who came to ARTHUR's court to obtain a hawk, two brachets and a scroll to give to his lover, who remains unnamed.

BRUTUS
Graeco-Romano-British and Arthurian
The legendary founder of the British people, the great-grandson of the Trojan AENEAS, he traditionally conquered BRITAIN from the giants and founded LONDON, naming it TROIA NOVA (New Troy).

Expelled from Italy for accidentally killing his father SILVIUS, Brutus first went to Greece, where he found a group of Trojan exiles enslaved by King PANDRASUS, whom he fought and defeated. He claimed the reluctant hand of Pandrasus' daughter IGNOGE (Anglicised as IMOGEN), and compelled Pandrasus not only to release his prisoners, but also to supply them with ships, provisions and bullion. Well equipped, Brutus and the Trojans sailed west and discovered another group of Trojan exiles under the leadership of CORINEUS. They joined forces and sailed to ENGLAND, landing at TOTNES,

Devon, where the giants who at that time inhabited the island attacked them. The giants were led by GOGMAGOG, whom Corineus defeated in single combat at Plymouth. Brutus then marched to the banks of the River THAMES, where he founded his capital city, Troia Nova, and where he was eventually buried.

GEOFFREY OF MONMOUTH, who recounts his story, makes Brutus the traditional founder of the British people, the progenitor of a line of kings and the eponym of Britain itself.

BRUYANT

Arthurian

Known as 'the Faithless', he was responsible for killing ESTONNE (a minor character in *PERCEFOREST*), LORD OF THE SCOTTISH WILDERNESS. Estonne's son, PASSALEON, an ancestor of MERLIN, later avenged his father's death.

BRYCHAN (BRYCHEINIOG)

Welsh and Arthurian

An early legendary King of POWYS, although some sources make him a fifth-century British chieftain. He is alleged to have been the father of as many as sixty-three saints, including Saint GWLADYS. He was also said to have been the grandfather of URIEN of RHEGED by way of his daughter NEFYN. His alleged grave is marked by an old stone with a ring cross on it in Llanspyddid church near Brecon, Powys.

BRYN GWYN

Welsh

'White Mount', the Welsh for the mount in LONDON on which the White Tower within the Tower of London now stands. Legends says that this is the place where the severed head of BENDIGEID VRAN was buried by the seven survivors of the disastrous expedition to IRELAND to avenge the cruelty shown to BRANWEN, Bendigeid Vran's sister, by her Irish husband MATHOLWCH.

BRYN MYRDDIN

Arthurian

A hill near CARMARTHEN, more popularly known as MERLIN'S HILL, containing a cave that is said to be one of the many possible locations for the last resting place of the great wizard.

BUAN

Irish

The daughter of SAMERA. She fell in love with CÚ CHULAINN but died when her head hit a rock as she fell in an attempt to leap onto Cú Chulainn's chariot.

BUDA

Irish

A shrewd old man who sometimes appears in translations of the *FLEDD BRICRENN* as one of the many judges of the right to be called Champion of all IRELAND that was being contested by CÚ CHULAINN, LOEGHAIRE BUADHACH and CONALL CERNACH. Buda arranged the contest whereby a giant should cut off the heads of each of the contestants after they had first cut off his own head. Loeghaire Buadhach and Conall Cernach obviously believed that the giant would be dead if they cut off his head, for they refused the giant his turn when he did not die as they expected. Cú Chulainn, however, duly knelt down and the giant proclaimed him the champion by right.

This story is usually associated with the judgements of AILILL, MEDHBHA and CÚ ROÍ MAC DÁIRI, although it may be that the usually accepted version of the *Fledd Bricrenn* is an abridged version and that this portion of the story belongs within the full rendition.

BUDIC(IUS)

Gaulish and Arthurian

According to GEOFFREY OF MONMOUTH, the name of two early Kings of BRITTANY. One is purely Arthurian in nature and was said to have married King ARTHUR's sister. The other was said to have been raised by the exiled AMBROSIUS AURELIUS and UTHER. Budic is, in all probability, identifiable with King Budic I of Cornouaille, who traditionally reigned in Brittany some time before 550.

BUGI

Arthurian

The husband of PERFERREN, ARTHUR's niece.

BUIC

Irish

The son of BANBLAI who was killed by CÚ CHULAINN as he escorted the captured DONN CUAILNGÈ to the camp of AILILL and MEDHBHA.

BUICHET

Irish

The foster mother to the six foster children of DERBRENN, who had turned them into six swine. Buichet craved to eat them, so they fled to OENGHUS MAC IN OG for help. He refused until a year later, but by that time five had been killed and the sole survivor lived a life of solitary grief.

BUINO

Irish

A son of FERGHUS MAC ROICH and brother of ILLAN. When his father was obliged to feast with BARUCH on his return from SCOTLAND with DERDRIU and the sons of UISNECH, he and his brother escorted the four to EMHAIN MHACHA. He was persuaded to desert his charges by CONCHOBAR MAC NESSA, who bribed him with a great estate, a desertion that led to the death of his brother when Conchobar mac Nessa attacked and killed the sons of Uisnech.

BULGARIA

Arthurian

Though the country of Bulgaria had not come into existence during the traditional Arthurian period, tradition and romance gave this country kings named NETOR and MADAN. Many such anachronisms exist throughout the confused web woven around the Arthurian tales.

BURLETTA DELLA DISERTA

Arthurian

The abductor of MORGAN Le Fay's daughter PULZELLA GAIA. She was rescued from him by LANCELOT.

BURY WALLS

Arthurian

Located in Shropshire, this is held by local legends to be where ARTHUR held his court.

BWLCH-Y-GROES

Welsh and Arthurian

A pass through the mountains on the highest road in north WALES above Tan-y Bwlch. Here lived the giant RHITTA, who had a penchant for collecting beards from the men he killed in order to make a cloak. One day, however, a man he picked on killed him and threw him down the hillside, where he was buried, presumably as he was too heavy to move and bury elsewhere. A path leads down the hill to Tan-y-Bwlch, which is known as RHIW BARFE, 'The Way of the Bearded One'. The giant's grave consists of a long, narrow trench surrounded by large boulders.

The alternative site for this battle, and for the giant's grave, is YR WYDDFA FAWR, or Mount SNOWDON. This tale was later embroidered to make the vanquisher of Rhitta none other than King ARTHUR himself, who obviously had no desire to part with his own beard, the fight occurring on the

occasion when King Arthur was travelling through the pass *en route* to visit MERLIN.

BWLCH-Y-SAETHU

Arthurian

According to Welsh legend, ARTHUR was killed by a flurry of arrows at this pass in Snowdonia, North WALES, where he had pursued his enemies following a battle at TREGALEN. When he fell, his men went to a cave called OGOF LANCIAU ERYRI to wait until he came back. A shepherd was once thought to have found the cave and seen the waiting warriors there. Over the years they seemed to have kept up with the times, for the shepherd reported they were armed with guns.

BWRDD ARTHUR

Arthurian

ARTHUR'S TABLE, the name of two prominent features in Clwyd, WALES. One is a circle of twenty-four indentations in a rock (cf. TWENTY-FOUR KNIGHTS) that is said to represent ARTHUR's knights at a table. The other feature is a barrow at Llanfair Dyffryn Ceiriog.

BYANOR

Arthurian

In the seventeenth-century unpublished poem *THE FAERIE KING* by Samuel Sheppard, Byanor is named as having received a sword that formerly belonged to King ARTHUR.

BYANU

Irish

A controversial name, which is found only in one OGHAM inscription of the eastern seaboard of the USA. It is possibly a derivation of DANU, but it is the location of the inscription that proves so controversial. To date, there has been no conclusive evidence that the Celts ever conquered the Atlantic, but existence of the Ogham inscription in America would seem to suggest that this was, indeed, the case. The problem remains, however, that, if the Celts did make the passage, why did they change the name of the goddess from Danu to Byanu? Until conclusive proof comes to light, the question of the Celts sailing the Atlantic will provide scholars with food for endless discussion and argument.

BYZANTIUM

Arthurian

The original name of CONSTANTINOPLE.

C

CABAL
Arthurian

ARTHUR's hound. NENNIUS says that while Arthur was pursuing the boar TROYNT, Cabal's footprint was left on a stone over which Arthur erected a cairn, which has become known as CARN CABAL. Another story has Cabal participating in the hunt for the boar YSGITHYRWYN.

CADAIR IDRIS
Welsh

A mountain in GWYNEDD. The name means the chair or seat of IDRIS, a legendary Welsh giant, although this may refer to his intellect rather than his physical size, for he was reputed to have been a poet, astronomer and philosopher. A chamber formed by massive rocks on the summit was thought to have been his 'observatory', while the hollow formed by LLYN CAU, a small lake on the south side of the mountain, was his 'chair'. Popular legend holds that anyone who dares to sleep on the summit of Cadair Idris, or, come to that, of Mount SNOWDON, will be found the next morning as a corpse, a madman or a brilliant poet.

Another small lake on the mountain is called *Llyn-y-tri graienyn*, 'The Lake of the Three Pebbles'. Its name is derived from three boulders standing near it, boulders that Idris found in his shoe that he emptied out where they now stand. One of these boulders is 24 feet long, 18 feet wide and 12 feet high, a measure of the size of Idris.

CADAIR, NEU CAR MORGAN MWYNFAWR
Welsh and Arthurian

The chair or car of MORGAN MWYNFAWR, which had the power to carry a person seated in it anywhere they desired to go. It numbered among the THIRTEEN TREASURES OF BRITAIN.

Cadair Idris, North Wales, the haunt of the local giant Idris. (© Genevieve Leaper; Ecoscene/Corbis)

Ruins of Cadbury Castle, Somerset, and one of the many possible locations of Camelot. (© Mick Sharp)

CADBURY CASTLE

Arthurian

A site in Somerset, midway between Yeovil and Wincanton, that is considered as one of the many possible locations of ARTHUR's capital, CAMELOT. The popular tradition that Cadbury Castle was the site of Camelot seems to date from the sixteenth century, though it could quite possibly, and in all probability does, pre-date that time. Archaeological excavations have revealed there was a fortified leader's dwelling at Cadbury Castle during the traditional Arthurian period. Many other places have been suggested as the site of Camelot, such as WINCHESTER, COLCHESTER and CAERLEON-ON-USK, but Cadbury Castle still remains the favourite option for many people.

A lesser-known theory puts forward Cadbury Castle, not as Camelot, but instead as one of the many possible locations for the last resting place of Arthur – that magical realm known as AVALON.

CADBURY HILL

Arthurian

A hill near Nailsea, Avon, that is the site of a cave from which, so local legend holds, King ARTHUR and his knights will one day ride forth.

CADELL

Welsh and Arthurian

A legendary king of the Welsh kingdom of POWYS, who was said to have reigned sometime during the fifth or sixth centuries, the traditional Arthurian period. His name appears on a pillar known as the Pillar of ELISEG near the ruins of Valle Crucis Abbey in CLWYD. This pillar, which was allegedly raised by CONCENN or CYNGEN FAB CADELL, the son of Cadell, gives a list of the legendary kings of Powys, although the entire inscription was not readable when Edward Llwyd examined the pillar in 1696. According to this inscription, Cadell was the son of BROCHMAIL and the father of Concenn.

CADO

Arthurian

Possibly identical with CADWY, the son of GEREINT, Cado appears in the medieval *LIFE OF SAINT CARANNOG*, where he is said to have co-ruled in the West Country alongside King ARTHUR. It seems more likely, however, that Cado is a simple corruption of CADOR, who is described as being either the ruler or the duke of CORNWALL.

CADOC, SAINT

Welsh and Arthurian

A Welsh saint who was said to be the son of King GWYNLLYM of Glamorgan and Saint GWLADYS of Brecon. In the *LIFE OF SAINT CADOC*, ARTHUR is said to have demanded that Cadoc hand over to him a man named LIGESSAC, who had sought and found sanctuary with Cadoc for ten years, after the killing of some of Arthur's followers. To settle the matter, Arthur was offered 100 kine (cattle) as compensation, which he demanded should be red before and white behind. With the help of God, Cadoc produced the required cattle, but they turned into bundles of fern the instant Arthur's men seized them.

CADOG

Arthurian

A knight who numbered among the TWENTY-FOUR KNIGHTS of King ARTHUR's court.

CADOR

(1) (*British and Arthurian*) Possibly to be identified with CADWY, the son of GEREINT, and identical to CADO, Cador was the ruler of CORN-WALL, being variously described as a king or a duke. He was an ally of ARTHUR, whom he helped in his battles against the SAXONS, defeating both BALDULF and CHELDRIC. His son CONSTANTINE was handed the crown by King Arthur following the King's final battle, this event reputedly occurring in the year AD 542. A Cador, the son of the King of Cornwall, brother of GUIGNIER and friend of CARADOC BRIEFBRAS, may be the same character, or even the son of this Cador. Some sources allege that this Cador was the guardian of GUINEVERE prior to her marriage to the young Arthur.

(2) (*Welsh and Arthurian*) A King of NORTHUMBRIA whose daughter ANDRIVETE circumvented the usurping plans of her uncle AYGLIN by marrying CEI. He passed into the Arthurian cycle when Cei became known, within those stories, as Sir KAY.

CADWALLAD(E)R

Welsh and Arthurian

A historical seventh-century hero, the son of CADWALLON, King of the VENDOTII in GWYNEDD. He defeated and killed Edwin (or Eadwine) of NORTHUMBRIA in 633 but, approximately one year later, was himself killed in battle. Cadwallader features in the *ARMES PRYDEIN*, which foretells that he will rise again and lead an army that will drive the SAXONS back into the sea. Welsh tradition makes him a saint who was active in and around ANGLESEY and CARMARTHEN.

CADWALLON

Welsh and Arthurian

Also CATWALLAUN

The father of CADWALLADER, according to GEOFFREY OF MONMOUTH, and King of the VENDOTII, who lived in North WALES, principally GWYNEDD.

CADWY

Arthurian

The son of GEREINT who was, according to a part of the *MABINOGION*, known as the *DREAM OF RHONABWY*, a contemporary of ARTHUR. It would appear that he was the original for both CADOR and CADO, though the latter is possibly a second-generation derivative.

CAELIA

Arthurian

The fairy queen who bore the FAERIE KNIGHT to TOM A'LINCOLN, the illegitimate son of ARTHUR, and eventually drowned herself.

CAER

(1) (*Welsh*) The Welsh for an earthen barrow, the equivalent of the Irish SÍDH. Where Caer appears as part of a name, either on its own or incorporated into a longer word, it is usually a reference to an OTHERWORLDLY abode.

(2) (*Irish*) The daughter of ETHAL ANUBAL, a TUATHA DÉ DANANN prince of CONNACHT. OENGHUS MAC IN OG fell in love with her after she had appeared to him in a dream, but no matter how hard he searched he could not find her. Turning for help to BODB, Oenghus Mac in Og had to wait a year before Bodb reported that he had found his 'dream maiden' on the banks of a lake along with her 149 sisters. Ethal Anubal refused to hand over his daughter, and he was taken prisoner by AILILL and the DAGHDHA. Still he refused to hand over his daughter, as he feared her magical powers.

Finally, Oenghus Mac in Og travelled to the lake and explained to Caer his love for her. She consented, her father was released, and the two, in the form of swans, flew away to BRUGH NA BÓINNE.

CAER ARIANRHOD
Welsh

The palace of ARIANRHOD, which legend locates on ANGLESEY, although folk tradition makes it a sunken and lost land in the centre of Caernarvon Bay. This folk tradition places the castle three-quarters of a mile offshore, near Dinas Dinlle, GWYNEDD, on the north-west side of the Lleyn Peninsula. It appears as a reef of stones that is laid bare at low tide, the sea having smothered her castle in revenge for her harsh treatment of LLEW LLAW GYFFES. A couple of miles further south MAEN DYLAN stands on a stretch of gravel. This marks the alleged grave of Arianrhod's first-born son, DYLAN EIL TON.

CAER DATHYL
Welsh

The court of MATH FAB MATHONWY, although some sources say that it is the home of GWYDION FAB DÔN.

CAER FEDDWID(D)
Welsh
Also CAER RIGOR, CAER SIDDI

The Fort of CAROUSAL, which is located in the Welsh OTHERWORLD realm of ANNWFN. Caer Feddwidd is a paradisiacal realm in which a fountain runs with wine and no one ever knows illness or old age. Later tradition says it was visited by King ARTHUR and his retinue.

CAER GAI
Arthurian

According to bardic tradition, Caer Gai is the place in Merioneth where ARTHUR was raised.

CAER L(L)UD(D)
Welsh

'Llud's Fort', the ancient name for the city of LONDON after LLUDD had rebuilt it, though some say that the name is derived from LUGH, the god of light. Later it became known as CAER LUNDEIN and still later as LUNDEIN or LWNDRYS.

CAER L(L)UNDEIN
Welsh

A later name for CAER LLUDD, or ancient LONDON. It is easy to see that the modern name London is a simple derivation of Lundein.

CAER LUEL
British

The name of the ancient Celtic city that is today known as CARLISLE. The Romans under Agricola seized the town in AD 80 and made it their regional capital, naming it *Luguvallium*. Caer Luel was located at the convergence of three rivers: the Eden, the Calder and the Petteril. Such places have a magical quality that tends to make them the centre of legendary landscapes. Legends abound in the region surrounding Carlisle about a former kingdom, known as RHEGED, that flourished in the seventh century.

CAER RIGOR
Welsh and Arthurian
Also CAER FEDDWID(D), CAER SIDDI

An alternative name for Caer Feddwid, which is also known as Caer Siddi, or the Fort of CAROUSAL. Though Welsh tradition states that Caer Feddwidd contains a fountain that runs with wine, and no one there knows old age, this variant would seem to suggest a realm of the dead from which there is no return.

CAER SIDDI
Welsh and Arthurian
Also CAER FEDDWID(D), CAER RIGOR

An alternative name for Caer Feddwid, the OTHERWORLD Fort of CAROUSAL, which shares the same attribute of having a fountain that runs with wine. Welsh tradition makes ARIANRHOD the ruler of Caer Siddi, though Arthurian legend does not seem to mention the name of the ruler on the occasion when ARTHUR and his men visited the mysterious fort.

CAER WYDYR
Welsh and Arthurian

A glass fort that is located in ANNWFN, the Welsh OTHERWORLD. Later tradition says that, like CAER FEDDWIDD, this fort was visited by King ARTHUR and his company, but they were unable to make its watchman talk to them.

CAERLAVERLOCK
Arthurian

'Fort Lark', the important harbour over whose ownership it is thought the Battle of ARTHURET was fought.

CAERLEON-ON-USK
Welsh and Arthurian

An important Celtic city located on the River Usk in GWENT, the site of a Roman fort and amphitheatre,

Caerleon-on-Usk was one of the most important cities within the realm of King ARTHUR. GEOFFREY OF MONMOUTH claims that it was called the CITY OF THE LEGION, was founded by King BELINUS (perhaps BELI MAWR), and had DUBRICIUS as the archbishop. If Caerleon-on-Usk is the City of the Legion, then it was here that Arthur held his plenary court at Whitsun, attended by representatives from all of Europe. Various sources name Caerleon-on-Usk as CAMELOT and the city where the KNIGHTS OF THE ROUND TABLE were first established.

CAI
Welsh
See CEI

CAIBELL
Irish

A supernatural king who had a beautiful daughter, a trait he shared with his ally ÉTAR. Two earthly kings sought the hands of the daughters and were offered battle for them. The battle took place at night so that there could be no distinction between earthly warriors and those of the two kings, who inhabited

Caerleon-on-Usk, Gwent, an important Celtic city where Arthur is alleged to have held a plenary court.
(© Photolibrary Wales, 2004)

neighbouring SÍDH. The battle was so ferocious that four hillocks were made from the antlers of those killed, for the two kings and their followers appeared as deer. Finally a lake had to be formed to quell the fighting. Caibell was killed, as were the two earthly kings. Only Étar survived.

CAILLEACH BEARA
Irish

'Hag of Beare', an ancient deity whose name is more recent. She appears to be a remembrance of an earlier MOTHER GODDESS or guardian spirit whose haunt is the wilds of the Beare peninsula from which she takes her name.

CAIRBR-E, -Y
Irish

The son of CORMAC MAC AIRT, whom he succeeded as King of IRELAND. The hand of his daughter SGEIMH SOLAIS was sought by an unnamed son of the King of the DECIES. The FIAN then claimed a tribute, which, so they claimed, was customarily paid to them on these occasions, but Cairbre refused to pay and went to war against the fian. At the Battle of GABHRA, when the majority of the fian were wiped out, Cairbre killed OSCAR, the son of OISÍN, in single combat, but himself received a number of mortal wounds from which he quickly expired.

CAIRBRE
Irish
See CAIRPRE NIAPER

CAIRENN
Irish

A SAXON from BRITAIN who married EOCHU MUGMEDÓN and, by him, became the mother of NIAL NOÍGIALLACH.

CAIRPRE (NIAPER)
Irish

The father of ERC. Cairpre Niaper was killed, along with CÚ ROÍ MAC DÁIRI during a fight with CÚ CHULAINN. Erc then marched against Cú Chulainn, one of the events that was to lead to the death of that great hero.

CAITHRÉIM CONGHAIL CLÁIRINGNIGH
Irish and Arthurian

An Irish romance that names ART AOINFHEAR as a son of King ARTHUR, though other Irish sources make him the son of King Conn of the Hundred Battles.

CALAD-BOLG, -CHOLG
Irish and Arthurian

The magical sword carried by CÚ CHULAINN, amongst others. Its name derives from *calad*, 'hard', and *bolg*, 'lightning', and has been linguistically linked with CALADVWLCH, the name given to EXCALIBUR in the *MABINOGION* story of *CULHWCH AND OLWEN*.

CALADVWLCH
Welsh and Arthurian

Linguistically linked to CALADBOLG, this sword appears in the *MABINOGION* story of *CULHWCH AND OLWEN*, where it is a representation of EXCALIBUR.

CALATIN
Irish

The father of twenty-seven sons who were, together with their father, killed by CÚ CHULAINN. His unnamed wife posthumously bore three monstrous sons and three daughters, who were cared for by MEDHBHA when they studied the magic arts in order to find a way to defeat Cú Chulainn. They later marched with ERC and his companions against Cú Chulainn and took part in the battle that was to lead to Cú Chulainn's death.

See also BAVE

CALEDON
British

An ancient name for SCOTLAND. Many authorities believe that this word was simply Latinised by the invading Romans (who, of course, never conquered Scotland), to give their name for the country, *Caledonia*.

CALEDON WOOD
Arthurian

The site of a battle fought against the SAXONS and won by King ARTHUR and his ally HOEL, being located either in the Scottish Caledonian Forest (CELYDDON or SILVA CALEDONIAE), or in CELIDON WOOD near LINCOLN.

CALIBURNUS
Arthurian

The name of one of King ARTHUR's swords, though GEOFFREY OF MONMOUTH specifically uses this name to refer to EXCALIBUR.

CALIN
Arthurian

According to LAYAMON, this FRISIAN King was subject to ARTHUR.

CALINAN
Arthurian
The son of GUIRON by his lover BLOIE.

CALIPH OF BAGHDAD
Arthurian
WOLFRAM VON ESCHENBACH, in *PARZIVAL*, specifically mentions that BARUC was the Caliph of Baghdad, though the reference to the Caliphate is an anachronism, since the traditional Arthurian period predates Muhammad and the foundation of the Caliphate.

CALLINGTON
Arthurian
One of the places that has been connected with KELLIWIC, the Cornish stronghold of ARTHUR. Some commentators have even tried to connect Kelliwic with CAMELOT, so Callington could also be so identified by connection.

CAM
Arthurian
A Somerset river that flows in the vicinity of CADBURY CASTLE. A nearby field, called WESTWOODS, has revealed a large number of skeletons that bear grim witness to a battle fought on that site, leading some to suggest that this is the site of ARTHUR's final Battle of CAMLANN. Other commentators have, however, identified this as the River Cam upon which CAMBRIDGE is situated, and this has subsequently led to the identification of that city with Camlann.

CAMAALIS
Arthurian
The pagan king who, according to the Arthurian romances, was the eponym of CAMELOT.

CAMAL
Arthurian
A suitor of HERMONDINE who was killed by MELIADOR.

CAMBENET
Arthurian
The Duke of Cambenet, EUSTACE, is numbered among the eleven leaders who rebelled against the youthful King ARTHUR at the outset of his reign.

CAMBOGLANNA
Arthurian
A Roman fort on Hadrian's Wall at Birdoswald that has been put forward as a possible site for the Battle of CAMLANN. Presumably it was in the north-western British kingdom of RHEGED at the time of the battle, so the siting of Camlann here would owe much to the associations between ARTHUR and URIEN.

CAMBRIA
General
An ancient name for WALES. It is still widely user to refer to items that come from, or are to be found in, Wales, such as the Cambrian Mountains.

CAMBRIDGE
Arthurian
A university city in the east of England, which was alleged to have received its charter from ARTHUR, at least according to Prior Nicholas Cantelupe, who died in 1441. Elizabethan tradition held that the university had been founded in Anno Mundi 3588 (since the creation of the world) by the Spanish Prince Cantaber. An obscure local tradition even said that Cambridge was the site of Arthur's final Battle of CAMLANN, though this would seem to stem from false etymology, and it could be said that any place-name having 'Cam' in it might be considered a worthy contender.

CAMEL
Arthurian
A Cornish river whose banks have been considered one of the many possible sites for the Battle of CAMLANN. The river runs through the town of CAMELFORD, which is another possible site.

CAMELFORD
Arthurian
A small town in north CORNWALL through which the River CAMEL runs, and which is given as yet another of the many possible sites for ARTHUR's final battle at CAMLANN.

Camelford, Cornwall, one of the many possible locations for the battle of Camlann. (Copyright © www.atlantic-highway.co.uk/Robin Rowling)

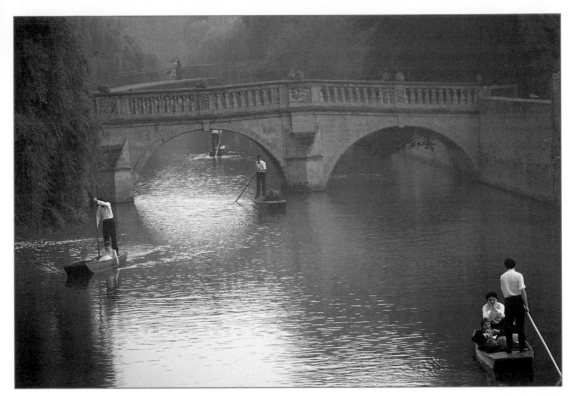

The River Cam running through the heart of the university city of Cambridge. (© Michael S. Yamashita/Corbis)

CAMELIARD

Arthurian

The kingdom of LEODEGRANCE, GUINEVERE's father. Various locations for the realm have been suggested, from SCOTLAND to the south-west of England, possibly having some association with the north Cornish town of CAMELFORD. One of its most important cities is named as CAROLHAISE.

CAMELOT

Arthurian

The name given to the place where ARTHUR had his main residence and held his court. Many places have been suggested for its location, which still remains a mystery. Among these are WINCHESTER, CAERLEON-ON-USK, COLCHESTER and, most commonly and popularly, CADBURY CASTLE in Somerset.

According to the romances, Camelot was named after a pagan King CAMAALIS, and, at the time when JOSEPH OF ARIMATHEA landed in BRITAIN, when AGRESTES was its King, it is cited as being the most important city in the country. Seemingly, Agrestes embraced Christianity, but, after Joseph of Arimathea had left, he persecuted the

Christians until he was sent mad by God. As such, the city of Camelot is first mentioned by CHRÉTIEN DE TROYES in *Lancelot*, while Sir Thomas MALORY, who identifies it with WINCHESTER, says that the name of its chief church was Saint Stephen's.

CAMILLE

Arthurian

A sorceress of SAXON ancestry who captured ARTHUR, who had become enamoured with her. LANCELOT rescued him, after which Camille committed suicide.

CAMLAN(N)

Arthurian

The site of the third and last battle between ARTHUR and his usurping nephew MORDRED, who was killed, and where Arthur was also mortally wounded. Both the date and location of the battle have caused considerable speculation. The *ANNALES CAMBRIAE* state quite clearly that the battle took place twenty-one years after BADON, but, as the date of that battle is also a mystery, this simply serves to confuse matters even further, leading to possible dates ranging from AD 515 to 539. GEOFFREY OF MONMOUTH, however, gives a date of AD 542, while the Irish *ANNALS OF TIGERNACH* date it to AD 541, and the Spanish *ANNALES TOLEDANOS* date it as late as AD 580. As to the site, there are many locations to choose from. Sir Thomas MALORY favours SALISBURY PLAIN, while SLAUGHTERBRIDGE on the River CAMEL in CORNWALL is a much-favoured and traditional site. The *DIDOT PERCEVAL* places it even further afield, this time in IRELAND, and even CAMBRIDGE has been suggested. Another suggested site, much favoured in Cumbria and the surrounding regions, is the Roman fort of CAMBOGLANNA on Hadrian's Wall.

Accounts of the battle, regardless of when and where it occurred, also vary. Sir Thomas Malory states that only Arthur, BEDIVERE and, for a very brief time, LUCAN survived. Welsh traditions usually speak of seven survivors, although *CULHWCH AND OLWEN* refers to any number of other survivors, including SANDAV, who was so beautiful that all mistook him for an angel, and MORFRAN, who was so hideous that he was mistaken for a devil. Other survivors, mentioned in other sources, include Saint DERFEL and Saint PETROC.

CAMULOS
British and Gaulish
A war deity whose name is to be found in inscriptions in SCOTLAND and GAUL. It is thought that he was the patron deity of COLCHESTER, after whom the Romans named the city *Camulodunum*. Camulos has been equated with the Roman god Mars, and some commentators have sought to make him the original of CUMHAILL, but there is no evidence to support any suggestion that Camulos was worshipped in IRELAND.

CANAN
Arthurian
The grandfather of EREC and father of LAC.

CANDACES
Arthurian
The son of King APOLLO of LIONES, who, during his lifetime, saw the unification of Liones and CORNWALL.

CANO
Irish
A historical figure whose death is recorded as having occurred in 688. The son of the Scottish King

GARTNÁN, Cano was exiled to IRELAND, where he was entertained by the elderly MARCÁN (Little Mark), whose beautiful young wife CRÉD had fallen in love with Cano even before she first saw him. During a feast given in Cano's honour, Créd drugged the entire company and begged Cano to take her as his mistress, but he refused to do this while he was still in exile. However, so taken with Créd was Cano that he pledged his undying love to her and gave her a stone that embodied his life.

Eventually, Cano was recalled to SCOTLAND following the death of his father, and he became the King. Every year he and Créd attempted to meet at Inber Colptha (the BOYNE estuary), but they were always forestalled by her stepson, COLCU, with a guard of one hundred warriors. Frustrated, the pair decided to give it one last go, this time arranging to meet at Lough Créde in the north. As they came within sight of each other, Colcu once again appeared and drove Cano away. Unable to withstand her suffering any longer, Créd jumped from her horse and dashed her brains out on a rock. During the fall from her horse Créd dropped the stone that Cano had given her. It smashed into tiny pieces, and three days later Cano died.

CANOLA
Irish
A mysterious Irish woman who appears in a story concerning the magic of the Irish harp. She fled from her husband, for reasons unknown, and was lulled to sleep by the sound of sinews clinging to the skeleton of a whale. Her husband found her on the beach and built a framework in which to house the sinews, the very first harp, whose music reconciled the couple.

CANOR
Arthurian
A King of CORNWALL who was aided in his battle by GONOSOR, an Irish king.

CANTERBURY
General
A cathedral city in KENT, which was called *Durovernum* by the Romans, and was the SAXON capital of Kent. The Celtic church was established at Canterbury in Roman times, but in the fifth century, when the Romans left and the heathen Saxons and JUTES replaced them as the rulers of south-east ENGLAND, Christianity was extinguished in the city.

Around 580 the local king, Aethelbert, married Bertha, a Christian princess. She brought a chaplain with her, and, though Aethelbert retained his pagan

Canterbury Cathedral, the home of British Christianity since 597. (© Bettmann, 1900/Corbis)

beliefs, he allowed his Queen to restore an ancient Christian church to the east of the city. The church, Saint Martin, is still there and claims to be the oldest Christian church in England.

Canterbury became the home of British Christianity after 597, when Pope Gregory sent Saint Augustine to England. Bertha welcomed the missionary to Canterbury, and before long her husband had accepted Christianity and was baptised in the church of Saint Martin. Augustine built an abbey in 598, to the east of the city wall, around Aethelbert's pagan temple, which became the church of Saint Pancras. A former Celtic Christian church was remodelled as a cathedral and on his death Saint Augustine was buried in his abbey.

In the Arthurian romances, the Archbishop of Canterbury was one of ARTHUR's advisers, though this is an anachronism as the archiepiscopal see was not founded until AD 597. The Archbishop was said to have been present at Arthur's final battle and to have survived it, only to be subsequently murdered by King MARK of CORNWALL. The Scandinavian *BRETA SOGUR* states that Arthur was buried at Canterbury, though this assertion is not found in any other Arthurian work.

CANTRE'R GWAELOD
Welsh

Also known as MAES GWYDDNO, Cantre'r Gwaelod is one of the three lost lands of popular Welsh tradition, the other two being LLYS HELIG and CAER ARIANRHOD. Cantre'r Gwaelod, or 'Lowland Hundred', lies in Cardigan Bay, and was supposedly inundated by the sea in the fifth century, when GWYDDNO GARANHIR, who was also known as DEWRARTH WLEDIG, was Prince of the Hundred.

CANVEL
Arthurian

The capital of PARMENIE, according to GOTTFRIED VON STRASSBURG.

CAOILTE MAC RONAN
Irish

One of the warriors, described as the 'fleetest of foot who could overtake the March wind', at the wedding feast of FIONN MAC CUMHAILL, his uncle, and GRÁINNE. He and four others, OISÎN, OSCAR, GOLL MAC MORNA and DIARMAID UA DUIBHNE, were not given the sleeping draught that Gráinne administered, and so witnessed the bond under which she placed Diarmaid ua Duibhne to elope with him, and were instrumental in making

sure that he complied, as he was honour bound to do. Later tradition says that Caoilte mac Ronan lived for many hundreds of years after the destruction of the FIAN and is reputed to have told their exploits to Saint PATRICK.

CAPALU
Gaulish and Arthurian

The continental name for the CATH PALUG, especially in FRANCE.

CARADAW-C, -G

1 (*Welsh*) A son of BENDIGEID VRAN. He headed the council left by his father when he and his troops invaded IRELAND to avenge the mistreatment of BRANWEN at the hands of MATHOLWCH. He was ousted during his father's absence by CASWALLAWN, who usurped Bendigeid Vran's kingdom.

2 (*British*) The son of BRENNIUS who, according to GEOFFREY OF MONMOUTH, lived with his father in Rome after Brennius and BELINUS had sacked the city. It is quite likely that this Caradawc is the same as the Welsh CARADAWC, for Brennius is often regarded as a variant of BENDIGEID VRAN.

CARADOC
Arthurian

The King of VANNES AND NANTES who married the niece of ARTHUR, the unfaithful YSAIVE, who, through one extramarital encounter with the wizard ELIAVRES, became the mother of CARADOC BRIEFBRAS.

CARADOC -VREICHVRAS, -BRIEFBRAS
Welsh and Arthurian

The son of LLYR MARINI, husband of TEGAU EUFRON, father of MEURIC and owner of the horse LLUAGOR. He is the legendary ancestor of a ruling dynasty, and it is thought that he may have founded the kingdom of GWENT during the fifth century. The epithet *vreichvras* (strong-armed) is usually misinterpreted as *briefbras* (short arm), and it is by this mistranslated epithet that he is most commonly known.

The later Arthurian romances made him the son of the philandering wife of King CARADOC of VANNES AND NANTES, the result of her affair with the wizard ELIAVRES. Caradoc Briefbras once confronted Eliavres about his parentage, and, when he did, his parents caused a serpent to twine itself around his arm. It took the combined efforts of his wife, GUIGNIER, and her brother, CADOR, to get rid of it. The fidelity of Guignier was proved to Caradoc Briefbras on the occasion when King MANGOUN of MORAINE sent him a horn from which to drink, such a drink being said to expose any infidelity on the part of the wife of him that drank from it.

CARADOS
Arthurian

Identified by some with the SAXON leader CERDIC, and also sometimes known as the King of Carados, which might indicate that Carados was his realm rather than his name. He was one of the eleven rulers who rebelled against ARTHUR at the start of his reign.

CARADOS OF THE DOLOROUS TOWER
Arthurian

The son of a sorceress and brother of Sir TURQUINE, he took GAWAIN captive and threw him into a dungeon. LANCELOT cut off his head with the only sword that could kill him – though we are not told what special properties the sword possessed – and so released Gawain and the other prisoners held in the dungeons.

CARANNOG, SAINT
Welsh and Arthurian
Also CARANTOC

Of Welsh origin, Carannog had a remarkable altar that had been sent from heaven. As he was travelling to Somerset from WALES, the altar fell into the sea, so Carannog came to ARTHUR to ask if it had been found. Arthur already had the altar in his possession, but would not return it until Carannog had performed a great deed for him, the capture of a violent serpent that lived on Ker Moor. Undaunted by this mammoth task, Carannog placed his stole around the serpent's neck and pacified it. Having then ordered it to do no more harm, the saint let it go again, and Arthur duly returned the altar. Carannog then built a chapel for the altar, which, so John Leland (chaplain to King Henry VIII) tells us, was at Carhampton, a short distance from Blue Anchor Bay, between Minehead and Watchet, though the church there today is not dedicated to the saint.

CARANTOC
Arthurian
A variant of CARANNOG.

CARATACUS
British and Arthurian
The son of CUNOBELINUS and brother of TOGODUMNUS, Caratacus was the King of the CATUVELLAUNI, a tribe of early Britons who lived near what is now known as Saint Albans at the time of the Roman invasion in AD 43. His historicity is unquestioned. Having led a hard-fought guerrilla campaign against the Roman invaders from his stronghold with the support of two Welsh tribes, the SILURES and the ORDOVICES, he was handed over to his enemies by CARTIMANDUA, Queen of the BRIGANTES, but was pardoned by the Emperor CLAUDIUS after he had been taken to Rome. It has been suggested that his story became legendary and that he should be considered as the original King ARTHUR. However, other commentators say that Caratacus should be regarded as identical with ARVIRAGUS, or at the very least with Arviragus' cousin.

CARBONEK
Arthurian
Also CORBENIC
The GRAIL CASTLE. Within its walls was the PALACE ADVENTUROUS, and within that palace was the Holy GRAIL itself.

CARDUEIL
Arthurian
Described as being one of King ARTHUR's palaces, or residences, Cardueil has been identified by some as CARLISLE.

CARDUINO
Arthurian
The son of DONDINELLO, he was raised in secret after his father had been poisoned. When grown up he travelled to ARTHUR's court, from where he embarked on a quest to aid Queen BEATRICE, who, along with all her subjects, had fallen under the enchantment of a wizard and been turned into animals. Carduino killed the wizard and, having restored Beatrice to her former shape with a kiss, married her.

CARELL
Irish
A late ruler of IRELAND and a contemporary of Saint PATRICK. He is not called 'King', but rather 'Chieftain'. His wife was said to have eaten whole the salmon that was the then incarnation of TUAN MAC STERN, the sole survivor of the invasion of Ireland led by PARTHOLÁN. The salmon turned into a baby within the woman, and nine months later Tuan mac Stern was reborn, thenceforth known as TUAN MAC CARELL.

CARHULES
Arthurian

A building near Castle DORE in CORNWALL that appears to have been named after a person called GOURLES, who was perhaps the original of GORLOIS.

CARIADO
Arthurian

Appearing in the romance *TRISTAN*, Cariado fell in love with ISEULT and told her that her lover, TRISTAN, had married ISEULT of the White Hands.

CARL OF CARLISLE
Arthurian

A giant because of a spell, he once welcomed and entertained GAWAIN, KAY and BALDWIN. At Carl's own request, Gawain broke the spell by cutting off the giant's head, and Carl was restored to his former size. Gawain subsequently married his daughter, and King ARTHUR knighted Carl, making him a KNIGHT OF THE ROUND TABLE and the Lord of Carlisle, hence his epithet, though some say he took the name Carl only after he had become Lord of Carlisle.

CARL OF CARLISLE, THE
Arthurian

Incomplete sixteenth-century English romance that is based on the earlier fourteenth-century English *SIR GAWAIN AND THE CARL OF CARLISLE*, which is also unfinished. It has been suggested that this work remains incomplete since it simply echoes the state of the earlier work on which it is based.

CARLACHS
Arthurian

The name of either a nation or a race of people. Appearing in Irish romance, the BLACK KNIGHT, son of the King of Carlachs, killed the KNIGHT OF THE LANTERN, having been accepted as one of ARTHUR's knights.

CARLISLE
General

A Cumbrian city situated at the western end of Hadrian's Wall on the confluence of the rivers EDEN, Calder and Petteril. Originally called *Luguvalium* by the Romans, during whose occupation it was a prosperous settlement, it was later raided successively by PICTS, Vikings and Scots. CHRÉTIEN DE TROYES makes Carlisle the seat of ARTHUR's court, but this connection is not made by GEOFFREY OF MONMOUTH, WACE or LAYAMON. Later writers mainly connect GAWAIN with Carlisle, especially in respect of the beheading, at his own request, of the CARL OF CARLISLE. The entire area surrounding the city is shrouded in legends concerning the ancient kingdom of RHEGED.

CARMAC
Irish

A legendary ancestor of Saint BRIDE. He appears in her genealogy as the son of CARRUIN and the father of CIS, and thus also an ancestor of the DAGHDHA.

CARMAN
Irish

The mother of the three sons who came from Athens, her home, to blight the TUATHA DÉ DANANN, who sent out AI, CRIDENBÉL, LUGH LAEBACH and BÉCHUILLE to do battle with them. The three were soundly beaten and left Carman behind as surety that they would never return. She died in captivity.

CARMARTHEN
Welsh and Arthurian

The town in DYFED that can rightly claim to be one of the oldest towns in WALES, probably beginning life as a Celtic hill fort that was obliterated by the Romans, who built a wooden fort there in AD 75. This was the most westerly of their large forts, but few traces remain. However, the discovery of an amphitheatre with a seating capacity of 500 would seem to suggest that the garrison at Carmarthen was not insignificant.

The town was the alleged birthplace of MYRDDIN and is actually known in Welsh as *Caerfyrddin*, 'the city of Myrddin'. Some suggest that Myrddin took his name from the town, while others say that it was named after him. Whatever the truth, the town certainly has many connections with this famous wizard, better known as MERLIN, and his prophecies. Probably the best known of these is that concerning the PRIORY OAK, or MERLIN'S TREE. Myrddin prophesied that the town would fall if this particular tree ever fell. Its remains now stand in the foyer of Saint Peter's Civic Hall, because the tree was moved in 1978 by the local authority from its site in the town, since it consisted mainly of concrete and iron bars and this constituted a hazard to traffic. Carmarthen, however, is still awaiting the fulfilment of the prophecy, but perhaps simply moving the tree was not enough to bring about the town's downfall.

Carmarthen, one of the oldest towns in Wales and the alleged birthplace of Merlin. (© Hulton-Deutsch Collection, *c*. 1910/Corbis)

CARN ARTHUR
Arthurian
Situated in the PRESELI HILLS, DYFED, below BEDD ARTHUR, is Carn Arthur, which has a stone perched precariously on its top. It was allegedly thrown by ARTHUR from Dyffryn, or from Henry's Moat, which lies about five miles distant.

CARN CABAL
Arthurian
A large heap of stones near Carngafallt, Powys, one of which is supposed to bear the impression of a hound's foot. This hound, so legend says, was owned by King ARTHUR and was called CABAL. Arthur himself is said to have gathered together this heap of stones, placing the magic stone with the paw print on the top. Anyone who takes this stone away cannot keep it, for it will always return itself to the pile.

CARNED(D) ARTHUR
Arthurian
A cairn in Snowdonia that local Welsh folklore states is the burial site of ARTHUR.

CARNEDD Y CAWR
Welsh and Arthurian
'The Giant's Carn', an alternative name for YR WYDDFA FAWR or Mount SNOWDON.

CARNUTE
Gaulish
The ancient Celtic name for the city of Chartres, FRANCE. JULIUS CAESAR reported that the DRUIDS used to meet at Carnute, while Aventius added that, when they were expelled from GAUL by the Emperor Tiberius, their sacred groves were felled. However, Carnute retained its holy and mystical

connections, which the new Christian faith was eager to absorb, and the site was thus chosen for the building of Chartres cathedral, which some authorities say covers the earlier meeting place of the Druids.

CARNWENNAN
Arthurian
The name of King ARTHUR's dagger.

CAROLHAISE
Arthurian
One of the most important cities that lay within CAMELIARD, the realm of King LEODEGRANCE.

CAROUSAL, FORT OF
Welsh and Arthurian
A literal translation of the OTHERWORLDLY castle of CAER FEDDWIDD.

CARRAS
Arthurian
The brother of King CLAUDAS and himself the King of RECESSE, he waged a bitter war against King ARTHUR until, finally, he was persuaded by GAWAIN to stop and sue for peace.

CARRAWBURGH
British
A Roman fort on Hadrian's Wall that lies between Chester and Housesteads. In Roman times a well was sunk and a shrine erected and maintained to a goddess whose name was revealed as COVENTINA during excavations at the site in 1876. It is unknown whether she was a local or imported deity, but she was obviously a deity of some importance from the sheer quantity of votive offerings that have been discovered in her well.

CARREG COETAN ARTHUR
Arthurian
Near Newport, GWENT, this cromlech is also known as ARTHUR'S QUOIT, supposedly one of the many thrown by King ARTHUR. Where this quoit was thrown from, however, remains a mystery.

CAR(R)IDWEN
Welsh and Arthurian
See CERRIDWEN

CARRUIN
Irish
The earliest ancestor of Saint BRIDE to be mentioned in a genealogy that makes Carruin the father of CARMAC.

CARTIMANDUA
British
The Queen of the powerful BRIGANTES, who was alleged to have handed CARATACUS, King of the CATUVELLAUNI, over to his enemies, the Romans.

CARVILIA
Arthurian
A daughter of the sorceress MORGAN Le Fay who appears in the works of the Italian poet Torquato Tasso (1544–95).

CASCORACH
Irish
The minstrel of the TUATHA DÉ DANANN. He is alleged to have lulled Saint PATRICK and his retinue to sleep with his music, a fact recorded by BROGAN, Saint Patrick's scribe.

CASNAR
Welsh
A British prince who is described as belonging to the same lineage as GWYNN GOHOYW, whose daughter, CIGFA, married PRYDERI.

CASSIVELAUNUS
British
The brother of LUD and NENNIUS, whom the Welsh call CASWALLAWN and make the brother of LLUDD, LLEFELYS and NYNNIAW. Because Lud's sons were too young to succeed their dead father, the throne passed to Cassivelaunus, who made the two young men, ANDROGEUS and TENUANTIUS, the Dukes of KENT and CORNWALL respectively. Twice Cassivelaunus repelled the Romans under the leadership of JULIUS CAESAR, but was defeated in a battle near CANTERBURY after Androgeus had betrayed his uncle to the Romans. Cassivelaunus capitulated and agreed to become a vassal king. After he died and was buried at YORK, he was succeeded by Tenuantius, as Androgeus had travelled to Rome, where he remained until he died.

History reveals that Cassivelaunus was the King of the CATUVELLAUNI, although his power drew respect from much further afield. His capital was later called *Verulamium* by the Romans, a city that is today known as Saint Albans.

CASTELLORS
Arthurian
According to the genealogies of JOHN OF GLASTONBURY, Castellors was the son of AMINABAD and an ancestor of King ARTHUR.

CASTLE-AN-DINAS

Arthurian

Situated near Saint Columb in CORNWALL, the largest Celtic hill fort in that county and a seat of Cornish kings after ARTHUR's time, it became associated in Cornish tradition with King Arthur himself, some sources even naming it as CAMELOT.

CASTLE EDEN

Arthurian

A village located in County Durham that is said to be haunted by the spirits of King ARTHUR's knights, who appear in the guise of chickens. It was also once thought that King Arthur's hall originally stood in the village.

CASTLE KEY

Arthurian

According to the medieval *History of Fulk Fitzwarin*, this earthwork in Shropshire (modern Caynham Camp) was allegedly built by Sir KAY.

CASTLE OF MAIDENS

Arthurian

GEOFFREY OF MONMOUTH says that EBRAUCUS, King of BRITAIN, founded this castle, which was originally known as the Castle of Mount AGNED. It may have been identified with EDINBURGH, which in the Middle Ages was known as Castellum (or Castra) Puellarum, though some of the tales associated with it put it in the vicinity of Gloucester. Ruled by Duke LIANOUR, it was said to contain young women, though why is not clear. Some think that they were prisoners. Seven unnamed brothers subsequently killed Lianour and took over the castle, but they were defeated by three of ARTHUR's knights, after which the daughter of Duke Lianour took charge.

CASTLE RUSHDEN

Arthurian

A castle on the Isle of MAN beneath which, in some caves, MERLIN was said to have imprisoned a number of giants he had defeated.

Castle-an-Dinas near Saint Columb, Cornwall, and one more possible site of Camelot. (Steve Hartgroves, Historic Environment Service/© Cornwall County Council)

CASTLEFORD

Arthurian

Called *Legiolium* by the Romans, this town in West Yorkshire has been identified by some with the CITY OF THE LEGION.

CASTRIS

Arthurian

According to WOLFRAM VON ESCHENBACH, Castris was the first husband of HERZELOYDE, from whom she inherited NORTHGALIS and WALES. Following his death, Herzeloyde married GAHMURET, by whom she became the mother of PERCEVAL.

CASWALLAWN

British and Arthurian

Traditionally the son of BELI and the conqueror of the ISLAND OF THE MIGHTY, thus disinheriting MANA-WYDAN FAB LLYR, the brother and heir of BENDIGEID VRAN (BRÂN THE BLESSED), and cousin of PRYDERI.

A separate Welsh tradition makes Caswallawn the brother of LLUDD, LLEFELYS and NYNNIAW, thus having his origin in CASSIVELAUNUS, the historical King of the CATUVELLAUNI at the time of the first Roman incursion led by JULIUS CAESAR.

CAT COIT CELIDON

Arthurian

The site of one of ARTHUR'S BATTLES. It is thought to be either in the southern part of SCOTLAND, in the area once known as SILVA CALEDONIAE (Wood of Scotland) or CELYDDON, or in CELIDON WOOD near LINCOLN.

CATH FI(O)NNTRA(GA)

Irish

The Battle of Ventry, a story in which the TUATHA DÉ DANANN helped the members of the FIAN in battle against an unnamed enemy, referred to simply as 'big men', presumably giants. Magical weapons were conveyed to FIONN MAC CUMHAILL by LABHRAIDH LAMFHADA, weapons that had been made by TADHG and that are recorded as shooting balls of fire. Other weapons were forged for the fian by the one-eyed, one-legged ROC, a smith god who appears only in this story.

CATH GODEU

Welsh

A mythical battle in which ARAWN was defeated by AMAETHON, one of the sons of DÔN, who was helped by the magic of his brother GWYDION FAB DÔN. The battle came about after Amaethon had brought up several animals from ANNWFN, the OTHERWORLD, the realm of ARAWN.

CATH MAIGHE TUIREDH

Irish

The Battle of Magh Tuiredh, an important part of the BOOK OF LEINSTER, which recounts the First and Second Battles of MAGH TUIREDH, and thus records much of the early mythological history of IRELAND.

CATH PALUG

Welsh and Arthurian

A monstrous member of the cat family whose name means 'clawing cat' (*palug* means 'clawing'). It was one of the vile offspring of the pig HÊN WEN and was thrown into the sea, from whence it was saved and raised by the sons of PALUG on ANGLESEY, where it grew to an enormous size and proceeded to devour at least 180 warriors. The Welsh poem *Pa Gur* tells how CEI (Sir KAY) travelled to Anglesey with a view to killing lions and especially prepared himself for a meeting with the Cath Palug. Unfortunately, this poem is incomplete, but it may have told how Cei defeated the animal. Welsh tradition also suggests that a leopard, kept as a pet by a Welsh king, may have given rise to the legend. Another Welsh tradition says that the Cath Palug was the offspring of CERRIDWEN, who was also sometimes known as Hên Wen.

ARTHUR was also said to have slain a giant cat near Lake BOURGET in the French Alps, an event that is celebrated in local names such as MONT DU CHAT (Cat's Mountain), DENT DU CHAT (Cat's Tooth) and COL DU CHAT (Cat's Neck). In the medieval French romance *Romanaz de Franceis*, Arthur fought a Capalu, the continental name for the Cath Palug, in a swamp, but it killed him and then invaded BRITAIN, where it became king. The character seems to have been expanded in later romances, for in the *BATAILLE LOQUIFER* a servant of MORGAN Le Fay appears who has the name KAPALU.

CATHB(H)A(D)(H)

Irish

The DRUID who foretold that DERDRIU, the daughter of FEDLIMID, FILI to CONCHOBAR MAC NESSA, would be exceptionally beautiful but the cause of much suffering and torment within ULSTER. He is also reputed to have told the youth SÉDANTA that his life would be short and glorious. Shortly afterwards this youth killed the hound of

CULANN, and thence became known as CÚ CHULAINN. Cathbhadh is the grandfather of Cú Chulainn according to a traditional genealogy that shows that DEICHTINE was his daughter by MAGA.

CATIGERN
British and Arthurian
A son of VORTIGERN. He fell in battle near Aylesford, KENT, in the fifth century and is supposedly buried in a Neolithic cromlech known as Kit's Coty House, though this cromlech pre-dates the death of Catigern by some considerable time.

CATUVELLA(U)NI
British
A tribe of Britons who inhabited a large area between the THAMES and Cambridgeshire at the time of the Roman invasion in AD 43, their capital perhaps being situated near what is today known as Saint Albans. At the time of the first unsuccessful invasion led by JULIUS CAESAR, their king was CASSIVELAUNUS, who led a fierce fight against the invaders before being captured and handed over to the Romans by CARTIMANDUA, Queen of the BRIGANTES. He was pardoned by CLAUDIUS.

CATWALLAUN LONGHAND
Arthurian
Possibly identical with CADWALLON, who ruled GWYNEDD in ARTHUR's time. According to GEOFFREY OF MONMOUTH, he was a North Welsh ruler who allegedly drove the Irish, led by Serigi, out of Anglesey some time around AD 500.

CAVERSHALL
Arthurian
The existing castle at Cavershall in Staffordshire dates from the thirteenth century, but local legend says that ARTHUR held court at Cavershall Castle, and also gave aid to a lady there.

CAW
Arthurian
The father of GILDAS, HUEIL and CYWYLLOG, according to Welsh tradition. He was himself regarded as a saint.

CÉATACH
Irish
A warrior who captured a maiden who then mysteriously disappeared. He set off in search of her and became embroiled in a lengthy battle on the side of her three brothers, who daily fought a foe that came back to life at night. One night Céatach remained with the dead and watched as a hag restored them to life with a potion from a small pot. He killed the hag and all those she had restored to life, but before she died she placed him under a bond to report his actions to a neighbouring king. He did this and was forced to fight the king, whom he killed, but not until the king had also placed Céatach under an oath to report what he had done. Again Céatach had to fight to prove his worth, which again he did, and again he was placed under an oath to report his deeds, but this time to a monstrous cat. The cat killed Céatach but fell onto the warrior's sword and died as well. Some time later, the maiden and her three brothers came looking for Céatach and, finding him dead, poured the potion from the cauldron of the hag onto him, and so restored him to life.

CEFN-Y-BRYN
Arthurian
A place in Gower, WALES, where there is a burial chamber known as ARTHUR'S STONE. Tradition has it that ARTHUR, on his way to his final battle at CAMLANN, felt a pebble in his boot and, after taking it out, flung it into the distance. It landed some seven miles away at Cefn-y-Bryn.

CEI
Welsh and Arthurian
Later to re-emerge under the guise of Sir KAY in the Arthurian legends, Cei was among the party assembled by CULHWCH in his quest to locate the maiden OLWEN, a story told in the *MABINOGION* story of *CULHWCH AND OLWEN*. Each of the party was chosen for a particular skill or attribute. Cei's talents were his ability to stay for nine days and nights without breathing or sleeping and to change his height at will. In addition, his body temperature was so high that he never got wet, and during the cold his companions could kindle a fire from him. The other members of the party were BEDWYR (BEDIVERE), CYNDDYLIG the Guide, GWRHYR the Interpreter, GWALCHMAI FAB GWYAR and MENW FAB TEIRGWAEDD.

CEITHIN
Irish
The uncle of LUGH and brother of CÚ and CIAN.

CELIDOINE
Arthurian
An ancestor of GALAHAD, he was the son of NASCIEN, who came to BRITAIN and was made King of SCOTLAND. His name appears to have been derived from the Latin name for Scotland, Caledonia, though this may be false etymology.

CELIDON WOOD

Arthurian

A wood to the north of LINCOLN that is considered by some to be the location of one of ARTHUR'S BATTLES that NENNIUS lists as having been fought at CALEDON WOOD.

CELL-Y-DEWINIAID

Welsh and Arthurian

'The Grove of the Magicians', a grove of oak trees, long since felled, near DINAS EMRYS. Within this grove, VORTIGERN's counsellors were said to meet to discuss the events of their times. They were buried in an adjoining field with each grave, at one time, marked by a stone. These, too, have long since vanished.

CELLIWIG

Arthurian

A place-name, and variant of CELLIWITH, mentioned in the early Welsh tradition of the Arthurian legends and possibly cognate with KILLIBURY. It is more likely that Celliwig was later transmuted into CAMELOT by the twelfth-century poets in their fanciful interpretations of the legends.

CELLIWITH

Arthurian

A variant of both CELLIWIG and KELLIWIC, and thus one of the many possible origins of CAMELOT.

CELTCHAR

Irish

The son of UTHECAR, the father of NIAMH, and one of the ULSTER warriors who belatedly came to the aid of CÚ CHULAINN towards the end of his epic defence of Ulster against the forces of MEDHBHA and AILILL. He was also one of the warriors who half-heartedly opposed the right of CET to carve the roast pig of MAC DÁ THÓ.

CELYDDON

Welsh

An ancient Welsh name for SCOTLAND. Many believe that the Welsh name gave rise to the more common Old English variant of CALEDON, which latter form possibly gave the Romans their name for Scotland, *Caledonia*. The later Arthurian cycle named Celyddon as one of the possible sites for one of ARTHUR'S BATTLES. In this guise is it possibly cognate with CAT COIT CELIDON, or SILVA CALEDONIAE, the Caledonian forest of southern SCOTLAND, or CELIDON WOOD to the north of LINCOLN.

CENCHOS

Irish

One of the FOMHOIRÉ. His name means 'The Footless', thus presumably indicating that, while he still had the single leg that was a feature of the Fomhoiré, his limb terminated in a stump.

CENEU

Welsh and Arthurian

According to Welsh tradition, the son of COEL GODEBOG, father of MOR and great-great-great-grandfather of MYRDDIN (MERLIN).

CENN CRÚIACH

Irish

'Head of the Mound', a deity, also known as CROM CRUACH, who was said to have been introduced to IRELAND by TIGERNMAS. Cenn Crúiach was undoubtedly a solar deity, but no trace of a being remotely like him has, as yet, been discovered in pagan literature or in the writings of Saint PATRICK. His purpose appears to have been the protection of the SÍDH. Offerings of children and small firstlings were sacrificed to him. Saint Patrick was alleged to have come across a statue of Cenn Crúiach that bowed down before him moments before the earth opened up and swallowed the pagan image.

CERDIC

Arthurian

The father of CYNRIC who is traditionally regarded as a SAXON leader, though it has also been suggested that he was a Jute. Most authorities maintain that he has a true place in history, though some consider him a fabrication. He is supposedly the founder of the kingdom of Wessex, but a problem exists in that his name is Celtic and not Teutonic. This has led to various speculations: that he was a rebellious British king; that he was a one-time ally of King ARTHUR who later changed his allegiances; that he was the original of the King CARADOS of Arthurian legend; and, most surprising of all, that he was a son of Arthur who gathered a mixed Celtic and Teutonic following on the continent.

CERNE ABBAS

British

A village approximately eight miles north of Dorchester, in the south of ENGLAND, that is famous for the gigantic figure carved in the side of a hill above the village that is, predictably, known as the Cerne Abbas Giant. The outline of the giant,

The fertility figure carved into the chalk hills of Dorset that is known as the Cerne Abbas Giant. (© Angelo Hornak/ Corbis)

which stands 180 feet tall, is formed by trenches cut through the turf to reveal the white chalk beneath. On the summit of the hill above the giant is a rectangular earthwork called the Trendle, or Frying Pan, which may have been the site of a temple dedicated to the giant that stands on the hillside below.

The date and origin of the giant remain unknown, but he was undoubtedly a fertility deity, as his huge erect phallus, some 30 feet in length, would indicate. Stylistically, the giant is ascribed to the first century AD and is thought, by some, to represent the Roman hero-god Hercules. This representation is supported by archaeological research that has revealed the outline of what might be a lion's skin, one of the usual attributes of Hercules, beneath the giant's outstretched left arm.

The ancient name of the giant is recorded in a thirteenth-century text by Walter of Coventry, which says that Cerne Abbas is in the pagan district of Dorset, where the god HELITH was once worshipped, although later this god was referred to as HELIS and HEIL. Helith was a solar deity, his name

possibly being derived from the Celtic word for 'sun', and as such this connection would fit the Cerne Abbas Giant, possibly the most striking representation of a fertility deity to be found in Europe.

CERNUNNOS
Widespread Celtic
The Lord of the Animals, the 'Horned One', whose image is found throughout the Celtic lands in Romano-Celtic worship sites, and whose role as an animal god and hunter is preserved in Celtic folklore and legend. As the guardian of the portal leading to the OTHERWORLD, Cernunnos became associated with wealth and prosperity, although his earlier function had been of a nature deity, the ruler of the active forces of life and death, regeneration and fertility. The name Cernunnos is known only from one damaged carving found at Notre Dame in Paris. This carving, which shows a deity with short horns, carries the incomplete inscription 'ERNUNNO'. Since that discovery the name has been used as a generic term for all occurrences of the 'Horned One'. Cernunnos

was, in all probability, a deity of Gaulish origin, and his worship was prominent in the areas settled by Belgic tribes that imported him to BRITAIN.

Cernunnos was of such importance to the Celts that the Christian Church made him a special target of abuse, taking his image to be that of the Devil, *deo falsus* or 'false god'. He was much maligned, even by his own worshippers, his cult opponents and even today by those who claim to be his revivalist supporters. The cult of Cernunnos was especially encouraged by the DRUIDS in their attempt to regularise the local Celtic deities into some form of pantheon and thus to establish Cernunnos as a national, rather than a local, deity. Cernunnos was possibly the nearest the Celts got to a universal father god within their fragmented system of worship.

His status as a fertility god is of much later origin, for Cernunnos has much less to do with sexuality than is held in popular belief. He is the god of hunting, culling and taking. His purpose is to purify through selection and sacrifice in order that the powers of fertility, regeneration and growth may progress unhindered. His image still survives in the figure of HERNE THE HUNTER, an antlered woodland being who dwells in Windsor Forest. He is also possibly the god originally worshipped in the surviving Abbots Bromley horn dance.

Cernunnos is usually represented holding a ram-headed serpent in his left hand, or a serpent with a ram's horn, while he himself sits, cross-legged. He has both animal and human ears, and carries a magnificent set of antlers from which hangs one torc, sometimes two. To his right stands a stag whose antlers are comparable to those of the god himself. Around him other woodland animals gather. The stag was, according to Celtic tradition, the oldest of all animals, and it played a major role in their culture as an OTHERWORLD creature, luring hunters into the tangled masses of the forests, the land of the gods, where it would allow itself to be eaten and then resurrected. One of the most remarkable images of Cernunnos is to be found on the GÜNDESTRUP CAULDRON. It is quite possible that the Irish CONALL CERNACH is a representation of Cernunnos.

The ram-headed serpent, representing the chthonic aspect of Cernunnos, is the totem creature of fire from within the earth, a creature that held special significance to the Celts as an emblem of power. Later Romano-Celtic images of the god, after he had adopted the role of god of wealth, sometimes show him with a sack of coins that he pours out onto the ground.

Later tradition made a tenuous relationship between Cernunnos and the Arthurian legends simply through the association of MERLIN with stags, thus leading to the suggestion that he had some connection with the cult of Cernunnos.

CER(R)IDWEN
Welsh and Arthurian
Also CARRIDWEN

The corn goddess and wife of TEGID VOEL. She is usually represented as a crone, the goddess of dark, prophetic powers, whose totem animal is the sow, which represents the fecundity of the OTHERWORLD. She is the keeper of the cauldron of the Otherworld, in which inspiration and divine knowledge are brewed, and it is this aspect that features most prominently in her story.

Like many Celtic goddesses, Cerridwen had two opposing children. One was the maiden CREARWY, the most beautiful girl ever to have been born, her very person radiating light and warmth. The other was the boy AFAGDDU, the ugliest boy to have lived, whose soul was dark and cold. A second son is also sometimes added to the list of Cerridwen's children. Named MORFRAN AB TEGID, he is said by some to be none other than Afagddu, for Afagddu may possibly be a derisive nickname for Morfran ab Tegid. Others say that they are two separate children, but no source gives any indication of Morfran ab Tegid's attributes. It seems most likely that Afagddu and Morfran ab Tegid are one and the same, for mythology tends to follow set patterns, and it would be extremely unlikely for a goddess such as Cerridwen to have had more than two children representing opposing forces.

To compensate her son for this misfortune, Cerridwen decided to brew a potion that would empower him with the gifts of inspiration and knowledge and would give him the ability to know all things past, present and future. Collecting together the magical herbs required, she placed them in her cauldron and set GWION BACH, the young son of GWREANG, to stir the potion for the required year and a day and the blind man MORDA to stoke the fire. At the end of the allotted time three drops of the hot liquid splashed onto Gwion Bach's thumb. As the little boy sucked his thumb to cool it, he was filled with the potency of the brew. Having now given up its essence, the remainder of the potion became poisonous, the cauldron split asunder and the contents poisoned the local waterways and killed the horses of GWYDDNO GARANHIR, which drank the contaminated water. The sucking of the thumb by Gwion Bach may enshrine an ancient divinatory practice that involved chewing the thumb. The practice was known in early IRELAND as

IMBAS FOROSNAI, and seems to have relied on the notion that chewing the raw flesh of the thumb imparted sagacity.

Gwion Bach immediately knew that his life was in danger and fled the site. When Cerridwen found the cauldron in pieces, she flew into a rage and beat Morda so cruelly about the head with a billet of wood that one of his eyes fell out onto his cheek. Realising that it was Gwion Bach who was responsible for the loss of her potion, Cerridwen dashed off after the boy in the guise of a fearful black hag and soon started to gain on him. Seeing Cerridwen gaining, Gwion Bach used his new-found powers to change himself into a hare so that he might run faster, but Cerridwen countered by changing herself into a greyhound. Gwion Bach saw Cerridwen gaining again and leapt into a river, changing into a fish as he did so. Cerridwen dived in after him and became an otter. Gwion Bach left the river and flew up into the air as a bird, with Cerridwen following as a hawk. Finally Gwion Bach saw a barn and, dropping onto the threshing floor, turned himself into a grain of wheat, thinking that he would be safe among the thousands of other grains that lay scattered all around. Cerridwen changed herself into a hen and, scratching around the floor, swallowed the hapless Gwion Bach.

Resuming her human form, Cerridwen discovered that she was pregnant. Nine months later she gave birth to Gwion Bach as a boy so beautiful that she could not bring herself to kill him. Instead she sewed him up inside a leather bag and threw him into a river. The bag caught on the fish weir of Gwyddno Garanhir, whose son ELPHIN found it and opened it. The first thing he saw was the forehead of the child and immediately exclaimed 'Radiant Brow', thus naming TALIESIN, for the name Taliesin means 'Radiant Brow'.

Cerridwen, whose name means 'White Grain', was also known as HÊN WEN, or 'old white one', the sow that supposedly gave birth to several monstrous offspring, one of which was the CATH PALUG, although this animal has another tale of its birth (see below). She was also the patroness of poetry, a just connection considering that the birth of the great bard Taliesin is a part of her story. She was, through her totem animal, connected with the sow goddess, as well as with ALBINE, the eponym of ALBION. Cerridwen lived at CAER SIDDI, also known as CAER FEDDWIDD, an Otherworldly

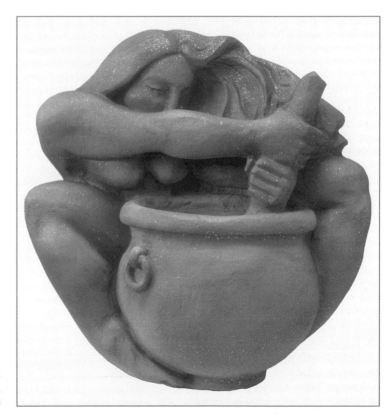

The goddess Cerridwen.
(By permission of artist Paul Borda/© Dryad Designs, www.dryaddesign.com)

kingdom that was represented in the stars as a spiral, although this realm is also sometimes associated with ARIANRHOD.

Not content with all these attributes and associations, Cerridwen was also said to have been given a kitten that grew up to become the Cath Palug. This connection led to Cerridwen being associated with a cat cult, although, quite perversely, she also had connections with wolves and was said, by some, to have been the centre of a Neolithic cult.

CERRIG MARCHOGION
Arthurian

'The Stones of Arthur's Knights' – a group of standing stones in DYFED that are located on a ridge above the CERRIG MEIBION ARTHUR. They are said to represent the knights of King ARTHUR who accompanied him in the hunt for the boar TWRCH TRWYTH.

CERRIG MEIBION ARTHUR
Arthurian

Two standing stones, separated by about 25 feet, in DYFED. They are said to be a monument to the sons of King ARTHUR who were killed by the boar TWRCH TRWYTH, which caused havoc in their encampment having swum over from IRELAND. The story is told in great detail in the *MABINOGION*. Located on a ridge above the stones are CERRIG MARCHOGION – 'The Stones of King Arthur's Knights'.

CES(S)AIR
Irish
Also KESAIR

The daughter of BITH, son of NOAH, who led the first invaders to the shores of IRELAND in a time before the Flood. Her party consisted of fifty women and just three men: Bith, LADRA and FINTAN. These three men shared the women among them, but, after Ladra died, Bith and Fintan took twenty-five women each, Cesair falling to Fintan. Bith died shortly before the Flood, which killed all the women and left Fintan as the sole survivor, for he had hidden in a cave that the waters of the Flood never reached. He lived on for many centuries as a shape-shifting immortal and witnessed all the subsequent invasions of Ireland.

CET
Irish
Also KET

The brother of ANLUAN. A warrior of CONNACHT, Cet claimed the right to carve the boar of MAC DÁ THÓ and cruelly derided all those who sought to challenge him until CONALL CERNACH arrived,

to whom he quickly gave way. However, Cet taunted Conall Cernach, saying that, had Anluan been present, he would have given him a run for his money. Conall Cernach then removed the bloody head of Anluan from a pouch and threw it onto the table in front of Cet.

CETHERN
Irish

A companion of CÚ CHULAINN who fought the combined armies of AILILL and MEDHBHA. He received numerous wounds in the conflict and retired to his camp for treatment. However, Cethern was a churlish man, and killed several of the physicians for saying that his wounds were fatal. Finally, one physician told him he could either lie around and await death or pull himself together and die with honour on the battlefield. Cethern chose the latter. In preparation, he lay for two days in a tub of bone marrow. He was then fortified with the ribs of a chariot wrapped around him to secure his own broken ribs and finally armed to the hilt. So frenzied was his attack that, on seeing him drawing close, the men of CONNACHT placed the crown of Ailill on a standing stone that Cethern simply split in half. So angry was he at the subterfuge that he made a captive Connacht warrior wear the crown and he split him in half. Cethern killed many hundreds of the Connacht warriors before he was outnumbered and killed.

CÉTHLIONN
Irish

The wife of BALAR, who told her husband that the arrival of his grandson LUGH among the ranks of the TUATHA DÉ DANANN would, as had been prophesied, bring about the downfall of the FOMHOIRÉ.

See also AIDED CHLAINNE TUIRENN.

CHASTEL MARTE
Arthurian

A castle whose master, according to *PERLESVAUS*, was an uncle of PERCEVAL. He seized the GRAIL CASTLE, but Perceval laid siege to him and he committed suicide.

CHASTIEFOL
Arthurian

The name of one of the swords that belonged to King ARTHUR.

CHÂTEAU DE LA CHARETTE
Arthurian

The castle of the QUEEN OF SORESTAN in which she, and three other associates of MORGAN Le Fay,

Chester, once known as the City of the Legion. (© Mick Sharp)

imprisoned Sir LANCELOT until he chose which of them he loved.

CHÂTEAU DE MORGAN LE FEE, LE
Arthurian
The French name for a mirage that appears in the Straits of Messina. Known as FATA MORGANA in Italian, this mirage distorts both horizontally and vertically, and is said to represent one of MORGAN Le Fay's fairy palaces.

CHELDRIC
Arthurian
According to GEOFFREY OF MONMOUTH, Cheldric was a SAXON leader who brought reinforcements with him from GERMANY to join COLGRIN, and took part in the battles of LINCOLN, CALEDON WOOD and BADON. Following the rout of the Saxons, he fled, but was finally defeated and killed by CADOR.

CHELINDE
Arthurian
The wife of SADOR, the son of BRONS.

CHESTER
Arthurian
Named *Deva* in classical times, Chester was, like CAERLEON-ON-USK, also known as the CITY OF THE LEGION. It has been suggested that Chester should replace Caerleon-on-Usk when considering the location of ARTHUR's principal city and the site of the battle at the City of the Legion.

CHEVREFUEIL
Arthurian
Arthurian romance written by the twelfth-century poetess MARIE DE FRANCE.

CHILDE ROWLAND
Arthurian
A medieval Scottish ballad that tells of how ELLEN, ARTHUR's daughter, was saved from an OTHERWORLD prison by her brother, and hence Arthur's son, ROWLAND.

CHLODOMER
Arthurian
The King of Orleans, FRANCE, who reigned

between AD 511 and 524, and was killed in a battle against Burgundian invaders. One theory put forward suggests that he was killed while fighting against ARTHUR.

CHOUGH
Arthurian

Although choughs are now extinct in CORNWALL, except for a few pairs in captivity, Cornish beliefs held that the spirit of ARTHUR used to fly over the cliffs in the form of this bird. This is just one bird that has become associated with the spirit of Arthur. Others include the PUFFIN and the RAVEN, the latter being related to the chough and possibly later replacing it, because of its rarity.

CHRAMM
Arthurian

The leader of a rebellion against CLOTHAIR, the King of the Franks, who was aided by CUNOMORUS; both leaders were allegedly killed in the course of the fighting.

CHRÉTIEN DE TROYES
Arthurian

A medieval French poet and troubadour who was born in Troyes, in the Champagne, some time during the middle of the twelfth century. The greatest of the French medieval poets, he was the author of the earliest romances dealing with King ARTHUR. He was a member of the court of the Countess Marie de Champagne, daughter of Louis VII, and to whom he dedicated his metrical romance of courtly love *Yvain et Lancelot*. He is probably best known for the number of Arthurian romances he wrote: *EREC ET ENIDE* (*c.* 1160); *Le Chevalier de Charette*, which is also simply known as *Lancelot*; *CLIGÉS* (*c.* 1164); *Le Chevalier au lion*, also called *Yvain*; *Le Conte de graal*, also called *PERCEVAL* (*c.* 1180), which he wrote for Philip, Count of Flanders, but which remained unfinished as he died *c.* 1183. His works are reputed to be the first to introduce the concept of the Holy GRAIL.

CHWIM-LEIAN, -BIAN
Welsh

The flower-maiden mentioned in the MYRDDIN (MERLIN) poem *AFOLLONAU*. She is thought to be identifiable with GUENDOLOENA and BLODEUWEDD.

CIABHAN
Irish
Also KEEVAN

Appearing in the *Acallamh na Senórach*, Ciabhan, one of the FIAN, journeyed over the seas to the land of MANANNÁN MAC LIR with LODAN and EOLUS. There the three persuaded the sisters CLIODNA, AEIFE and EDAEIN to elope with them, Cliodna travelling with Ciabhan. They had just reached shore when a huge wave rolled in and engulfed the lovers, drowning the three maidens, as well as ILDÁTHACH and his sons, who, themselves in love with Cliodna, had set off in pursuit of her. Some sources, however, say that the wave did not drown the sisters, but rather carried them back to TÍR TAIRNGIRI.

CIAN
Irish
Also KIAN

The brother of CÚ and CEITHIN and the earthly father of LUGH. He had been involved in a long-standing blood feud with the sons of TUIRENN – BRIAN, IUCHAR and IUCHARBA – by whom he was killed. His death was avenged by his son Lugh, who made the three murderous men collect a number of items required by the TUATHA DÉ DANANN for the forthcoming Second Battle of MAGH TUIREDH. Brian, Iuchar and Iucharba completed all the tasks set them, but died as a result of the injuries they received performing the last task.

CIGFA
Welsh
Also KICVA

The daughter of GWYN GOHOYW and the wife of PRYDERI. She was left alone with MANAWYDAN FAB LLYR after Pryderi had been magically imprisoned within a CAER.

CIMBAOTH
Irish
Also KIMBAY

According to the eleventh-century historian Tierna of Clonmacnois, Cimbaoth ruled *c.* 300 BC and was responsible for the foundation of the kingdom of ULSTER and the building of EMHAIN MHACHA. Legend says that Cimbaoth was the son of RED HUGH and the brother of MACHA and DITHORBA. On the death of their father, Macha refused to yield the throne to Dithorba, who went to war with her. He was killed, and Macha then compelled Cimbaoth to marry her, and so ruled as Queen of all IRELAND. The five sons of Dithorba were captured by Macha and made to build the ramparts of her fortress, which has, since that time, been known as Emhain Mhacha.

CIRCE
Arthurian

A sorceress of classical Graeco-Roman mythology, appearing in Homer's *Odyssey* and Apollonius of Rhodes's *Argonautica*. In the Arthurian romance *PERCEFOREST*, she marries BETHIDES and brings the Romans to BRITAIN.

CIS
Irish

An ancestor of Saint BRIDE according to an oral genealogy of that saint that forms part of a protective prayer. This genealogy makes Cis the son of CARMAC and the father of CREAR.

CISSA
Arthurian

A son of AELLE, he accompanied his father when his SAXON forces defeated the Britons.

CIST ARTHUR
Arthurian

A burial chamber, mentioned in a survey of 1737, on MOEL ARTHUR, a hill in Clwyd, WALES. This chamber has been cited as being yet another of the numerous possible last resting places of King ARTHUR.

CITY OF SOULS
Arthurian

According to *PERLESVAUS*, an OTHERWORLD city, haunted by spirits, that was visited by LANCELOT.

CITY OF THE LEGION(S)
Arthurian

According to NENNIUS, the City of the Legion was the site of one of ARTHUR'S BATTLES. GEOFFREY OF MONMOUTH identifies it with CAERLEON-ON-USK, which was called ISCA LEGIONIS and ISCA LEGIONUM in early times. It has also been identified with CHESTER, called URBS LEGIONIS in Latin, and also with CASTLEFORD, which the Romans called *Legiolium*. If the City of the Legion is to be identified with Caerleon-on-Usk, then it was here that ARTHUR once held a plenary court that was allegedly attended by representatives from all of Europe.

CLAIRE
Arthurian

The sister of SAGREMOR, she was saved by GUINGLAIN from two giants.

CLAMADEUS
Arthurian

A king who was defeated in single combat and killed by PERCEVAL after he had laid siege to BLANCHEFLEUR's castle.

CLARENCE, DUCHY OF
Arthurian

The duchy of which GALESCHIN was said to have been made duke by ARTHUR after his defeat of the SAXONS, who were besieging the city. This is an anachronism, since the duchy of Clarence was not created until 1362, and the place to which it relates, the small wool town of Clare in Suffolk, can hardly be called a city.

The Duchy of Clarence, Suffolk.
(© Michael S. Yamashita/Corbis)

CLARETTE
Arthurian

The maiden whose hand was won by the KNIGHT OF THE SLEEVE at a tournament at ARTHUR's court, according to the Dutch romance *Ridder metter Mouwen*.

CLARINE
Arthurian

The wife of King PANT of GENNEWIS, Clarine is made the mother of LANCELOT in a Germanic version of his story.

CLARION
Arthurian

The SAXON King who was, according to some sources, the owner of the horse GRINGALET, which GAWAIN took from him.

CLARIS
Arthurian

The hero of the romance *CLARIS ET LARIS*. He rescued his companion LARIS from the King of DENMARK, TALLAS, married LIDOINE, Laris's sister, and became a KNIGHT OF THE ROUND TABLE.

CLARIS ET LARIS
Arthurian

A thirteenth-century French verse romance concerning the adventures of CLARIS and his companion LARIS.

CLARISSANT
Arthurian

The mother of GUIGENOR by GUIROMELANT, she was the daughter of MORGAUSE and LOT.

CLARISSE
Arthurian

Simply mentioned as being the sister of GAWAIN.

CLAS MYRDDIN
Welsh

'Merlin's Precinct or Enclosure', which is, according to the *Trioedd Ynys Prydein*, one of the earliest names for ENGLAND.

CLAUDAS
Arthurian

Possibly having an origin in Clovis I, King of the Franks between AD 481 and 511, Claudas is described as King of the Desert Land, his realm being identified with Berry, since *berrie* in Old French signifies a desert. He was the opponent of King BORS, whose kingdom he seized after that king's death. Bors's sons fell into the hands of Claudas's lover PHARIEN, but, when Claudas had them brought to him, they escaped in the guise of greyhounds, killing his son DORIN in the process. Claudas imprisoned GUINEVERE after insulting one

of her ladies-in-waiting, and war broke out between Claudas, who was supported by the Romans, and BRITAIN, the latter finally being victorious.

CLAUDIA
British

Claudia has the distinction of being the only Briton to be mentioned in the Bible (2 Timothy 4: 21). She is described as the child of blue-painted parents (Celts), yet in Rome, where she lived, she had acquired every civilised grace.

CLAUDIUS
General

The fourth Roman Emperor (40 BC–AD 54), who ruled between AD 10 and AD 54 and was born in Lyons. He was the younger son of Drusus senior and brother of the Emperor Tiberius. He inaugurated the conquest of BRITAIN, taking part in the opening campaign in person (AD 43). GEOFFREY OF MONMOUTH claims that ARVIRAGUS became the King of Britain during the Roman invasion. Peace was established between Arviragus and Claudius when the former married GENVISSA, Claudius' daughter. Arviragus later revolted, but Genvissa interceded and peace was once more established.

CLEENA
Irish

A queen of the SÍDH of south MUNSTER. Her name is sometimes said to be a variant of CLIODNA.

CLERIADUS
Arthurian

A descendant of ARTHUR; he was the successor to PHILIPPON, the father of his wife, MELIADICE, as the King of England.

CLIACH
Irish

A harper who is mentioned in an incidental reference as having sought the hand of the daughter of BODB but was kept at bay for a year by the magic power of that deity and then died when a DRAGON appeared from beneath the ground.

CLIGÉS
Arthurian

The hero of the romance *CLIGÉS* by CHRÉTIEN DE TROYES, he was the son of ALEXANDER, then Emperor of CONSTANTINOPLE, and of SOREDAMOR, the daughter of LOT. While his uncle ALIS was Emperor, he married FENICE, with whom Cligés also fell in love. Unable to make his feelings known, he left the court at Constantinople and travelled to that of ARTHUR. When Alis subsequently died, Cligés returned out of his self-enforced exile and duly married Fenice.

CLIGÉS
Arthurian
Romance by CHRÉTIEN DE TROYES concerning the exploits of the hero after whom the work is named. Written *c.* 1164, the romance is based mainly around the imperial family of CONSTANTINOPLE, genealogical evidence within the work illustrating a connection between CLIGÉS and LOT.

CLI(O)DNA
Irish
The most beautiful woman in the world. A divine maiden who is accompanied by three brightly coloured magical birds, whose song is so sweet that they soothe the sick and the wounded to sleep, and feed on the fruit of the apples of the LAND OF PROMISE, TÍR TAIRNGIRI.

Another story concerning Cliodna appears in the *Acallamh na Senórach*. CIABHAN, one of the FIAN, journeyed over the seas to the land of MANANNÁN MAC LIR with LODAN and EOLUS. There they persuaded the sisters Cliodna, AEIFE and EDAEIN to elope with them, Cliodna travelling with Ciabhan. They had just reached shore when a huge wave rolled in and engulfed the lovers, drowning the three maidens, as well as ILDÁTHACH and his sons who, themselves in love with Cliodna, had set off in pursuit of her. Some versions of this story say that, rather than drowning the three sisters, the great wave simply carried them back to the land of Manannán mac Lir. Yet another version says that she left the Land of Promise with IUCHNA to travel to OENGHUS MAC IN OG, and it was on that occasion that the wave carried her back to the realm of Tír Tairngiri.

CLITON
Welsh and Arthurian
One of the nine sisters of MORGEN (MORGAN Le Fay).

CLODION
Arthurian
A son of PHARAMOND who was killed in single combat by TRISTAN.

CLOGWYN CARNEDD YR WYDFFA
Welsh and Arthurian
'The Precipice of the Carn of Yr Wydffa', a name sometimes used to refer to YR WYDFFA FAWR or,

alternatively, to the cairn that used to be situated on the top of the mountain that is today known as Mount SNOWDON.

CLOTEN
British
The ruler of CORNWALL after the death of PORREX, and the father of MOLMUTIUS. The name of his wife or partner remains unrecorded.

CLOTHAIR
Arthurian
The King of SOISSONS, who later became King of all the Franks. It is claimed by some sources that CUNOMORUS died during an uprising against him in AD 560.

CLOTHRU
Irish
The sister of MEDHBHA and EITHNE. Her brothers were BRES, NÁR and LOTHAR. All three sisters were at one stage the wife of CONCHOBAR MAC NESSA, Clothru and Eithne becoming successive wives after Medhbha had left the King for AILILL. Clothru remained childless until she had an incestuous relationship with each of her three brothers. From each affair she bore a son named LUGAID, although some sources name but one son with this name, and give him the three brothers as his joint father. She subsequently had an affair with one of her sons and bore him a son named CRIMTHANN NIA NÁIR.

CLOVIS
Arthurian
Merovingian ruler of the Franks, born AD 465, the grandson of Merovich. In AD 481 he succeeded his father, Childeric I, as King of the Salian Franks, and spent his entire life expanding the Frankish kingdom. When he died in AD 511, in his capital, Paris, the kingdom was divided equally between his four sons, who eagerly continued the expansion begun by their father. The anonymous romance *Palamedes* says that Clovis was a direct ancestor of GUIRON.

CLUD
Welsh
A shortened and popularised form of GWAWL FAB CLUD.

CLUTARIUS
Welsh
The father of MAELGWYN.

CLWYD

General

An ancient Welsh kingdom that is the equivalent of the county of the same name today. The kingdom was once closely aligned with POWYS, as is illustrated in the Pillar of ELISEG, which is situated in Clwyd and yet gives a list of the early kings of Powys.

CLYDNO

Arthurian

One of ARTHUR's warriors who was, in Welsh tradition, the father of CYNON.

CLYDNO EIDDYN

Welsh and Arthurian

The owner of a cauldron that was considered one of the THIRTEEN TREASURES OF BRITAIN.

CNOC AINÉ

Irish

A small hillock in MUNSTER that is said to be the home of the supernatural woman AINÉ.

COBA

Irish

A trapper to EREM, son of MÍL. He was the first to prepare a trap and pitfall in IRELAND. However, he tested it by putting his leg into it and, having broken his shin bone and his arms, he died.

COBTHACH COEL

Irish

In order to usurp the Irish throne, Cobthach Coel killed his brother LOEGHAIRE LORC, King of IRELAND, along with his nephew, AILILL AINE, King of LEINSTER. At the same time he drove LABHRAIDH LOINGSECH, Ailill Aine's son, into exile. With the help of the Men of MUNSTER, Labhraidh Loingsech regained his kingdom and went on to make peace with Cobthach Coel, even inviting the usurper to his court, although this was a trick. Labhraidh Loingsech had an iron house prepared for his visitor and his thirty vassal knights, who accepted the invitation in all innocence. When they were all inside the iron house, Labhraidh Loingsech had the door fastened and ordered fires to be kindled all around it, thus roasting Cobthach Coel and his supporters to death.

See also COVAC, LOEGHAIRE

CODAL

Irish

The foster father of ÉRIU. He appears in a very early story concerning the creation of the landscape of IRELAND. One day he was feeding Ériu on the side of a small hillock, and, as she grew, so too did the hillock on which she was standing. It would have continued to grow until it had swamped Ireland had not Ériu complained to her foster father of the heat of the sun and the coolness of the wind. He immediately led her off what by now was a mountain, which stopped growing the moment she left its slopes.

COEL

British and Arthurian

Possibly a historical figure in the north country in the early fifth century, who successfully defended his kingdom against the PICTS and Scots. He is almost certainly the Old King Cole of nursery-rhyme fame, as the adjective *hen* ('old') was applied to him. A fourth-century manuscript says that Coel was King of all BRITAIN, dying in AD 267, while a sixteenth-century manuscript draws him into the Arthurian cycle saying that, through his mother, he was an ancestor of King ARTHUR.

Tradition names his wife as STRADAWL and his daughter as GWAWL, who may have been the wife of CUNEDDA. He was regarded as the founder and ruler of COLCHESTER. Legend says that this city was besieged by the Roman Emperor Constantius Chlorus for three years and that, after peace had been restored, the Emperor married Coel's daughter HELENA, who is better known as Saint Helena. Their son, Constantine the Great, was born in AD 265.

COEL GODEBOG

Welsh and Arthurian

The father of CENEU and great-great-great-great-grandfather of MYRDDIN (MERLIN) in Welsh tradition.

COETAN ARTHUR

Arthurian

A round barrow with burial chamber and very large capstone at Saint David's Head in DYFED. It is one of the numerous locations where King ARTHUR is said to be buried.

CÓIGEDH

Irish

Literally meaning 'one-fifth', this is the collective name for the five provinces of IRELAND into which the country was divided by the invading FIR BHOLG. These five provinces were ULSTER, LEINSTER, MUNSTER, CONNACHT and MEATH.

CÓIR ANMANN
Irish

'Fitness of Names', which gives an account of the adventures of CONNLA, although it differs from the normal by saying that Connla was slain by his enemies rather than departing in a boat to a divine kingdom from which he never returned.

COIR-BRE, -PRE
Irish

The FILI of the TUATHA DÉ DANANN who so skilfully and magically satirised BRES that that tyrannical king broke out in boils, abdicated the throne and defected to the FOMHOIRÉ, the people of his father.

COIRPRE
Irish

The son of DOEL. He once fought with CÚ CHULAINN but was forced to yield and, having carried Cú Chulainn into his castle, gave the hero his daughter, who remains unnamed.

COL DU CHAT
Arthurian

'Cat's Neck'. This name is found in the vicinity of Lake BOURGET in the French Alps, and celebrates the fact that near that lake ARTHUR was said to have slain a huge cat.

COLCHESTER
Arthurian

Reputedly founded by COEL and called *Camulodunum* in Roman times, Colchester has been identified by some with CAMELOT, this association coming from the similarity of the Roman name, though this could also be said about any place-name that has 'Cam' in it, whether Roman or British.

COLCU
Irish

The stepson of CRÉD who was always on hand when she attempted to meet with CANO. Eventually his intervention led to the suicide of Créd and the death, three days later, of Cano.

COLE, OLD KING
Arthurian

It is almost certain that the Old King Cole of nursery rhyme had his origins in COEL, for this possibly historical character had the adjective *hen* (old) applied to him. Whether he was actually a 'merry old soul' though is open to speculation.

The traditional rhyme is as follows:

Old King Cole was a merry old soul,
And a merry old soul was he.
He called for his pipe, and he called for his bowl,
And he called for his fiddlers three.

Every fiddler had a fiddle fine,
And a very fine fiddle had he, had he.
Tweedle dum, tweedle dee, went the fiddlers three,
Tweedle dum dee, dum dee deedle dee.

Tweedle dum, tweedle dee, went the fiddlers three,
Tweedle dum dee, dum dee deedle dee.

COLGREVANCE
Arthurian

A native of the realm of GORE, he became a KNIGHT OF THE ROUND TABLE. Accounts of his death vary. In one he was killed by LIONEL, but in another he was among those who surprised LANCELOT and GUINEVERE together and was killed by the escaping, yet unarmed, Lancelot.

COLGRIN
Arthurian

According to GEOFFREY OF MONMOUTH, the SAXON leader after the death of UTHER. He was defeated by ARTHUR at the Battle of the River DOUGLAS, after which he fled to and took refuge in YORK, where he was joined by his brother BALDULF. Arthur laid siege to the city, and Colgrin was subsequently defeated by Arthur at both LINCOLN and CALEDON WOOD (some authorities make these one battle), even though he had been joined by CHELDRIC, who had brought reinforcements with him from the continent. Fleeing to GERMANY, they regrouped and came back, this time to be utterly routed at BADON, where Colgrin was killed.

COLLEN, SAINT
Welsh

An early Welsh saint who once lived in a hermitage on the slopes of GLASTONBURY TOR. One day he heard two men speaking of GWYNN AP NUDD, and he reproached them for speaking of pagan beliefs. They replied that he had offended Gwynn ap Nudd and would have to suffer the consequences. The following day a messenger arrived from Gwynn ap Nudd and invited Collen to visit the King, but Collen refused. The messenger arrived again the following day, this time making thinly disguised threats. For several more days the messenger arrived, each day increasing the severity of the threats. Finally, Collen consented to visit Gwynn ap Nudd and, armed with holy water, climbed

Glastonbury Tor, where he entered a magical castle on its summit. Gwynn ap Nudd offered him food, but Collen refused, knowing that if he ate he would be condemned to spend the rest of his days in the OTHERWORLD. Collen sprinkled holy water all around him and in an instant the castle and all its inhabitants vanished, leaving Collen quite alone on the summit of the hill. From that day to this the fairy castle of Gwynn ap Nudd has never been seen again.

This story, although based on a seventh- or eighth-century tradition, was not written down until the sixteenth century, and it appears to have been much altered over the years.

See also TOLLEN

COLMCILLE
Irish
See COLUMBA

COLOMBE
Arthurian
The lover of LANCEOR, the son of the King of IRELAND, who killed herself when Lanceor was killed by BALIN.

COLUM CUALLEINECH
Irish
A smith, described as 'of the three processes', employed by the TUATHA DÉ DANANN at the time of the arrival of LUGH. It seems quite probable that Colum Cualleinech is a composite figure representing the three smith gods GOIBHNIU, CREIDHNE and LUCHTAINE, although this is by no means certain.

COLUMBA, SAINT
Irish
The famous early Irish monk, who is said to have lived from 521 to 597. Born in Gartan in County Donegal, Columba attended a school that was run by Saint Finnian at Molville on Strangford Lough. He founded numerous monasteries in IRELAND, before leaving to preach to the PICTS in 563 following a dispute with his old mentor.

Numerous legends exist surrounding the character of Saint Columba, who is also known as Saint Colmcille. One particular legend says that Columba was responsible for driving the last remnants of the FOMHOIRÉ from their home on TORY Island with the aid of his cloak, which spread out underneath him as he sat on it, causing the Fomhoiré to flee in case they were smothered. They leapt off the island and were never heard of again.

Columba left Ireland in a curragh with twelve followers and landed first on the island of IONA.

The King of DÁL RIADA gave Columba the island, and he founded a monastery there that was to become one of the most famous and influential in all Christendom. It was from this base that Columba and his disciples set out on missions among the Picts and Scots.

On one occasion he was travelling to visit BRIDEI, a son of MAELGWYN, who had become King of the Picts. As he travelled down the Great Glen, he stopped to rest for the night on the slopes of one side of the valley. While he slept, a local woman forgot to recap an inexhaustible well that lay in the valley, and when Columba and the local people awoke the following morning the valley had become a deep lake. The locals exclaimed '*Tha loch nis ann!*' ('There is a lake there now!'), which is how Loch Ness came into being and got its name. Shortly afterwards a huge monster surfaced in the lake and chased the boat carrying his disciples. Columba commanded it to do them no harm, and the monster slid beneath the surface of the lake. This is the first alleged report of the Loch Ness Monster.

CONAIRE MÓR
Irish
The incestuously conceived son of EOCHAIDH AIREMH and his daughter ÉDÁIN. His conception occurred after MIDHIR gave Eochaidh Airemh the choice of fifty women, all of whom appeared to be his wife ÉDÁIN ECHRAIDHE. The one Eochaidh Airemh chose was in fact his own daughter, and it was not until after Conaire Mór had been born that the girl's true identity was revealed. However, some sources say that Conaire Mór was Eochaidh Airemh's grandson by MESS BUACHALLA, the daughter of Eochaidh Airemh and his own daughter ESS, for it was Ess whom he had chosen thinking that she was his wife Édáin Echraidhe.

CONALL
Irish
The son of CÚ CHULAINN and his mistress AÍFE. Born in SCOTLAND, Conall remained there after his father had returned to IRELAND. Under the tutorage of SCÁTHACH, Conall grew to be a mighty warrior and sorcerer. Finally, he was sent to Ireland with strict instructions that he should not reveal his true identity to any who challenged him. As Conall approached the coast of Ireland in his bronze boat, the heroes of that land were so amazed by his magical deeds that they sent a champion, CONALL CERNACH, to challenge the newcomer. Conall Cernach was quickly defeated, so Cú Chulainn himself went out to meet the lad, despite

the pleas of EMER, Cú Chulainn's wife, who warned him that the boy could only be his son.

When Conall refused to give his name, Cú Chulainn attacked him. They fought long and hard, and it was only with great difficulty that Cú Chulainn at last managed to inflict a mortal wound. As Conall lay dying, he revealed his identity to his father. Cú Chulainn was filled with remorse and, taking his son's corpse, showed the men of ULSTER his son.

CONALL CE(A)RNACH
Irish

The son of AMORGIN and one of the three champions who persuaded BRICRIU to claim the champion's right to carve the roast at a feast. (The other claimants were LOEGHAIRE BUADHACH and CÚ CHULAINN; some sources make Cú Chulainn the foster son of Conall Cernach.) The right to carve the roast was awarded to Cú Chulainn twice, firstly by MEDHBHA of CONNACHT, and subsequently by CÚ ROI MAC DÁIRI. On both occasions the judgement was refused by the two losers, but they were finally made to accept it.

Conall Cernach also appears in the story of MAC DÁ THÓ's boar, in which he is portrayed as the champion. On this occasion the Connacht champion CET was about to carve the pig when Conall Cernach appeared. Cet grudgingly gave way to the superiority of Conall Cernach, but not before he had taunted him, saying that, if ANLUAN (Cet's brother) were present, he would give Conall Cernach a sound thrashing. At this Conall Cernach removed the severed head of Anluan from a pouch and threw it onto the table in front of Cet. He then set about carving and devouring the pig.

Conall Cernach met his end at the hands of CONALL, whom he challenged as the magical youth approached the shores of IRELAND in search of his father Cú Chulainn. When Conall Cernach asked Conall his name, the youth refused to tell him, following the instructions of SCÁTHACH, so Conall Cernach attacked him, but was quickly overcome. The youth was finally killed by his own father.

CONAN MAC LIA
Irish

The son of LIA, Lord of LUACHAR. After his father had been killed by FIONN MAC CUMHAILL, Conan mac Lia took his revenge by harrying the FIAN for seven years. Finally, he was captured and brought before Fionn mac Cumhaill, to whom Conan mac Lia swore an oath of allegiance and served faithfully for the next thirty years.

CONAN MAC MORNA
Irish

A son of MORNA. A fat, bald character, Conan mac Morna was derisively known as 'Conan the Bald'. On one occasion he and several other members of the FIAN entered a SÍDH where they found a wondrous feast. They sat down to devour the food, but, as they did so, the door began to shrink. Realising they had been tricked by the gods, Conan mac Morna's comrades bolted for the exit, but Conan mac Morna simply continued to eat. Eventually he was alerted to their predicament, but he found himself stuck fast to his chair. Several of the fian grabbed hold of him and tugged him loose, but he left a large portion of his flesh behind. To cover the open wound, the skin of a black sheep was hurriedly slapped into place, where it stayed until Conan mac Morna died.

The cowardice of Conan mac Morna is clearly demonstrated on the occasion when the fian put him forward to fight LIAGAN. Liagan mocked the choice of Conan mac Morna, who retorted that Liagan was in more peril from the man that stood behind him than from the one who stood in front of him. Liagan turned around, and Conan mac Morna cut off his head, an act of cowardice that amused the rank and file of the fian, but annoyed FIONN MAC CUMHAILL.

See also MIDAC

CONÁN (MAOL)
Irish

A member of the FIAN and a close friend of DIARMAID UA DUIBHNE. He was present with his friend, together with OSCAR and GOLL MAC MORNA, when Diarmaid ua Duibhne received from a young lady the mark on his forehead, his BALL-SEIRC or 'love-spot', that would thenceforth cause any maiden who saw it to fall instantly in love with him.

CONAN (MERIADOC)
Arthurian

According to GEOFFREY OF MONMOUTH, the ruler of BRITTANY who is claimed, by some commentators, to be an ancestor of ARTHUR.

CONANN
Irish

One of the two kings of the FOMHOIRÉ during the time of the people of NEMHEDH. He was the ruler on the occasion of the revolt of Nemhedh and his people, and was killed during their storming of TORY island.

CONARAN

Irish

A King of the TUATHA DÉ DANANN in the time of FIONN MAC CUMHAILL. He had his three hag-like daughters punish Fionn mac Cumhaill for hunting the deer he considered to be his exclusive property. However, two of the daughters were killed by GOLL before they could exact their punishment on Fionn mac Cumhaill. The third appeared to restore her sisters to life, but Goll took her prisoner and burned Conaran's SÍDH.

CONCENN

Welsh

An alternative name for the last King of POWYS, who is more usually known as CYNGEN FAB CADELL. This name appears on the Pillar of ELISEG that was erected by Cyngen fab Cadell near the ruins of Valle Crucis abbey in CLWYD. The inscription on this pillar gives a short genealogy of the Kings of Powys, in which Concenn is the son of CADELL and thus great-grandson of Eliseg, to whom he erected the pillar.

CONCHEANN

Irish

After Concheann's wife had been seduced by AED, a son of the DAGHDHA, Concheann killed the youth, whereupon the Daghdha made Concheann carry the corpse until he found a stone large enough to cover the grave.

CONCHENN

Irish

A daughter of BODB. When the harper CLIACH came to her father's home to court her, Bodb's magic kept him at bay for a whole year, after which the earth opened, a DRAGON appeared and Cliach died of fright.

CONCHOBAR (MAC NESSA)

Irish

The son of NESSA by the giant FACHTNA and one of the greatest Kings of ULSTER, whose reign is alleged to have been at the very beginning of the Christian era. Conchobar mac Nessa was the father, brother or half-brother of DEICHTINE, the mother of CÚ CHULAINN, although some accounts make Conchobar mac Nessa that hero's father, yet these sources do not hint at an incestuous relationship. Conchobar mac Nessa's traditional genealogy shows a bloodline connection between Conchobar mac Nessa and the sons of UISNECH, whom he was to have treacherously murdered.

Conchobar mac Nessa held his court at EMHAIN MHACHA, where, as his first heroic deed, Cú Chulainn defeated all fifty youths in the King's service. His FILI, FEDLIMID, was the father of the maiden DERDRIU. At her birth it was prophesied that she would be very beautiful, but would cause untold suffering in Ulster. Some wanted to kill her at birth, but Conchobar mac Nessa refused to do this, saying that he would marry her when she came of age. However, as Derdriu reached maturity, she fell in love and eloped with NAOISE. Conchobar mac Nessa took his revenge some time later by killing Naoise and his brothers, after which Derdriu committed suicide. Conchobar mac Nessa also plays a role in the ribald story of MAC DÉ THÓ's boar, although only as an observer to the events, and also in the later version of this story known as *Fledd Bricrenn*.

Conchobar mac Nessa's death occurred after he had made an unjust and cruel attack on MESGEDRA, King of LEINSTER, who was killed by CONALL CERNACH. Conall Cernach removed the dead King's brain and mashed it up and mingled it with lime to form a small ball known as a 'brain ball', one of the deadliest of all weapons. It was kept in the treasure house of EMHAIN MHACHA, from where it was stolen by CET. Some time later, Cet used the 'brain ball' in battle and struck Conchobar mac Nessa full in the forehead. His physicians advised him that to remove it would mean his death, and they sewed up the wound with golden thread. Conchobar mac Nessa was told that he had nothing to fear provided he managed to keep his cool. Unfortunately he was unable to do this. In the heat and excitement of battle the lethal 'brain ball' exploded through his skull and Conchobar mac Nessa died instantly.

CONDATIS

Gaulish

A generic name given to the deities of river confluences, though what they look like is not recorded.

CONDERY

Irish

The messenger sent by CÚ CHULAINN to ask the name of the magical youth approaching Ireland. The youth refused to answer the question, so CONALL CERNACH was sent out against him, but was quickly killed. Cú Chulainn then fought the youth himself and, having inflicted a mortal wound on the young man, discovered that it was none other than his son CONALL.

CONDWIRAMURS

Arthurian

The Queen of BROBARZ and wife of PERCEVAL, according to WOLFRAM VON ESCHENBACH.

CONL-AÍ, -AOCH

Irish

Alternative name(s) for the magical warrior CONALL, the son of CÚ CHULAINN and AÍFE.

CONMARCH

Welsh

The painter or sculptor in the employ of CONCENN, who inscribed the Pillar of ELISEG at the command of his employer.

CONN

Irish

1 An ancestor of Saint BRIDE according to the genealogy recorded in an early protective prayer, which makes Conn the son of CREAR and father of ART. One legend tells of the time he was bewitched by BÉCUMA, who eventually left him after his son Art had returned from the dead with DELBCHAEM.
2 The son of LIR and AOBH, and brother to FIONUALA, HUGH and FIACHTRA.

CONN CÉTCHATHLACH

Irish

'Conn of One Hundred Battles', the father of CONNLA and grandfather of CORMAC MAC AIRT. His son went to live with an OTHERWORLDLY maiden and was never seen again.

One day, while Conn Cétchathlach stood on the ramparts of TARA with his DRUIDS and FILIDH, a horseman approached out of the swirling mists and invited the company to visit his home. The horsemen led them to MAGH MELL. There, in a house built next to a golden tree and having a golden ridge pole, they found the god LUGH and the SOVEREIGNTY OF IRELAND. Beside the deities, there was a golden bowl and cup, and a silver vat. As the vision faded, these items remained, and Conn Cétchathlach returned to Tara with the godly gifts.

CONNACHT

Irish

One of the five CÓIGEDH, or provinces, into which the leaders of the invading FIR BHOLG divided IRELAND, the other four being ULSTER, LEINSTER, MUNSTER and MEATH. Traditionally Connacht and Ulster were great rivals. Connacht is the ancient name for the county that is today known as Connaught.

CONNLA

Irish

1 The husband of ACHTLAND. A giant, he slept on his island home with his head on a stone in the west, and his feet against another in the east.
2 The son of CONN CÉTCHATHLACH. He fell in love with an OTHERWORLDLY maiden who came from TÍR NA MBÉO, went to live with her there and was never seen again.

CONON

Arthurian

The father of EMMELINE who was loved by ARTHUR in John DRYDEN's *KING ARTHUR*.

CONRAD

Arthurian

A bishop who unsuccessfully, and unwisely, had MERLIN charged with heresy.

CONSTANCE

Arthurian

In Italian romance, the wife of King BAN of BRITTANY and the mother of LANCELOT.

CONSTANS

British and Arthurian

According to GEOFFREY OF MONMOUTH, Constans was the son of King CONSTANTINE and the brother of both AMBROSIUS AURELIUS and UTHER. After CONSTANTINE had died, Constans was installed as a puppet king by VORTIGERN, though first he had to be persuaded to leave the monastery in which he had taken refuge. Finally, Vortigern had himself proclaimed king after having Constans killed by PICTS in his pay. Later tradition makes Constans the uncle of King ARTHUR through his brother UTHER, who was, of course, Arthur's father.

CONSTANTINE

British and Arthurian

(1) The grandfather of ARTHUR. The brother of ALDROENUS or AUDRIEN, King of BRITTANY, he was made King of BRITAIN at the Britons' own request and had three sons, AMBROSIUS AURELIUS, UTHER and CONSTANS. He was stabbed to death by a PICT and was succeeded by Constans, who was no more than a puppet of VORTIGERN, until he too was killed by a Pict. In the Welsh genealogies, his father is named as KYNNVOR, but he is also thought to have been the son of SOLOMON, King of Brittany, in which case he is the grandson of URBIEN. His origin has been

suggested as lying with the Roman Emperor Constantine III, and there are many similarities between the two, not least the fact that they both had sons named Constans who had immured themselves in monasteries.

(2) A sixth-century King of DUMNONIA who appears in the Arthurian romances as ARTHUR's cousin, the son of Duke CADOR of CORNWALL. Arthur passed the crown to this Constantine following the final battle at CAMLANN, before being borne away to AVALON, the year being recorded as AD 542. Following his ascension, the sons of MORDRED rebelled against him, but he defeated them, killing each of them separately, and each before an altar where they had desperately sought sanctuary.

CONSTANTINOPLE
Arthurian

Formerly called BYZANTIUM, this city became, at the time when the ROMAN EMPIRE was divided into two, the capital of the Eastern or Byzantine Empire. During the traditional Arthurian period there were a number of Byzantine emperors: Marcian (AD 450–7), Leo I (AD 457–74), Leo II (AD 474), Zeno (AD 747–75 and again AD 476–91), Basiliscus (AD 475–6), Anastasius I (AD 491–518), Justus I (AD 518–27) and Justinian I (AD 527–67). The Emperor considered contemporary with Arthur was simply named as Leo by GEOFFREY OF MONMOUTH, and if Leo II ruled only in AD 474 it seems that this refers to Leo I.

Constantinople appears in a number of the Arthurian romances. In *PEREDUR* the Empress was the lover of PEREDUR (PERCEVAL), with whom she was said to have lived for fourteen years, and had previously given him an enchanted stone that made him invisible to the AFANC. In *FLORIANT ET FLORETE*, the Emperor is named as FILIMENIS. However, most interesting of all is *CLIGÉS*, which gives the genealogy of the imperial family, showing its relationship to LOT.

CONTE DE GRAAL, LE
Arthurian

An unfinished, pre-thirteenth-century work by the French poet CHRÉTIEN DE TROYES, the 484-line-long prologue to the work being known as the *ELUCIDATION*. It is considered the earliest work that enhances the legends of King ARTHUR and introduces the concept of the Holy GRAIL. Its unfinished state gave rise to a lengthy series of *CONTINUATIONS*, the first of these appearing *c.* 1200.

CONTINUATION(S)
Arthurian

Since CHRÉTIEN DE TROYES left his *Le CONTE DE GRAAL* unfinished, it inspired various other writers to continue where Chrétien left off. These works are referred to as 'Continuations'. The first 'Continuation' appeared *c.* 1200, the second sometime during the thirteenth century. GERBERT and Manessier also produced *Continuations* during the same century.

COOLEY
Irish

The southern half of the province of ULSTER. It was the home of a bull known as the DONN CUAILNGÈ, or 'Dark One of Cooley'. The quest of MEDHBHA and AILILL to capture this bull is told in the *Taín Bó Cuailngè*.

COPHUIR IN DÁ MUCCIDA
Irish

'The Two Swineherds', an introductory story to the *Taín Bó Cuailngè*. It tells of friendly relationships between two swineherds, one from CONNACHT and one from ULSTER, whose friendship was spoiled by the people. They go through a shape-shifting saga and end up as worms that are eaten by two cows. These cows subsequently give birth to FINNBHENNACH and the DONN CUAILNGÈ.

CORAN-IEID, -IADS
British

A mysterious people, said to have infected (*sic*) BRITAIN during the reign of LLUDD. They could overhear every conversation, and they used magical money to undermine the fragile economy, because, although the money appeared to be real, it would turn into mushrooms if kept for any time. They were killed after Lludd had discussed the matter out at sea with his brother LLEFELYS. Llefelys gave Lludd large numbers of an insect, never before seen in Britain, that should be crushed and fed to everyone. Normal humans would feel only a slight discomfort, but the Coranieid would be poisoned.

The Coranieid may be Breton in origin, for their name is similar to KORRIGANED, a Breton name for supernatural beings. However, one of the *Trioedd Ynys Prydein* states that the Coranieid came from Arabia.

CORBENIC CASTLE
Arthurian

A variant of CARBONEK Castle, the castle where the FISHER KINGS, descendants of JOSEPH OF ARIMATHEA, guarded the Holy GRAIL.

CORBON

Arthurian

In the obscure medieval romance *BATAILLE LOQUIFER*, which contains a few Arthurian references, Corbon appears as the son of RENOART and MORGAN Le Fay, thus making him ARTHUR's nephew.

CORDELIA

British and Arthurian

The youngest daughter of the mythical King LEIR and the sister of GONERIL and REGAN. Cordelia married AGANIPPUS, King of the FRANKS, after she had been dispossessed by her two scheming elder sisters. Her husband later restored Leir to the throne for the last three years of his life. Cordelia buried her father in an underground chamber beneath the River Soar in Leicestershire. This chamber, to which all the local craftsmen used to come at the beginning of each year to perform their first act of labour, was later dedicated to the Roman god Janus. It has been suggested that she has her origins in CREIDDYLAD.

CORINEUS

Graeco-Romano-British and Arthurian

An exiled Trojan leader, who came to BRITAIN in the company of BRUTUS. Renowned as a soldier and a giant killer, GEOFFREY OF MONMOUTH makes Corineus a giant himself and says that when he landed in Britain his party found the country inhabited by a tribe of giants with whom they engaged in battle. Eventually the quarrel was decided by single combat in which Corineus defeated the giant GOGMAGOG, the battle between the two giants occurring, according to legend, on Plymouth Hoe. Even though Gogmagog managed to break three of Corineus' ribs, this served only to madden him, and he finally flung Gogmagog to his death. Two huge figures commemorating the giants were carved in the white limestone overlooking Plymouth harbour. These were destroyed in 1671. In return for Corineous' magnanimous deeds ridding the country of the giants, Brutus gave him the land of CORNWALL, which he named after himself.

CORMAC MAC AIRT

Irish

Possibly a historical character and traditionally the King of IRELAND in 227–66, Cormac mac Airt, son of ART and thus a grandson of CONN CÉTCHATHLACH, ascended to the throne after having his predecessor MAC CON stabbed. He was not able to become king immediately, however,

because a relative of Mac Con had set fire to his hair, and he had to wait for it to grow again, as no person with any imperfection could become king. He died in 266 after a salmon bone caught in his throat, and he was ceremoniously buried at RELIGH NA RIGH. Legend makes Cormac mac Airt the father of GRÁINNE.

One particularly interesting story concerning this king says that Cormac mac Airt was once lured to visit TÍR TAIRNGIRI by MANANNÁN MAC LIR, who assumed the guise of a warrior and appeared to the King so disguised at dawn on May Day morning as the King stood on the ramparts of TARA. Manannán mac Lir told the King that he came from a realm where decay, falsehood, old age and death were unknown. So entranced was Cormac mac Airt with the warrior's description that he readily agreed to exchange three wishes with the stranger for a bough of three golden apples that produced a healing music when shaken.

Exactly a year later Manannán mac Lir reappeared to claim his three wishes, and in so doing stole away with Cormac mac Airt's wife and family. The King set off in hot pursuit, even though he had no idea where he was heading. *En route* he was overtaken by a strange, thick mist, which seemed to guide him. As it cleared, Cormac mac Airt came to a wondrous palace standing in the middle of a beautiful plain. Entering, he was entertained by a handsome warrior and a charming girl to whom he told his story of the loss of his wife and children. Lulled to sleep by the wonderful singing of the warrior, Cormac mac Airt awoke the following morning to find his wife and children restored to him.

The warrior then revealed himself as Manannán mac Lir, saying that he had lured the King to Tír Tairngiri to reward him, upon which he gave Cormac mac Airt a wonderful golden cup. Next morning Cormac mac Airt, his wife, and his children awoke to find themselves lying on the grass outside their home at Tara. Beside them were the golden apples and the cup presented to him by Manannán mac Lir. This cup would break into three pieces if three lies were spoken over it, but three truths told over the pieces would make it whole again. It is this cup that led to the wisdom of Cormac mac Airt, but it mysteriously vanished upon his death. An annalist records that Cormac mac Airt disappeared for seven months in 284, which is supposedly when he visited Manannán mac Lir.

This story bears obvious comparison with that of Conn Cétchathlach, although in that story the godly gifts were given by LUGH and the SOVEREIGNTY OF IRELAND.

CORMAC MAC CUILENNÁIN
Irish

A historical medieval Irish writer (*fl.* 900), who states that MANANNÁN MAC LIR was a wonderful navigator and a merchant of incomparable ability, who hailed from the Isle of MAN. Because of these skills he had, according to Cormac mac Cuilennáin, become regarded as a god by both the Irish and the Welsh. While the story itself is undoubtedly a fabrication, it obviously lends weight to the possibility that the Irish Manannán mac Lir and the Welsh MANAWYDAN FAB LLYR are simply the Irish and Welsh aspects of the same deity.

CORMAC MAC DUBTHACH
Irish

The son of DUBTHACH – his name literally means 'Cormac son of Dubthach'. He was sent to SCOTLAND with his father and FERGHUS MAC ROICH by CONCHOBAR MAC NESSA to guarantee the safety of NAOISE, DERDRIU, ARDÁN and AINNLE if they returned to IRELAND from their self-imposed exile. Unaware of the treachery that awaited their return, the exiles travelled back to Ireland with the three messengers. When Derdriu and the sons of UISNECH arrived at EMHAIN MHACHA, Conchobar mac Nessa went back on his word and had the young men killed by EOGHAN MAC DURTHACHT and his company. Furious at this act, Ferghus mac Roich, Dubthach and Cormac mac Dubthach attacked and burned Emhain Mhacha, killing three hundred of the Men of ULSTER before they deserted to AILILL and MEDHBHA of CONNACHT, the enemies of Conchobar mac Nessa.

CORM-ORAN, -ILAN
British and Arthurian

A uniquely Cornish character, the most famous of all English giants. He was popularly disposed of by JACK THE GIANT-KILLER, who, in Sir Thomas MALORY's *Morte d'Arthur* and earlier in GEOFFREY OF MONMOUTH'S *Historia Regum Britanniae*, fought the prototype of the later popular giant, whose home was on SAINT MICHAEL'S MOUNT, off Penzance, CORNWALL. Jack the Giant-killer, who is English rather than Cornish, illustrates the popularisation of the tale as it spread from its origins in Cornwall to the rest of the country. He remains, uniquely, the only European hero to triumph over a giant by his own natural dexterity and wit rather than relying on force of arms. Later legends replace Jack the Giant-killer as the killer of Cormoran with King ARTHUR.

Cormoran has become immortalised in the fairy-tale of 'Jack and the Beanstalk', for he is none other than the giant who lives in the wonderful land Jack stumbles across when he climbs the beanstalk that has magically appeared outside his house. Cormoran is, in this instance, possibly based on an earlier tradition, which would replace 'Englishman' with 'Cornish-man', said to have rejoiced in the familiar cry:

> Fee, fi, fo, fum,
> I smell the blood of an Englishman:
> Be he alive, or be he dead,
> I'll grind his bones to make my bread!

Identification has also been made between this giant and GOGMAGOG through the variant GOURMAILLON, which has been applied to both. If this is the case, then Jack the Giant-killer would seem to be a commemoration of CORINEUS, the giant Trojan ally of BRUTUS, who was said to have flung Gogmagog into the sea at Plymouth, which is not too far distant from Saint Michael's Mount.

CORN BRANGALED
Welsh and Arthurian

A drinking-horn owned by BRANGALED and numbered among the THIRTEEN TREASURES of BRITAIN. It was said to be able to provide any drink that its holder desired.

CORNUBAS
Arthurian

A Welsh earl whose daughter married ARTHUR's son, the KNIGHT OF THE FAIR COUNTRY.

CORNUBIA
Romano-British

The name given by the Romans to CORNWALL, then the western portion of the kingdom of DUMNONIA.

CORNWALL
British

A county in the west of southern ENGLAND. Legend says that it gained its name from CORINEUS, upon whom the land was bestowed by BRUTUS. Part of the county was, at one time, within the ancient realm of DUMNONIA, and called CORNUBIA by the Romans. The tribal rulers of Cornwall were united under a high king, but from the fifth to the ninth centuries it was gradually taken over by the invading SAXONS. It is the resistance of the Cornish people to these invaders that has led to the many legends associated with the county, none more potent than the belief that King ARTHUR held the Saxons at bay and will one day return from the dead to drive them from the land. In the body of Arthurian legends the kingdom was said to be the realm of King MARK, and it is by no means impossible that someone named Mark did indeed rule some territory within the region. To this day the county is remarkably Celtic in nature, and visiting the ancient sites to be found dotted all over the county is a worthwhile and satisfying experience.

COUDEL
Arthurian
The *ESTOIRE DEL SAINTE GRAAL* described Coudel as an early king of NORTHGALIS who was killed fighting against the Christians.

COURECHOUSE
Arthurian
The sword owned by King BAN.

COVAC
Irish
The son of UGAINY and brother of LOEGHAIRE. When Ugainy died, Loeghaire inherited the throne, which consumed Covac with envy. His DRUID advised him to feign death and then took news of his death to Loeghaire. When Loeghaire arrived and bent over the supposed corpse to kiss his brother, Covac stabbed him through the heart and thus ascended to the throne. As a young boy MAON, son of AILILL AINE, was brought into the presence of Covac, who made him eat a portion of his father's and his grandfather's hearts, along with a mouse and all her young. The disgust Maon felt left him dumb, and, fearing nothing from a boy who had lost the power of speech, Covac let him go. Many years later Maon returned and killed Covac. Having recovered his powers of speech, he was known as LABHRAIDH LOINGSECH.
See also COBTHACH COEL

COVENTINA
British
The goddess of springs and waters, who is depicted as floating on a leaf with a water plant in one hand and a flowing cup in the other. Her most famous association is with the spring at CARRAWBURGH. Her shrine here, near a fort on Hadrian's Wall, has revealed large numbers of coins, bronze votive offerings and even a human skull, although it is unlikely that the latter was the result of a human sacrifice.

CRADELMENT
Arthurian
A King of NORTHGALIS and one of the eleven leaders who rebelled against King ARTHUR at the start of his reign.

CRAFTINY
Irish
The harper of King SCORIATH, who was sent by the King's daughter, MORIATH, to Gaul with a magic harp that restored the speech of MAON, who was thenceforth known as LABHRAIDH LOINGSECH, which means 'The Mariner who speaks'.

CRAIG-Y-DINAS
Arthurian
A mount near SNOWDON, North WALES, that is one of the many locations regarded as the last resting place of King ARTHUR, who, in a story told by Iolo MORGANNWG (the bardic name of Edward Williams, 1747–1826), rests there, along with his knights and his treasure. He was found, according to the story, by a Welshman who was led there by a magician, though a variant account makes the visitor a Monmouthshire farmer. As Iolo Morgannwg was a bard, his material is not regarded as a reliable source, for he had doubtless simply enhanced an earlier tale, feeling that his version would be the better. Similar tales of the sleeping Arthur are found in England, notably at ALDERLEY EDGE (*see also* THOMPSON). A cave near to Llandebie with the similar-sounding name of OGO'R DINAS has also been mooted as one of the last resting places of Arthur.

CRANN BETHADH
Irish
The 'Tree of Life', an icon found in pagan cultures. The human world lies amid the tree, beside its trunk while the OTHERWORLD lies within its roots, and the heavens within its branches. The best-known tree of this nature is the Norse-Teutonic version, Yggdrasil.

CRANN BUIDHE
Irish
The deadly, yellow-shafted spear of DIARMAID UA DUIBHNE, although it was not powerful enough to save him from being killed by the boar BEANN GHULBAN.

CREAR
Irish
An ancestor of Saint BRIDE, found in a genealogy of that saint contained within a chanted protective prayer that makes Crear the son of CIS and father of CONN.

CRE-ARWY, -IRWY

Welsh

The daughter of the goddess CERRIDWEN and TEGID VOEL, and sister to AFAGDDU. She is described as the fairest women in the world, light and beautiful, in contrast to her brother, the darkest and ugliest of all men. It is common for goddesses to have two children who reflect both sides of nature, a notion that has carried through into Christian times in the concept of good and evil.

CRÉD

Irish and Arthurian

The daughter of King GUAIRE of CONNACHT, and the beautiful young wife of the ageing MARCÁN. She fell in love with the exiled CANO even before she had set eyes on him, and at a feast drugged all those present so that she might implore Cano to take her as his mistress. Cano refused to do so while he was still in exile from his native SCOTLAND, but he pledged his undying love for Créd and gave her a stone that embodied his life. Eventually, Cano was recalled to Scotland, where he was made king. Remembering their pledge, Cano and Créd attempted to meet each year at Inber Colptha (the BOYNE estuary). However, each attempt was foiled by Créd's stepson COLCU with a guard of 100 warriors. Finally, frustrated by their numerous failures, the two illicit lovers decided to meet at Lough Créde in the north (the Lough gained its name from Créd and the events that were about to occur there). As the two came within sight of each other, Colcu once again appeared and drove off Cano. In desperation, Créd threw herself from her horse and dashed out her brains against a rock, although some say that this was accidental. In falling she dropped the stone that Cano had given her. It smashed into tiny pieces, and three days later Cano himself died. This is thought to have been one of the sources for the TRISTAN story.

CREIDDYL-AD, -ED

Welsh

The daughter of LLUD LLAW EREINT, although some name her father as the god LLYR, and the original of CORDELIA, the youngest daughter of King LEIR, who has his origins in Llyr, thus suggesting that the god was her most likely father. Her hand was fought over by GWYNN AP NUDD, and GWYTHR, son of GREIDAWL. First one, then the other, would have the upper hand, the contest being fated to continue at each May Day until Doomsday. The story is undoubtedly inspired by some earlier, now lost, legend concerning divine combatants. Later stories say it was King ARTHUR who ruled how the contest was to be fought.

CRE(I)D(H)NE

Irish

A god of metalworking, a brazier or *cerd*, one of the brothers, or aspects, of the great GOIBHNIU, the divine smith, his other brother/aspect being LUCHTAINE, the divine wheelwright. As a triad deity the three smiths were collectively known as the TRÍ DÉ DÁNA. Together they worked at the speed of light to keep the TUATHA DÉ DANANN supplied with weapons for the Second Battle of MAGH TUIREDH. No one who was wounded by these weapons ever recovered.

Creidhne, on this occasion on his own, helped the great leech DIAN CÉCHT to fashion NUADHA an artificial arm from silver after he had lost one during the First Battle of MAGH TUIREDH. Once the arm had been fitted, Nuadha became known as Nuadha Airgedlámh, which translates as 'Nuadha of the Silver Hand'.

See also COLUM CUALLEINECH

CREIRWY

Welsh

See CREARWY.

CREUDYLAD

Welsh

A little used variant of CREIDDYLAD.

CRIDENBÉL

Irish

A lampooner. He occupied the house in which the DAGHDHA was forced to live by BRES and demanded the best of the ration every night. OENGHUS MAC IN OG heard of this and told the Daghdha to put three gold coins in Cridenbél's portion, for these would kill him. Before this, Cridenbél had been employed by the TUATHA DÉ DANANN when he was sent out to help rid IRELAND of the monstrous children of CARMAN. At that stage he appears to have been an accepted member of the Tuatha dé Danann, but his head seems to have been turned by Bres, with whom he possibly thought he might curry favour.

CRIMMAL

Irish

The uncle of DEIMNE, whose fortunes were restored after Deimne, later known as FIONN MAC CUMHAILL, killed LIA and gave his uncle the treasure of the FIAN he had stolen from Lia.

CRIMTHAN(N) (NIA NÁIR)
Irish

A historical King of IRELAND who reigned for a solitary year (*c*. AD 74). Legend says he was the son of LUGAID and was married to a supernatural woman by the name of NÁIR, whom he met on a military campaign. Among the gifts she gave him and that he brought back with her to his fort on the Hill of Howth to the east of Dublin were a gilt chariot, a multicoloured cloak embroidered in gold, a golden chessboard inlaid with gems, a silver shield and a sword decorated with serpents. None of these, nor his magical wife, was enough to save his life when he fell from his horse a short time later.

CRÓCHAN
Irish

A handmaiden of ÉDÁIN. She accompanied Édáin and MIDHIR to BRÍ LEITH.

CROM CRUACH
Irish
See CENN CRÚIACH

CRONNCHU
Irish
See CRUNDCHU

CROP-EARED DOG
Arthurian

One of the main characters of the Irish *EACHTRA AN MHADRA MHAOIL*, this ear-less and tail-less creature, while obviously canine, also had the power of human speech. Originally the Crop-eared Dog had been the Prince ALEXANDER, the son of the King of India. However, his stepmother had changed him and his brothers into various canine creatures in order to ensure that her own son, the KNIGHT OF THE LANTERN, received a handsome inheritance. The Knight of the Lantern was admitted to ARTHUR's court, but while there he insulted the King and the court. GAWAIN and the Crop-eared Dog went to track him down, and, when they had at length captured him, the Knight of the Lantern removed his mother's spell, and restored Alexander to his original shape. He eventually went on to become the ruler of India.

CRUITHNE
Irish

1 According to some sources, the wife of FIONN MAC CUMHAILL; elsewhere, however, his wife is named as SAAR or Sabia.
2 The name given by the IRISH to the PICTS.

CRUNDCHU
Irish
Also CRONNCHU

A wealthy peasant, the son of AGNOMAN, who boasted at a feast held by the men of ULSTER that his second wife, MACHA, who had appeared at his house soon after his first wife had died and remained there ever since as his wife, could easily outrun any of their horses. He was ordered to bring her before them by CONCHOBAR MAC NESSA to prove this boast. Macha, however, was heavily pregnant at the time, and begged to be let off until after she had given birth. The men of Ulster refused, but she easily won the race. Just then she went into labour and, giving birth to twins, cursed the men of Ulster that they too, for the next nine generations, should feel the pangs of labour whenever they were called upon to go into battle. Macha died shortly afterwards.

CÚ
Irish

The brother of CIAN and CEITHIN, and thus an uncle of LUGH.

CÚ CHULAIN(N)
Irish
Also CUCHULAINN

The best known and greatest of all the Irish heroes and the guardian of the sacred land of ULSTER. He was son of DEICHTINE (the sister or daughter of CONCHOBAR MAC NESSA). Some say that his father was the god LUGH, others that it was none other than Conchobar mac Nessa himself, although the husband of Deichtine is usually named as SUALTAM. The inclusion of the possibility that his father was the god Lugh enables him to fulfil the role of the archetypal hero whose parents bridge the two worlds, their offspring being at once human and divine. Twin foals born at precisely the same time as Cú Chulainn were later to become his famous steeds: Black of SAINGLIU and Grey of MACHA.

Cú Chulainn was not the original name of this hero. His mother gave him the name SÉDANTA. It was while still known by this name that he undertook his first heroic deed, the defeat of the fifty youths in the service of Conchobar mac Nessa at EMHAIN MHACHA. Later, though still a youth, he was attacked by the fierce hound of CULANN the smith. Sédanta threw his ball down the animal's gaping throat and seized the animal before it had regained its senses, dashing out its brains on a rock. Culann complained about the loss of his hound, which elicited a promise from Sédanta that he would act as Culann's guard dog for as long as he required one. It was this act that

Celtic bronze bit, first century AD, from the collections of the National Museum of Dublin.
(© Werner Forman/Corbis)

earned him his popular name, Cú Chulainn, which means 'Culann's Hound'. Now known as Cú Chulainn, the hero was offered the chance of either a long life or fame. He chose the latter. Having assumed his new name, he made a magical obligation, or *geis*, which was never to eat the flesh of a dog or hound, for that animal became his totem beast and to taste such meat would bring about his downfall. As he made the promise to Culann, he underwent a magical transformation, during which a fountain of terrible power erupted from his head and he went through a frenzy of shape-changing. As Cú Chulainn regained his human form, he took up arms and went out to do battle with the three monstrous sons of NECHTA SCÉNE. He leapt into his scythed chariot, which was equipped with iron points having thin edges and hooks, and hard spit-spikes, with sharp nails that studded over the axles and straps and the tackle that harnessed his two steeds, Black of Saingliu and Grey of Macha. Setting forth, he drove the chariot with such force that its iron-shod wheels sank into the earth and made ruts that were of an equal depth to the wheels themselves. Having killed the three sons of Nechta Scéne with relative ease, he decapitated them and hung their heads from his chariot. On his way home again, he captured a stag and tethered a whole flight of swans that flew overhead as he approached Emhain Mhacha, his body still seething with the indiscriminate fury of battle.

Seeing him approach, and in order to calm his frenzy, MUGHAIN, Queen of Ulster, led her women out to meet him, every one of them completely naked. Overcome with embarrassment, Cú Chulainn cast his eyes aside, which allowed the King's warriors to capture him and dip him into three tubs of icy cold water they had ready. The first tub immediately burst, the water in the second boiled, but the water in the third merely became warm. Now calm, and having been clothed by Mughain herself, Cú Chulainn entered the royal household.

Cú Chulainn wanted to take EMER, the daughter of FORGALL, to be his wife. To prove his worth he travelled from IRELAND to a land that is described as having been far to the east beyond the country of ALBA, or SCOTLAND. In this country, which remains nameless, Cú Chulainn became the pupil of the prophetess SCÁTHACH. While there he fought and overcame AÍFE, the great rival of Scáthach, and took her as his mistress. She later bore him a son named CONALL or CONLAÍ. He also failed to capture two magic birds for his wife-to-be, a failure that was punished by two dream-women, LI BAN and FAND, who lashed him with whips, a lashing that was so severe that it disabled him for a year.

After Cú Chulainn had returned to Ireland, his son Conall came under the tutorage of Scáthach, tutorage that enabled him to grow into a mighty, magical warrior of almost equal power to his father. As a young man Conall was sent to Ireland to seek out his father, though Scáthach made him promise never to reveal his identity to any who challenged him. Approaching the Irish coast in his bronze boat, Conall so amazed the people there that they sent out their champion, CONALL CERNACH, to challenge him. Conall quickly overcame the champion, and, when news of this was taken to Cú Chulainn, he himself came to challenge the youth, even though his wife EMER warned him that the youth could only be his own son.

When challenged by Cú Chulainn, Conall refused to give his name, and he and his father fought long and hard before Cú Chulainn succeeded in inflicting a mortal wound. As Conall lay dying, he revealed his true identity to his father, who, grieving at the sad loss of the son he had never known, took his corpse and showed the body of his son to the men of Ulster.

In sharp contrast to the tragic story of Cú Chulainn and Conall is the tale of *Fledd Bricrenn*. Based on a much earlier ribald tale *Scéla Mucce Maic Dá Thó*, this tells of the occasion on which Cú Chulainn was twice adjudged the champion of all Ireland, although chronologically this story must fall before that of Cú Chulainn and Conall, for in it Conall Cernach is still very much alive. The malicious BRICRIU organized a feast for all the men of Ulster and CONNACHT, the two great traditional rival provinces. At this feast the privilege of carving the roast, as was the custom, would fall to the greatest warrior there present. Bricriu had bribed three great warriors all to claim the honour for themselves, these three being Cú Chulainn, LOEGHAIRE BUADHACH and Conall Cernach. As each claimed the honour, a brawl broke out, and it was eventually decided that all three must seek the judgement of MEDHBHA of Connacht. She decreed that the most worthy recipient of the honour was Cú Chulainn, but the other two refused to accept the decision, saying that Cú Chulainn must have bribed the Queen. All three were then sent to CÚ ROÍ MAC DÁIRI, King of MUNSTER. He, too, chose Cú Chulainn, and once again the two others refused to accept the verdict, leaving the feud unsettled.

At Emhain Mhacha, when all the men of Ulster were assembled in the great hall, a rough giant entered and challenged Loeghaire Buadhach, Conall Cernach and Cú Chulainn first to cut off his head, and then, the following evening, to allow him to return and retaliate in kind. Loeghaire Buadhach agreed the challenge and swiftly beheaded the giant with an axe. The giant calmly picked up his head and left the hall, returning the next evening to fulfil the pact he had made. Loeghaire Buadhach, who had obviously thought that the giant would have been dead after he had cut its head off, welched on their agreement. Now Conall Cernach took his turn, but he, too, reneged on the bargain when the restored giant returned the following evening. Cú Chulainn then took his turn and, when the giant returned to fulfil their pact, Cú Chulainn knelt down and calmly awaited the blow. The giant lifted his axe, but only touched Cú Chulainn gently on the nape of his neck with the blade. Lifting Cú Chulainn to his feet, he proclaimed him champion of all Ireland.

The giant then revealed himself to the three he had challenged. He was none other than Cú Roí Mac Dáiri, who had chosen this method to reaffirm the judgement he had previously made, and that the two cowards had refused to accept.

Cú Roí mac Dáiri appears in another episode in the life of Cú Chulainn. On this occasion the hero had taken his men to raid the OTHERWORLD, here depicted as Scotland, when Cú Roí mac Dáiri appeared in disguise and offered to help them. With his aid they managed to capture a magical cauldron, three magic cows, and the beautiful Otherworldly maiden BLÁTHNAD. However, when Cú Chulainn and his men failed to keep their promise to share the spoils with Cú Roí mac Dáiri, he simply seized the lot, and, when Cú Chulainn attempted to prevent him from leaving, Cú Roí mac Dáiri buried the hero up to his armpits and shaved off all his hair. After this Cú Chulainn had to go into hiding for a year to hide his shame. On the feast of SAMHAIN, Cú Chulainn planned to take his revenge and conspired with Bláthnad, whom Cú Roí mac Dáiri had married. Cú Chulainn killed Cú Roí mac Dáiri and took Bláthnad to be his mistress. However, FERCHERDNE, the FILI of the dead King, avenged the death of his master when he noticed Bláthnad standing near the edge of a cliff. Launching himself at her, he caught her around the waist and plummeted with her to their deaths on the rocks below.

Cú Chulainn, having chosen fame over a long life, was foredoomed to an early death. In the *Taín Bó Cuaílngè*, Cú Chulainn single-handedly protected Ulster from the armies of AILILL and Medhbha but came into conflict with the powers of the MÓRRÍGHAN, whom he failed to recognise. He was forced into a situation whereby he ate the flesh of a dog, an act that broke his *geis* and immediately

weakened his previously invincible skills and energy. Overcome by the magic powers of his enemies, he tied himself to a pillar so that he might die honourably while still erect. When his enemies saw three hooded crows land on Cú Chulainn's shoulders, they recognised the presence of the Mórríghan in her three aspects and calmly walked up to Cú Chulainn and cut off his head.

CÚ ROÍ MAC DÁIR-I, -E
Irish

A King of MUNSTER and a great sorcerer. He appears in two episodes of the life of the hero CÚ CHULAINN. The first occasion is when he is called upon to settle the dispute between LOEGHAIRE BUADHACH, CONALL CERNACH and Cú Chulainn, each of whom has, in the *Fledd Bricrenn*, claimed the honour of carving the roast, and after MEDHBHA of CONNACHT's judgement in favour of Cú Chulainn has been refused by the two losers. Cú Roí mac Dáiri makes the same judgement, which is again refused by the losers.

During a feast at EMHAIN MHACHA, to which all the men of ULSTER had come, a rough giant entered and challenged Loeghaire Buadhach, Conall Cernach and Cú Chulainn first to cut off his head, and then to allow him to return the following evening to retaliate in kind. Both Loeghaire Buadhach and Conall Cernach cut off the giant's head, but welched on their bargain when the giant, fully restored, returned to complete their bargain. Only Cú Chulainn knelt to accept the blow that would decapitate him. The giant, however, simply touched the blade against Cú Chulainn's neck and, helping the hero to his feet, proclaimed him champion of all IRELAND. That giant was none other than Cú Roí mac Dáiri, the challenge being his way of reaffirming the judgement he had earlier made in favour of Cú Chulainn.

The second appearance of Cú Roí mac Dáiri in the life of Cú Chulainn occured when that hero was, with his men, raiding the OTHERWORLD, which is in this instance portrayed as SCOTLAND. The King appeared to Cú Chulainn and his men in disguise and offered to help them. They accepted and agreed to share any plunder equally with the stranger. However, having captured a marvellous cauldron, three magical cows and the beautiful maiden BLÁTHNAD, the heroes broke their promise and refused to share the booty. Cú Roí mac Dáiri simply retaliated by making off with the lot. When Cú Chulainn attempted to stop him, he buried the great hero up to his armpits and shaved off all his hair, an act that forced Cú Chulainn into hiding for a year to hide his shame.

Cú Chulainn plotted his revenge at the feast of SAMHAIN with the aid of Bláthnad, whom Cú Roí mac Dáiri had married. Cú Chulainn killed the King and took the Otherworldly maiden as his mistress. The death of Cú Roí mac Dáiri was avenged by his FILI, FERCHERDNE, who saw Bláthnad standing close to the edge of a cliff. Rushing at her, he caught her around the waist, and together they plunged headlong to their deaths on the rocks below.

CUA(I)LNGÈ

Irish

1 The owner of the bull known as the DONN CUAILNGÈ that is the subject of the *Taín Bo Cuailngè*; the owner of this beast is also known as DARA.
2 A variant of CULANN, the divine smith of the TUATHA DÉ DANANN.

CU(A)L(L)ANN

Irish

Also CUAILNGÈ

The divine smith of ULSTER whose hound attacked the youth SÉDANTA. Unperturbed, the youth threw his ball down the animal's gaping throat and killed it by dashing out its brains before it could regain its senses. When Culann complained at the loss, Sédanta promised to act as a guard dog for Culann for as long as the divine smith had need of him. This promise led to the youth being known as CÚ CHULAINN, which means 'Culann's Hound'.

Culann had two daughters, AINÉ and MILUCH-RADH, both of whom loved FIONN MAC CUMHAILL, but neither of whom had their love requited.

CUARE

Irish

A son of SCÁTHACH.

CUCHULAIN(N)

Irish

A simple variant of CÚ CHULAINN.

CUCULATTI

Romano-British

'Hooded Ones', protective spirits who appear in carvings near Hadrian's Wall as well as in the Cotswolds. They appear to be male, and usually appear in groups of three. They wear hoods and cloaks that reach to either their knees or their ankles. They are possibly a Roman interpretation of the triad deities common among the Celtic peoples, but Romanised to suit their own beliefs.

CULANN

Irish

See CU(A)L(L)AN

CÚLDUB

Irish

A mischievous supernatural being who, on three successive nights, stole the food of the FIAN and took it back to his SÍDH. FIONN MAC CUMHAILL followed him one night, but got his thumb caught in a doorway. Removing it with difficulty he sucked it and on doing so found that he knew all that had passed and all that would occur. This is not the usual account of how Fionn mac Cumhaill gained the thumb that could be sucked to give wisdom, and appears to have been a local story.

CULHWCH

Welsh and Arthurian

Also KILHWCH, KULHWCH

The hero of the *MABINOGION* story of *CULHWCH AND OLWEN*, although this story undoubtedly owes its origins to a much earlier legend.

Culhwch was the son of KILWYDD and GOLEUDDYDD and the sister of EIGYR. During the course of her pregnancy Goleuddydd went insane and wandered aimlessly around the countryside. The pains of labour restored her sanity just as she was in the middle of a herd of swine, the shock of her returning senses causing her to give birth immediately. She named the child Culhwch to reflect the fact that he had been born in a pig run, for *hwch* means 'pig'.

After Goleuddydd died, Kilwydd remarried, although the name of his second wife remains unknown. She told Culhwch that he would only love OLWEN, the daughter of the chief giant YSPADDADEN. Culhwch set out on his quest to locate the girl and formed a party, each chosen for a particular skill, to help him. The members of this party were CEI, BEDWYR, CYNDDYLIG the Guide, GWRHYR the Interpreter, GWALCHMAI FAB GWYAR and MENW FAB TEIRGWAEDD. At length the party came to a shepherd whose wife proved to be the aunt of Culhwch. Although she had lost twenty-three of her twenty-four sons to Yspaddaden, she vowed to help Culhwch meet Olwen, who came to wash her hair at the woman's cottage every Saturday.

Olwen came as the woman had said that Saturday, and when she met Culhwch she agreed to become his wife on condition that he ask her father for her hand, warning him not to flinch from any condition he might set. On three successive days Culhwch and his companions went to Yspaddaden's castle. On each occasion the giant told them to come back the following morning and, as they turned their backs on the castle, hurled a poisoned stone at them. Culhwch and his friends were always too quick and caught the stone and threw it back. On the fourth day, as the poisoned stones had taken effect on the giant, Yspaddaden agreed to Culhwch's suit, provided he complete three tasks. The first of these involved the felling and burning of a thicket, ploughing its ashes into a field, and sowing that new field with flax. The second involved the collection of a variety of provisions for the wedding feast, while the third was to obtain various preparations and pieces of equipment, among them a razor and comb from between the ears of the great boar TWRCH TRWYTH, with which to barber Yspaddaden.

The giant imposed innumerable conditions, and, as Yspaddaden mentioned each, he added that it would be impossible to fulfil. Culhwch, remembering the advice of Olwen, simply replied that he could accomplish any task with ease. Finally, unable to stand the continual opposition of the giant, even though he had completed all the tasks set him, Culhwch gathered together all the giant's enemies, returned to his castle, and killed Yspaddaden. Culhwch married Olwen, and the two remained faithful to each other throughout their lives.

Arthurian legend sticks fairly closely to the Welsh roots, though, as is always the way, the story was enhanced to fit the theme the writers sought to follow. The principal facts of Culhwch's birth remain the same as in the original Welsh version, though now he is said to be the cousin of King Arthur, his mother now being made the sister to IGRAINE.

After Goleuddydd had died, Culhwch's father remarried, though the name of Culhwch's stepmother remains unknown. She put Culhwch under an obligation to marry none other than OLWEN, the daughter of the chief giant YSPADDADEN. Realising the enormity of his task, Culhwch went to the court of his cousin, King Arthur, to ask for his help in winning the hand of Olwen. When Culhwch arrived at Arthur's court, he was met by GLEWLWYD, the gatekeeper, who declared that Culhwch was the most handsome youth he had ever laid eyes on.

Arthur agreed to help his cousin, though he confessed that he had never heard of Olwen or her father. He sent messengers to seek them out, but, after a year, they all returned unsuccessful. A new party was formed to help Culhwch in his quest, this party being made up of exactly the same participants

of the original Welsh quest, though now Cei becomes Sir KAY, and Bedwyr becomes Sir BEDIVERE. Each was chosen for his own particular skill. Kay could stay for nine days without either sleeping or breathing. He could alter his height at will and had a body temperature that was so high that during a storm he never got wet, and in cold weather his companions could kindle their fires from him. Bedivere, though he had only one arm, was faster with his sword than three others fighting together. Gwalchmai fab Gwyar never gave up on any quest he had started, and Menw fab Teirgwaedd was a master of spells that would preserve the company in heathen lands. The final two, Cynddylig and Gwrhyr, were chosen for the talents their titles imply.

After some time the party came across a shepherd whose wife turned out to be an aunt of Culhwch. Even though she had already lost twenty-three of her twenty-four sons to the giant Yspaddaden, she agreed to help Culhwch meet Olwen, who came to the woman's cottage every Saturday to wash her hair.

When they met, Olwen asked Culhwch to come to their castle and request her hand. However, she warned him not to flinch from any conditions her father might set. For three days Culhwch and his companions went to Yspaddaden's castle. On each occasion the giant told them to return the following morning and then, as they turned their backs, threw a poisoned stone at them. The party, however, were always too quick and, catching it, they threw it back, which greatly concerned the giant. On the fourth day he agreed to Culhwch's suit, but imposed on him three monumental tasks. The first of these involved felling and burning a thicket, ploughing its ashes into a field and sowing it with flax. The second was to obtain a variety of items for the wedding feast, and the third was to obtain various items and preparations necessary to barber the giant, among which was a razor and comb from between the ears of the great boar Twrch Trwyth.

Innumerable other conditions were imposed, each of which Yspaddaden told Culhwch was impossible to fulfil. Each time Culhwch simply replied that he could complete the task with ease. Finally, with the help of King Arthur, who was most notably present in the hunt for Twrch Trwyth, he completed all the tasks set him and returned to the giant's castle in the company of all the giant's enemies. There the giant was killed and Olwen became Culhwch's wife, the couple remaining faithful for the rest of their lives.

As can be seen, the later Arthurian version closely follows the Welsh origins, the most notable differences being the relationship to King Arthur, and that monarch's participation in some, if not all, of the tasks set by the giant Yspaddaden.

CULHWCH AND OLWEN

Welsh and Arthurian

The complex and possibly incomplete pre-eleventh-century romance, part of the *MABINOGION*, that tells the story of CULHWCH, ARTHUR's cousin, and OLWEN, the daughter of the chief giant YSPAD-DADEN. This section of the *Mabinogion* is perhaps the most important for the Arthurian student. Within its complex structure many of the characters who were later developed into the leading lights of the Arthurian legends can be found in possibly their original form.

CULAAN

Irish

See CU(A)L(L)AN

CUMHA(I)L(L)

Irish

The father of the great hero of the FIAN, FIONN MAC CUMHAILL, by MUIRNE, daughter of TADHG. Fionn mac Cumhaill was born posthumously after Cumhaill had been killed by AODH.

CUNDRIE

Arthurian

This name only appears in the works of WOLFRAM VON ESCHENBACH, where it is used for two women.

1 The daughter of ARTHUR's sister SANGIVE and LOT, she married LISCHOIS.

2 A GRAIL maiden who told PERCEVAL that his wife and sons had been summoned to the GRAIL CASTLE. There she told him the GRAIL QUESTION should be asked to free both AMFORTAS, the GRAIL KING, and his own family.

CUNEDAGIUS

British

The brother of MARGANUS, their mother being either GONERIL or REGAN, the elder daughters of LEIR. Five years after the death of Leir, the two brothers usurped CORDELIA's throne and took her prisoner. Cordelia, in despair, took her own life.

CUNEDDA

British

With a pedigree suggesting that he originated from a Roman family, Cunedda was a ruler of the Votadini of north BRITAIN who emigrated to WALES, and rid a large part of that country of Irish settlers, some time around AD 430. According to the medieval Welsh history *Brut y Brenhinedd,* he was the father of GWEN, the mother of EIGYR (IGRAINE), who was in turn ARTHUR's mother, thus making him Arthur's great-grandfather. This, however, is a confusion, for Eigyr was usually regarded as the sister of CULHWCH, whose parents were KILWYDD and GOLEUDDYDD. It has been suggested that his wife may have been GWAWL, the daughter of COEL.

CUNOBELINUS

British

'The Hound of Belinus', the son of TENUANTIUS and ruler of the CATUVELLAUNI who, some time during the first century, made himself the King over a considerable part of southern BRITAIN and ruled for thirty years in peace. Welsh tradition made him a relation of ARTHUR, whilst he was called CYMBELINE by SHAKESPEARE.

CUNOMORUS

British and Gaulish and Arthurian

A historical ancient ruler of CORNWALL and BRITTANY. Warned that one of his sons would kill him, Cunomorus murdered each of his wives as soon as they announced that they were pregnant. However, one wife, TREPHINA, the daughter of WAROK, chief of the VENETII, managed to avoid him until after she had given birth to JUDWAL or TREMEUR. Cunomorus then had her decapitated, and her son exposed and left to die. GILDAS restored Trephina to life and sent her back to the castle with her head neatly tucked under her arm. The battlements promptly fell on Cunomorus and killed him.

It has been suggested by several commentators that Cunomorus is the historical origin of King MARK of Cornwall, or that Cunomorus at least contributed to the tyrannical aspect of Mark.

CUR

Irish

A warrior of CONNACHT, the son of DALY. He went out to fight CÚ CHULAINN, obviously unaware of the prowess of the youth he was to be pitted against. Cú Chulainn was eating an apple as Cur approached and, turning to face his attacker, he threw it with such force that it smashed straight through Cur's head.

CURCOG

Irish

The daughter of MANANNÁN MAC LIR. Her handmaiden was EITHNE, who had been born at the exact same moment as she had.

CURETANA

Arthurian

The name of the sword that had been owned by TRISTAN and that was presented to OGIER by Charlemagne.

CUSCRID
Irish

The son of CONCHOBAR MAC NESSA. He appears in the story of MAC DÁ THÓ's pig as one of those warriors who challenges CET and is ridiculed by him.

CUSTENNIN
Welsh and Arthurian

According to the pedigree of Anlawdd that has been postulated by T.W. Rolleston, Custennin was the son of Anlawdd and brother of YSPADDADEN and GOLEUDDYDD. The same author prepared a genealogy for King ARTHUR in which Custennin appears to be a simple variant of KUSTENNIN.

CYLEDYR THE WILD
Welsh and Arthurian

In the *MABINOGION* romance *CULHWCH AND OLWEN*, one of those involved in the quest to locate OLWEN and the one who managed to snatch the shears required to barber YSPADDADEN from between the ears of the boar TWRCH TRWYTH.

CYLLEL LLAWFRODEDD
Welsh and Arthurian

A DRUID sacrificial knife, said to have numbered among the THIRTEEN TREASURES OF BRITAIN that MERLIN took with him when he sailed away, never to be seen again, in his glass boat.

CYMBELINE
Arthurian

The name used by SHAKESPEARE for CUNOBELINUS.

CYMEN
Arthurian

A son of the SAXON leader AELLE who accompanied his father when his forces defeated the Britons.

CYNAN
Welsh

The son of EUDAF and brother of GADEON and ELEN. He and his brother later came to the help of MACSEN, whom Elen had married, and brought an army of Britons to help Macsen retake Rome. In return, Cynan was given the province of ARMORICA, where his men killed all the men but kept the women for themselves, cutting out their tongues so that they could not speak their native, alien language.

CYNDDYLIG (THE GUIDE)
Welsh and Arthurian

One of the party who were to help CULHWCH locate and win the hand of the maiden OLWEN, daughter of the chief giant YSPADDADEN. The other members of the party were CEI (KAY), BEDWYR (BEDIVERE), GWRHYR, GWALCHMAI FAB GWYAR and MENW FAB TEIRGWAEDD. Each member of the party was chosen for a particular skill, that of Cynddylig being obvious from his epithet.

CYN-FARCH, -VARCH
Welsh and Arthurian

The father of URIEN.

CYNGEN (FAB CADELL)
Welsh and Arthurian
Also CONCENN

A legendary King of POWYS, who was said to have reigned some time between the fifth and sixth centuries, although the Pillar of ELISEG puts his death in Rome somewhat later – 854.

CYNON
Welsh and Arthurian

In Welsh tradition, the lover of OWAIN's twin sister, MORFUDD.

CYNRIC
Arthurian

A son of CERDIC.

CYON
Arthurian

A knight who is named as being one of the TWENTY-FOUR KNIGHTS of King ARTHUR's court.

CYWYLLOG
Arthurian

Welsh tradition makes Cywyllog the daughter of CAW and wife of MORDRED who, after her husband's death, became a nun and founded the church of Llangwyllog on Anglesey.

D

DA CHICH NANANN
Irish

'The Paps of Anu', two hills in Kerry that resemble breasts and are named after DANU, although here under her variant ANU. The naming of these hills after that goddess reflects her chthonic nature as an earth and fertility deity.

DA DERGA
Irish

A Lord of LEINSTER, whose home is described as a hostel, a place where travellers were always welcome. This home is the subject of the lengthy *Da Derga's Hostel*, which tells of the arrival of CONAIRE MÓR at the hostel, his death there after he had broken all the bonds placed on him at his birth and the destruction of the home of Da Derga.

DÁ THÓ
Irish

A wealthy Lord of LEINSTER and the father of MESRODA. His son owned a magnificent pig, or boar, the ownership of which became the subject of the ribald *SCÉLA MUCCE MAIC DÁ TIIÓ*. Because of this story, his son is better known simply as MAC DÁ THÓ.

DAG(H)D(H)A
Irish and Arthurian

The son of ELADU, the Daghdha was an earth and father god and one of the two greatest kings of the TUATHA DÉ DANANN, although he was, on one occasion, forced to build the tyrant BRES a fort. He originally lived at BRUGH NA BÓINNE, County MEATH. A hugely successful military leader of superhuman capacity, he owned a harp that played by itself and that could invoke the seasons, a wondrous cauldron of plenty called UNDRY, and a massive club, one end of which brought death to the recipient of the blow, while the other would restore a dead person to life. His wife had three names: BRENG meaning 'lie', MENG meaning 'guile' and MEABEL meaning 'disgrace'. She bore him three daughters, all of whom were named BRIGHID. His wife and daughters are yet further examples of the triad goddess that is common among Celtic and other pagan cultures, the most famous Celtic example being the MÓRRÍGHAN. The Daghdha is known as DUGAL the Brown in a traditional genealogy of Saint BRIDE.

With a name meaning 'Great God', the Daghdha was destined, if only by name, to become the greatest of all the Irish gods, although the description is principally meant to signify that he was not simply the master of one trade, but more a godly 'Jack of all trades' and master of all of them. He was also known as EOCHAIDH OLLATHAIR ('Eochaidh the Great Father') and RUADH ROFHESSA ('red one of great knowledge' or 'Mighty and Most Learned One'). His principal association appears to have been with the DRUIDS as the god of wisdom, a primal father deity of enormous power, combining elements of the sky father, war god and a chthonic fertility deity with those of a powerful sorcerer. His attributes of a club and a cauldron are potent spiritual and magical icons to the Celts. These two primal and pagan magical implements were later to resurface in the Arthurian legends, having been much refined, as the Holy GRAIL and the LANCE OF LONGINUS.

His cauldron gave a perpetual supply of food, much of which he gave away to the needy, and had the power, just as one end of his club did, to restore the dead to life, although it could also heal those who had been merely wounded. It appears to have provided not simply physical nourishment but also nourishment of a spiritual nature. The dual polarity of the club signifies power, and the control of such a wonderful cauldron rightly asserts the position of the Daghdha as a god of fertility and abundance. His club was so massive that eight men could not lift it, and it had to be mounted on wheels for ease of transport, and yet the Daghdha had no trouble in wielding it. If he simply dragged it along the ground behind him, it would leave a furrow that was as deep as a frontier ditch.

The Daghdha is usually, although not always, described as a giant wearing short peasant's clothing that revealed his buttocks. This mode of dress may have been an attempt to portray the sexuality of the god, for his sexual prowess was, even among the Celtic gods, outstanding. On one notable occasion he was said to have mated with the Mórríghan on the eve of SAMHAIN, this feat being accomplished while the goddess was straddling the river UNIUS, in which she continued to wash the armour of those who would die in the forthcoming Second Battle of MAGH TUIREDH. This theme of a god of life mating with a goddess of death is found in many pagan cultures, although not all of them adopt such an uncomfortable position. The Daghdha was also said to have been the father of OENGHUS MAC IN OG through an illicit union with BOANN, this time in a position that is not specified, although usually this coupling is said to have taken place on the same day as he had straddled the River Unius with the Mórríghan. The Daghdha is also said to have been the father of, among others, OGHMA, MIDHIR and BODB.

His presence at the Second Battle of Magh Tuiredh led to an attempt by the FOMHOIRÉ to disable him. The Daghdha had an insatiable appetite, an appetite that resulted in his having an ugly and portly figure, quite often the butt of derisive remarks, his waddling walk causing much amusement. Before the battle that was finally to establish the Tuatha Dé Danann as the rulers of IRELAND, the Fomhoiré boiled a huge cauldron of porridge, which they encouraged the Daghdha to eat. The cauldron they used was nothing more than a gaping hole in the ground, but the Daghdha easily finished the porridge, which consisted of eighty normal cauldrons full of oats, milk and fat that had been stuffed with whole sheep, pigs and goats. His spoon on this occasion was big enough to hold both a man and a woman. Having scooped out all he could with his spoon, he ran his finger around the gravel lining of the hole to make sure he had not missed a single drop. His physical appetite then satisfied, he sought to satisfy his sexual one with one of the Fomhoiré women, who was so impressed by his prowess that she agreed to use her magical powers against her own people during the forthcoming battle. Following the victory of the Tuatha Dé Danann over the Fomhoiré, brought about when LUGH killed BALAR with a slingshot, he, Lugh and Oghma recovered the stolen harp, thus restoring the seasons to their rightful order. Later, after the Tuatha Dé Danann had been conquered by the invading Sons of MÍL ÉSPÁINE, he gave each of the Tuatha Dé Danann a SÍDH in which to live after they had been awarded the underground half of Ireland by their conquerors. His own sídh contained a magical pig that could be eaten one day, but that would reappear the following day, whole again, and ready and willing to be eaten again.

Although the Daghdha is normally treated as a grotesquely comic figure, just as the god Thórr is in Norse–Teutonic tradition, there is little doubt about his ultimate authority, and the manner in which the Daghdha is portrayed seems to be little more than light-hearted ribaldry.

See also AINGE

DAGONET
Arthurian
ARTHUR's fool, but none the less knighted by ARTHUR himself.

DAHUT
Gaulish and Arthurian
Also AHES
A MORGAN (a Breton class of water-fairy), a variant of AHES and the name by which she is known as the daughter of GRADLON, who threw her into the sea after she had caused the sea to engulf YS, a domain she is still said to inhabit, luring sailors to their death in the drowned city. It is thought by some that her class of fairy, also known as MARI-MORGAN(S), was the origin of MORGAN Le Fay.

DAIRE
Irish and Arthurian
A son of FIONN MAC CUMHAILL. He was swallowed by a monster but hacked his way out from inside the creature, thus setting free the other inhabitants of the monster's stomach. It is quite possible that this Daire is the same as the Pictish King shown in the genealogies as being the father of the OTHERWORLD woman AILLEANN.

DAIRE MAC FIACHNA
Irish
A son of FIACHNA and one of the guardians of the DONN CUAILNGÈ, whom he led, in the company of the MÓRRÍGHAN, past CÚ CHULAINN, although that hero failed to recognise the Mórríghan, a mistake that was to cost him his life.

DÁL NARAIDI
Irish
The Irish kingdom from which a group emigrated to found the kingdom of DÁL RIADA on the west coast of SCOTLAND. Close links remained between the two kingdoms, FIACHNA LURGAN, King of Dál nAraidi, remaining a close ally of AEDÁN MAC GABRÁIN, King of Dál Riada.

DÁL RIA-DA, -TA
Irish and Arthurian
An ancient Hiberno-Scottish kingdom on the west coast of SCOTLAND, which today covers Argyllshire,

although it also included a small region in the north of IRELAND. It was founded by a group of emigrants from the kingdom of DÁL NARAIDI, and it is the alleged homeland of the Scottish people. The King of the newly founded domain, AEDÁN MAC GABRÁIN, maintained close links with the parent kingdom and was a close ally of FIACHNA LURGAN. The son of Aedán mac Gabráin, known as ARTHUR OF DÁL RIADA, has been suggested as the historical origin of King ARTHUR.

DALAN
Irish

A DRUID who was employed by EOCHAIDH AIREMH to discover the whereabouts of his wife ÉDÁIN ECHRAIDHE after she had been abducted by MIDHIR. After a year Dalan reported to Eochaidh that he had located his wife at the SÍDH of BRÍ LEITH.

DALI
Irish

The father of PHELIM MAC DALL, the court story-teller of CONCHOBAR MAC NESSA. The son is better known as FEDLIMID.

DALNY
Irish

An Anglicisation of DEALGNAID, the wife of PARTHOLÁN.

DALY
Irish

An inhabitant of CONNACHT and the father of CUR.

DAMAN
Irish

One of the FIR BHOLG and the father of FERDIADD.

DAMART
Arthurian

A magician who was killed by BETIS who thereafter became known as PERCEFOREST.

DAMAS
Arthurian

The brother of Sir ONTZLAKE, whom he used to make fight other knights he had trapped, a practice that was stopped by ARTHUR.

DAMONA
Gaulish

'Divine Cow', the goddess of a cow cult with whom the god BORMO is paired, a pairing that represents a plentiful supply of nourishment.

DAMOSEL DEL GRANT PUI DE MONT DOLEROUS, LA
Arthurian

According to some sources, the daughter of MERLIN.

DANAIN THE RED
Arthurian

The name of the Lord of MALEHAUT.

DANAND
Irish

A variant of DANU, in which form she is mentioned in connection with BÉCHUILLE and was made a foster mother to the gods.

DANANN
Irish

A mistaken variant of DANU. It comes about from a misunderstanding of the TUATHA DÉ DANANN, which, as this variant illustrates, was once thought to mean the 'People of Danann'. However, the correct translation is the 'People of the Goddess Danu'.

DANIEL
Arthurian

According to the *TAVOLA RITONDA*, the brother of DINADAN and the leader of the company of knights who trapped GUINEVERE and LANCELOT together in the Queen's bedchamber. A knight of this name also appears in a thirteenth-century German poem written by Der Stricker. As BREUNOR is also named as the brother of DINADAN, it seems that Daniel and BREUNOR were also brothers. Alternatively, it has been suggested that they were simply different names for the same character.

DAN-U, -A
Irish

A mother goddess, the daughter of the DAGHDHA and mother of a brood of gods who were collectively known as the TUATHA DÉ DANANN, or literally the 'People of the Goddess Danu'. A shadowy figure, about whom little is known, and possibly having OTHERWORLDLY connections, she also appears to have been known as BRIGHID, for her remembrance survives in the Christian calendar as Saint Brighid. The mother of BRIAN, IUCHAR and IUCHARBA, she is usually conceived of as a benevolent goddess, though she is sometimes, perversely, under her variant name of ANU, included within the malevolent triad that is the MÓRRÍGHAN, her partners in this association being BADHBH and MACHA. She also has connections with the moon goddess AINÉ, patroness of crops and cattle.

Some authorities have suggested that the Tuatha Dé Danann are a relatively late idea, their original name having been Danu, and it was only the later concept of a single MOTHER GODDESS that led to their subsequent naming.

DANU, THE PEOPLE OF THE GODDESS
Irish
The literal translation of TUATHA DÉ DANANN.

DARA
Irish
1 The son of FACHTNA and the owner of the DONN CUAILNGÈ, the great Brown Bull that is the subject of the *Taín Bó Cuailngè*. The owner of the beast is also known as Cuailngè.
2 The DRUID of CORMAC MAC AIRT. During the wedding feast of GRÁINNE and FIONN MAC CUM-HAILL, it was Dara who told Gráinne about DIARMAID UA DUIBHNE, and about his BALLSEIRC (love-spot), which made him irresistible to women.

DARERCA
Irish and Arthurian
According to Jocelyn's *Life of Saint Patrick*, Darerca was that saint's sister and had no fewer than seventeen sons. Her sister, TIGRIDIA, was said to have married GRALLO, the grandson of CONAN, thus also connecting her with ARTHUR, for Darerca was said to have married Conan himself.

DATHI
Irish
A historical ruler of IRELAND, one of the last Celtic kings to rule at TARA before the arrival of Saint PATRICK. He led a military campaign into BRITAIN, and from there into the continent, that was said to have been ordained by his DRUIDS. The campaign foundered when Dathi was struck by lightning while storming a tower in the Rhine valley. His body was carried back to Ireland and he was buried in the royal cemetery of RELIGH NA RIGH at RÁTH CRUACHAN. There, a 7-foot-high stone pillar still marks his grave among the numerous earthworks.

DATIS
Arthurian
The King of Tuscany who was killed by GARETH during ARTHUR's campaign against the ROMAN EMPIRE.

DAUGHTER OF THE KING OF LOGRES
Arthurian
According to *Tyolet*, this maiden challenged a knight

to cut the foot off a white stag, which TYOLET, the hero of the romance, succeeded in doing, afterwards becoming her husband. Her name remains a mystery, as she is not named in the romance.

DAVID, SAINT
Welsh and Arthurian
Also DEWI, SAINT
The patron saint of WALES, who, unsurprisingly, is linked with ARTHUR in a number of Welsh sources. GEOFFREY OF MONMOUTH makes him Arthur's uncle; the medieval Welsh history *Brut Y Brenhinedd* makes him Arthur's second cousin; another Welsh manuscript of uncertain date makes him Arthur's grandnephew. As the date of David's death remains unknown, it is certainly not impossible that there was some tangible link between him and Arthur.

DAVID'S SWORD
Arthurian
Though some commentators make this sword the one-time property of Saint DAVID, it is more widely accepted as having belonged to the biblical David. It appears in the Arthurian tales as the sword used by VARLAN to kill King LAMBOR in one account of the DOLOROUS STROKE.

DE EXCIDIO ET CONQUESTU BRITANNIAE
British and Arthurian
This famous text, probably written between 516 and 547 by the British writer GILDAS, is the only extant history of the Celts and the only contemporary version of events from the Roman invasion to his own time. An invaluable source to the Celtic researcher, the text mentions many of the events and places later to become associated with King ARTHUR, but does not actually mention him by name. It can therefore be considered a far truer account than those of writers such as NENNIUS or GEOFFREY OF MONMOUTH.

DE GABAIL INT SÍDA
Irish
The Conquest of the Fairy Mound, one of the eight manuscripts that together form the *Book of Leinster*. This tells how the DAGHDHA apportioned the SÍDH among the TUATHA DÉ DANANN, although his son, OENGHUS MAC IN OG, was omitted, as he was with his foster father MIDHIR. Returning, he claimed the sídh of BRUGH NA BÓINNE from his father, but his request was refused. Oenghus Mac in Og then asked to be allowed to stay the night, which he was, along with the following day. However, when the Daghdha asked him to leave, he refused, as he had stayed in the sídh for a night and a day, and

thus the sídh was rightfully his. The Daghdha had to agree and was thus dispossessed.

DE ORTU WALUUANII
Arthurian

A Latin romance of undetermined date that concerns the adventures of the young GAWAIN.

DE TROYES, CHRÉTIEN
Arthurian
See CHRÉTIEN DE TROYES

DEA CAELISTIS
Romano-British

A Roman high goddess whose name appears in an inscription found on Hadrian's Wall that associates BRIGANTIA with Dea Caelistis, thus raising the status of the local deity to the highest ranking and ensuring her worship by both the native population and the Roman invaders.

DEALGNAID
Irish

The wife of PARTHOLÁN, whom she accompanied to IRELAND, and the mother of RURY, although the true father of Rury may have been TOPA, manservant to Partholán, rather than Partholán himself, for Dealgnaid is said to have seduced Topa and thus instigated the first legal proceedings ever. She, her husband and her son all died in the pestilence that ended the occupation of Ireland by the people of Partholán, the sole survivor being Partholán's nephew TUAN MAC STERN.

DECA(I)R
Irish

An inhabitant of TÍR TAIRNGIRI, who brought a magical steed from that land to FIONN MAC CUMHAILL and the FIAN.

This miserable-looking animal reacted wildly when it was placed among the horses of the fian and bit them. CONAN MAC MORNA was ordered to ride the horse to its death, but it refused to move. Thirteen other members of the fian leapt on the animal's back, whereupon it fled, with another member of the fian swinging from its tail, back to Tír Tairngiri, whence Decair returned by running under the sea. The members of the fian were later rescued by Fionn mac Cumhaill.

DECIES
Irish

A mysterious people who appear only briefly in the story of the death of FIONN MAC CUMHAILL and the end of the FIAN. A son of the King asked for the hand of SGEIMH SOLAIS in marriage, which led the fian to ask for a customary tribute. Sgeimh Solais's father, CAIRPRE, was having none of this and went to war against the fian.

DECTER-A, -E
Irish
See DEICHTINE

DEERHURST
British

A small village seven miles north of Gloucester and the ancient capital of the Celtic kingdom of HWICCE. Traces of a Roman settlement and a Celtic monastery have been discovered here. Various pagan and Christian kings ruled from Deerhurst until the seventh century, when Deerhurst was claimed for the Roman Church.

DEICHTINE
Irish

The sister or daughter of CONCHOBAR MAC NESSA, wife of SUALTAM, and the mother of the hero CÚ CHULAINN, whose father was said to have been the god LUGH, although others say that it was none other than her father, Conchobar mac Nessa. Other sources call her Dectera and make her the daughter of CATHBHADH.

DE(I)MN-E, -A
Irish

The name by which FIONN MAC CUMHAILL was first known. He received the name by which he is better known at the age of ten, when he was described as 'fair', both in looks and in play, after which it was ordered that he should be known as Fionn, for *fionn* means 'fair'.

See also MUIRNE

DEIRDRE
Irish

An alternative, modern spelling of DERDRIU.

DELBAETH
Irish

The brother of the DAGHDHA and, according to some, the father of the goddess DANU, although this relationship seems highly improbable, as it would be impossible for Danu to be the mother of the gods if she were not born until after the gods themselves. Another story makes Delbaeth a FOMHOIRÉ and the father of LUGH by ÉRI.

See also ANU

DELBCHAEM

Irish

The mysterious female being whom BÉCUMA sent ART to fetch to TARA while she bewitched Art's father CONN CÉTCHATHLACH. Very little is said about Delbchaem other than that she lived in one of the Irish OTHERWORLDs. By sending Art to fetch her to Tara, Bécuma thought that she would be killing the youth, but he returned triumphant and Bécuma left in disgust.

DELGNAT

Irish

See DEALGNAID

DEMETIA

Welsh and Arthurian

The ancient name for the kingdom of DYFED in the south of WALES. According to GEOFFREY OF MONMOUTH, the kingdom was ruled by STATER during the fifth or sixth century, the traditional time attributed to the reign of King ARTHUR, but history knows nothing of a king of this name.

DEMETRUS

Welsh and Arthurian

The maternal grandfather of MYRDDIN (MERLIN), whose name appears to be a simple variant of DEMETIA, the kingdom in southern WALES that was the home of MYRDDIN's mother.

DEMOGORGON

Arthurian

The primeval being of classical mythology who appears in *La Caccia* by Erasmo de Valvasone when ARTHUR enters his cave *en route* through a mountain to reach the palace of MORGAN Le Fay.

DENMARK

Arthurian

Denmark and its rulers appear in several places in the Arthurian tales, but historically speaking very little is known about the Danish kings during the traditional Arthurian period. GEOFFREY OF MONMOUTH states that ASCHIL, the King of Denmark, was an ally of ARTHUR at CAMLANN, but the *MORTE ARTHURE* makes the Danish the allies of MORDRED. The kings themselves are also variously named. The twelfth-century Welsh writer Geoffrey Gaimar says that, in Arthurian times, the King was called GUNTER, while elsewhere he is called TRYFFIN. In *DURMART LE GALLOIS* he is JOZEFANT, while in the *LIVRE D'ARTUS* he is called AMINADUC and described as a SAXON.

CLARIS ET LARIS gives us still further variation, stating that it was first ruled by HELDINS, who was succeeded by TALLAS. He was defeated by Arthur and subsequently LARIS ascended to the throne.

DENT DU CHAT

Arthurian

'Cat's Tooth'. A place-name in the vicinity of Lake BOURGET in the French Alps that commemorates the fact that ARTHUR was said to have slain a huge cat, possibly a CATH PALUG or CAPALU, near there.

DENW

Arthurian

The daughter of ANNA, ARTHUR's sister, and LOT, who, according to Welsh tradition, became the wife of OWAIN.

DEOCA

Irish

A princess of MUNSTER who became betrothed to a CONNACHT chief called LAIRGNEN. She begged him to bring her the four marvellous singing swans she had heard of, these swans being the four children of LIR, who had been condemned to take that form for 900 years by their stepmother AOIFE. Lairgnen duly trapped the four swans and brought them to his intended, but as soon as they arrived a dreadful transformation began, the sight of which made Lairgnen flee from the palace, never to be seen again. Their 900 years had come to an end and they began to revert back to their original form, though now they were old and withered. They were quickly baptised into the Christian faith, for death was near. FIONUALA, the only one of them to speak, asked that upon their death they should be buried in one grave with CONN at her right, FIACHTRA at her left, and HUGH in front of her. Moments later they died and were buried as requested.

DERBRENN

Irish

The first love of OENGHUS MAC IN OG, and the foster mother to the six children whose natural mother turned them into swine, after which Oenghus Mac in Og sent them to be cared for by BUICHET.

DERDRIU

Irish and Arthurian

The daughter of FEDLIMID, the FILI of CONCHOBAR MAC NESSA. The DRUID CATHBHADH prophesied that she would be exceptionally beautiful but that she would cause much suffering in ULSTER. At her birth, and remembering the prophecy, many wanted to have her killed, but Conchobar mac Nessa decreed that she should live and that he would marry her when she came of age.

Derdriu was raised in the strictest seclusion by the wise woman LEBHORCHAM. One day, while she watched her foster father flay a newly killed calf in the snow, she saw a raven land and drink the blood. Remarking that she would love a man whose hair was as black as the raven, whose blood was as red as that of the calf and whose skin was as white as the snow, she learnt from Lebhorcham that just such a man was NAOISE, one of three brothers who were known as the sons of UISNECH. Immediately she contrived a plan that would allow her to meet him, which she did as he rode through the woods.

Naoise was everything Derdriu had hoped for, but he, remembering the prophecy of Cathbhadh and knowing of her betrothal, was reluctant to respond, even though he found Derdriu exceptionally beautiful. She countered by saying that if he did not become her lover she would make him a laughing stock. Caught in a hopeless trap, Naoise fled to SCOTLAND with Derdriu and his two brothers, ARDÁN and AINNLE. Conchobar mac Nessa was furious, and it was some time before the men of Ulster managed to persuade him to call a truce and ask the fugitives to return home. Finally, Conchobar mac Nessa sent FERGHUS MAC ROICH, DUBTHACH and Dubthach's son, CORMAC MAC DUBTHACH, to ask them to return and to guarantee their safety. However, when Derdriu and her companions returned, Conchobar mac Nessa reneged and had the young men killed by EOGHAN MAC DURTHACHT and his men. Furious at this deceit, Ferghus mac Roich, Dubthach and Cormac mac Dubthach stormed and razed EMHAIN MHACHA, killed 300 of the men of Ulster, and defected to AILILL and MEDHBHA of CONNACHT, the great enemies of Conchobar mac Nessa.

For a whole year Derdriu pined, never once lifting her head. Finally, Conchobar mac Nessa asked her what she disliked most in the world. She replied that it was Conchobar mac Nessa himself, with Eoghan mac Durthacht a close second. Conchobar mac Nessa decreed that, since she had spent a year with him, she would spend the next with Eoghan mac Durthacht. The very next day, as she was travelling to Eoghan mac Durthacht, Derdriu threw herself from the chariot and dashed her brains out against a rock.

Her story is thought to have been one of the sources for the story of TRISTAN and ISEULT.

DERFEL, SAINT
Arthurian
The founder of Llanderfel in GWYNEDD, who, according to Welsh tradition, participated in, and survived, the Battle of CAMLANN.

DERMOT (O'DYNA)
Irish
The Latinised form of DIARMAID (UA DUIBIINE).

DERUVIAN
Arthurian
Named as one of the missionaries who were sent in *c.* AD 166 from Rome by Pope ELUTHERIUS at the request of the then British King LUCIUS, and founded the abbey at GLASTONBURY. The name of the other missionary is given as PHAGAN.

DESA
Irish
The father of the monstrous sons who laid siege to the hostel of DA DERGA while CONAIRE MÓR was staying there.

DESTRUCTIVE ONE
Arthurian
The name of the servant of MERLIN who was employed in the imprisonment of ORLANDO at the request of MADOR, who was jealous because MELORA, whom he loved, showed her preference for the hapless Orlando.

DETORS
Arthurian
Simply mentioned as being an alleged King of NORTHUMBERLAND.

DEVORGILLA
Irish
The princess who was to be given to the FOMHOIRÉ as tribute by her father but was rescued by CÚ CHULAINN, who was returning to IRELAND from his time with SCÁTHACH. Devorgilla was awarded to Cú Chulainn, but he gave her to LUGAID, as he was to be married to EMER. Devorgilla and her handmaiden changed themselves into birds to seek out Cú Chulainn, who fired a slingshot at them and wounded them, whereon they resumed their true form. Cú Chulainn sucked out the shot with which he had wounded them, but this made it impossible for Devorgilla even to entertain the thought of marriage to Cú Chulainn, as he had swallowed her blood, which made him her brother.

DEWI, SAINT
Welsh and Arthurian
Saint DAVID, the patron saint of WALES.

DEWRARTH WLEDIG
Welsh
An alternative for GWYDDNO GARANHIR.

DIAN (CÉCHT)
Irish
The god of healing, depicted as a huge leech, and the mythical author of *The Judgements of Dian Cécht*, a tract concerning the legal responsibilities of one who has caused another injury or illness. The aggressor is held responsible for paying the bills incurred for the cure of the person hurt, with wounds being measured in grains of corn, so that even the smallest wound has its price.

Dian Cécht has, in later Romano-Celtic tradition, been assimilated with the Roman god Apollo, for he, like that god, slew a giant serpent that threatened the land. This serpent came from MEICHE, the son of the MÓRRÍGHAN, whom Dian Cécht killed. Cutting open the body, he discovered three hearts, one for each aspect of his triad mother, each being a snake's head. He immediately burned two hearts, but the third escaped and grew into the serpent he later killed. Dian Cécht threw the ashes of the burned hearts into the River Barrow, whose waters became corrosive.

With the serpent comes the undeniable iconography of the healer, for to this day a staff entwined by a serpent, the staff or *caduceus* of Asclepios, the Graeco-Roman god of medicine, remains in use as a symbol employed by numerous medical bodies. Again this further links Dian Cécht and Apollo, for Apollo was also considered a god of healing.

Dian Cécht was most notably active during the two battles of MAGH TUIREDH. After the first, and with the help of the divine smith CREIDHNE, he fashioned and fitted an arm made out of silver to replace the one that NUADHA had lost in that battle. The Second Battle of Magh Tuiredh kept Dian Cécht particularly busy, for he revived the fallen and wounded TUATHA DÉ DANANN by plunging them into a magic well or bath. He had three sons, all of whom were healers and who helped him in this enormous task. Following the battle, he killed one of them, MIDACH, for he was becoming too skilful and thus represented a threat to his father's reputation and position.

Dian Cécht could also replace lost eyes or cure blindness by using the eyes of cats. This operation, however, had one distinct disadvantage in that the replacement eye would sleep during the day and be wide awake during the night, alert to every movement or sound and responsive to the slightest noise.

DIANA
Arthurian
The classical Roman goddess who, in the mighty *VULGATE VERSION*, is the goddess of the wood, the mother of DYONAS (Dione) and hence grandmother of VIVIENNE.

DIARMAID UA DUIBHNE
Irish
The foster son of OENGHUS MAC IN OG, Diarmaid ua Duibhne received a spot on his forehead from a mysterious maiden, who informed him that any woman who saw that spot would instantly fall in love with him. It was this spot, his BALL-SEIRC, that made GRÁINNE become besotted with him, even though she was betrothed to the ageing FIONN MAC CUMHAILL, of whom Diarmaid ua Duibhne was a loyal subject. On the night of her wedding feast, Gráinne drugged Fionn mac Cumhaill and most of those present and then, casting a GESSA spell on Diarmaid ua Duibhne, forced him to elope with her to a wood in CONNACHT, where they were besieged by Fionn mac Cumhaill.

Gráinne was rescued from the wood by Oenghus Mac in Og, and Diarmaid ua Duibhne escaped by jumping, in a single tremendous bound, straight over the heads of the attackers. Safe from attack, Diarmaid ua Duibhne still refused to break his oath to Fionn mac Cumhaill and to take the maiden as his mistress, and it was only after she had derided him wickedly that he was driven to be disloyal.

Gráinne bore Diarmaid ua Duibhne four sons and finally, with the help of Oenghus Mac in Og, they were reconciled with Fionn mac Cumhaill. With their quarrel patched up, Diarmaid ua Duibhne accompanied Fionn mac Cumhaill when he went to hunt the magical boar of BEANN GHULBAN, even though it had been prophesied that the boar, Diarmaid ua Duibhne's foster brother, would kill him. During the hunt, Diarmaid ua Duibhne was mortally gored, seconds before he struck the killing blow to the boar. His life could be saved only if Fionn mac Cumhaill, who had the gift of healing, would give him water out of his own hands. Fionn mac Cumhaill fetched some water but, remembering Diarmaid ua Duibhne's treachery, allowed it to trickle away through his fingers. Again he fetched some water, and again allowed it to seep away. By the time he returned the third time Diarmaid ua Duibhne had died.

DIARMUID MAC CEARBHAILL
Irish
A historic sixth-century King of IRELAND whose Latinised name is Dermot MacKerval. His reign marked the progress of the Irish towards true national unity. Diarmuid mac Cearbhaill upheld all the laws of the land, but this led him into trouble with the clergy, who had sought to shelter a chief by the name of Hugh Guairy, who had murdered one of the King's officers. The King sought him out and dragged him from the sanctuary he had been offered in order to stand trial at TARA. This offended the clergy, who gathered at Tara and, through their prayers, cursed the royal court, which was thenceforth abandoned by subsequent kings of Ireland.

DIDOT PERCEVAL
Arthurian
A French prose romance that dates from *c.* 1200 and tells of PERCEVAL's quest for the Holy GRAIL. Although the author of this work remains unknown, it has been suggested that he is ROBERT DE BORON.

DIL
Irish
The daughter of LUGMANNAIR who was loved by TULCHAINDE, DRUID to CONAIRE MÓR. Tulchainde wanted Dil to elope with him from the Isle of FALGA (Isle of MAN). Dil loved two magically conceived oxen, FEA and FERNEA, and begged Tulchainde to take them with her. He managed this with the help of the MÓRRÍGHAN, who magically conveyed them from Falga to MAGH MBREG.

DILLUS
Welsh and Arthurian
In the *MABINOGION* story of *CULHWCH AND OLWEN*, Dillus's beard was required by the giant YSPADDADEN as one of the conditions he set CULHWCH if he were to marry OLWEN. The task was completed by CEI (Sir KAY), who cast Dillus into a hole in the ground and pulled out the hairs of his beard with a pair of tweezers.

DINABUTIUS
Welsh and Arthurian
The name of a young boy who taunted the youthful MYRDDIN (MERLIN) for not knowing his father's name. This taunting brought Myrddin to the attention of VORTIGERN's counsellors, for Vortigern was looking for a fatherless child to sacrifice in an attempt to cure the problem he was having with building his tower at DINAS EMRYS, which, every time he built it, promptly fell down again.

DINADAN
Arthurian
The brother of BREUNOR the Black and a KNIGHT OF THE ROUND TABLE. He is recorded as having seen no purpose in fighting for fighting's sake, and was finally killed by MORDRED and AGRAVAIN.

DINAS
Arthurian
The seneschal (steward) of King MARK who was a KNIGHT OF THE ROUND TABLE but none the less felt sorry for TRISTAN, whom he thought had been ill-treated, and who became the latter's companion. Dinas accompanied LANCELOT when that knight ran off with Queen GUINEVERE and duly became Duke of ANJOU. After the death of King Mark, Dinas, according to the *TAVOLA RITONDA*, became King of CORNWALL.

DINAS DINNLLEV
Welsh
The home of GWYDION FAB DÔN in which he raised LLEU LLAW GYFFES from his birth until the second curse of ARIANRHOD.

DINAS EMRYS
Welsh and Arthurian
Situated two miles north-east of Beddgelert, GWYNEDD, lies a wooded hill known as Dinas Emrys, just below Llyn Dinas. It was here that VORTIGERN had repeatedly attempted to build his tower, but every night the stones fell down again. His counsellors advised him that he needed to sacrifice a fatherless child, for which MYRDDIN (MERLIN) was considered ideal, for he was supposed to have been born without a father, the offspring of an incubus. However, Merlin advised Vortigern that the real problem lay in the fact that there were two dragons – one white and one red – confined beneath the site in a subterranean lake. Merlin subsequently dealt with the dragons and built his own fortress on the hill-top.

Details of how the dragons came to be below the hill are to be found in the *MABINOGION* story of *LLUD AND LLEFELYS*. During LLUD's reign a scream, whose origin could not be found, was heard every year on the eve of May Day. LLEFELYS, the King of FRANCE, told Llud that it was caused by fighting dragons, which were subsequently captured and buried at Dinas Emrys.

Dinas Emrys, North Wales, where Vortigern built his tower and where Merlin fought two dragons.
(© Mick Sharp)

There are still some earthworks of the ancient fort to be seen on this site, which has its main entrance on the northern side of the hill. Traces of a ruined tower some 36 feet by 24 feet have been found on the summit, though whether these are the ruins of Vortigern's tower or Merlin's fort remains open to speculation. Nearby lies a circle of tumbled stones roughly 30 feet in diameter, which is said to be a mystic ring in which the battling dragons were contained. At one time the fort was known as DINAS FFORAN – 'the Fort with High Powers'. Merlin's treasure is apparently hidden in a cave at Dinas Emrys, having been placed in a golden vessel in the cave, along with his golden chair. Merlin then rolled a huge stone over the entrance of the cave and covered it with earth and grass. Tradition states that the discoverer of the treasure will be 'golden-haired and blue-eyed'. When that person comes near to Dinas Emrys, a bell will be heard, inviting him, or her, into the cave, which will open of its own accord the instant that person's foot touches the stone covering the entrance.

A youth living near Beddgelert once searched for the treasure, obviously wanting to give himself a head start in life. Taking a pickaxe with him, he climbed to the top of the hill and started to dig on the site of the tower. As soon as he did, unearthly noises began to rumble beneath his feet and the whole of Dinas Emrys began to rock like a cradle. The sun clouded over and day became as night. Thunder roared over his head and lightning flashed all around him. Dropping his pickaxe, he ran for home, and, when he arrived, everything was calm, but he never returned to retrieve the pickaxe.

Not far from Dinas Emrys is CELL-Y-DEWINIAID – 'the Grove of the Magicians'. There was once a grove of oak trees at the northern end of a field here under which Vortigern's counsellors were said to meet to discuss the events of their times. They were buried in an adjacent field, at one time each grave being marked by a stone, a white thorn tree annually decorating each with falling white blossoms.

DINAS FFORAN
Arthurian
'The Fort with High Powers', the name by which the fort atop DINAS EMRYS was once known.

DINDRANE
Arthurian
The sister of PERCEVAL who was known as AGRESTIZIA in Italian romance. She accompanied her brother on the quest for the Holy GRAIL, and, when the questers came to a castle where it was the custom to demand the blood of passing women to cure the leprous mistress, Dindrane voluntarily gave her blood and died by so doing.

DINNSHENCHAS
Irish
The Lore of the Prominent Places, a twelfth-century Christian collection of Irish legends concerning the origins of local place-names, which has been described as 'mythological geography'. In places it echoes the stories of the *Taín Bó Cuailngè*, and mentions sacred trees that were alleged to have been planted by the gods as they passed.

DINSUL
British
'Mount of the Sun', the pre-Christian Celtic name for SAINT MICHAEL'S MOUNT.

DIONES
Arthurian
Possibly cognate with DYONAS, Diones was the father of NIMUE, whose godmother was said to be none other than the goddess DIANA.

DIONETA
Arthurian
The name of two maidens in the *BIRTH OF ARTHUR*, a fourteenth-century Welsh work.
1 A daughter of LLEU (LOT) and GWYAR, the sister of GWALCHMAI and MORDRED.
2 A daughter of GORLOIS and IGRAINE, thus a half-sister to ARTHUR.

DIONISE
Arthurian
The enchanted mistress of a castle whom GAWAIN freed but refused to marry.

DIRAC
Arthurian
The brother of LAC and hence the uncle of EREC.

'DIS PATER'
Romano-Gaulish
Originally an unnamed deity who was given his name by the Romans to equate him with their own god Dis Pater, the god of death. JULIUS CAESAR wrote that the Celts of GAUL regarded this deity as the divine ancestor of mankind and not a god of death at all. It has been suggested that the association was made so that the indigenous Gauls would come to believe that even their divine ancestor could not save them from the Romans.

Some authorities state that the original of 'Dis Pater' was the god SUCELLOS.

DITAS
Arthurian

The King of HUNGARY, who was said to have been numbered among the followers of the Roman Emperor THEREUS when the latter attacked ARTHUR.

DITHORBA
Irish

The brother of MACHA and CIMBAOTH. When his sister Macha refused to give up the throne after the death of their father, Dithorba was fought and killed, and Cimbaoth was forced to marry his sister, who ruled all IRELAND as queen. The five sons of Dithorba fled to the west of Ireland and plotted their revenge. They were caught and forced to build the ramparts of EMHAIN MHACHA.

DIU CRÔNE
Arthurian

Thirteenth-century GRAIL romance by HEINRICH VON DEM TURTIN in which GAWAIN features as the hero, and which names King GARLIN of GALORE as the father of GUINEVERE and GOTEGRIM.

DIURAN
Irish

One of the companions of MAIL DÚIN.

DIWRNACH
Welsh and Arthurian

The Irish owner of a wondrous cauldron, which he refused to hand over to CULHWCH or ARTHUR during the expedition to help CULHWCH. An expedition was mounted to IRELAND during which Diwrnach was slain and the cauldron seized. Subsequently this cauldron became one of the THIRTEEN TREASURES OF BRITAIN. The appearance of a wondrous Irish cauldron in this tale leads to a possible identification between Diwrnach and the DAGHDHA and, latterly, with the Holy GRAIL.

DO
Arthurian

The son of ARES and father of GRIFLET and LORETE, he was employed as a forester by UTHER.

DODINEL
Arthurian

The son of BELINANT and EGLANTE, though one story makes his mother the Lady of MALEHAUT.

A KNIGHT OF THE ROUND TABLE, he was known as 'The Savage', as he liked to hunt wild game in the forests. He is perhaps originally identical with PERCEVAL.

DOEL
Irish

The father of ACHTLAND and COIRPRE, as well as several other unnamed sons. The story of the disappearance of his sons from IRELAND, and their subsequent rescue by CÚ CHULAINN, is told in the *Longes mac nDuil Dermait*.

DOGSHEADS
Arthurian

In the poem *PA GUR*, the Dogsheads are the opponents of ARTHUR who were fought by either Arthur himself or KAY. It has been suggested that they might, in origin, be a recollection of a legendary Irish people, the *Conchind* – Dog-heads. Identifications with the *Cunesioi*, or *Concani*, both said to inhabit the Iberian peninsula, have also been made. They are not fully described in *Pa Gur*, and this has led to some speculation about what exactly the Dogsheads were – man or beast.

DOLDAVIUS
Arthurian

The King of Gotland who, along with GUNPHAR, the King of the ORKNEYS, came to pay homage to ARTHUR, having heard of his prowess and fearing his might.

DOLLALLOLLA
Arthurian

The ridiculous name of ARTHUR's queen in Henry Fielding's parody *Tragedy* of *Tragedies* (1730).

DOLOROUS GARD
Arthurian

The name by which LANCELOT'S castle, JOYOUS GARD, was originally known, and to which it later reverted. It has been identified with BAMBURGH castle in NORTHUMBERLAND.

DOLOROUS STROKE
Arthurian

The name given to the blow that rendered the WASTE LAND barren and that made the quest for the Holy GRAIL necessary. The *ESTOIRE DEL SAINTE GRAAL* makes this the occasion when VARLAN, or BRULAN, killed LAMBOR with DAVID'S SWORD. However, Sir Thomas MALORY places the event later in the Arthurian chronology, and states it was the occasion when BALIN stabbed PELLAM with the LANCE OF LONGINUS, destroying three entire countries as a result.

DOMNAL
Irish

A warlike inhabitant of SCOTLAND whom FORGALL urged CÚ CHULAINN to seek out in the hope that he would be killed and thus not return to claim the hand of EMER. Domnal, however, recognised the power of Cú Chulainn and taught him all manner of wonderful feats before dispatching him to learn even more from SCÁTHACH. During his time with Domnal, Cú Chulainn had rebuffed the amorous advances of DORNOLLA. In revenge she caused Cú Chulainn's companions to feel so homesick that Cú Chulainn was left alone in Scotland.

DÔN
Welsh and Arthurian

MOTHER GODDESS, daughter of MATHONWY, sister of MATH FAB MATHONWY and wife of BELI. She is the Welsh equivalent of the Irish DANU. Her children, known collectively as the Children of Dôn, included gods of the sky, sea and poetry, all of whom were locked in eternal battle with the children of LLYR, their opposites, the powers of darkness. Traditionally she was the mother of GILFAETHWY, ARIANRHOD and GWYDION FAB DÔN, as well as several others, as illustrated in her traditional genealogy. It has been suggested that Dôn was the original of DO, even though this would mean a change of gender.

DONDINELLO
Arthurian

The father of CARDUINO who was killed by poison.

DONN
Romano-Gaulish

A form of 'DIS PATER'.

DÔN(N)
Irish

(1) The discourteous leader of the Sons of MÍL ÉSPÁINE. He was drowned shortly after they had arrived and, after he had been buried on the island of TECH DUÍNN, where he had been shipwrecked, became god of the dead. He still welcomes dead warriors to the island. His name means 'Dark' or 'Brown One', and some authorities have sought to identify him with the DAGHDHA, but the two are clearly different characters. Modern Irish folklore sees Dônn not only as the god of the dead, but also as the ambivalent god of storms and shipwrecks, and a patron of crops and cattle.

(2) Sometimes identified with DONN, this Dônn first appears in the form of a swineherd in the *Taín Bó Cuailngè* who, after a multitude of animal reincarnations, was reborn as the DONN CUAILNGÈ. Dônn is possibly to be identified with the Gaulish TARVOS TRIGARANOS.

(3) The father of DIARMAID UA DUIBHNE. He killed the boy born to his wife after she had an affair with ROC. This child was reincarnated as the monstrous BEANN GHULBAN.

DONN BO
Irish

A famous story-teller and minstrel at the court of King FERGAL. Although he was killed in battle, he continued to sing the praises of his King, who had also been killed in the battle. His head was cut off and taken back to a feasting hall, where it continued to sing with such sweetness that it moved those attending to tears and caused many of them to renounce their pagan faith and accept Christianity.

DONN CUAILNGÈ
Irish

Donn Cuailngè was the name of the brown bull that belonged to CUAILNGÈ or DARA. This bull was the centre of attraction to MEDHBHA, who swore to own it whatever the cost. The epic story of her quest to locate and then take the bull is contained in the *Taín Bó Cuailngè*, a remarkable early text that tells of the heroic stance adopted by CÚ CHULAINN, who defended ULSTER single-handedly against the armies of Medhbha and AILILL but was eventually killed after he had failed to recognise the presence of the MÓRRÍGHAN. The Donn Cuailngè was finally captured, but it destroyed FINNBHENNACH before returning to Ulster to die.

DONN TETSCORACH
Irish

The brother or son of MIDHIR. He entertained FIONN MAC CUMHAILL and the FIAN in the SÍDH of his father.

DOR(E) CASTLE
Arthurian

Cornish castle where there is an ancient, and partially unintelligible, inscription thought to link CUNOMORUS with King MARK. This is said to read *Drustans hic iacit cunomori filius* – 'Here lies Tristan, son of Cunomorus'. If this is indeed the true meaning of the inscription, it would seem to imply that the relationship between King Mark and TRISTAN was far closer than later writers were prepared to allow.

DORIN
Arthurian
The son of CLAUDAS, he was killed in a fight with BORS and LIONEL.

DORNAR
Arthurian
A son of King PELLINORE, the brother of DRIANT. He and his brother were both KNIGHTS OF THE ROUND TABLE.

DORNOLLA
Irish
The ugly daughter of DOMNAL. Her love for CÚ CHULAINN was unrequited while that hero was in SCOTLAND, and in revenge she caused his companions to feel so homesick that they left him to travel on to SCÁTHACH alone.

DOUGLAS, RIVER
Arthurian
The river in LINNIUS that was the site of four of ARTHUR'S BATTLES, when the new king, aged just fifteen and having newly ascended the throne, defeated the SAXON leader COLGRIN and a mixed force of SAXONS, Scots and PICTS. Colgrin took refuge after the fourth battle in YORK, and ARTHUR then laid siege to him there.

DOZMARY POOL
Arthurian
A body of water lying on Bodmin Moor, just to the east of Colliford Lake, about six miles from SLAUGHTERBRIDGE, the traditional Cornish location for CAMLANN. Dozmary Pool is just one of many possible locations for the episode where EXCALIBUR was returned to the LADY OF THE LAKE.

DRAGON
General
The usual form of dragon that appears in Celtic legend is that represented on the modern Welsh flag, a scaly lizard-like animal, with wings, that can breath fire. It is the symbolic image of the Celtic chief. Although the appearance of a dragon in Celtic myth is somewhat rarer than in other pagan cultures, particularly Chinese and Slavonic, those that do appear are all OTHERWORLDLY creatures, and all are usually dealt with in a heroic manner. Welsh myth is the most common place to find a dragon, but even here they do not leap out from every nook and cranny, being more usually confined to later folklore.

See also DINAS EMRYS

Dozmary Pool on Bodmin Moor, where Excalibur may have been returned to the Lady of the Lake.
(© Mick Sharp)

Sir Lancelot kills a dragon. (Mary Evans Picture Library/Arthur Rackham Collection)

DRAIDECHT

Irish

The title used to refer to the DAGHDHA as the god of magic and Druidism.

DREAM OF RHONABWY, THE

Arthurian

A Welsh romance that forms an important part of the *MABINOGION*, and concerns the adventures dreamt of by the hero of the story, RHONABWY.

DRIANT

Arthurian

A son of King PELLINORE and the brother of DORNAR. Both he and his brother were KNIGHTS OF THE ROUND TABLE. He died after receiving a mortal wound in combat against GAWAIN.

DRUDWAS

Arthurian

The son of King TRYFFIN of DENMARK who, while supposedly one of ARTHUR's followers and one of the TWENTY-FOUR KNIGHTS of Arthur's court, was once to meet the King in single combat. A cunning knight, he told his three pet griffins to go ahead of him and kill the first man who came on to the field of combat, fully expecting it to be Arthur. Drudwas, however, was the first to arrive, as his sister, Arthur's mistress, delayed the King. The griffins, not recognising their master, killed him.

DRUID(S)

General

The name given to the common priesthood of the Celtic peoples, although Druids were much more than simple priests – they were also teachers, seers, poets, judges, doctors, diviners and magicians. Their name is thought to come from *drus*, the ancient name for an oak tree, which was sacred to them. The Druids were the unifying force between different Celtic tribes, their efforts preserving common culture, religion, history, laws, scholarship and science. Because Druids represented the most powerful force within the Celtic society and because their office was sacred, they had freedom to move as they wanted, being instrumental in stopping battles and forcing opposing factions to settle their disputes by arbitration. The Druids managed the higher legal systems and established colleges where pupils would receive up to twenty years' oral instruction before being admitted to their order. They were also responsible for the education of minstrels and bards, who received a similarly lengthy tuition.

Knowledge of the ancient Druids comes directly from contemporary writers, although little can be gleaned from these sources of their rituals and customs, which remain shrouded in mystery. JULIUS CAESAR wrote that they had an intimate knowledge of the stars and their motions and of the universe and its size. They knew about the powers and authority of the gods, and taught the doctrine of the immortality of the soul. It appears that they also accepted the principles of reincarnation, for it was recorded that they allowed debts incurred in this lifetime to be repaid in the next.

Caesar significantly remarks that the first Druids came from BRITAIN, and it is quite possible that this is a factual comment, for Druidism retains the appearance of an insular religion. It seems increasingly likely that the first Celts to arrive in Britain found there a religion controlled by a priesthood. They simply adopted that religion and its priests, a supposition possibly supported by the religious importance placed by the Druids on ancient megalithic monuments such as STONEHENGE. Yet there is a fundamental difference between the Celtic Druids and the megalithic priesthood. The Druids abandoned the great stones and reverted to natural shrines, a change that implies religious reformation, a reformation that may have come about with the first influx of Celtic peoples and a realisation by the priesthood that, if it were to retain its position of importance, it had to adapt its religion to match the beliefs of the new population.

It is almost impossible to put a date to this reformation, but it seems likely that the megalithic priests were in existence prior to 2000 BC. They appear to have enjoyed almost 1400 years of independence before the accepted date for the arrival of the first Celtic people in Britain, 600 BC. They then enjoyed a further 700 or 800 years of this independence before the first Christians arrived in Britain, and it was not until several centuries later that the pagan rituals of the Druids were finally eradicated from the Celtic Church when that was taken over by the Church of Rome.

The regularisation of the Celtic pantheon by the Druids was brought to an abrupt end by the Roman invasion, during which the priesthood and holy places were destroyed with systematic savagery. It was obvious to the Romans that the Druids represented the driving force behind Celtic power, and they thought that the only answer to such power was the sword. The *nemeton*, or holy groves, were put to the axe, and the Druids and their families slaughtered. Evidence of this massacre is to be found in the writings of Tacitus, although he refers to the slaughter of innocent women and children as 'heroism'. Having annihilated the religious order of the Celts, the Romans turned to the pen and assigned foreign and inappropriate names to the Celtic gods. This single act destroyed the Celtic way of life, but, more importantly for the student of Celtic times, made it impossible to determine the characteristics of many of the Celtic deities and their position within any pantheon that the Druids had devised.

If the Druids are indeed a priesthood that underwent a reformation with the arrival of the Celts in Britain, they must surely represent one of the oldest religions to have survived to the present, for there is today a great resurgence of the Druidic culture worldwide.

DRUIDAN
Arthurian

When YDAIN tried to leave her lover GAWAIN, the latter bestowed his mistress on this dwarf.

DRUMELZIER
Arthurian

A place in SCOTLAND that numbers among the possible locations for the burial site of MERLIN.

DRYDEN, JOHN
Arthurian

An English poet (1631–1700). His opera *King Arthur* (1691), with music by Henry Purcell, has little actual Arthurian content. In this version ARTHUR is in love with a blind girl called EMMELINE, but she is also loved by OSWALD, the SAXON enemy of the King.

DRYNOG
Welsh and Arthurian

The owner of a cauldron, known as PAIR DRYNOG, that numbered among the THIRTEEN TREASURES of BRITAIN and was said to boil no meat save that of a brave man.

DU
Welsh

The horse of GWYNN AP NUDD, although some sources say that this horse was rather the one given by Gwyn ap Nudd to CULHWCH to enable the latter to catch the great boar TWRCH TRWYTH.

DUB
Irish

The husband of ENNA. He once caused the seas to swell and drown AIDE, the wife of AED, and her family.

DUBRIC(IUS), SAINT
Arthurian
Also DYFRIG

An important Celtic saint who died *c.* AD 550. He was the Bishop, and possibly also the Abbot, of Caldey and, according to GEOFFREY OF MONMOUTH, was also the Archbishop of CAERLEON-ON-USK who crowned the young King ARTHUR. Modern thinking has sought to identify him with MERLIN.

DUBSAINGL-U, -END
Irish

The true name of Black of SAINGLIU, one of the two horses that were born at the same time as CÚ CHULAINN and that were later to become his famous steeds. The other horse was known as Grey of MACHA.

DUBTHACH
Irish

The father of CORMAC MAC DUBTHACH (literally 'Cormac son of Dubthach') and the owner of a spear that had to be kept in a brew of soporific herbs if it were not to fly forth on its own, eager for massacre. Dubthach was sent with his son and FERGHUS MAC ROICH to SCOTLAND by CONCHOBAR MAC NESSA to bring the fugitive DERDRIU, along with ARDÁN, AINNLE and NAOISE, back to IRELAND.

When Conchobar mac Nessa reneged on his truce and had the three young men killed, Dubthach, Ferghus mac Roich and Cormac mac Dubthach attacked and burned EMHAIN MHACHA, killed 300 of the men of ULSTER and then defected to AILILL and MEDHBHA of CONNACHT, the great enemies of Conchobar mac Nessa.

DUE TRISTANI
Arthurian

An Italian romance dating from 1551 that gives details about the son and daughter of TRISTAN and ISEULT.

DUGAL
Irish

A variant name for the DAGHDHA. A chanted protective hymn giving the genealogy of Saint BRIDE names the Daghdha as 'Dugal the Brown', making him the son of AODH, son of ART, son of CONN, son of CREAR, son of CIS, son of CARMAC, son of CARRUIN.

DUMBARTON
Arthurian

A Scottish town whose Roman name was *Alclud*, and in which HOEL was besieged by an army of PICTS and Scots until he was relieved by his ally King ARTHUR. According to Gaelic tradition, Dumbarton was also the birthplace of MOROIE MOR, the son of Arthur.

DUMNONIA
British and Arthurian

A considerable ancient Celtic kingdom, which survived the Roman invasion. It was said to have covered Devon, CORNWALL, and other sizeable areas of south-west ENGLAND, its most westerly portion being known as CORNUBIA to the Romans. ARTHUR's successor, CONSTANTINE, was said to be the king of this realm. Its name undoubtedly comes from the DUMNONII, a British tribe who were more than likely related to the Irish Fir Dhomhnann.

DUMNONII
British

An ancient Celtic tribe that probably gave their name to the large kingdom of DUMNONIA. They were possibly related to the Irish FIR DHOMHNANN.

DUN STALLION
Arthurian

One of ARTHUR's horses. Its spirit is said to haunt the village of CASTLE EDEN in County Durham.

DUNADD
Irish

The capital of DÁL RIADA in the Kintyre peninsula near Crinan.

DUNATIS
Gaulish

A generic name given to the deities of strongholds.

DURMART
Arthurian

The hero of the French romance *DURMART LE GALLOIS*, he fell in love with the Queen of IRELAND, FENISE (FENICE).

DURMART LE GALLOIS
Arthurian

A thirteenth-century French romance concerning the love of the hero, DURMART, for the Queen of IRELAND.

DUSIUS
General

The Celtic name for an *incubus*, a demon believed to have intercourse with sleeping women, who thereby conceive demonic children. The mother of MYRDDIN (MERLIN) was alleged by VORTIGERN's counsellors to have been visited by just such a being.

DWYFACH
Welsh

One of the two survivors, named in the *Trioedd Ynys Prydein*, of a flood that wiped out the entire population of WALES. The other survivor is named as DWYFAN. They escaped in a boat, and later repopulated Wales, but the individual genders of the survivors are not recorded. This story would appear to be a Welsh version of NOAH and the biblical Flood.

DWYFAN
Welsh

One of the two survivors, named in the *Trioedd Ynys Prydein*, of a flood, perhaps even the biblical Flood, that wiped out the entire population of WALES. The other survivor is named as DWYFACH. They escaped in a boat, here echoing the biblical Ark, and following the flood the pair repopulated Wales.

DYFED
Welsh

The modern name for DEMETIA, a kingdom in the south of WALES which GEOFFREY OF MONMOUTH says was ruled by STATER during the Arthurian period.

DYFRIG
Arthurian

The Welsh name for Saint DUBRICIUS.

DYLAN (EIL TON)
Welsh and Arthurian

The first baby to be born to ARIANRHOD as she undertook the rite to attest her virginity after she had been put up for a maiden's post at the court of MATH FAB MATHONWY. A golden-haired boy, he was immediately named Dylan. Growing to maturity in an instant, he set out for the sea, whose nature he assumed, thereafter being known as Dylan Eil Ton, or 'Dylan, Son of the Wave'. Some have sought to explain this curious tale by saying that the boy was drowned in the sea, and that is how he came to adopt the sea's nature. However, this is pure supposition, as no evidence, legendary or otherwise, exists to support the theory. His grave is said to be MAEN DYLAN, a stone that stands on a gravel bank approximately two miles south of CAER ARIANRHOD, about three-quarters of a mile offshore, and thus visible at low tide only.

DYLAN, SON OF THE WAVE
Welsh and Arthurian

The literal translation of DYLAN EIL TON.

DYNEVOR CASTLE
Arthurian
A castle in the vicinity of Llandeilo, DYFED. A cave in the park surrounding the castle is said to be one of the many possible sites for the confinement of MERLIN.

DYONAS
Arthurian
Possibly cognate with DIONES, Dyonas was the father of VIVIENNE, according to the *VULGATE VERSION*.

DYRNWYN
Welsh and Arthurian
The sword of RHYDDERCH HAEL, which would instantly burst into flame from the point to the cross if any man, save the true owner, drew it. It always numbered among the THIRTEEN TREASURES OF BRITAIN.

DYSGYFDAWD
Welsh and Arthurian
The father of GALL.

DYSGYL A GREN RHYDDERCH
Welsh and Arthurian
The platter of RHYDDERCH HAEL upon which any meat desired would appear. It always numbered among the THIRTEEN TREASURES OF BRITAIN.

DYWEL
Arthurian
The brother of GEREINT.

E

EACHTACH

Irish

One of the two daughters of DIARMAID UA DUIBHNE and GRÁINNE. She attacked FIONN MAC CUMHAILL and wounded him so severely that it took four years for him to be fully healed.

EACHTRA AN MHADRA MHAOIL

Arthurian

An Irish prose romance regarding a hapless Indian prince, ALEXANDER, who was enchanted and transformed into a doglike creature known as the CROP-EARED DOG.

EACHTRA MHELÓRA AGUS ORLANDO

Arthurian

A sixteenth-century Irish romance regarding ARTHUR's daughter MELORA that was perhaps inspired by the Italian school of chivalrous romances, particularly those of ARIOSTO.

EAGLE OF GWERNABWY

Welsh and Arthurian

The oldest living creature in the world. The Eagle of Gwernabwy is said to have helped CULHWCH and his companions by introducing them to the SALMON OF LLYN LLW, although some sources make the Salmon of Llyn Llw older than the eagle.

EANNA

Irish

The husband of one of MANANNÁN MAC LIR's daughters and the father of the maiden SCÁTHACH, whom FIONN MAC CUMHAILL, having been lured to Eanna's SÍDH, said he would marry for a year. The following morning, however, Fionn mac Cumhaill woke up to find himself far away from the sídh with no way back.

EBER (DONN)

Irish

One of the Sons of MÍL ÉSPÁINE to whom the

TUATHA DÉ DANANN King MAC CUILL fell in battle. His surname, which is not usually used in the source texts, seems to link him with the character of DONN, the churlish King of the Míl Éspáine who was drowned shortly after they had arrived in IRELAND, his death possibly being a punishment for killing Mac Cuill. His brother was EBER FINN.

EBER FINN

Irish

One of the leaders of the Sons of MÍL ÉSPÁINE and the brother of EBER DONN. After the death of his brother, he was involved in a struggle with EREMON, another of the leaders of the invasion, over who should rule IRELAND. AMHAIRGHIN decreed that Eremon should rule first, and that, upon his death, Eber Finn should rule. However, Eber Finn refused to accept this, and Ireland was split into two realms, Eber Finn taking the southern half, and Eremon the northern. Peace did not last long before war broke out. Eber Finn was killed and Eremon became the sole King of Ireland, which he ruled from TARA.

EBISSA

Arthurian

One of the sons of HENGIST, brother to AESC, OCTA, HARTWAKER, RONWEN and SARDOINE.

EBRAUC(US)

British and Arthurian

A legendary King of BRITAIN and the sixth king after BRUTUS. His rule was said to have started in 944 BC, when he founded the city of YORK. The Romans called this city *Eboracum* when they captured it from the BRIGANTES in AD 71 and made it their northern headquarters. Ebrauc was also alleged to have founded Edinburgh and to have had twenty wives, twenty sons and thirty daughters. Arthurian legends made him the founder of the CASTLE OF MAIDENS, which was originally known as the Castle of Mount AGNED.

ECHID

Irish

The father of NESSA, by whom he became the grandfather of CONCHOBAR MAC NESSA through Nessa's marriage to the giant FACHTNA.

ECHTRA CONDLA CHAIM MAIC CUIND CHETCHATHAIG

Irish

The section of the *Leabhar na hUidhre* (*The Book of the Dun Cow*) that tells the story of CONNLA and his elopement with a supernatural maiden. It was certainly written prior to 1106, for that is the recorded date of the murder of its scribe Maelmori ('Servant of Mary').

ECHTRA NERAI

Irish

The *Adventures of Nera*, an introductory tale to the *Taín Bó Cuailngè* in which the gods are regarded as demons that appear on the eve of SAMHAIN. NERA was the only one of AILILL's warriors brave enough to tie a withe around the leg of a hanged corpse, but the corpse came to life and asked Nera for a drink. He carried the corpse to a house and gave it some water, but it squirted that water in the faces of those sleeping there, and then died. Nera returned the corpse to the gallows. He then discovered the fort of Ailill burnt to the ground and a heap of human ashes nearby. Travelling to the SÍDH of Cruachan, Nera was told that what he had seen was a premonition that would come true unless he could persuade Ailill to destroy the sídh. This he did, and Ailill's forces promptly proceeded to flatten the sídh.

ECHTRAI

Irish

One of the two classifications of ancient Irish literature, the other being the IMMRAM. The *echtrai* are accounts of visits made by humans to supernatural lands, either by crossing endless tracts of water, or by entering one of the many SÍDH. The *immram* on the other hand is an account of a fantastic voyage to an island realm, either human or supernatural.

ECNE

Irish

The name of the three sons, or of the grandsons, of DANU, who is, in this instance, the daughter of the DAGHDHA. Ecne means 'knowledge' or 'poetry'. Some sources further complicate what is already a confused picture by saying that the three sons of Danu, all called Ecne, each had a single son, whom they also called Ecne. However, as Danu is often considered the goddess of light and knowledge, it may be that Ecne was simply an aspect of the goddess, and the story of the three or six young men carrying the same name was a later invention.

ECTOR

Arthurian

The father of KAY and foster father to ARTHUR, his name being the Welsh form of HECTOR. The baby Arthur was delivered to him by MERLIN and was raised by Ector until, when Arthur was fifteen, Ector took him and his son Kay to London for a tournament at which Kay was to be knighted, with Arthur acting as his squire. When, having found that he had forgotten Kay's sword, Arthur returned with the enchanted sword that had been placed in a stone to test who should become King of all England, Kay tried to claim that it was he who had drawn it. Ector, however, made Kay tell the truth, and so Arthur became king.

ECTOR DE MARIS

Arthurian

The son of King BAN of BENWICK (more commonly known as Ban of BRITTANY), whom he succeeded, and brother of Sir LANCELOT. He was in love with PERSE and rescued her from ZELOTES, to whom she had been promised by her father.

ECUNAVER

Arthurian

The King of KANEDIC, who was conquered by GAREL after he had declared that he intended to attack ARTHUR.

EDA ELYN MAWR

Arthurian

The name of ARTHUR's killer is not usually given. However, the Harlcian MS 4181 in the British Library (entry 42) gives the name of Eda Elyn Mawr as the man who inflicted Arthur's mortal wound at CAMLANN.

EDAEIN

Irish

The sister of CLIODNA and AEIFE. She and her sisters eloped from TÍR TAIRNGIRI with CIABHAN, LODAN and EOLUS, but MANANNÁN MAC LIR sent a huge wave after them, which engulfed the boat in which they had been travelling seconds after it had landed in IRELAND and either drowned the three sisters or carried them back to Tír Tairngiri.

ÉDÁIN

Irish

The daughter of EOCHAIDH AIREMH and ÉDÁIN ECHRAIDHE. She was mistakenly chosen by Eochaidh Airemh when the King was presented with fifty identical women, all of whom were the exact likeness of Édáin Echraidhe. She subsequently bore her father a son, the hero CONAIRE MÓR, long before the King realised his mistake.

ÉDÁIN (ECHRAIDHE)
Irish

The daughter of King AILILL who was described as the most beautiful woman in all IRELAND. Her name means 'Horse-riding Edain', and she is possibly the Irish equivalent of the Welsh RHIANNON and the Gaulish EPONA. Her hand was sought by OENGHUS MAC IN OG on behalf of his foster father MIDHIR, a god who lived in TÍR TAIRNGIRI. Although he lived in the SÍDH of BRÍ LEITH in County Longford, Midhir was a god associated with rebirth, rather than with the OTHERWORLD.

FUAMHNACH, the first wife of Midhir, was so jealous of the beauty of Édáin Echraidhe that she turned the girl into a pool of water. That pool changed into a worm, and the worm into an enormous and incredibly beautiful fly whose music filled the air. Although she was no longer the maiden he had longed to make his wife, Midhir was more than content to have Édáin Echraidhe remain in this unusual, but equally beautiful form. Seething with resentment, Fuamhnach conjured up a huge wind, which blew Édáin Echraidhe away to the rocky coastline, where she lay, buffeted by the waves, for seven years. At last Oenghus Mac in Og found the beautiful fly that was Édáin Echraidhe and placed her carefully in a crystal bower. Once again Midhir and Édáin Echraidhe had to endure the wrath of Fuamhnach, who thought she had seen the last of the girl. This time the wind that carried the unfortunate girl away deposited her in a wine glass and she was swallowed. However, being swallowed was not the end of Édáin Echraidhe, for the woman who swallowed her became pregnant, and, so some accounts say, ten or twelve years after her first birth, she was once more reborn, this time as Édáin, daughter of the daughter of the ULSTER hero ÉDAR.

At about the time Édáin came of age this second time around EOCHAIDH AIREMH became the King of Ireland, but as he was unmarried his warriors would not follow him. Learning of the uncompromising beauty of Édáin, he set out to claim her to be his wife. News of the girl's beauty reached Midhir, and he set out to TARA to reclaim the girl who could only be the reincarnation of his long lost wife. When Midhir claimed her, Édáin refused to leave Eochaidh Airemh without his permission. He at first refused, but swore to give up the girl if

Midhir could beat him in a chess contest. The god allowed Eochaidh Airemh to win the early round and accepted any forfeits the King might impose, one of which was to build a great causeway across the bogs of MEATH.

Having completed the causeway, Midhir returned to TARA to fight the deciding match. This he won and chose as his prize a kiss from Édáin. A month later, when Midhir returned to claim his fairly won prize, he found all the doors of Tara barred against him, while inside the King sat feasting with all his warriors. Unperturbed, the god simply appeared in their midst, seized Édáin and the pair flew out of the great hall, in the shape of swans, through the central smoke hole.

Eochaidh Airemh and his company set out in hot pursuit, and, when they reached the sídh of Brí Leith, they began to dig it up. Midhir appeared to them and promised to return Édáin to the King, upon which he produced fifty women, all of whom were the exact likeness of Édáin. Although Eochaidh Airemh chose carefully, the Édáin he chose was actually his own daughter, also called Édáin, although some call her ESS. It was quite a considerable time before the King realised his mistake, and by that time Édáin had borne the King a son, the hero CONAIRE MÓR.

ÉDAR
Irish

The hero of ULSTER whose daughter swallowed ÉDÁIN ECHRAIDHE (in the shape of a fly) when Édáin was blown into the glass of wine she was drinking on a wind conjured up by the jealous FUAMHNACH. The girl subsequently gave birth to Édáin Echraidhe for the second time.

EDEN
Arthurian

The name of an unidentified river. It would seem to be the river of that name to be found in Cumbria, for local legend says that UTHER, a giant in this instance, founded the kingdom of MALLERSTANG and tried to form a moat around his castle by diverting a river of this name.

EDINBURGH
Arthurian

During the Middle Ages this city was known as *Castellum Puellarum*, which has led to its being identified with the CASTLE OF MAIDENS. It is also the site of ARTHUR'S SEAT, a volcanic plug where ARTHUR was alleged to have watched his forces defeat the PICTS and Scots.

Edinburgh, Scotland, whose famous castle sits atop a volcanic plug where Arthur was alleged once to have sat.
(William Daniell, 1814. © Stapleton Collection/Corbis)

EDOR
Arthurian
An ancestor of LOT.

EFFLAM, SAINT
Arthurian
An Irish saint who is mentioned by the hagiologist Le Grand. However, Le Grand is not considered wholly reliable, as it appears that he may have altered some of his source material. He says that Efflam travelled to BRITTANY, where he found himself face to face with a decidedly unfriendly dragon. ARTHUR, badly equipped with just a club and a lionskin shield, came to his assistance, but to no effect. Efflam blessed Arthur for his help, and then put the monster to flight.

EFNISIEN
Welsh and Arthurian
The son of PENARDUN and EUROSSWYD, brother to NISIEN and half-brother of BENDIGEID VRAN. While MATHOLWCH, King of IRELAND, was in WALES seeking the hand of BRANWEN, daughter of LLYR and sister to Bendigeid Vran, Efnisien cruelly disfigured the hundreds of horses Matholwch had brought with him, an insult so bad that Matholwch took his revenge on Branwen by treating her cruelly after they had returned to Ireland. When Bendigeid Vran learnt of the suffering of his sister, he set out with his host to rescue her.

The Irish at first attempted to placate Bendigeid Vran by housing him in a splendid palace, but they had hidden one hundred warriors inside bags of provisions. Efnisien suspected the trick and circumvented it by crushing the heads of each of the hidden warriors while they were still in hiding. Matholwch and Bendigeid Vran met and decided that the best way to settle their argument was to bestow the kingship of Ireland on GWERN, the boy who had been born to Branwen and Matholwch. On hearing this, Efnisien cast the unfortunate boy into the fire and war broke out.

Because of the cauldron Bendigeid Vran had given Matholwch as a wedding gift, the Irish at first had

141

the upper hand, for they could restore their dead to life. Efnisien changed the fortunes of the Welsh when he managed to destroy the cauldron, but he was killed in the attempt. So absolute was the carnage that only five pregnant Irish women remained hidden in a cave, and only seven of the invaders returned across the Irish Sea.

EFRAWG
Welsh and Arthurian
Also EVRAWG
In the *MABINOGION* story of *PEREDUR*, the father of PEREDUR (PERCEVAL). Because the name means 'York', it would seem that this was not his true name, but was instead a title indicating the city he ruled.

EFRDDF
Welsh and Arthurian
The twin sister of URIEN, ruler of RHEGED.

EGLANTE
Arthurian
The mother of DODINEL the Savage.

EHANGWEN
Arthurian
This was the name of ARTHUR's hall, built by GWLYDDYN the carpenter, though its precise location remains a mystery. Some authorities say that it was situated at CAMELOT (wherever that might be), while others place it in various locations around the country, including CARLISLE and CASTLE EDEN in County Durham.

EIAN
Arthurian
The son of NASCIEN, father of JONAANS, and great-great-great-grandfather of GALAHAD.

EIDDILIG
Arthurian
Named in the Welsh *PEDWAR MARCHOG AR HUGAN LLYS ARTHUR* as one of the TWENTY-FOUR KNIGHTS of King ARTHUR's court.

EIGYR
Welsh and Arthurian
The Welsh form of IGRAINE. Her parentage in Welsh tradition is somewhat confused, although all the various pedigrees that exist tend to agree that she married GORLOIS, the Duke of CORNWALL. She then passed into the realm of Arthurian legend as the mother of King ARTHUR by UTHER.

EILHART VON OBERGE
Arthurian
The twelfth-century author of *Tristant*, which gives just one of the many variations on the story of TRISTAN and ISEULT.

EINION
Welsh and Arthurian
The hero of the Welsh folktale *EINION AND OLWEN*, in which he travels to the OTHERWORLD to marry OLWEN, the daughter of the chief giant YSPADDADEN. They had a child whom they named TALIESIN. Einion would appear to be a localised direct replacement for CULHWCH, the hero of the *MABINOGION* story of *CULHWCH AND OLWEN*, who is usually connected with the quest to marry Olwen. However, as *Culhwch and Olwen* is generally considered an Arthurian story, the reverse may be true, with Culhwch replacing Einion, whose story would then be the earlier.

EINION AND OLWEN
Welsh and Arthurian
A Welsh folktale in which the hero, EINION, undertakes to travel to the OTHERWORLD to marry OLWEN, the daughter of YSPADDADEN. It seems without doubt that Einion was a local hero who was a direct replacement in the region of Wales (where the tale originated) for CULHWCH, the hero normally associated with the quest to locate and marry Olwen, although the reverse could also be true, and Einion was replaced by Culhwch in a later Arthurian rendition of the story.

EIRE
General
The correct Gaelic name for IRELAND. It is derived from ÉRIU, one of the triad of goddesses who met the invading Sons of MÍL ÉSPÁINE. She promised that Ireland would forever be theirs, and they replied that the country would be named in her honour.

EISIRT
Irish
The FILI of IUBDAN, the King of FAYLINN. He told his King about a race of giants who lived in ULSTER (humans) and was clapped in irons for his audacity at challenging the power of the people of Faylinn, whose warriors were said to be able to fell a thistle with a single stroke, for Faylinn was the realm of elfin beings. Eisirt said that he would gather proof for the King, and was sent on his way. He later returned from the court of FERGHUS MAC LEDA with AEDA, a dwarf at the court of that

King, and placed Iubdan and his wife, BEBO, under a bond to visit Ferghus mac Leda. They did so but were taken captive, only to be released after Eisirt had led the people of Faylinn against the men of Ulster and plagued their land.

E(I)THNE
Irish

(1) The daughter of BALAR and, by CIAN, mother of LUGH, whom she conceived while imprisoned by her father, who had been told of a prophecy that any child of Eithne's would lead to his death and the end of the FOMHOIRÉ. She conceived triplets, but all but one of them was drowned on the instructions of Balar, the surviving child being conveyed to Cian, who raised the boy.

(2) The wife of ELCMAR. She was coveted by the DAGHDHA, who sent Elcmar on a diplomatic mission and then caused the sun to remain in the sky for nine months and Elcmar not to feel hungry for the same period. During his absence Eithne was seduced by the Daghdha and conceived a son, OENGHUS MAC IN OG, who was sent to be fostered by MIDHIR hours before Elcmar returned. Midhir subsequently sent the boy back to be fostered by Elcmar, who obviously believed that Oenghus Mac in Og was the son of Midhir.

This story is possibly later than the better-known story of Oenghus Mac in Og's conception and birth. In that version no mention is made of a maiden by the name of Eithne, for Oenghus Mac in Og's mother is BOANN, the sister of Elcmar, with whom she goes to stay, and it is while she is staying there that the Daghdha disposes of Elcmar for the nine months while Oenghus Mac in Og gestates and is subsequently born.

(3) The mistress of CÚ CHULAINN, whom he offended by omitting her when he distributed a flock of beautiful birds he had captured to the maidens of ULSTER. To appease her, he went in search of two more beautiful birds he had heard of, but fell foul of LI BAN and FAND, daughters of AED ABRAT, at whom he aimed his slingshot while they were in the form of birds. He lay almost dead for a year until Li Ban and Fand healed him. The story does not say whether he ever managed to appease Eithne.

(4) The daughter of the steward of ELCMAR, who remained in service after OENGHUS MAC IN OG had taken the SÍDH of BRUGH NA BÓINNE. At the same time as she was born, CURCOG was born to MANANNÁN MAC LIR, who sent his daughter to be fostered by Oenghus Mac in Og. Eithne later became her attendant. Eithne grew up into a beautiful young lady, but one day it was discovered that she neither ate nor drank, as she had been insulted by one of the TUATHA DÉ DANANN, and was instead sustained by an angel of God.

However, Manannán mac Lir and Oenghus Mac in Og brought two sacred cows to the sídh from a foreign land, and, since they had nothing to do with the Tuatha Dé Danann, Eithne was thenceforth sustained by their milk. She continued to thrive in this manner for 1,500 years until she was christened by Saint PATRICK, and subsequently died in that saint's arms after he had administered the last rites to her.

This story plainly owes its origins to a Christianisation of the earlier pagan tales, a process that often leaves the pagan myths in a confused state.

ELADU
Irish

The Father of the DAGHDHA, and possibly the husband of DANU, although this is by no means certain.

ELAINE
Arthurian

A form of Helen, this name is borne by at least six ladies in the Arthurian tales.

1 The daughter of King PELLES, who, with the aid of an enchanted potion administered by BRISEN, tricked LANCELOT into sleeping with his daughter, their night of enchanted passion leading to the conception and subsequent birth of Sir GALAHAD. Lancelot was said to have lain with her on a second occasion when he thought she was his beloved GUINEVERE, again under an enchantment, but this time at CAMELOT.

2 Elaine the White, the daughter of BERNARD OF ASTOLAT, and better known as the LADY OF SHALOTT. She fell in love with LANCELOT, who carried her sleeve during a joust, but when her love went unrequited she died for love of him. She was brought up the Thames in a boat to ARTHUR's court, bearing with her a letter explaining the circumstances of her death.

3 The daughter of PELLINORE who took her own life after the death of her lover, Sir MILES of the Laundes.

4 The wife of King NENTRES of GARLOT. She was the daughter of IGRAINE, sister to MORGAN Le Fay and MORGAUSE, and half-sister to ARTHUR.

5 The wife of BAN of BENWICK (Ban of BRITTANY) and mother of Sir LANCELOT.

6 Variously described as the daughter of either LOT or NENTRES, this Elaine was a niece of ARTHUR and fell in love with Sir PERCEVAL.

ELATHA(N)
Irish
A FOMHOIRÉ chieftain who had a relationship with ÉRI, a TUATHA DÉ DANANN woman. This led to the subsequent birth of BRES, who later become a tyrannical King of the Tuatha Dé Danann.

ELCM(H)A(I)R(E) OR ELKMAR
Irish
The foster father of OENGHUS MAC IN OG, who was the son of Elcmar's wife by the DAGHDHA, although other possibly earlier stories make Oenghus Mac in Og the son of Elcmar's sister, BOANN. The boy had originally been fostered by MIDHIR, but he subsequently returned the youth to his natural mother, with Elcmar still unaware of the child's true parentage. Oenghus Mac in Og subsequently succeeded in expelling Elcmar from his SÍDH, BRUGH NA BÓINNE, which then passed into his ownership. The earlier version of this story says that Brugh na Bóinne was originally the sídh of the Daghdha, and it was from him that Oenghus Mac in Og took possession.

ELEN
Welsh
The daughter of EUDAF and sister to CYNAN and GADEON. She accepted the marriage proposal of MACSEN, but said that she would not leave BRITAIN and that if he wanted to marry her he must come to her. This he did and stayed, thus neglecting Rome. A popular queen, she embarked on a road-building plan that earned her the name Elen Luyddogg ('Elen-of-the-Hosts'), which referred to the numbers of workmen she employed.

Seven years after their marriage, her husband received notice from Rome that, as he had been absent for so long, a new emperor had been chosen. She marched with her husband and her brothers to Rome at the head of a large British army, which succeeded in sacking Rome and reinstating Macsen as emperor, with Elen as empress. Cynan returned to Britain where he became king, while Gadeon settled in ARMORICA.

ELERGIA
Arthurian
A witch who imprisoned ARTHUR and from whom the King was rescued by TRISTAN, according to the Italian romance *TAVOLA RITONDA*.

ELF
Arthurian
The offspring of Prometheus, the classical Greek hero who stole fire from the gods, and a fairy from the gardens of Adonis. The inhabitants of FAIRYLAND, or FAERIE, claimed their descent from him. His son, ELFIN, ruled over both England and America.

ELFANT
Arthurian
A ruler of FAIRYLAND.

ELFAR
Arthurian
A ruler of FAIRYLAND who was said to have killed two giants, one of which had two heads, the other three.

ELFERON
Arthurian
A ruler of FAIRYLAND.

ELFICLEOS
Arthurian
A ruler of FAIRYLAND.

ELFILINE
Arthurian
A ruler of FAIRYLAND who built a golden wall around the city of Cleopolis, which had been founded by his predecessor ELFINAN.

ELFIN
Arthurian
The son of ELF, whom he succeeded as the ruler of FAIRYLAND, as well as ruling over both England and America.

ELFINAN
Arthurian
A ruler of FAIRYLAND who founded the city of Cleopolis.

ELFINELL
Arthurian
A ruler of FAIRYLAND who was said to have defeated the goblins in battle.

ELFINOR
Arthurian
A ruler of FAIRYLAND who built a brazen bridge upon the sea.

ELFLAND
Arthurian
An OTHERWORLD realm with whose king ROWLAND did battle and, by defeating him, so secured the release of his sister and brothers.

ELIABEL

Arthurian

Also ELIABELLA

Presumably identical with the ELIZABETH of Sir Thomas MALORY's works, she was the mother of TRISTAN in Italian romance.

ELIABELLA

Arthurian

Also ELIABEL

A cousin of ARTHUR who was, according to Italian romance, the mother of TRISTAN, and presumably identical with ELIZABETH, the sister of King MARK. She married King MELIODAS of LIONES to bring about peace between her new husband and Arthur, who had been at war.

ELIAVRES

Arthurian

A knight with magical powers or, more simply, a wizard. He fell in love with ARTHUR's niece YSAIVE, who was the wife of King CARADOC of VANNES AND NANTES. While Eliavres slept with Ysaive, resulting in the birth of CARADOC BRIEFBRAS, the wizard enchanted Caradoc and made him sleep with a bitch, a sow and a mare. When Caradoc Briefbras discovered the truth regarding his parentage, he told Caradoc, who, in wild fury, made Eliavres lie first with a bitch, by which he became the father of GUINALOT, then with a sow, by which he became the father of TORTAIN, and finally, in full reflection of the same partners forced on him by the wizard, Caradoc made Eliavres lie with a mare, by which he became the father of LORIGAL.

ELIAZAR

Arthurian

A son of PELLES, brother to ELAINE the White, and hence an uncle of GALAHAD.

ELIDUS

Arthurian

A King of IRELAND.

ELIEZER

Arthurian

A son of EVELAKE.

ELIS

Arthurian

The son of a duke who, thanks to a misprint in Caxton's original edition of Sir Thomas MALORY's *LE MORTE D'ARTHUR*, has also been regarded as having this name. The duke is in fact unnamed, and simply referred to as an uncle of ARTHUR.

ELISEG

Welsh

The son of GUAILLAUC and father of BROCHMAIL. A pillar, known as the Pillar of Eliseg, was erected in his honour by CONCENN, the last King of Powys, who died in Rome in 854. The pillar is located near the ruins of Valle Crucis abbey in CLWYD, and was examined in 1696 by Edward Llwyd, who made an invaluable record of the inscription, which was just visible at that time, although the crosshead had disappeared and the shaft of the pillar was broken in two. The inscription consisted of thirty-one lines divided into paragraphs, each of which was marked with a cross. The translation made by Llwyd of this inscription reads as follows

+ Concenn son of CADELL, Cadell son of Brochmail, Brochmail son of Eliseg, Eliseg son of Guaillauc.
+ And so Concenn, great-grandson of Eliseg, erected this stone for his great-grandfather Eliseg.
+ This is that Eliseg, who joined together the inheritance of Powys . . . out of the power of the ANGLES with his sword of fire.
+ Whosoever repeats the writing, let him give a blessing on the soul of Eliseg.
+ This is that Concenn who captured with his hand eleven hundred acres which used to belong to his kingdom of Powys . . .
+ [Illegible]
+ [Illegible]
+ BRITU son of VORTIGERN, whom GERMANUS blessed, and whom SEVIRA bore to him, daughter of MAXIMUS the King, who killed the King of the Romans.
+ CONMARCH painted this writing at the request of King Concenn.
+ The blessing of the Lord upon Concenn and upon his entire household and upon all the region of Powys until the day of doom.

Although it is quite obvious that the pillar was erected some time after the Welsh had been converted to Christianity, the inscription provides researchers with a valuable genealogy of the kings of Powys and confirms the historicity of the likes of Vortigern, his wife, father-in-law and son.

ELIVRI

Arthurian

The head groom in ARTHUR's stables, so presumably responsible for looking after the King's horse.

ELIWLOD

Arthurian

The son of MADOG, who was, in turn, the son of UTHER, thus making Eliwlod ARTHUR's nephew. Suggested as the original of Sir LANCELOT, he was named as one of the TWENTY-FOUR KNIGHTS of Arthur's court and, after his death, he appeared to Arthur in the guise of an eagle, according to the early Welsh poem *Ymddiddan Arthur a'r Eryr*.

ELIZABETH

Arthurian

Probably to be identified with ELIABEL or ELIABELLA from Italian romance, Elizabeth was the sister of King MARK of CORNWALL, wife of King MELIODAS of LIONES (LYONESSE) and mother of TRISTAN. While heavily pregnant, she entered the woods to search for her husband, went into labour and delivered Tristan, but died in so doing.

ELLEN

Arthurian

Referred to as Burd Ellen, *burd* meaning 'lady', in the Scottish ballad *CHILDE ROWLAND*, she was, according to that ballad, the daughter of ARTHUR.

ELLYLL

Welsh

The name given to an elf in Welsh tradition, elves being one class of the *Plant* (or 'children of') ANNWFN.

ELMET

British and Arthurian

An ancient Celtic kingdom, centred on Leeds, that certainly existed prior to the fifth century, and continues during the Arthurian period, but whose exact extent remains undetermined.

ELPHIN

Welsh and Arthurian

The son of GWYDDNO GARANHIR. He rescued the child from the leather bag that CERRIDWEN had thrown into the sea, naming the radiant child within TALIESIN. In return, he was rescued by the bard when he was held captive by MAELGWYN.

ELSA (OF BRABANT)

Arthurian

The daughter of the Duke of BRABANT. When she was besieged by Frederick de TELRAMUND, LOHENGRIN came to her aid and defeated her attacker. Lohengrin then married Elsa, but cautioned her that she was never to ask his name. Having borne him two children, she at length asked the forbidden question, upon which Lohengrin immediately departed.

ELUCIDATION

Arthurian

A 484-line-long prologue, in French, to the *CONTE DE GRAAL* by CHRÉTIEN DE TROYES.

ELUNED

Welsh and Arthurian

The owner of a ring that was numbered among the THIRTEEN TREASURES OF BRITAIN, and that made the wearer invisible.

ELUTHERIUS

Arthurian

The POPE who, at the request of King LUCIUS, sent the two emissaries DERUVIAN and PHAGAN to invigorate the work on the abbey at GLASTONBURY. This was said to have been in *c*. AD 166.

ELVA

Irish

The daughter of CATHBHADH and MAGA, she married UISNECH and by him became the mother of NAOISE, ARDÁN and AINNLE, collectively known as the sons of Uisnech.

ELVES

Arthurian

Although these Teutonic creatures do not figure elsewhere in Celtic mythology, they do appear in LAYAMON's works, in which they were said to have bestowed gifts upon ARTHUR at his birth, arranging for him to be long-lived, valiant and rich.

ELYADUS

Arthurian

The King of Sicily and father of FLORIANT, who was raised by MORGAN Le Fay.

ELYAN (THE WHITE)

Arthurian

The son of Sir BORS and the unnamed daughter of King BRANDEGORIS, who later became the Emperor of CONSTANTINOPLE.

ELYAS ANAIS

Arthurian

The proper name of the HERMIT KING, though that title was also applied to King PELLES. He was either a maternal or a paternal uncle of PERCEVAL, though the sources cannot agree on the actual lineage.

ELYZABEL

Arthurian

A cousin of GUINEVERE who was imprisoned by CLAUDAS on a charge of espionage. ARTHUR, at the behest of his queen, requested Elyzabel's release, and when this was refused he waged war on Claudas. It is possible that she is the original of ELIZABETH and ELIABEL, for etymologically the names are similar.

EMER

Irish

The daughter of FORGALL and sister of FIALL. She was wooed by CÚ CHULAINN, who travelled beyond ALBA to become a pupil of the prophetess SCÁTHACH to prove his worth. Having conceived a son with AÍFE, Cú Chulainn returned to IRELAND and, having killed Forgall, married Emer. Many years later a mysterious, magical youth appeared off the Irish coast in a bronze boat. This youth quickly disposed of CONALL CERNACH, so Cú Chulainn himself went to challenge him, even though Emer warned him that the youth could only be his own son. Cú Chulainn mortally wounded the boy, whereupon he revealed his name, CONALL, his son by Aífe.

EMHAIN ABHLACH

Irish and Arthurian

'Emhain of the Apple Trees', a paradisiacal land that is usually identified as the Isle of ARRAN. It also has associations with MANANNÁN MAC LIR, god of the sea, whose home was said to have been the Isle of MAN. Both islands have equal claim to be Emhain Abhlach, and, as is usual, no evidence exists to support the claim of one over the other. GEOFFREY OF MONMOUTH later associated this realm with AVALON.

EMHAIN MHACHA

Irish

The chief court of ULSTER, or ULAIDH, situated approximately two miles west of Antrim. Legend says that it was built by the five sons of DITHORBA, the brother of MACHA and CIMBAOTH. After the death of their father at the hands of Macha, who compelled her other brother, Cimbaoth, to marry her so that she became sole ruler of IRELAND, the five sons of Dithorba attacked Macha. She easily captured them and, tracing the outline of a great fort on the ground with the pin of her brooch, made the brothers build Emhain Mhacha, which means 'Brooch of Macha'.

It is most famous as the court of the treacherous CONCHOBAR MAC NESSA. As his first heroic act, CÚ CHULAINN defeated all fifty of the youths in the King's service while he was still a boy and known as SÉDANTA. The court was attacked and razed by FERGHUS MAC ROICH, DUBTHACH and CORMAC MAC DUBTHACH in response to the treachery of Conchobar mac Nessa, who had had the three emissaries travel to SCOTLAND to elicit the return of DERDRIU and the sons of UISNECH, promising them safety, but instead having the three young men, NAOISE, ARDÁN and AINNLE, killed by EOGHAN MAC DURTHACHT and his men.

EMMELINE

Arthurian

A blind girl, the daughter of Duke CONON of CORNWALL, who in DRYDEN's opera *KING ARTHUR* was betrothed to the King but was carried off by Oswald, the SAXON King of KENT. Her sight was restored to her by MERLIN while she was still Oswald's prisoner. Arthur eventually defeated Oswald, thus rescuing her.

EMPRESS OF CONSTANTINOPLE

Arthurian

Unnamed, this member of the imperial family of CONSTANTINOPLE gave a magical stone to PERCEVAL that rendered him invisible, and thus helped him in his fight against the AFANC.

EN MAC ETHOMAIN

Irish

The poet and *senchaid* (historian, genealogist and folklorist) at TARA when LUGH came to the court.

ENBARR

Irish

See AONBARR

ENDELIENTA, SAINT

Arthurian

The god-daughter of ARTHUR who owned a cow that was, by tradition, killed by the Lord of TRENTENY. Arthur either had him killed, or performed this deed himself, but, whatever the means of his death, Endelienta restored him to life.

ENEUAVC

Welsh

The daughter of BEDWYR (BEDIVERE) and sister of AMREN.

ENEYD

Welsh

According to some translations of the *MABINOGION*, Eneyd is one of the sons of DÔN, and thus a brother to the likes of ARIANRHOD, GWYDION FAB DÔN and GILFAETHWY.

ENFACES GAUVAIN
Arthurian

A French Arthurian poem that dates from the thirteenth century concerning the life of GAWAIN. This work is unusual in that it makes LOT, Gawain's father by MORGAUSE, a page at ARTHUR's court.

ENGLAND
General

The largest division of BRITAIN, lying off the north coast of FRANCE from which it is separated by the English Channel. The first Celts to land in England are traditionally thought to have arrived *c*. 600 BC. England remained a Celtic stronghold until the Roman invasion, although even then the English Celts retained a fair degree of autonomy. After the departure of the Romans, the country was laid open for invasion by the ANGLO-SAXONS, who pushed the Celts further and further west until they were confined to CORNWALL in the south-west or in WALES. Very little of the Celtic way of life in England has survived, except in these small areas.

ENGRES
Arthurian

A king, the brother of ISEULT, according to the Icelandic *SAGA OF TRISTRAM*, who offered his sister's hand to whomsoever managed to kill a dragon.

ENID(E)
Arthurian

The heroine of *EREC ET ENIDE* by CHRÉTIEN DE TROYES and the Welsh variant *GEREINT AND ENID*. In both versions she is the wife of the hero, either EREC or GEREINT. *Erec et Enide* says that she was the daughter of LICONAUS and TARSENESYDE, while *Gereint and Enid* gives her father as YNWYL, her mother remaining unnamed.

ENNA
Irish

The wife of DUB who caused the seas to swell and drown AIDE, wife of AED, and her family, although usually the casting of the spell is attributed to her husband.

ENYGEUS
Arthurian

The sister of JOSEPH OF ARIMATHEA who married BRONS and became the mother of ALAN.

EOCHAID(H)
Irish

1 'Beautiful', the name originally given to BRES, although this may have simply been a title, for he is also given the title GORMAC, 'dutiful son', to which he certainly did not live up.
2 An alternative name, sometimes used for EREMON.
3 The son of ERC. Eochaidh became King of the FIR BHOLG and was killed during the First Battle of MAGH TUIREDH.

EOCHAIDH AIREMH
Irish

The King of IRELAND who married the reincarnated ÉDÁIN ECHRAIDHE. When news of this reached MIDHIR, the god travelled to TARA to reclaim the woman who could only be his former, and long lost, second wife. Édáin Echraidhe accepted Midhir's account, but would not leave without the consent of Eochaidh Airemh. The King refused, but accepted the challenge of Midhir to a chess match, the winner being granted a boon. Midhir lost the early game, his forfeit being to build a huge causeway for the King across the bogs of MEATH, but he won the final match and claimed his former wife, returning one month later to collect her. However, Eochaidh Airemh had barred all the doors of Tara against Midhir, so the god simply appeared among the company, took hold of Édáin Echraidhe and flew up with her through the smoke hole of the great hall in the guise of a pair of swans.

Eochaidh Airemh set out in hot pursuit, and, when he reached the SÍDH of BRÍ LEITH, began to dig it up. Midhir appeared to the King and said that he would return Édáin Echraidhe, although he then produced fifty identical women, all of whom were the exact likeness of Édáin Echraidhe. Eochaidh Airemh chose carefully, but he chose his own daughter, ÉDÁIN, and did not realise his mistake until well after that girl had borne him the son CONAIRE MÓR.

Other accounts of this story say that the child born to Eochaidh Airemh and his daughter, here named as ESS to save confusion, was a girl by the name of MESS BUACHALLA. She then became the mother of Conaire Mór through her union with ETERSCEL, when that king flew into the house in which she was living in the guise of a bird and left again afterwards in the same manner.

EOCHAIDH BRES
Irish

'Beautiful Bres', the name by which BRES was

originally called by his parents, although his later actions caused the 'Eochaidh' to be dropped so that he became simply known as Bres.

EOCHAIDH OLLATHAIR
Irish

'Eochaidh, the Great Father', one of the terms of reverence given to the DAGHDHA, another being RUADH ROFHESSA ('Mighty and Most Learned One').

EOCHO GLAS
Irish

Possibly the brother of EOCHO ROND, Eocho Glas was responsible for the imprisonment of the sons of DOEL whom CÚ CHULAINN was cursed to find by Eocho Rond in the *Longes mac nDuil Dermait*. When Cú Chulainn and his companions arrived at the SÍDH of Eocho Glas, he succeeded in fending off Cú Chulainn several times before he was killed and the sons of Doel were freed.

EOCHO MUMHO
Irish

Quite possibly a historical character, Eocho Mumho was the alleged tenth king in succession from EREMON. The county of MUNSTER is said to have derived its name from this king, for Munster in Irish is *Mumhan*.

EOCHO ROND
Irish

The father of FINDCHOÉM. Eocho Rond is a mysterious character who appears in the *Longes Mac nDuil Dermait* in which he curses CÚ CHULAINN, a curse that will remain on him until he has discovered the whereabouts of the missing sons of DOEL. His brother appears to have been EOCHO GLAS, whom Cú Chulainn kills and then returns to EMHAIN MHACHA, where it becomes apparent that Eocho Rond had cursed Cú Chulainn because the hero loved his daughter Findchoém, whom he was now compelled to hand over as Cú Chulainn had completed the set task.

EOCHU MUGMEDÓN
Irish

The husband of the SAXON CAIRENN and, by her, the father of NIAL NOÍGIALLACH.

EOGABAL
Irish

The father of AINÉ and AILLEANN. He was killed by FERCHESS.

EOG(H)AN
Irish

Mentioned in the *Leabhar Gabhála* as being hostile to the TUATHA DÉ DANANN. Later tradition makes him the son of OILILL. He killed LUGAID MAC CON, which led to the Battle of MAGH MUCRIME, in which Quill's seven sons, Eoghan among them, perished.

EOGHAN MAC DURTHACHT
Irish

A vassal of CONCHOBAR MAC NESSA, who, on that King's orders, killed the sons of UISNECH – ARDÁN, AINNLE and NAOISE – when they returned from exile in SCOTLAND.

EOL
Irish

A supernatural being who appears in a fragmentary text as an ally of MANANNÁN MAC LIR who, on one occasion, fought CÚ CHULAINN. The outcome, regrettably, is not known, but it seems likely that Eol perished.

EOLUS
Irish

One of the two companions of CIABHAN, the other being LODAN, who travelled to TÍR TAIRNGIRI and eloped from there with the sisters CLIODNA, AEIFE and EDAEIN. One account of the story says that all six, along with some men from the LAND OF PROMISE, were drowned by a huge wave sent after them by MANANNÁN MAC LIR. Another says that only the three sisters drowned, while a third says that the three maidens were carried back to Tír Tairngiri by the wave.

EOPA
Arthurian

The SAXON who, at the casual instigation of VORTIGERN's son PASCHENT, poisoned AMBROSIUS AURELIUS and later fell in battle against UTHER.

EPONA
Gaulish

'The Great Mare', the goddess of a horse cult who is most likely to be identified with the Irish ÉDÁIN ECHRAIDHE or MACHA and the Welsh RHIANNON. As goddess of horses, she was of great importance within a horse-based culture such as that of the Celts. Her image appears on over 300 stones in GAUL, although rarely in BRITAIN, and she is usually depicted riding side-saddle. In Romano-

Celtic imagery she is constantly associated with corn, fruit and, strangely, serpents – strangely because serpents are natural enemies of horses. These associations led to her also being considered a goddess of fertility and nourishment.

ÉRAINN
Irish

The eponymous ancient rulers of IRELAND. Their name undoubtedly comes from the goddess ÉRIU, the eponym of EIRE or Ireland.

ERBIN
Arthurian

The father of GEREINT, although according to the Life of Saint Cyby this role is reversed and Gereint is given as the father of Erbin.

ERC
Irish

1 The father of EOCHAIDH and thus one of the FIR BHOLG.
2 The son of CAIRPRE, who appears in the *Taín Bó Cuailngè*. He joined forces with the three monstrous sons of CALATIN and LUGAID, the son of CÚ ROÍ MAC DÁIRI, and marched against CÚ CHULAINN. During the fight that was to result in the death of Cú Chulainn, Erc used that hero's infallible spear, the GAE BOLGA, to kill Grey of MACHA.

ERCOL
Irish

The husband of GARMNA. According to one account of the *Fledd Bricrenn*, CÚ CHULAINN and his competitors for the right of champion were sent to Ercol to be judged. He challenged them to attack him and his steed. LOEGHAIRE BUADHACH's horse was killed by Ercol's horse and he fled to EMHAIN MHACHA and said that the others had been killed. CONALL CERNACH also fled, but Cú Chulainn fought on until Grey of MACHA killed Ercol's horse, and Cú Chulainn carried Ercol back to Emhain Mhacha, where he found the entire company lamenting his death. The judgement of champion was awarded to Cú Chulainn, but the others refused to accept it, so CONCHOBAR MAC NESSA sent them to CÚ ROÍ MAC DÁIRI.

EREC
Arthurian

Usually given as the son of LAC, King of NANTES, whom he succeeded, although the Norse version of his story, *EREX SAGA*, names his father as ILAX.

The hero of *EREC ET ENIDE* by CHRÉTIEN DE TROYES, he first encountered his future wife, ENIDE, when he gave chase to someone who had insulted Queen GUINEVERE. He gave up his knightly adventures when he married Enide, but when she later scolded him for doing so, he undertook some more.

EREC
Arthurian

Late twelfth- or early thirteenth-century Middle High German romance by HARTMANN VON AUE concerning the exploits of EREC that closely follows the earlier work of CHRÉTIEN DE TROYES.

EREC ET ENIDE
Arthurian

French romance, written *c.* 1160, by CHRÉTIEN DE TROYES. Introducing the characters of EREC and ENIDE, the work was followed very closely by HARTMANN VON AUE in his work *EREC*, which was probably written within forty years of the original. Welsh romancers substituted their own hero for Erec in their version of the story, *GEREINT AND ENID*.

EREM
Irish

A son of MÍL. His trapper, COBA, was said to have been the first to set a trap and pitfall in IRELAND.

EREMON
Irish

One of the Sons of MÍL ÉSPÁINE, he became the first King of all IRELAND after the death of EBER DONN and EBER FINN, his joint leaders in the expedition from Spain to Ireland. Eber Donn died before landing, although according to some he may have died shortly afterwards. AMHAIRGHIN then decreed that Eremon should rule until he died, when the kingship would pass to Eber Finn. Eber Finn refused, and so the country was divided into two, Eremon ruling over the northern half, and Eber Finn over the southern portion. Peace did not last long, and the two sides went to war. Eber Finn was killed, and Eremon ruled as sole King of Ireland from his court at TARA. Sometimes known as EOCHAIDH.

EREX SAGA
Arthurian

Norse saga concerning EREC that is undoubtedly based on *EREC ET ENIDE* by CHRÉTIEN DE TROYES.

The ruins of Tintagel Castle, Cornwall, where Uther was said to have lain with Igraine, the union leading to the birth of King Arthur. (© Jean Williamson/Mick Sharp)

Mount Snowdon, the highest peak in Wales. (© Jean Williamson/Mick Sharp)

Winchester, Hampshire, which has many Arthurian connections, including being one of the possible locations for Camelot. (By R. Ackermann, 1816. © Historical Picture Archive/Corbis)

Bamburgh Castle, Northumberland, possibly once known as Joyous Gard, the home of Sir Lancelot. (© Mick Sharp)

Below: *Sewingshields, Northumberland, one of the many locations where King Arthur and his knights are said to be sleeping.* (© 2000 Graeme Peacock)

Above: *The ill-fated lovers:* Dido and Aeneas, *by Nicolas Verkolye.* (Courtesy of the J. Paul Getty Museum, Los Angeles)

Left: *Sir Galahad receiving the keys to the Castle of the Maidens.* (Edwin Austin Abbey, 1895. © Burstein Collection/ Corbis)

St Joseph of Arimathea, the uncle of Jesus who was said to have traded for tin in Cornwall. Detail from Pietà *by Raphael.* (© Burstein Collection/Corbis)

Parsifal participates in the Quest for the Holy Grail. (Ferdinand Leeke, nineteenth century. © Christie's Images/Corbis)

Above: The Battle of the Amazons *by Peter Paul Rubens (c. 1617), depicting the ferocity with which these classical warrior maidens fought.* (Bridgeman Art Library/Alte Pinakothek, Munich, Germany)

Opposite page: *Oberon and Titania, King and Queen of the Fairies, from* A Midsummer Night's Dream. (© Bettmann/Corbis)

Left: *Isolde asks for the protection of Guinevere. From* Roman de Tristan, *fifteenth century.* (© Archivo Iconografico. S.A./Corbis)

Below: *The Bayeux Tapestry, which depicts the Norman invasion of England.* (© Gianni Dagli Orti/Corbis)

ERFDDF
Welsh and Arthurian
The daughter of CYNFARCH by NEFYN and twin sister of URIEN, according to the Welsh *Trioedd Ynys Prydein*.

ÉRI
Irish
Possibly a variant of ÉRIU, Éri is recorded as the TUATHA DÉ DANANN mother of LUGH by DELBAETH, one of the monstrous FOMHOIRÉ. However, there appears to be a confusion here, as Éri is also recorded as one of the Fomhoiré, the sister of ELATHA by whom she became the mother of BRES.

ERIES
Arthurian
A son of LOT, perhaps originally identical with GAHERIS, he became one of King ARTHUR's knights.

ERIN
Irish
A mythical Irish queen whose name is also the ancient Gaelic name for IRELAND, a name still in use poetically.

ÉRIU
Irish
One of the three aspects of the SOVEREIGNTY OF IRELAND, the other two being BANBHA and FÓDLA. The wife of MAC GRÉINE, she was wooed by AMHAIRGHIN, who promised her that the land would bear her name for all time. In turn, she promised that IRELAND would belong to the invading Sons of MÍL ÉSPÁINE until the end of time. However, she also warned DONN, the discourteous King of the Sons of Míl Éspáine, that neither he nor his heirs would enjoy the land. He drowned soon after this encounter and was buried on the island of TECH DUÍN, to which he still welcomes dead warriors. It is quite possible that Ériu is the same as the earlier ÉRI.

ERLAN
Arthurian
An ancestor of LOT of LOTHIAN.

ERMALEUS
Arthurian
The son of the King of ORKNEY and GAWAIN's cousin, he was defeated by BIAUSDOUS and sent as a captive to ARTHUR. He appears in the romance *Beaucilous*.

ERMID
Arthurian
A brother of GEREINT.

ERMINE
Arthurian
A sister of ARTHUR who is identifiable with ANNA. Some sources say that she married BUDIC while her sister married LOT, but it is more normal to equate Anna/Ermine with the wife of Lot.

ERMINIA
Arthurian
The realm of ROULAND, the father of TRISTAN by BLANCHEFLEUR, according to one medieval romance.

ERYRI
Arthurian
The name by which GEOFFREY OF MONMOUTH refers to YR WYDDFA FAWR or, more usually nowadays, Mount SNOWDON. He states that it was on this mountain that ARTHUR slew the giant RITHO.

ESCANOR
Arthurian
The name of at least three knights from the Arthurian tales.
1 A knight whose strength grew to its peak at noon, and then lessened. Appearing in *L'Atre Perileux*, he absconded with ARTHUR's female cupbearer, but was pursued and eventually killed by GAWAIN.
2 Escanor Le Beau. Appearing in the obscure French romance *Escanor*, this knight fought a duel with GAWAIN, after which the two became firm friends.
3 Escanor Le Grand. The son of a giant and a witch, and the uncle of ESCANOR Le Beau, he also appears in *Escanor*, and held GRIFLET prisoner.

ESCAVALON
Arthurian
The King of this realm is named as the father of FLORIE, who married GAWAIN and became the mother of WIGALOIS by him.

ESCLABOR
Arthurian
Also ASTLABOR
A nobleman from BABYLON and the father of PALAMEDES. Sent to Rome as part of a tribute, he saved the Roman Emperor's life. In due course he

arrived in LOGRES, saved the life of King PELLINORE, and then hurried on to CAMELOT.

ESCLADOS
Arthurian

The defender of a wondrous fountain in the forest of BROCELIANDE, he was killed by OWAIN, who married his widow, LAUDINE. This marriage of the victor to the widow of the vanquished is thought to encapsulate a pagan custom whereby the victor was ritually married to the territory of whomsoever he defeated.

ESCLARIMONDE
Arthurian

A fairy who was the lover of both ESCANOR Le Beau and BRIAN DES ILES.

ESCLARMONDE
Arthurian

The wife of HUON. She was taken by MORGAN Le Fay to the TERRESTRIAL PARADISE, bathed there in the FOUNTAIN OF YOUTH and was changed by Jesus into a fairy. This story appears in *Le Chanson d'Esclarmonde*, a sequel to *HUON DE BORDEAUX*, which gives, as a reason for this episode, the fact that HUON's right to the throne of the kingdom of FAERIE was disputed by ARTHUR, who had resided there since his earthly days had come to an end. The fairy folk refused to obey Huon because he had not married one of their people and so, by changing Esclarmonde into a fairy, the problem was resolved, and Huon could ascend the throne.

ESCOL
Arthurian

The son of the King of IRELAND, he is simply described as a follower of ARTHUR.

ESCORDUCARLA
Arthurian

The Lady of VALLONE, who became enamoured of MERLIN and planned to make him her prisoner. The plan, however, backfired, and Escorducarla ended up as Merlin's prisoner instead.

ESIAS
Irish

A wizard who lived in GORIAS. He is one of the four wizards said to have taught the TUATHA DÉ DANANN their magical arts. He is also said to have presented them with the invincible spear of LUGH. His three co-teachers were MORFESSA of FALIA, USCIAS of FINDIAS and SIMIAS of MURIAS.

ESS
Irish

According to some sources, the daughter of EOCHAIDH AIREMH by the mortal ÉDÁIN was called Ess, although this name seems to have been derived, or even invented, as an attempt to avoid obvious confusion between mother and daughter. Under this name she is said to have born MESS BUACHALLA to her father, and it was Mess Buachalla, rather than Ess herself, who became the mother of CONAIRE MÓR. The more usual version of this story makes Conaire Mór the son of Eochaidh Airemh and Édáin. In the variant where Ess is the mother of Mess Buachalla, it is recorded that, after Eochaidh Airemh realised his mistake, he attacked MIDHIR, who restored the true Édáin Echraidhe to him. Later Midhir's loss was avenged by his son SIUGMALL, who killed Eochaidh Airemh.

ESTE, HOUSE OF
Arthurian

Italian family who were historical rulers of Ferrara between 1000 and 1875. According to ARIOSTO, BRADMANTE, a female warrior of the Carolingian era (AD 751–987), was told that the House of Este would descend from her.

ESTOIRE DEL SAINTE GRAAL
Arthurian

A thirteenth-century French romance that forms a part of the *VULGATE VERSION*. It is unusual in identifying the WASTE LAND of the GRAIL legends with WALES, an association that is found in no other source, the connection possibly being made by means of a transliterative error.

ESTONNE
Arthurian

The father of PASSALEON and LORD OF THE SCOTTISH WILDERNESS, he was killed by BRUYANT the Faithless.

ESTORAUSE
Arthurian

The pagan King of SARRAS who, when dying, asked forgiveness of BORS, PERCEVAL and GALAHAD for imprisoning them, forgiveness that was forthcoming, which seems to suggest that Estorause was converted on his deathbed.

ESTRANGOT
Arthurian

A variant name applied to ILLE ESTRANGE, the kingdom of VAGOR.

ESTREGALES

Arthurian

The kingdom of LAC, who was also the ruler of the Black Isles and the father of EREC, BRANDILES and JESCHUTÉ.

ESTRILDIS

British

A beautiful German maiden who was taken captive by LOCRINUS, who wanted to make her his wife. However, Locrinus was already betrothed to GWENDOLEN, the daughter of CORINEUS, who made Locrinus honour his promise by force. After his marriage, Locrinus installed Estrildis in a house in TROIA NOVA and made her his mistress. During the seven years Estrildis was kept in hiding, she bore him a daughter, HABREN, while Gwendolen bore him a son, MADDAN.

After the death of Corineus, Locrinus deserted Gwendolen and made Estrildis his queen. Gwendolen raised an army in CORNWALL and marched against her estranged husband, killing him in a battle near the River Stour. Gwendolen then commanded that Estrildis and Habren be drowned in a river, which she also decreed would thenceforth be named Habren in honour of Locrinus' daughter. Habren became SABRINA in Latin, the river today being known as the River SEVERN.

ESUS

Gaulish

A mysterious deity who appears to be connected to a lost myth involving the ritual felling of trees, and whose totem animals appear to be three cranes and a bull. A Romano-Celtic altar to Esus depicts a man cutting down a tree. He seems to have connections with TARANIS and TEUTATES to form a triad of powerful deities. Human sacrifices are said to have been made to all three gods. See also AESUS.

ÉTAIN

Irish

See ÉDÁIN ECHRAIDHE.

ÉTAIN (OIG)

Irish

A variant of ÉDÁIN. The epithet 'Oig' means 'the younger', and is applied as a means of identifying this Édáin from ÉDÁIN ECHRAIDHE.

ETAN

Irish

The sister of LOEG with whom CÚ CHULAINN spent one night, giving her a ring as a token, *en route*

to discover the whereabouts of the sons of DOEL, this story appearing in the *Longes mac nDuil Dermait*.

ÉTAR

Irish

The father of the mortal ÉDÁIN, his wife becoming pregnant after she had swallowed the fly into which ÉDÁIN ECHRAIDHE had been transformed. Étar also appears in a story about two kings who had incredibly beautiful daughters, the other king being CAIBELL. The hands of the kings' daughters were sought in marriage, and the two kings offered battle to test the worthiness of the suitors. The battle raged long and hard, but finally Caibell and the two suitors were killed, Étar alone surviving.

ETER-SCEL, -SKEL

Irish

One of the possible fathers of CONAIRE MÓR, the more usual father being EOCHAIDH AIREMH. In the version where Eterscel is the father, he is married to MESS BUACHALLA, the daughter of Eochaidh Airemh and the reincarnated ÉDÁIN, although a further version makes Mess Buachalla the daughter of Eterscel and ESS and thus introduces the incestuous conception of Conaire Mór in a different form.

ETHAL ANUBAL

Irish

A prince of CONNACHT, father of CAER, and thus the father-in-law of OENGHUS MAC IN OG. When Oenghus Mac in Og came to him to ask for his daughter's hand, he replied that his daughter was more powerful than he was and that Oenghus Mac in Og would have to persuade her without his help. He did, however, explain to Oenghus Mac in Og how he might win his daughter, who spent alternate years in the form of a beautiful maiden and a magnificent swan.

ETHLINN

Irish

One of the names given to the daughter of BALAR who became the mother of LUGH. She is better known as EITHNE.

ETHNEA

Irish

A variant of EITHNE, the mother of LUGH.

ETNA, MOUNT

Arthurian

More normally associated with classical mythology, this active volcano on Sicily is considered by some to be one of the possible last resting places of

ARTHUR. It seems likely that the Arthurian tales were carried to Sicily during the Norman occupation of that island.

ETTARD

Arthurian

The beloved of PELLEAS, she did not reciprocate his feelings. NIMUE cast an enchantment over her and she fell in love with Pelleas, but, under another enchantment cast by Nimue, Pelleas no longer loved her, having transferred his feelings to Nimue herself. Ettard died of her then unrequited love for Pelleas.

EUDAF

Welsh and Arthurian

The father of CYNAN, GADEON and ELEN. He became King of BRITAIN after MACSEN, Elen's husband, removed BELI, son of MANOGAN, and placed Eudaf on the throne.

EUGENIUS

Arthurian

A King of SCOTLAND and an ally of MORDRED, according to the *SCOTORUM HISTORIAE* of BOECE, he captured GUINEVERE, who remained a prisoner of the PICTS.

EURIC

Arthurian

A historic King of the Visigoths between AD 466 and 484. He was opposed by the Emperor ANTHEMIUS, who counted RIOTHAMUS among his supporters.

EUROSSWYD

Welsh

The father of EFNISIEN and NISIEN by PENARDUN, which makes his children the half-brothers of MANAWYDAN FAB LLYR, and the stepbrothers of BRANWEN and BENDIGEID VRAN.

EUSTACE

Arthurian

The Duke of CAMBENET, he was one of the eleven leaders who rebelled against the youthful ARTHUR at the outset of his reign.

EVADEAM

Arthurian

A man who fell under an enchantment and was transformed into a dwarf. GAWAIN, who had been told that he would assume the shape of the next person he met, came across Evadeam and, while Evadeam regained his original form, Gawain became a dwarf. Eventually Gawain was restored to his former self and Evadeam was made a KNIGHT OF THE ROUND TABLE.

EVAINE

Arthurian

The sister of ELAINE, wife of BAN. She became the wife of BORS and mother of LIONEL and the younger Bors. Following the death of her husband, she became a nun, having left her children in the care of PHARIEN.

EVANDER

Arthurian

One of the various kings that were said to have ruled SYRIA during the traditional Arthurian period.

EVDAF

Arthurian

Also EUDAF

According to the paternal pedigree of ARTHUR in *BONEDD YR ARWR*, Evdaf was the son of KRADOC and the father of KYNAN. GEOFFREY OF MONMOUTH makes him OCTAVIUS, Duke of GWENT. The uncle of CONAN MERIADOC, he subsequently became King of BRITAIN.

EVELAKE

Arthurian

A king who was born in FRANCE. Sent to Rome as part of a tribute, he afterwards travelled to SYRIA, but there he slew the governor's son and had to flee to BABYLON, where he helped the King, THOLOMER, and as a reward was given land. He became the king of SARRAS and was baptised by JOSEPH OF ARIMATHEA, at which time he took the name MORDRAIN. He had two sons, ELIEZER and GRIMAL. He is associated with the stories of the Holy GRAIL, for it was said that he lived with un-healing wounds, sustained only by the Sacred Host, and would remain that way until the knight who would achieve his quest for the Holy Grail should release him. Evelake might, in origin, have been the father of MODRON, who is named as AVALLOC in the Welsh *TRIADS*. This further leads him to an association with AVALON, as Avalloc is thought to have been a god associated with apples, and Avalon is sometimes referred to as the Isle of APPLES.

EVGEN

Arthurian

According to the sixteenth-century maternal pedigree for ARTHUR of Grufudd Hiraethog, Evgen is said to have been among his ancestors.

EVRAIN

Arthurian

One of the wizards who was responsible for changing BLONDE ESMERÉE into a serpent.

EVRAWG

Arthurian

According to Welsh tradition, the father of PEREDUR (PERCEVAL).

EXCALIBUR

British and Arthurian

The romanticized magical sword of ARTHUR that was given to him by the LADY OF THE LAKE. The story goes that MERLIN was often afraid that Arthur would fall in battle, and so decided that he should have his own special sword. Therefore, Merlin took Arthur on a journey to the shores of a wide and still lake. There, in the middle, Arthur saw an arm, clothed in rich samite (silk), rise from the calm waters, the hand clasping a fair sword.

Merlin advised Arthur that he must speak kindly to the Lady of the Lake in order to obtain the sword. Sure enough, she invited Arthur to row out to the centre of the lake to take the sword and its scabbard. Returning to the shore, Merlin asked which he preferred, sword or scabbard? Arthur considered the question, and then replied that he preferred the sword, to which Merlin added that the scabbard was worth ten of the sword, for while Arthur carried the scabbard he would never lose blood, no matter now sorely wounded he might be.

Some sources say that, knowing he was dying, Arthur passed Excalibur on to GAWAIN. However, the most popular end to the life of Excalibur is that it was returned to the Lady of the Lake by Sir BEDIVERE after Arthur's last battle at CAMLANN. On the first occasion that Bedivere returned from the lake, having hidden Excalibur, meaning to keep the sword for himself, Arthur asked him what he had seen. Bedivere's answer, that he had seen nought but wind and waves, told Arthur that his instructions had not been carried out. The second time Bedivere carried out Arthur's orders and hurled the sword out over the lake. As it fell towards the water, an arm appeared and, having caught the sword, drew it back under the waters. Returning once again to Arthur, Bedivere recounted what he had seen and this time Arthur knew all was well.

Some sources incorrectly state that Excalibur was the SWORD IN THE STONE, but, even though this is not the accepted state of affairs, they do make partial amends by saying that it was placed in the stone by the Lady of the Lake.

Sir Thomas MALORY does not name the sword in his *LE MORTE D'ARTHUR*. In the early Welsh story of *CULHWCH AND OLWEN*, the sword is called CALADVWLCH, which can be linguistically linked with the magical sword CALADBOLG (derived from *calad* – 'hard' – and *bolg* – 'lightning'), a sword borne by Irish heroes, and in particular CÚ CHULAINN. GEOFFREY OF MONMOUTH calls the sword CALIBURNUS, and so derives the Excalibur of the romances.

F

FACHTNA (FATHACH)
Irish
The giant King of ULSTER, the husband or lover of NESSA, and, according to some, the father by Nessa of CONCHOBAR MAC NESSA. His son, DARA, was the owner of the DONN CUAILNGÈ, the huge brown bull, to gain possession of which MEDHBHA and AILILL attacked Ulster. The mother of Dara is not named, but it seems reasonable to assume that it was not Nessa.

FAEBOR BEG-BEOIL CUIMDIUIR FOLT SCENBGAIRIT SCEO UATH
Irish
The second ridiculous name that the MÓRRÍGHAN used when her identity was asked by CÚ CHULAINN in his defence of ULSTER against the forces of MEDHBHA and AILILL. The first name she gave was UAR-GAETH-SCEO LUACHAIR-SCEO.

FAERIE
Arthurian
Alternative name for FAIRYLAND, the allegorical realm that is SPENSER's vision of England.

FAERIE KING, THE
Arthurian
An unpublished seventeenth-century poem by Samuel Sheppard that tells how BYANOR received a sword that had once belonged to King ARTHUR.

FAERIE KNIGHT, THE
Arthurian
The son of CAELIA and TOM A'LINCOLN, ARTHUR's illegitimate son, and thus the grandson of ARTHUR himself.

FAERIE QUEENE, THE
Arthurian
The epic, unfinished, allegorical work of Edmund SPENSER that features the uncrowned King ARTHUR, and remains the poet's most famous work. In the poem, England is represented as FAIRYLAND, where Arthur had adventures before being crowned and where he became enamoured with GLORIANA (representing Queen Elizabeth I), the daughter of OBERON and TITANIA.

FAIRYLAND
Arthurian
Also FAERIE
The allegorical vision of the England of SPENSER's day as used in his poem *THE FAERIE QUEENE*, and a realm in which ARTHUR had adventures before becoming king. The inhabitants of this land claimed their descent from ELF, a creation of Prometheus, the classical Greek hero who stole fire from the gods, and a fairy from the gardens of Adonis, also a hero from classical Greek mythology. Elf's son was called ELFIN and ruled both England and America. Other rulers of Fairyland were called ELFINAN, who founded the city of Cleopolis; ELFILINE, who built a golden wall around Cleopolis; ELFINELL, who defeated the goblins in battle; ELFANT; ELFAR, who killed two giants, one of which had two heads, the other three; and ELFINOR, who built a brazen bridge upon the sea. Other kings mentioned are ELFICLEOS, ELFERON and OBERON, the latter being the husband of TITANIA and the father of GLORIANA, with whom ARTHUR became enamoured.

FÁL
Irish
One of the four great treasures that were brought with the TUATHA DÉ DANANN when they returned from exile in the north to IRELAND. This stone, which came from the mythical city of FALIA, was said to cry out when a true king sat upon it. The stone was later sent to SCOTLAND and is today said to be the Stone of SCONE, which is housed within Westminster Abbey, although whether this is the original mythical stone is a matter of debate. The remaining three wondrous treasures were the invincible spear of LUGH, the inescapable sword of NUADHA and the inexhaustible cauldron of the DAGHDHA.

FALGA
Irish
An ancient name for the Isle of MAN.

FALIA(S)
Irish

A mythical city that was the home of MORFESSA, one of the four wizards who taught the TUATHA DÉ DANANN their magical arts. From this city came the LIA FÁIL or Stone of FÁL.

FALKIRK
Arthurian

Town in SCOTLAND near which there used to stand a Roman temple that has become known as ARTHUR'S O'ON. The temple was destroyed in 1743, but an exact copy was built at nearby Penicuick House to serve as a dovecote. It has been suggested that ARTHUR used the original temple and that it, in turn, was the original of the ROUND TABLE.

FALSE GUINEVERE, THE
Arthurian

In French romance, the identical half-sister of Queen GUINEVERE, whom her father, King LEODEGRANCE, fathered on the same night. Championed by BERTHOLAI, this Guinevere claimed that she was the true Guinevere and enticed ARTHUR into giving up her half-sister. The true Guinevere then took refuge in SORLOIS. In the end she and her champion admitted their deception and, after two and a half years, Arthur and the real Guinevere were reunited.

FAN-D, -N
Irish

(1) A daughter of FLIDHAIS.

(2) A daughter of AED ABRAT and sister of LI BAN. The consort of MANANNÁN MAC LIR, she and her sister once so soundly thrashed CÚ CHULAINN that he lay immobile for a year until they relented and healed him. It seems that this thrashing was in revenge for Cú Chulainn having refused the love of Fand, although one version states that Fand and Li Ban were 'dream-women' who punished Cú Chulainn for failing to capture two magical birds for his intended wife EMER. Some sources, however, say that Cú Chulainn spent a month with Fand, whereupon his wife Emer came to hunt him out. He left Fand for his wife, while she returned to her husband. Cú Chulainn pined for the love of Fand, and it was this that laid him low for a year until Manannán mac Lir caused him to fall asleep, and when he awoke he no longer remembered Fand.

FARAMOND
Arthurian

A variant of PHARAMOND.

FATA MORGANA
Arthurian

The Italian form of MORGAN Le Fay who was believed to live in Calabria, a region of southern Italy. Legends concerning Morgan Le Fay, the sister of ARTHUR, under this name are found in Sicily, possibly being introduced by the Normans, who settled on the island. The Italian term 'Fata Morgana' is still applied to a mirage, often seen in the Straits of Messina, which is traditionally ascribed to the sorcery of Morgan Le Fay. This mirage magnifies both vertically and horizontally, so that buildings appear like Morgan Le Fay's fairy palaces.

FAUSTUS
British and Arthurian

A son of VORTIGERN.

FAYLINN
Irish

The mythical land inhabited by elfin people, whose king was IUBDAN and their queen BEBO.

FEA
Irish

The red ox that was loved by DIL and whose companion, FERNEA, was a black ox.

FEB(H)AL
Irish

The father of BRÂN.

FEDELM(A)
Irish

The prophetess wife of LOEGHAIRE BUADHACH, who came to MEDHBHA while she was on the way to ULSTER in search of the DONN CUAILNGÈ, and gloomily foretold of the disaster that was witing for her and her forces at the hands of CÚ CHULAINN.

FEDLIMID
Irish

The father of the beautiful DERDRIU and FILI to CONCHOBAR MAC NESSA.

FÉINN
Irish

An alternative name for the FIAN.

FEIMURGAN
Arthurian

A variant of MORGAN Le Fay.

FEIREFIZ

Arthurian

The son of GAHMURET and BELCANE in WOLFRAM VON ESCHENBACH's *Parzifal* who, because his parents were of different colours, was piebald. He met his half-brother PERCEVAL, and the pair went to ARTHUR's court, where Feirefiz fell in love with the GRAIL damsel REPANSE DE SCHOIE. He converted to Christianity and he and Repanse de Schoie went to India, where they became the parents of PRESTER JOHN.

FEIS TEMHRACH

Irish

A ritual marriage feast held at TARA at which the king mated with a beautiful virgin who was considered the personification of a goddess, the SPIRIT OF IRELAND, their union symbolically binding sovereign to realm and sanctifying his reign.

FELIX

Arthurian

According to the *TRISTANO RICCARDIANO*, the father of MELIODAS and King MARK, and thus the grandfather of TRISTAN. In another Italian romance, *TAVOLA RITONDA*, Felix was the King of CORNWALL and LIONES, while according to Sir Thomas MALORY Meliodas and King Mark were brothers-in-law.

FENICE

Arthurian

Also FENISE

1 According to CLIGÉS, the wife of the Emperor of CONSTANTINOPLE, ALIS.
2 In *DURMART LE GALLOIS*, the Queen of IRELAND, though here her name is spelt FENISE.

FENISE

Arthurian

A variant of FENICE found in *DURMART LE GALLOIS*.

FER FIDAIL

Irish

The son of EOGABAL, a divine DRUID in the service of MANANNÁN MAC LIR who sent him in the form of a woman to gain access to TUAG, whom the god desired. Fer Fidail spent three nights with Tuag before conveying her by boat back towards TÍR TAIRNGIRI. On the way their boat was swamped by Manannán mac Lir, who could not stand the treacherous behaviour of Fer Fidail. Tuag drowned and Fer Fidail was killed by the angry god after he had landed in Tír Tairngiri.

FERAMORC

Irish

A mythical kingdom within MUNSTER. It appears in the story of MAON, at which time SCORIATH was said to be king.

FERCHERDNE

Irish

The FILI of CÚ ROÍ MAC DÁIRI who avenged the death of his master at the hands of CÚ CHULAINN and BLÁTHNAD. Fercherdne saw Bláthnad standing alone near the edge of a cliff. Flinging himself at her, he caught her around the waist and plummeted with her to their deaths on the rocks below.

FERCHESS

Irish

An ally of OILILL and the killer of EOGABAL.

FERDIA(D(D))

Irish

The son of DAMAN, a FIR BHOLG, a member of the RED BRANCH and the foster brother of CÚ CHULAINN, Ferdiadd was a terrible, yellow-haired, monstrous hero who did battle with Cú Chulainn. His magical armour is well described. First, there was a kilt of striped silk with a border of spangled gold. Over this went an apron of brown leather to protect the lower, more delicate, parts of his body. For added protection he also hung a large stone over the apron. Finally, his lower half was protected by a further apron, this time made of purified iron. Ferdiadd thought this would protect him from the GAE BOLGA, the terrible, inescapable spear of Cú Chulainn.

On his head he wore a huge, crested battle helmet, each quarter embellished with a flashing gem, its entire surface encrusted with crystals and rubies. He hung his curved battle sword, with a golden hilt and red pommel of pure gold, on his left side, and slung a huge shield upon his back, this shield consisting of fifty bosses, each of which would bear the weight of a full-grown boar, with a central boss of red gold. Finally, he took his sharp pointed spear in his right hand.

The preparations completed, he stepped out to meet Cú Chulainn. The battle raged long and hard. The first day neither could inflict even a single wound. The second day each fared a bit better, but not much. The third day both warriors received horrible wounds, cutting away huge chunks of each other's flesh. The fourth day saw Cú Chulainn call for his invincible spear, the Gae Bolga, and, although he had been terribly wounded himself, he let fly with the Gae Bolga, which easily penetrated the armour of Ferdiadd, who died in his arms.

FERGAL
Irish

Possibly the historical King of ULSTER who was killed in a battle along with DONN BO. The head of Fergal was cut off and taken to the hall of the King whose army had defeated Fergal's. There it was treated with great respect. The King combed its hair and washed the face, before setting it on a velvet cloth and positioning it in the place of honour at a feast to commemorate the battle. Afterwards the head was taken away for burial. *The Yellow Book of Lucan* records that the eyes opened and the head gave thanks to God for the respect with which the head had been treated.

FERGAR
Irish

One of the three great-grandsons of DESA, the foster father of CONAIRE MÓR, with whom that hero grew up. The names of the other great-grandsons of Desa are recorded as FERLEE and FERROGAN.

FERGUS
Arthurian

1 Having witnessed the splendour of ARTHUR and his knights, this ploughboy aspired to become a knight. On his horse ARONDIEL, he had various adventures, finally marrying GALIENE, the Lady of LOTHIAN.
2 A KNIGHT OF THE ROUND TABLE of Cornish provenance. He was said to have slain the BLACK KNIGHT, who guarded a wimple and a horn on an ivory lion.

FERG(H)US
Irish

One of the people of NEMHEDH who, during the uprising against the FOMHOIRÉ, managed to kill CONANN, one of the Fomhoiré kings, but was himself killed by MORC, another Fomhoiré ruler.

One of the three sons of ERC, he left IRELAND to establish a kingdom in SCOTLAND, this settlement being the nucleus of DÁL RIADA, the kingdom that was ruled over from DUNADD and is considered the realm from which present-day Scots are descended. He borrowed the LIA FÁIL, or Stone of FÁL, from his brother MURTAGH MAC ERC, King of Ireland, and apparently forgot to return it,

for this is now the Stone of SCONE to be found in Westminster Abbey.

FERG(H)US MAC LEDA
Irish

A King of ULSTER and a contemporary of CONCHOBAR MAC NESSA, and possibly a vassal king. He features in a story that brings him into contact with the elfin inhabitants of FAYLINN. The King of Faylinn, IUBDAN, had always thought his warriors to be the strongest of all living beings, but his bard, EISIRT, told him of a giant race living in Ulster of which but a single man could destroy an entire battalion of the people of Faylinn. Iubdan refused to believe this, so Eisirt said he would bring him evidence, which he did in the form of AEDA, a dwarf at the court of Ferghus mac Leda, although, as Eisirt explained, he was not a true representation of the men of Ulster, for those men could carry Aeda as if he were a child.

Eisirt now placed Iubdan under a bond to travel to Ulster and see for himself. Iubdan took his wife BEBO with him and sneaked into the palace of Ferghus mac Leda at night. However, they were captured, and Ferghus mac Leda refused to let them go. Led by Eisirt, the people of Faylinn attacked Ulster, ruined crops and dried up the milk of cows. Still Ferghus mac Leda would not release his tiny captives, but agreed to ransom them against some of the finest of the treasures of Faylinn. Iubdan and Bebo were released after Ferghus mac Leda had been presented with a cauldron that could never be emptied, a harp that played itself and shoes with which a man could walk on water.

This story seems to represent an early incarnation of the LEPRECHAUN of popular Irish folk belief.

FERG(H)US MAC ROI-CH, -GH
Irish

A son of ROSS and ROICH, and the tutor of CÚ CHULAINN, Ferghus mac Roich is perhaps best known as the leader of the RED BRANCH, and one of the three heroes dispatched by CONCHOBAR MAC NESSA to SCOTLAND to offer a truce to NAOISE, ARDÁN, AINNLE and DERDRIU who had fled there after DERDRIU, the betrothed of Conchobar mac Nessa, had forced Naoise to elope with her. The other two heroes who went were DUBTHACH and his son CORMAC MAC DUBTHACH.

However, when the three returned with the exiles. Ferghus mac Roich was placed under bond to feast with BARUCH, another member of the Red Branch. Without the protection of Ferghus mac Roich, the exiles travelled on to EMHAIN MHACHA, where Conchobar mac Nessa broke his word, and had EOGHAN MAC DURTHACHT and his company kill the three young men. Outraged by this deceit, Ferghus mac Roich, Dubthach and Cormac mac Dubthach attacked and razed Emhain Mhacha, killing 300 of the men of ULSTER in the process, before defecting to AILILL and MEDHBHA of CONNACHT, the traditional enemies of Conchobar mac Nessa.

FERGN-A, -E
Irish
An ally of BODB. A cunning leech (physician) who diagnosed the love-sickness that plagued OENGHUS MAC IN OG for a year after he had dreamt of, but been unable to locate, a beautiful maiden. Fergna then had his mother BOANN search for a second year, but still she could not be found. Finally, Fergna suggested the intervention of the DAGHDHA, who advised his son to ask the advice of Bodb.

FERLEE
Irish
One of the three great-grandsons of DESA, the foster father of CONAIRE MÓR, with whom that hero grew up. FERGAR and FERROGAN are recorded as the names of the other great-grandsons of Desa.

FERNEA
Irish
The black ox of DIL whose companion, FEA, was a red ox.

FERRAGUNZE
Arthurian
A knight who, among other declarations, asserted to ARTHUR and MELIODAS that he was never jealous of VERSERIA, his beautiful wife. Deciding to test him over his claim, they arranged for Verseria to be discovered in the embraces of GAWAIN. True to his word, Ferragunze showed no signs of jealousy.

FERREX
British
A son of GORBODUC and JUDON, and brother of PORREX. As the two brothers came of age, Porrex plotted to ambush Ferrex. Ferrex got wind of this and fled to GAUL, where he raised an army for his return. Porrex succeeded in killing his brother shortly after he had returned. However, as Ferrex had been his mother's favourite, his death unhinged

her, and she hacked the sleeping Porrex to pieces. As neither Ferrex nor Porrex left an heir, the line of descent from BRUTUS died out with the death of Gorboduc.

FERROGAN
Irish
One of the three great-grandsons of DESA, the foster father of CONAIRE MÓR, with whom that hero grew up. The names of the other great-grandsons of Desa are recorded as FERLEE and FERGAR.

FÉTH FIADA
Irish
The mantle of invisibility that was worn by the gods so that they might remain unseen by mortals. Some sources say that the Féth Fiada was a spell that might be cast to cover a whole group of beings and thus make them invisible. In this form it was said to be a power used by the DRUIDS and later by the Christian saints, who could use it not only to make themselves invisible but also to change their form.

FFRWDWR
Arthurian
According to *BONEDD YR ARWR*, a maternal ancestor of ARTHUR.

FFYNNON CEGIN ARTHUR
Arthurian
The oily appearance of the water in this well in Caernarvon is said to have been acquired from animal fat from ARTHUR's kitchens.

FIACHNA
Irish
(1) The son of FIRABA. He joined MEDHBHA and AILILL after the treacherous murder of the sons of UISNECH by CONCHOBAR MAC NESSA. Later he came to the aid of CÚ CHULAINN when that hero had been outnumbered by the sons of CALATIN and killed all twenty-eight of them, although some sources say he simply cut off their hands, and then Cú Chulainn finished them off.

(2) An inhabitant of MAGH MELL who came to seek the help of LOEGHAIRE to release his wife, who was the prisoner of GOLL. Loeghaire and fifty of his men followed Fiachna to the underwater realm of Magh Mell, and there released Fiachna's wife. In return, Fiachna gave each of the men of CONNACHT a wife, giving his own daughter SUN TEAR to Loeghaire. Loeghaire and his men stayed a year in Magh Mell before briefly returning to

Connacht. However, none of them could forget the wonders they had beheld, and soon returned, Loeghaire becoming the joint ruler of Magh Mell beside Fiachna.

FIACHNA LURGAN
Irish

The King of DÁL NARAIDI who went to SCOTLAND to join his ally AEDÁN MAC GABRÁIN, the King of DÁL RIADA, in his fight against invading SAXONS. While in ALBA, a stranger arrived at Fiachna Lurgan's court and informed his wife that, unless she would bear him a son, her husband would die the very next day. Convinced that the stranger had prophesied truthfully, the Queen consented to lie with the man that night. The following morning he had disappeared, and was seen that day on the battlefield in Alba, where his prowess enabled Fiachna Lurgan and Aedán mac Gabráin to rout the Saxon forces.

When Fiachna Lurgan returned home, his wife immediately told him all that had happened in his absence, for she had, by that time, determined that the stranger she had lain with and who had subsequently protected her husband and his ally was none other than MANANNÁN MAC LIR, for the god had left the Queen a poem that enabled her to determine whose son she was to bear. Legend says that the child born of this union was MONGÁN.

FIACHTRA
Irish

A daughter of LIR and AOBH, and sister to FIONUALA, HUGH and CONN. She was one of the four children of Lir who were condemned to spend 900 years as swans by their jealous stepmother AOIFE. They regained their human form during the time of Saint PATRICK and died shortly afterwards.

FIAL(L)
Irish

A daughter of FORGALL and elder sister of EMER.

FIAN
Irish

(pl. *fiana*) A generic name for a roving band, or bands, of warriors. This name is said, by some, to be the root of the name of FIONN MAC CUMHAILL. The *Annals of Tigernach*, which date from the eleventh century, say that the fian was a hireling militia defending IRELAND, this militia being made up of seven legions each of 3,000 men under a single commander. It is worth noting that, during the time of Fionn mac Cumhaill and the fian, Ireland was not invaded once.

FIANNUIGEACHT
Irish

The title adopted by the leader of the FIAN, although it was also used to describe the leading battalion, or clan, within the fian.

FIDCHELL
Irish

A symbolic board game, often called 'chess' in the translations of the Irish myths and legends. Fidchell has its Welsh equivalent in GWYDDBWYLL.

FIGOL
Irish

A DRUID at TARA during the preparations for the Second Battle of MAGH TUIREDH. He is recorded as having promised to rain showers of fire on the FOMHOIRÉ during the battle and to reduce their strength by two-thirds, their loss of strength being transferred to the TUATHA DÉ DANANN, whose strength would increase proportionally.

FILI
Irish

(pl. *filidh* or *file*) The Gaelic for a bard or poet. They were normally found, in this position, within a royal court, examples of royal filidh being AMHAIRGHIN, FERCHERDNE and FEDLIMID.

FILIMENIS
Arthurian

The Emperor of CONSTANTINOPLE, according to *FLORIANT ET FLORETE*.

FINBEUS
Arthurian

A knight who had obtained a magical stone from his fairy mistress that made its owner beautiful, wise and invincible. He lent this stone to GUINEVERE, but, having returned it to Finbeus, she still coveted it and asked GAWAIN to retrieve it for her, which he did by defeating Finbeus in combat.

FINCHORY
Irish

The sunken island to which the sons of TUIRENN were sent by LUGH to retrieve a magical cooking spit as part of their punishment for having killed CIAN.

FIND
Irish

'The Fairhaired One', a title that was most likely applied to LUGH. His continental equivalent was VINDONNUS.

FINDABA(I)R
Irish

The daughter of MEDHBHA and AILILL who loved FRAOCH. Ailill, fearing Fraoch's divine parentage, attempted to kill him, but he overcame the obstacles placed in his path, and Ailill could no longer refuse the betrothal of his daughter. In return, Fraoch agreed to fight on the side of Medhbha and Ailill in the forthcoming attack on ULSTER to secure the DONN CUAILNGÈ. During the course of this battle Medhbha offered Findabair to FERDIADD as his wife, even though by this time she was married to Fraoch, although she may have been widowed, for the *TAÍN BÓ CUAILNGÈ* does not record what happened to Fraoch.

FIN(D)CH-OÉM, -OOM
Irish

The daughter of CATHBHADH and MAGA, sister of DEICHTINE and ELVA, mother of CONALL CERNACH by AMORGIN, and aunt of CÚ CHULAINN, whom she helped to raise while he was still known as SÉDANTA. Some sources call Findchoém the daughter of EOCHO ROND, which leads to the supposition that Eocho Rond and Cathbhadh are one and the same.

FIN(D)IAS
Irish

A mythical city that was the home of USCIAS, one of the four wizards who taught the TUATHA DÉ DANANN their magical arts. From this city came the invincible sword of NUADHA. The other three mythical cities and their associated wizards are: FALIA (MORFESSA), GORIAS (ESIAS) and MURIAS (SIMIAS).

FINEGAS
Irish
See FINNÉCES.

FINGAL
British

The name given by the Irish living in SCOTLAND to FIONN MAC CUMHAILL. Under this name he is supposed to have constructed the Giant's Causeway in Northern IRELAND, the legend saying that he built it to walk across to Scotland. Fingal's Cave on Staffa is so called because the hero was alleged to have used that island as his base for the defence of the Hebrides against Norse invaders.

FINGEN
Irish

The physician to CONCHOBAR MAC NESSA. He told that king that the 'brain ball' that had become lodged in his forehead could not be removed, otherwise he would die. Instead he simply sewed it into place with golden thread and told Conchobar mac Nessa that he had nothing to worry about provided he did not become agitated. Conchobar mac Nessa died when he could not control his emotions and the 'brain ball' burst from his head.

FINN MAC -COOL, -CUMHAL
Irish

Popular versions of FIONN MAC CUMHAILL.

FINNABAIR
Irish

The wife of RIANGABAIR and mother of LOEG and of three beautiful daughters. She and her husband were visited twice by CÚ CHULAINN, Loeg and LUGAID on their quest to discover the whereabouts of the sons of DOEL, once on their way from EMHAIN MHACHA and once on the way back again. On the first occasion ETAN, one of the daughters, spent the night with Cú Chulainn, who gave her a ring as a token.

FINNB(H)ENNACH
Irish

'The White-horned', a bull owned by AILILL, although it had been calved among the herds of MEDHBHA. It was the adversary of the DONN CUAILNGÈ, the brown bull of Cuailngè in the final conflict of the saga *Taín Bó Cuailngè*. The two bulls fought for a day and a night, a fight that was so fierce that it shook the mountains. The following morning the Donn Cuailngè trotted back into the camp of Medhbha and Ailill with all that remained of Finnbhennach hanging from his horns.

FIN(N)ÉCES
Irish
Also FINEGAS

A DRUID to whom FIONN MAC CUMHAILL was sent to learn science and poetry. Finnéces lived on the banks of the River BOYNE. Near his home a hazel tree dropped its Nuts of Knowledge into a stream, where there were eaten by a salmon. This salmon, known as the SALMON OF WISDOM, had long been sought by Finnéces, but he could never catch it. Fionn mac Cumhaill caught it at the first attempt and took it to Finnéces, who told him to cook it. As it was cooking, Fionn mac Cumhaill accidentally touched it with his thumb, which he sucked to soothe it, and he was immediately filled with the potency of the fish; when he reported this to Finnéces, the Druid said that it had been prophesied that he should eat the fish. In this way Fionn mac

Cumhaill was able to chew his thumb and know of all events, past and future. Finnéces then sent the youth on his way, for he already knew more than he could possibly be taught.

See also BLACK ARCAN

FINNEN
Irish

A sixth-century abbot who is reputed to have sought the hospitality of TUAN MAC CARELL, who dwelt not far from his monastery in County Donegal. Tuan mac Carell at first refused him entry, but, after Finnen had fasted for a day and a night on his doorstep, he relented and admitted him.

Some time later, Tuan mac Carell visited Finnen, and it was then that he revealed that, although he was now known as Tuan mac Carell, he had first been incarnated as TUAN MAC STERN, one of the people of PARTHOLÁN who had been the first humans to set foot on IRELAND. Tuan mac Carell told Finnen the history of Ireland, and lived with Finnen and his monks until his death during which time Finnen and his company wrote down all Tuan mac Carell told them.

FINNILENE
British

One of the four ALAISIAGAE, war goddesses who originated in the Teutonic heartland but whose worship was possibly brought to BRITAIN by the Romans. The names of all four of the Alaisiagae – the other three being BEDE, BAUDIHILLIE and FRIAGABI – appear on three stones at Housesteads on Hadrian's Wall, where they are connected with Mars, the Roman god of war.

FINTAN
Irish

(1) The only survivor of the early settlers of IRELAND who were led to the island by CESAIR, although some name the leader of the expedition as BANBHA. Of this expedition, only three were men – Fintan, BITH and LADRA – the other fifty members all being women who were shared out among the three, Fintan obtaining Cesair. After Ladra died, the women were reapportioned, and Fintan and Bith received twenty-five each. Shortly after the death of Bith, all his surviving compatriots were killed during the biblical Flood. Fintan survived and lived on, first as a falcon, then an eagle and then a hawk, and he saw all that came to pass in later days. Later tradition says it was this Fintan who became the SALMON OF WISDOM, cooked and eaten by FIONN MAC CUMHAILL.

(2) The father of CETHERN.

(3) The name of the SALMON OF WISDOM according to a late tradition. This magical fish, which was cooked and eaten by FIONN MAC CUMHAILL, is thought by some to have been the final form taken by FINTAN, the sole survivor of the first people to land in IRELAND under the leadership of CESAIR. If this is the case, it would certainly explain why Fionn mac Cumhaill instantly knew all that had passed before, because Fintan would have been the oldest living thing in Ireland and a veritable historical encyclopaedia.

FI(O)NN MAC CUMHAILL
Irish

The legendary Irish hero who has been identified with a general or chieftain who organized the first regular Irish army in the middle of the third century. He was called FINGAL by James Macpherson (1736–96) in his popular epics (1762–3), which were supposedly translations of the writings of a third-century bard named OSSIAN, although Ossian is actually a variant of OISÎN, the son of Fionn mac Cumhaill. Fionn mac Cumhaill is most popularly known as FINN MAC COOL, and is, from his possession of a shield that had belonged to LUGH, which was given to that god by MANANNÁN MAC LIR, possibly a degenerate version of the god Lugh himself.

The son of CUMHAILL and MUIRNE, Fionn mac Cumhaill was born posthumously at the home of BODHMHALL, Muirne's sister, and was originally called DEIMNE. At a very early age he was judged to be 'fair' in looks as well as in play, and from this judgement he received his name Fionn, for 'fionn' means fair. A poet (FILI) and seer, Fionn mac Cumhaill became the leader of a famous warrior troop, or FIAN, at the age of just eight (ten according to some sources) by defeating the monstrous AILLÉN MAC MIDHNA, who, every year on the feast of SAMHAIN, came to TARA and, having first bewitched the entire company with beautiful music, burned down the court. Fionn mac Cumhaill remained immune to the magical music of Aillén mac Midhna by pressing the point of his spear into his forehead. As Aillén mac Midhna drew near to Tara, belching smoke and fire, Fionn mac Cumhaill calmly stepped out and beheaded the monster. He later killed whole hordes of monstrous serpents throughout IRELAND, each of which had various attributes of fire and water.

Fionn mac Cumhaill was blessed with a supernatural wisdom, some saying that this came from his drinking an OTHERWORLDLY brew.

However, most accounts say that it came about after he accidentally touched the SALMON OF WISDOM with his thumb while staying with his mentor FINNÉCES. Thenceforth, all he had to do was bite his thumb to learn what the future held. This ritual biting of the thumb was known as IMBAS FOROSNAI, and it appears to have carried across the Irish Sea to WALES, where it resurfaces in the story of CERRIDWEN and GWION BACH.

Fionn mac Cumhaill had many wives and mistresses. One wife was CRUITHNE, while another was SAAR or SABIA, the daughter of BODB DEARG and the mother, by Fionn mac Cumhaill, of Oisîn.

His two famous hounds, BRÂN and SGEOLAN, were in fact his nephews, for their father ILLAN married TUIREANN, the sister of Fionn mac Cumhaill's wife, but Illan's supernatural mistress changed Tuireann into a wolfhound, in which form she bore the two famous dogs.

As an ageing widower, Fionn mac Cumhaill became betrothed to the beautiful, and much, much younger GRÁINNE. Unfortunately for Fionn mac Cumhaill, she loved DIARMAID UA DUIBHNE so deeply that, on the night of their wedding feast, she drugged most of the guests and her new husband, and, casting a GESSA spell on Diarmaid ua Duibhne, eloped with him to a wood in CONNACHT. When they had recovered from the effects of the drug, Fionn mac Cumhaill and his men went after the lovers and surrounded the wood in which they were hiding. Diarmaid ua Duibhne's foster father, OENGHUS MAC IN OG, carried Gráinne to safety, while Diarmaid ua Duibhne made good his escape by bounding over the heads of the besieging horde in a single leap. However, Diarmaid ua Duibhne remained loyal to his former master and would not take Gráinne as his lover. It was only after he had endured her intolerable derision that he eventually broke his oath to Fionn mac Cumhaill.

Fionn mac Cumhaill, Gráinne and Diarmaid ua Duibhne were finally reconciled through the efforts of Oenghus Mac in Og. So complete was the reconciliation that Fionn mac Cumhaill invited Diarmaid ua Duibhne to accompany him in the hunt for the great boar BEANN GHULBAN. Diarmaid ua Duibhne accepted, even though it had been foretold that Beann Ghulban, his foster brother, would bring about his end. Sure enough, seconds before he delivered the killing blow, Diarmaid ua Duibhne was mortally gored by the boar. Only Fionn mac Cumhaill, who had the divine gift of healing, could save the dying man if he would give him water from his own hands. Fionn mac Cumhaill went to fetch water, but on the way back he remembered the treachery of Diarmaid ua Duibhne and allowed the water to trickle away. By the time he had done this for the third time, Diarmaid ua Duibhne was dead.

Fionn mac Cumhaill was said to have died at the age of 230, his death causing the decline and eventual disbanding of the fian. He was later alleged to have been reincarnated as the seventh-century Irish chieftain MONGÁN, whose death is recorded as AD 625.

See also AINÉ, MILUCHRADH

FION(NGH)UALA
Irish

The eldest daughter of LIR, and one of his four children who were transformed into swans by Lir's second wife AOIFE, a form they were condemned to retain for 900 years. At the end of the allotted time, in the time of Saint PATRICK, Fionuala, her sister, and her brothers regained their human form, but now as ancient, white-haired beings on the verge of death. They were accepted into the Christian faith and baptised moments before they died. Fionuala was the only one to speak, and she gave precise details of how they were to be buried, saying that CONN should be laid at her right, FIACHTRA at her left and HUGH at her face.

FIR BHOLG
Irish

The leaders of the fourth invasion of IRELAND, which consisted of three parties, the Fir Bholg, the GAILIÓIN and the FIR DHOMHNANN. The Fir Bholg were said to have been descended from SEMION, son of STARIAT. All three were made up of the survivors of an earlier Irish people known as the people of NEMHEDH, who had been forced to flee to Greece. Having successfully landed and taken Ireland, the Fir Bholg divided the country into the five CÓIGEDH, or provinces, of ULSTER, LEINSTER, MUNSTER, CONNACHT and MEATH. The Gailióin became known as the LAIGHIN after they settled in Leinster, while the Fir Dhomhnann settled in Connacht. The other three provinces were occupied by the Fir Bholg, who ruled Ireland until they were beaten by the TUATHA DÉ DANANN at the First Battle of MAGH TUIREDH, when their King EOCHAIDH MAC ERC was killed, and they were forced into exile among the FOMHOIRÉ.

FIR DEA
Irish

'Men of the god' or 'the divine tribe'. This was possibly the original name of the TUATHA DÉ DANANN, although it is open to speculation.

FIR DHOMHNANN

Irish

One of the two parties, survivors of the people of NEMHEDH, who came, from Greece to IRELAND under the leadership of the FIR BHOLG. The other company to invade Ireland on this occasion, the fourth such invasion in the early history of the island, was the GAILIÓIN. The Fir Dhomhnann settled in CONNACHT, the Gailióin in LEINSTER, whereafter they became known as the LAIGHIN, while the Fir Bholg occupied the remaining three CÓIGEDH, or provinces, ULSTER, MUNSTER and MEATH. Some authorities believe that the Fir Dhomhnann may have moved across the Irish Sea to become the origins of the DUMNONII.

FIR SÍDH

Irish

The name by which the inhabitants of the SÍDH were sometimes referred. Meaning 'men of the sídh', the expression was used when there was no better way to refer to supernatural beings that lived within the boundaries of IRELAND, rather than in the OTHERWORLDLY realms, which usually lay overseas. It is possibly a relatively late term, coming into use after the power of the TUATHA DÉ DANANN had started to decline.

FIRABA

Irish

The father of FIACHNA.

FISH-KNIGHT

Arthurian

Closely resembling a mounted knight, this 'fishy' monster was fought by ARTHUR, who sought to release a fairy by the name of the LADY OF THE FAIR HAIR.

FISHER KING(S)

Arthurian

The descendants of JOSEPH OF ARIMATHEA who guarded the Holy GRAIL in CARBONEK Castle. In early versions of the Grail stories, the Grail itself is said to have been the vessel in which the blood of Christ was collected after Jesus' side had been pierced with a lance by the centurion LONGINUS (John 19:34). Later versions made the Grail the cup from which Jesus and his disciples drank at the Last Supper.

This wondrous relic is housed in the GRAIL CASTLE, where it is guarded by the GRAIL KEEPER, the wounded Fisher King. Maimed 'through the thighs' (*sic*), a wound said to have been caused by the DOLOROUS STROKE, he feeds only from a magical dish. His land has become infertile as a result of his wound, and will revive only if the King himself is cured. The cure will come about only if there is a knight brave enough to travel on the perilous journey through the 'land of wailing women' to the Grail Castle and, once there, wise enough to ask the GRAIL QUESTION. This would then break the enchantment under which both King and land are held captive.

The Fisher King is given various names and associations in the Arthurian tales. Sometimes, though not always, identified with the MAIMED KING, he is called PELLES in the *VULGATE VERSION*, which names the Maimed King as PARLAN or PELLAM. In Manessier's *CONTINUATION*, his wound was said to have been inflicted by fragments of the sword that killed his brother, GOON DESERT, while CHRÉTIEN DE TROYES himself says that he could not ride as a result of his infirmity, and so took to fishing as a pastime – hence his title.

ROBERT DE BORON names him BRONS and says that the title Fisher King came from the fact that he supplied fish for Joseph of Arimathea, though another early commentator derives his name from the Christian fish symbol. WOLFRAM VON ESCHENBACH identifies him as ANFORTAS, while the *Sone de Nausay* states that the Fisher King is none other than Joseph of Arimathea himself.

It is generally agreed that the story of the Fisher King is derived from an ancient fertility myth and has associations with the sea god, the ruler of the mysterious OTHERWORLD. The *PREIDDEU ANNWFN* describes a journey made to this Otherworld by King ARTHUR in search of a magic cauldron, and this story is regarded as one of the sources of the Grail stories.

FLEDD BRICRENN

Irish

Bricriu's Feast, a quasi-tragic, even comedic tale, which was based on the much earlier ribald tale, *Scéla Mucce Maic Dá Thó*. The story tells of the maliciousness of BRICRIU, who, during a feast, bribed three great heroes to claim the honour of carving the roast, which led to an unseemly brawl. The matter was first judged by MEDHBHA and subsequently by CÚ ROÍ MAC DÁIRI. Both judges came out in favour of CÚ CHULAINN.

See also BUDA

FLIDHAIS

Irish

The goddess of forest animals to whom the deer was sacred, roaming herds being seen as her 'cattle'.

Some sources name her as the mother of FAND and LI BAN. In the *Taín Bó Cuailngè*, Flidhais is named as the wife of AILILL, although his wife is usually named as MEDHBHA, and she is here called the owner of a magnificent cow that could feed a whole army for seven days on the results of one milking.

FLOREE
Arthurian
A variant of FLORIE.

FLORENCE
Arthurian
The son of GAWAIN, he was among the company of knights who surprised GUINEVERE and LANCELOT together in the Queen's bedchamber, and was killed by the escaping yet unarmed Lancelot.

FLORETE
Arthurian
The daughter of the Emperor of CONSTANTIN-OPLE and the wife of FLORIANT. She is the heroine of the romance *FLORIANT ET FLORETE*.

FLORIANT
Arthurian
The hero of *FLORIANT ET FLORETE*, the son of ELYADUS, King of Sicily, who was raised by MORGAN Le Fay. He was said to have been brought by a WHITE STAG to his foster mother. A member of ARTHUR's court, he supported the latter in his war against the Emperor of CONSTANTINOPLE, falling in love with that emperor's daughter, FLORETE, whom he married.

FLORIANT ET FLORETE
Arthurian
A thirteenth-century French poetic romance concerning FLORIANT, the fosterling of MORGAN Le Fay who, during ARTHUR's war against FILIMENIS, the Emperor of CONSTANTINOPLE, fell in love with the Emperor's daughter, FLORETE, and duly married her.

FLORIE
Arthurian
Also FLOREE
The name of at least two ladies from Arthurian tales.
1 The Queen of KANADIC, she raised ARTHUR's son ILINOT, who fell in love with her. As a result she sent him away, and he died of a broken heart.
2 The niece of King JORAM and daughter of the King of ESCAVALON. She married GAWAIN and became the mother of WIGALOIS by him.

FLORISDELFA
Arthurian
Learning her magic arts under the tutorship of MERLIN, this enchantress sent her master a herd of magic swine and a crystal tower seated on a chariot that was drawn by fire-breathing dragons. She committed suicide when she perceived the beauty of ISEULT.

FLOWER FACE
Welsh
The literal translation of BLODEUWEDD, the magically made wife of LLEU LLAW GYFFES.

FLURATRONE
Arthurian
A realm whose queen married GAURIEL. She deserted him, saying that she would return only when her husband had captured three of ARTHUR's knights, a task that was successfully completed.

FLURENT
Arthurian
According to the Icelandic *SAGA OF TRISTRAM*, the mother of ISEULT.

FLYING HORSE
Arthurian
According to the French romance *The Fair Magalona and Peter, Son of the Count of Provence*, this fabulous beast was made by MERLIN.

FÓDLA
Irish
The wife of MAC CÉCHT and one of the triad of goddesses known as the SOVEREIGNTY OF IRELAND. She and her other aspects, ÉRIU and BANBHA, were encountered by the Sons of MÍL ÉSPÁINE while they were on their way to TARA.

FOILL
Irish
A son of NECHTA SCÉNE. He was killed by CÚ CHULAINN, along with his two brothers, while Cú Chulainn was travelling to EMHAIN MHACHA. He cut off the brothers' heads and tied them to his chariot, along with a stag and sixteen wild swans he had caught and tethered.

FOLLAMAN
Irish
The son of CONCHOBAR MAC NESSA. He led the youth of EMHAIN MHACHA to the aid of CÚ CHULAINN, who stood alone protecting ULSTER

against the forces of MEDHBHA and AILILL. He and his companions were all killed.

FOM(H)OIRÉ
Irish

One of the great tribes of Celtic IRELAND and the sworn enemies of the TUATHA DÉ DANANN. The Fom(h)oiré came to Ireland after the time of the biblical Flood; their name means, literally, 'sea giants'. They were a race of half-human monsters, each of whom had a single leg, a single hand, one eye in the centre of the forehead and three rows of razor-sharp teeth. Having enjoyed free reign of Ireland for a considerable time, they were eventually defeated by PARTHOLÁN and forced into exile on the Hebrides and the Isle of MAN. They returned many years later, after Partholán had himself been conquered by NEMHEDH, and set about reclaiming the island. They quickly reduced the people of Nemhedh to subserviency, compelling them to pay a tribute of two-thirds of their wine, corn and children; it was not too long before the people of Nemhedh rebelled. Only one boatload of the people of Nemhedh survived the rebellion, and they fled to Greece from whence they were later to return as the FIR BHOLG, GAILIÓIN and FIR DHOMHNANN.

When the Fir Bholg, Gailióin and Fir Dhomhnann returned and invaded Ireland, they quickly established the five CÓIGEDH (provinces) and settled down. However, the Tuatha Dé Danann then arrived and shattered their peace. They met the forces of the Tuatha Dé Danann at the First Battle of MAGH TUIREDH, when they were soundly beaten and forced into exile among the Fomhoiré, their earlier enemies.

The Fomhoiré and Tuatha Dé Danann settled into an uncomfortable peace, each keeping to their own territory, although that of the Fomhoiré was but a small corner of the country. A strange relationship between the two enemies occurred with the birth of BRES, whose parents were the Fomhoiré ELATHA and a Tuatha Dé Danann woman. When Bres was forced to abdicate as the leader of the Tuatha Dé Danann, he carried off the magic harp of the DAGHDHA, an act that shattered the fragile truce and led to the Second Battle of Magh Tuiredh.

Bres had mustered an army against the Tuatha Dé Danann when LUGH sent the Daghdha to attempt to reclaim the harp and call a truce. The Fomhoiré, well aware of the power of the Daghdha, attempted to incapacitate him by feeding him an enormous meal, finished off by a bout of love-making with a Fomhoiré maiden. The plan backfired, for the Daghdha had an insatiable appetite, and his sexual prowess so impressed the Fomhoiré maiden that she agreed to use her magical powers against her own people.

The Second Battle of Magh Tuiredh, during which the sea god TETHRA was said to have fought alongside the Fomhoiré, was brought to an abrupt end when Lugh aimed a slingshot into the single monstrous eye of BALAR with such force and accuracy that it exploded Balar's brains to the four winds, then carried on to decimate the Fomhoiré army. The remnants of the monstrous race were then driven from the country.

See also AIDED CHLAINNE TUIRENN

FOMOIRI
Irish

A variant sometimes used to refer to the FOMHOIRÉ in the plural form, although Fomhoiré is both singular and plural.

FOMORIAN(S)
Irish

A semi-Latinised variant of FOMHOIRÉ.

FOOL OF THE FOREST
Arthurian

According to Gaelic tradition, the name by which MOROIE MOR, the son of ARTHUR who was born at DUMBARTON, was known.

FORBAY
Irish

The son of CONCHOBAR MAC NESSA. He is said to have killed MEDHBHA with a slingshot as she bathed in a lake on the island to which she had retired after the death of AILILL.

FOREST OF ADVENTURE
Arthurian

Unidentified forest, appearing in *EREC ET ENIDE*, where a WHITE STAG was reputedly hunted down.

FORGALL
Irish

The father of FIALL and the maiden EMER, who was later to marry the hero CÚ CHULAINN after he had proved his worth by becoming a pupil of the prophetess SCÁTHACH. Forgall did not welcome the union between his daughter and Cú Chulainn, and sending the hero beyond ALBA was his attempt to ensure that the unworthy suitor of Emer never returned. Cú Chulainn did, of course, return, and Forgall was killed in his vain attempt to protect his home.

FORT OF GLASS
Welsh and Arthurian
CAER WYDYR, an OTHERWORLDLY city that has become associated with both GLASTONBURY and AVALON. Some sources have identified the Fort of Glass with CAER FEDDWIDD or CAER SIDDI, another Otherworldly realm, but that mysterious fort is better known as the Fort of CAROUSAL.

FORTUNE
Arthurian
A maiden whom ARTHUR dreamt he saw spinning her wheel in the *MORTE ARTHURE*. The King was strapped to the wheel, which was spun until he was smashed to smithereens. His dream was explained as foretelling his downfall.

FOTHAD (AIRGLECH)
Irish
A king slain in the third century by FIONN MAC CUMHAILL, although it was later revealed that Fothad was actually killed by KEELTA.

FOUNTAIN OF THE TRUTH OF LOVE
Arthurian
According to *Astrée*, a seventeenth-century novel started by Honoré d'Urfe (1567–1625) and finished by his secretary, Baro, this fountain was created by MERLIN and guarded by lions that would not eat people who were pure and honest. The fountain makes its appearance in the section of the novel written by Baro.

FOUNTAIN OF YOUTH
Arthurian
The fountain located in the TERRESTRIAL PARADISE in which ESCLARMONDE was bathed by MORGAN Le Fay.

FRAGARACH
Irish
'The Answerer', the invincible sword owned by LUGH.

FRANCE
General
This large European country is sometimes, in the Arthurian tales, referred to by its older name of GAUL. During the Arthurian period, France was a Frankish kingdom, that race having established themselves there *c*. AD 457. Indeed, the present name of France derives from their name. Clovis I, who came to the throne in AD 481, is possibly the original of CLAUDAS, while in some Arthurian sources PHARAMOND, who is also possibly Frankish in origin, is the King of France. The *MABINOGION* story of *CULHWCH AND OLWEN* tells of two French kings at ARTHUR's court named IONA and PARIS.

FRANCHISE TRISTAN
Arthurian
Formerly called SERVAGE, this country changed its name when it was conquered by TRISTAN, though some sources say that the country was given to him by its previous ruler.

FRANKS
General
A Germanic people who were influential in Europe between the third and eighth centuries. Believed to have originated in Pomerania on the Black Sea, they had settled on the Rhine by the third century, spread into the Roman Empire by the fourth, and gradually conquered most of GAUL and Germany under the Merovingian (481–751) and Carolingian (768–987) dynasties. The kingdom of the western Franks became FRANCE, to which they gave their name, while that of the eastern Franks became Germany.

FRAOCH
Irish
The subject of the *Táin Bó Fraich*, the son of BÉBIND, which makes him the nephew of BOANN. He was loved by FINDABAIR, the daughter of AILILL and MEDHBHA, whom Fraoch travelled to see with a vast hoard of treasure for her parents. Fraoch was entertained regally until he asked Ailill and Medhbha to allow him to marry their daughter. They refused and thought of a way to kill Fraoch so that he did not seek to bring divine retribution upon them.

While Fraoch was swimming in a lake, Ailill had him fetch a branch from a rowan tree that hung over the water. On the second trip to the tree the guardian monster of the tree attacked Fraoch, but, although he was horribly wounded, he managed to behead the beast with the sword his beloved Findabair threw him. Fraoch was carried back to the SÍDH of his mother, from whence he appeared the following day fully healed. Ailill and Medhbha could not refuse him now, and agreed to the betrothal on the condition that Fraoch helped them in the coming battles with ULSTER to secure the DONN CUAILNGÈ.

FREDERICK
Arthurian
The King of the FRISIANS, according to the *ALLITERATIVE MORTE ARTHURE*, and an ally of MORDRED.

FREDERICK DE TELRAMUND
Arthurian
See TELRAMUND, FREDERICK DE

FRIAGABI
British
One of the four Teutonic ALAISIAGAE, the others being BEDE, BAUDIHILLIE and FINNILENE, to whom an altar was dedicated at Housesteads on Hadrian's Wall. Her name may mean 'Ruler of Battle'. It seems quite likely that the four goddesses were brought to BRITAIN by the invading Romans, who introduced their worship to the warlike Celts.

FRIMUTEL
Arthurian
The father of AMFORTAS, the GRAIL KING, according to WOLFRAM VON ESCHENBACH.

FRISIAN(S)
Arthurian
A Germanic people who have given their name to the islands off the coast of GERMANY and the Netherlands. They were numbered among the barbarian invaders of BRITAIN by the Byzantine historian Procopius, whose writings date from the traditional Arthurian period. King CALIN of Friesland – that is, the land of the Frisians – was subject to ARTHUR, according to LAYAMON, though the *ALLITERATIVE MORTE ARTHURE* makes the king, FREDERICK, an ally of MORDRED.

Frisian is today spoken as a lesser-used language in Germany and in the Netherlands. There are three main varieties of Frisian: West Frisian (Frysk), which is spoken in Friesland/Fryslan (Netherlands), North Frisian (Friisk), which consists of nine different dialects in Schleswig-Holstein (Germany), and Sater Frisian (Seeltersk), which is spoken in Niedersachsen (Germany).

FRIUCH
Irish
'Bristle', a swineherd of MUNSTER, in the employ of BODB. He appears in the COPHUIR IN DA MUCCIDA along with RUCHT ('Grunt'), a swineherd in CONNACHT, in the employ of OCHALL OICHNI. The two were on the best of terms, leading their respective herds of swine to feed with each other depending on where the pasture was best, and both were well versed in the pagan arts, being able to transform themselves at will. However, the people of Munster and Connacht conspired to make the two fall out, which they eventually did, each casting spells on the other's herd. Friuch and Rucht turned themselves into ravens and fought for a year in Munster and a year in Connacht. Next, they became water-beasts, then demons and finally worms or maggots, though some sources also include a transformation into dragons. These worms, or maggots, were subsequently swallowed by cows and reborn as FINNBHENNACH and the DONN CUAILNGE. Although there is some confusion as to which great bull represented which swineherd, it is generally agreed that Friuch was reborn as the mighty Donn Cuailngè.

FROCIN
Arthurian
A dwarf whom King MARK had beheaded for betraying the secret that the King had horse's ears.

FROLLO
Arthurian
The Roman tribune who ruled GAUL for the emperor Leo and whose weak army was defeated by ARTHUR when the latter first invaded Gaul at the start of his Roman campaign. Frollo fled and took refuge in Paris, where Arthur besieged the city. Realising that the city could not hope to withstand a lengthy siege, Frollo challenged Arthur to a single combat to decide the fate of Gaul. Though Frollo managed to inflict a wound on Arthur, the tribune was killed and Paris surrendered to Arthur, with Gaul capitulating shortly afterwards.

This is, at least, the conventional view of Frollo. The *PROSE TRISTAN* does not differ from this view, but adds that Frollo had a son named SAMALIEL, who went on to become a renowned knight. The *VULGATE VERSION*, *Prose Lancelot*, says he was an ally of King CLAUDAS and a claimant to the throne of FRANCE (GAUL). Elsewhere he is said to have been a German who became the Gaulish king.

FUAMHNACH
Irish
The first wife of MIDHIR. Her jealousy at the beauty of Midhir's second wife, ÉDÁIN ECHRAIDHE, knew no bounds, and her first act was to turn the beautiful young woman into a pool of water. That pool became a worm, and that worm became a huge and astoundingly beautiful fly (some say butterfly), whose perfume filled the air. Midhir was quite contented to have Édáin Echraidhe around him, even in this unusual form. This once more enraged Fuamhnach, so she conjured up a strong wind, which blew the fly over a cliff to lie helpless on the rocky coast for a total of seven years before

OENGHUS MAC IN OG found her, placed her in a crystal bower surrounded by flowers and herbs, cured her of her injuries, and brought her back to Midhir. Fuamhnach finally, in her lifetime, managed to dispose of Édáin Echraidhe when she once again called up a strong wind, which this time blew the fly into a goblet of wine, which was subsequently drunk by the daughter (some sources say wife) of the warrior ÉDAR, the fly subsequently being born as that woman's daughter.

FULGENTIUS
Arthurian
Listed by GEOFFREY OF MONMOUTH as an early King of BRITAIN, he was also said by the Scottish historian John of Fordun to have been an ancestor of LOT. It is highly likely that Fulgentius was none other than Fabius Planciades Fulgentius, the Latin mythographer and allegorist who flourished *c*. AD 500, and who simply found his way into the Arthurian cycle at the whim of the various authors.

FYFNNON FAWR
Arthurian
'Our Lady's Well', a spring that lies below ARTHUR'S STONE at CEFN-Y-BRYN, near Reynoldstone, Gower, WALES. The waters of this spring are supposed to run according to the ebb and flow of the nearby sea. The water used to be drunk from the palm of one hand while a wish was made. It is said that the spectral figure of King ARTHUR appears from beneath the stone on nights with a full moon, though this seems to be true about almost all the many stones associated with Arthur.

GABAN

Arthurian

The maker of a sword, according to the *Polistoire del Eglise de Christ de Caunterbyre*, in the days when Christ was just fourteen years old. The sword was reputedly later wielded by GAWAIN. This ancient metalworker may represent a survival of the ancient Celtic smith god GOFANNON or GOIBHNIU.

GABHRA

Irish

A mythical battle, known popularly as the Battle of GOWRA, was fought between two opposing factions within the FIAN and was ultimately to lead to the end of the supremacy of the fian within IRELAND.

See also CAIRBRE, DECIES, SGEIMH SOLAIS.

GADDIFER

Arthurian

The brother of BETIS who, when Betis was make King of England following the conquest of BRITAIN by ALEXANDER THE GREAT, was made the King of SCOTLAND.

GADELIUS

Irish

An ancestor of the Sons of MÍL ÉSPÁINE. He was said to have been bitten by a venomous snake and then to have been cured by Moses.

GADEON

Welsh

The son of EUDAF and brother of CYNAN and ELEN. After Elen had married MACSEN, he and Cynan mustered an army and marched with Macsen against Rome, which had chosen a new emperor to replace Macsen. Triumphant after having reinstated Macsen as emperor, Cynan and Gadeon conquered ARMORICA. Cynan returned to BRITAIN, while Gadeon and a large number of the British troops settled in Armorica, where they killed all the men and cut out the tongues of the women so that they could not talk a foreign language.

GAE BOLGA

Irish

The invincible spear of CÚ CHULAINN. It was launched, as Cú Chulainn had been taught by SCÁTHACH, from between his toes. The hero used the spear on two memorable instances, when he used it to kill his son CONALL and his foster brother FERDIADD.

GAELS

Irish

The name by which the human inhabitants of IRELAND, and latterly SCOTLAND, are properly known, their name giving rise to the Gaelic language. The definition was first used to describe the Sons of MÍL ÉSPÁINE, the first human inhabitants of Ireland.

GAHERIS

Arthurian

The name of two KNIGHTS OF THE ROUND TABLE. Nothing else is known about one of them, but the other was a son of LOT and MORGAUSE. He surprised LAMORAK and Morgause in bed together and killed his mother, an act for which ARTHUR banished him. In the company of AGRAVAIN he hunted down and killed Lamorak. During LANCELOT's rescue of Queen GUINEVERE, Gaheris was killed by Lancelot.

GAHMURET

Arthurian

According to WOLFRAM VON ESCHENBACH, the father of PERCEVAL. Travelling to the Orient, he entered the service of the BARUC of Baghdad, during which time he rescued BELCANE, Queen of ZAZAMANC, from a Scottish army and married her. His son by Belcane was the piebald FEIREFIZ. Returning to Europe, he married again, this time HERZELOYDE, the Queen of WALES and NORTHGALIS, by whom he became the father of Perceval. He left to help the Baruc of Baghdad and was killed.

GAÍ DEARG

Irish

The magical, red-shafted spear owned by DIARMAID UA DUIBHNE. GRÁINNE advised him to take it on the hunt for BEANN GHULBAN, but he thought that this gave him an unfair advantage. His refusal to take his magical weapon, once owned according to some by MANANNÁN MAC LIR, cost him his life.

GAIBHDE

Irish

A variant of GOIBHNIU that is commonly used in Irish folklore.

GAIBLE

Irish

The son of NUADHA. He once stole a bundle of twigs that AINGE, a daughter of the DAGHDHA, had gathered to build herself a tub that did not leak. Gaible threw away the twigs, and where they landed a mature wood sprang out of the ground.

GAILHOM

Arthurian

The capital of the ancient kingdom of GORE.

GAILIÓIN

Irish

One of the three companies made up of the descendants of the survivors of the people of NEMHEDH, who came from Greece and invaded IRELAND, settling in LEINSTER, where they became known as the LAIGHIN. The other two companies were the FIR BHOLG, the leaders of the invasion, and the FIR DHOMHNANN. It has been suggested that the FIAN were descended from the Gailíóin.

GALACHIN

Arthurian

A variant of GALESCHIN.

GALAGANDREIZ

Arthurian

One of the fathers-in-law of Sir LANCELOT.

GALAHAD

Arthurian

The name of at least three characters from the Arthurian stories.

(1) The grandson of BAN and the natural son of LANCELOT whose mother is variously given as ELAINE, AMITE or PEREVIDA. Possibly simply the creation of the author of the *QUESTE DEL SAINTE GRAAL*, as this is where he first appears, he may also be derived from either the Palestinian place-name Gilead or the Welsh character of

GWALHAFED, who is mentioned in the *MABINOGION* story of *CULHWCH AND OLWEN*. It has even been suggested that he derives from Saint ILLTYD. As a child he was placed in a nunnery, where his paternal great-aunt was the abbess, later being knighted there by his father, LANCELOT. His story is almost entirely concerned with the quest of the Holy GRAIL and is, basically, as follows.

One day a sword in a marble and iron stone was spotted in a river by a company of ARTHUR's knights and taken back to CAMELOT. Galahad was brought into the presence of the King and the KNIGHTS OF THE ROUND TABLE.

There he sat in the SIEGE PERILOUS, the place reserved for the purest knight, and, no calamity befalling him, he easily drew the sword from the stone, which, according to an inscription, could be done only by the world's best knight. Joining the Knights of the Round Table, Galahad was present when the vision of the Grail appeared and was one of the knights chosen to go on the quest in search of this most magnificent and mysterious of relics. Before leaving, he was given a white shield that had been made by EVELAKE and that had a red cross on it that had been painted in blood by JOSEPH OF ARIMATHEA.

During the course of his quest, he met and joined up with PERCEVAL, BORS and Perceval's sister, gaining for himself DAVID'S SWORD as they travelled aboard SOLOMON's ship. Following the death of Perceval's sister, the remaining trio parted company, and, for a while, Galahad journeyed with his father. They visited Evelake, who afterwards died, and, having parted from his father, Galahad once again joined up with Perceval and Bors. These three knights came to Castle CARBONEK, where they achieved their quest by finding the Holy Grail.

When Galahad repaired the broken sword, which neither Perceval nor Bors had managed to do, Joseph of Arimathea appeared and celebrated mass with them, after which Jesus appeared to the three knights and told Galahad that he would see the Grail more openly in SARRAS. Before leaving Carbonek, Galahad anointed the MAIMED KING with blood from the GRAIL SPEAR, thus curing him of his ailment. Having left Carbonek, the three knights came to a ship on board which they once again found the Grail and in this vessel they sailed to Sarras. There the pagan King ESTORAUSE cast them into a prison, where they were sustained by the Grail. As Estorause lay dying, the three gallant knights forgave him for having imprisoned them, and, following his death, Galahad became the new King of Sarras.

Sir Galahad draws the sword from the floating stone, which only the best knight in the world could do.
(Mary Evans Picture Library/Arthur Rackham Collection)

One year later Galahad came across Joseph of Arimathea celebrating mass and once again beheld the Holy Grail. Having done so, he asked that he should be allowed to die, which he did in peace. He was also said, at some stage in his life, to have saved the kingdom of LOGRES. Various commentators have given Galahad any number of lines of descent.

(2) A son of JOSEPH OF ARIMATHEA who was born in BRITAIN, ascended to the throne of WALES, when he became known as HOCELICE, and was an ancestor of URIEN.

(3) The original name of the father of GALAHAD, better known as LANCELOT. He is named as one of the TWENTY-FOUR KNIGHTS of King ARTHUR's court.

GALEGANTIS
Arthurian
The maternal grandfather of LANCELOT and also the name of one of ARTHUR's knights.

GALEHAUT
Arthurian
'The High Prince' who ruled the District Isles, SURLUSE and various other kingdoms. The son of BRUNOR and the giantess BAGOTA, he invaded BRITAIN. He became a firm friend of Sir LANCELOT and, through that friendship, also a friend of ARTHUR, being made a KNIGHT OF THE ROUND TABLE. When he thought that his great friend Lancelot was dead, he fasted until the sickness, caused by doing so, killed him.

GALENTIVET
Arthurian
The brother of GRIFLET who once participated in a treacherous attack on ESCANOR that was blamed on GAWAIN.

GALERON
Arthurian
A Scottish knight of Galloway who became a KNIGHT OF THE ROUND TABLE, even though his lands had been confiscated by ARTHUR.

GALES
Arthurian
A kingdom that is usually identified with WALES.

GALES LI CAUS
Arthurian
A KNIGHT OF THE ROUND TABLE who was, according to GERBERT, the husband of PHILOSOPHINE and father of PERCEVAL.

GALESCHIN
Arthurian
Also GALACHIN
The son of King NENTRES of GARLOT, and BELISENT, ARTHUR's sister. A supporter of Arthur in his battle against the SAXONS, who were laying siege to the city after the Saxons had been defeated. However, this story is an anachronism, as the Duchy of Clarence was not created until 1362, and the place to which it related was the small wool town of Clare in Suffolk, which can hardly be called a city by anyone's standards.

GALIAN
Arthurian
According to the *Gallians tattur*, a Faeroese ballad that was written down during the eighteenth century, Galian was a son of OWAIN.

GALIENE
Arthurian
The Lady of LOTHIAN who married FERGUS.

GALIHODIN
Arthurian
A KNIGHT OF THE ROUND TABLE, a cousin of GALEHAUT and sub-king of SURLUSE, one of the kingdoms ruled by GALEHAUT. When LANCELOT fled ARTHUR's court, Galihodin joined him and was made the Duke of SENTOGE as a reward.

GALL
Welsh and Arthurian
The son of DYSGYFDAWD who was said to have killed the birds of GWENDDOLAU.

GALLAFER
Arthurian
The grandson of GADDIFER who, having been converted to Christianity, went to preach to his ancestors who still inhabited the ISLE OF LIFE.

GALORE
Arthurian
The kingdom of King GARLIN, whom the German *DIU CRÔNE* makes the father of GUINEVERE.

GALVARIUN
Arthurian
Depicted on the MODENA archivolt, the underside of an arch in Modena cathedral, this knight of ARTHUR appears nowhere else, in either literature or art.

GANDIN

Arthurian

The grandfather of PERCEVAL, according to WOLFRAM VON ESCHENBACH.

GANIEDA

Welsh and Arthurian

The twin sister of MYRDDIN (MERLIN), she appears in Welsh poetry as GWENDYDD, and under this name in the *VITA MERLINI*, which says she was the adulterous wife of RHYDDERCH, whose philandering was spotted by her brother, Merlin. The Welsh poems do not say for definite that she was married to Rhydderch. In origin, Ganieda would appear to be LANGUORETH, the wife of Rhydderch in Jocelyn's *LIFE OF SAINT KENTIGERN*, who became enamoured with a soldier.

GANNES

Arthurian

The kingdom ruled over by King BORS.

GARADIGAN

Arthurian

The domain from which LORE, called the Lady of Garadigan, hailed.

GARANWYN

Welsh and Arthurian

In Welsh tradition, a son of CEI (Sir KAY).

GARCELOS

Arthurian

According to the sixteenth-century Welsh writer Gruffudd Hiraethog, Garcelos was a maternal ancestor of ARTHUR. It would seem that Garcelos is a simple corruption of CASTELLORS, who appears in the pedigree of JOHN OF GLASTONBURY.

GAREL

Arthurian

The hero of the romance *GAREL VON DEM BLÜHENDEN TAL* by Der Pleier, Garel was an Arthurian knight who conquered KANEDIC after its king, ECUNAVER, had announced his intention to attack ARTHUR. He married Queen LAUDAME of ANFERE.

GAREL VON DEM BLÜHENDEN TAL

Arthurian

A thirteenth-century German poetic romance recounting the exploits of GAREL. It was written by an obscure author, simply known as Der Pleier, who may have been Austrian.

GARETH

Arthurian

A son of LOT and MORGAUSE. Coming to ARTHUR's court in disguise, he was put to work in the kitchens and, attracting the attention of the impertinent KAY, he was given the nickname 'Beaumains' – 'Fair Hands', indicating that his hands were unsullied and unused to hard work. When LYNETTE came to Arthur's court looking for someone to help her sister LYONESSE, who was being besieged by the RED KNIGHT of the Red Lands, Gareth went with her, accompanied by a dwarf who knew his real identity. Throughout their journey Gareth had to endure the caustic tongue of Lynette, who had no wish to have her cause championed by a mere kitchen worker. However, Gareth prevailed against Black, Green and Red Knights before finally defeating the Red Knight of the Red Lands and subsequently marrying Lyonesse.

During Arthur's war against the Roman Emperor THEREUS, Gareth killed King DATIS of Tuscany, but was himself killed by the fleeing yet unarmed LANCELOT, on the occasion when the latter was discovered in Queen GUINEVERE's bedchamber. His story, recounted by Sir Thomas MALORY, seems French in origin, and it is quite possible that it was based on a now lost French romance.

GARGAMELLE

Arthurian

A giantess who was created by MERLIN from the unlikely ingredients of the bones of a cow whale and ten pounds of GUINEVERE's nail clippings. Her mate was called GRANDGOUSIER, also created by Merlin, and their offspring named GARGANTUA.

GARGANTUA

Arthurian

The giant son of GRANDGOUSIER, whom MERLIN had made from a bull whale's bone and a phial of LANCELOT's blood, and GARGAMELLE, likewise created by Merlin from the bones of a cow whale and ten pounds of GUINEVERE's nail clippings. This impossible being, born of impossible parents, was obviously a simple derivation of the word 'gargantuan', but was said to have saved ARTHUR who furnished him with a 60-foot-long club. Gargantua also once had an encounter with the minuscule TOM THUMB, the latter managing to place him under an enchantment.

GARLIN

Arthurian

The King of GALORE who was, according to the German *DIU CRÔNE*, the father of GUINEVERE and GOTEGRIM.

GARLON

Arthurian

The brother of King PELLAM, this evil and invisible knight was killed by BALIN.

GARLOT

Arthurian

The realm of King NENTRES, who was married to one of ARTHUR's sisters. It was also said to have been the kingdom of URIEN, and is possibly identifiable with Galloway.

GARMAN

Irish

The son of GLAS. From his grave a lake was said to have formed.

GARMANGABI

British

A goddess whose name is known only from an inscription found at Lanchester near Durham. Her name appears to mean 'Giving' or 'Generous', thus connecting her with the later goddess GEFION as a bestower of gifts. It is thought that her name may be Teutonic in origin and that she was introduced to BRITAIN during the Roman invasion.

GARMNA

Irish

The consort of ERCOL to whom MEDHBHA and AILILL sent CÚ CHULAINN, LOEGHAIRE BUADHACH and CONALL CERNACH to be judged during the aftermath of the feast thrown by the malicious BRICRIU.

GARTNÁN

Irish and Arthurian

A King of SCOTLAND and the father of CANO, who, after a period in exile, succeeded him. His historicity is slightly doubtful, although if he did live it was certainly prior to AD 688, as this is the recorded date for the death of his son.

GARWEN

Arthurian

According to the Welsh *TRIADS*, the daughter of HENIN THE OLD and one of ARTHUR's three mistresses.

GARWY

Arthurian

Given the epithet 'the Tall', Garwy was the father of INDEG, who was, according to the Welsh *TRIADS*, one of the three mistresses of ARTHUR.

GASCONY

Arthurian

A region of south-west FRANCE. In *CLARIS ET LARIS*, it was ruled by King LADON, while in Welsh tradition the king is the elder BORS. The Irish romance the *VISIT OF GREY HAM* makes the HUNTING KNIGHT the son of the king of this region.

GASOZEIN

Arthurian

Appearing in *DIU CRÔNE*, this character claimed that GUINEVERE was his wife prior to her marrying ARTHUR, and that she should leave the King and return with him to his home. Even though the choice was left with Guinevere, and she chose to stay with Arthur, her brother GOTEGRIM considered she was wrong. In anger Gotegrim carried her off and intended to kill her. Gasozein rescued her and then fought GAWAIN over her. He eventually admitted that his claim had been fictitious.

GASTE FOREST

Arthurian

The realm of King PELLINORE, it was probably identical with the WASTE LAND.

GAUL

General

A Roman province in western Europe, which stretched from what is now northern Italy to the southern part of the Netherlands. The name is most commonly used nowadays to refer to FRANCE, but this is not strictly accurate. The Gauls themselves were divided into several distinct groups, but united under a common religion that was controlled by the DRUIDS. One group of Gauls invaded Italy *c.* 400 BC, sacked Rome and settled between the Alps and the Apennines. This region, known as Cisalpine Gaul, was conquered by Rome *c.* 225 BC. The Romans conquered southern Gaul between the Mediterranean and the Cevennes *c.* 125 BC, the remaining Gauls as far as the Rhine being conquered by JULIUS CAESAR between 58 and 51 BC.

GAURIEL

Arthurian

A warrior who had a pet ram that he had taught to fight and who features in a German romance written by Konrad von Stoffeln. He married the ruler of FLURATRONE, but she abandoned him, saying that she would return only after he had captured three of ARTHUR's knights for her, a task Gauriel accomplished. Having done so, he spent a year with Arthur.

GAU-VAIN, -WAIN

Arthurian

Variants of GAWAIN.

GAVIDA

Irish

An alternative name applied to GOIBHNIU in his role as foster father to his nephew LUGH.

GAWAIN

Arthurian

Also GAUVAIN, GAUWAIN, GAYAIN, WALGA(I)NUS, WALEWEIN, BALBHUAIDH, GWALCHMAI

(1) One of the most prominent of ARTHUR's knights, Gawain was the eldest son of LOT and MORGAUSE, though in Welsh tradition there appears to be some confusion over his parentage. Sometimes GWYAR is given as his father, sometimes as his mother. In French romances his name is variously given as Gauvain, Gauwain, Gayain, etc.; in Latin he is *Walganus* (GEOFFREY OF MONMOUTH calls him Walgainus); in Dutch *Walewein* and in Irish *Balbhuaidh*. Welsh tradition calls him Gwalchmai – 'hawk of May' or 'hawk of the plain'– but it has been argued, some think successfully, that Gwalchmai and Gawain were originally different characters, the Welsh simply identifying their Gwalchmai with the continental Gawain. Others have, with almost equal success, argued that the two have always been identical. In origin, if Gwalchmai and Gawain were always the same character, he appears to be the *MABINOGION* character GWRVAN GWALLT-AVWY, which in turn seems to have been derived from the Welsh *gwalltavwyn* (hair like rain) or *gwalltaclvwyn* (fair hair). He is also possibly to be identified with UALLABH, the hero of a Scottish tale.

His story is variously given, but aside from minor differences it is as follows.

He was the son of King Lot of LOTHIAN, who was, in his early days, a page to Arthur's sister Morgause, and on whom he fathered Gawain. The *DE ORTU WALUUANII* makes his mother ANNA rather than Morgause. Having been baptised, he was set adrift in a cask, eventually rescued by fishermen, made his way to Rome and was knighted by Pope SULPICIUS. Arriving at Arthur's court, he became one of that King's most prominent knights, depicted in early romance as a great champion but less likeable in later works that were influenced by the writing of Sir Thomas MALORY, who seems to have taken a particular dislike to him. French romances, on the whole, portray Gawain as promiscuous in the extreme.

Various tales give him different wives, including AMURFINE, RAGNELL, the daughter of the King of SORCHA and the daughter of the CARL OF CARLISLE. Italian romance made him the lover of PULZELLA GAIA, the daughter of MORGAN Le Fay, while he was the husband or lover of YSABELE in *WALEWEIN*. His sons are named as FLORENCE, GUINGLAIN and LOVEL.

Following Arthur's argument with LANCELOT, and the latter's departure from the court, Gawain became violently opposed to Lancelot, and accompanied Arthur on his continental expedition against the ROMAN EMPIRE. Landing back in BRITAIN, he was killed with a club, though according to Breton tradition he survived the last battle of CAMLANN and actually succeeded Arthur, who abdicated in his favour. His death did not mark his last appearance, for his ghost was reputed to have advised Arthur in the run-up to Camlann.

The owner of a horse named GRINGALET, Gawain had the strange power of becoming stronger towards noon, while his strength diminished again during the afternoon. This same trait has also been attributed to ESCANOR, one of Gawain's enemies. This peculiar gift appears to be Welsh in origin, as this is the special skill attributed to GWALCHMAI, who was one of the party picked to help CULHWCH in his quest to locate OLWEN. He may, therefore, have a solar origin, possibly being a memory of some ancient solar deity. Connection has also been made between Gawain and CÚ CHULAINN, the archetypal Irish warrior who, like Gawain, owned an enchanted belt that rendered the wearer invulnerable.

William of MALMESBURY reports that his grave was discovered during the reign of King William II (1087–1100) at Ros, though this location cannot be determined with any certainty. His skull was supposed to have been held in Dover Castle.

Gawain participated in a beheading contest with a giant, the story appearing in the tales of *SIR GAWAIN AND THE GREEN KNIGHT*, *SIR GAWAIN AND THE CARL OF CARLISLE* and *TURK AND GAWAIN*. This story, which is paralleled in the Irish story of Cú Chulainn, possibly represents a memory of some earlier pagan hero who was the prototype of Gawain. Some have maintained that Gawain is identical with Cú Chulainn, this association being drawn not just from the similarity of the stories but also from the fact that the tales seem to come from the north of England, and in ancient times a tribe known as the Setantii lived in this region, and the original name of Cú Chulainn was SÉTANTA. It is not very hard to see how this association was made. The anonymous but famous *Sir Gawain and the*

Green Knight gives possibly the best-known account of this episode.

During Arthur's Christmas Feast the festivities were interrupted by the arrival of a GREEN KNIGHT, who challenged the knights present to cut off his head, setting as the only condition that he be allowed to retaliate in the same manner the following year. Only Gawain dared accept the challenge.

Another story concerning Gawain comes from the vicinity of CARLISLE during the days when Arthur was alleged to have held his court there, and is related in a traditional Border ballad. Outside the city walls Arthur was overpowered by a local knight who spared his life on the condition that within a year he would return with the answer to the question 'What is it that women most desire?' No one at his court could supply the answer, so Arthur was honour-bound to return to the knight when the year had elapsed and forfeit his life. On his way to the meeting, Arthur was approached by a hideous woman who told him that she would give him the answer, provided the King found a husband for her. Arthur agreed, and the hag told him that the one thing women desire most is to have their own way. The answer was related to the knight and, proving correct, Arthur's life was spared. Returning to his court, he appointed Sir Gawain to be the ugly woman's husband, thus fulfilling his promise

Though she was hideous beyond comprehension, Gawain always treated her with knightly courtesy, and in return the woman offered Gawain a reward. She would become beautiful either by day or by night, the choice was his. Remembering the answer she had given Arthur, Gawain told her that she might have her own way and bade her choose for herself. His chivalrous answer broke the enchantment under which she had been held, and she immediately became beautiful by both day and night.

Commentators seeking the origins of the Arthurian characters have suggested that Gawain was originally Arthur's son, as the story of Gawain's birth and his subsequently being set adrift mirrors that of MORDRED. This version of events suggests that Gawain was the incestuous son of Arthur and his sister, who was MORGAN Le Fay in the original story. Again Morgan Le Fay to Morgause does not take much imagination. It has also been suggested that Gawain was originally one of the GRAIL questers, but was later replaced by GALAHAD because of the former's pagan origins and continuing associations. Similarly, PERCEVAL has been mooted as the replacement character.

(2) 'The Brown', a knight who had the baby GAWAIN baptised.

GAWAYNE
Arthurian
Variant spelling of GAWAIN that appears in the original title of the famous fourteenth-century *SIR GAWAYNE AND THE GREENE KNIGHT*.

GAYAIN
Arthurian
A variant of GAWAIN.

GEF(IO)N
British
A chthonic goddess of giving whose name is thought to have derived from GARMANGABI and is possibly the ANGLO-SAXON form of that name.

GEIS
Irish
A variant of GESSA.

GENDAWD
Arthurian
The father of GWYL who was, according to the Welsh *TRIADS*, one of ARTHUR's three mistresses.

GENERON
Arthurian
Thomas HEYWOOD's *Life of Merlin* makes this a castle belonging to VORTIGERN, replacing the tower that refused to stand in other versions of the story.

GENITI GLINNE
Irish
'Damsels of the Glen'. Although it is not clear what, or who, these beings were, it is thought that they may be a resemblance of a pre-Celtic nature spirit. They appear in the Celtic literature as being associated with the TUATHA DÉ DANANN. In the *Taín Bó Cuailngè* the Geniti Glinne are associated with NEMHAIN or BODB, and they wreak confusion on the forces of MEDHBHA, but they appear to have been afraid of the DONN CUAILNGÈ, for they would not go near him.

GENNEWIS
Arthurian
The realm of King PANT, who married CLARINE, the mother of LANCELOT in a Germanic version of the latter's story.

GEN-VISSA, -UISSA
British and Arthurian
According to GEOFFREY OF MONMOUTH, the daughter of the Roman Emperor CLAUDIUS. She

married ARVIRAGUS and, when her husband revolted against her father, restored the peace.

GEOFFREY OF MONMOUTH
General

The twelfth-century chronicler (*c.* 1100–*c.* 1154) who wrote two important Latin works. Thought to be the son of Breton parents, he studied at Oxford and was archdeacon of Llandaff or Monmouth (*c.* 1140), being appointed Bishop of Saint Asaph in 1152. His totally fictitious *HISTORIA REGUM BRITANNIAE* (*History of the Kings of Britain*) deals with a pseudo-mythical history of BRITAIN. Although worthless as history, it is notable for its substantial section on King ARTHUR. According to Geoffrey of Monmouth, this work was based on an earlier Welsh work that he alone had seen and was the first to contain a coherent narrative account of King Arthur. The second, *VITA MERLINI* (*Life of Merlin*), is wholly Arthurian and, in verse, tells of the madness and adventures of MERLIN (MYRDDIN).

GERAINT
Arthurian

A variant of GEREINT.

GERBERT
Arthurian

The thirteenth-century author of a *CONTINUATION* to *PERCEVAL* by CHRÉTIEN DE TROYES.

GEREINT
Arthurian
Also GERAINT

The King of DUMNONIA, he married ENID, their adventures being told in the Welsh romance *GEREINT AND ENID*, a version of *EREC ET ENIDE*, the hero of the earlier French version being substituted with Gereint, a local Welsh hero. Listed as a contemporary of ARTHUR, even being made a cousin, Gereint may be older, for the *MABINOGION* story of *THE DREAM OF RHONABWY* calls his son CADWY, and makes that son the contemporary of Arthur. Another *Mabinogion* story, *CULHWCH AND OLWEN*, names two of his brothers as ERMID and DYWEL. His father's name is usually given as ERBIN, but the *Life of Saint Cyby* makes this character his son.

GEREINT AND ENID
Arthurian

A Welsh romance, possibly dating from the twelfth century, that features in the *MABINOGION*. It is based on the French romance *EREC ET ENIDE* by CHRÉTIEN DE TROYES, but substitutes a local Welsh hero for EREC.

GERENTON
Arthurian

Mentioned in one of the numerous pedigrees of ARTHUR as one of his ancestors, the father of CONAN.

GERMAN
Irish

A companion of MAÍL DÚIN.

GERMANUS
British and Gaulish

A Gallic bishop who came to BRITAIN in AD 429 to regulate the Church, which had been divided by Pelagian heresy. News reached him of a combined SAXON and PICT raid, which he met with a British force that lay in ambush until Germanus rose and shouted 'Hallelujah!' three times, a cry that was, apparently, sufficient to cause the Saxons and the Picts to turn tail and flee.

The name Germanus appears on the Pillar of ELISEG in the eighth paragraph of the inscription on that pillar. This states that Germanus blessed BRITU, son of VORTIGERN, but, seeing that Germanus was sided against the Saxons, this would seem to indicate that his blessing was not of a kindly nature but one that would today be called a curse.

GERMANY
Arthurian

During the traditional Arthurian period this country was the domain of various tribes. However, the romance *CLARIS ET LARIS* makes its ruler the Emperor HENRY, father of LARIS.

GERONTIUS
Arthurian

A Roman leader, he overthrew the rule of the historical Roman Emperor Constantine III in BRITAIN.

GESSA
Irish
Also GEIS

A form of magical spell, or enchantment. It was famously used during the wedding feast of GRÁINNE and FIONN MAC CUMHAILL, when Gráinne used it to induce DIARMAID UA DUIBHNE to elope with her.

The gessa appears to have originated as a form of bond that, if broken, would lead to dishonour or even death. The Celtic people were very honourable and lived by the motto that a 'man's word is his bond'. CONCHOBAR MAC NESSA used the gessa of FERGHUS MAC ROICH that he might not refuse the hospitality of another to good effect when he wanted to dispose of the sons of UISNECH, who were being escorted back to EMHAIN MHACHA under Ferghus mac Roich's protection. Conchobar mac Nessa simply had a member of the RED BRANCH, BARUCH, invite Ferghus mac Roich to feast with him, knowing that Ferghus mac Roich dare not refuse. This left the sons of Uisnech without their guardian, and they were easily disposed of.

Tradition embroidered the gessa into a magical spell that embodied the life forces of the individual. The death of CÚ CHULAINN was attributed to his breaking the gessa (here plural) that governed his very existence. To break the gessa was to break a promise, and to the Celts this would mean dishonour and death, either at their own hand or by the hand of another. It has even been suggested that a Celt so dishonoured would commit suicide rather than live, but this has never been proved or disproved.

GEST OF SIR GAUVAIN
Arthurian

A thirteenth-century English verse romance that survives only in a fragmentary condition, and includes details of the combat between GAWAIN and BRANDILES.

GEWISSEI
Welsh

An ancient people who inhabited the south-east of WALES and who were at one time ruled by Octavius, who made himself King of BRITAIN and chose MACSEN as his successor.

G(H)ULBAN
Irish

The owner or, more correctly, the foster father of the monstrous BEANN GHULBAN.

GIANT
General

Many giants are to be found in Celtic mythology and legend. BRITAIN was said to have been ruled by a race of giants before the arrival of BRUTUS, who defeated them, though even he was accompanied by a 'giant', CORINEUS. Later giants tended to be portrayed as clumsy, greedy cannibals who dominated whole districts. Traditionally, a giant could not be overcome by sheer strength but could be defeated by trickery and cunning. One of the best known of all children's fairy tales is 'Jack and the Beanstalk', in which a giant is defeated by JACK THE GIANT-KILLER. This giant is none other than the Cornish giant CORMORAN.

GIANT OF MONT SAINT MICHEL
Arthurian

A giant, living on the Mont SAINT MICHEL off the coast of BRITTANY, who seized HELENA, the niece of HOEL, King of Brittany. ARTHUR, KAY and BEDIVERE set off after him, but found that Helena was already dead. They slew the giant none the less.

GIANTS' -RING, -ROUND, -DANCE
British and Arthurian

(Latin *Chorea Gigantum*) The legendary name given to STONEHENGE in Wiltshire. According to legend it was a memorial commissioned by AMBROSIUS AURELIUS to honour the British warriors slain by the SAXONS under the command of HENGIST. The ring of stones was transported from Mount KILLARAUS in County Kildare, IRELAND, to be re-erected on SALISBURY PLAIN by MYRDDIN (MERLIN) and 15,000 men. Each of the stones of the ring was said to have medicinal qualities and was alleged to have been originally carried to Ireland by giants who originated in Africa, giants whom some say were the first inhabitants of the earth and who were the forefathers of ALBION. This is, of course, pure fantasy, as Stonehenge pre-dates the time of the Saxons by several thousand years.

GIDOLIN
Welsh

A dwarf who was said to keep flasks of hag's blood warm on the 'hearth of hell'. CULHWCH was set the task of fetching these flasks as one of the conditions imposed on him by YSPADDADEN in his quest to marry OLWEN.

GILAN
Arthurian

Duke of SWALES and the original owner of the dog PETITCRIEU, which he gave to TRISTAN.

GILANEIER
Arthurian

The name given to ARTHUR's queen in the romance *Jaufré*.

GILBERT
Arthurian

A knight and the father of BRANDILES.

Giant with human figures, thought to be the Giant of Mont St Michel, whom King Arthur was said to have defeated. Illustration for the Inferno *from* The Divine Comedy *by Dante. (© Corbis)*

GILDAS JUNIOR
British and Arthurian
An alternative name for TREMEUR, the son of
TREPHINA and CUNOMORUS.

GILDAS, SAINT
British and Arthurian
A Romano-British historian and monk working in the
traditional Arthurian period. Born in STRATHCLYDE,
he fled the strife that raged in his neighbourhood and
went to WALES, where he married. He became a monk
only after his wife had died. His famous work, *DE
EXCIDIO ET CONQUESTU BRITANNIAE*, probably
written between AD 516 and 547, and most likely
written while Gildas was still quite a young man, does
not mention ARTHUR by name, but it does mention
the Battle of BADON. It is the only extant contemporary history of the Celts, and the only contemporary
British version of events from the invasion of the
Romans to his own time. The *MABINOGION* story of
the *DREAM OF RHONABWY* makes him Arthur's
counsellor. Other stories make him the son of CAW,
brother of HUEIL and friend of Arthur. While in
IRELAND he learned that Arthur had killed his
brother, but he appears to have remained on friendly
terms with him.

GILFAETHWY
Welsh and Arthurian
The son of DÔN and brother of GWYDION FAB
DÔN. Gilfaethwy fell for the beautiful GOEWIN, who
held the post of foot-holder at the court of MATH FAB
MATHONWY, a post that could be held only by a
virgin. Learning of his brother's desire, Gwydion fab
Dôn used his magic arts to conjure up a quarrel
between Math fab Mathonwy and PRYDERI. While
Math fab Mathonwy was away fighting Pryderi,
Gilfaethwy and Gwydion fab Dôn abducted Goewin,
whom they took turns in ravishing. When Math fab
Mathonwy returned and discovered what had
happened, he punished the brothers by condemning
them to spend three years in animal forms, the first as
male and female deer, the second as swine and the third
as wolves. At the end of each year, when Gilfaethey
and Gwydion fab Dôn had produced an offspring, Math
fab Mathonwy changed them into their next form. At
the end of the three years, each having been male and
female, he considered their punishment to be complete
and changed them back into human form. Gilfaethwy is
the Celtic origin of GRIFLET.

GILIERCHINS
Arthurian
One of the various names given to the father-in-law

of TRISTAN. He was called HAVELIN by
EILHART and JOVELIN by GOTTFRIED VON
STRASSBURG, while this variation appears in the
Italian *TAVOLA RITONDA*.

GILLOMANIUS
Irish and Arthurian
A King of IRELAND who sided with, and aided,
PASCHENT when the latter invaded BRITAIN.

GILMAURIUS
Arthurian
Although no such King of IRELAND is known by
this name, GEOFFREY OF MONMOUTH asserts
that he was the King of Ireland whom ARTHUR
defeated when he invaded that country.

GIOMAR
Arthurian
The nephew of ARTHUR who became the subject of
MORGAN Le Fay's attentions while she was a lady-
in-waiting to GUINEVERE. The Queen separated
them, and as a result Morgan Le Fay was said by
some sources to have sown the first seeds of doubt
in Arthur's mind regarding the fidelity of his wife.

GIRALDUS CAMBRENSIS
Welsh and Arthurian
The Norman–Welsh chronicler and ecclesiastic (*c.*
1146–*c.* 1223). Of noble birth, he was born in
Manorbier Castle, DYFED, his father being Gerald
de Barn, Lord of Manorbier, and his mother being
Angharad, daughter of Gerald of Windsor by the
Welsh Princess Nest. He was educated at the abbey
of Saint Peter, Gloucester, and later studied in Paris.
He became Archdeacon of Saint David's, but when
his uncle the bishop died (1176), he was overlooked
for the position because he was a Welshman. He was
again overlooked for the same vacancy in 1198, and
after that time concentrated on his studies and
writing, although his important *Itinerarium
Cambriae* was written after he had travelled the
length and breadth of WALES in 1188 in the
company of Baldwin, then Archbishop of
CANTERBURY. Though not usually referred to as a
major Arthurian source, he did, however, comment
on MERLIN, stating the reason for his period of
madness, but also saying that there were two
Merlins, one a wizard, the other a wild man.

GIRFLET
Arthurian
A variant of GRIFLET that would appear to be a
simple spelling error.

GISMIRANTE

Arthurian

A little-known knight who appears in a fourteenth-century *cantare* by the Italian poet Antonio Pucci. In this he is one of ARTHUR's knights who heard of a land where, every year, the King's daughter went naked to church, anyone seeing her being beheaded. Gismirante travelled to that land and abducted the girl, though later he had to rescue her from a savage man who ran off with her.

GLAIN

Arthurian

A magic snake egg that MERLIN sought. It appears only in an early Cornish poem.

GLAS

Irish

The father of GARMAN.

GLASTONBURY

General

A small town in Somerset, England, arguably one of the most magical towns in BRITAIN, around which a multitude of legends has arisen, particularly its famous tor (hill) and ruined abbey. It is the home of countless legends, Celtic, ANGLO-SAXON and Christian, and even today it is a magical, mystical place with an air of mystery about it. Even the noise and fumes of modern-day traffic cannot detract from the unique atmosphere of Glastonbury. According to tradition, the abbey was founded by missionaries from Rome *c.* AD 166, named by some as DERUVIAN and PHAGAN, to the then British King, LUCIUS. Others say it was founded by Saint Patrick prior to his mission to the Irish, or, most popularly, by JOSEPH OF ARIMATHEA. However, there is no real evidence to suggest that there was an abbey on this site prior to the seventh century, although there is evidence of a much smaller and older church on the site, and it is perhaps this that has become elevated to the status of abbey prior to the true date for the foundation of the abbey church itself.

According to medieval traditions, Glastonbury was visited by Jesus as a boy, in the company of his uncle, Joseph of Arimathea, a tin trader, who came to the West Country for Mendip lead and Cornish tin. This particular trip is said to have been the inspiration for William Blake's poem 'Jerusalem', which begins:

> And did those feet in ancient time
> Walk upon England's mountains green?

Joseph of Arimathea, who took Jesus' body down from the Cross and placed it in his sepulchre, is said to have returned to BRITAIN some years later – AD 37 or 63 – bringing the Christian message with him. With eleven followers, he made his way to Glastonbury, wishing to be among the friendly and influential Druids he had met during his earlier visits. On arrival, he stuck his wooden staff into the ground, and it immediately took root and blossomed as a young tree. He took this as a divine sign that he had reached his journey's end. This tree is now immortalised as the HOLY THORN or GLASTONBURY THORN, which has the special attribute of blossoming twice a year, in the spring and at Christmas.

Joseph of Arimathea was alleged to have brought the Chalice Cup of the Last Supper with him, as well as two cruets containing the blood and sweat of Christ. Although the latter two were said to have been later buried with him in his Glastonbury grave, the whereabouts of the Chalice Cup was, and still remains, unknown, though some commentators have said that it too was buried with Joseph of Arimathea. It has become entangled in myth, and is identified with the Holy GRAIL of Arthurian fame.

The local king, ARVIRAGUS, gave Joseph of Arimathea and his disciples twelve hides of land – a hide being a medieval measure of land equal to the area that could be tilled with one plough in a year. On this land they built their wattle-and-daub church, dedicated to the Virgin Mary, which has its traditional site as the location of the Lady Chapel within the abbey. It had the name *Vetusta Ecclesia*, or Old Church, and, though dilapidated in later years, did not disappear until a tragic fire swept through the abbey on the night of 25 May 1184.

The legends continued in the century following Joseph of Arimathea's arrival. Pope ELUTHERIUS, at the request of King Lucius, Arviragus' grandson, sent two emissaries, Deruvian and Phagan, to invigorate the work of Glastonbury. These two are credited with the foundation of the abbey, though other accounts say that it was founded in the fifth century by Saint Patrick, who was the abbot at Glastonbury before leaving to convert the Irish people to Christianity. The patron saint of WALES, Saint DAVID, is said to have travelled to Glastonbury at a later date, accompanied by seven bishops to dedicate the Old Church, but was warned in a dream that the Lord had already done so. Instead, David added another church and dedicated that.

The town remains most famous for its Arthurian connections, which started to appear during the seventh century. The legends regarding King ARTHUR and Glastonbury really start with his death. If CAMELOT is indeed to be identified with CADBURY CASTLE, across the moors, it seems perfectly reasonable to equate Glastonbury with AVALON, which is how many people saw the association. In 1191 the monks at Glastonbury claimed to have uncovered the bodies of both Arthur and GUINEVERE just south of the Lady Chapel. Their relics were said to have been 16 feet down in the hollowed-out trunk of an oak tree. With them was a leaden cross with the Latin inscription *Hic jacet sepultus inclitus Rex Arturius in insula avalonia* (Here lies Arthur, the famous King of the Isle of Avalon); or, alternatively, the inscription *Hic jacet Arthurus, rex quondam, rex futurus* (Here lies Arthur, king that was, king that shall be). When the political and domestic background of the times is considered, this 'finding' of Arthur seems extremely convenient. King Henry II was having immense problems with the Welsh, who believed that Arthur was sleeping and would return to lead them to victory. To prove that Arthur was dead by exposing his grave made sound and prudent political sense. Excavations at the same spot have revealed a break in the charred earth resulting from the fire, and the base of a pyramid that was said to have been next to the graves. These at least confirm a part of the monks' story.

Also, as the abbey had experienced its terrible fire in 1184, the additional kudos brought to the abbey through this 'discovery' ensured many more pilgrimages would be undertaken, thus bringing in the huge sums of money needed for the rebuilding work. After 600 years Arthur was becoming a cult figure, and the monks obviously saw no harm in attaching his cult status to the abbey. Some eighty-seven years after the remains of Arthur and Guinevere had been 'uncovered', they were reburied in front of the abbey's high altar in 1278. Obviously they had lost none of their romantic or political importance, for this reinterment was attended by King Edward I and Queen Eleanor. The tomb into which Arthur and Guinevere were supposedly placed was made of black marble and survived until the Dissolution in 1539. Its position was rediscovered during the excavation in 1934 and is now clearly marked within the ruins. The inscription at Glastonbury today reads:

The site of King Arthur's Tomb

In the year 1191 the bodies of King Arthur and his queen were said to have been found on the south side of the Lady Chapel.

On 19 April 1278 their remains were removed in the presence of King Edward I

and Queen Eleanor to a black marble tomb on this site. This tomb survived until the dissolution of the Abbey in 1539.

Legend also says that Glastonbury is connected with the returning of EXCALIBUR to the LADY OF THE LAKE, though in this instance it is a river and not a lake into which Excalibur is said to have been thrown. On the main road between Street and Glastonbury lies the POMPARLES BRIDGE (*Pons Perilis*) over the River Brue. It is from this bridge that Excalibur was said to have been thrown and, as it tumbled towards the waters of the River Brue, a hand reached out and caught it, drawing it into safekeeping beneath the water. Another story links Arthur with the little chapel on the island of Beckery (now unfortunately located adjacent to the town sewage works). Told to go to the chapel by an angel, Arthur saw Mary and the infant Jesus there.

The quest for the Holy Grail would have involved Arthur at Glastonbury. One supposed hiding place of the Grail was at the bottom of a well that is known as the Chalice Well. This is an unlikely story, for the name was a medieval transplant and did not come into local use until after 1306. Its alternative name, 'blood spring', which some say equates it with the blood of Christ, which was supposedly caught in the chalice, comes from the high concentration of iron in the water, which leaves a blood-red deposit on the stones it passes over. Arthur has also been associated with the GLASTONBURY ZODIAC, being identified as Sagittarius, while the zodiac itself has been regarded as the ROUND TABLE.

GLASTONBURY CROSS
Arthurian
The leaden cross that was unearthed when the grave of ARTHUR and GUINEVERE was supposedly uncovered by the monks at GLASTONBURY in 1191. It was the inscription on this cross that led to the identification of the bodies, for it read, in Latin, *Hic jacet sepultus inclitus Rex Arturius in insula avalonia* (Here lies Arthur, the famous King of the isle of Avalon). Alternatively, the inscription was said to read: *Hic jacet Arthurus, rex quondam, rex futurus* (Here lies Arthur, king that was, king that shall be). The cross was subsequently lost, but in recent times a pattern-maker named Derek Mahoney claimed to have found it and reburied it.

GLASTONBURY THORN
British and Arthurian
A thorn tree situated within the grounds of GLASTONBURY Abbey. It was said to have grown

Glastonbury Abbey, where Arthur and Guinevere's remains were allegedly discovered in 1191.
(© Jean Williamson/Mick Sharp)

from the staff of JOSEPH OF ARIMATHEA, although some sources state that the original tree grew on Weryall Hill. The thorn had the special attribute of flowering twice a year, in the spring and at Christmas. The tree is first mentioned in the *Lyfe of Joseph of Arimathea*, which dates from *c.* 1500, but only its descendants remain alive today, for the original thorn was cut down in 1643 by a Puritan zealot. The best-known surviving tree is that in front of the Church of Saint John the Baptist in Glastonbury, from which a sprig is sent every Christmas to the reigning monarch.

Various other legends exist about this Holy Tree. Some accounts say that the original tree, from which Joseph of Arimathea's staff had been cut, grew from a thorn from the Crown of Thorns worn by Christ. Local Somerset legends also tell of those who wished the tree harm. Usually the Puritans were blamed in these stories, but the tree always seemed to get the better of them. One particular assailant attacked the thorn with an axe, but it slipped from the trunk and embedded itself in the man's leg, while wood chips flew into his eyes.

An alternative legend says that the Glastonbury Thorn was not a thorn tree at all but a walnut tree. Early writers described this tree, again said to have sprung into life from the staff of Joseph of Arimathea, saying that it budded on Saint Barnabas' Day (11 June) and never before. It seems that, until this tree was cut down, it was held in the same degree of reverence as the Glastonbury Thorn, for both trees, walnut and thorn, were thought, by some, to have once existed in the town.

GLASTONBURY TOR

British

The hill at GLASTONBURY, Somerset, around which various legends have arisen. The Tor is said to be the home of GWYNN AP NUDD, Lord of the Dead, and is thus regarded as a portal between the world of the living and the OTHERWORLD. The summit of the Tor is reached by a man-made, labyrinthine spiral path that winds its way around the side of the hill, which, according to some, was also man-made and should thus be considered alongside such places as SILBURY Hill. The tower that stands at the summit is all that remains of the Church of Saint Michael, a fourteenth-century church that replaced a much earlier building. Celtic hermits occupied cells on the summit and slopes of the hill, and traces of a prehistoric settlement have also been found. It seems natural for the Celts, and later the Christians, to have maintained the sanctity of the Tor, for the survival of a few ancient stones

around the Tor indicates that the hill also had a religious significance to the megalithic peoples.

See also COLLEN

GLASTONBURY ZODIAC

Arthurian

According to the theory postulated by Kathryn Maltwood in her 1930s book *A Guide to Glastonbury's Temple of the Stars*, the zodiac consists of giant figures in the landscape surrounding GLASTONBURY, their outlines being delineated by such things as field edges, roads, streams, etc. These figures supposedly correspond to the heavenly signs above them, and each figure has been equated with episodes in the quest for the Holy GRAIL, ARTHUR himself being said to be represented by Sagittarius. While the theory has attracted some following, many people consider the zodiac's existence to be pure fantasy.

GLEIN, RIVER

Arthurian

Located at the mouth of either of the English rivers having this name was the site of one of ARTHUR'S BATTLES.

GLENTHORNE

Arthurian

Place on the Devon coast where, in stormy weather, JOSEPH OF ARIMATHEA, with the young Christ on board, was said to have run his ship ashore. In need of fresh water, Joseph of Arimathea and Jesus went on a fruitless search. As a result, Jesus caused a spring to rise and it has never failed since.

GLENVISSIG

Welsh and Arthurian

The realm of ATHRWYS, which has been identified by some with GWENT.

GLEWLWYD (GAFAELFAWR)

Welsh and Arthurian

Also GLWELWYD

Featuring in Welsh tradition, Glewlwyd appears in the *MABINOGION* story of *CULHWCH AND OLWEN* as ARTHUR's porter, and has the epithet *gafaelfawr* (great grasp) applied to him, a logical epithet for a porter, though he is also referred to as one of the TWENTY-FOUR KNIGHTS of King Arthur's court. In the poem *PA GUR*, he appears as the gatekeeper to Arthur's court who refuses to admit CULHWCH and his companions until they have identified themselves, though he declared that never in all his long and varied career had he seen so handsome a man as the youthful Culhwch.

The Glastonbury Thorn, which allegedly grew from the staff of Joseph of Arimathea.
(© Jean Williamson/Mick Sharp)

GLIFIEU
Welsh and Arthurian
Also GLUNEU EIL TARAN
One of the seven survivors of the expedition to
IRELAND mounted by BENDIGEID VRAN to
avenge the cruelty being dealt out to his sister
BRANWEN by the Irish King MATHOLWCH. He
and his six compatriots carried the severed head of
Bendigeid Vran back from Ireland and, following
Bendigeid Vran's instructions, after a lengthy
journey, buried it under the WHITE MOUNT in
LONDON. Glifieu's companions are named as
PRYDERI, MANAWYDAN FAB LLYR, TALIESIN,
YNAWC (YNAWAG), GRUDYEN (GRUDDIEU)
and HEILYN, Glifieu himself sometimes being called
GLUNEU EIL TARAN. They brought the
unfortunate Branwen home with them, but, when she
sat down and thought of the destruction wreaked on
her behalf, she died of a broken heart.

GLIGLOIS
Arthurian
The son of a German noble who served as Sir
GAWAIN's squire. Both he and his master fell in
love with GUINEVERE's maid, BEAUTE. She
chose Gliglois.

GLITEN
Welsh and Arthurian
The name of one of the nine sisters of MORGEN
(MORGAN Le Fay).

GLITONEA
Welsh and Arthurian
The name of one of the nine sisters of MORGEN
(MORGAN Le Fay), and thus co-ruler of an OTHER-
WORLD kingdom that is usually identified with
AVALON. She is possibly the same character as
GLITEN.

GLOIER
Arthurian
The King of SORELOIS.

GLORIANA
Arthurian
In SPENSER's allegorical *FAERIE QUEENE*,
Gloriana is the allegorical representation of Queen
Elizabeth I of England. ARTHUR saw her in a
dream and fell in love with her.

GLORIANDE
Arthurian
The wife of King APOLLO of LIONES.

GLUNEU EIL TARAN
Welsh and Arthurian
Named in some sources as one of the seven
survivors of the expedition to IRELAND mounted
by BENDIGEID VRAN. He is more usually referred
to as GLIFIEU.

GLWELWYD
Arthurian
Also GLEWLWYD
The gatekeeper at King ARTHUR's court who was
the first to meet CULHWCH as he came to the court
to ask for help in locating OLWEN. He declared that
Culhwch was the most handsome youth he had ever
laid eyes on.

GLWYD(D)YN
Arthurian
Also GWLYDDYN
The carpenter who built ARTHUR's feasting hall,
EHANGWEN. His name may be a remembrance of
GWYDION, a Celtic god, the son of NODENS.

GOBAN
Irish
See GOIBHNIU

GOBBÁN (SAER)
Irish
'Gobbán the Wright', a miraculous builder and
marvellous mason who is an aspect of the divine smith
GOIBHNIU, although some authorities simply give
Gobbán Saer as a more modern variant of Goibhniu.

GODFREY
Arthurian
A Danish duke and the father of OGIER, he appears
in the Carolingian romance *OGIER LE DANOIS*.

GODODDIN, THE
Arthurian
Traditionally composed by Aneurin, a Welsh court
poet who flourished in the late sixth and early
seventh centuries, this poem can claim to contain the
first literary allusion to ARTHUR, unless, of course,
the relevant line is a later addition. A contemporary
of TALIESIN, and similarly supposed to have
courtly connections with URIEN of RHEGED,
Aneurin celebrated the British heroes from
Gododdin, which stretched from the Forth to the
Tees, who were annihilated by the SAXONS in the
bloody Battle of Cattraith (Catterick in Yorkshire)
c. AD 600. In the poem the prowess of a British
warrior is compared to that of Arthur:

He stabbed over three hundred of the finest,
He glutted black ravens on the ramparts of the fort,
Although he was no Arthur.

This reference, if in fact included in the original poem, indicates that Arthur was already widely known in the north by that time.

GOEMAGOT
British

A variant of GOGMAGOG, although it is possible that this is the original name of that particular giant, and that Gogmagog is a later Christianisation taken from the Gog and Magog who appear in the Bible (Revelation 20:8).

GOEWIN
Welsh

The beautiful daughter of PEBIN. She held the post of foot-holder, a post that could be held only by a certified virgin, at the court of MATH FAB MATHONWY. There she came to the attention of GILFAETHWY, the brother of GWYDION FAB DÔN. Gwydion fab Dôn magically contrived a quarrel between Math fab Mathonwy and PRYDERI, and, while Math fab Mathonwy was away fighting Pryderi, Gilfaethwy abducted Goewin. The two brothers ravished the maiden, but were made to suffer a humiliating punishment for this crime on the return of Math fab Mathonwy, who made them spend three years in animal form and have three offspring as a result.

GOFANNON
Welsh and Arthurian
Also GOVANNON

The divine smith whose honour it was, according to ancient Welsh law, to have the first drink or toast at any feast held in a chieftain's court. Gofannon was said to have struck the blow that killed DYLAN EIL TON. Gofannon may have his origins in the Welsh father god GWYDION and is undoubtedly the Welsh version of the Irish GOIBHNIU.

GOG
British

A legendary giant whose companion was MAGOG, although this pair are perhaps none other than the giants of the same name that appear in the Bible (Ezekiel 38, *passim*; Revelation 20:8). The pair are usually combined into one giant named GOGMAGOG, but in this form they were said to have been defeated by BRUTUS and chained to a palace that once stood on the site of the Guildhall in

LONDON, the palace possibly being the one established by BRUTUS in his capital of TROIA NOVA.

Legends from the Middle Ages said that Gog and Magog led similarly named nations that had been confined behind an immense range of mountains by Alexander the Great after he had conquered BRITAIN. This is, of course, a complete fabrication, for Alexander the Great never landed anywhere on the British Isles.

GOG AND MAGOG
British and Arthurian

During the Middle Ages these two characters were thought to be nations that were confined behind mountains, having been imprisoned there by ALEXANDER THE GREAT, who had used 6,000 iron and bronze workers to build a huge gate to hold them back. In the Arthurian tales it seems that they escaped their confinement and attacked ARTHUR, but the latter was helped by the giant GARGANTUA, and Gog and Magog were overcome. They were then said to have been chained to a palace on the site of London's Guildhall.

Not all tales make Gog and Magog separate giants, referring instead to a single gigantic character known as GOGMAGOG. It is said that he led twenty others against BRUTUS at TOTNES, Devon, but was engaged in single combat by CORINEUS, Brutus' ally, who threw him over the cliffs to his death, though some accounts place this battle at Plymouth. This legendary giant is still remembered today in Cambridgeshire, where his name is given to a range of low-lying hills to the west of Cambridge.

GOGMAGOG
British and Arthurian

A legendary giant, one of the original inhabitants of BRITAIN, he led twenty others against BRUTUS when he landed at TOTNES, Devon. Gogmagog, who also appears as the two giants GOG and MAGOG, was engaged in single combat by CORINEUS, who overcame him and hurled him from Plymouth Hoe to his death. His name possibly derives from the Bible (Ezekiel 38, *passim*; Revelation 20:8), and may probably be considered as a depaganisation by later Christian writers.

GOGVRAN
Welsh and Arthurian

One of the various names, along with OCVRAN, that is given to the father of GUINEVERE in Welsh tradition.

The legendary giants Gog and Magog, who were said to have been chained to a palace on the site of London's Guildhall. (© Elio Ciol/Corbis)

GO(I)B(H)NIU

Irish

Also GOBAN

The divine smith and leader of the triad TRÍ DÉ DÁNA. He was accompanied by two other deities, or aspects, sometimes referred to as his brothers, these aspects being CREIDHNE, the god of metalworking, and LUCHTAINE, the divine wheelwright. His name is thought to come from the Old Irish *goba*, 'smith'. All three were particularly active during the Second Battle of MAGH TUIREDH when they worked at lightning speed to make and repair the weapons of the TUATHA DÉ DANANN, these weapons being magically empowered and thus causing wounds from which none could recover.

In the OTHERWORLD Goibhniu once hosted a feast at which his guests, through a magical, highly intoxicating drink, were rendered immortal. He is known in WALES as GOFANNON.

See also AN GLAS GHAIBHLEANN, COLUM CUALLEINECH

GOLDEN ISLAND

Arthurian

The realm of PUCELLE AUX BLANCHE MAINS, the fairy lover of GUINGLAIN.

GOLEUDDYDD

Welsh and Arthurian

The wife of KILWYDD. During her pregnancy, she lost all reason and aimlessly wandered the countryside. As the first labour pains started, her sanity returned, although this happened while she was standing in the middle of a herd of swine. So frightened was Goleuddydd that she immediately delivered the child, a boy, who was named Culhwch to commemorate the place of his birth, for in Welsh *hwch* means 'pigs'. Later Arthurian legend additionally made Goleuddydd the sister of Igraine and the aunt of King ARTHUR. Though she is normally given as the sister of Igraine, one genealogy for Arthur unusually makes her the sister of CUSTENNIN and YSPADDADDEN, and the aunt of Igraine.

GOLISTANT

Arthurian

A son of MARHAUS, the daughter of King ANGUISH of IRELAND and the brother of AMOROLDO.

GOLL

Irish

The son of the King of MAGH MELL, and the

nephew of FIACHNA. Coil abducted the wife of Fiachna and staved off all attempts made to release his captive. Fiachna travelled from the OTHERWORLD and secured the help of LOEGHAIRE, who accompanied him back to Magh Mell and released Fiachna's wife.

GOLL MAC MORNA
Irish
Also AODH
The son of MORNA, leader of the FIAN before the arrival of FIONN MAC CUMHAILL, and a friend of DIARMAID UA DUIBHNE. He was out hunting with Diarmaid ua Duibhne and two other members of the fian when, as night fell, they came to a small hut where they were welcomed and entertained by an old man and his beautiful young daughter. That night each of the four men propositioned the girl, but she turned each of them down, saying that she was the personification of Youth, and that, though once she had belonged to them, they might never have her again.

Goll mac Morna was also present at the wedding feast of Fionn mac Cumhaill and GRÁINNE and was one of those not drugged by Gráinne when she sought to make off with Diarmaid ua Duibhne, for she needed witnesses to the bond under which she placed Diarmaid ua Duibhne. The other witnesses were OISÎN, OSCAR and CAOILTE MAC RONAN.

GOLWG HAFDDYDD
Arthurian
In the Welsh version of the TRISTAN legend, *Ystoria Trystan*, this character is the maid of ISEULT.

GOMERET
Arthurian
The kingdom of BAN, which is alternatively known as BENWICK. Most commonly, though, Ban is called the King of BRITTANY, leading to the assumption that Gomeret and Benwick were either alternative names for Brittany or sub-kingdoms within the realm of Ban.

GONERIL(LA)
British
One of the two older daughters of the mythical King LEIR, her sister of comparable age, some say her twin, being REGAN. The two played upon the vanity of their father to give them a quarter of his kingdom each as their dowries. Their younger sister CORDELIA refused to be a part of this deceit, and so received nothing. Subsequently Goneril and Regan, along with their respective husbands, MAGLAURUS, Duke of ALBANY, and HENWINUS,

Duke of CORNWALL, seized the rest of Leir's kingdom. Maglaurus initially allowed Leir to keep a retinue of 140 men, but Goneril reduced that to eighty, then Regan reduced it to five, before Goneril once more reduced it to a single man.

GONOSOR
Arthurian
A King of IRELAND who was converted to Christianity by JOSEPH OF ARIMATHEA. In respect of the help he had given King CANOR of CORNWALL, a tribute was paid by Cornwall to Ireland until TRISTAN killed MARHAUS.

GOON DESERT
Arthurian
The brother of the FISHER KING, he was killed by PARTINAL. The sword used to kill him broke in the process, and its rejoining became one of the feats involved in achieving the Holy GRAIL.

GORBODUC
British
A King of BRITAIN, the husband of JUDON and the father of FERREX and PORREX. Because neither of his sons left an heir, Porrex killing Ferrex, and Porrex being killed by Judon, the line of descent from BRUTUS died out when Gorboduc himself died.

GORDDU
Welsh
The 'Hag of Hell', the collection of whose blood was one of the tasks set CULHWCH by YSPADDADEN.

GORE
Arthurian
Variously described as the kingdom of URIEN, and thus possibly preserving a memory of RHEGED, or BAGDEMAGUS. It lay on the borders of SCOTLAND, from which it was separated by the River TEMPER, crossable only by one of two bridges, one like the edge of a sword, the other under water. If one of ARTHUR's knights entered the realm, only LANCELOT could rescue him.

GOREU
Arthurian
The son of CONSTANTINE by an unnamed daughter of AMLAWDD WLEDIG. His name, meaning 'best', was earned for managing to gain entrance to WRNACH's stronghold with his followers. He was a cousin of ARTHUR, whom he is said to have rescued on three occasions from imprisonment. One curious family tree for Arthur,

that prepared by T. W. Rolleston, makes Goreu the brother of ERBIN and IGRAINE, and thus the uncle of Arthur. Furthermore, this peculiar genealogy names Goreu's father as CUSTENNIN.

GORIAS
Irish
A mythical city, the home of ESIAS, one of the four wizards who taught the TUATHA DÉ DANANN their magical arts. The city was the origin of the invincible sword of LUGH.

GORLAGON
Arthurian
Featuring as the hero of the thirteenth-century Latin romance *ARTHUR AND GORLAGON*, Gorlagon was the husband of a faithless wife who, with the aid of a magic wand, turned him into a wolf, that wolf subsequently becoming ARTHUR's pet. ARTHUR obtained the wand and restored Gorlagon to his former shape.

GORLOIS
British and Arthurian
Duke of CORNWALL and husband of EIGYR (IGRAINE), the beautiful woman who became the subject of the infatuation of UTHER. Helped by MYRDDIN (MERLIN), who magically altered Uther's appearance so that he resembled Gorlois, Uther was able to enter Gorlois's castle at TINTAGEL, Cornwall, and lie with Eigyr. That very same night the real Gorlois was killed in battle with Uther's troops, so Eigyr later married Uther. Later legend has extended what was obviously a local legend to the point where this story relates the magical conception of King ARTHUR. A building named CARHULES near Castle DORE in Cornwall appears to have been named after a person named GOURLES, who was, perhaps, the original of Gorlois.
   See also IGRAINE

GORMAC
Irish
'Dutiful son', one of the names of BRES and one to which he certainly did not live up.

GORMANT
Arthurian
According to the *MABINOGION* story of *CULHWCH AND OLWEN*, a brother of ARTHUR on his mother's side, his father being named as RICA, the chief elder of CORNWALL. In Welsh tradition it seems as if Rica occupies the position normally associated with GORLOIS.

GORMUND
Arthurian
An African King who conquered IRELAND and established his realm there, according to GEOFFREY OF MONMOUTH. It would seem that his name has given rise to GURMUN, who, according to GOTTFRIED VON STRASSBURG, was the son of an African king who became the King of Ireland and the father of ISEULT.

GORNEMANT DE GOORT
Arthurian
A KNIGHT OF THE ROUND TABLE and Prince of GRAHERZ. He trained PERCEVAL in all the knightly skills in the hope that he would marry LIAZE, his daughter, but that did not come about. His three sons, GURZGI, LASCOYT and SCHENTEFLEURS, all met violent deaths.

GORSEDD
General
The name given to a meeting place of bards, augurs and DRUIDS.

GORVENAL
Arthurian
Born in GAUL, Gorvenal started out as the tutor and later servant of TRISTAN. He married BRANGIEN, ISEULT's maidservant, and ascended to the throne of LIONES when Tristan left. He and Tristan were said to have been given refuge by PHARAMOND following the death of MELIODAS.

GOSWHIT
Arthurian
Meaning 'goose white', this was the name given to ARTHUR's helmet in the works of LAYAMON.

GOTEGRIM
Arthurian
The brother of GUINEVERE, according to the German *DIU CRÔNE*, whom he abducted when she refused to leave ARTHUR in favour of GASOZEIN, who claimed already to be her husband.

GOTTFRIED VON STRASSBURG
Arthurian
The thirteenth-century author (*fl.* 1200) of the masterly German romance *TRISTAN AND ISOLDE*, based on the Anglo-Norman poem by THOMAS. Very little is actually known about his life, but he was famous as an early exponent of literary criticism, having left numerous appraisals of the poets of the period.

GOURLES

Arthurian

Cornish person after whom it is thought that CARHULES, a building near DORE CASTLE, CORNWALL, is named and who, it has been suggested, was the original of Gorlois.

GOURMAILLON

British and Arthurian

An alternative name that has been applied to both CORMORAN and GOGMAGOG. This has led to a possible identification between these gigantic figures, making the giant disposed of by CORINEUS, Gogmagog, the same as the one disposed of by JACK THE GIANT-KILLER and commonly known through nursery rhyme as Cormilan or, more correctly, Cormoran. Further, the application of this variant to both giants leads to the supposition that Jack the Giant-killer is a memory of the gigantic Trojan Corineus.

GOVANNON

Welsh

See GOFANNON

GOWRA

Irish

The popular name for GABHRA, the site of the mythical battle between opposing factions within the FIAN.

GRACIA

Arthurian

One of ARTHUR's nieces, according to the fourteenth-century *BIRTH OF ARTHUR* (cf. GRAERIA).

GRADLON

Gaulish

A historical sixth-century King of BRITTANY, whose statue today stands between the towers of the medieval cathedral at Quimper. His daughter was DAHUT, also called AHES, who was said to have been responsible for the inundation of the legendary city of YS.

GRAERIA

Arthurian

One of ARTHUR's nieces, according to the fourteenth-century *BIRTH OF ARTHUR* (cf. GRACIA).

GRAHERZ

Arthurian

GORNEMANT DE GOORT was described as being a prince of this domain.

GRAIL

British and Arthurian

Possibly the most widely known of all the Arthurian legends is the Quest for the Holy Grail. The Grail itself was thought to be the Chalice used by Christ at the Last Supper, or, according to some sources, the cup used to catch the blood of Christ from the wound inflicted upon him by the centurion LONGINUS while Christ hung upon the Cross.

When JOSEPH OF ARIMATHEA came to GLASTONBURY in either AD 37 or 63, he was said to have brought with him two cruets containing the blood and sweat of Christ, as well as the Chalice. It is this Chalice that has become embroiled in the legends concerning the Holy Grail. In essence the legend is as follows.

Each year the KNIGHTS OF THE ROUND TABLE gathered at CAMELOT for the feast of Pentecost, to relate their deeds and the marvels they had beheld. Each year, however, their company remained incomplete, for the last place, the SIEGE PERILOUS, remained empty. According to custom, they had, each year, found their names were written in gold around the ROUND TABLE, but one year they found new words written above the Siege Perilous. These read: 'Four hundred winters and four and fifty accomplished after the passion of our Lord Jesu Christ ought this siege be fulfilled.'

LANCELOT stated that he had accounted for the time since the Crucifixion, and said that the siege ought to be fulfilled that very day. All the other knights agreed, and they covered the Siege Perilous with a silk cloth so that the words could not be seen until the rightful knight came to them. They did not have long to wait. As they seated themselves at their own respective places at the Round Table, an old man entered the hall at Camelot accompanied by a fresh-faced young knight who was unarmed, save for an empty scabbard at his waist.

As the entire company watched, the old man led the boy up to the Round Table, and then to the Siege Perilous beside Lancelot. Lifting the silk cloth off the siege, the gathered knights saw that the lettering had changed, and now read: 'This is the siege of Galahad the haut prince.' Sitting the young knight on the Siege Perilous, the old man departed, leaving the boy as the centre of attention. Many marvelled that one so young should dare sit in the siege, but Lancelot recognised him as his son, and knew that all that had been prophesied had been fulfilled.

The following day Arthur led GALAHAD to a lake near Camelot where his knights had found a sword set in a stone. Here accounts vary, for some say the stone, complete with sword, was taken to

Camelot, though others say it was left where found. This sword was inscribed with lettering that pronounced that only the best knight in all the world would pull it clear. Many thought that this surely meant Sir Lancelot, but he declined even to try, for he remembered his sin of loving his Queen. Sir GAWAIN and Sir PERCEVAL both tried, and failed. Arthur, sure that Galahad was the rightful owner, bade him attempt, and he easily and cleanly lifted the sword from the stone. Placing it in his empty scabbard, Galahad found it a perfect fit.

At a great jousting tournament arranged so that Galahad might test his skills against the other knights, he acquitted himself superbly, managing to unhorse a good many of the Knights of the Round Table, save two whom he did not fight, Lancelot and Perceval. That evening the knights once again gathered in the hall at Camelot and scarcely had they sat down when there was a monstrous roar of thunder that shook the very walls. Amidst this clamour, the hall was flooded with a brilliant light that was described as being 'seven times' clearer than daylight, and all the knights present felt themselves filled with the grace of the Holy Ghost. They all appeared fairer than they ever were before, and they were all struck dumb by the presence they felt.

Then a golden centre appeared to this light, and, when the knights became accustomed to the brilliance of this new light, they perceived a dish, covered in white samite cloth, so that they could not see the dish itself. This was the Holy Grail, and with it came all manner of meat and drink that the knights loved best. Slowly the Grail crossed over the length of the hall, and then vanished as suddenly as it had appeared. In the sudden emptiness of the hall the entire company burst into one voice.

Sir Gawain was the first to his feet, pledging that he would go out in quest of the Holy Grail, promising to labour 'for a year and a day or longer if needs be', not resting until he had seen the Grail more openly than it had been seen that night. Each of the other knights made similar promises, but Arthur remained silent. He remembered the prophecies and teachings of MERLIN and knew that many of his knights would never return, and the Round Table would never again be complete.

The quest continued for many years, and all the knights who set out to seek this holiest of vessels had many wondrous adventures, but none more than Lancelot, who was to see the Grail at Castle CARBONEK, or Galahad, whose destiny it was to fulfil the quest.

Lancelot rode hard for several days until he came to an old chapel where he thought he might rest. He tried to enter, but found he could reach only the altar, richly covered in silk and set with six great candles in a silver candlestick. He found no way into the chapel and at last, tired and dismayed, laid himself on his shield at a stony cross outside.

Later he was half wakened when two white palfreys (saddle horses) rode up to the cross, bearing a sick knight who moaned in pain for the Grail to come to heal him. Still half asleep, for it seemed that he could not fully awaken, Lancelot stirred and witnessed the candlestick from the altar float to the cross. It was followed by a silver table and the shining holy vessel of the Grail, though Lancelot could not see anyone bearing it aloft. He heard the sick knight sit up and welcome the Grail, and he saw him kneel on the ground to touch and kiss the vessel. Having done so, the knight rose up again, healed. The Grail remained at the cross for some time, with Lancelot looking upon it, then it glided back into the chapel. Yet Lancelot found he had no power to follow it, and drifted back off to sleep.

When, some hours later, Lancelot properly awoke, he recalled all that he had seen and heard, but it seemed as if a dream. As he pondered on his recollections, a voice spoke to him and told him to remove himself from that holy place, for he was unworthy of being there. Lancelot was greatly troubled by these words, but knew the reason behind them, for, on a holy quest, his earthly sins, his lust for his queen, had made him unworthy. He was even more troubled when he found that the knight, whom he had witnessed being so miraculously cured, had taken his horse, helm (helmet) and sword.

Removing himself from the chapel, his heart leaden with sorrow, Lancelot went to a hermitage, where the hermit heard his confession and absolved him of his sins. With the hermit's blessing, Lancelot renewed his quest and, after many months, came to the water of MORTAISE, where he laid down to sleep. In his sleep Lancelot received a vision that told him to enter the first ship he came to. Arising, he went to the strand, where he found a ship that had neither sail nor oar and he entered. Upon doing so, he was overwhelmed by a great peace and joy. He remained with the ship for more than a month.

Growing somewhat weary of the small ship, Lancelot was seated on the shore one day when he heard the thundering of a horse's hoofs and saw a fair knight ride up and dismount. Taking his saddle and bridle with him, this knight went straight to the ship. Curious about this self-assured young knight, Lancelot followed and made himself known. The young knight was none other than Galahad, Lancelot's own son. The two embraced and told each other of their various adventures.

Sir Perceval and the Holy Grail. (© Bettmann/Corbis)

Upon leaving Camelot, Galahad had ridden into strange lands unknown to him. Many adventures had befallen him, but he was always successful in his endeavours and gained much in knightly experience. He had defeated many knights in fair combat, had given support to the defenders in a great siege and, with their comrades BORS and Perceval, had been set adrift in a boat, which had beached them in the marshes of SCOTLAND, there to be challenged and do battle with many knights.

Lancelot revelled in hearing of these adventures and felt proud of his son. For a full six months, father and son voyaged together in that boat and encountered many perilous adventures, but they never came near to the Holy Grail. Finally Galahad left his father to seek the Grail, as he was ordained.

Sorry to see his son depart, Lancelot placed his trust in the boat, and, after a month at sea, it beached at midnight beside a fine castle. A door opened out towards the sea and a voice bade Lancelot enter.

Arming himself for the adventure he knew lay ahead, Lancelot approached the gate. As he did, he saw two lions on guard and immediately drew his sword in readiness. As he did so, it was struck from his hand by some unseen force, and a voice chided his evil faith that he put more trust in his weapons than his Maker.

Without further challenge, Lancelot entered the castle, but once inside he could find no door that would open. Behind one door he heard sweet and reverent singing and he knew full well that the Grail was within. Dropping to his knees, he prayed to God that he should be shown at least some part of the Grail. Looking up from his prayers, he watched as the chamber door swung slowly open. A green light shone out from the room, a light that was the cleanest and purest Lancelot had ever seen. Within the light coming from that room was a silver table, the Holy Grail covered in red samite cloth and all the ornaments of the altar, along with a priest who seemed to celebrate mass. Lancelot could no longer bear to remain outside the room and, taking a deep breath, he strode into the room.

Reaching out to touch the holy vessel, Lancelot was thrown to the ground by a scorching wind. Unable to move, he felt hands all around him that carried him out of the room, leaving him in the passageway. The following morning the people of the castle found Lancelot's inert body and carried him to a bedchamber, where he lay without stirring. On the twenty-fifth day, he woke and, realising that he had achieved as much of the Grail quest as he was to be allowed, gave thanks to the Lord.

Elsewhere, Galahad, since leaving his father, had had many adventures, before meeting up with Bors and Perceval again. The three knights rode together until they came to Castle Carbonek, which they entered, to be received courteously by King PELLES, who knew that the quest for the Holy Grail would now be achieved.

King Pelles, his son ELIAZAR and the three knights sat down to dine, but before they could eat a voice came to them, saying: 'There are two among you that are not in the quest for the Holy Grail, and therefore you both should depart.' Pelles and his son stood up and, with a single glance at Galahad, they slipped away. Scarce had they gone when a man and four angels appeared before the knights. The angels set the man down before a table of silver, and on that table the Holy Grail appeared. The man, who was dressed in the robes of a bishop, started to celebrate mass. He kissed Galahad and directed Galahad to kiss his fellow knights, which he did. The man then disappeared.

Looking up, the three knights saw a man come out of the Grail, a man with open wounds that bled freely, as did those of Jesus Christ. He offered the Holy Grail to Galahad, who knelt and received his Saviour, who told him that he must depart with Bors and Perceval the following morning and put to sea in a boat they would find ready and waiting for them.

The following day the three knights set out and, after three days, they came to a ship, on board which they found a table of silver and the Holy Grail covered in red samite. They fell to their knees and prayed. The ship put to sea and took them to the pagan city of SARRAS. There they disembarked, taking the table of silver with them. They remained in that city for twelve months (some accounts make this year follow a period of imprisonment during which the Holy Grail sustained them). On that day, at the year's end, a man in the likeness of a bishop came to them, carrying the Holy Grail. They celebrated mass, and the man revealed himself to the knights as JOSEPHE, son of JOSEPH OF ARIMATHEA, and Galahad realised that his time on earth was near an end.

Galahad knelt before the table that held the Holy Grail and prayed. As he did so, his soul departed his body, and Galahad, having achieved his destiny, passed away. The watching Bors and Perceval beheld a host of angels take Galahad's soul to heaven, while a great hand came down and took the vessel and bore that up to heaven as well. That was the last that any earthly man saw of the Holy Grail.

The basis of the quest appears to come from Celtic traditions, and, although the story given here forms possibly the best-known version of the tale, there are innumerable variations. The word Grail is derived from the Old French *graal*, meaning a type of dish. The Grail is first mentioned in the works of CHRÉTIEN DE TROYES, in which Perceval is the hero, and the Grail itself is simply referred to as a 'grail', a common noun. It was not until later that it became '*the* Grail'.

At first Perceval fails to achieve the Grail, thanks to his not asking the GRAIL QUESTION – What is the Grail? Whom does it serve? – thereby restoring the MAIMED KING to health and the land to fertility. Even though in its final form the Grail has become the Chalice Cup of the Last Supper, its origins are not so simple to determine. Connection has been sought between the Grail of Arthurian legend and the Chalice supposedly brought to BRITAIN by Joseph of Arimathea, but the magical qualities of the Grail stories suggest a much older, OTHERWORLD connection.

Arthur's expedition to the Otherworld to obtain a magical cauldron, as recorded in the *PREIDDEU*

ANNWFN, seems to reflect the ability of the Grail to provide unending sustenance. This story has a direct parallel in the *MABINOGION* story of *CULHWCH AND OLWEN*. Both have aspects that directly relate to the Grail quest as we know it today, so either or both may have been used as the originals; thus the magical cauldron of Celtic tradition becomes transformed into the symbolic cup of the Eucharist. The romanticised events surrounding the quest itself are, however, without doubt purely the inventions of the various authors who have related the tale.

The FISHER KINGS, not mentioned as such in the above rendition of the Grail story, were said to be the descendants of Joseph of Arimathea who guarded the Grail in Castle Carbonek. Also associated with the Grail was a bleeding lance, usually identified with the LANCE OF LONGINUS, said to be that with which Jesus' side was pierced by the centurion (John 19: 34). In the instances where this connection is made, the Grail is also mentioned as having been used to catch Christ's blood as it flowed from this wound. It seems that this alone is the earlier use for the Grail, the association with the Last Supper (Matthew 26: 27–8) coming later.

In the early version of the Grail myth by Chrétien de Troyes, the mysterious and wondrous vessel is housed in the GRAIL CASTLE, where it is guarded by the GRAIL KEEPER. This guard, the wounded Fisher King, has been maimed 'through his thighs' (*sic*) and feeds only from a magical dish – the Grail. As a result of the injury, caused by the DOLOROUS STROKE, the land around the castle has become infertile and will revive only if the King himself is healed. This, however, can happen only if there is a knight brave enough to face all the perils on the dangerous journey through the 'land of wailing women' to the Grail Castle, and then be wise enough to ask the Grail Question. This will then break the enchantment under which the King and his land are held.

This curious tale is generally agreed to have derived from an ancient fertility myth, and it is interesting that the Christian symbol of a fish (Christ) appears to have been the origin of the Fisher King. The 'land of wailing women' is obviously a reference to the Otherworld, so again associations with the Celtic Otherworld of ANNWFN are not hard to make.

Even though Galahad is usually portrayed as being the sole knight to achieve the Grail, other sources beg to differ. The *CONTINUATIONS*, WOLFRAM VON ESCHENBACH and *PERLESVAUS* name the successful knight as Perceval. The *DIU CRÔNE* names GAWAIN and Sir Thomas MALORY names Galahad, Bors and Perceval as having all been

successful. The *QUESTE DEL SAINTE GRAAL* and its derivatives name Galahad, and it is this work that is alone in saying that the Grail was, after Galahad had completed his quest, carried up to heaven by a hand.

The Grail episode remains one of the most fascinating and enigmatic of all the Arthurian legends, and has found almost universal appeal, its underlying theme of seeking mystical union with God being appropriate to many religious beliefs, not solely Christianity.

GRAIL CASTLE
Arthurian
The castle, known as CARBONEK or CORBENIC, in which the Holy GRAIL was housed and where it was guarded by the FISHER KINGS.

GRAIL KEEPER
Arthurian
The MAIMED KING, GRAIL KING or injured FISHER KING who guards the Holy GRAIL in the GRAIL CASTLE. The Holy Grail sustains him while he waits for the purest knight to ask the GRAIL QUESTION, thus releasing him from his enchantment and achieving the goal of the quest.

GRAIL KING
Arthurian
Another name for the GRAIL KEEPER, MAIMED KING or FISHER KING, who is the custodian and guardian of the Holy GRAIL.

GRAIL PROCESSION
Arthurian
According to several versions of the GRAIL story, this procession was witnessed by PERCEVAL at the GRAIL CASTLE. According to CHRÉTIEN DE TROYES, the Grail was carried in a procession led by a squire with the bleeding LANCE. He was followed by two squires carrying ten-branched candlesticks, a damsel carrying the Grail itself and a final damsel carrying a plate. The *DIDOT PERCEVAL* describes the order of the procession as a squire with a lance, a damsel with two silver plates and cloths, and finally a squire with a vessel (the Grail) containing the blood of Christ. The Welsh *PEREDUR* says that the procession consisted of two youths carrying a large spear from which blood freely flowed, followed by a damsel carrying a salver on which there was a head swimming in blood. It is worth noting that the Grail Procession only ever appears in works where it is Perceval who achieves the Grail.

GRAIL QUESTION

Arthurian

The question to be asked of the wounded FISHER KING in order to break the enchantment under which he and his lands are held. The question is really twofold: 'What is the Grail? Whom does it serve?' At first PERCEVAL did not achieve the GRAIL simply because he forgot to ask this question. He did not make the same mistake twice.

GRAIL SPEAR

Arthurian

An alternative way of referring to the LANCE OF LONGINUS, or the BLEEDING LANCE.

GRAIL SWORD

Arthurian

Made by TREBUCHET, this sword shattered when it was used to strike down GOON DESERT, the brother of the FISHER KING. Making it whole again featured in some sources as a condition of the quest for the Holy GRAIL.

GRÁINNE

Irish and Arthurian

The beautiful daughter of CORMAC MAC AIRT. The ageing FIONN MAC CUMHAILL became betrothed to her, some accounts saying that he first saw Gráinne in the form of a deer into which she had been transformed, although this deer is usually called SAAR. Gráinne, however, loved DIARMAID UA DUIBHNE. During the wedding feast Gráinne drugged most of the company and then cast a GESSA spell on Diarmaid ua Duibhne and induced him to elope with her to a wood in CONNACHT, where they were besieged by Fionn mac Cumhaill. Gráinne was rescued by OENGHUS MAC IN OG, the foster father of Diarmaid ua Duibhne, who escaped himself by leaping over the heads of Fionn mac Cumhaill and the FIAN in a single, tremendous bound. Even at this stage Diarmaid ua Duibhne did not break his oath to Fionn mac Cumhaill and take Gráinne as his mistress. It was only after suffering the considerable derision of Gráinne that he finally committed this disloyal act.

Gráinne bore Diarmaid ua Duibhne four sons, and, at length, having been forced to live the life of fugitives, they were reconciled with Fionn mac Cumhaill through the good offices of Oenghus Mac in Og. However, the reconciliation was not perfect, for after Diarmaid ua Duibhne had been mortally gored by his foster brother, the boar BEANN GHULBAN, his only hope was to be given water out of the hand of Fionn mac Cumhaill. Three times Fionn mac Cumhaill let the life-giving water spill from his hands as he remembered the treachery of Diarmaid ua Duibhne and Gráinne. By the time the third lot of water had spilled away Diarmaid ua Duibhne was dead.

As with the stories of CANO and DERDRIU, the story of Gráinne is thought to be one of the origins of the TRISTAN story.

GRALLO

Irish and Arthurian

The grandson of CONAN MERIADOC, he was said to have married TIGRIDIA, sister of DARERCA.

GRAMOFLANZ

Arthurian

The brother-in-law of GAWAIN following his marriage to the latter's sister, ITONJE.

GRANDGOUSIER

Arthurian

The father of GARGANTUA, this giant had been created by MERLIN from a bull whale's bones and a phial of LANCELOT'S blood. His mate, GARGAMELLE, was also created by the wizard, this time from the bones of a cow whale and ten pounds of GUINEVERE's nail clippings.

GRANLAND

Arthurian

The territory ruled by the AMANGONS in the Old French *Le Chevalier as deus espées*, which is thought by some to have either been the original of Greenland or derived from that country's name.

GRANNUS

Gaulish

A healing deity who was possibly assimilated with the Graeco-Roman Apollo and who appears to have associations with the Irish GRIANAINECH, a title applied to the god OGHMA that means 'Sun-face'. His consort appears to have been the goddess SIRONA, whose name means 'star', a connection that is reminiscent of the major concept that underpins Celtic mythology, the Three Worlds of star, sun and moon. Historical records show that Grannus was invoked by the Emperor Caracalla in AD 215 in association with the Roman deities Aesculapius and Serapis, both healing deities, a record that confirms the medical attributes of Grannus.

GRATILLE

Arthurian

One of the two possible mothers of GRIMAL by EVELAKE, the other suggested mother being FLORIE.

GREAT FOOL

Arthurian

An unnamed nephew of ARTHUR and the hero of the Irish romance *Eachtra an Amadán Mor*. He was raised in obscurity in the woods following his brother's unsuccessful plot against Arthur. Having grown up, he proved to be a mighty champion, defeating many knights, including GAWAIN, the RED KNIGHT, the PURPLE KNIGHT and the SPECKLED KNIGHT.

GREAT GODDESS

Arthurian

Common to many cultures and beliefs was the concept of a Great Goddess, at once benevolent and malevolent. It has been suggested that ARTHUR was the last of a long line of hereditary priests of the Great Goddess, though this concept has not acquired a great following.

GREAT SPIRITS SPRING

Arthurian

Located at Windfall Run, USA, a spring to which, according to an unlikely American legend, ARTHUR went to drink of its healing waters.

GREEN CHAPEL

Arthurian

The chapel to which GAWAIN went in order to fulfil his promise to meet the GREEN KNIGHT one year after he had been challenged in ARTHUR's court to trade blows and had struck off the Green Knight's head.

GREEN KNIGHT

Arthurian

At least two knights in the Arthurian legends were simply known by this title.

(1) The most famous Green Knight features in one of the best known of all Arthurian poems, the anonymous fourteenth-century *SIR GAWAIN AND THE GREEN KNIGHT*, and its derivative the GREEN KNIGHT (*c.* 1500). This knight, whose name was BERTILAK and who lived at Castle HUTTON, came to ARTHUR's court and challenged any of the knights there present to trade blows. GAWAIN accepted and, being allowed to strike first, cut off the Green Knight's head. Calmly, that knight picked up his severed head and told Gawain to meet him on New Year's morn for his turn.

On his way to keep his appointment, Gawain lodged with a lord, and they agreed to give to each other what they had obtained every day during Gawain's stay. On the first day, while his host was out hunting, Gawain received a kiss from his host's wife, which was duly passed on. The second day Gawain received two kisses, and again he duly passed these on. The third day saw Gawain receiving three kisses and some green lace that would magically protect him. Only the kisses were passed on.

Having left his host's home, Gawain made his way to the GREEN CHAPEL, where he was to meet the Green Knight. He knelt to receive the blow. Three times the Green Knight aimed his sword at Gawain. The first two failed to make contact, while the third but lightly cut Gawain on the neck. Revealing himself, the Green Knight turned out to be none other than his host of previous days, who told him that he would not have cut Gawain at all had he been told about the lace.

This tale obviously has its origins in Celtic mythology, as it accurately reflects the legend of CÚ CHULAINN and CÚ ROÍ, where the former becomes translated into Gawain and the latter into the Green Knight.

(2) The epithet of Sir PERTOLEPE, who was defeated in combat by GARETH.

GREEN KNIGHT, THE

Arthurian

Based on the anonymous, fourteenth-century *SIR GAWAIN AND THE GREEN KNIGHT*, this work dates from *c.* 1500, but it is a much inferior telling of the famous incident between GAWAIN and the GREEN KNIGHT.

GREENAN CASTLE

Arthurian

Built on the site of an Iron Age fort and situated about three miles from Ayr, SCOTLAND, this has been suggested as the original CAMELOT, or even BADON.

GREENLAND

Arthurian

Called KALAALLIT NUNAAT in the native Greenlandic tongue, this island was allegedly conquered by ARTHUR, according to William Lambard in his *Archaionomia* (1568). The famous sixteenth- and seventeenth-century travel writer Hakluyt was of the opinion that Greenland was GROCLAND, while it also seems possible that Greenland may in fact be a derivation of GRANLAND, the territory ruled by the AMANGONS in the Old French *Le Chevalier as deus espées*.

GREGORY

Arthurian

A POPE who once brought MERLIN's orthodoxy into question. During his pontificate a bishop named

CONRAD was reported to have charged Merlin with heresy, possibly at the instigation of Gregory, but the wizard was acquitted. If this was indeed the correct name of the pope, it is possible that Pope Gregory I (pope from AD 590 to 604) is meant, but his pontificate falls too late to have been contemporary with the traditional Arthurian period.

GREIDAWL
Welsh and Arthurian
The father of GWYTHR.

GRELOGUEVAUS
Arthurian
In the First *CONTINUATION* to CHRÉTIEN DE TROYES's *PERCEVAL*, Greloguevaus is named as PERCEVAL's father.

GREY LADY
Arthurian
A ghost said to haunt MOEL ARTHUR in Llanwist, Clwyd, who, it has been suggested, is guarding the treasure of ARTHUR allegedly buried there.

GRIAN(AINECH)
Irish
A title, applied to the god OGHMA, that means 'sun-face'. It is this title that has led to the association between Oghma and the Gaulish GRANNUS.

GRIFFITH
Arthurian
Having obtained the throne of WALES by murdering the true king, Griffith was later ousted by the rightful heir, MERIADOC.

GRIFLET
Arthurian
Also GIRFLET
The son of DO, his name is also sometimes rendered as GIRFLET, and may be cognate with JAUFRÉ, the hero of a Provençal romance. In one version of the Battle of CAMLANN it was he, and not BEDIVERE, who was charged by the dying ARTHUR with returning EXCALIBUR to the LADY OF THE LAKE. Having seen Arthur's tomb, Griflet became a hermit, but died shortly afterwards. In origin Griflet is Celtic, a derivation of GILFAETHWY, who was described as the brother of GWYDION and son of the goddess DÔN in the *MABINOGION* story of *Math, Son of Mathonwy*. Griflet's father, Do, appears to have come from Dôn, even though this would mean a change of gender, for Dôn was Gilfaethwy's goddess mother in British tradition.

GRIMAL
Arthurian
The illegitimate son of EVELAKE, his mother being either GRATILLE or FLOREE.

GRINGALET
Arthurian
Also KINCALED
The name given to GAWAIN's horse, which is called Kincaled in Welsh tradition. The account of how he came to own Gringalet varies. One story says that he took it from the SAXON King CLARION, while another says he won it in a duel from ESCANOR Le Grand, even though at that time Gringalet was owned by Escanor's nephew, to whom it had been given by the fairy ESCLARIMONDE.

GRISANDOLE
Arthurian
The name used by the maiden AVENABLE when she went to the court of JULIUS CAESAR disguised as a page. She introduced MERLIN to the imperial court and eventually married JULIUS CAESAR.

GROCLAND
Arthurian
According to the *Itinerary* of Jacob Cnoyen, Grocland was an island in the polar regions, possibly cognate with GREENLAND, that was colonised by ARTHUR *c.* AD 530. The inhabitants of this land were alleged to have been 23 feet in height. Surrounding the Pole was a range of mountains through which four channels passed, forming four INDRAWING SEAS. Four thousand of Arthur's men were said to have gone to the Pole via these channels, but none returned. In 1364, it was alleged that seven of the men, plus one of Flemish descent, presented themselves to King Magnus of NORWAY. If true, then the date is wrong, for at that time Norway was ruled by King Haakon VI, and it would appear that the Magnus referred to was his predecessor, Magnus VII, who ruled between 1319 and 1355.

GROMER
Arthurian
A knight who, under an enchantment, was made to resemble a Turk, his story being told in the poem *TURK AND GAWAIN*, which dates from about *c.* 1500. He and GAWAIN travelled to the Isle of MAN, where, after various adventures, they killed the King and Gromer took his place, having been decapitated at his own request in order to break the spell.

GROMER (SOMER JOURE)
Arthurian
Better known simply as Gromer, this knight once captured ARTHUR and kept him prisoner.

GRONOIS
Arthurian
A son of Sir KAY.

GRONW -BEBYR, -PEBYR
Welsh and Arthurian
The hunter whom BLODEUWEDD took as her lover. Together the lovers plotted the death of Blodeuwedd's husband LLEU LLAW GYFFES. At Gronw Bebyr's suggestion, Blodeuwedd set about discovering how Lleu Llaw Gyffes might be killed, and at length managed to persuade him to reveal that he could be killed only by a spear that had been worked for a year and a day at mass time on Sundays, and then only if he were standing with one foot in a bathtub and the other on the back of a billygoat.

At length Blodeuwedd persuaded Lleu Llaw Gyffes to demonstrate the position to her. Gronw Bebyr, furnished with the necessary spear, hid in some nearby bushes and, when Lleu Llaw Gyffes adopted the ridiculous position, stood and hurled the spear at him but managed only to inflict a wound. Lleu Llaw Gyffes changed into an eagle and flew away to die from his wound, but was sought out and healed by GWYDION FAB DÔN. Lleu Llaw Gyffes returned to kill Gronw Bebyr, while Gwydion fab Dôn dealt with the infidelity of Blodeuwedd by changing her into an owl.

GRUD-DIEU, -YEN
Welsh and Arthurian
One of the seven survivors of the expedition to IRELAND mounted by BENDIGEID VRAN to avenge the treatment of his sister BRANWEN by MATHOLWCH. He and his six compatriots carried the severed head of Bendigeid Vran back from Ireland and buried it, after a lengthy journey, under the WHITE MOUNT in LONDON. Gruddieu's companions are named as PRYDERI, MANAWYDAN, TALIESIN, YNAWC (YNAWAG), GLIFIEU (GLUNEU EIL TARAN) and HEILYN. They brought the unfortunate Branwen home with them, but she died of a broken heart when she sat down and thought of the destruction wreaked on her behalf.

GUAILLAUC
Welsh
According to an inscription found on the Pillar of ELISEG, Guaillauc was the father of Eliseg, and the founder of the line of descent of the Kings of POWYS.

GUAIRE
Irish and Arthurian
A King of CONNACHT and the father of the beautiful CRÉD, who became the wife of the elderly MARCÁN, and the ill-fated lover of CANO.

GUENDOLOENA
Welsh and Arthurian
A flower-maiden who, in the medieval *VITA MERLINI*, is married to MYRDDIN (MERLIN). It is possible that she is to be identified with CHWIMLEIAN, who is mentioned in *AFOLLONAU*, although she may also be identified with that other famous Welsh flower-maiden, BLODEUWEDD. She is said to have been divorced by Myrddin. It seems quite likely that this Guendoloena is an immediate forerunner of the ill-fated GUINEVERE of the later Arthurian cycle.

GUENEVER(E)
Arthurian
A little-used variant of GUINEVERE.

GUENGASOAIN
Arthurian
He was guarded by a bear, for he knew that he could be slain only by a pair of knights. This came to pass when, to avenge RAGUIDEL, the knights GAWAIN and YDER slew him, the latter then marrying his daughter.

GUENLOIE
Arthurian
The wife of YDER. It is possible that she was the unnamed daughter of GUENGASOAIN whom YDER married after he and GAWAIN had slain Guengasoain to avenge RAGUIDEL.

GUIDERIUS
British and Arthurian
According to GEOFFREY OF MONMOUTH, this King of BRITAIN was killed during the Roman invasion that was led by CLAUDIUS. He was succeeded by his brother ARVIRAGUS.

GUIGENOR
Arthurian
A grandniece of ARTHUR, daughter of CLARISSANT and granddaughter of LOT and MORGAUSE, she married AALARDIN.

GUIGNIER
Arthurian
The pure wife of King CARADOC BRIEFBRAS

whose fidelity was tested and proved by a mantle that a boy had brought to ARTHUR's court, stating that it would fit only faithful wives. Various ladies tried it on, but it fitted only Guignier. She lost one of her breasts while dealing with a magical serpent that had entwined itself around her husband's arm. This was replaced by a magical golden shield boss, made for her by AALARDIN, who had once been in love with her. Guignier is identifiable with the Welsh TEGAU EUFRON.

GUINALOT
Arthurian

The offspring of ELIAVRES and a bitch with which the wizard had been forced to copulate.

GUINEBAUT
Arthurian

The brother of BAN and the elder BORS. He was an accomplished wizard who made a magic chessboard and caused a dance to continue perpetually.

GUINEVERE
Arthurian

Also GUENEVER(E), GWENHWYFAR, GWENHWYVAR

The wife of King ARTHUR and, according to Sir Thomas MALORY, the daughter of King LEODEGRANCE of CAMELIARD. Welsh tradition calls her Gwenhwyfar (Guinevere is simply a straight translation into English), and calls her father GOGVRAN or OCVRAN. She has a sister named GWENHWYFACH in the Welsh *MABINOGION* and she may have been preceded by GUENDOLOENA, who was said to have been married to, and subsequently divorced by, MERLIN (MYRDDIN). The German *DIU CRÔNE* makes her father King GARLIN or GALORE, and gives her a brother named GOTEGRIM. In French romance she had an identical half-sister who, for a while, took her place (*see* FALSE GUINEVERE). WACE says she was MORDRED's sister, while GEOFFREY OF MONMOUTH says she was of noble Roman descent and the ward of Duke CADOR.

Early versions of the Arthurian legends make no mention of the famous love affair between her and LANCELOT, and instead give the reason for Arthur's absence, leaving Mordred the chance to seize the throne and Guinevere, as Arthur's campaign against the ROMAN EMPIRE. It is the later version of the legends that most are familiar with, and in these she is the mistress of Lancelot. This version of her story is basically as follows.

Arthur wished to marry the daughter of King Leodegrance of Cameliard the very first time he saw her, thinking her the fairest and most valiant lady in all the land. However, as ever in these early years of his reign, he asked for the counsel of Merlin, for he was still guided by this wise wizard's words.

Merlin agreed that she was above all women in beauty and fairness, but warned Arthur that she would fall in love with Lancelot, and that this love would ultimately bring about the King's downfall. Arthur's heart was set and nothing Merlin said would make him change his mind. Finally Merlin went to King Leodegrance to tell him that Arthur wanted his daughter for his wife.

Naturally, King Leodegrance was overjoyed and immediately gave his consent, adding that he would send a gift to Arthur that would be far more pleasing than any land, for Arthur already had land enough. Instead he sent the ROUND TABLE, given to him by UTHER, which was capable of seating 150 knights, along with a company of 100 of the most noble knights in his realm. Arthur was rightly delighted with this gift and, while he made preparations for the coming wedding, he dispatched Merlin to find another fifty knights to complete the company that would become known as the KNIGHTS OF THE ROUND TABLE. When Merlin returned from his mission, there was but one remaining place to be filled, the SIEGE PERILOUS.

As the knights assembled in CAMELOT for the wedding of Arthur to Guinevere, the Knights of the Round Table had their duties set out for them by Arthur. He charged them never to commit murder or treason, never to be cruel, never to enter into battle for a wrongful reason whatever the reward, but ever to grant mercy when it was asked for, and ever to help ladies, whether gentlewomen or damsels, whenever help was needed. Every knight was sworn to this oath, and every year at Pentecost they returned to Camelot to reaffirm it.

Lancelot was a latecomer to the Knights of the Round Table, and, almost immediately after his arrival, it became clear that he was attracted to Guinevere, and she likewise. In clandestine meetings they affirmed their love, but, even though other members of his court knew of the affair, Arthur would hear nothing against his queen unless proof could be given to him. This played straight into the hands of the scheming Mordred, who wanted the throne as his own. In the company of twelve other knights, he trapped Lancelot and Guinevere in the Queen's bedchamber, but Lancelot, even though unarmed, managed to fight his way to freedom, killing all but one of the knights who sought to capture him.

GURZGI

Arthurian

One of the three sons of GORNEMANT DE GOORT, all of whom met with violent deaths.

GWADYN ODYEITH

Welsh

A seldom mentioned companion of CULHWCH in his quest to locate OLWEN. Gwadyn Odyeith's particular skill was to be able to strike as many sparks from the soles of his feet as would fly from a hammer striking white hot metal. He, like GWADYN OSSOL and several others, appears to have been dropped from later traditions, which altered the story to give it an Arthurian content.

GWADYN OSSOL

Welsh

A seldom mentioned member of the party formed to help CULHWCH in his quest to locate OLWEN. Each member was chosen for a particular skill, that of Gwadyn Ossol being that under his feet even the highest mountain would become a plain.

GWAELOD

Welsh

A legendary drowned kingdom, better known as CANTRE'R GWAELOD, said to lie beneath the waters of Cardigan Bay.

GWAL-CHAFED, -CHAVED

Welsh and Arthurian

'Falcon of Summer'. Suggested by some sources as originally being identifiable with GWALCHMAI, this character is thought, by a few, to have been the original of the Arthurian Sir Galahad.

GWALCHMAI (FAB GWYAR)

Welsh and Arthurian

Son of GWYAR, as indicated by his epithet, and one of the party formed to help CULHWCH locate the maiden OLWEN. His companions were CEI (KAY), BEDWYR (BEDIVERE), CYNDDYLIG the Guide, GWRHYR the Interpreter and MENW FAB TEIRGWAEDD. Gwalchmai fab Gwyar later resurfaced in the Arthurian cycle as the knight Gawain.

GWALES

Welsh and Arthurian

A stopping place in Pembroke mentioned in the *MABINOGION* of the seven survivors of the expedition to IRELAND mounted by BENDIGEID VRAN to avenge the ill-treatment of BRANWEN at the hand of the Irish King MATHOLWCH. They remained in a great hall at Gwales for a total of eighty years, the severed and uncorrupted head of Bendigeid Vran keeping them company, until one member of the seven opened a door facing towards CORNWALL. At once, all seven were filled with memories of what had passed and left to continue their journey to LONDON, where they fulfilled the last orders of Bendigeid Vran and buried his head, face towards FRANCE, under the WHITE MOUNT.

The seven survivors are named as PRYDERI, MANAWYDAN FAB LLYR, GLIFIEU, TALIESIN, YNAWAG, GRUDDIEU and HEILYN.

GWALHAFED

Welsh and Arthurian

Mentioned in the *MABINOGION* story of *CULHWCH AND OLWEN*, Gwalhafed was the brother of GWALCHMAI FAB GWYAR and thus one of the sons of GWYAR. His name should, perhaps, more correctly be Gwalhafed fab Gwyar. Later tradition seems to suggest that he is the original of the Arthurian knight Sir GALAHAD.

GWARTHEGYDD

Arthurian

The son of CAW and a counsellor to ARTHUR.

GWAWL

Arthurian

The daughter of COEL, who, possibly, married CUNEDDA.

GWAWL FAB CLUD

Welsh

The rejected suitor of RHIANNON who, disguised as a handsome, richly dressed youth, came to HEFEYDD's house and asked a boon of PWYLL, a boon that was unthinkingly granted. Gwawl fab Clud asked for Rhiannon. Although horrified by the boon, both Pwyll and Rhiannon were honour-bound to comply, Rhiannon suggesting that they should postpone her meeting with Gwawl fab Clud for a year, a suggestion that was accepted by both parties.

Rhiannon advised Pwyll that he should, on the night in question, have ready one hundred of his men hiding in the orchard. He himself was to enter her wedding feast in the guise of a shabbily dressed beggar carrying a sack. He should then ask for enough food to fill the sack, a request to which she would accede. They would trick Gwawl fab Clud into treading the food down into the sack, and thus capture him. Everything went as planned, and, as the sack was tied around Gwawl fab Clud, Pwyll blew his horn and summoned his men, who began to kick the sack around the hall until Gwawl fab Clud was forced to beg for mercy and to withdraw his claim to Rhiannon. Only when he had also promised never to seek vengeance was Gwawl fab Clud released and sent on his way.

GWEIR

Arthurian

Variously described as an adviser of ARTHUR and a knight, he was the son of GWESTYL.

GWEIR GWRHYD ENNWIR

Arthurian

According to the *MABINOGION* story of *CULHWCH AND OLWEN*, a maternal uncle of ARTHUR.

GWEIT PALADYR HIR

Arthurian

According to the *MABINOGION* story of *CULHWCH AND OLWEN*, a maternal uncle of ARTHUR.

GWENDDOL-AU, -EU

Welsh and Arthurian

A British prince who fought the Battle of ARFDERYDD against his cousins GWRGI and PEREDUR. He was killed during the battle. The Welsh MYRDDIN poems say that he was Myrddin's (MERLIN's) lord at the battle, his retinue being described as one of the six faithful companies of BRITAIN, for it continued to fight on for six weeks after the death of Gwenddolau. One of the *TRIOEDD YNYS PRYDEIN* elaborates the story, saying that he had birds that were tethered by a yoke of gold and that ate two corpses for dinner and supper. They were killed by GALL, the son of DYSGYFDAWD. The *VITA MERLINI* contradicts all the earlier sources by saying that Gwenddolau was a British prince who fought on the opposing side to Merlin at Arthuret. Fighting against his cousins Gwrgi and Peredur, he was killed in the fracas. Gwenddolau was said to have owned a GWYDDBWYLL board that was one of the THIRTEEN TREASURES OF BRITAIN.

GWENDOLEN

British and Arthurian

The daughter of CORINEUS whom LOCRINUS married, although he had to be forced to do this by her father after Locrinus had captured the beautiful German maiden ESTRILDIS, whom he would much rather have married. For seven years Locrinus kept Estrildis as his mistress, and during that time she bore him a daughter, HABREN, while Gwendolen gave him a son and heir, MADDAN. It is not known whether Gwendolen knew of the relationship between Estrildis and her husband.

After the death of Corineus, Locrinus deserted Gwendolen and installed Estrildis as his new queen. Gwendolen went to CORNWALL and raised an army. During a battle near the River Stour, Locrinus was killed by an archer. Gwendolen then commanded that Estrildis and Habren be drowned in a river, but in honour of the fact that Habren was Locrinus' daughter she ordered that the river should thenceforth carry her name. That river became known as the SABRINA to the Romans, and is today known as the River SEVERN.

Gwendolen reigned as queen for fifteen years before she abdicated in favour of her son Maddan and retired to Cornwall.

According to Sir Walter Scott's *The Bridal of Triermain* (1813), Gwendolen was the half-fairy mother of GYNETH by ARTHUR, and it seems reasonable to assume that Scott simply picked the name from the earlier legends.

GWENDYDD

Welsh and Arthurian

The name under which GANIEDA appears in Welsh poetry as well as in the *VITA MERLINI* by GEOFFREY OF MONMOUTH, in which she appears as the philandering wife of RHYDDERCH HAEL, whose infidelities were spotted and reported to her husband by her twin brother, MYRDDIN (MERLIN).

GWENHWY-FACH, -VACH

Arthurian

In Welsh tradition, the sister of GUINEVERE, whom she struck, thus leading to the Battle of CAMLANN. A more modern story, Thomas Love Peacock's *Misfortunes of Elphin* (1829), makes her the wife of MORDRED.

GWENHWY-FAR, -VAR

Welsh and Arthurian

The Welsh name for GUINEVERE. It is a late name that does not appear to have been in use prior to the establishment of the Arthurian cycle. In one version of the story of *CULHWCH AND OLWEN*, however, a character named as Gwenhwyfar, who may be the same, is said to have had two servants named YSKYRDAW and YSEUDYDD, who could run as rapidly as their thoughts, both of whom joined the expedition mounted by CULHWCH to locate OLWEN.

GWEN(N)

Welsh and Arthurian

1 In the *MABINOGION* story of the *DREAM OF RHONABWY*, Gwenn is the name given to a mantle that made its wearer invisible. In other sources it is simply referred to as MANTELL, or as the Mantle of Invisibility, and was said to number among the THIRTEEN TREASURES OF BRITAIN. Later tradition made King ARTHUR the owner of this treasure.

2 In Welsh tradition, the daughter of CUNEDDA and maternal grandmother of ARTHUR.

  See also EIGYR.

GWENT

Welsh and Arthurian

The kingdom of southern WALES that is thought to be identifiable with GLENVISSIG, the realm of MEURIG, father of ATHRWYS.

GWENWYNWYN

Arthurian

ARTHUR's chief fighter in the *MABINOGION* story of *CULHWCH AND OLWEN*.

GWERN

Welsh

The son of BRANWEN and MATHOLWCH. After BENDIGEID VRAN had mounted his expedition to IRELAND to avenge the cruelty being shown to Branwen, his sister, by Matholwch, the two sides entered into discussions, and they decided that the best way to solve the dispute was to make the infant Gwern King of Ireland. All seemed to be agreed until EFNISIEN picked up the infant and threw him onto the fire. Fighting broke out, which eventually left only five pregnant women alive in Ireland and all but seven of Bendigeid Vran's forces dead.

GWESTYL

Arthurian

The father of ARTHUR's adviser GWEIR.

GWEVYL

Welsh

A seldom listed member of the expeditionary force led by CULHWCH on his quest to locate the maiden OLWEN. Gwevyl was chosen as he was able, when sad, to let one of his lips fall to his stomach, and raise the other as a hood over his head.

GWIAWN

Welsh

One of the many seldom mentioned members of the party formed to help CULHWCH find OLWEN. Gwiawn became a member as he was skilled enough to remove a speck of dirt from the eye of a gnat without injuring it.

GWINAM GODDWF HIR

Arthurian

The horse of Sir KAY.

GWION (BACH)

Welsh and Arthurian

The tiny son of GWREANG. He was given the job of tending the cauldron in which CERRIDWEN was brewing a divine potion of inspiration and knowledge for her son AFAGDDU. At the end of the allotted time, a year and a day, three drops of the magical brew splashed out of the cauldron onto Gwion's thumb. He sucked the thumb to cool it and immediately knew all that had passed and all that was to happen in the future. This knowledge filled him with dread, for it told him that, aftger he had ingested the potency of the brew, Cerridwen would kill him. Gwion Bach thus took to his heels.

When Cerridwen found the potency of her potion had been stolen, she set off in hot pursuit of the fleeing Gwion Bach. He first changed into a hare in order to be able to run faster, but Cerridwen countered by becoming a greyhound. Gwion Bach leapt into a river and became a salmon, but the hag followed assuming the form of an otter. Gwion Bach rose out of the river as a bird, but Cerridwen followed as a hawk. Finally, Gwion Bach settled on a threshing floor and became one of the thousands of grains lying there, but even there he was not safe, for Cerridwen became a hen and swallowed him. Nine months later he was reborn as a beautiful boy, whom Cerridwen set adrift in a leather bag. This boy was rescued by ELPHIN and named TALIESIN.

Certain similarities may be seen between this story and that of FIONN MAC CUMHAILL, who, in Irish legend, accidentally touched the SALMON OF WISDOM, and gained knowledge and inspiration by simply biting the thumb that had touched that wonderful fish. It has even been suggested that Gwion Bach was a historical character who studied the Druidic arts and, filled with inspiration by what he had learned, began to compose poetry under the name of Taliesin.

GWLADYS, SAINT

Arthurian

In Welsh tradition, the daughter of BRYCHAN who was abducted by GWYNLLYM FILWK, King of GWYNLLYWG. ARTHUR saw Brychan giving chase, but gave his help to Gwynllym Filwk, as they had reached his realm. Gwladys and Gwynllym Filwk, according to Welsh tradition, became the parents of Saint CADOC.

GWLYDDYN
Arthurian
Variant of GLWYD(D)YN.

GWRAGEDD ANNW(F)N
Welsh
The name sometimes used to refer to supernatural women who lived in lakes. It means 'Dames of the Lower Regions' or 'Dames of Annwfn'.

GWREANG
Welsh and Arthurian
The father of GWION BACH.

GWRFODDHU HÊN
Arthurian
According to the *MABINOGION* story of *CULHWCH AND OLWEN*, a maternal uncle of ARTHUR.

GWRGI
Welsh and Arthurian
One of the cousins of the British prince GWENDDOLAU, the other being PEREDUR, who fought against the Prince at the Battle of ARTHURET.

GWRGI GWASTRA
Welsh
A vassal of PRYDERI who was, along with twenty-three others, at one stage offered as a hostage to MATH FAB MATHONWY if he would put an end to the war between them that had been caused when GWYDION FAB DÔN tricked Pryderi out of the swine his father had been given by ARAWN.

GWRHYR (GWALSTAWD IEITHEODD)
Welsh and Arthurian
Usually known with the epithet 'the Interpreter', Gwrhyr was one of the party formed to help CULHWCH in his quest to locate OLWEN. Each of the party, which consisted of CEI (KAY), BEDWYR (BEDIVERE), CYNDDYLIG the Guide, GWALCHMAI FAB GWYAR and MENW FAB TEIRGWAEDD, was chosen for their particular skills. Gwrhyr was chosen because he could interpret the language of animals. During the quest to locate Olwen, Gwrhyr first asked for directions from the BLACKBIRD OF CILGWRI. That bird sent them to the STAG OF RHEDYNFRC, who in turn passed them on to the OWL OF CWN CAWLWYD, who passed them on to the EAGLE OF GWERNABWY, who finally sent them to the SALMON OF LLYN LLW. Later Gwrhyr was cited as acting as an interpreter at the court of King ARTHUR when the story of Culhwch and Olwen had been adapted to suit the Arthurian romances.

GWRI
Welsh and Arthurian
The name given to the child born to PWYLL and RHIANNON after it had mysteriously disappeared one night from its crib. TEYRNON TWRYF LIANT took the child in and treated him as his own. A year later, learning of the loss of the child and because of the child's uncanny likeness to Pwyll, Teyrnon Twryf Liant concluded that the boy must be none other than the lost child of Pwyll and Rhiannon. He took the child back to his parents, who subsequently named him PRYDERI. It is thought that this legendary Welsh character is the origin of BORS.

GWRVAN GWALLT-AVWY
Welsh and Arthurian
A character who appears in the *MABINOGION*, and is thought, by some, to be the origin of the Arthurian knight Sir GAWAIN.

GWRVAWR
Arthurian
According to the pedigree contained in *BONEDD YR ARWR*, a maternal ancestor of ARTHUR.

GWYAR
Welsh and Arthurian
The father of GWALCHMAI FAB GWYAR and GWALCHAFED. Later tradition made him the father of Gawain in the Arthurian cycle. Gwyar appears to have also been the father of Gwalchmai's sister DIONETA. However, when the Welsh came into contact with the continental tales that made LOT the father of Gawain, it seems that they simply changed Gwyar's gender, and made this character Gawain's mother instead. This is certainly the case in later Welsh stories. However, since Lot is not really a name, rather a title that means 'Lothian-ruler', it is not impossible that his real name was Gwyar.

GWYDDAWG
Arthurian
In Welsh tradition, the slayer of KAY, who was in turn slain by ARTHUR.

GWYDDBWYLL

Welsh and Arthurian

An early Celtic board game that is, in essence, the same as the Irish FIDCHELL, meaning 'wood sense'. The board was seen as the world in miniature, and games played, particularly in the legends, may have been a ritualistic combat with the sole purpose of deciding an argument or quarrel without having to resort to bloodshed. On one occasion ARTHUR played OWAIN in what was possibly a ritual match, but the outcome remains unclear. The Gwyddbwyll board of GWENDDOLAU numbers among the THIRTEEN TREASURES OF BRITAIN.

GWYDDNO GARANHIR

Welsh and Arthurian

The father of ELPHIN who possessed a fish-weir that yielded many salmon. He also owned a *mwys*, or basket, which could feed one hundred people at a time. In origin, Gwyddno Garanhir may have been a god whose purpose appears to be either agricultural, as the *mwys* signifies, or with a more watery association, as reflected in the fish-weir. His basket or hamper was said to have been one of the THIRTEEN TREASURES OF BRITAIN.

Under the name of DEWRARTH WLEDIG, Gwyddno Garanhir was said to have been, during the fifth century, the King of the lost realm of CANTRE'R GWAELOD or the Lowland Hundred, which is said to lie under the waters of Cardigan Bay.

See also MAES GWYDDNO.

GWYDION (FAB DÔN)

Welsh and Arthurian

An all-powerful British father god, magician and poet, a son of DÔN and brother of GILFAETHWY and ARIANRHOD.

While he was in the service of MATH FAB MATHONWY, Lord of GWYNEDD, Gwydion fab Dôn learned of a herd of magic swine in the possession of PRYDERI, whose father had received them as a gift from ARAWN. Gwydion fab Dôn told his master of the swine and promised to obtain them for him. He disguised himself as a bard and, in the company of eleven others all similarly disguised, travelled to DYFED, where they were hospitably received by Pryderi.

Gwydion fab Dôn told Pryderi of his errand and promised to show him a fair exchange for the swine the very next morning. That night Gwydion fab Dôn secretly created, by magic, twelve magnificent stallions, twelve greyhounds with golden collars and twelve golden shields. Pryderi was shown the magically created animals and shields and, after consulting his lords, agreed to the exchange. Gwydion fab Dôn made off quickly with the herd of swine, for he knew that after two days his spell would fail. When the enchantment wore off and Pryderi was left with nothing, he set off in hot pursuit of Gwydion fab Dôn. Math fab Mathonwy mustered an army against Pryderi and after two bloody battles agreed that Gwydion fab Dôn should meet Pryderi in single combat to settle the issue. However, the whole issue of the herd of swine was nothing more than a smoke screen, invented by Gwydion fab Dôn to help his brother, Gilfaethwy, who had fallen for Math fab Mathonwy's foot-holder, the virgin GOEWIN. While Math fab Mathonwy was absent fighting Pryderi, the two brothers abducted Goewin and took turns in ravishing her. Gwydion fab Dôn then met Pryderi at MAEN TYRIAWG, where he used his magic to overcome and kill Pryderi.

Although the acquisition of the swine should have placed Gwydion fab Dôn in high favour with Math fab Mathonwy, his behaviour towards Goewin led to him and his brother being humiliated by a punishment in which they were, for three years, forced to live in the shape of animals, each carrying out the role of male and female, and each year mating and producing an offspring. At the end of the three-year period Math fab Mathonwy considered they had been humiliated enough and restored them to their human form.

The position of foot-holder, which had to be filled by a virgin, was still vacant, so Gwydion fab Dôn put forward his sister ARIANRHOD. However, during the rite to attest her virginity, two bundles dropped from her, for Arianrhod had been pregnant, and her time came during the test, which is referred to as stepping over the wand. The first was a golden-haired baby, who was named DYLAN. Immediately reaching maturity, Dylan set off for the sea, whose attributes and nature he adopted, whereafter he was known as Dylan Eil Ton, or 'Dylan Son of the Wave'. Some have suggested that this story was concocted to cover the drowning of the first baby in the sea.

Gwydion fab Dôn quickly snatched up and concealed the second baby in a chest. He subsequently adopted the boy, but four years later could not resist showing him to his mother. Embarrassed by the reminder of her shame, Arianrhod cursed the boy, saying that he should bear no name until she herself gave him one. Gwydion fab Dôn circumvented this curse by disguising himself and the boy and tricking Arianrhod into calling the boy LLEU LLAW GYFFES. Gwydion fab Dôn could not resist boasting to his sister on how he had tricked her. Furious, she cursed the boy for the second time, this time saying that he would not bear arms until she herself armed him. Again Gwydion fab Dôn found a way around the curse. Finally Arianrhod cursed Lleu Llaw Gyffes for a third time, saying that he would never have a mortal wife.

Gwydion fab Dôn and Math fab Mathonwy worked together to evade this third curse by making Lleu Llaw Gyffes a wife from the flowers of oak, broom and meadowsweet, whom they named BLODEUWEDD ('Flower Face'). However, she was unfaithful to Lleu Llaw Gyffes with the hunter GRONW BEBYR, the lovers unsuccessfully trying to kill Lleu Llaw Gyffes. Gwydion fab Dôn found the wounded Lleu Llaw Gyffes and healed him before changing Blodeuwedd into an owl. Lleu Llaw Gyffes himself dealt with Gronw Bebyr. Later tradition says that Gwydion fab Dôn was responsible for the magical creation of TALIESIN, although in the *MABINOGION* he simply appears as a shape-shifter, an obvious reference to his magical abilities.

GWYDRE
Arthurian
According to the *MABINOGION* story of *CULHWCH AND OLWEN*, a son of ARTHUR who was killed by the boar TWRCH TRWYTH.

GWYL
Arthurian
The daughter of GENDAWD who, according to the Welsh *TRIADS*, was one of ARTHUR's three mistresses.

GWYN AP NUDD
Welsh and Arthurian
See GWYNN AP NUDD

GWYN GLOYW
Welsh
See GWYN GOHOYW

GWYNEDD
Welsh and Arthurian
A medieval kingdom of North WALES, and still the name of a county or region within that country. In Latin it was known as VENDOTIA, the home of the VENDOTII. While early kings are legendary, the names of the rulers around the traditional Arthurian period were thought to have been Einion (*c.* AD 443),

CADWALLON I (AD 443–517) and MAELGWYN (AD 517–47). GEOFFREY OF MONMOUTH makes Cadwallon the contemporary of ARTHUR.

GWYNLLYM (FILWK)
Arthurian
The King of GWYNLLYWG and abductor of Saint GWLADYS. Her father, BRYCHAN, gave chase, but GWYNLLYM was helped to escape by ARTHUR. In Welsh tradition, he and Gwladys are the parents of Saint CADOC.

GWYNLLYWG
Arthurian
The realm of GWYNLLYM FILWK.

GWYN(N) (AP NUDD)
Welsh and Arthurian
The son of NUDD, Lord of the Dead of the UNDERWORLD (rather than of the OTHERWORLD) and Master of the WILD HUNT. Some sources name his father as LLUDD LLAW EREINT, in which case he is to be considered as the Welsh equivalent of the Irish FIONN MAC CUMHAILL. In later tradition he was said to have resided beneath GLASTONBURY TOR, which acted as a portal to his realm. He was also said to have fought GWYTHR, son of GREIDAWL, for the maiden CREIDDYLAD, a contest that was ruled should take place every May Day until Doomsday, when the winner would claim the hand of the maiden. The Arthurian cycle adds to the stories of Gwynn ap Nudd, saying that it was ARTHUR who made the judgement regarding the contest over Creiddylad and that it was also Arthur who made Gwynn ap Nudd Lord of the Dead, ruler over the demons of ANNWFN, though this combines the Otherworld and the Underworld in an entirely non-Celtic union. Yet another story says that he was defeated by Saint TOLLEN on GLASTONBURY TOR, though this fabrication undoubtedly owes its origins to the thought that Glastonbury Tor was a supernatural portal to the Underworld.

GWYN(N) GOHOYW
Welsh
Also GWYN GLOYW
Euphemistically referred to as the 'Great', the father of CIGFA, who became the wife of the heroic PRYDERI.

GWYNN (HÊN)
Welsh and Arthurian
The father of HEILYN.

GWYRANGON
Arthurian
During the reign of VORTIGERN, Gwyrangon ruled KENT, though Vortigern subsequently gave Kent to HENGIST.

GWYTHR
Welsh and Arthurian
The son of GREIDAWL who, with his followers, entered into a battle against GWYNN AP NUDD and the latter's followers over the maiden CREIDDYLAD. To end the senseless bloodshed, it was arranged that each leader should fight until Doomsday on each May Day, the eventual winner gaining the hand of Creiddylad. This arrangement was later said to have been made by none other than King ARTHUR himself.

GYNETH
Arthurian
In a fairly modern work, Sir Walter Scott's *Bridal of Triermain* (1813), Gyneth is the daughter of ARTHUR by GWENDOLEN, who is half-fairy. MERLIN caused her to fall into an enchanted sleep on account of her cruelty, from which she was awakened by Sir Roland de VAUX.

HABREN

British

The daughter of LOCRINUS by his mistress ESTRILDIS. After Locrinus had been killed in a battle against his estranged wife GWENDOLEN, Habren and her mother were drowned by Gwendolen in a river. Gwendolen, however, decreed that the river should, thenceforth, carry Habren's name in honour of the fact that she was Locrinus' daughter. The River Habren became known as the River SABRINA to the Romans, and is today known as the River SEVERN.

HA-FGAN, -VGAN

Welsh

The enemy of ARAWN who was disposed of by PWYLL while he spent a year in ANNWFN in the form of Arawn, Arawn having adopted Pwyll's form to rule over DYFED for the year. Pwyll was instructed by Arawn that Hafgan could be killed only by a single blow, for he had the ability to recover instantly upon receiving a second blow. When Pwyll met Hafgan, he struck a mortal blow. As Hafgan lay dying, he beseeched Pwyll to finish him off, but Pwyll refused and left Hafgan to die of his wounds.

HAG OF HELL

Welsh

A mysterious, supernatural woman whose blood had to be obtained by CULHWCH as one of the tasks set him by YSPADDADEN if he were to be allowed to marry OLWEN.

HAGS OF GLOUCESTER

Arthurian

Collective term for nine witches who lived in Gloucester with their father and mother. They killed PERCEVAL's cousin, whose head was subsequently seen by Perceval on a platter, but one of their number trained Perceval in the use of arms. Perceval, with the help of ARTHUR's men, destroyed all nine of them.

HALSTATT

General

An Austrian town, near Salzburg, in whose salt-mines the first examples of Celtic art were unearthed in 1846. These, coupled with the discoveries at LA TÈNE, Switzerland, a few years later, were the first indicators of the richness of the Celtic culture. The site at Halstatt revealed a number of rich burials that were subsequently dated at between 700 and 400 BC. The term 'Halstatt' was then employed to refer to any artefacts discovered that fell within this broad date range. The Halstatt findings proved that the early continental Celts had traded with Etruria and Greece and were also capable of producing their own 'works of art' that were impressive in their individuality.

HAM

Irish

The son of NOAH from whom the FOMHOIRÉ were alleged to have been descended.

HANLON

Irish

See ANLUAN

HARLEQUIN

Arthurian

Also ARLECCHINO

The name by which HELLEKIN became known in the Italian *commedia dell'arte*, and under which guise he appeared in the Arthurian pantomime *Merlin* (1734) by Lewis Theobald.

HART FELL

Arthurian

A mountain in SCOTLAND that has been proposed by N. Tolstoy as the dwelling place of MERLIN.

HARTMANN VON AUE

Arthurian

A German poet (*c.* 1170–1215) of the Middle High German period and a participant in the Crusade of 1197. He is the author of two Arthurian romances, *Erec* and *Iwain*, both of which closely follow the works of CHRÉTIEN DE TROYES.

HARTWAKER

Arthurian

The son of HENGIST, whom he may have succeeded as the ruler of German Saxony, reigning

Celtic bronze fitting, first century AD. (© Werner Forman/Corbis)

between AD 448 and 480. His brothers are named as AESC, OCTA and EBISSA, his sisters as RONWEN and SARDOINE.

HAVELIN
Arthurian
A variant for HOEL.

HAYDN
Welsh
See HYDWN

HEBRON
Arthurian
An alternative name given to BRONS that is thought to have been the invention of ROBERT DE BORON, who wanted to make Brons sound more Hebrew. Hebron is a well-known name from the Holy Bible, being a place-name in Palestine.

HECTOR
Arthurian
According to the Old French romance *Roman de*

Troie, this famous classical Trojan hero, the son of Priam and defender of Troy during the Trojan War, who was slain by Achilles, was loved by MORGAN Le Fay. Spurned by him, she turned against him.

HEFEYDD (HÊN)

Welsh

With his epithet *Hên*, meaning 'the Old', Hefeydd was the ageing father of the beautiful RHIANNON, who became the wife of PWYLL.

HEIDYN

Welsh

According to some sources, the name of TALIESIN's murderer.

HEIL

British

One of the later names applied to the obscure sun god HELITH, who was apparently only worshipped in a small region of Dorset.

See also CERNE ABBAS

HEILYN

Welsh and Arthurian

The son of GWYNN HÊN and one of the seven Britons to survive the battles between BENDIGEID VRAN and MATHOLWCH and return to BRITAIN, carrying the head of Bendigeid Vran, which had been cut off at the King's own bequest to be buried at the WHITE MOUNT in London, the face towards FRANCE, forever acting as a guardian over the country. The others that returned with him were PRYDERI, MANAWYDAN, TALIESIN, YNAWC (YNAWAG), GRUDYEN (GRUDDIEU) and GLUNEU EIL TARAN (GLIFIEU), along with BRANWEN, the unfortunate maiden who was the cause of the battles.

HEINRICH VON DEM TURTIN

Arthurian

The thirteenth-century German poet and author of *DIU CRÔNE*, a GRAIL romance that makes GAWAIN the hero.

HEITHIURUN

Irish

A curious British idol mentioned in the *Dinnshenchas* that is possibly cognate with the continental TARANIS.

HEL TOR

Arthurian

On top of this peak, near Moretonhampstead, Devon, is a circular stone, said to be a quoit thrown by the Devil in the course of a fight with King ARTHUR. The Devil lost and crept, sulking, back to Northlew, where he died of cold.

HELAIN THE WHITE

Arthurian

The son of the daughter of King BRANDEGORIS and BORS who eventually became the Emperor of CONSTANTINOPLE.

HELAIUS

Arthurian

According to the pedigree of JOHN OF GLASTONBURY, the nephew of JOSEPH OF ARIMATHEA and a maternal ancestor of ARTHUR.

HELDINS

Arthurian

The first ruler of DENMARK; according to *CLARIS ET LARIS*, he was succeeded by TALLAS.

HELENA

British

(1) The daughter of COEL who, legend says, married the Roman Emperor Constantius Chlorus after peace had been restored between her father and the Emperor, who had been besieging his city of COLCHESTER for three years. Their son, born in AD 265, was Constantine the Great. Helena is better known as Saint Helena, her dates being given as *c.* AD 255–330. Tradition makes her the daughter of an innkeeper in Bithynia. She was divorced, for political reasons, in AD 292, but whenConstantius Chlorus was declared emperor by his army in YORK, he made her the Empress Dowager. In AD 312, when toleration was extended to Christianity, she was baptised and in AD 326, according to tradition, she visited Jerusalem and founded basilicas on the Mount of Olives and at Bethlehem. Her feast day is 18 August.

(2) The niece of HOEL, King of BRITTANY, who was seized by the GIANT OF MONT SAINT MICHEL. ARTHUR, KAY and BEDIVERE came to her aid, but, finding her already dead, they killed the giant.

HELI

British

A little-used variant of BELI, the variant occurring in the works of GEOFFREY OF MONMOUTH, whose chronology was all wrong, and thus placed Beli well out of the normally accepted line of descent. To counter this he simply appears to have changed the first letter of Beli to make Heli.

HELIADES
Arthurian

An ally of MORDRED to whom the latter awarded the kingdom of SCOTLAND.

HELIE
Arthurian

The name of the damsel who brought GUINGLAIN to the aid of her mistress, BLONDE ESMERÉE. At first she despised Guinglain, thinking him unworthy to champion her mistress, but as time passed her contempt turned into respect for his prowess.

HELIG (VAEL) AP GLAN(N)O(W)G
Welsh

A legendary sixth-century ruler of a lost kingdom, which is said to lie approximately two miles out to sea in Conwy Bay. Even today it is claimed that the sunken ruins of his palace may be seen at the lowest of tides. The first recorded sighting of the ruins was in 1864, and subsequent sightings estimated that the palace would have occupied no less than $5^1/2$ acres. Earlier, however, in 1816, Edward Pugh wrote that he had floated over the ruins of the palace and is said to have also identified a causeway beneath the water.

See also TRWYN YR WYLFA

HELIS
Arthurian

The son of ARDAN, an uncle of ARTHUR and hence his cousin.

HEL-ITH, -IS
British

An ancient sun god who appears only to have been worshipped in Cerne, an ancient name for a district of modern Dorset. His name has been connected with the giant figure that lies on the hills overlooking CERNE ABBAS, although this is purely conjectural, and is not based on any evidence, historical or archaeological. The variant Helis appears to have been a later invention, for it is first reported in 1746 by William Stukeley, who says that the Cerne Abbas giant was known locally as Helis.

HELLEKIN
Arthurian

In the thirteenth-century *LI JUS ADEN*, Hellekin appears as a fairy king who became the lover of MORGAN Le Fay. An established figure in Teutonic lore, he is first mentioned in the eleventh- or twelfth-century *Ecclesiastical History* by Ordericus Vitalis. In this he is described as a giant with a club who leads the WILD HUNT. Later, in Italy, Hellekin became the HARLEQUIN (ARLECCHINO) of the *commedia dell'arte*, and in this guise appears in the Arthurian pantomime *Merlin* (1734) by Lewis Theobald.

HELM WIND
Arthurian

A miniature hurricane that occurs in the Lake District and that, in Cumbrian tradition, is associated with ARTHUR.

HEMISON
Arthurian

A knight who was the lover of MORGAN Le Fay but was killed by TRISTAN. In Italian romance he was said to have been the father of PULZELLA GAIA by Morgan Le Fay.

HÊN WEN
Welsh and Arthurian

A pig whose offspring were, according to tradition, going to cause untold trouble for BRITAIN. Later she entered the Arthurian cycle, which said that she was pursued, while heavily pregnant, by ARTHUR, and gave birth to various progeny. She was eventually forced to dive from a cliff into the sea at Penryn Awstin. It has been suggested that Hên Wen was the mother of the CATH PALUG, but that particular animal is also said to have been a kitten raised by CERRIDWEN, the witch who was also known as Hên Wen. Her name is sometimes spelled as a single word: Hênwen.

HENGIST
Arthurian

A semi-legendary SAXON leader who, with his brother HORSA, settled in KENT *c.* AD 449, the first ANGLO-SAXON settlers/invaders in BRITAIN. Hengist was originally a leader of the Jutes, and thus he and his brother are said to have come from Jutland.

According to legend, the brothers became allies of VORTIGERN, and Hengist's daughter RONWEN became Vortigern's queen, Hengist receiving Kent as the bride price. Defeated in battle by VORTIMER, he fled to GERMANY, but Vortigern recalled him and he returned with 300,000 men and persuaded Vortigern to summon all the British leaders to a meeting at Salisbury. There he had the entire company massacred. Hengist was eventually defeated by AMBROSIUS AURELIUS, his actual death being attributed to Count Eldol. The *ANGLO-SAXON CHRONICLE* places his death in AD 448, but neglects to say how he died. His story is told by BEDE and GEOFFREY OF MONMOUTH.

Hengist, who is nowadays generally regarded as a historical figure, is usually credited with sons named HARTWAKER (who may have succeeded him as the ruler of German Saxony and reigned between AD 448 and 480), AESC, OCTA and EBISSA. His daughters are given as SARDOINE and RONWEN. However, the latter appears to be a Latinisation of her true name, for, in various sources that appear to adhere to accepted Anglo-Saxon spellings, the name of Hengist's daughter who became Vortigern's queen is given as HROTHWINA.

HENIN THE OLD
Arthurian

The father of GARWEN, according to the Welsh *TRIADS*, his daughter being named as one of the three mistresses of ARTHUR.

HENRY
Arthurian

1 Referred to as 'The Courtly', he appears in the *PROPHÉCIES DE MERLIN*, where he was the leader of a force sent to give aid to a beleaguered Jerusalem.
2 The Emperor of Germany and father of LARIS and LIDOINE, according to the romance *CLARIS ET LARIS*.

HENRY OF HUNTINGDON
Arthurian

English chronicler (*c.* 1084–1155) and archdeacon of Huntingdon from 1109. In 1139 he visited Rome and compiled his famous *Historia Anglorum (History of England)* down to 1154.

HENWINUS
British

The Duke of CORNWALL and one of the husbands of REGAN, one of the older daughters of the mythical King LEIR, the other being MAGLAURUS, who, along with another of Leir's daughters, GONERIL, seized the remainder of the ageing King's domain that had not already been seized by their scheming. Leir's youngest daughter CORDELIA, who married AGANIPPUS, had nothing to do with the underhand usurping of her father's kingdom and welcomed her father to FRANCE after he had been deposed, and later helped him regain his throne.

HERI
Arthurian

In the Icelandic *SAGA OF TRISTRAM*, the informer who told King MARK about the affair between TRISTAN and ISEULT.

HERMESENT
Arthurian

The daughter of IGRAINE and HOEL, a sister to ARTHUR. It is thought that she may be identifiable with BELISENT, who appears in *ARTHOUR AND MERLIN*, or BLASINE.

HERMIT KING
Arthurian

Proper name ELYAS ANAIS, though the title was also applied to King PELLES, this character was either a maternal or a paternal uncle of PERCEVAL, whom the latter visited. The sources remain divided as to the correct lineage he belongs in.

HERMONDINE
Arthurian

The daughter of the King of SCOTLAND. She became the wife of MELIADOR after he had slain her other suitor, CAMAL.

HERN(E) THE HUNTER
British

The leader of the WILD HUNT. He was a legendary antlered giant who is said still to live in the forests of Windsor Great Park and who probably owes his existence to the cult of CERNUNNOS, of whom he is undoubtedly a lingering memory. He has even been linked with Robin Hood, some making the link as that hero's father, although this is extremely tenuous, for Herne the Hunter is, without doubt, a far older figure.

HEROWDES
Arthurian

Having gone blind, this Emperor of Rome consulted MERLIN. His advice was that the Emperor should kill the Seven Sages, who were the imperial counsellors. When he did this his sight was restored to him.

HERZELOYDE
Arthurian

According to WOLFRAM VON ESCHENBACH, the mother of PERCEVAL. Her first husband was CASTRIS, from whom she inherited NORTHGALIS and WALES. Following his death, she married GAHMURET, Perceval's father.

HESPERIDES
Arthurian

The daughters of Atlas in classical Graeco-Roman mythology who had fabulous gardens, located either on the slopes of Mount Atlas or on islands, where trees with golden apples grew. In Irish romance they became the domain of MADOR's father.

HEVEYDD (HÊN)
Welsh
See HEFEYDD

HEYWOOD, THOMAS
Arthurian
The seventeenth-century (*c.* 1574–1641) author of *Life of Merlin*. Born in Lincolnshire, the son of a clergyman, he was educated at Cambridge and was writing plays by 1596. Up to 1633 he had a large share in the composition of 220 plays. Twenty-four of them have survived.

HIND OF THE FAIRIES
Arthurian
In the Arthurian romance *La Caccia* by Erasmo de Valvasone, this deer-like animal led ARTHUR through a mountain to MORGAN Le Fay's palace, where the King was shown the heavens and the earth in order to guide his future destiny.

HIR ATRYM
Welsh
The brother of HIR ERWN. Mentioned in the story of *CULHWCH AND OLWEN*, the two brothers were said to have gigantic, insatiable appetites, which meant they would eat all that was provided for them and, still being hungry, would then leave the land bare as well.

HIR ERWN
Welsh
The brother of HIR ATRYM.

HISTORIA BRITONUM
British and Arthurian
This clumsily put together Latin work is ascribed to NENNIUS, and it dates from, perhaps, the ninth century. The work purports to give an account of British history from the time of JULIUS CAESAR to towards the end of the seventh century. It gives a mythical account of the origins of the British people and recounts the Roman occupation, the settlement of the SAXONS and King ARTHUR's twelve victories. Although it contains fanciful material of doubtful historical significance, its real value lies in its preservation of material needed for the study of early Celtic literature in general and the Arthurian legends in particular.

HISTORIA MERIADOCI
Arthurian
A Latin romance that tells of the adventures of MERIADOC, the foster son of KAY.

HISTORIA REGUM BRITANNIAE
Arthurian
History of the Kings of Britain, the eleventh-century Latin work by GEOFFREY OF MONMOUTH that gives the first coherent narrative of the legends surrounding King ARTHUR as they are still known today.

HOCELICE
Arthurian
The name by which GALAHAD, a son of JOSEPH OF ARIMATHEA, became known after he had ascended to the throne of WALES.

HOEL
Arthurian
(1) The King of BRITTANY, a cousin (or possibly nephew) of ARTHUR, who landed at SOUTHAMPTON with a large army in response to Arthur's request for help. Together they defeated the SAXONS at LINCOLN, at CALEDON WOOD and at BADON. They put down the Scots, PICTS and Irish in Moray, and toured Loch Lomond. Next they raised the siege of YORK, where COLGRIN, the defeated Saxon leader, had taken refuge, and, having defeated him, Arthur restored that city to its former glory, and returned their lands to the three dispossessed Yorkist princes, LOTH, URIAN and AUGUSELUS. Hoel also helped Arthur to defeat the whole of GAUL within nine years, and to establish his court and a proper legislative government in the city of Paris.

GEOFFREY OF MONMOUTH says that he was the son of BUDICIUS, but does not name his mother. Some commentators have suggested that she was the sister of AMBROSIUS rather than Arthur, thus leading to the ambiguity of his relationship to Arthur. Traditional Breton dating places his rule between AD 510 and 545. He is possibly best known as the father of ISEULT of the White Hands and her brother KAHEDRIN, but the *PROSE TRISTAN* makes him the father of RUNALEN. The fourteenth-century Welsh *BIRTH OF ARTHUR* gives him a pedigree that makes him the son of Arthur's sister GWYAR by YMER LLYDAW.

(2) An alternative name for IGRAINE's first husband, more normally given as GORLOIS, according to *ARTHOUR AND MERLIN*. Their daughters are named in this work as BLASINE, BELISENT and HERMESENT. This Hoel is also mentioned in the *Vulgate Merlin Continuation*, where he is given the title Duke of TINTAGEL. He is also named as being among the TWENTY-FOUR KNIGHTS of King Arthur's court.

Hogalen Tudno

Welsh and Arthurian

The whetstone of TUDNO. It numbered amongst the THIRTEEN TREASURES OF BRITAIN, being said to sharpen none but the weapon of a brave man.

Holger

Arthurian

A Danish hero whom the Danes hold is to be identified with OGIER.

Hok-Braz

Gaulish

A Celtic giant who inhabited the coastline of BRITTANY, where he was said to swallow three-masted ships for his breakfast. What he had for his dinner and his supper remains unrecorded.

Holy Grail

British and Arthurian

See GRAIL

Holy Thorn

British and Arthurian

See GLASTONBURY THORN

Honoree

Arthurian

BIAUSDOUS, the son of GAWAIN, unsheathed this sword and by so doing gained the right to marry BIAUTEI.

Honorius

Arthurian

The fifth-century Roman Emperor of the Western Empire. The second son of Theodosius I, at whose death the empire was divided between his sons Arcadius and Honorius, the latter, then only ten years old, receiving the western division.

Horn of Brangaled

Welsh and Arthurian

Also CORN BRANGALED

One of the THIRTEEN TREASURES OF BRITAIN. MERLIN had to acquire it before he could be given any of the others. Originally it had belonged to a centaur that was slain by Hercules, its particular property being that it was capable of containing any drink one wished it to.

Horsa

Arthurian

The brother of HENGIST who accompanied him to BRITAIN and was killed by a cousin of VORTIGERN.

His memorial is thought to have been a flint pile near Horsted in KENT (his brother's realm).

Hrothwina

Arthurian

Alternative spelling for RONWEN, the daughter of HENGIST who married VORTIGERN. This appears to be the original ANGLO-SAXON form of her name, Ronwen simply being the Latinised version.

Hu Gadarn

Arthurian

Hero of a story by Iolo MORGANNWG who was said to have killed an AFANC. It would appear that Hu Gadarn was simply the invention of the bard, for his name appears nowhere else.

Huail

Arthurian

Variant of HUEIL.

Hudibras

British and Arthurian

According to GEOFFREY OF MONMOUTH, an early King of BRITAIN (ninth century BC), the ninth ruler after BRUTUS, the legendary founder of WINCHESTER and the father of the magical BLADUD. He sent his son to Athens to study philosophy, but while he was there his father died, and he returned to claim the throne.

Hueil

Arthurian

Also HUAIL

A son of CAW and brother of GILDAS. An opponent of ARTHUR, their feud beginning when Arthur stabbed GWYDRE, Hueil's nephew. They fought and Arthur was wounded in the knee, but said he would not kill Hueil on condition the wound was never mentioned. Some time later Hueil forgot his promise and Arthur had him executed. Another version of this story says that Arthur and Hueil, son of KAW of Brydyn, fought over the favours of a lady. They were both wounded and went their separate ways, but Arthur always limped after this incident. Some years later they met again, and, even though Arthur was in disguise, Hueil recognised him by the limp. They fought again over the same lady. Arthur managed to throw Hueil against a large stone and, drawing his sword, cut off his head.

Hueil's Stone

Arthurian

The stone in Ruthin, Clwyd, on which ARTHUR was said to have beheaded HUEIL.

HUGH

Irish

A son of LIR and AOBH and one of the four children of Lir who were transformed into swans by AOIFE, a shape in which they were condemned to stay for 900 years. The other three are named as FIONUALA, FIACHTRA and CONN. They regained their human form in the time of Saint PATRICK and died shortly afterwards.

HUMBER

British and Arthurian

The leader of a mythical invasion of Huns who killed ALBANACTUS but were routed by KAMBER and LOCRINUS. Humber drowned in the river that still carries his name. It has been suggested by Scottish writers that ARTHUR fought his last battle, CAMLANN, on the shores of this east of England river that empties into the North Sea.

HUNBAUT

Arthurian

When ARTHUR sent GAWAIN on a mission to the KING OF THE ISLES, Hunbaut went as his companion, and tended to proceed with much greater caution than Gawain in the course of the adventures the pair had together.

HUNBAUT

Arthurian

A thirteenth-century French verse romance that deals with the adventures of HUNBAUT and, more particularly, his companion GAWAIN.

HUNCAMUNCA

Arthurian

The name of ARTHUR's daughter in Henry Fielding's *Tom Thumb* (1730).

HUNGARY

General

Though the inclusion of Hungary in the Arthurian romances is an anachronism – it did not exist as a single country until about the ninth century, much later than the traditional Arthurian period – several kings are assigned to it. *CLARIS ET LARIS* names the King as SARIS, saying he captured Cologne, but was subsequently killed by LARIS. Elsewhere a king named JEREMIAH is mentioned, the father-in-law of GAWAIN, while SAGREMOR is called the son of the King of Hungary. King DITAS of Hungary was said to have been among the followers of the Roman Emperor THEREUS when the latter attacked ARTHUR.

HUNTING CAUSEWAY

British and Arthurian

The route between Cadbury Castle and GLASTONBURY that, local Somerset legend says, King ARTHUR rides each Christmas Eve in the company of his knights. Usually he remains invisible except for the glint of silver horse shoes, but the sounds made have reputedly been heard by many people. This legend is obviously a variant of the much older legends of the WILD HUNT that occur throughout the ancient Celtic lands.

A local variant of this story says that, rather than Christmas Eve, the spectral ride occurs on 24 June, Saint John the Baptist's Day, when Arthur and his knights ride to Glastonbury to do homage to the abbot there.

HUNTING KNIGHT

Arthurian

This son of the King of GASCONY came to ARTHUR's court to learn valour and all the various aspects of chivalry.

HUON

Arthurian

The hero of the thirteenth-century romance *HUON DE BORDEAUX*, which is set in Carolingian (AD 751–987) times. This tale, from which SHAKESPEARE obviously drew a great deal of material, names OBERON as the King of the fairies who assigned his kingdom to Huon. ARTHUR, who had lived in FAIRYLAND since the end of his earthly reign, thus making Fairyland cognate with AVALON, had come to think that the realm would be passed to him and was greatly troubled. However, Oberon threatened Arthur and thus ensured that there would be peace between him and Huon.

HUON DE BORDEAUX

Arthurian

Thirteenth-century French romance concerning the ascension of HUON to the throne of FAIRYLAND, called MOMUR in this work, in preference to ARTHUR.

HUTH-MERLIN

Arthurian

An alternative name for the *SUITE DU MERLIN*.

HUTTON, CASTLE

Arthurian

The home of BERTILAK, the GREEN KNIGHT of the famous poem *SIR GAWAIN AND THE GREEN KNIGHT*.

HWICCE

British

An ancient Celtic kingdom that had its capital at DEERHURST, and once covered the modern counties of Gloucestershire and Worcestershire.

H(W)YCHDWN

Welsh

The name of the second boy born to GWYDION FAB DÔN and GILFAETHWY during the year they spent as wild pigs, part of their three-year punishment by MATH FAB MATHONWY for the rape of his foot-holder GOEWIN. His brothers, also conceived as animals but turned into human boys by Math fab Mathonwy, were BLEDDYN and HYDWN.

HY-BR(E)ASIL

Irish

An enchanted OTHERWORLDLY island that, according to legend, is visible off the west coast of IRELAND once every seven years and that, if once touched by fire, would remain above the surface of the sea as an accessible paradise. MANANNÁN MAC LIR was thought to have condemned this once earthly realm to its watery grave, although he gave its inhabitants the right to breathe fresh air once every seven years.

HYDWN

Welsh

The name given to the boy who was born to GWYDION FAB DÔN and GILFAETHWY during their year as deer, the first of three years they spent in animal form as punishment for the rape of the maiden GOEWIN. MATH FAB MATHONWY named the boy after he had turned him into a human child from the fawn he had been born as. His brothers, HWYCHDWN and BLEDDYN, were also originally born as young animals, Hwychdwn as a wild pig, and Bleddyn as a wolfcub.

HYGWYDD

Arthurian

When ARTHUR captured the cauldron of DIWRNACH, this servant of his carried it on his back.

I

IALONUS
Gaulish

An agricultural deity with special responsibility for cultivated fields.

IATH N'ANANN
Irish

An ancient name for IRELAND. It appears to be derived from ANA, one of the variants of DANU.

IBERT
Arthurian

According to WOLFRAM VON ESCHENBACH, a character, possibly cognate with IWERET, who had a wife named IBLIS and who castrated KLINGSOR.

IBHELL
Irish

The beautiful wife of AED. The King of LEINSTER, who had previously abducted the wife of MONGÁN, fell in love with Ibhell. Seeing this, Mongán magically changed himself to appear in the form of Aed, and changed a hag into the beautiful Ibhell. The deception worked. The King of Leinster exchanged the woman he had abducted for the disguised hag, whereupon Mongán and his wife disappeared, and the hag returned to her original hideous form.

IBLIS
Arthurian

The wife of IBERT, according to WOLFRAM VON ESCHENBACH, though that author also names LANCELOT as her husband. It would appear that he simply invented the name, using *Sibile* (a Sibyl) as the root.

ICELAND
Arthurian

Part of ARTHUR's kingdom, whose King AELENS, at least according to LAYAMON, voluntarily submitted to Arthur and sent his son ESCOL by the King of RUSSIA's daughter to Arthur's court. GEOFFREY OF MONMOUTH names the King of Iceland as MALVASIUS.

ICENI
British

An ancient British tribe that lived in Norfolk. Their most famous rulers were BOUDICCA and her husband PRASUTAGUS. After the death of Prasutagus, the Iceni and the TRINOVANTES, allied under the leadership of Boudicca, attacked the Roman invaders but, after three notable successes, were routed, when Boudicca took her own life.

IDDAWC
Arthurian

In the *MABINOGION* story of the *DREAM OF RHONABWY*, Iddawc was the companion of RHONABWY when they encountered KAY.

IDDAWG
Arthurian

A messenger sent by ARTHUR to MORDRED before the final battle at CAMLANN. Iddawg, however, delivered the message in such a way that it enraged Mordred, and as a result Iddawg became known as the 'Embroiler of Britain'.

IDRES
Arthurian

A King of CORNWALL who was among the eleven leaders who rebelled against the youthful ARTHUR at the start of his reign.

IDRIS
Welsh

A giant said to have his home on the appropriately named mountain of CADAIR IDRIS in GWYNEDD. He is said to have been a poet, astronomer and philosopher, which leads to the conjecture that his description as a giant related to his intellect rather than his physical size.

IDUMEAN(S)
Arthurian

An alternative name for the Edomites, an ancient people inhabiting a region south of the Dead Sea. Traditionally descended from the biblical Esau, they appear in the Arthurian legends of later writers, who said that the Queen of the AMAZONS was rescued from their King by TRISTAN THE YOUNGER. They were also said to have done battle with GAWAIN, their own Queen being killed by the CROP-EARED DOG.

IGERN-A, -E
British and Arthurian
See IGRAINE

IGNOGE
Graeco-British and Arthurian
The daughter of the Greek King PANDRASUS. She became the reluctant bride of BRUTUS after he had fought and defeated her father, compelling the King to release his Trojan captives and to supply them with ships, provisions and bullion to enable them to leave Greece. She travelled to BRITAIN with Brutus and the Trojan slaves, and subsequently became known as IMOGEN.

IGRAINE
British and Arthurian
Also EIGYR, IGERNA, IGERNE, YGERNA
(1) The mother of ARTHUR, who has her roots in the Welsh character EIGYR. The daughter of AMLAWDD, she married GORLOIS (sometimes called HOEL) and had a number of daughters by him. UTHER became infatuated with her and, while at war with her husband, had MERLIN make him resemble her absent husband by magic. On the very night that Gorlois was killed in a battle against Uther's troops, the latter lay with her, the resulting child of their union being Arthur. Uther later married her but, even though she had grown to love him, their happiness was short-lived, for Uther died within two years.
(2) The sister of ARTHUR with whom he had an incestuous relationship, according to the *VULGATE Merlin Continuation*.

ILAX
Arthurian
The father of EREC, according to the Norse version of the story of Erec, the *EREX SAGA*.

ILDÁNACH
Irish
A little-used variant of SAMILDÁNACH.

ILDÁTHACH
Irish
An inhabitant of the realm of TÍR TAIRNGIRI who was, along with his sons, drowned by the wave sent by MANANNÁN MAC LIR after the sisters CLIODNA, AEIFE and EDAEIN. Ildáthach and his sons were in love with Cliodna.

ILINOT
Arthurian
According to WOLFRAM VON ESCHENBACH, this son of ARTHUR ran away as a child and was raised by Queen FLORIE of KANADIC. He fell in love with her, but she expelled him from her realm and he died of a broken heart.

ILLAN
Irish and Arthurian
Also ULLAN
A traditional king of LEINSTER, who was thought to have led raids into BRITAIN, and who traditionally reigned between AD 495 and 511. The history of Leinster at this time is obscure, and Illan may have reigned on either side of these dates, or not at all. Legend makes him the husband of TUIREANN, the sister-in-law of FIONN MAC CUMHAILL. Shortly before the birth of Illan's two sons, his supernatural mistress changed Tuireann into a wolfhound, and it was in that form that she gave birth to BRAN and SGEOLAN, the two famous hounds of Fionn mac Cumhaill. After Illan had promised to desert Tuireann, Illan's mistress restored her human form. Arthurian commentators have sought to argue that he was a historical enemy of ARTHUR.

ILLE ESTRANGE
Arthurian
Otherwise known as ESTRANGOT, this kingdom was ruled by VAGOR, who kept LIONEL a prisoner. Lionel was due to fight MARABRON, Vagor's son, but, being injured, was unable to do so and LANCELOT acted as his substitute, successfully defeating Marabron and so earning Lionel's release.

ILLTYD, SAINT
Arthurian
The daughter of RIEINGULID, according to Welsh tradition, Illtyd was said to have been related to ARTHUR and to have served as a warrior under him. She founded the monastery of Llanilltud Fawr (now Llantwit Major) in WALES.

IMBAS FOROSNAI
Irish
A pagan rite that implied that chewing the raw flesh of the thumb imparted sagacity. FIONN MAC CUMHAILL was said to have been blessed with this ability after he accidentally touched the SALMON OF WISDOM, which he was cooking for FINNÉCES.

The rite appears to have crossed the Irish Sea to reappear in the story of GWION BACH and the witch CERRIDWEN.

IMBOL-C, -G
General

The spring festival celebrated on 1 February, it later became the feast day of Saint BRIGHID, the Christian feast of Candlemas. Imbolc was one of the four main festivals of the Celtic calendar, the others being SAMHAIN, BELTANE and LUGHNASADH.

IMMRAM
Irish

(*pl. immrama*) The name given to 'a voyage tale', one of the two main branches of early Irish literature, the other being the ECHTRAI. The earliest of these was the *Immram Curaig Maíle Dúin.*

IMMRAM CURAIG MAÍLE DÚIN
Irish

The earliest of the *immrama*, or 'voyage tales', which was later to inspire the famous story of Saint Brendan. It concerns the travels of one MAÍL DÚIN, who is bent on revenge after the murder of his father, but discovers that it is better to forgive those who have transgressed. The account of this voyage names numerous island realms, which may be found under the heading ISLANDS OF MAÍL DÚIN.

IMOGEN
British

The wife of BRUTUS according to some sources. The name is a simple variant of IGNOGE, the daughter of PANDRASUS, whom Brutus brought to BRITAIN with him from Greece.

IN DAGHDHA
Irish

The full title of the Irish father god, who is more usually known simply as the DAGHDHA.

INDECH
Irish

The co-ruler of the FOMHOIRÉ, along with ELATHA and TETHRA, and father of the Fomhoiré maiden with whom the DAGHDHA had intercourse before the Second Battle of MAGH TUIREDH.

INDEG
Arthurian

The daughter of GARWY the Tall, she was, according to the Welsh *TRIADS*, one of the three mistresses of ARTHUR.

INDRAWING SEAS
Arthurian

The name given to four channels that passed through the mountains that surrounded the North Pole on the island of GROCLAND. Four thousand of ARTHUR's men were supposed to have gone to the Pole via these channels, but none returned. In 1364, it was alleged that seven of the men, plus one of Flemish descent, presented themselves to King Magnus of NORWAY.

INEEN
Arthurian

A kingdom that appears in the Scottish Gaelic folktale of UALLABH. It is said that the son of the King of Ineen, who was also the brother of the Queen (which, if taken literally, would mean that he had married his daughter, or stepdaughter), imprisoned Uallabh, but he was rescued by the Queen's younger sister.

INGCEL
Irish

A monstrous being, described as the son of the King of BRITAIN, whose single eye was said to have three pupils. He appears in the legend of CONAIRE MÓR and the hostel of DA DERGA, in which, together with a band of outlaws, he storms the hostel and razes it to the ground.

INIS MANANN
Irish

A name for the Isle of MAN as the home of MANANNÁN MAC LIR. It literally means 'Isle of Manann(án)'.

INNIS EALGA
Irish

'The Noble Isle', one of the first names that was given to IRELAND by the Sons of MÍL ÉSPÁINE after they had arrived there.

INNIS FAIL
Irish

'The Isle of Destiny', the name allegedly given to IRELAND as the Sons of MÍL ÉSPÁINE first spotted the island, which they also called INNIS EALGA.

INOGEN
Arthurian

In Richard Hole's *Arthur* (1789), Inogen is named as a daughter of MERLIN with whom ARTHUR fell in love.

St Martin's Cross on the island of Iona. (© Mick Sharp)

IONA

(1) (*Arthurian*) The name of a King of FRANCE who, according to the *MABINOGION* story of *CULHWCH AND OLWEN*, came to ARTHUR's court.

(2) (*General*) A tiny island, 3½ miles long by 1½ miles wide, which was a pagan stronghold for centuries before the Christians arrived and claimed it as their own. COLUMBA landed there on 12 May 563 and quickly set about establishing his famous monastery. The island's Gaelic name is *Innisnam Druidbneach*, which translates as 'Island of the Druids', reflecting its long Celtic history. However, within a century of the landing of Saint COLUMBA, Iona was pre-eminently Christian.

IORUAIDH

Arthurian

The son of the King of ICELAND, father of RATHLEAN and, through her, according to the Irish romance *VISIT OF GREY HAM*, the grandfather of AILLEAN.

IRELAND

(1) (*General*) A large island lying to the west of Great BRITAIN, from which it is separated by the Irish Sea. It consists of the provinces of ULSTER, LEINSTER, MUNSTER and CONNACHT and is, today, divided between the Republic of Ireland, or EIRE, which occupies the south, central and north-west of the island, and Northern Ireland, which occupies the north-east corner and forms a part of the United Kingdom.

(2) (*Arthurian*) Traditionally a part of ARTHUR's kingdom. His conquest of the island and defeat of its king, GILMAURIUS, is described by GEOFFREY OF MONMOUTH. Other sources name the king as ANGUISH, ELIDUS, MARHALT and GURMUN, while *DURMART LE GALLOIS* names a Queen of Ireland as FENISE (FENICE), and says that the royal standard-bearer of Ireland was PROCIDES, governor of Limerick.

The country features most prominently in ancient myths that later became embroidered into the Arthurian sagas, such as the battles between BENDIGEID VRAN and MATHOLWCH, and CULHWCH and OLWEN. It seems possible that, thanks to the OTHERWORLD themes of the Irish stories incorporated into Arthurian legend, the inclusion of Ireland in Arthur's domain was intended to signify his rule over not just the land of the living but also the land of the dead.

IRION

Arthurian

A king who was the father of MARTHA and father-in-law of YSAIE THE SAD, TRISTAN's son.

IRNAN

Irish

One of the three sorceress daughters of CONARAN. She and her two sisters took a large number of the fian captive on the order of their father because the fian had trespassed onto his land. Her two sisters were slaughtered by GOLL MAC MORNA, but Irnan was spared on condition that she released the members of the fian who were held by her enchantment. As the last of the men was released, she vanished, but later reappeared and demanded single combat to avenge the death of her sisters. FIONN MAC CUMHAILL was about to go into battle when Goll mac Morna stepped forward and took his place. After a long battle Goll mac Morna ran Irnan through, after which the fian sacked the home of Conaran.

IRONSIDE

Arthurian

A KNIGHT OF THE ROUND TABLE. This was the more common name of the RED KNIGHT of the Red Lands. He was the father of Sir RAYNBROWN and was defeated by GARETH.

IS ELFYDD

Welsh

'Beneath the World', a name sometimes used to refer to ANNWFN.

ISAIAH

Arthurian

Son of EIAN and father of JONAANS, according to the traditional lineage of GALAHAD.

ISCA LEGIONIS, -UM

Arthurian

The name by which CAERLEON-ON-USK was known in early times, which has led to its identification with the CITY OF THE LEGION.

ISEO

Arthurian

The daughter of TRISTAN who married King JUAN of Castile in Spanish Arthurian romance. The romances also say that TRISTAN THE YOUNGER, Iseo's brother, married MARIA, the sister of King Juan, though some sources make Maria the King's daughter.

ISEULT

Arthurian

Also ISODD, ISOLDE

The name of at least four ladies from the Arthurian legends.

The Rock of Cashel, Ireland. (© Mick Sharp)

(1) The fated daughter of King ANGUISH of IRELAND. She cured the poisoned wounds of TRISTAN which he had sustained fighting the Irish King MORAUNT and his ally, the giant Sir MORHOLT. He told his uncle, King MARK, of her beauty, and was sent to woo her on Mark's behalf. She consented to the marriage and returned with Tristan, but, as the result of drinking a love potion, became hopelessly enamoured of Tristan rather than Mark. So began their famous and unfortunate love affair. Having already lain with Tristan, she substituted her maid for herself on her wedding night so that King Mark would not learn the truth. Subsequently, their affair uncovered, Tristan fled to BRITTANY, where he married ISEULT of the White Hands. When Tristan died, Iseult's heart broke and she died as well. Although she is said to be the daughter of the King of IRELAND, her name derives from the ancient British *Adsiltia* – 'She who is gazed on'.

(2) Iseult of the White Hands, who married TRISTAN after he had left ISEULT. She is variously described as the daughter of HOEL or JOVELIN, Duke of Arundel. Even though married, the union was never consummated, for Tristan still loved Iseult, something she very naturally resented. When Tristan was fatally wounded he sent for Iseult, believing that she could heal him, making the captain of the ship that was to fetch her agree to hoist black sails if she had refused to return with him and white sails if she was on board. When the ship returned, it was showing white sails, but Iseult of the White Hands lied to her husband, saying the sails were black, and he died before Iseult arrived. Some sources say Iseult did refuse to come, and so Tristan died, while others say that the jealous King Mark killed Tristan. Classical influences obviously play a very important part here, particularly the story concerning Aegeus and his son Theseus with regard to the white and black sails. An Icelandic version of the Tristan story says that this Iseult was Spanish, being given to Tristan when he defeated the King of SPAIN.

(3) Queen of IRELAND, wife of ANGUISH and mother of ISEULT.

(4) TRISTAN's god-daughter.

ISLAND OF THE MIGHTY
Irish and Welsh
A term commonly used in both Irish and Welsh stories to refer to BRITAIN, although the term could quite equally apply to WALES, ENGLAND or SCOTLAND in the Irish tales. The Welsh used the term more correctly to refer to England.

ISLANDS OF MÁIL DÚIN
Irish
The *Immram Curaig Maíle Dúin* tells the story of a voyage undertaken by MAÍL DÚIN and three companions to discover the identity and whereabouts of the murderers of Maíl Dúin's father. During their voyage, they visit a large number of mysterious island realms. These are briefly described below in the order in which they appear in the text.

(1) **The Island of the Slayer:** A day and a half into the voyage Maíl Dúin and his crew came across two small, bare islands, each having a fort on it. One of these islands was the home of the murderer of Maíl Dúin's father, AILILL, who was boasting of this to his neighbour in a loud voice. Maíl Dúin was about to land when GERMAN and DIURAN cried out that God had guided them. A high wind then sprang up and blew the small boat out to sea again. Maíl Dúin chided them for speaking of God, but it was of little use, for the islands had disappeared from sight.

(2) **The Island of the Ants:** Having drifted for three days and three nights, Maíl Dúin came to a small island where a swarm of ferocious ants, each the size of a new-born foal, swarmed down to the beach to meet him. Needless to say, he hurriedly put back to sea.

(3) **The Island of the Birds:** This heavily wooded island was the first land on which Maíl Dúin set foot since departing from IRELAND. He and his companions killed and ate a large number of the birds inhabiting the island, and took many more on board to re-provision themselves.

(4) **Island of the Fierce Beast:** A large, sandy island, inhabited by a ferocious horse-like beast that had clawed feet. Maíl Dúin and his companions quickly shoved off, but were pelted with pebbles thrown by the beast as they drew away.

(5) **The Island of the Giant Horse:** A large, flat island that German and Diuran set out to explore. They discovered a huge racecourse, which was pock-marked with hoof prints, each hoof being the size of the sail on their boat. They quickly turned tail and set out to sea again. As they sailed away, they heard the roar of a crowd at a horserace and turned to see massive horses that ran like the wind competing against each other.

(6) **The Island of the Stone Door:** A week after leaving the Island of the Giant Horses, they came to a smaller island, where a single house stood on the shore. A stone door with an opening into the sea received hordes of salmon, which the rolling surf hurled into the house. Maíl Dúin and his crew entered the house, which they found unoccupied, although four massive beds stood ready for the giant

Iseult writes a letter to her beloved Tristan. (Aubrey Beardsley, 1893–4/Mary Evans Picture Library)

owners. Maíl Dúin and his companions ate from the feast they found laid out on the vast table, and then sailed away.

(7) **The Island of the Apples:** An island surrounded by insurmountable cliffs, which the boat reached after all supplies had been exhausted. Over the edge of these cliffs hung the branch of a tree, which Maíl Dúin broke off. For three days and three nights they circled the island unable to find a place to land. However, by that time the branch of Maíl Dúin had grown three apples, each apple being sufficient to maintain the crew for forty days.

(8) **The Island of the Wondrous Beast:** An island with a stone fence around it that retained a huge beast that ran round and round in a frenzy. Shortly it ran to the top of the hill and made its skin revolve around its body while it held that body quite still, and then caused its body to revolve within its stationary skin. Maíl Dúin and his companions hurriedly left that island, but were pelted with stones by the beast, one stone lodging itself in the keel of their boat.

(9) **The Island of the Biting Horses:** An island that housed a herd of monstrous horse-like beasts, which continually gnawed huge chunks of flesh from each other, so that the island ran with blood. Needless to say, Maíl Dúin and his crew did not bother to land.

(10) **The Island of the Fiery Swine:** With all their provisions once again exhausted, Maíl Dúin arrived at an island inhabited by huge red beasts that kicked the trees that grew on the island and ate the apples they knocked down. At night they retired into caverns beneath the island. Maíl Dúin and his crew came ashore at night and felt the ground hot with the heat of the fiery swine sleeping underground. They quickly replenished their stores with the apples that grew on the island and put back out to sea.

(11) **The Island of the Little Cat:** An island that was like a tower of chalk that reached almost to the clouds. Atop were several great white houses. Maíl Dúin and his crew entered the largest of these and found a small cat leaping in play from pillar to pillar. The cat ignored them as they ate from the feast they found laid out. They then took as much food as they could carry and made ready to leave. As they did, one member of Maíl Dúin's crew sighted a wonderful necklace and picked it up. The small cat immediately changed into a ball of fire and reduced that member of the crew to ashes. Maíl Dúin spread those ashes on the water as they left the island.

(12) **The Island of the Black and White Sheep:** An island containing two flocks of sheep, one black and the other white, which were divided by a bronze fence. They were tended by a huge shepherd, who periodically took one of the white sheep and placed it in with the black ones, whereupon it immediately changed colour, and vice versa. Maíl Dúin threw a white stick amongst the black sheep, and, when it, too, immediately changed colour, they changed course and did not attempt to land.

(13) **The Island of the Giant Swine:** A wide island on which there lived a herd of huge swine. Maíl Dúin and his crew killed a small one and roasted it on the spot because it was too large for them to carry. Later, German and Diuran explored the island and located a herd of cattle being tended by a huge man on the far side of a wide river. To test the depth of the water German dipped his spear into it and it was instantly dissolved. After that they set sail again.

(14) **The Island of the Mill:** The location of a grim-looking mill, inside which they found a huge miller grinding, as he said, half the grain of Ireland. He also told them that he was sent to grind all that men begrudge each other. Maíl Dúin and his companions crossed themselves and sailed away.

(15) **The Island of the Black Mourners:** An island full of black people who constantly mourned and wept. As soon as Maíl Dúin's companions set foot on shore, they, too, turned black and started to mourn. Maíl Dúin rescued them by shrouding his head so that he could not look on the place, nor breathe its air, and they quickly left the island.

(16) **The Island of the Four Fences:** An island divided into four by fences of gold, silver, brass and crystal, one region being occupied by kings, the second by queens, the third by warriors and the fourth by maidens. Maíl Dúin and his companions were welcomed by the maidens, who gave them cheese that tasted to each man exactly as he wanted it to. They were then given a drink that made them sleep for three days and nights. When they woke they found themselves back at sea, with no trace of the island to be seen.

(17) **The Island of the Glass Bridge:** An island on which there stood a fort with a brass door and a glass bridge leading to it. When they tried to cross the bridge, it threw them off. For four days they attempted to gain entrance to the fort, each day watching as a maiden came out and filled her pail from the moat that ran below the bridge. On the fourth day she crossed the bridge and bade them follow her into the fort. Inside, she fed each man with what he most desired, each meal coming from her pail. For three days they were entertained in this manner. However, when they woke on the fourth morning there was no trace of the maiden, the fort or the island, as they found themselves far out at sea again.

(18) **The Island of the Shouting Birds:** An island full of black birds and speckled brown ones that spoke to and shouted at each other. They sailed past without landing.

(19) **The Island of the Anchorite:** An island covered in trees, full of birds and inhabited by a man whose only clothing was his own hair. This man told them that he had sailed from Ireland on a sod of turf that God had turned into the island. Each year God added a foot's breadth and one tree to the island where he and the birds were to remain until Doomsday, being nourished by the angels. The hermit entertained them for three days before they set sail again.

(20) **The Island of the Miraculous Fountain:** An island crowned by a golden castle, within which they found another hermit clothed only in his hair. The castle housed a fountain that gave water on Fridays and Wednesdays, milk on Sundays and the feast days of martyrs, and ale and wine on the feast days of the Apostles, Mary and John the Baptist, and the high tides of the year.

(21) **The Island of the Smithy:** An island they did not land on, for they heard a giant smith talking about their approach. As they sailed away, he emerged from his forge and cast a huge lump of red-hot metal after them, which made the sea boil.

(22) **The Sea of Clear Glass:** Not an island, but one of the events of the voyage that is best left in its correct order. The sea was so clear that it was said to resemble 'green glass'. For a whole day they sailed across its surface, marvelling at the clarity of the water and the formation of the seabed, which was clearly visible.

(23) **The Undersea Island:** An island viewed through a sea whose waters seemed to be only just capable of supporting their boat. Through the water they saw roofed fortresses and a monstrous beast lodged in a tree, with droves of cattle around it and an armed warrior beneath it. Despite the warrior, the beast continued to stretch down and devour the cattle. Sorely afraid that they might sink in the thin waters, they hurriedly sailed away.

(24) **The Island of the Prophecy:** An island around which the sea built up into a wall so that Maíl Dúin and his crew looked down on the people, who seemed to be expecting them but were afraid of them. One woman pelted them, from below, with large nuts, which they collected to replenish their stores. Then they sailed away, sure that they would not be received warmly if they landed.

(25) **The Island of the Spouting Water:** A stream on this island spouted its water in a great arc from one side to the other. Maíl Dúin had only to thrust his spear through the water to catch great numbers of salmon. Having filled their boat with the fish, they sailed on.

(26) **The Island of the Silver Column:** Not so much an island, but rather a huge, square, silver pillar that rose from the sea. Each side was as wide as two oar-strokes of the boat. It rose straight from the seabed, with its top lost in the clouds. As they looked on, a huge silver net was cast down into the sea, through which Maíl Dúin steered the boat, and from which Diuran cut away a section said to have weighed 2½ ounces. They sailed away, as they were unable to find any way of landing or ascending the pillar.

(27) **The Island of the Pedestal:** This island was suspended above the sea on a huge pedestal in which there was a locked door. Unable to gain entry, Maíl Dúin sailed away.

(28) **The Island of the Women:** On this island was a mansion housing seventeen maidens. They watched those maidens prepare a bath. At length, a rider approached. One of the maidens took the horse and led the rider, a woman, into the mansion, where she entered the bath. After a while one of the maidens came out to Maíl Dúin and his comrades and bade them enter. Inside they were bathed and sat down to eat, each man having a maiden in close attendance. After the meal, Maíl Dúin was married to the queen of the island, and each of his comrades to the most comely of the maidens. For three contented months during the winter they lived on the island, where no one ever knew old age or sickness.

At the end of the three months Maíl Dúin and his companions sailed away in their boat while the queen was away on business. However, they had not gone far when the queen appeared on the shore and threw Maíl Dúin a ball of thread that stuck to his hand. Thus, the queen pulled Maíl Dúin and the boat back to the shore. For a further three months Maíl Dúin and his crew lived with the maidens.

Twice more they attempted to make their escape, and twice more they were hauled back by the queen and her clew of thread. Diuran suspected that Maíl Dúin loved the queen so much that he caught and held onto the thread on purpose. Therefore, the next time the queen threw the ball of thread at them, Diuran leapt in front of Maíl Dúin and caught it instead. The clew stuck to his hand, so he cut it off with his sword, and it fell into the sea. It was only because Diuran had severed his hand that they were finally able to make their escape.

(29) **The Island of the Red Berries:** This island contained trees upon which grew red berries that yielded a highly intoxicating juice. They mixed it with water to moderate its power and sailed on.

(30) **The Island of the Eagle:** An island on which there lived an ageing anchorite, clad only in his hair. While they were there, a monstrous eagle alighted near a lake and started to preen itself. It was joined by two others, and all three bathed in the lake for three days before flying away again, their flight stronger than it had been when they had arrived. Seeing this, Diuran, against the advice of Maíl Dúin, plunged into the lake, and from that day until he died he never had a day's illness.

(31) **The Island of the Laughing Folk:** On this island they discovered a great company of men who laughed and played incessantly. They drew lots as to who should set foot on the island, but, as soon as one foot touched the beach, that man also began to laugh and had to be quickly hauled back onto the boat. Some accounts say that the man could not be rescued and was left on the island as Maíl Dúin sailed away.

(32) **The Island of the Flaming Rampart:** A flaming wall of fire circled this island. Through an opening in the fire they could see the wonders of the island, but could not land.

(33) **The Island of the Monk of Tory:** A rock in the sea on which lived a monk who had come from the monastery on TORY Island off the coast of Donegal. Dressed only in white, the monk told Maíl Dúin of his adventures in reaching the island. He had gathered together a vast treasure and set sail, meaning to keep the plunder for himself. However, his boat was becalmed, and an angel told him to throw all his booty over the side and then to dwell wherever his boat took him. This he did, and he came to the rock on which he had been living, nourished by otters who brought him salmon and even flaming firewood, for seven years. Maíl Dúin and his men were fed in the same manner and then prepared to leave. The monk advised Maíl Dúin where he would find the killer of his father, and told him to forgive him his crime.

(34) **The Island of the Falcon:** The last island on the epic voyage of Maíl Dúin. This was inhabited by no humans, only herds of sheep and oxen. They landed and ate their fill when one of the sailors saw a large falcon. Commenting that the falcon was like those seen in Ireland, they vowed to follow it.

At the end of the epic voyage, Maíl Dúin ran his boat ashore on a small island off the coast of Ireland, where he discovered the man who had killed his father. Remembering the words of the monk, he forgave him his crime and then made his way back to his own home.

Cross of the Scriptures and the ruins at Conmacnoise, County Offlay, Ireland (© Tim Thompson/Corbis)

ISLE OF HONEY
Welsh and Arthurian
An early name for BRITAIN, according to the
WHITE BOOK OF RHYDDERCH.

ISLE OF LIFE
Arthurian
Possibly to be identified with the Isle of Wight and
where the ancient British Kings GADDIFER and
PERCEFOREST were said to have enjoyed a
lengthy existence. This life-prolonging island seems
to have connections with the Isle of APPLES, which
GEOFFREY OF MONMOUTH makes AVALON,
and, by association with Irish mythology, might
possibly be identified with the Isle of MAN.

ISODD
Arthurian
Norse and Icelandic variant of ISEULT.

ISOLDE
Arthurian
Variant of ISEULT used in the thirteenth century by
GOTTFRIED VON STRASSBURG, and in the
nineteenth century by Richard Wagner.

ITH
Irish
One of the Sons of MÍL ÉSPÁINE, who were to
become the first human inhabitants of IRELAND. A
descendant of BREGON, Ith is alleged to have spied
the far-off land of Ireland from the top of the tower
his ancestor had built in Spain. Ith set off with ninety
followers and landed in Ireland, where he was
warmly welcomed by the TUATHA DÉ DANANN,
who had just lost their king, NEIT, in a battle with
the FOMHOIRÉ. The Tuatha Dé Danann asked Ith
to judge the rights of MAC CUILL, MAC CÉCHT
and MAC GRÉINE to rule, but, as Ith spoke so
favourably about the island, the Tuatha Dé Danann
began to suspect that he had designs on their
homeland and killed him. His body was recovered
and carried back to Spain, from where a second,
better-prepared expedition set out, this second
expedition conquering the Tuatha Dé Danann and
thus making Ireland a home of mortal men for the
first time.

ITHER
Arthurian
The son of UTHER's sister and therefore a cousin of
ARTHUR. He was raised by his uncle and became
the King of KUKUMARLANT, but later claimed
Arthur's throne and stole a golden goblet from him.
He was slain by PERCEVAL.

ITINERARIUM CAMBRIAE
Welsh
Itinerary of Wales, an important source text by
GIRALDUS CAMBRENSIS. It was written after he
had travelled through WALES in the company of
Baldwin, Archbishop of CANTERBURY, in 1188
preaching the Third Crusade. He recorded everything
he saw or heard and appeared to believe even the most
outrageous stories that the people of Wales told him.
This text is fascinating, because it records details of
saints, sunken forests and kingdoms, miracles, strange
lakes and mountains, and a host of other mythological
and quasi-historical or legendary material.

ITONJE
Arthurian
Sister of GAWAIN who married King
GRAMOFLANZ.

IUBDAN
Irish
The elfin King of the realm of FAYLINN and
husband of BEBO. He and his wife were taken
captive by FERGHUS MAC LEDA, but released
after they had been ransomed by EISIRT.

IUBHAR
Arthurian
The Irish name for the father of ARTHUR. However,
one Irish romancer misunderstood this name and
made Iubhar Arthur's grandfather, calling Arthur's
father UR.

IUCHAR
Irish
A son of TUIRENN and brother of BRIAN and
IUCHARBA, some accounts naming BRIGHID as
their mother. The three brothers were responsible for
the murder of CIAN, the father of LUGH, who made
them pay for their crime by obtaining magical
implements the TUATHA DÉ DANANN needed for
the Second Battle of MAGH TUIREDH against the
FOMHOIRÉ. The three brothers succeeded in all the
tasks set them, but died from the wounds they
received in accomplishing the final one.

IUCHARBA
Irish
A son of TUIRENN and brother of BRIAN and
IUCHAR.

IUCHNA
Irish

In some versions of the legend of CLIODNA, Iuchna is named as the mortal who persuades Cliodna to elope with him from TÍR TAIRNGIRI, this time, however, as the emissary for OENGHUS MAC IN OG, who was apparently in love with her. The outcome of the elopement remains the same as in the main versions of the legend.

IVOINE
Arthurian

In French romance, the original name of MOINE or CONSTANS, the former being the most likely contender based purely on etymological grounds.

IVOIRE
Arthurian

The sister of BAN who was married to King CONSTANTINE of BRITAIN and had three sons: UTHER, IVOINE (MOINE or CONSTANS) and PANDRAGON (AMBROSIUS).

IVOR
Arthurian

The huntsman who raised MERIADOC, but about whom nothing else is known.

IWAIN
Arthurian

Middle High German romance by the late twelfth- and early thirteenth-century poet HARTMANN VON AUE that clearly follows the earlier works of CHRÉTIEN DE TROYES. The hero of this work is usually known as OWAIN.

IWERET
Arthurian

According to WOLFRAM VON ESCHENBACH, the father of IBLIS and hence father-in-law of LANCELOT. The Lord of BEFORET, he raided the territories of Lancelot's foster brother MABUZ, as a result of which Lancelot killed him. He appears to be of Celtic origin, possibly from YWERIT, the father of BRAN, though he may also be identified with IBERT.

IWERIADD
Welsh

According to a traditional genealogy of BENDIGEID VRAN, Iweriadd was the mother of both Bendigeid Vran and BRANWEN by LLYR, although her attributes and characteristics remain unknown. It has been suggested that she personifies IRELAND and thus explains the connection between Llyr and LIR, but this theory is somewhat suspect.

J

JACK THE GIANT-KILLER
British and Arthurian

The famous giant-killer from nursery stories who is perhaps best known for his exploits with a beanstalk and a goose that laid a golden egg. Thought to have flourished during the traditional Arthurian period, Jack started his career by killing the giant CORMORAN, whom he trapped in a large pit and then hacked to pieces. He was then himself captured, by the giant BLUNDERBOAR, but managed to escape and killed Blunderboar and his brothers. He was also said to have tricked a Welsh giant into killing himself. His first appearance in the Arthurian saga says that he became the servant of ARTHUR's son and, in the course of this service, obtained a wonderful sword, shoes of swiftness, and caps of knowledge and invisibility. He continued to rid the land of giants, married a duke's daughter and was given a noble residence by Arthur himself. There is no evidence that Jack was a hero of early tales and he is possibly a composite of several, being invented some time around the end of the eighteenth or beginning of the nineteenth century. Classical influences may have played some part in his creation, for there are marked similarities between his character and that of Perseus, who killed the Gorgon Medusa and married Andromeda. Even his attributes are similar.

JAPHETH
British

According to a few early English chroniclers, the first inhabitants of BRITAIN were descendants of Japheth, one of the sons of NOAH. However, all trace of these people vanished by the time the country came to be inhabited by the giants whose king was ALBION.

JAUFRÉ
Arthurian

Possibly cognate with GRIFLET, Jaufré appears in a romance that carries his name and tells how

TAULAT came to ARTHUR's court, killed a knight in front of the Queen and promised to return each year to do exactly the same again. Jaufré was dispatched after him and, following a variety of adventures, killed him, marrying BRUNISSEN, whom Taulat had made suffer.

JEREMIAH
Arthurian

An alleged King of HUNGARY during the Arthurian period.

JESCHUTÉ
Arthurian

A character appearing in the story of PERCEVAL. Named by WOLFRAM VON ESCHENBACH only as the daughter of King LAC, and thus the sister of EREC, she was the wife of ORILUS, Duke of LALANDER. Perceval's mother had told her son to demand a jewel or a kiss from any lady he met. He came upon a girl in a tent and demanded both, this story appearing in works by both Wolfram von Eschenbach and CHRÉTIEN DE TROYES.

JOAN GO-TO-'T
Arthurian

In the play *The Birth of Merlin*, published in 1662 but written at an earlier date, Joan go-to-'t is the mother of MERLIN. Although anonymous, the play may have been written by W. Rowley (d. 1626), though the style indicates that Shakespeare may have had a hand in it.

JOHFRIT DE LIEZ
Arthurian

During LANCELOT's stay in MAIDENLAND, this character was responsible for training the knight as a mighty warrior.

JOHN OF GLASTONBURY
Arthurian

The fourteenth-century author of a Latin history of GLASTONBURY that includes some Arthurian material, most notably genealogical information.

JONAANS
Arthurian

A virtuous ancestor of LANCELOT who emigrated from BRITAIN to GAUL, where he married the daughter of King MARONEX, from whom he inherited his kingdom.

JONAS

British and Arthurian

The first husband of TREPHINA, daughter of WAROK, and father by her of JUDWAL or TREMEUR. It is possible that the couple remained childless, for Tremeur is also named as the son of CUNOMORUS, who was also, at some stage, married to Trephina.

JORAM

Arthurian

In the medieval *Wigalois* by WIRNT VON GRAFENBERG, Joram was a king who left GUINEVERE a magic girdle, saying either she could regard it as a gift or he would come and fight for the right to present it to her. She asked him to do the latter, which he did, successfully defeating several champions, but to one, GAWAIN, he presented the girdle. Gawain subsequently married FLORIE, the niece of King Joram.

JOSA, SAINT

Arthurian

According to Coptic tradition, the daughter of JOSEPH OF ARIMATHEA.

JOSEPH D'ARIMATHIA

Arthurian

Important work by the twelfth-century Burgundian ROBERT DE BORON that deals with the GRAIL legends, particularly those surrounding the biblical associations of JOSEPH OF ARIMATHEA.

JOSEPH OF ARIMATHEA

British and Arthurian

A biblical character who was either the uncle of Jesus and a tin trader who regularly visited the West Country for Mendip lead and Cornish tin, on one occasion allegedly accompanied by Jesus, or a soldier of Pilate, who gave him the Chalice Cup used at the Last Supper. The former version is possibly the better known of the two.

The tradition that he was the uncle of Jesus also says that, following the Crucifixion, he travelled to BRITAIN in either AD 37 or 63, bringing the Christian Gospel with him and accompanied by eleven or twelve disciples. Arriving at GLASTONBURY, he pushed his staff into the ground and it immediately rooted, a divine sign that his journey had come to an end. The local king gave him and his followers twelve hides of land, and on that land they founded the Old Church, later to be incorporated into Glastonbury Abbey. The sprouting staff grew into a thorn tree, the GLASTONBURY THORN, that had the special distinction of flowering twice a year, once in the spring and again at Christmas. Tradition also says that Joseph brought three holy relics with him, the first two being cruets containing the blood and sweat of Jesus, while the third, and the most famous, was the Chalice Cup used by Christ at the Last Supper, and also, according to some sources, used to catch the blood of Christ while on the Cross from the wound in his side made by the LANCE OF LONGINUS. This vessel has become known as the Holy GRAIL, the subject of the quest by ARTHUR's knights.

The alternative tradition makes Joseph a soldier of Pontius Pilate. After the Resurrection, and having been thrown into a dungeon, Joseph was visited by Jesus, who returned to him the Chalice Cup of the Last Supper, which Pilate had originally given Joseph but which had become lost. Joseph was set free when Jerusalem fell to the armies of Vespasian and, with his sister ENYGEUS and her husband, BRONS or HEBRON, went into exile with a group of companions. When suffering from famine, those among them who had not sinned were sustained by the Chalice Cup – the Grail. Brons and Enygeus had twelve sons, eleven of whom married, but the twelfth, ALAN, did not. Placed in charge of his brothers, he sent them out to preach Christianity. His father, Brons, was told to become a fisherman, thus becoming known as the RICH FISHER. Joseph himself meanwhile travelled to Britain, most sources saying that he brought the Grail with him, though ROBERT DE BORON says that Brons was entrusted with the holy vessel. His journey to Britain is variously described, and in one version he crosses the sea on a miraculous shirt (*sic*), the property of his son JOSEPHE.

Joseph and his followers were also said to have converted the pagan city of SARRAS to Christianity, though this does not correspond to the later Grail legends, which still make Sarras a pagan city. Its king, EVELAKE, having adopted the Christian faith, was then able, with divine help, to defeat his enemy, King THOLOMER. Sarras, from which the SARACENS are sometimes said to have derived their name, but which is not known outside romance, is variously located either in the East, meaning Asia, or in Britain itself.

Other legends exist concerning Joseph of Arimathea. The romance *Sone de Nausay* relates how he drove the Saracens out of NORWAY, married the daughter of the pagan king and became king himself. God then made him powerless and the land became infertile. Fishing was his only pleasure, which led to his becoming known as the FISHER

KING, though he was finally cured of his ailments by a knight. This is a curious version of the story of the Fisher King, who is usually described as one of Joseph's descendants, and appears to have been lifted directly from the Grail legends. He was then said to have provided for the foundation of the GRAIL CASTLE, though monastery would be a better description, for it was to have thirteen monks in charge to reflect Christ and his twelve apostles.

JOHN OF GLASTONBURY provides us with some information about Joseph's arrival in Britain. He mentions the cruets of blood and sweat, but does not mention the Grail. He also says that Joseph was dispatched to Britain by Saint Philip, who was preaching in GAUL. Gallic tradition states that he was placed in an oar-less boat in the company of Lazarus, Martha, Mary Magdalene and others, which was then guided by the divine hand to Marseilles. Another tale, Spanish in origin, says that this party went to Aquitaine, while an Aquitainian story says that Joseph and his party landed at Limoges. All these seem to be an attempt to claim Joseph for Gaul, but most are now not seriously regarded by hagiologists.

The *Sone de Nausay* says that Joseph had a son named ADAM, while the *ESTOIRE DEL SAINTE GRAAL* says his son was called Josephe. Coptic tradition claims that he had a daughter, Saint JOSA. Attempts have been made to connect Joseph with Joachim, the father of the Virgin Mary, or with Joseph the father of Jesus. These attempts have found no following, for biblical information alone is sufficient to prove their invalidity.

JOSEPHE
Arthurian
The son of JOSEPH OF ARIMATHEA who is first mentioned in the *ESTOIRE DEL SAINTE GRAAL*. When his father and his followers crossed the sea to BRITAIN, it was said that the pure ones did so on Josephe's outstretched shirt (*sic*). He became the first GRAIL KEEPER of Arthurian legend, and consecrated ALAN as his successor before he died and was buried in SCOTLAND. However, the *QUESTE DEL SAINTE GRAAL* had him living long enough to administer Communion to GALAHAD.

JOSHUA
Arthurian
The name of at least three characters from Arthurian legend.
1 The son of BRONS and ENYGEUS, brother of ALAN and nephew of JOSEPH OF ARIMATHEA. He married the daughter of King KALAFES of TERRE FORAINE, later inheriting that kingdom. He succeeded Alan as the GRAIL KEEPER, following the normal line of descent for the FISHER KINGS.
2 According to the pedigree of JOHN OF GLASTONBURY, the son of HELAIUS and an ancestor of ARTHUR.
3 According to the pedigree of Grufudd Hiraethog, the son of EVGEN, father of GARCELOS, and an ancestor of IGRAINE.

JOVELIN
Arthurian
According to GOTTFRIED VON STRASSBURG, the Duke of Arundel (Sussex) who was the father of ISEULT of the White Hands.

JOYOUS GARD
Arthurian
Originally called DOLOROUS GARD, presumably because the DOLOROUS STROKE was delivered there, this castle was captured by and became the property of LANCELOT, who changed its name. Located in the north of England and identified by many with BAMBURGH Castle, it was to this castle that Lancelot took GUINEVERE once he had rescued her from being burnt alive. The castle later reverted to its original name.

JOZEFANT
Arthurian
According to *DURMART LE GALLOIS*, the King of DENMARK.

JUAN
Arthurian
The King of Castile in Spanish romance who married ISEO, the daughter of TRISTAN. His sister, or daughter, MARIA, married TRISTAN THE YOUNGER.

JUDON
British
The wife of GORBODUC who, following the murder of her favourite son FERREX by his brother PORREX, became insane. In her insanity she hacked Porrex to pieces in his sleep. Because neither son had left an heir and because she and Gorboduc were too old to have further children, the line of descent from BRUTUS died along with Gorboduc.

JUDWAL
British and Arthurian
The alternative name for TREMEUR, the son of TREPHINA and either CUNOMORUS or JONAS.

Julius Caesar, who led three invasions of Britain and paved the way for the later Roman conquest led by Claudius. (© Archivo Iconografico, S.A./Corbis)

JULAIN
Arthurian

The husband of YGLAIS and mother of PERCEVAL, according to *PERLESVAUS*.

JULIUS CAESAR
General

A famous Roman statesman, born 100 or 102 BC, made ruler of Rome in 49 BC, and assassinated in the Forum in 44 BC. He led three expeditions to BRITAIN, the first two of which were unsuccessful. The third invasion laid the foundations for the later invasion of CLAUDIUS. He appears in several of the Arthurian sources. The *VULGATE VERSION* calls him 'emperor', though he never actually was, and makes him the contemporary of ARTHUR, though some 500 years too early for the traditional Arthurian period.

MERLIN was introduced to the imperial court and told Caesar that a dream he had had could be interpreted only by the Wild Man of the Woods. The latter was captured by Merlin and GRISANDOLE, and told Caesar that his dream was about his wife's infidelities. Even more fantastically, the romance *HUON DE BORDEAUX* makes Julius Caesar the father of OBERON by MORGAN Le Fay.

JUPITER OPTIMUS MAXIMUS TANARUS
Romano-British

A Celticised form of the Roman sky god Jupiter. The only evidence that remains of this deity is a worn altar dedicated to him that was found at Chester. The last part of the name comes from the Celtic thunder god known from GAUL and further afield.

JUTES
General

A Germanic people who originated in Jutland but later settled in Frankish territory. They occupied KENT about AD 450 and conquered the Isle of Wight and the opposite coast of Hampshire in the early sixth century.

K

KADIEN(N)
Arthurian
According to the Welsh *BONEDD YR ARWR*, both a maternal and a paternal ancestor of ARTHUR, directly descended, on both occasions, from LLYR.

KADWR
Arthurian
A paternal ancestor of ARTHUR in the line of descent from LLYR, as found in the Mostyn MS 117.

KAERBADUS
British
The original name of BATH.

KAERLEIR
British
'Leir's Fort', the original name of the city of Leicester, which was founded by King LEIR.

KAHEDRIN
Arthurian
The son of King HOEL of BRITTANY and brother of ISEULT of the White Hands. His good friend TRISTAN married his sister, but Kahedrin fell in love with ISEULT and wrote poems and love letters to her. She replied in all innocence, but Tristan misunderstood, and Kahedrin had to jump from a window to avoid being killed by the enraged Tristan. He landed on a chess game that King MARK was playing below the window, and eventually died of his love for Iseult. Some people say that this story led to the belief that King Mark killed Tristan in jealousy, believing that it was he, and not Kahedrin, who had been corresponding with his wife.

KAI
Welsh and Arthurian
A variant of CEI. Kai was later to resurface in the Arthurian cycle, his name only slightly altered, as the knight Sir KAY. This variant of the name is used when the knight of ARTHUR was said to have been encountered in a dream by IDDAWC and RHONABWY, a tale related in the *MABINOGION* story of the *DREAM OF RHONABWY*.

KALAALLIT NUNAAT
Arthurian
The native name for GREENLAND.

KALAFES
Arthurian
The King of TERRE FORRAINE who, following his cure from leprosy by ALAN, became a Christian and took the name ALFASEIN at his baptism. His daughter married Alan's brother JOSHUA, another son of BRONS. He died after having been speared through the thighs (a common wound in the GRAIL legends) for watching the GRAIL PROCESSION.

KALEGRAS
Arthurian
The name of TRISTAN's father in the Icelandic *SAGA OF TRISTRAM*, and also the name given to Tristan's son by ISEULT of the White Hands. This younger Kalegras was eventually said to have become the King of England.

KAMBER
British
The son of BRUTUS and brother of LOCRINUS and ALBANACTUS. After the death of his father, Kamber became the King of WALES, while Locrinus ruled over ENGLAND and Albanactus over SCOTLAND. Kamber later helped his brother Locrinus to defeat the Huns after the invaders had killed Albanactus. The leader of the Huns, HUMBER, was drowned in a river that has ever since carried his name.

KAMELIN
Arthurian
The son of the Irish King ALVREZ, a KNIGHT OF THE ROUND TABLE and brother of MIROET, also a Knight of the Round Table.

KANADIC
Arthurian
The domain over which FLORIE was queen.

KANAHINS
Arthurian
The squire of Sir LANCELOT.

KANEDIC

Arthurian

The realm of ECUNAVER, who was conquered after he had stated that he intended to attack ARTHUR. It is possible that Kanedic is to be identified with KANADIC, the realm of FLORIE.

KAPALU

Arthurian

A servant of MORGAN Le Fay who appears in the *BATAILLE LOQUIFER*. It seems as if this character has his origins in CAPALU, the continental name for the monstrous cat, the CATH PALUG.

KARADAN

Arthurian

The husband of an unnamed sister of ARTHUR, and father by her of AGUISANT.

KARADAWC

Arthurian

Presumed to be a variant of KARADOC and KRADOC, this name appears in a paternal pedigree found in the Mostyn MS 117, which gives the descent of ARTHUR from LLYR.

KARADOC

Arthurian

According to two pedigrees found in the Welsh *BONEDD YR ARWR*, an ancestor of ARTHUR. It is thought that he is to be identified with KRADOC and KARADAWC, names that appear in other manuscripts and pedigrees, and that are illustrated under LLYR.

KARDEIZ

Arthurian

According to WOLFRAM VON ESCHENBACH, one of the twin sons of PERCEVAL.

KAW

Arthurian

A variant of CAW.

KAY

Arthurian

Also CAI, CEI, KAI, KEI

The son of ECTOR and foster brother of ARTHUR. Though he appears in the earlier romances as a model of chivalry, later stories made him a troublesome and somewhat childish character who believed that his relationship to Arthur gave him the right to behave in any way he chose. Originally he claimed that it was he, not Arthur, who had withdrawn the SWORD IN THE STONE, but Ector compelled him to tell the truth. He married ANDRIVETE, the daughter of King CADOR of NORTHUMBERLAND, and is credited with a daughter named KELEMON, and two sons called GARANWYN and GRONOIS. His horse was known as GWINAM GODDWF HIR.

Many different stories are told about Kay, some obscure and some well known. In Welsh tradition he was a member of the party formed to help CULHWCH in his quest to locate OLWEN. PERLESVAUS recounts how he killed LOHOLT, Arthur's son, and joined BRIAN DES ILES in a rebellion against the King. The accounts of his death vary. Throughout Welsh literature and tradition he was said to have been killed by GWYDDAWG, who was in turn killed by Arthur. He was also said to have been killed during Arthur's campaign against the ROMAN EMPIRE, or in the war against MORDRED. One source lists him among the knights killed by the escaping yet unarmed LANCELOT when the latter had been caught in compromising circumstances in GUINEVERE's bedchamber.

KEELTA (MAC RONAN)

Irish

A leading member of the FIAN, one of the house-stewards of FIONN MAC CUMHAILL, a strong warrior and an unrivalled story-teller. He was said to have lived for a long time after the fian had died out and to have been christened by Saint PATRICK, to whom he told the stories of the fian. In one notable instance, King MONGÁN called upon the spirit of Keelta to prove a wager, and it was during the course of this that it was revealed that Keelta was the killer of FOTHAD, rather than Fionn mac Cumhaill, who had, until that time, been held responsible.

KEEPER OF THE FOREST

Arthurian

A character who is possibly to be identified with CERNUNNOS and is referred to in the Welsh poem *OWAIN*.

KEEVAN

Irish

A Latinised variant of CIABHAN.

KEHYDIUS

Arthurian

A variant form of KAHEDRIN that was used by Sir Thomas MALORY.

KEI

Arthurian

A variant of KAY.

KELEMON

Arthurian

The daughter of Sir KAY, according to Welsh tradition.

KELLIW-IC, -IG

Arthurian

A Cornish stronghold of ARTHUR. Possibly to be identified with Castle KILLIBURY, it has also been connected with CALLINGTON, CELLIWITH and KELLY ROUNDS.

KELLY ROUNDS

Arthurian

A place in CORNWALL that, it has been suggested, is identifiable as KELLIWIC.

KELTCHAR

Irish

See CELTCHAR

KELTOI

General

The term used by both the Greeks and the Romans to refer to the northern barbarians who at times posed a considerable threat to the Mediterranean countries from their western and central European heartland. This name is possibly the origin of the word Celt.

KENT

General

The kingdom of GWYRANGON during VORTIGERN's time, which the latter gave to the SAXON leader HENGIST. During the traditional Arthurian period the county seems to have been under ANGLO-SAXON rule and may have been ruled by AESC, Hengist's son, who traditionally reigned between AD 488 and 512. William of MALMESBURY says that Aesc had to defend the kingdom, implying that he had a formidable enemy, such as ARTHUR. BEDE says that Kent was originally settled by the JUTES, and this has led to an association between Hengist, his brother HORSA, and Jutland, the homeland of the Jutes.

KENTIGERN, SAINT

Arthurian

The son of THANEY (the daughter of LOT), according to the account given in the *LIFE OF SAINT KENTIGERN*. Also called Mungo, Saint Kentigern was a Celtic churchman and the apostle of Cumbria. According to his own legend, he was the son of a Princess Thenew, which is not too dissimilar to Thaney, who was cast from TRAPRAIN LAW,

then exposed on the Firth of Forth in a coracle and set adrift to die. This carried her to Culross, where she bore a son (*c.* AD 518). Mother and child were baptised, an anachronism, by Saint Serf, who reared the boy in his monastery, where he was so loved that his name, Kentigern ('chief lord'), was often exchanged for Mungo ('dear friend'). He founded a monastery at Cathures (Glasgow) and in AD 543 was duly consecrated Bishop of Cumbria. In AD 553 he was driven to seek refuge in WALES, where he visited Saint DAVID, and where he founded another monastery and a bishopric, which still bears the name of his disciple Saint Asaph. In AD 573 he was recalled by a new king, RHYDDERCH HAEL, and about AD 584 was visited by Columba. He died in AD 603 and was buried in Glasgow Cathedral, which is named after him as Saint Mungo's, his tomb today lying in the centre of the Lower Choir.

KESAIR

Irish

See CESAIR

KET

Irish

See CET

KEVA

Irish

The daughter of FIONN MAC CUMHAILL. He gave her to GOLL MAC MORNA after Goll mac Morna had taken the place of Fionn mac Cumhaill and killed IRNAN, the third of the sorceress daughters of CONARAN, having earlier killed her two sisters.

KIAN

Irish

See CIAN

KICVA

Welsh

See CIGFA

KILHWCH

Welsh and Arthurian

A little used variant of CULHWCH.

KILLARAUS, MOUNT

Irish and Arthurian

The mount in IRELAND from where MYRDDIN (MERLIN) was said to have transported the GIANTS' RING that was re-erected on Salisbury Plain as STONEHENGE.

KILLIBURY

Arthurian

Place in CORNWALL that, it has been suggested, is identifiable as CELLIWIG, and thus CAMELOT.

KIL(W)YDD

Welsh and Arthurian

The father of CULHWCH and GOLEUDDYDD, ARTHUR's aunt.

KIMBAY

Irish

A Latinisation of CIMBAOTH.

KINCALED

Arthurian

The name by which GAWAIN's horse GRINGALET is known in Welsh tradition.

KING ARTHUR

Arthurian

An opera written in 1691 by John DRYDEN, with music by Henry Purcell, which has little actual Arthurian content. In it, ARTHUR is in love with the blind EMMELINE, daughter of Duke CONON of CORNWALL. She is carried off by OSWALD, the SAXON King of KENT and Arthur's enemy. While she is held captive, her sight is restored to her by MERLIN, and she is eventually rescued when Arthur finally defeats Oswald.

KING ARTHUR AND (THE) KING (OF) CORNWALL

Arthurian

A sixteenth-century English ballad that featured ARTHUR and the sorcerer King Cornwall.

KING OF THE ISLES

Arthurian

The father of BIAUTEI, whose hand was won by GAWAIN when the latter managed to unsheathe the sword HONOREE.

KING WITH A HUNDRED KNIGHTS

Arthurian

One of the eleven leaders who rebelled against the youthful ARTHUR at the start of his reign. He has been variously identified with BERRANT LES APRES, AGUYSANS and MALEGINIS, though the *DUE TRISTANI* implies that he originated from Piacenza and had a wife called RICCARDA.

KLINGSOR

Arthurian

The Duke of TERRE LABUR, according to WOLFRAM VON ESCHENBACH, who, after being emasculated by King IBERT of Sicily, became a wizard. It would appear that his realm was in Italy, as its capital is named as Capua. In Wagner's opera *Parsifal* he is portrayed with a black character, but this is not usually how he is seen; normally he is shown as courteous and a man whose word was his bond, one tradition making him a bishop rather than a sorcerer. He was said to have kept ARTHUR's mother (named by Wolfram Von Eschenbach as ARNIVE) and several other queens captive, but they were released by GAWAIN.

KLUST

Welsh

One of the seldom-mentioned members of the party formed to help CULHWCH locate OLWEN. His special skill, for which he was chosen, was the acuteness of his hearing, for, even if he were buried deep underground, he could hear an ant leave its nest 50 miles away.

KNIGHT OF THE DRAGON

Arthurian

The name by which SEGURANT THE BROWN, a knight of the OLD TABLE and UTHER's mightiest warrior, was known. He was also sometimes known as the KNIGHT OF THE OLD TABLE.

KNIGHT OF THE FAIR COUNTY

Arthurian

The brother of King ARTHUR who married the daughter of Earl CORNUBAS of WALES and became the father of the GREAT FOOL.

KNIGHT OF THE LANTERN

Arthurian

The title of the son of LIBEARN. This knight was also the son of the King of the CARLACHS, who slew the BLACK KNIGHT, thus suggesting that Libearn was either married to, or had an affair with, the King of the CARLACHS.

KNIGHT OF THE LION

Arthurian

A title given to OWAIN, who was usually accompanied by a lion.

KNIGHT OF THE OLD TABLE

Arthurian

A name by which SEGURANT THE BROWN, a knight of the OLD TABLE and UTHER's mightiest warrior, was known. He was also sometimes known as the KNIGHT OF THE DRAGON.

KNIGHT OF THE SLEEVE
Arthurian
Winning the hand of CLARETTE at a tournament at ARTHUR's court, this knight is the hero of the Dutch romance *Ridder metter Mouwen*.

KNIGHT OF THE TWO SWORDS
Arthurian
Honorific title given to BALIN.

KNIGHTS OF THE FRANC PALAIS
Arthurian
An order of knights, eventually wiped out by the Romans, that was founded by PERCEFOREST.

KNIGHT(S) OF THE ROUND TABLE
Arthurian
The most chivalrous order of knights ever to have been formed. They obtained their name from the table at which they were seated, so that none had precedence over the other. They vowed to uphold a code of ethics laid down by ARTHUR, and reasserted this oath every year at the feast of Pentecost, meeting in the great hall at CAMELOT.

The number of knights in the order varies greatly, but those specifically mentioned in this book as being Knights of the Round Table are:

ADRAGAIN, AGRAVAIN, ALON, ARTEGALL, ARTHUR (whom most forget), BAGDEMAGUS, BANIN, BEDIVERE, BELLEUS, BLAMORE DE GANIS, BORRE, BORS, BRANDILES, CARL OF CARLISLE, CLARIS, COLGREVANCE, DINADAN, DINAS, DODINAL, DORNAR, DRIANT, EVADEAM, FERGUS, GAHERIS, GALAHAD, GALEHAUT, GALERON, GALES LI CAUS, GALIHODIN, GAWAIN, GORNEMANT DE GOORT, IRONSIDE, KAMELIN, LAC, LAMORAK, LANCELOT, LOHOLT, MADOR, MARROK, MERAUGIS, MIROET, MORDRED, NENTRES, OWAIN THE BASTARD, PELLEAS, PERCEVAL, POLIDAMAS, PRIAMUS, SAGREMOR, TOR, TRISTAN, TRISTAN THE YOUNGER and YDER.

KORRIGANED
Gaulish
The Breton name for a supernatural woman. It is thought that these beings gave rise to the CORANIEID, who were said to have invaded and plagued BRITAIN during the reign of LLUDD, although one of the *TRIOEDD YNYS PRYDEIN* specifically states that the Coranieid came from Arabia.

KRADOC
Arthurian
Thought to be identifiable with KARADAWC or KARADOC, an ancestor of ARTHUR.

KUKUMARLANT
Arthurian
The realm of which ITHER became King before claiming ARTHUR's throne, though related to him, and finally being killed by PERCEVAL.

KULHWCH
Welsh and Arthurian
A little-used variant of CULHWCH.

KUSTENHIN
Arthurian
Also CUSTENNIN, KUSTEN(N)IN, MUSTENNIN
The early Welsh form of CONSTANTINE, it was used to designate the Constantine who was ARTHUR's grandfather, and is found in this form, or its alternative Kustenin, in the paternal descent of Arthur from LLYR in the Mostyn MS 117 and in the Welsh *BONEDD YR ARWR*. The curious variant of Mustennin appears in one version of Arthur's paternal pedigree found in the *Bonedd yr Arwr*. It seems most probable that this variant is simply a transcriptive error.

KUSTEN(N)IN
Arthurian
Variant of KUSTENHIN.

KYMBELIN
British
The seventy-first British king after the time of BRUTUS. His reign was said to have lasted just one year, 22 BC. William Shakespeare later calls this possibly historical character Cymbeline, in his play of the same name.

KYMIDEU KYMEINVOLL
Welsh
The giantess wife of the giant LLASSAR LLAESGYVNEWID, both of whom hailed from IRELAND but were expelled as they spread panic wherever they went owing to their great size. They crossed the Irish Sea and were received hospitably by BENDIGEID VRAN. In return for his kindness, the two giants gave him an inexhaustible cauldron that had the power instantly to rejuvenate anyone placed into it. This cauldron later found its way back to Ireland when Bendigeid Vran gave it to MATHOLWCH as part of the peace offering to

appease the insult of EFNISIEN. This cauldron may later have resurfaced as the HOLY GRAIL.

KYNAN
Arthurian
According to the paternal pedigrees that may be found in the Welsh *BONEDD YR ARWR*, as well as in the Mostyn MS 117, a maternal and paternal ancestor of King ARTHUR in his line of descent from LLYR.

KYN-FARCH, -VARCH
Welsh and Arthurian
According to popular Welsh tradition, Kynfarch was the father of URIEN of RHEGED by NEFYN, the daughter of BRYCHAN.

KYNNVOR
Arthurian
The father of CONSTANTINE and grandfather of King ARTHUR, according to the paternal pedigree of Arthur that may be found in the Welsh *BONEDD YR ARWR*.

KYNOR
Arthurian
Variant form of KYNUAWR that is found in ARTHUR's line of descent from LLYR, as contained in the *BONEDD YR ARWR*.

KYNOTUS
Arthurian
The rector of CAMBRIDGE who was installed by none other than King ARTHUR himself.

KYNUAWR
Arthurian
Also KYNOR
According to the pedigree in the Mostyn MS 117, the paternal great-grandfather of ARTHUR in his line of descent from LLYR.

KYNWAL
Arthurian
According to the pedigree found in the Welsh *BONEDD YR ARWR*, a maternal ancestor of King ARTHUR.

L

LA TÈNE
General

A settlement at the north-eastern end of Lake Neuchâtel, Switzerland, that revealed a large number of metal Celtic relics when the site was excavated in 1858. These are thought to have been votive offerings that date from 400 BC. They represent the next stage of the development of the Celtic art form after the artefacts found at HALSTATT, and as a result the name La Tène has come to be used as a term to describe the post-400 BC Celtic period.

LABEL
Arthurian

A King of Persia whose daughter married CELIDOINE following her conversion to Christianity. Label died either in retreat at a hermitage or in battle.

LABHRAIDH
Irish

The brother of LI BAN and FAND.

LABHRAIDH LAMFHADA
Irish

A Druidic sorcerer who appears in the *Cath Finntrága*, delivering the magical weapons forged by Tadhg to FIONN MAC CUMHAILL and the FIAN.

LABHRAIDH LOINGSECH
Irish

A King of LEINSTER, the son of AILILL AINE. He was originally named MAON, and is traditionally said to have reigned *c*. 268 BC. Driven into exile by COBTHACH COEL, who made him eat a portion of his father's and his grandfather's hearts, along with a mouse and all her young, he lost his voice and travelled to GAUL, where he mustered his forces and returned. With the additional help of the men of MUNSTER, he later reclaimed his kingdom and made a false peace with Cobthach Coel. Unsuspecting, Cobthach Coel accepted the invitation proffered and

visited Labhraidh Loingsech at his court with his thirty vassal kings. There Labhraidh Loingsech had an iron chamber readied for his visitors and, after they had retired for the night, had the door closed and a huge fire lit underneath it, thus roasting Cobthach Coel and his supporters to death. He then sought out and married MORIATH, the daughter of SCORIATH, whom he had loved before his enforced exile.

Labhraidh Loingsech had a secret that none but his barber knew, and that was that he had horse's ears. Each year he would have his hair cropped, and each year he made his barber swear to keep the secret. Eventually the strain of keeping the secret made the barber unwell, and he sought the advice of a DRUID, who told him to tell the secret to a tree. This he did and soon became well again. However, CRAFTINY cut down that very tree to make a new harp and, to his amazement, the first time he played it at the royal court it sang out about Labhraidh Loingsech's ears. Labhraidh Loingsech stood up and revealed his ears, and never tried to conceal them again. This story has a parallel in the story of the classical Greek King Midas.

LABIANE
Arthurian

The niece of King MARK and mother of MERAUGIS following her rape by her uncle. Mark subsequently murdered her.

LAC
Arthurian

A KNIGHT OF THE ROUND TABLE, the son of CANAN and brother to DIRAC. He was King of ESTREGALES and ruler of the Black Isles, and father of EREC, BRANDILES and JESCHUTÉ.

LADIS
Arthurian

The ruler of LOMBARDY in the Arthurian romances.

LADON
Arthurian

The elderly King of GASCONY who was married to LIDOINE, the sister of LARIS.

LADRA
Irish

The pilot who led CESAIR and her party to the shores of IRELAND. Ladra was one of just three

Ceramic urn discovered at the important early Celtic site at Le Tène, Switzerland. (© Werner Forman/Corbis)

men among the expedition, the others being BITH and FINTAN. They were accompanied by fifty women whom they shared among themselves, but Ladra died from excessive sexual activity, leaving Bith and Fintan with twenty-five women each.

LADY OF SHALOTT
Arthurian
The name by which ELAINE, the daughter of BERNARD OF ASTOLAT, is possibly best known, appearing under this title in Alfred, Lord Tennyson's famous poem *The Lady of Shalott.*

LADY OF THE FAIR HAIR
Arthurian
A fairy whom ARTHUR saved from the FISH-KNIGHT and subsequently became her lover.

LADY OF THE LAKE
Arthurian
The mysterious lady from whom ARTHUR received EXCALIBUR, and to whom it was returned on his death. Very little is said about her in the Arthurian romances, except that she took LANCELOT while still a child to raise him (hence his title Lancelot of the

Lake), and later cured him when he lost his senses. She is sometimes identified with VIVIENNE, or NIMUE, though usually remains nameless. According to ULRICH VON ZARZIKHOVEN, the fairy who raised Lancelot was the mother of MABUZ and, as Mabuz is thought to be identical with the Celtic god MABON, this would suggest that the Lady of the Lake in this instance was none other than MORGAN Le Fay, for she was, in origin, Mabon's mother, MATRONA. It seems highly likely, therefore, that the Lady of the Lake has her origins in a Celtic lake divinity, a possibility further supported by the fact that some sources say that she was one of the three queens aboard the ship that ferried the dying Arthur to AVALON.

BALIN was said to have killed a Lady of the Lake, though not necessarily the one who delivered and received Excalibur.

LAEG(H)
Irish
See LOEG

LAERY
Irish
A Latinised form of LOEGHAIRE.

Elaine, the Lady of Shalott, lies dead. (Mary Evans Picture Library/Arthur Rackham Collection)

Arthur, Merlin and the Lady of the Lake, the guardian of the sword Excalibur. (© Stapleton Collection/Corbis)

LAHELIN

Arthurian

The German form of the Welsh Llewelyn. The brother of ORILUS, he stole the kingdoms of WALES and NORTHGALIS from HERZELOYDE following the death of GAHMURET.

LAIGHIN

Irish

The name that the GAILIÓIN adopted after they had settled in LEINSTER, although some say that this name was used only by their descendants. The Gailióin were one of the three companies that invaded IRELAND from Greece, the other two being the FIR DHOMHNANN and the FIR BHOLG.

LAILOKEN

Welsh and Arthurian

Celtic tradition makes Lailoken a wild man whose career closely resembles that of MYRDDIN (MERLIN). He spent some time at the court of RHYDDERCH HAEL, revealed that the wife of King MELDRED was adulterous, and made several prophecies regarding his own death. It seems likely that Lailoken was simply a nickname for Merlin, as the name closely resembles the Welsh word for a twin, and tradition states that Merlin had a twin sister, GANIEDA.

LAIRGNEN

Irish

The chief of CONNACHT who became betrothed to DEOCA. She begged him to obtain four marvellous singing and talking swans whose fame had spread far and wide. This he did, but as he brought them before her they began a hideous transformation, for these swans were the four children of LIR, whom AOIFE had condemned to remain as swans for 900 years. That time was now up and they changed from beautiful swans into decrepit old people on the verge of death. Lairgnen fled, and nothing more was heard of him.

LAKE DISTRICT

Arthurian

Picturesque region of Cumbria that has been suggested (by S. G. Wildman) as the birthplace of ARTHUR or, failing that, the region in which he was raised. The most famous Lakeland legend concerning King Arthur is that of the HELM WIND, though local Lake District folklore almost unreservedly claims that Arthur was King in that region.

The Lake District, Cumbria, suggested as the birthplace of King Arthur. (© Kim Sayer/Corbis)

LALANDER

Arthurian

The duchy of ORILUS, the husband of JESCHUTÉ.

LAMBOR

Arthurian

The King of either TERRE FORRAINE or LOGRES, he was killed by BRULAN (VARLAN), following which both his realm and that of his slayer were diseased, thus originating the WASTE LAND of the GRAIL stories. It is possible that he may be identical with LAMBORD.

LAMBORD

Arthurian

The maternal great-grandfather of ARTHUR, according to the pedigree of JOHN OF GLASTONBURY.

LAMORAK

Arthurian

The son of King PELLINORE, brother of PERCEVAL and a KNIGHT OF THE ROUND TABLE. He was killed by GAWAIN after sleeping with the latter's mother, MORGAUSE.

LANCE OF LONGINUS

Arthurian

The lance with which the centurion LONGINUS was said to have pierced the side of Jesus while the latter hung on the Cross following the Crucifixion (Saint John 19: 34). This has led to its also being known as the BLEEDING LANCE. It has become associated with the Holy GRAIL, being carried in the GRAIL PROCESSION and being sought by MELORA, the warrior daughter of ARTHUR.

LANCELOT

Arthurian

The name of two related characters from the Arthurian legends and, aside from ARTHUR, possibly the best known of all the Arthurian characters.

(1) The grandfather of LANCELOT, he married the daughter of the king of IRELAND and, by her, became the father of BAN and BORS.

(2) The most famous of all Arthur's knights, the King's champion, friend and confidant. He was a KNIGHT OF THE ROUND TABLE and a most complex character. Different commentators are still undecided on his origin. Was he Celtic or merely the invention of the continentals? His name is generally regarded as a double diminutive of the German word *Land*, though it has been argued, some feel

successfully, that LLWCH LLEMINAWC, a character who accompanies Arthur to the OTHERWORLD in *PREIDDEU ANNWFN*, is his original. By the same token, this journey has been identified with the expedition Arthur makes to IRELAND in the *MABINOGION* story of *CULHWCH AND OLWEN* and, if this is indeed the case, Lancelot appears to number among the accompanying party as LLENLLEAWC, though in this instance an Irishman. These identifications have been called into doubt through the appearance of the names LANSLOD and LAWNSLOT, which seem to have been used to translate Lancelot from other languages into Welsh. This is certainly possible, and may be a retranslation of Lancelot back into Welsh when those writers who came across the name Lancelot failed to recognise its origins in Llwch Leminawc or Llenlleawc.

Celtic origins certainly figure in the version of Lancelot's story told by ULRICH VON ZARZIKHOVEN. Here, Lancelot is the son of King PANT of GENNEWIS, and CLARINE. As his father had been killed during an uprising, Lancelot was taken away by a fairy and raised in MAIDENLAND, but she would not tell him his name until he had fought IWERET of BEFORET. He was trained as a knight and in the use of all manner of weapons by JOHFRIT DE LIEZ and married the daughter of GALAGANDREIZ. The fairy had a son, MABUZ, whose lands were being invaded by IWERET, whom Lancelot fought and killed, thus learning his name. He married IBLIS, Iweret's daughter, and had four children by her, and eventually won back the kingdom of his father, Pant. The appearance of Mabuz, who is thought to have originated in the Celtic god MABON, certainly indicates that Lancelot had a Celtic origin. Parts of this story are common with the more normal story of Lancelot as related in French and German sources, as well as by Sir Thomas MALORY.

The more usual version of Lancelot's story is, in essence, as follows.

The son of King BAN and ELAINE was left on the shores of a lake by his mother after Ban had died. He was found by the LADY OF THE LAKE, who raised him, and because of this he became known as Lancelot of the Lake. Having grown to manhood, he joined ARTHUR's court, became a KNIGHT OF THE ROUND TABLE, and Arthur's most trusted companion. However, just as MERLIN had foretold, he fell in love with GUINEVERE, who reciprocated his feelings, and so began the famous, and sometimes stormy, love affair between them. Guinevere was not the only lady to love Lancelot,

Elaine ties her sleeve round Sir Lancelot's helmet. (© Bettmann/Corbis)

Four queens discover the sleeping Lancelot. (Aubrey Beardsley, 1893–4/Mary Evans Picture Library)

for he was also loved by ELAINE of Astolat (the LADY OF SHALOTT), who died of her love for him, her body being brought up the Thames on a barge along with a note saying why she had died.

During his many adventures, Lancelot visited Castle CARBONEK, and there rescued Elaine from a bath of boiling water, though some say that this rescue happened in a brazen tower some distance from the castle itself. However, some further describe the tower itself as the fairest Lancelot had ever seen. Entertained by King PELLES, Elaine's father, the king and BRISEN, Elaine's handmaiden (or, alternatively, an enchantress), conspired to have Lancelot sleep with Elaine, for it had been prophesied that he should father the purest knight on her. At a feast in Lancelot's honour, during which, according to some sources, Lancelot witnessed the GRAIL PROCESSION, Brisen administered a love potion and Lancelot, enchanted into thinking that Elaine was Guinevere, lay with Elaine. As a result GALAHAD was conceived. Later the two slept together again (once more with the help of Brisen's magic), this time at CAMELOT, but they were discovered by the furious Guinevere, who banished her lover from the court. He went mad, running wild in the forests, sometimes tended by hermits and village folk. Only after many years was he restored to sanity by the GRAIL, the holy vessel he subsequently quested for.

He returned to Arthur's court, but the King still refused to believe that the rumours he was hearing about Lancelot and his wife were true. Lancelot championed the Queen's cause when she was abducted by MELEAGAUNCE, the son of King BAGDEMAGUS. The only mode of transport that was available to Lancelot was a cart, in which he was most reluctant to travel but did, none the less, crossing a 'sword bridge' to reach the castle in which Meleagaunce had taken refuge. The two fought, but Bagdemagus pleaded with Guinevere to save his son, so the fight was stopped, on the condition it be taken up in one year's time. Later Meleagaunce accused Guinevere of committing adultery with KAY, and once again Lancelot championed her cause. Again Bagdemagus had to plead for his son's life, which was on this occasion spared, but Lancelot finally killed him in combat at Arthur's court.

Lancelot's adultery with Guinevere was now brought to Arthur's attention, but he refused to believe it unless conclusive evidence was brought before him. Finally Lancelot and Guinevere were trapped together in the Queen's bedchamber, but Lancelot, though unarmed, managed to fight his way to freedom, killing all but one of the knights who had caught him and Guinevere together. Lancelot fled and Guinevere was sentenced to be burnt at the stake, being rescued in the nick of time by Lancelot, who secreted her in his castle, JOYOUS GARD. Even now Arthur, wary of Merlin's prophecies, wanted nothing more than to make peace with his old friend, but he mistakenly took the advice of his nephew MORDRED, who had designs on the throne, and Arthur went to war against Lancelot. While absent, Mordred seized the throne and Arthur cut off his fight with Lancelot to return to deal with the situation at home. Lancelot followed some time later, but arrived one month after the final Battle of CAMLANN, and thus too late to help his old friend. He travelled to AMESBURY, where Guinevere had taken the veil, and, realising that she was lost to him, he went to GLASTONBURY, where he became a monk, then returning to Amesbury following a dream that told him to ride there as fast as he could. He arrived too late, for Guinevere had died not half an hour earlier. Grief-stricken, Lancelot could neither eat nor sleep and within a matter of a few short weeks he too had died.

LANCELOT OF THE LAIK
Arthurian
An anonymous fifteenth-century Scottish verse romance.

LANCELOT OF THE LAKE
Arthurian
The full title by which LANCELOT was known, for he was, allegedly, raised by the LADY OF THE LAKE, who was identified, in thirteenth-century sources, as VIVIENNE.

LANCEOR
Arthurian
The son of the King of IRELAND who was sent by ARTHUR to slay BALIN, for the latter had killed the LADY OF THE LAKE. Balin, however, killed him, and his lover, COLOMBE, took her own life. It is alleged that subsequently King MARK rode by and, seeing their bodies, buried them.

LANCIEN
Arthurian
Now known as LANTYAN, CORNWALL, this was the site of King MARK's palace.

LAND FROM WHICH NO ONE RETURNS
Arthurian
A mysterious realm that was ruled over by GUNDEBALD. MERIADOC did, however, manage

to escape from this realm, having rescued the daughter of the German Emperor.

LAND OF PASTURES AND GIANTS
Arthurian
One of the various realms ascribed to the rule of RIENCE. The name of this domain would seem to connect RIENCE with the giant of Welsh tradition RHITTA, RHICCA or RITHO, who was associated with YR WYDDFA FAWR (Mount SNOWDON).

LAND OF PROMISE
Irish
The literal translation of TÍR TAIRNGIRI.

LAND OF THE LIVING
Irish
The literal translation of TÍR INNA MBÉO.

LAND OF -THE YOUNG, -YOUTH
Irish
The literal translation of TÍR NA NOC.

LAND OF WOMEN
Irish
See WOMEN, LAND OF

LANGUORETH
Welsh and Arthurian
In Jocelyn's *LIFE OF SAINT KENTIGERN*, the wife of RHYDDERCH who became enamoured with a soldier. It seems that she may be identifiable with GANIEDA, MYRDDIN's (MERLIN's) twin sister.

LANSDOWN HILL
Arthurian
Called Mons Badonicus in early times, this hill, near BATH, has become associated with the site of the Battle of BADON. During the Middle Ages it was reported that the skeleton of King ARTHUR had been found there.

LANSLOD
Arthurian
A name that, along with LAWNSLOT, seems to have been used to translate LANCELOT into Welsh.

LANTRIS
Arthurian
The brother of ISEULT, though this is a later name for ALCARDO. Under the name of Lantris, Alcardo is said to have been a squire, possibly to TRISTAN, and was killed in his attempt to rescue his sister from King MARK.

LANTYAN
Arthurian
Place in CORNWALL, formerly called LANCIEN, that is said to have been the site of King MARK's palace.

LANVAL
Arthurian
One of ARTHUR's knights who became the lover of a mysterious woman, having solemnly promised to keep their affair secret. GUINEVERE subsequently attempted to seduce Lanval, but, when he would have nothing to do with her, she falsely accused him of making advances to her. He was put on trial and told to prove he was enamoured of someone other than the Queen, but, true to his promise, he refused. However, when all seemed lost, the mysterious lady arrived, and together they left for AVALON. He was given the fairy horse BLANCHARD by his lover, TRYAMOUR.

Lanval's story is recounted several times, first of all in the twelfth-century *Lanval* by MARIE DE FRANCE, and subsequently in English in the fourteenth-century *Sir Landeval*, and in two sixteenth-century works *Sir Lambewell* and *Sir Lambwell*.

LAOGHAIRE
Irish
A historical King of IRELAND, who was reigning at the time of the arrival of Saint PATRICK. It was not long before Saint Patrick thought it necessary to attack the pagan religion practised by Laoghaire and his subjects. On the eve of May Day the DRUIDS were assembled at TARA, awaiting the lighting of the royal fire, when they were amazed to see smoke rising from the nearby hill of Slane, the smoke coming from a fire lit by Saint Patrick. The DRUIDS brought him before King Loeghaire, whom he challenged to a magic contest to see whose God was the more powerful.

The official Christian account of this event says that two huts were set alight. Inside one was a Christian youth, wearing the robe of a royal magician, while in the other was a DRUID wearing Saint Patrick's own cloak. From the ashes of one hut the boy emerged unscathed although the magician's cloak had been burnt to a cinder, while from the ashes of the second hut Saint Patrick's cloak was retrieved unharmed, but the Druid had been incinerated.

From that day Christianity became popular throughout Ireland, although Loeghaire remained a pagan until he died, appropriately enough from a bolt of lightning. He was buried standing up, sword in hand, facing LEINSTER, the county from which his enemies had come.

LAPIS EXILLIS
Arthurian
Meaning 'worthless stone', and probably owing its origin to the alchemists' philosopher's stone, this was the name given to the GRAIL by WOLFRAM VON ESCHENBACH, who thought it not a holy vessel but rather a stone.

LAPLAND
Arthurian
This region of Scandinavia was said to have formed the eastern border of ARTHUR's territories by Hakluyt in his sixteenth-century *Travels*.

LAR
Arthurian
The husband of Queen AMENE. When Amene was besieged by the evil ROAZ after Lar's death, his ghost guided WIGALOIS to help his widow.

LARIE
Arthurian
The daughter of LAR and AMENE, she married WIGALOIS after the latter had defeated ROAZ.

LARIS
Arthurian
The son of HENRY, Emperor of GERMANY and one of the heroes of *CLARIS ET LARIS*. He loved MARINE, the daughter of URIEN, but had a rival in the form of King TALLAS of DENMARK, who laid siege to Urien. ARTHUR arrived and defeated the Danes, but Laris had been taken prisoner and had to be rescued by CLARIS and others. He became King of Denmark in place of the defeated Tallas.

LASCOYT
Arthurian
One of the three sons of GORNEMANT DE GOORT, he, like his brothers, met with a violent death.

LAUDAME
Arthurian
The Queen of ANFERE whom GAREL married.

LAUDINE
Arthurian
The lady of the fountain. First married to ESCLADOS, she married OWAIN after the death of her first husband.

LAUFRODEDD
Welsh
Also LLAWFRODEDD

The owner of a knife that was considered one of the THIRTEEN TREASURES OF BRITAIN.

LAUNCELOT
Arthurian
A variant of LANCELOT.

LAUNDES
Arthurian
The Earl of Laundes was BELLANGERE, the son of ALISANDER THE ORPHAN and the killer of King MARK of CORNWALL.

LAUREL
Arthurian
The niece of LIONORS and LYNETTE, she married AGRAVAIN.

LAVAINE
Arthurian
The son of BERNARD OF ASTOLAT and brother of ELAINE (the LADY OF SHALOTT). He became a follower of Sir LANCELOT.

LAVARCHAM
Irish
See LEBHORCHAM

LAWNSLOT
Arthurian
A name that, along with LANSLOD, seems to have been used to translate LANCELOT into Welsh.

LAYAMON
Arthurian
A Worcestershire poet and priest (*fl. c.* 1200) at Ernley (now Areley Regis) on the Severn near Bewdley. In *c.* 1200 he wrote an alliterative verse chronicle, the ANGLO-SAXON *BRUT*, a history of England that contains much Arthurian material, and that was an amplification of WACE's slightly earlier *ROMAN DE BRUT* or *BRUT D'ANGLETERRE*. It is an important work in the history of English versification, as it is the first poem written in Middle English.

LAZILIEZ
Arthurian
Named as an ancestor of PERCEVAL.

LE COTE MALE TAILÉE
Arthurian
'The badly cut coat', a nickname given to BREUNOR by the ever-impertinent KAY when Breunor arrived at ARTHUR's court in a badly tailored coat.

LE MORTE D'ARTHUR
Arthurian

Completed in 1470 and published by Caxton in 1485 as one of the first books to use modern printing, this fifteenth-century work by Sir Thomas MALORY comprises a series of episodes from the legendary life of King ARTHUR. It is regarded as the first great prose work in English literature, but in actual fact only the last eight books of the series are titled *Le Morte d'Arthur*. The series omits a few of the tales, and contains many inconsistencies, particularly its multitude of women named ELAINE and wounded kings. However, it still remains the main English source on the Arthurian legends and is an undoubted literary masterpiece.

LE TORNOIMENT DE L'ANTICHRIST
Arthurian

A French poem by Huon de Mery that tells how he, the poet, went to an enchanted spring in BROCELIANDE, where BRAS-DE-FER, the chamberlain of the Antichrist, rode up. Together they rode to the scene of a mighty battle, where the forces of Heaven, which included ARTHUR and his knights, were fighting the forces of Hell.

LEABHAR GABHÁLA ÉIREANN
Irish

The Book of the Conquest of Ireland, popularly known as *The Book of Invasions,* is a twelfth-century pseudo-history that embodies and embroiders earlier tradition. It places emphasis on the prestige of the late Gaelic ruling classes and remains one of the essential sources concerning early Irish legend. It lists six successive invasions, as briefly detailed below.

(1) **The First Invasion – The people of Cesair:** In a time before the biblical Flood a company of people came to IRELAND either under the leadership of CESAIR, daughter of BITH, a son of NOAH, or led by BANBHA, the SPIRIT OF IRELAND. Of these people, all but one, FINTAN, perished in the Flood, but he lived on in various forms to oversee all that later befell the country.

(2) **The Second Invasion – Partholán:** Between the death of the people of Cesair and the coming of this second group, Ireland had become inhabited by the monstrous FOMHOIRÉ, a race of half-human monsters that each had a single leg, hand and eye and three rows of razor sharp teeth. The Fomhoiré were defeated by PARTHOLÁN and his people and forced into exile to the Hebrides and the Isle of MAN. Ireland itself was nothing like a recognizable country at this time, so Partholán had his people clear four plains and create seven lakes, thus starting to create a recognisable landscape. Partholán also built the first guest house, brewed the first beer and established laws and crafts. Partholán's people were wiped out by a plague, leaving Ireland open once more.

(3) **The Third Invasion – Nemhedh:** Arriving from an unknown place, NEMHEDH and his people quickly settled in Ireland, as there was no one to resist them. They cleared twelve plains and created four more lakes. Following the death of Nemhedh, the Fomhoiré returned from their exile and quickly suppressed the people. Every SAMHAIN they compelled the people to pay them a tribute of two-thirds of their corn, wine and children. Finally the people rebelled and attacked the Fomhoiré. The rebellion failed, and only one boatload of people survived, some of them settling in Greece, others in unnamed northern lands.

(4) **The Fourth Invasion – the Fir Bholg:** The remnants of the people of Nemhedh who had settled in Greece multiplied sufficiently so that they could return to Ireland and reclaim it from the Fomhoiré. During their exile they had split into three tribes, the FIR BHOLG, who led the return expedition, the GAILIÓIN and the FIR DHOMHNANN. Their invasion was successful, and the Fir Bholg divided the land into five CÓIGEDH, or provinces, ULSTER, LEINSTER, MUNSTER and CONNACHT with MEATH in the centre. The Gailióin settled in Leinster, whence they became known as the LAIGHIN, and the Fir Dhomhnann in Connacht. The Fir Bholg inhabited the remaining three provinces.

(5) **The Fifth Invasion – the Tuatha Dé Danann:** The remnants of the people of Nemhedh who had fled to the north now returned. During their time in exile they had learned much magical lore and now called themselves the TUATHA DÉ DANANN. Led by the DAGHDHA, they brought four great treasures with them: the stone of FÁL, the invincible spear of LUGH, the inescapable sword of NUADHA and the inexhaustible cauldron of the Daghdha. There followed the two battles of MAGH TUIREDH, the first against the Fir Bholg, whom they utterly routed, and the second against the Fomhoiré, whom they also defeated.

(6) **The Sixth Invasion – the Sons of Míl Éspáine:** The last invasion came from Spain, as the name of the invaders would suggest. They landed on the feast of BELTANE (1 May), their leader being AMHAIRGHIN, the FILI. They defeated a massive Tuatha Dé Danann army and marched towards TARA, the capital. On the way they encountered three goddesses, BANBHA, FÓDLA and ÉRIU, the wives of the Tuatha Dé Danann kings MAC CUILL,

MAC CÉCHT and MAC GRÉINE respectively. These goddesses disputed the right of the Sons of MÍL ÉSPÁINE to Ireland, but they proved their right by overcoming the Tuatha Dé Danann at the Battle of TAILTIU, having completed a magical test. The Tuatha Dé Danann still refused to accept their defeat and used their magic to deprive the invaders of milk and corn. Finally, their two companies agreed to divide the land, the Tuatha Dé Danann receiving the underground half.

The *Leabhar Gabhála Éireann* demonstrates that, like the mythology of early BRITAIN, the island was originally inhabited by a race of giants, but those of Irish origin are far more mysterious and terrible than those that were said to have been the mythical inhabitants of Britain. The landscape of Ireland was successively shaped by human invaders, until it resembled something akin to the geography of Ireland that would have existed in Celtic times. Finally, the gods were suppressed by human inhabitants who sought not to annihilate them, but rather to subjugate them and have them near at hand should their help ever be needed. It is, however, worth mentioning that, as this work dates from the twelfth century, a long time after Christianity had arrived in Ireland, it cannot be taken as a true representation of the early mythology of Ireland, but a more romanticised version that has its grounding in the Celtic oral tradition.

LEABHAR NA HUIDHRE
Irish
The Book of the Dun Cow, an eleventh- or twelfth-century text that is, without doubt, based on material of a much earlier date. It was certainly written before 1106, because this is the recorded date for the murder of its scribe Maelmori. It is one of the main sources for the study of Irish mythology, along with *The Book of Leinster*. One of the most famous stories contained in the *Leabhar na hUidhre* is that of ÉDÁIN ECHRAIDHE and the god MIDHIR, although it is also notable for its version of the battle in which CUMHAILL, the father of FIONN MAC CUMHAILL, was killed, and for the story of CONNLA, which is told in a section of the book known as the *Echtra Condla chaim maic Cuind Chetchathaig*.

LEAPACHA DHIARMADA AGUS GHRÁINNE
Irish
'Beds of Diarmaid and Gráinne', a popular name throughout IRELAND for dolmens, which are believed to have once sheltered the fugitives DIARMAID UA DUIBHNE and GRÁINNE.

LEAR
Arthurian
The Shakespearian variant of LEIR.

LEBHORCHAM
Irish
Also LAVARCHAM
The wise woman who raised the infant DERDRIU in the strictest seclusion. She told Derdriu that NAOISE, son of UISNECH, had the attributes that Derdriu desired most in a man, even though, from birth, Derdriu had been betrothed to CONCHOBAR MAC NESSA. She is also said to have been at EMHAIN MHACHA on the occasion when CÚ CHULAINN approached, still seething with the frenzy of battle, and is alleged to have devised the plan by which he was cooled down sufficiently to be allowed entry to the court. A woman of extraordinary powers, considered by some a prophetess, Lebhorcham was said to cross all IRELAND every day, though whether she physically did this or let her mind travel is open to speculation.

LEINSTER
Irish
One of the five original provinces into which IRELAND was divided by the FIR BHOLG and still one of the provinces of that country. Situated in the south-east of Ireland, Leinster today covers the counties of Carlow, Dublin, Kildare, Kilkenny, Laoighis, Longford, Louth, MEATH, Offaly, Westmeath, Wexford and Wicklow.

LEINSTER, BOOK OF
Irish
One of the major sources of Irish mythology, the *Book of Leinster* was written before 1160 and is now one of the most prized possessions of Trinity College Library, Dublin. This book contains an ancient list of saga titles that refer to mythological tales that, sadly, no longer exist.

LEIR
British and Arthurian
A legendary early British king who was the prototype of William SHAKESPEARE's tragic King LEAR. The son of King BLADUD, Leir ruled for sixty years and founded the town of KAERLEIR or Leicester. He had three daughters – CORDELIA, REGAN and GONERIL. The two eldest, Regan and Goneril, played on his vanity and persuaded him to give them each one-quarter of his kingdom as their dowries. Cordelia refused to have any part of this and remained faithful to her father until his death.

Goneril and Regan, along with Regan's two husbands, MAGLAURUS, Duke of ALBANY, and HENWINUS, Duke of CORNWALL, then seized the remainder of Leir's kingdom. Maglaurus allowed Leir to keep a retinue of 140 men, but Goneril reduced this to eighty. Regan then had her turn and reduced it to just five, before Goneril finally reduced it to just one man. Leir exiled himself to FRANCE, where he was greeted and treated as an honoured guest by Cordelia and her husband AGANIPPUS, who equipped an army and sailed back to BRITAIN and restored Leir to the throne. Three years later Leir died. Cordelia buried him in a vault dedicated to the Roman god Janus, which lay beneath the River Soar, downstream from Leicester, the town her father had founded.

LÉN LINFIACLACH
Irish
The brazier of BODB. He lived in Loch Lein, which was named after him, where he made wonderful vessels for FAND, the daughter of FLIDHAIS. Every evening he threw his anvil far eastwards to the grave-mound at Indéoin na nDése. He then threw a shower of water, then one of fire and finally one of purple gems at the grave-mound.

LENA
Irish
The grandson of MAC DÁ THÓ who had been responsible for the raising of the huge boar owned by his grandfather and then for slaughtering it for a feast. The goings-on at the feast are described in the ribald *Scéla Mucce Maic Dá Thó*.

LENDAR
Irish
The wife of CONALL CERNACH. During the feast thrown by BRICRIU she was persuaded to challenge the right of EMER, wife of CÚ CHULAINN, and Fidelma, wife of LOEGHAIRE BUADHACH, to be regarded as the premier woman of ULSTER.

LENUS OCELUS VALLAUNUS
Romano-British
The name by which the Roman god Mars was known in South WALES, where he was perhaps worshipped as a healing deity rather than as a god of war.

LEODEGRANCE
Arthurian
The King of CAMELIARD and father of GUINEVERE. Some sources say he presented the ROUND TABLE to ARTHUR.

LEPRECHAUN
Irish
A small, roguish elf, often thought of as a cobbler, who possesses a huge buried treasure, although this treasure is popularly thought to be hidden at the end of a rainbow. If caught, a leprechaun can be made to tell his secrets and grant wishes, but if his captor stops looking at him, even for a split second, he will vanish. Leprechauns were said to guard the gold mines of County Wicklow, which, to this day, have not been found, and yet golden ornaments of ancient Irish design, and dating back to at least 1500 BC, have been discovered throughout Europe. Leprechauns are popularly referred to as Fairyfolk, or the 'wee people'.

LER
Irish
See LIR

LESTOIRE DE MERLIN
Arthurian
A part of the *VULGATE VERSION* that gives one version of the history of MERLIN.

LEUDONUS
Arthurian
An early form of the name LOT, both meaning 'LOTHIAN-ruler'.

LEVAINE
Arthurian
The daughter of BERNARD OF ASTOLAT and sister to ELAINE the White.

LEVANDER
Arthurian
A servant of the King of Africa who was sent, by that King, to give assistance to MELORA, ARTHUR's daughter, on her quest.

LI BAN
Irish
The daughter of AED ABRAT. A dream-woman who, with her sister, FAND, whipped CÚ CHULAINN and disabled him for a year after he had failed to capture two magical birds for his wife.

LI JUS ADEN
Arthurian
Thirteenth-century French romance that says that HELLEKIN, already an established figure in Teutonic lore, was a fairy king who became the lover of MORGAN Le Fay, whose companions are named as ARSILE and MAGLORE.

LIA
Irish

A lord of LUACHAR in CONNACHT and the treasurer of the FIAN. He kept the hereditary treasures of the fian, said to have been passed down to them directly from the TUATHA DÉ DANANN, in a bag made of crane's skin. Lia was killed by DEIMNE.

LIA FÁIL
Irish

The Stone of Destiny, otherwise known as the stone of FÁL and today as the Stone of SCONE. It was allegedly brought to IRELAND by the TUATHA DÉ DANANN, to whom it had been given, in FALIA, by the wizard MORFESSA.

LIAGAN
Irish

A member of an unnamed band of warriors who chose to pick a fight with the FIAN. He faced the cowardly CONAN MAC MORNA in single combat, laughing heartily at the poor champion the fian had put forth. Conan mac Morna nervously replied that Liagan was in more danger from the man behind him than he was from the man in front of him. As Liagan turned, Conan mac Morna cut off his head and rushed back to the security of the fian, where he was met with derision.

LIANOUR
Arthurian

The ruler of the CASTLE OF MAIDENS who is described as a duke.

LIATH
Irish

The young prince of the TUATHA DÉ DANANN who loved BRÍ, the daughter of MIDHIR, a love she welcomed. Her father did not approve, however, and so, when Liath came to meet Brí, Midhir had his servants fire their slingshots at Liath. So heavy was the bombardment that Liath had to turn away, and Brí died of a broken heart.

LIAZE
Arthurian

The daughter of GORNEMANT DE GOORT whom her father wanted PERCEVAL to marry, but this did not come about. Her three brothers, GURZGI, LASCOYT and SCHENTEFLEURS, all met violent deaths.

LIBAN
Arthurian

A daughter of King BAN and the mother of illegitimate twins by PANDRAGUS.

LIBEARN
Arthurian

The stepmother of ALEXANDER, Prince of India, who turned him into the CROP-EARED DOG by magic.

LICAT ANIR
Arthurian

An earthen mound at ARCHENFIELD said to mark the burial place of ARTHUR's son AMR. Each time the length of the mound was measured, it allegedly gave a different reading.

LICONAUS
Arthurian

The father of ENIDE by TARSENESYDE, according to *EREC ET ENIDE*.

LIDDINGTON CASTLE
Arthurian

Near Swindon, Wiltshire, Liddington Castle is one of the various locations suggested as the site of the Battle of BADON.

LIDOINE
Arthurian

The sister of LARIS and the daughter of HENRY, Emperor of Germany, according to *CLARIS ET LARIS*. At first married to the ageing King LADON of GASCONY, she was captured by SAVARI, King of SPAIN, after his death. She was rescued by ARTHUR, after which she married her brother Laris's companion, CLARIS.

LIFE OF SAINT CADOC
Arthurian

According to this work, which details the life of the eponymous Saint CADOC, the son of GWYNLLYM and Saint GWLADYS, LIGESSAC sought and found sanctuary from ARTHUR with Saint Cadoc for ten years after he had killed some of Arthur's followers.

LIFE OF SAINT CARANNOG
Arthurian

A medieval work which states that CADO, who is possibly cognate with CADWY, co-ruled the West Country alongside King ARTHUR.

LIFE OF SAINT KENTIGERN
Arthurian

According to this work by Jocelyn, which details the life of Saint KENTIGERN, LOT was the father of THANEY, and thus Kentigern's grandfather.

LIGESSAC
Arthurian

A fugitive from King ARTHUR who sought, and found, refuge with Saint CADOC for ten years.

LILE
Arthurian

A mysterious lady from AVALON who brought a great sword to ARTHUR's court. Only BALIN managed to withdraw it from its scabbard, but when asked to return it he refused. Lile then foretold that the sword would bring about his own destruction and kill his dearest friend.

LIMOUSIN
Arthurian

Former province and modern region of central FRANCE. Arthurian legend says that, when ARTHUR quarrelled with LANCELOT, BLAMORE DE GANIS and BLEOBERIS both supported their father (Lancelot) in the dispute, Blamore de Ganis being made the Duke of Limousin.

LINCOLN
Arthurian

County town of Lincolnshire, England. Known as *Lindum* to the Romans, Lincoln had a flourishing wool trade in medieval times. Paulinus built a church in Lincoln in the seventh century, and the eleventh–fifteenth-century cathedral has the earliest Gothic work in BRITAIN. The twelfth-century High Bridge in the High Street is the oldest in Britain still to have buildings on it.

As to Arthurian connections, Lincoln is cited as the birthplace of ANDRED, TRISTAN's cousin and a resident at MARK's court. It is also used as a surname for TOM A'LINCOLN (Tom of Lincoln), the RED ROSE KNIGHT, the illegitimate son of ARTHUR and ANGELICA. However, Lincoln is possibly best known in connection with CAT COIT CELIDON, a wood slightly to the north of the city that is cited by NENNIUS as the location of one of ARTHUR'S BATTLES.

LINCOLN, BATTLE OF
Arthurian

The site of a battle at which ARTHUR and HOEL defeated the SAXON hordes. It is possible that this battle is cognate with the Battle of CALEDON WOOD.

LINNÉ
Irish

A friend of OSCAR, by whom he was mistakenly killed.

Lincoln Cathedral, which sits atop a hill overlooking the city. (© Michael Maslan Historic Photographs/Corbis)

LINNIUS

Arthurian

The scene of four battles fought by ARTHUR in the catalogue of battles found in the works of NENNIUS. It is possibly to be identified with Lindsey (Lincolnshire), and might therefore also be considered identical with the Battle of Lincoln.

LION

Arthurian

Though the lion is not native to BRITAIN, it appears in several Arthurian stories. The sixteenth-century Scottish historian BOECE claimed that lions were once native to SCOTLAND. Both GAWAIN and BREUNOR were said to have killed lions, while OWAIN was said to have had a lion as a companion. KAY was also, in *PA GUR*, said to have killed some lions of Anglesey, but it is thought that this is rather a reference to animals of a supernatural nature.

LION THE MERCILESS

Arthurian

The name of the person from whom ARTHUR won his pet PARROT.

LIONEL

Arthurian

One of the two sons of BORS, his brother having the same name as their father. A fearsome character, he was given the throne of GAUL by ARTHUR, but, following the latter's death, he was killed by MORDRED's son, MELEHAN.

LIONES

Arthurian

Thought by some commentators to be identical with LYONESSE, this kingdom was that ruled by MELIODAS, the father of TRISTAN. The early history of the realm is supplied by the *PROSE TRISTAN*, which says that one of its kings, PELIAS, was succeeded by his son LUCIUS, who was in turn succeeded by APOLLO. This king unwittingly married his own mother, but later married GLORIANDE, by whom he became the father of CANDACES, later King of both Liones and CORNWALL. The *VULGATE VERSION* makes LOT one of the early Kings of Liones, which would seem to suggest that Liones and LOTHIAN are one and the same.

LIONORS

Arthurian

The daughter of SEVAIN and mother of LOHOLT by ARTHUR. Sir Thomas MALORY makes her the mother of BORRE, the illegitimate son of Arthur who is possibly identical with Loholt.

LIR

Irish

Also LER

An ancient god of the sea who has his Welsh equivalent in LLYR. Not much is said about Lir himself, other than that he was the father of MANANNÁN MAC LIR, as well as four other children, by his first wife AOBH, who were condemned to spend 900 years in the form of swans by his second wife AOIFE.

LISCHOIS

Arthurian

The husband of CUNDRIE, the daughter of SANGIVE and LOT.

LISTINOISE

Arthurian

The kingdom of King PELLEHAN that, following the delivery of the DOLOROUS STROKE, became the WASTE LAND of the GRAIL legends.

LIT MERVEILE

Arthurian

A marvellous bed that GAWAIN, having travelled to rescue the captives held in a certain castle, saw moving around on its own. He jumped on to it and it darted from wall to wall, smashing itself against them. As it came to rest, some 500 pebbles were shot at Gawain from sling-shots, following which numerous crossbow bolts were fired at the knight, but his armour proved sufficient to protect him.

LIVRE D'ARTUS

Arthurian

A French *CONTINUATION* to ROBERT DE BORON's work *MERLIN*.

LIZ

Arthurian

The realm of King MELJANZ, who declared war on Duke LYPPAUT after OBIE, the Duke's daughter, had refused him.

LIZABORYE

Arthurian

A kingdom of which BELAYE, LOHENGRIN's second wife, was a princess. However, her parents, and presumably rulers of Lizaborye, sent mercenaries to kill Lohengrin, for they believed their daughter was under his spell.

LLACHEU

Arthurian

According to Welsh tradition, a son of ARTHUR who became identified with LOHOLT, though the two were probably originally different characters.

LLALLAWC

Welsh and Arthurian

A Welsh variant for the wizard MYRDDIN (MERLIN).

LLALLOGAN VYRDIN

Welsh and Arthurian

A Welsh variant for the wizard MYRDDIN (MERLIN).

LLAMREI

Arthurian

The mare owned by King ARTHUR.

LLASAR LLAESGYWYDD

Welsh

Possibly a variant of LLASSAR LLAES-GYVNEWID, this character is said to have taught MANAWYDAN FAB LLYR the arts of saddle-making, which he was later able to employ to provide a living for himself and PRYDERI, along with their respective wives, RHIANNON and CIGFA.

LLASSAR LLAESGYVNEWID

Welsh

A giant, the husband of KYMIDEU KYMEINVOLL and the father of countless riotous children, who were apparently born once every six weeks as fully grown and clad warriors. These children wreaked havoc in their native IRELAND, so MATHOLWCH devised a plan to rid his kingdom of them. He had an iron house made and enticed the entire giant family into it. He then slammed the door and lit huge fires around the house in an attempt to roast them alive. However, as soon as the walls became pliable, the giant and his wife burst through and escaped, although all their children perished.

They travelled from Ireland to WALES, where they were hospitably greeted by BENDIGEID VRAN. They brought with them a wonderful cauldron that had the power to heal the wounded or to bring the dead back to life. With the aid of this cauldron the realm of Bendigeid Vran became a wonderfully prosperous place.

Some years later the cauldron returned to Ireland. Matholwch married BRANWEN and was given the cauldron as recompense for EFNISIEN's insult. It was subsequently destroyed by Efnisien during the expedition mounted by Bendigeid Vran to Ireland to avenge the cruelty shown by Matholwch towards Branwen, even though the effort killed Efnisien. What happened to Llassar Llaesgyvnewid and his wife is not recorded, but some suggest that they accompanied Bendigeid Vran to Ireland and were killed there.

LLAWFRODEDD

Welsh and Arthurian

Also LAUFRODEDD

According to some sources, the owner of CYLLEL LLAWFRODEDD, a Druidic sacrificial knife that is numbered among the THIRTEEN TREASURES OF BRITAIN.

LLEFELYS

Welsh and Arthurian

Also LLEVELYS

A King of FRANCE, son of BELI and brother of LLUDD, CASWALLAWN and NYNNIAW, who, in the *MABINOGION* story of *LLUD AND LLEFELYS*, told Lludd that a scream heard on the eve of every May Day, and whose source could not be found, was actually caused by fighting DRAGONS. These were subsequently caught and interred at DINAS EMRYS.

LLEN ARTHUR

Arthurian

The veil of ARTHUR, which would render the wearer invisible. It is numbered among the THIRTEEN TREASURES OF BRITAIN.

LLENLLEAWC

Arthurian

An Irishman who appears as a companion of ARTHUR in the *MABINOGION* story of *CULHWCH AND OLWEN* and helped in the seizure of the cauldron of DIWRNACH. He is normally identified with LLWCH LLEMINAWC, who appears in a similar role of companion to Arthur in the *PREIDDEU ANNWFN*, and it is possible that both Llenlleawc and Llwch Lleminawc formed the prototype character of Sir LANCELOT.

LLEU

Arthurian

Thought by some commentators to be an early form of LOT, possibly deriving from LEUDONUS.

LLEU LLAW GYFFES

Welsh and Arthurian

A Welsh hero god who is, perhaps, a degenerative version of the Irish LUGH, and who is, curiously, depicted as being a skilled cobbler. He was the second son born to ARIANRHOD, much to her shame, as she was being put through a rite that would attest her virginity. This rite was being carried out because her brother, GWYDION FAB DÔN, had put Arianrhod forward for the post of foot-holder, a post that could be held only by an accredited virgin, at the court of MATH FAB MATHONWY. Her first-born son was immediately named DYLAN.

Gwydion fab Dôn snatched up Arianrhod's second child and hid him in a chest, later adopting the boy as his own. Four years later, and still without a name, the child was shown by Gwydion fab Dôn to his sister Arianrhod. Reminded of her shame, she cursed the child, saying that he would never bear a name until she herself gave him one. Some time later Gwydion fab Dôn managed to circumvent this curse by disguising himself and the young boy and travelling to Arianrhod's castle, where she was tricked into calling the boy Lleu Llaw Gyffes, which means 'Bright One with the Nimble Hand'. Gwydion fab Dôn could not resist revealing their true identity to his sister, and in her fury she cursed the boy a second time, this time saying that he would never bear arms until she herself armed him.

Later Gwydion fab Dôn and the now maturing Lleu Llaw Gyffes travelled to Arianrhod's castle, placed in these legends on the isle of ANGLESEY, and by use of magic made it seem as if the castle was under attack. In her fright, Arianrhod armed Lleu Llaw Gyffes, but again Gwydion fab Dôn could not resist boasting of the deception, and Arianrhod cursed the youth for a third time, saying that he would never marry a mortal woman.

Enlisting the help of Math fab Mathonwy, Gwydion fab Dôn also bypassed this final curse, for together the two magically created a woman of the flowers of oak, broom and meadowsweet whom they named BLODEUWEDD. Lleu Llaw Gyffes married Blodeuwedd, and this time at least Gwydion fab Dôn appears to have resisted the temptation of boasting to his sister.

All did not go well with Lleu Llaw Gyffes's marriage, however, for after a short time Blodeuwedd started an affair with the hunter GRONW BEBYR. Together, the lovers plotted to kill Lleu Llaw Gyffes, but they knew that this could not be accomplished before their victim had revealed the exact manner in which he could be dealt a mortal blow. Finally, Blodeuwedd managed to persuade her husband to reveal that he could be killed only by a spear that had been worked for a year and a day at Mass time on Sundays, and then only if he had one foot in a bathtub and the other on the back of a billygoat. Gronw Bebyr immediately set about forging the required weapon. A year and a day later,

with the spear ready, Blodeuwedd managed to convince Lleu Llaw Gyffes to demonstrate to her the ridiculous position he would need to adopt to be killed. As he took up the stance, Gronw Bebyr rose from his hiding place, but managed only to wound Lleu Llaw Gyffes, who changed into an eagle and flew away to die from his injury.

Gwydion fab Dôn tracked down Lleu Llaw Gyffes by following a sow that fed on the maggots that dropped from the eagle's festering wound. He found the dying hero perched in the branches of a tree and cured his wound before changing Blodeuwedd into an owl for her infidelity. Lleu Llaw Gyffes resumed his human form and killed Gronw Bebyr.

LLEVELYS
Welsh and Arthurian
See LLEFELYS

LLEW
Welsh and Arthurian
An Anglicised and shortened variant of LLEU LLAW GYFFES.

LLIGWY CROMLECH
Arthurian
Located near Moelfre on the east side of Anglesey, GWYNEDD, this cromlech is also known as ARTHUR'S QUOIT, though just where ARTHUR was meant to have thrown this quoit from is unknown.
See also CARREG COETAN ARTHUR

LLOEG(Y)R
Welsh
The ancient Welsh name for ENGLAND. It was later thought to have given rise to the naming of England as LOGRES in the Arthurian legends.

LLONGAD GRWRM FARGOD EIDYN
Welsh and Arthurian
The killer of ADDAON, son of TALIESIN.

LLONGBORTH
Arthurian
The site of a battle in which ARTHUR's men fought. The *RED BOOK OF HERGEST* says that GEREINT was killed during this battle, but the preferred *BLACK BOOK OF CARMARTHEN* makes no mention of this.

LLUAGOR
Welsh and Arthurian
The horse belonging to CARADOC VREICHVRAS (CARADOC BRIEFBRAS).

LLUD AND LLEFELYS
Welsh and Arthurian

A part of the *MABINOGION* that tells how every May Day eve a scream was heard, the source of which could not be located. LLEFELYS, the King of FRANCE, told LLUD that the scream was caused by fighting dragons. These were eventually caught and interred at DINAS EMRYS.

LLUDD
Welsh and Arthurian

The father of GWYNN AP NUDD and brother of LLEFELYS and NYNNIAW, he is the equivalent of the Irish LUGH. He is of great mythical importance for, along with his brother, he appears in a legend concerning three 'plagues' that infected ENGLAND. One of these was a scream, heard every May Day eve, whose source could not be located. Llefelys told Lludd that the scream came from two DRAGONS battling for supremacy. These dragons were finally captured in an underground chamber, a plan devised by Llefelys, and subsequently imprisoned beneath DINAS EMRYS in WALES. A direct comparison can be made between this tale and that concerning the dragons found in an underground lake, as foretold by MYRDDIN, on the site where VORTIGERN was attempting, without success, to erect his tower. It seems safe to assume that these were the same dragons.

LLUD(D) LLAW EREINT
Welsh and Arthurian

The father of CREIDDYLAD whose name means 'Llud of the Silver Hand', perhaps betraying his generous nature. The Welsh equivalent of NUADHA AIRGEDLÁMH, and the British NUDD or NODENS. His daughter was the original of CORDELIA, while his son was GWYNN AP NUDD, the Welsh equivalent of the Irish hero FIONN MAC CUMHAILL.

LLWCH LLEMINAWC
Arthurian

A companion of ARTHUR in the *PREIDDEU ANNWFN*. It is possible that both LLENLLEAWC, with whom he is normally identified, and Llwch Lleminawc formed the prototype character of Sir LANCELOT.

LLWYD FAB -CIL COED, -KILCOED
Welsh

The magician who cast a spell on CIGFA, RHIANNON, MANAWYDAN and PRYDERI to avenge PWYLL's treatment of his friend GWAWL FAB CLUD.

LLYCHLYN
Welsh and Arthurian

The Welsh name for Scandinavia, which, like the similar Irish Lochlann, may originally have signified an OTHERWORLD realm. The character of BLAES, who appears in the Welsh *TRIADS* and is apparently identical with MERLIN'S master, BLAISE, is described as being the son of the Earl of Llychlyn.

LLYFR DU CAERTYDDIN
Welsh

The Black Book of Carmarthen, written prior to 1105. This work was written by the black-robed monks of CARMARTHEN, hence its name, and it is today housed in the National Library of WALES at Aberystwyth. Along with the *Red Book of Hergest*, it is one of the most important sources of Welsh mythological and legendary beliefs.

LLYGADNUDD EMYS
Arthurian

A maternal uncle of King ARTHUR.

LLYN BARFOG
Arthurian

A lake located in GWYNEDD, where ARTHUR was alleged to have done battle with an AFANC.

LLYN CAU
Welsh

A small lake situated on the south side of CADAIR IDRIS in GWYNEDD. Legend claims that it is bottomless and the home to a monster. This legend was embellished some time during the eighteenth century when it is said a young man attempted to swim across Llyn Cau when suddenly, as the man reached the mid-point, the monster appeared, took him in its mouth and disappeared.

See also IDRIS

LLYN EIDDWEN
Welsh and Arthurian

A lake in DYFED that, according to legend must never be allowed to dry up. MYRDDIN (MERLIN) prophesied that, if it did, CARMARTHEN would suffer a catastrophic disaster.

LLYN LLECH OWEN
Arthurian

Located one mile north of Gorslas in west Glamorgan, WALES, this pool now covers the site of a magic well that never ran dry so long as the stone slab covering it was replaced after water had been drawn from it. One day, one of King ARTHUR's knights stopped to drink from the well, but dozed off to sleep and forgot to replace the slab. When he awoke, he found that the well had overflowed and was flooding the surrounding countryside. He hurriedly mounted his waiting horse and quickly rode around the edge of the flood waters, which stopped encroaching over the land when they touched his horse's hoofs. The resulting lake is still there to be seen today.

LLYN TEGID
Welsh

The largest natural lake in WALES and the legendary home of TEGID VOEL and his wife CERRIDWEN. A familiar legend surrounds its creation, the same form of legend that is associated with many other lakes, including Loch Ness in SCOTLAND. Local people used to draw their water from a well that had to be capped after use. One night, however, the well-keeper neglected his duties, and the water gushed out of the well while the local people slept. By morning, having had to flee their houses in the night, the local people looked down from the surrounding hills to see a lake some three miles long and one mile wide. Today Llyn Tegid is five miles long, and local belief holds that it will continue to grow.

LLYN-Y-FAN FACH
Welsh

A small lake at the foot of Bannau Sir Gaer near Llanddeusant in DYFED. It is the site of a fascinating legend, thought to have been one of the inspirations for the later Arthurian character of the Lady of the Lake. Regrettably, the lake was dammed to form a reservoir early in the twentieth century. A maiden left the allegedly bottomless lake to marry a local farmer's son, bringing with her herds of sheep, goats, cattle and horses. However, after several years of marriage, the lady's husband broke the condition that he must refrain from giving her three blows, and she returned to the lake with all the animals she had brought with her. The farmer followed, but was drowned as he attempted to find her.

LLYR
Welsh and Arthurian

A King of BRITAIN, the father of BENDIGEID VRAN, BRANWEN and MANAWYDDAN. In origin he was the Welsh sea deity (Welsh *llyr* = 'sea'). He is listed in two paternal pedigrees found in *BONEDD YR ARWR* as the direct descendant of ARTHUR, though the genealogies themselves differ

quite markedly. However, when studied more closely, it becomes obvious that the pedigree that appears first in the work has skipped three generations. Another interesting paternal pedigree for Arthur, which names his descent as direct from Llyr, is to be found in the Mostyn MS 117. When the three lines of descent are compared, it is not hard to see that all three are obviously based on the same source material.

LLYR MARINI
Welsh and Arthurian

According to ancient Welsh pedigrees, an ancestor of ARTHUR on both his maternal and his paternal sides, most sources making him the father of CARADOC BRIEFBRAS (CARADOC VREICHVRAS). In origin he may have been LLYR, a sea deity, and the legendary ancestor of a number of royal houses. He would also seem to have some tenuous connection with the King LEAR of SHAKESPEARE. Though this character is normally associated with LEIR, he may have originated from Llyr.

LLYS HELIG
Welsh

The lost realm of HELIG AP GLANNOWG, which is alleged to lie beneath the waters of Conwy Bay, approximately two miles out. It is still claimed that the sunken ruins of his palace can be seen at the lowest of tides. Llys Helig joins CANTRE'R GWAELOD and CAER ARIANRHOD to form a triad of legendary lost kingdoms off the coast of WALES.

LLYWARCH HÊN
Welsh and Arthurian

A celebrated Welsh poet, who is thought to have flourished about AD 600. Said to have been the cousin of URIEN of RHEGED, he is sometimes, incorrectly, identified with TALIESIN. Various traditions place him in POWYS, or among the North Briton tribesmen. He is later listed as one of the TWENTY-FOUR KNIGHTS of King ARTHUR but appears to have been a reasonably late addition to the Arthurian tales.

LOCH
Irish

The son of MOFEBIS, Loch was a warrior of CONNACHT who refused the order of MEDHBHA to fight CÚ CHULAINN, saying that he would not fight a beardless youth. Cú Chulainn stuck some dried grass to his chin to resemble a beard and then disposed of Loch when he eventually came to fight him, even though he also had to battle against the magical powers of the MÓRRÍGHAN at the same time.

LOCHLANN
Irish

An ancient realm, whose king was killed by FIONN MAC CUMHAILL, although the hero spared his son, MIDAC, who later took his revenge on the members of the FIAN.

LOCRINUS
British

A son of BRUTUS and brother of ALBANACTUS and KAMBER. After the death of his father, Locrinus became the ruler of ENGLAND, Kamber the ruler of WALES and Albanactus the ruler of SCOTLAND. After Albanactus had been killed by invading Huns, Locrinus and Kamber joined forces and routed the Huns. Among the captives taken was a beautiful maiden by the name of ESTRILDIS. Locrinus wanted to marry her, but he was already betrothed to GWENDOLEN, the daughter of CORINEUS.

Forced to honour his commitment to Gwendolen, Locrinus took Estrildis as his mistress and hid her in LONDON. For seven years he visited her in secret, during which time Estrildis bore him a daughter, HABREN, while Gwendolen bore him a son, MADDAN.

After the death of Corineus, Locrinus deserted Gwendolen and made Estrildis his queen. Gwendolen went to CORNWALL and mustered an army, which she led into battle against Locrinus near the River Stour. Locrinus was killed, and Gwendolen had Estrildis and Habren drowned in a river that she decreed would thenceforth carry the name of Locrinus' daughter. This river became the SABRINA to the Romans, and is today known as the River SEVERN.

LOCRIS
British

According to GEOFFREY OF MONMOUTH, this early name for ENGLAND derived from LOCRINUS. This is false etymology, for the name Locris is actually an Anglicisation of the Welsh LLOEGYR.

See also LOGRES

LODAN
Irish

(1) The son of the King of India, India here being used to signify a foreign land. He, along with EOLUS, son of the King of Greece (used in the same manner), accompanied CIABHAN on his journey to TÍR TAIRNGIRI, where they met the sisters CLIODNA, AEIFE and EDAEIN, whom they persuaded to elope with them. However, MANANNÁN MAC LIR sent a huge wave after them, which engulfed the three sisters, as well as ILDÁTHACH and his sons who were pursuing them, and either drowned them or carried them back to the LAND OF PROMISE.

(2) The son of LIR, brother of Manannán mac Lir and father of Sinend. Some have sought to equate this Lodan with the LODAN above, but if this were the case Lodan would not have needed to persuade Cliodna and her sisters to elope with him and his companions, for inhabitants of the same OTHERWORLDLY kingdom could come and go as they pleased.

LODONESIA
Arthurian

A early name for LOTHIAN, the realm of LOT, who is sometimes referred to as LOTH of Lodonesia.

LOEG
Irish
Also LAEG

The charioteer of CÚ CHULAINN. He was killed by LUGAID, who used the GAE BOLGA, the invincible short spear of Cú Chulainn.

LOEGHAIRE
Irish

(1) A son of UGAINY and KESAIR and the brother of COVAC. After the death of Ugainy the kingdom passed to Loeghaire, which consumed Covac with jealousy. He sought the advice of a DRUID, who told him to feign death and have word sent to his brother. This he did, and, when Loeghaire bent over the supposed corpse, Covac thrust his knife into Loeghaire's heart and killed him. He also had to kill Loeghaire's son AILILL, who had accompanied his father. In this way Covac ascended to the throne he so desired.

See also COBTHACH COEL, LOEGHAIRE LORC.

(2) The son of the King of CONNACHT who went to the aid of FIACHNA, whose wife had been taken captive by GOLL, the son of the King of MAGH MELL. Loeghaire and fifty of his men followed Fiachna to his OTHERWORLDLY land and there succeeded in freeing Fiachna's wife. Fiachna gave Loeghaire his daughter, SUN TEAR, in thanks. After a year Loeghaire and his men briefly revisited their families in Connacht, but they then returned to Magh Mell and were never seen again.

LOEGHAIRE BUADHACH

Irish

One of the three champions who were persuaded by the mischievous BRICRIU to claim the honour of carving the roast at a feast he had thrown, the other claimants being CONALL CERNACH and CÚ CHULAINN. The decision went in favour of Cú Chulainn on two occasions, the first at the judgement of MEDHBHA of CONNACHT, and the second by decree of CÚ ROÍ MAC DÁIRI. On both occasions the two losers refused to accept the judgement, but they were later forced to concede after Cú Roí mac Dáiri had proved his judgement to be correct.

LOEGHAIRE LORC

Irish

A King of IRELAND and father of AILILL AINE, King of LEINSTER. He and his son were killed by Loeghaire Lorc's brother COBTHACH COEL when he usurped the throne.

   See also COVAC, LOEGHAIRE

LOEGHAIRE MAC NEILL

Irish

A pagan King of IRELAND who appears in a late Christian legend found in the twelfth-century *Book of the Dun Cow*. Saint PATRICK summoned CÚ CHULAINN from Hell to prove the truths of Christianity and the horrors of damnation to the king. Sure enough, Cú Chulainn rode up from Hell on his chariot, converted Loeghaire mac Neill, and then prayed for admittance to heaven, a prayer that was apparently answered, thus conveniently allowing Christianity to claim the spiritual conversion of one of the most powerful and popular figures of the pagan Irish tradition.

LOGISTILLA

Arthurian

According to the *ORLANDO FURIOSO* of ARIOSTO, a sister of MORGAN Le Fay, and possibly one of the nine co-rulers of AVALON.

LOGRES

British and Arthurian

The archaic name given to England in Arthurian romance. It derives from *Lloegr*, the Welsh for England, but may have originally come from *legor*, an ANGLO-SAXON element found in the place-name of Leicester. The name Logres was used throughout the Arthurian legends to refer not just to England, but to the entire British realm of King ARTHUR.

LOHENGRIN

Arthurian

The story of Lohengrin and his adventures are told by WOLFRAM VON ESCHENBACH, where he is the son of PERCEVAL and a member of the GRAIL community. He sailed to BRABANT in a boat drawn by an angel, disguised as a swan, to help ELSA, the daughter of the Duke of Brabant, who was besieged by Frederick de TELRAMUND, who claimed that Elsa had promised to marry him. Lohengrin defeated this unworthy suitor in combat, and duly married Elsa, but made her promise never to ask his name. They had two children. Eventually, Elsa asked the forbidden question and Lohengrin immediately left her. Subsequently he married Princess BELAYE of LIZABORYE, but was murdered by mercenaries sent by her parents, who believed that their daughter was under his spell. Belaye died of grief and the country had its name changed to Lothringen (Lorraine) in his honour. Lohengrin also appears in *Rigomer*, a later, anonymous poem.

LOHOLT

Arthurian

A KNIGHT OF THE ROUND TABLE and the son of ARTHUR, though his mother is not so definitely named, being either GUINEVERE or LIONORS. In *PERLESVAUS*, he was murdered by KAY, but this episode, which does not appear elsewhere, seems to have been concocted by the author of this work.

LOMBARDY

Arthurian

The realm of King LADIS, which had not, in reality, been conquered by the Lombard people by the traditional Arthurian period.

LONDON

General

The capital city of Great Britain. It was allegedly founded by BRUTUS, who named the city TROIA NOVA, which means 'New Troy'. The city subsequently became the capital of LLUDD, the sixty-eighth ruler after Brutus, who fortified the walls, at which time it was known as CAER LLUDD, 'Lludd's Fort', or CAER LUNDEIN. Some time later the 'Caer' was dropped, and the city simply became known as LUNDEIN, of which the modern name is a simple derivation.

LONE

Arthurian

The mistress of GAWAIN in the anonymous *RIGOMER*.

LONG MEG

British

A semi-mythical giantess who, according to the historian John Hale (*c.* 1640), was said to be buried on the south side of the cloisters of Westminster Abbey, LONDON, a site that had held a sacred status long before the arrival of Christianity. Long Meg is immortalised in a megalithic stone circle at Little Salkeld, north-east of Penrith in Cumbria.

LONGES MAC NDUIL DERMAIT

Irish

The Exile of the Sons of Doel the Forgotten, a text that tells the story of EOCHO ROND's bonding of CÚ CHULAINN to discover the whereabouts of the sons of DOEL and of Cú Chulainn's adventures and his ultimate success.

LONGINUS

Arthurian

The name of the Roman centurion who was said to have pierced the side of Jesus while Christ hung on the Cross following the Crucifixion (John 19: 34).

LORD OF THE SCOTTISH WILDERNESS

Arthurian

The title of ESTONNE, a minor character in *PERLESVAUS*. He was killed by BRUYANT, his death being avenged by his son PASSALEON.

LORE

Arthurian

The Lady of GARADIGAN, she brought a sword belt with her when she arrived at ARTHUR's court and challenged anyone to unfasten it, a task that only MERIADOC was able to accomplish.

LORETE

Arthurian

The sister of GRIFLET.

LORIGAL

Arthurian

The offspring of ELIAVRES and the mare with which he had been forced to mate.

LOT(H)

Arthurian

The King of LOTHIAN (LODONESIA), ORKNEY and NORWAY, and brother-in-law of ARTHUR, his wife being named as ANNA by GEOFFREY OF MONMOUTH and MORGAUSE by Sir Thomas MALORY. He was the father of five sons, GAWAIN, GAHERIS, AGRAVAIN, GARETH and MORDRED,

and two daughters, SOREDAMOR and CLARISSANT. Geoffrey of Monmouth makes Lot a supporter of Arthur, already the King of Lothian. He was one of the three dispossessed Yorkist princes, the others being URIAN and AUGUSELUS, to whom Arthur restored their lands after he and HOEL had raised the siege of YORK. Arthur gave Lot the kingdom of Norway after he had defeated that country. His kingship of Orkney appears to be a later development of the stories. Other sources, however, state the opposite, making Lot one of the eleven rebellious leaders who revolted against Arthur at the start of his reign. He was killed by King PELLINORE, which resulted in a continuing feud between his sons and those of his slayer. The *ENFACES GAUVAIN* makes Lot a page at Arthur's court, becoming the father of GAWAIN following an affair with Morgause. The *LIFE OF SAINT KENTIGERN* makes him the father of THANEY, KENTIGERN's mother – provided, of course, that it is the same Lot that is being referred to. BOECE further claimed that he was the King of the PICTS.

The name Lot appears to mean simply 'Lothian-ruler' (taken from its early form of LEUDONUS). It has been suggested that his personal name may have been GWYAR, though it seems certain that here the truth will remain a mystery. It would seem that there was indeed a king in the Lothian region during the fifth century who had his headquarters near EDINBURGH at TRAPRAIN LAW.

His ancestry has also been variously described. The *Chronica Gentis Scotorum* by John of Fordun claims his descent from FULGENTIUS, an early King of Britain according to Geoffrey of Monmouth. His more accepted ancestry is that described by JOHN OF GLASTONBURY, who gives a line of descent from PETRUS, one of the companions of JOSEPH OF ARIMATHEA. Welsh tradition, on the other hand, almost always makes ANNA his wife.

LOTHAR

Irish

A brother of BRES, NÁR, MEDHBHA, CLOTHRU and EITHNE, the latter two both being said to have been the wife of CONCHOBAR MAC NESSA after MEDHBHA had left him for AILILL. Clothru once bewailed her childlessness to her three brothers, and as a result had a child by each of them, each child being given the name LUGAID.

LOTHIAN

Arthurian

The realm of LOT, which is also known as LODONESIA. Historically speaking, Lothian comprised all the eastern part of the Lowlands of SCOTLAND from the Forth to the Cheviots, and between the seventh and eleventh centuries it was a part of Northumbria.

LOTTA
Arthurian

The Queen of IRELAND and mother of ISEULT, according to the *TAVOLA RITONDA*.

LOUGH NEAGH
Irish

The lake in which MOYLINNY is situated, and from where MONGÁN ruled in the early seventh century.

LOVEL
Arthurian

One of the sons of GAWAIN, he was among the party that caught LANCELOT and GUINEVERE together, and one of those killed by the escaping though unarmed Lancelot.

LUACHAR
Irish

A kingdom within CONNACHT over which LIA, the keeper of the treasure of the FIAN, ruled.

LUCAN
Arthurian

The Duke of Gloucester, brother of BEDIVERE, ARTHUR's butler and one of his knights. After Arthur's final battle at CAMLANN, he attempted to help his brother lift the dying king, but Arthur was so badly wounded that the effort killed him. A variant of this story says that the dying king embraced him, and the strength of this embrace finished him off.

LUCHORPÁIN
Irish

A form of LEPRECHAUN that lives under the sea. They are said to be able to guide humans beneath the sea either by placing a cloak over their head or by stuffing herbs into the humans' ears.

LUCHTA(INE)
Irish

One of the TRÍ DÉ DÁNA, the three divine smiths, the others being GOIBHNIU and CREIDHNE, although Luchtaine is sometimes described as a carpenter rather than a smith. The three are most famous for their efforts during the Second Battle of MAGH TUIREDH, when they worked at lightning speed to make and repair the weapons of the TUATHA DÉ DANANN, weapons magically empowered so that none wounded by them would ever recover.

See also COLUM CUALLEINECH

LUCIUS
Arthurian

The son of PELIAS, father of APOLLO and an early King of LIONES.

LUCIUS HIBERIUS
Arthurian

The name of the Roman Emperor whose empire ARTHUR attacked. Lucius summoned Arthur to Rome but was defeated. Both WACE and Sir Thomas MALORY emphatically refer to him as 'Emperor', though GEOFFREY OF MONMOUTH calls him the 'procurator' (governor), and implies that he was inferior to the Emperor of CONSTANTINOPLE, Leo.

LUD
British

A mythical early British King, who is an Anglicised version of the Welsh LLUDD, and thus also of the Irish LUGH. His mythical exploits are the same as those of Lludd in connection with the city of LONDON.

LUFAMOUR
Arthurian

In the English verse romance *SIR PERCEVAL OF GALLES*, the lover of the hero of that work, PERCEVAL.

LUG
Gaulish

The Gaulish variant of the Irish LUGH.

LUGAID
Irish

(1) Three sons of CLOTHRU were given this name, their fathers being Clothru's brothers BRES, NÁR and LOTHAR. The Lugaid born to Nár also bore Clothru a son who was named CRIMTHANN NIA NÁIR.

(2) The son of CÚ ROÍ MAC DÁIRI, who marched with ERC and the monstrous sons of CALATIN against CÚ CHULAINN. Lugaid took possession of the GAE BOLGA and with it wounded both Grey of MACHA and Cú Chulainn, who tied himself to a pillar so that he might die standing up. Realising that Cú Chulainn was beaten, Lugaid strode boldly up to him and cut off his head, but as he did so Cú Chulainn's sword fell from his hand

and cut off Lugaid's own hand. CONALL CERNACH and Grey of Macha pursued Lugaid and caught him up, whereupon Grey of Macha took great bites of his flesh before Conall Cernach cut off his head.

LUGAID MAC CON
Irish

The companion of EOGHAN, the son of OILILL, with whom he discovered a tiny magical harper concealed within a yew tree that had been conceived as part of the vengeance planned by AINÉ after she had been outraged by Oilill. The Harper caused a quarrel between Eoghan and Lugaid mac Con, which resulted in the death of Lugaid mac Con. His death led to the Battle of MAGH MUCRIME, in which all seven of Oilill's sons were killed.

LUGH
Irish

The Irish god of light, the patron of the festival of LUGHNASADH and often associated with the Roman god Mercury. His cult spread as far as Spain and Switzerland. His Gaulish name was LUG or LUGUS, while in WALES he was LLUDD. His name means 'shining one', and JULIUS CAESAR referred to him as the Gaulish 'MERCURY'. Reputedly coming to IRELAND from across the sea, he is said to have spoken with a 'stammer', meaning that he did not speak native Erse. One story says that his mother was the wife of one of the TUATHA DÉ DANANN, and it was she who trained him to bear arms, most notably the slingshot. Another source says that he was born in the OTHERWORLD, the sole survivor of divine triplets, and was raised by MANANNÁN MAC LIR, who acted as his foster father and armed him with four wonderful weapons – an inescapable spear, a great sling (his favourite weapon), a helmet of invisibility and the wondrous shield that was later owned by the hero FIONN MAC CUMHAILL.

Lugh's most unlikely relation was the FOMHOIRÉ giant BALAR, although this relationship may explain Lugh's ownership of his inescapable spear. This spear appears in the story of the DAGHDHA, who is said to have brought it to Ireland when the Tuatha Dé Danann first arrived on that island. The spear was carried by the Daghdha in the First Battle of MAGH TUIREDH, where it was, so it would seem, lost to the Fomhoiré as a spoil of war. As Balar is said to be the grandfather of Lugh, it would appear that he passed the spear, which had come into his possession, on to his grandson.

Lugh arrived at the gates of the royal palace of NUADHA, King of the Tuatha Dé Danann, and asked for a job, claiming that he was a carpenter. However, when he learned that there was already a carpenter at the court, he said that he was a harpist, then a FILI, a historian, a hero, a magician, an astrologer, a cook and a great many other things. It was his ability to turn his hand to anything that rightfully earned him the honorific title SAMILDÁNACH, which means 'of many skills', skills that are said to have become his on the death of his two divine siblings. It was his multitude of abilities that led to his being admitted to the court of the Tuatha Dé Danann, and to Nuadha, who immediately recognised his superiority, resigning in his favour. With Lugh enthroned as their king, the Tuatha Dé Danann prepared for the coming Second Battle of Magh Tuiredh. They went into combat armed with the magical weapons forged for them by the TRÍ DÉ DÁNA, and reinforced by a battery of powerful charms obtained by Lugh. During the battle Lugh appeared, in characteristic sorcerer's form with a single leg and single eye, everywhere among the forces of the Tuatha Dé Danann, chanting words of magic and putting new strength into every man. Those who were wounded or killed were speedily restored to full vitality by DIAN CÉCHT and his three sons, who cast them into a magic bath, cauldron or well.

As a last, desperate measure the Fomhoiré called for single combat between Balar and the Tuatha Dé Danann's champion. Lugh stepped forward and faced the hideous monster, his own grandfather. Like his compatriots, Balar had but a single eye in the middle of his forehead, an eye that was so powerful that a single glance could kill an entire army. It took four men to lift the eyelid, and as they did the Tuatha Dé Danann took cover. Lugh, however, stood his ground and, once the eye was fully open, aimed his slingshot with such accuracy that the shot passed straight through Balar's eye and continued on through his head to force his brains out of the back. The slingshot had been fired with such power that it continued its path of destruction and decimated the Fomhoiré army. The few survivors of the Fomhoiré then fled the country and were never heard of again, though where they then escaped to still remains unknown.

This myth described two very important events in early Irish mythology. The first was the establishment of a single deity whose skills were not singular, a concept that was revolutionary at the time. The second was the establishment of a new order of gods and goddesses who drove the primal beings from the land and brought skill and order to the sacred land.

LUGH LAEBACH
Irish
A wizard, possibly an aspect of LUGH, who was sent out against the monstrous CARMAN and her sons by the TUATHA DÉ DANANN.

LUGH LAMFHADA
Irish
A name given to LUGH that means 'Lugh of the Long Arm'. It does not mean that Lugh possessed unusually long arms, but rather signified the magical power of his sling and spear as typical attributes of a god of light and victory.

LUGHNASADH
General
One of the four great Celtic festivals, the Celtic harvest festival. It was celebrated on 1 August and was later to become Christianised as Lammas, the feast day of Saint BRIGHID. The other three major Celtic festivals were SAMHAIN, IMBOLC and BELTANE. The major sites for the observance of Lughnasadh were those that had associations with fertility goddesses, associations that are entirely appropriate for a festival that celebrates the fertility of the earth.

LUGMANNAIR
Irish
The father of DIL and an inhabitant of the Isle of FALGA (the Isle of MAN).

LUGUAIN
Arthurian
The servant of YDER whose loyalty was rewarded when he was made a knight.

LUGUS
Gaulish
A variant of LUG, the Gaulish version of the Irish god of light LUGH. The continental Romans quickly identified Lugus with Mercury.

LUNDEIN
British
One of the ancient names of LONDON and one from which the modern name may be seen to be directly derived. Its origin is slightly confused. Some say that it comes from the Old English Lud-Dun, a name given to the capital after LUD, mythical King of BRITAIN, had fortified the walls, Lud-Dun meaning 'Lud's Fortress'. Others, however, say that it comes from CAER LLUDD, a name of obviously Welsh origin, and that it was this name that degenerated into Caer Llundein, the 'Caer' later being dropped and the spelling slightly altered, both changes being made to eliminate the Welsh influence.

LUNETE
Arthurian
The cousin of NIMUE, from whom she learned her magic arts, using them to create a fountain in the forest of BROCELIANDE to be defended by her lover.

LWNDRYS
British
Another obviously Welsh name that was, at some point, applied to the capital LONDON. The source of this name is uncertain, but some say that it is a derivative form of CAER LLUDD.

LYBIUS DESCONUS
Arthurian
'The Fair Unknown One', an illegitimate son of GAWAIN whose mother kept his ancestry a secret. He came to ARTHUR's court, where he was made a knight, later to be sent to rescue the Lady of SINADONE, being accompanied on the journey by the damsel ELLEN. Lybius Desconus is actually a nickname, the character being the same as GUINGLAIN.

LYBIUS DESCONUS
Arthurian
The fourteenth-century English poem concerning the adventures of a hero having the same name.

LYNETTE
Arthurian
The sister of LYONESSE who was besieged by the RED KNIGHT of the Red Lands when she came to ARTHUR's court to seek help. She was given the services of GARETH, but her manner towards him was at first derisory, improving only as their adventure progressed and Gareth proved himself to her.

LYONESSE
(1) (*Arthurian*) The sister of LYNETTE. Her realm was being attacked by the RED KNIGHT of the Red Lands when Lynette went to ARTHUR's court to seek help. She returned with Gareth, who rescued and subsequently married her.

(2) (*British*) A lost land said to have existed in CORNWALL, or to have lain off the coast. It is possible that it was the realm of LYONESSE. Some commentators have suggested that it is to be identified with LIONES, though this may have

The Lady Lyonesse, whose realm was besieged by the Red Knight. (Mary Evans Picture Library/Arthur Rackham Collection)

originally been LOTHIAN (Leoneis). Later confusion identified this fabled realm with a region of BRITTANY (Leonais).

Legend states that, following the death of ARTHUR at CAMLANN, MORDRED's forces pursued the remnants of Arthur's army to Lyonesse. The ghost of MERLIN appeared and the land sank, destroying Mordred's army, but Arthur's men reached what are now the Isles of Scilly. Local legend says this fabled land sank in 1099, but the bells of its churches are still said to be heard sometimes, ringing beneath the waters.

Reference is made to Lyonesse in William Camden's *Britannia* (1586) and in George Carew's *Survey of Cornwall* (1602). Before that the medieval Arab geographer Idrisi used the word Dns for a place that is perhaps the Scilly Isles, Dns possibly being a scribal mistake for *Ens* (Lyonesse). The origin of the legend seems to stem from Roman times, when the Isles of Scilly appear to have been a single island that was partially submerged by the sea. More recently, Lyonesse was mentioned by Alfred, Lord Tennyson as the site of Arthur's final battle.

LYPPAUT
Arthurian
The Lord of BEAROSCHE and the father of OBIE and OBILOT.

M

MABINOGION
Welsh and Arthurian

One of the most important of all Welsh and Arthurian source texts, although it was not compiled until the mid-nineteenth century. The name comes from the Welsh word *mabinogi*, which means 'instruction for young poets'. Drawing on two much earlier manuscripts, the *WHITE BOOK OF RHYDDERCH* (1300–1325) and the *RED BOOK OF HERGEST* (1375–1425), the *Mabinogion* is a collection of medieval Welsh myths and folk tales. Strictly speaking the *Mabinogion* consists of four branches or tales, three of which concern the hero PRYDERI. The four stories are those of PWYLL, BRANWEN, MANAWYDAN FAB LLYR and MATH FAB MATHONWY. Later editions of the *Mabinogion* have been extended to include much Arthurian material, although these undoubtedly draw on earlier and entirely relevant material. The extensions include the stories *GEREINT AND ENID*, *CULHWCH AND OLWEN*, *OWAIN*, *PEREDUR* and the *DREAM OF RHONABWY*. The most famous translation of the *Mabinogion*, that made by Lady Charlotte Guest, also includes the story of TALIESIN.

MABON
Welsh and Arthurian

(1) This Celtic god of liberation, harmony, unity and music, also known as MAPONOS, was undoubtedly the original of the Arthurian characters having the same name, as well as several others. He was possibly one of the most universally worshipped of all the Celtic deities, the centre of the Druidic cosmology, the original Being, pre-existent, the Son of the Great Mother. In mythology he is represented as both a prisoner and a liberator. Many other heroic and divine figures, and not just those in the Arthurian legends, are related to Mabon.

As Maponos, this deity was worshipped in the north of BRITAIN and GAUL, and is widely associated with therapeutic springs. In the most common Welsh tradition he is Mabon, son of MODRON ('son of the Mother'), held captive since he had been stolen from his mother aged just three days. He is equated in a Romano-Celtic inscription with Apollo Citharoedus – 'the player of the lyre'. This would indicate that Mabon was a youthful god of the Apollo type, connected to therapy, music and a ritual hunt. His Irish equivalent appears to have been OENGHUS MAC IN OG. Furthermore, his legends suggest that he was linked to the order of creation, for an increasingly complex cycle of animals lead the Arthurian warrior to rescue him.

(2) The Welsh poem *PA GUR* names two of ARTHUR's followers as Mabon. One is the son of MODRON (the most common association for Mabon), who is described as the servant of UTHER. The other is called the son of MELLT.

Some sources say that these two are one and the same, with Modron being the mother (derived from the Celtic goddess MATRONA), and Mellt the father (possibly derived from a god called MELDOS). The MABINOGION story of CULHWCH AND OLWEN says that he was stolen away from his mother when just three nights old and taken to Caer Loyw (Gloucester), which here is used to symbolise the OTHERWORLD. It became a necessary part of CULHWCH's quest to find and rescue him. Arthur attacked his prison while KAY and BEDIVERE rescued him. Subsequently he took part in the hunt for the magic boar TWRCH TRWYTH and succeeded in taking the razor that Culhwch required from between the beast's ears. Mabon appears to have had several variants within the Arthurian sagas – MABONAGRAIN in EREC ETENIDE and MABUZ in Lanzelet by ULRICH VON ZARZIKHOVEN.

It has been argued that MERLIN acted as prophet to MABON, thus bringing a direct connection to the Arthurian tradition, and leading some to refer to Mabon himself as a sorcerer. In later tradition the story of Mabon seems to have been replaced by that of GAWAIN.

MABONAGRAIN
Arthurian

In French romance, Mabonagrain appears as the opponent of EREC in EREC ET ENIDE, in which he was kept as a prisoner in a castle with an 'airy' (sic) wall, and was the lover of the lady of that mysterious OTHERWORLD place. When Erec defeated him, he told Erec to blow a horn, and this freed him from his magical imprisonment. Identification has been made between this character and MABON, and through that to the Celtic deity of the same name – Mabon.

MABUZ
Arthurian

The son of the LADY OF THE LAKE, according to ULRICH VON ZARZIKHOVEN. In his story, *Lanzelet*, LANCELOT comes to the aid of Mabuz, whose territory is under attack from IWERET, and defeats the invader. Connection has been made between Mabuz and both the characters known as MABON. This would, in turn, identify his mother, the Lady of the Lake, with MODRON/MATRONA.

MAC AN DAIMH
Irish

A child born at the same time as MONGÁN to one of the attendants of FIACHNA LURGAN's wife. As Mongán is said to be the son of MANANNÁN MAC LIR, it is thought that Mac an Daimh is also one of the offspring of this amorous god.

MAC CÉCHT
Irish

One of the three TUATHA DÉ DANANN kings at the time of the invasion by the Sons of MÍL ÉSPÁINE, by whom they were conquered. His co-rulers at TARA were MAC CUILL and MAC GRÉINE. Mac Cécht's wife was FÓDLA, while Mac Cuill's was BANBHA and Mac Gréine's was the goddess ÉRIU. He was killed by AIREM, one of the leaders of the Sons of Míl Éspáine.

MAC CON
Irish

Possibly a historical predecessor of CORMAC MAC AIRT, who traditionally gained the throne in the year AD 227 by having Mac Con stabbed.

MAC CUILL
Irish

One of the three TUATHA DÉ DANANN kings at the time of the invasion by the Sons of MÍL ÉSPÁINE, by whom they were conquered. His co-rulers at TARA were MAC CÉCHT and MAC GRÉINE. Mac Cuill's wife was BANBHA, while Mac Cécht's was FÓDLA and Mac Gréine's was the goddess ÉRIU. Mac Cuill was killed by EBER, one of the leaders of the Sons of Míl Espáine.

MAC DÁ THÓ
Irish

A King of LEINSTER and the owner of the pig that is the central character in the ribald story *Scéla Mucce Maic Dá Thó*. This story later formed the basis of *Fledd Bricrenn*, which tells how the hero CÚ CHULAINN came to be regarded, after two judgements in his favour, as the champion of all IRELAND.

Mac Dá Thó owned not just the famous pig, but also a wondrous hunting dog, which was famed throughout the land, being able to run all around Leinster in a single day. This dog was sought both by MEDHBHA and AILILL of CONNACHT and by CONCHOBAR MAC NESSA of ULSTER. Mac Dá Thó promised it to both and invited both monarchs and their retinues to a feast, sincerely hoping that he would be able to escape the argument that was bound to arise. The chief dish at this feast was the pig that Mac Dá Thó's grandson LENA had raised, nurturing it for seven years on the flesh of fifty cows. After it had been killed by Lena, it took sixty oxen to drag its carcass, and its tail alone required sixty men to carry it.

Nothing more is said of this wonderful animal in the story, apart from the quarrel that arose over who should have the right to carve it. CET originally claimed the right, but he was eventually made to cede in favour of CONALL CERNACH. Mac Dá Thó did indeed escape the quarrel, but by promising his dog to both monarchs he lost not only that dog, which fled the scene, but also his marvellous pig.

MAC ERC
Irish

The leader of the FIR BHOLG forces in their battle with the TUATHA DÉ DANANN at the First Battle of MAGH TUIREDH, during which he was killed.

MAC GRÉ(I)NE
Irish

One of the three TUATHA DÉ DANANN kings at the time of the invasion by the Sons of MÍL ÉSPÁINE, by whom they were conquered. His co-rulers at TARA were MAC CUILL and MAC CÉCHT. Mac Gréine's wife was the goddess ÉRIU, while Mac Cuill's was BANBHA and Mac Cécht's was FÓDLA. He was killed by AMHAIRGHIN, the FILI.

MAC IN(D) O-C, -G
Irish

A shortened variant of OENGHUS MAC IN OG.

MAC LUGACH
Irish

A prominent member of the FIAN, although he is mentioned only in passing.

MAC MHAOL
Irish

A giant whom CÚ CHULAINN fought in single combat for the unlikely trophy of the two front teeth of the King of Greece, Greece in this instance being used as a name to suggest an OTHERWORLDLY kingdom. Mac Mhaol was easily overcome and led his vanquisher to where he might obtain the trophy he required.

MAC ROTH
Irish

The steward of MEDHBHA who told her of the existence of the DONN CUAILNGÈ and who may thus be considered responsible for the quest undertaken by that Queen against ULSTER to secure that marvellous animal and thus also for the eventual death of CÚ CHULAINN.

MACGNÍMARTHA FINN
Irish

The Boyish Deeds of Finn, a story copied from the tenth-century Psalter of Cashel. It tells of the boyhood of FIONN MAC CUMHAILL, from his posthumous birth to his becoming the head of the FIAN.

MACHA
Irish

A daughter of MIDHIR, an Irish fertility and mother goddess, and a formidable warrior, who built the fortress named after her, EMHAIN MHACHA, the ancient capital city of ULSTER, a prehistoric and probably ritual site, which is today known as Navan Fort. She is also associated with the city of Armagh, or Ard Macha, which was later to become the centre of Celtic Christianity. Legend says that Macha had two brothers, DITHORBA and CIMBAOTH. She fought and killed Dithorba for the right to become Queen of IRELAND and forced her other brother to marry her. The five sons of Dithorba attacked her, but she easily overcame them, and, having drawn the outline of a massive fort in the earth with the pin of her brooch, she made her five captives build her fort, which became known as Emhain Mhacha or 'Brooch of Macha'.

The wife of CRUNDCHU, she was, while pregnant, forced by the men of Ulster to run a race against the horses of CONCHOBAR MAC NESSA. The race brought on her labour, and she gave birth to twins. Although she died as a result of childbirth, she remained alive long enough to curse the men of Ulster so that, at critical moments in any battle from that day forth, they would suffer the labour pains of women in childbirth. Her race against the horses of Conchobar mac Nessa led to Macha becoming regarded as the patroness of ritual games and festivals but, more importantly, as the horse goddess, who was also known as ÉDÁIN ECHRAIDHE in Ireland, RHIANNON in WALES and EPONA in GAUL.

Following her untimely death, Macha became connected with BADHBH and NEMHAIN in the triple aspect goddess the MÓRRÍGHAN, her guise now being that of a war goddess, who foretold war, fire and slaughter. She, and her companions, were sometimes said to have been witnessed actually on the field of battle in the form of birds of carrion.

MACHA, GREY OF
Irish

One of twin foals, the other being Black of SAINGLIU, that were born at exactly the same time as the hero CÚ CHULAINN. The two horses later became the famous steeds of that warrior. Grey of Macha was killed by ERC, one of the warriors who had taken part in the hunt for the DONN CUAILNGÈ.

MACSEN (WLEDIG)
Welsh and Arthurian

The name by which the Roman Emperor MAXIMUS was known in Welsh tradition. In this guise he is said to have married ELEN, daughter of EUDAF, and to have been later restored as emperor with the help of Elen's brothers CYNAN and GADEON.

MADAGLAN
Arthurian

Following the death of GUINEVERE, this King, whose story appears in *PERLESVAUS*, demanded that, as he was the dead Queen's relation, ARTHUR should give him the ROUND TABLE. If Arthur refused, he further demanded that the King marry his sister. Arthur refused on both counts, and Madaglan was twice defeated by LANCELOT – presumably once for each demand.

MADAN
Arthurian

The King of BULGARIA in Arthurian romance.

MADDAN
British

The son of LOCRINUS and GWENDOLEN, and thus grandson of CORINEUS. His right to the accession was upheld by his mother, who, after Locrinus had abandoned her for his mistress

ESTRILDIS, mustered an army in CORNWALL and, in a battle near the River Stour, killed her wayward husband. Gwendolen then reigned for fifteen years before abdicating in favour of her son.

MAD-OC, -UC
Arthurian
This name appears on several occasions in the Arthurian tales. Welsh legend makes him a legendary Prince of GWYNEDD, who was supposed to have discovered the Americas and been the ancestor of a group of light-skinned, Welsh-speaking Indians in the American west. French romance names a Madoc or MADUC as an opponent of ARTHUR. He also makes an appearance as the son of UTHER in the *Book of Taliesin*, though this reference would seem to be simply a translator's error. In the Welsh poem *Ymddiddan Arthur a'r Eryr*, ELIWLOD, Arthur's nephew, appears in the guise of an eagle. This character's father is named as Madoc, which would imply that he was King Arthur's brother-in-law.

MADOG MORFRYN
Welsh and Arthurian
According to Welsh genealogies, the father of MYRDDIN (MERLIN), although some sources name MORGAN FRYCH as Myrddin's father.

MADOR
Arthurian
One of the KNIGHTS OF THE ROUND TABLE who also partook in the Quest for the Holy GRAIL (as indeed did most of this company of knights, if the Grail legend is to be taken literally). He is given the epithet, or surname, *de La Porte* ('of the Door'). In the sixteenth-century Irish romance *EACHTRA MHELÓRA AGUS ORLANDO*, he is referred to as the son of the King of the HESPERIDES.

MAELGWYN
Welsh and Arthurian
A sixth-century ruler of GWYNEDD. The son of CLUTARIUS, he has been tenuously identified with MELKIN.

MAEN ARTHUR
Arthurian
The name of a stone that allegedly had a hollow in it made by the hoof of ARTHUR's horse. This stone, which was in the vicinity of Mold, Clwyd, can no longer be identified – perhaps it has been stolen. Another stone having the same name is in Maen Arthur Wood near Llanafan, DYFED.

MAEN DYLAN
Welsh
The Stone of Dylan, which stands on a stretch of gravel approximately two miles south of a reef of stones off the coast of GWYNEDD that is known as CAER ARIANRHOD. Maen Dylan is alleged to mark the grave of DYLAN EIL TON, the first of the two children mysteriously born to ARIANRHOD.

MAEN TYRIAWG
Welsh
An ancient name for Maentwrog, where GWYDION FAB DÔN used his magical powers to overcome and kill the good King PRYDERI.

MAES GWYDDNO
Welsh
An alternative name for CANTRE'R GWAELOD, the lost realm of GWYDDNO GARANHIR in Cardigan Bay. The name is also sometimes used to refer to the fish-weir of Gwyddno Garanhir, this weir appearing in the story of CERRIDWEN and the birth of TALIESIN.

MAEVE
Irish
An alternate name for MEDHBHA, Queen of CONNACHT.

MAGA
Irish
The daughter of OENGHUS MAC IN OG and the mother of FACHTNA by ROSS, and thus the grandmother of CONCHOBAR MAC NESSA. However, she was married for a second time, to the DRUID CATHBHADH, and by him became the mother of FINDCHOÉM, Elva and DEICHTINE, and was therefore also the grandmother of CÚ CHULAINN, the sons of UISNECH and CONALL CERNACH. Maga is also said to have been the mother of CET and ANLUAN, but by whom is unrecorded.

MAG(H) MBREG
Irish
A supernatural realm, mentioned in the story of DIL and TULCHAINDE as being the place to which the MÓRRÍGHAN, here benevolent rather than malevolent, arranged to have the oxen loved by Dil transported so that she and her lover might elope from the Isle of FALGA (Isle of MAN).

MAG(H) MEL-L, -D
Irish
An OTHERWORLDLY realm, whose name means

'The Delightful Plain'. It is a paradisal land of the righteous dead, the home of FIACHNA, and the land to which LOEGHAIRE travelled with fifty of the men of CONNACHT to release Fiachna's wife from the clutches of GOLL. It is also the realm in which CONNLA, the son of CONN CÉTCHATHLACH, was enticed to live by a beautiful maiden.

MAGH MOR

Irish

A supernatural kingdom, the 'Great Plain', a paradise where the gods were entertained with magical music. The inhabitants are described as graceful, and nothing belongs to any one person. There is a choice between wine and mead to drink. Conception is considered without crime or sin, and the people live on salted pork and new milk, such dishes being confined to the gods. In the *Leabhar na hUidhre* it is the realm to which MIDHIR attempts to entice the reincarnated ÉDÁIN.

MAGH MUCRIME

Irish

The scene of a battle ultimately caused by the outrage or rape of AINÉ by OILILL. Ainé swore revenge and caused LUGAID MAC CON and EOGAN (who was one of Oilill's sons) to fall out over a diminutive harper she had created. Lugaid mac Con was killed, and his family went to war against the family of Oilill, whose seven sons were killed in the resulting battle.

MAGH TUIREDH

Irish

Pronounced MOYTURA, Magh Tuiredh was the location of two major battles between the TUATHA DÉ DANANN and the then inhabitants of IRELAND. However, the name is slightly misleading, for the First Battle of Magh Tuiredh took place in County Mayo and the second in County Sligo. The First Battle of Magh Tuiredh was fought after the Tuatha Dé Danann demanded that the FIR BHOLG, the then rulers of Ireland, resign their kingship or fight for it. They chose to fight, but were utterly defeated and forced into exile among the terrible FOMHOIRÉ.

In the course of the battle, the King of the Tuatha Dé Danann, NUADHA, lost an arm and was forced to abdicate because no physically blemished king might rule. He passed the kingship to BRES, a slightly strange choice when it is considered that his mother was a Tuatha Dé Danann woman, but his father a Fomhoiré warrior. Bres was not the best of kings, proving tyrannical beyond belief and even

forcing the DAGHDHA and OGHMA to be his slaves. Finally, COIRBRE satirised Bres so savagely that he broke out in boils and had to abdicate. He fled to the Fomhoiré and there mustered an army against the Tuatha Dé Danann.

Nuadha was restored to the kingship after the giant leech (physician) DIAN CÉCHT, with the help of the smith CREIDHNE, manufactured and fitted the King with an artificial arm made of silver. Thenceforth he was known as Nuadha Airgedláhm. He then prepared to lead the Tuatha Dé Danann against the Fomhoiré forces mustered by Bres at the Second Battle of Magh Tuiredh.

Shortly before the battle, however, LUGH arrived at the royal palace, and Nuadha abdicated in his favour. Under new leadership, the Tuatha Dé Danann made their preparations for the forthcoming battle, which they entered armed with the magical weapons forged for them by the TRÍ DÉ DÁNA and the spells and charms of Lugh, who appeared instantaneously all over the battlefield to encourage and invigorate his men, appearing to them in typical sorcerer's guise with a single leg and a single eye. All those who were killed or wounded were restored to full vitality by Dian Cécht and his three children, who immersed them in a magic cauldron or well.

Sensing defeat, the Fomhoiré demanded that the outcome of the battle be decided in single combat between BALAR and the Tuatha Dé Danann's champion. They put forward Lugh, who stood his ground as the Fomhoiré raised the huge eyelid of the monstrous Balar to expose his single eye, an eye that had the power to kill an entire army at a glance. As the eyelid was opened, Lugh fired his slingshot with such accuracy and force that it smashed straight through Balar's eye and scattered his brains to the four winds as it continued out of the back of his head and decimated the Fomhoiré, the remnants of whom were forced to flee the land.

Bres was taken captive during the battle and pleaded for his life, promising that in return he would ensure four harvests a year and a continual supply of milk from the cows. The Tuatha Dé Danann rejected these offers, although they did spare his life in return for his advice on the best times for ploughing, sowing and reaping.

MAGH TUIREDH, THE BATTLE OF

Irish

An epic poem that tells the stories of the first and second Battles of MAGH TUIREDH. It is an important source text because it also records the names and attributes of numerous Irish Celtic deities.

The Roman de Tristan, *which tells of the tragic love of Tristan and Iseult.* (© Archivo Iconografico, S.A./Corbis)

Saint David, the patron saint of Wales.
(Bridgeman Art Library/British Library,
London)

*Opposite page: The Tower of London, where
Guinevere was said to have hidden herself
away when Mordred planned to marry her.*
(© Historical Picture Archive/Corbis)

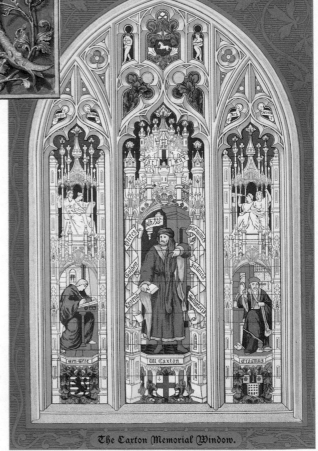

*The Venerable Bede, whose historical
importance is indicated by his inclusion here
within the design of a stained-glass window.*
(Mary Evans Picture Library)

Above: *Jack and the Beanstalk, a children's story based on the exploits of Jack the Giant-killer.* (© Swim Ink, 1935/Corbis)

Tom Thumb, who often accompanied King Arthur and the Knights of the Round Table, but died during a battle with an adder. (© Bettmann, *c.* 1800/Corbis)

A leprechaun, that mischievous and famous legendary Irish character. (© Bettmann/Corbis)

Erin go Bragh

Hurrah for mother Erin, St Patrick's Day
For her sons and daughters scattered far away
For her harp and her emblem–the shamrock green
and for the best of all–her Irish Colleen.

Herne the Hunter, the legendary antlered giant said to live in Windsor Great Park. (Photograph by Tim Hawkins. By permission of artist Michael Rizzello/© Garden of England Sculpture)

The tragic Tristan and Iseult take the love potion that is the cause of their ill-fated love. (Mary Evans Picture Library/Arthur Rackham Collection)

Merlin and Vivian, the Lady of the Lake. (Mary Evans Picture Library/Arthur Rackham Collection)

Lohengrin, the son of Perceval and a member of the Grail community. (© Gianni Dagli Orti/Corbis)

MAGLAURUS

British

The Duke of ALBANY, one of the husbands of REGAN, who was one of the older daughters of King LEIR, her sister of a comparable age being GONERIL. Together with Regan's other husband, HENWINUS, Duke of CORNWALL, and Regan, he helped Goneril seize what remained of Leir's kingdom after he had given each of these daughters one-quarter as their dowry. Their younger sister CORDELIA, who had nothing to do with the deceit, remained faithful to her father, went to FRANCE and married AGANIPPUS. Maglaurus originally allowed Leir to retain a retinue of 140 men, but Goneril reduced this to eighty. Regan had her turn and reduced it to five, before Goneril finally reduced it to just one man. Leir left for France, where Cordelia and her husband raised an army and restored him to the throne for the last three years of his life.

MAGLORE

Arthurian

According to the thirteenth-century French romance *LI JUS ADEN*, a companion of MORGAN Le Fay.

MAGOG

British

One of two giants said to be among the earliest inhabitants of BRITAIN, although they are usually combined into a single gigantic being known as GOGMAGOG. If the two were originally separate beings, their combination might have been a later Christian attempt to remove them from the biblical characters of Gog and Magog (Ezekiel 38, *passim*; Revelation 20:8).

MAIA

Gaulish

A little-used alternative name for ROSMERTA.

MAID OF THE NARROW WOOD

Arthurian

A maid who fell in love with GAWAIN but subsequently tried to kill him when he did not return her feelings.

MAIDENLAND

Arthurian

The home of the foster mother of LANCELOT, and where that knight was raised. As Lancelot was raised by the LADY OF THE LAKE, this would seem to draw its origin from the Irish TÍR INNA MBAN, the Land of Women, an OTHERWORLD realm.

MAÍL DÚIN

Irish

The central character of the IMMRAM, or voyage tale, *IMMRAM CURAIG MAÍLE DÚIN*. The story, which possibly dates from the eighth century, although the text is from the tenth century, tells how Maíl Dúin, the son of a nun, set out on a voyage to find the murderer of his father, who was said to have come from the Isle of ARRAN. After a long time he came to a hermit who told him and his travelling companions that, even though they would eventually locate the murderer, they should spare his life as a token of the gratitude they felt to God for sparing them from so many dangers during their long voyage. Eventually, having found and forgiven his father's murderer, Maíl Dúin and his companions were guided by a falcon back to their home.

The many islands visited by Maíl Dúin and his companions may be found under the heading ISLANDS OF MAÍL DÚIN.

MAÍL FOTHARTAIG

Irish

The handsome son of RÓNÁN, whose stepmother fell in love with him and attempted to seduce him. He repulsed her advances, so she accused him of rape. At first Rónán refused to believe that his son could be capable of such an act, but finally, convinced of Maíl Fothartaig's guilt, he had the boy killed.

MAIMED KING

Arthurian

Named PARLAN, PELLEAM, PELLEHAN or PELLES, this character parallels the FISHER KING and was, according to the *VULGATE VERSION*, a being created when the Fisher King divided into two. His injury, usually described as a 'wound through the thighs' (*sic*), has been variously explained: as being inflicted by Balin, or as a punishment for his drawing the SWORD OF THE STRANGE HANGINGS.

MAINE

Irish

A son of AILILL who fought, and was killed by, CÚ CHULAINN during the hunt for the DONN CUAILNGÈ.

MAIR

Irish

The wife of BERSA. She fell in love with FIONN MAC CUMHAILL and sent him nine enchanted nuts that, if he had eaten them, would have caused him to fall for her. Instead, he simply buried the nuts.

MALDUC

Arthurian

A wizard who promised to rescue GUINEVERE from VALERIN, provided he was given GAWAIN and EREC as prisoners. He duly freed Guinevere and received his captives, but they were subsequently rescued from him by LANCELOT.

MALEDISANT

Arthurian

The damsel helped by BREUNOR the Black. At first Maledisant was abusive to Breunor, presumably as he refused to remove his ill-fitting coat, which had earned him the nickname LE COTE MALE TAILÉE, until he had avenged his father. However, Maledisant obviously changed her opinion of him, for she subsequently married him.

MALEGINIS

Arthurian

One of the possible names of the KING WITH A HUNDRED KNIGHTS, one of the eleven rebellious leaders at the outset of ARTHUR's reign, though he has also been identified with BERRANT LES APRES and AGUYSANS.

MALEHAUT

Arthurian

A city of Arthurian BRITAIN, supposedly in the realm of the KING WITH A HUNDRED KNIGHTS, whose location remains a mystery. The lord of this city was called DANAIN THE RED, while his wife, BLOIE, was the lover of GALEHAUT and the mother of DODINEL. Elsewhere, Bloie is known as EGLANTE.

MALLERSTANG

Arthurian

A kingdom supposedly founded by UTHER, according to local Cumbrian legend, which also made Uther a giant.

MALMESBURY, WILLIAM OF

British and Arthurian

An English chronicler (*c.* 1090–*c.* 1143) who became a monk in the monastery at Malmesbury and, in due course, became librarian and precentor. He took part in the council at WINCHESTER in 1141 against King Stephen. His *Gesta Regum Anglorum* provides a lively history of the Kings of England from the SAXON invasion until 1126, and the *Historia Novella* brings down the narrative to 1142. His *Gesta Pontificum* is an ecclesiastical history of the bishops and chief monasteries of England to 1123. Other works are an account of the church at GLASTONBURY and lives of Saint Dunstan and Saint Wulfstan.

MALORY, SIR THOMAS

Arthurian

A fifteenth-century knight about whose life little can be said with any certainty. He is most famous as the author of the *LE MORTE D'ARTHUR*, printed by Caxton in 1485, and for many the classic Arthuriad. Caxton's preface to this work states that Malory was a knight, that he finished the work in the ninth year of the reign of King Edward IV (1470), and that he 'reduced' it from a French book. It is possible that he was the Sir Thomas Malory of Newbold Revel, Warwickshire, whose quarrels with a neighbouring priory and (probably) Lancastrian politics led to his imprisonment. Of Caxton's black-letter folio, only two copies now exist. An independent manuscript was discovered at Winchester in 1934. *Le Morte d'Arthur* is the best prose romance in English and was a happy attempt to give epic unity to the whole mass of French Arthurian romance.

MALVASIUS

Arthurian

The King of ICELAND, according to GEOFFREY OF MONMOUTH.

MAN, ISLE OF

Irish, British and Arthurian

A large island in the Irish Sea with a long Celtic history. Irish legend says that it was the island to which some of the FOMHOIRÉ were exiled after their defeat by the people of PARTHOLÁN, other exiles going to the Hebrides. Later tradition made it the home of MANANNÁN MAC LIR. CORMAC MAC CUILENNÁIN (*fl.* 900) attempted to establish Manannán mac Lir as a historical person by declaring him a magnificent navigator and merchant who hailed from the island, and by saying that it was these skills that led both the Irish and the British to regard him as a god. The island was, during the traditional Arthurian period, ruled by a number of Celtic kings about whom very little is known. The enchanted knight GROMER became king with the help of GAWAIN. The island also figures in a tale concerning MERLIN, who allegedly defeated a number of giants and interred them in caves beneath Castle Rushden on the island. Recent works have attempted to connect the Isle of Man with AVALON, perhaps because of the naming of Avalon as the Isle of APPLES by GEOFFREY OF MONMOUTH and the Irish connection of the island with EMHAIN

Morgan gives Tristan a shield. (Aubrey Beardsley, 1893–4. © Archivo Iconografico, S.A./Corbis)

ABHLACH ('Emhain of the Apple Trees'), the home of the Irish sea god Manannán mac Lir.

MAN-A, -U
Irish
The Irish name for the Isle of MAN, the equivalent of the Welsh MANAW.

MANAEL
Arthurian
According to the pedigree of JOHN OF GLASTONBURY, the son of CASTELLORS and an ancestor to ARTHUR.

MANANNÁN MAC LIR
Irish and Arthurian
The son of LIR, god of the sea, who lived in TÍR NA NOC or TÍR TAIRNGIRI, both OTHERWORLDLY realms, although the Isle of MAN has also been named as his home. He is also associated with the paradisal EMHAIN ABHLACH, 'Emhain of the Apple Trees', a realm that is usually identified with the Isle of ARRAN. He is said to have raised LUGH in the Otherworld when he acted as that god's foster father. In WALES he became known as MANA-WYDAN FAB LLYR, while later tradition has also connected him with the shadowy character of BARINTHUS. The Welsh connection between Manannán mac Lir and Manawydan fab Llyr has always been a tenuous one, although the medieval chronicler CORMAC MAC CUILENNÁIN attempted to reconcile the connection by declaring that Manannán mac Lir was a historical navigator and merchant who traded on both sides of the Irish Sea, leading to his being regarded as a god by both Irish and Welsh. Manannán mac Lir is a primal god of the depths of the ocean, with associations with stellar navigation. He was clearly an important deity, because IRELAND had a long tradition of having been invaded from the sea. He remains the only Irish sea deity about whom much information is recorded. There was another, named TETHRA, who fought on the side of the FOMHOIRÉ, but little more is known about him.

Manannán mac Lir is usually depicted dressed in a green cloak fastened with a silver brooch, a satin shirt, a gold fillet and wearing golden sandals. He has the ability to adopt various forms and to calm the waters or to whip them into a frenzy. On one occasion, when BRAN set out for TÍR INNA MBAN, he was encountered driving his chariot across the waters, which he had turned into a beautiful flowery plain. Singing a wondrous song, Manannán mac Lir was accompanied by salmon that appeared as calves and lambs, the waves as flowering shrubs and the seaweed as fruit trees. Once Manannán mac Lir had passed, the sea returned to its normal state.

In his attempt to lure CORMAC MAC AIRT to his realm in order to reward that King, Manannán mac Lir assumed the guise of a warrior and appeared to the King on the ramparts of TARA at dawn. He told Cormac mac Airt that he came from a kingdom where decay, old age, death and falsehood were unknown, and, in exchange for the promise of three wishes, gave the King a branch that held three golden apples that would regrow when the branch was shaken. A year later, as had been agreed, Manannán mac Lir returned to claim his three wishes and made off with Cormac mac Airt's wife and children. The King set off in hot pursuit, but was enveloped in a thick mist. This cleared to reveal a beautiful plain in the middle of which stood a wondrous palace. Entering, the King and his company were entertained by a warrior and a beautiful maiden, whom he told of his quest. Lulled to sleep by the singing of the warrior, Cormac mac Airt awoke the following morning to find himself beside his wife and children. The warrior then revealed himself as Manannán mac Lir, and he presented the King with a beautiful golden cup. Intending to set off for Tara the following day, Cormac mac Airt, his wife and children awoke to find themselves on the grass outside their home, the cup and bough of golden apples beside them.

Manannán mac Lir used his shape-changing ability for a number of purposes. Some believed that he used this skill to control reincarnation. He also fathered mortal children, who thus became his personifications, and one such occasion was the fathering of a son on the wife of FIACHNA LURGAN, King of DÁL NARAIDI. Manannán mac Lir came to Fiachna Lurgan's Queen in the guise of a nobleman and forced her to lie with him, saying that if she did not her husband would die the very next day. The following morning she awoke to find the nobleman had gone, leaving only a poem behind by which she identified him as Manannán mac Lir. Later the same day he was seen on the battlefield in ALBA, where he overcame all the SAXON forces and thus enabled Fiachna Lurgan and AEDÁN MAC GABRÁIN to win an outstanding victory.

When Fiachna Lurgan returned home, the Queen told him all that had happened. Three days after her child MONGÁN had been born, Manannán mac Lir came and took him to Tír Tairngiri, where the boy remained until he was either twelve or sixteen, when he was returned. The taking of the boy to an

The Irish sea god Mannanan mac Lir. (By permission of artist Paul Borda/© Dryad Designs, www.dryaddesign.com)

Otherworldly realm, and the boy's subsequent rebirth, is just one example of Manannán mac Lir's associations with reincarnation, an attribute he shares with MIDHIR.

His connection with Arthurian legend is tenuous, to say the least. He is, however, said to have met BENDIGEID VRAN when the latter set out to journey to TÍR INNA MBAN (Land of Women). His main connection is through the part played by his Welsh counterpart, MANAWYDAN FAB LLYR. In the *VITA MERLINI*, Barinthus, an alternative name for Manannán mac Lir, is the ferryman on the barge that transports the dying ARTHUR to AVALON, accompanied by MERLIN and TALIESIN.

MANAW

Welsh

The Welsh name for the Isle of MAN, the equivalent of the Irish MANA.

MANAWYD(D)AN (FAB LLYR)

Welsh and Arthurian

A Welsh sea god, the son of LLYR, as his epithet shows, and perhaps the Welsh aspect of the Irish MANANNÁN MAC LIR. The *MABINOGION* makes him the brother and heir of BENDIGEID VRAN and a cousin of PRYDERI, while the story of *CULHWCH AND OLWEN* makes him a follower of King ARTHUR.

Following the destructive expedition led by Bendigeid Vran to IRELAND, PRYDERI found that his cousin Manawydan fab Llyr had been disinherited by CASWALLAWN, son of BELI. Pryderi compensated for the loss by giving Manawydan fab Llyr his mother RHIANNON to be his wife together with the seven *cantrefs* of DYFED (literally meaning 'one hundred', a *cantref* was an administrative district).

The most famous story concerning Manawydan fab Llyr is that of the curse of LLWYD FAB CIL COED. One night, as Pryderi, Manawydan fab Llyr and their wives were feasting, they heard a loud clap of thunder. This was followed by a dark cloud from which there emanated a brilliant light that enveloped them all. When the light disappeared, they found that all their men, houses and beasts had disappeared, leaving only the four of them alone in the entire realm. For two years they lived quite happily, hunting the game that freely roamed the forests and catching the fish that filled the streams and rivers. At length, growing tired of their solitary life, Pryderi and Manawydan fab Llyr decided to go from town to town to earn a living.

A short time later, while they were out hunting in the forest, their dogs disappeared into a CAER. Against Manawydan fab Llyr's advice, Pryderi entered to bring them out, but he could not leave because he was bound fast by an enchantment. Manawydan fab Llyr waited until dusk for his cousin to reappear before returning to Rhiannon. She immediately went to the caer and, seeing a door in it, a door that remained invisible to Manawydan fab Llyr, she too entered the caer and was trapped. That night the caer vanished, taking Rhiannon and Pryderi with it.

When CIGFA, Pryderi's wife, realised that they had been left alone, Manawydan fab Llyr promised to provide for her and, having neither dogs to hunt nor any other means of support, set himself up as a cobbler. So skilful was he that they soon prospered

and were, within a year, able to return to establish three crofts. These Manawydan fab Llyr sowed with wheat. When the time came to reap the first, he found that the entire crop had been eaten. The same happened when the second ripened, so he kept a watch on the third. As it ripened he saw a host of mice appear and start to devour every last ear. He caught one of the mice and took it home, vowing that he would solemnly hang it the following day for theft. Cigfa tried to dissuade him from carrying out such a ridiculous punishment, but Manawydan fab Llyr insisted.

The next day, as he was preparing the tiny gallows, a poor clerk came by, then a richly dressed priest and finally a bishop with all his retinue, the first people either Manawydan fab Llyr or Cigfa had seen in over a year. Each offered Manawydan fab Llyr a purse of money to save the life of the mouse. All their offers were refused, but the bishop raised his offer, saying that, in return for the life of the mouse, he would grant Manawydan fab Llyr whatever he wished. Manawydan fab Llyr demanded the return of Pryderi and Rhiannon and that the spell over their land be lifted. The bishop agreed, adding that the mouse was his wife and that he was Llwyd Fab Cil Coed, who had cast the spell to avenge PWYLL's treatment of his friend GWAWL FAB CLUD. The spell was lifted the moment Manawydan fab Llyr handed the mouse to the bishop. Pryderi and Rhiannon reappeared and the lands of Dyfed were miraculously restored to their former prosperous state of affairs.

Later Arthurian connections say that Manawydan fab Llyr was among the party that accompanied his brother to Ireland to rescue BRANWEN, and one of the seven who returned with Bendigeid Vran's head for burial under the WHITE MOUNT in London. The others who returned with him were PRYDERI, GLUNEU EIL TARAN (GLIFIEU), TALIESIN, YNAWC (YNAWAG), GRUDYEN (GRUDDIEU), the son of MURYEL, and HEILYN, the son of GWYNN HÊN, along with the unfortunate and heart-broken Branwen.

MANES

Irish

The collective name for the seven sons of AILILL and MEDHBHA.

MANGOUN

Arthurian

The King of MORAINE who sent King CARADOC a horn that was capable of exposing any infidelity on the part of his wife.

MANOGAN
Welsh
The father of BELI.

MANTELL
Welsh and Arthurian
A robe that was one of the THIRTEEN TREASURES OF BRITAIN and had the ability to keep the wearer warm, no matter how severe the weather. Some sources say that this robe was owned by ARTHUR and, rather than keeping the wearer warm, would render that person invisible. It was also known as GWENN.
See MANTLE OF INVISIBILITY

MANTLE OF INVISIBILITY
Arthurian
The loose-fitting cloak of ARTHUR that became one of the THIRTEEN TREASURES OF BRITAIN.

MAOL
Irish
One of the FOMHOIRÉ. He and his companion, MULLOGUE, were sent by BALAR to the mainland from TORY Island every time one of Balar's tenants married to demand the right to spend the first night with the bride. On one such occasion GOIBHNIU was at the wedding feast, and he killed both Maol and Mullogue to put a stop to the evil custom.

MAON
Irish
The son of AILILL. Maon was made to eat a portion of his father's and his grandfather's hearts, along with a mouse and all her young, by his uncle COVAC after Covac had killed Ailill. The disgust Maon felt struck him dumb. Maon travelled to MUNSTER and stayed for a while with SCORIATH, whose daughter MORIATH fell in love with him, before going to GAUL. CRAFTINY, the FILI to Scoriath, followed him at the behest of Moriath and serenaded him so wondrously that his voice returned.

Maon now gathered together an army and returned to IRELAND, where he killed Covac and all his retinue save one DRUID who questioned one of the Gauls as to the identity of their leader, for he had begun to suspect that this was Maon returned. The Gaul replied that their leader was the mariner ('Loingsech'). Now the Druid asked if he could speak. The Gaul replied that he could ('Labraidh'). From that day forth Maon became known as LABRAIDH LOINGSECH, and he married Moriath, whose love had restored his voice.

MAPON-OS, -US
Gaulish, British and Arthurian
The divine youth. An early Celtic deity, the son of MATRONA, he later became known as MABON the son of MODRON. In northern BRITAIN he was especially revered as a hunter, whilst in Arthurian legend he was known as Mabon, MABONAGRAIN and MABUZ.

MARABRON
Arthurian
The son of King VAGOR of the ILLE ESTRANGE who was defeated in battle by Sir LANCELOT.

MARAGOZ
Arthurian
The steward of King ELYADUS of Sicily. He killed his master and thus caused the Queen to flee, for her own safety was in doubt. In exile she gave birth to FLORIANT, who was reared as the foster son of MORGAN Le Fay.

MARC
Arthurian
The son of YSAIE THE SAD and so the grandson of TRISTAN. He married ORIMONDE, the daughter of the Emir of Persia.

MARCÁN
Irish
'Little Mark'. The ageing husband of the beautiful, and young, CRÉD. He entertained the exiled CANO, with whom his wife had fallen in love before setting eyes on him and who attempted to conduct a love affair following Marcán's death.

MARCH
Arthurian
The son of MEIRCHIAUN, King of Glamorgan, and identified by some commentators with King MARK.

MARDOC
Arthurian
Possibly to be identified with MORDRED, this character appears on the battlements of the Arthurian bas-relief in MODENA cathedral, alongside WINLOGEE, who is thought identifiable with GUINEVERE.

MARFISA
Arthurian
A female knight who appears in *ORLANDO FURIOSO* and is thought to have been the inspiration for BRITOMART in SPENSER's allegorical *FAERIE QUEENE*.

MARGANTE

Arthurian

An alternative name for ARGANTE, a queen who appears in *BRUT* by LAYAMON, and, in this work, an alias for MORGAN Le Fay.

MARGANUS

British

One of the nephews of CORDELIA, the other being CUNEDAGIUS. Following the death of LEIR, Cordelia reigned in peace for five years. However, her nephews, having by that time inherited their fathers' kingdoms, resented female rule, so rose up against her and took her prisoner. Cordelia took her own life. Marganus and his brother divided the kingdom between them, but the peace lasted only two years before Marganus tried to overturn his brother. His attempt was unsuccessful, because he was killed by his brother, who went on to rule for thirty-three years as the sole monarch.

MARHALT

Arthurian

According to Sir Thomas MALORY, the King of IRELAND and father of MARHAUS. However, the chronology in Malory is a little peculiar. When Marhaus fought with TRISTAN, he was the brother-in-law of the then King, ANGUISH, his father, Marhalt, only ascending the vacant throne some time later.

MARHAUS

Arthurian

The son of MARHALT and brother of ISEULT who was slain in combat by his sister's lover, TRISTAN. Prior to this, according to Sir Thomas MALORY, Marhaus had been a supporter and follower of ARTHUR and had killed the giant TAULURD. Married to the daughter of ANGUISH, the King of Ireland before Marhalt ascended the throne, he had two sons named AMOROLDO and GOLISTANT. The works of GOTTFRIED VON STRASSBURG supply the information that Marhaus was a duke, but of where remains a mystery.

MARI-MORGAN(S)

Gaulish and Arthurian

A class of water-fairy of Breton origin. It has been suggested that they gave rise to MORGAN Le Fay, because they are sometimes simply referred to as MORGANS. One in particular is of interest. Called either AHES or DAHUT, this fairy was held responsible for the destruction of the legendary city of YS.

MARIA

Arthurian

The sister of King JUAN of Castile in Spanish romance. She was taken captive by an African potentate, but was rescued by TRISTAN THE YOUNGER, whom she subsequently married.

MARIE DE FRANCE

Arthurian

A twelfth-century (*fl. c.* 1160–90) French poetess and authoress of two Arthurian romances – *Chevrefueil* and *Lanval*. Born in Normandy, she spent most of her life in England, where she wrote her *Lais* some time before 1167 and her *Fables* some time after 1170. She translated into French the *Tractatus de Purgatorio Sancti Patricii* (*c.* 1190), and her works contain many classical allusions. The *Lais*, her most important work, comprises fourteen romantic narratives in octosyllabic verse based on Celtic material.

MARINAIA

Arthurian

MERLIN'S mother, according to Pieri's fourteenth-century *Storia de Merlino*.

MARINE

Arthurian

The daughter of URIEN who was loved by LARIS.

MARIUS

British and Arthurian

An early King of BRITAIN who was the son of ARVIRAGUS, according to GEOFFREY OF MONMOUTH. He soundly defeated the PICTS under SODRIC, but still bestowed Caithness on them.

MARJODOC

Arthurian

The steward of King MARK who was at first friendly towards TRISTAN. However, when he discovered the affair between Tristan and ISEULT, he turned against his old friend.

MARK

Arthurian

(1) King of Glamorgan who is possibly to be identified with MEIRCHIAUN, his son, MARCH, being identified, by some, with the Mark below, King of CORNWALL.

(2) The brother to ELIZABETH/ELIABEL or BLANCHEFLEUR, King of CORNWALL, uncle of TRISTAN and husband of the unfortunate ISEULT.

Tristan is discovered. (Mary Evans Picture Library/Arthur Rackham Collection)

He was generally portrayed as something of a tyrant, Sir Thomas MALORY referring to him as 'bad King Mark'. It seems that this tyrannical aspect derives from his association with an ancient and historical ruler, CUNOMORUS, who reigned in both Cornwall and BRITTANY. Cunomorus, warned that one of his sons would kill him, murdered each of his wives as soon as they announced that they had fallen pregnant. However, one wife, TREPHINA, the daughter of WAROK, chief of the VENETII, managed to escape him until after she had given birth. When she had given birth to JUDWAL, or TREMEUR, Cunomorus had her decapitated, and her son was left to die. GILDAS restored Trephina to life, and she went back to the castle, neatly carrying her head, whereupon the battlements fell on Cunomorus and killed him.

The Mark known from Arthurian legend is usually depicted as the injured party in the tragic love affair between Iseult, his wife, and Tristan. His name in Welsh, March, means 'horse', and BÉROUL says that he had horse's ears, a trait shared with many other legendary and mythological characters. The *MABINOGION* story of the *DREAM OF RHONABWY* makes him the cousin of ARTHUR, while his nephew, Tristan, is lowered to the status of a swineherd in the Welsh *TRIADS*. Not much is said of Mark during the life of his wife and her lover, the emphasis being placed firmly on that famous affair. It is generally stated that he remained ignorant of the events occurring around him for some time. One version says that on the death of the lovers Mark had them buried in a single grave, though in MALORY Mark is said to have actually killed Tristan in a blind rage when he caught him playing the harp to Iseult.

The story of Tristan and Iseult appears in the romances of many countries, and so, by association, does the character of Mark. His family tree, however, differs greatly. That most commonly referred to is the pedigree given by Sir Thomas Malory. The Italian romance TRISTANO RICCARDIANO gives a version that has great similarity to the details given by Sir Thomas Malory.

There are several versions of what actually happened to Mark following Tristan's death. The Italian romance *La vendetta che fe messer Lanzelloto de la morte de miser Tristan* states that LANCELOT invaded Cornwall and killed him. Other sources say that he was defeated and killed by TRISTAN THE YOUNGER, or that he was placed in a cage that overlooked the graves of Tristan and Iseult. Another says that the son of ALISANDER THE ORPHAN, BELLANGERE, killed him, while yet one more says that when Lancelot died he invaded LOGRES and subsequently destroyed much of CAMELOT, including the ROUND TABLE. He fell at the hands of PAMLART, a direct descendant of BAN.

The origin of Mark remains somewhat obscure, the most tenable link being made with Cunomorus. The writer Wrmonoc says that Cunomorus was also called Mark, though this may be an identification with MARCH, the son of the King of Glamorgan, Meirchiaun. A further link between Mark and Cunomorus may lie in an ancient, and partially unintelligible, inscription at DORE CASTLE in Cornwall. This may read *Drustans hic iacit cunomori filius* – 'Here lies Tristan, son of Cunomorus'. If this is indeed the true meaning of the inscription, it would seem to imply that the relationship between Mark and Tristan was far closer than later writers were prepared to allow. Even in those fairly amoral times, an affair between son and stepmother may have been a little too strong to stomach.

Breton tradition carries the name of King Mark to this day, for it is said that he rides a winged horse, named Mormarc'h, when the sea off Penmarc'h, Mark's Head (a headland in Brittany), is rough.

MARLBOROUGH
Arthurian

A town in Wiltshire whose borough arms bear the motto *Ubi nunc sapientis ossa Merlini* – 'Where are the bones of MERLIN now?' Until the fourteenth century, tradition stated that Merlin was buried under an earthen mound at the western end of the town, which now lies in the grounds of Marlborough College.

MARMYADOSE
Arthurian

A sword, said to have belonged once to Hercules and to have been made by the god Vulcan. It was won by ARTHUR from RIENCE, a giant whom the King killed when that giant demanded Arthur's beard to add to his cloak, which was made from the beards of those men he had conquered and killed.

MARONEX
Arthurian

A King of GAUL whose daughter married JONAANS, the latter inheriting Maronex's kingdom following his death.

MARPESIA
Arthurian

Medieval legend claimed that this King of the Goths formed an army of women, among them the

Marlborough, Wiltshire, where tradition said Merlin was buried in the grounds of Marlborough College.
(© Jason Hawkes/Corbis)

AMAZON warriors of classical mythology, and journeyed, by way of the Caucasus, to Africa.

MARRION

Arthurian

According to the romance *BATAILLE LOQUIFER*, one of MORGAN Le Fay's sisters.

MARROK

Arthurian

One of the KNIGHTS OF THE ROUND TABLE, he was changed into a werewolf by his wife for a total of seven years.

MARSIQUE

Arthurian

A fairy who obtained the enchanted scabbard of EXCALIBUR for GAWAIN after that knight had fought the wizard MABON over her.

MARTHA

Arthurian

The daughter of King IRION who married TRISTAN's son, YSAIE THE SAD.

MART(IN)ES

Gaulish

A peculiarly Breton class of fairy, akin to the MARI-MORGAN(S). Martes, or Martines, were huge women with masses of brown hair and huge breasts, who would rush after passers-by so that they could suckle them.

MARTYN

Arthurian

The son of OGIER and MORGAN Le Fay and hence a nephew of King ARTHUR.

MATH (FAB MATHONWY)

Welsh and Arthurian

The lord of GWYNEDD and the magical son of MATHONWY. GWYDION FAB DÔN brought to his attention the herd of magic swine owned by PRYDERI and sought his permission to bring them back for him. Math fab Mathonwy agreed, and Gwydion fab Dôn set off, returning with the swine, originally the property of ARAWN, which he had magically acquired. Two days later the enchantment wrought by Gwydion fab Dôn wore off, and Pryderi marched against Math fab Mathonwy, who mustered his army and went out to meet the attack.

This was exactly what Gwydion fab Dôn wanted, for he had caused the quarrel between Pryderi and his master solely for the purpose of getting Math fab Mathonwy out of the way, his intention being to help his brother, GILFAETHWY, ravish the maiden GOEWIN, who held the post of foot-holder. Gwydion fab Dôn and Gilfaethwy abducted Goewin and took turns in raping her.

The battle between Math fab Mathonwy and Pryderi was at stalemate, so it was agreed that Gwydion fab Dôn, who had caused the argument in the first place, should meet Pryderi in single combat. He did, and at MAEN TYRIAWG quickly overcame and killed Pryderi by using his magical powers. Returning triumphant to the court of Math fab Mathonwy, Gwydion fab Dôn and his brother were punished for their rape of Goewin. Math fab Mathonwy decreed that the two should spend the next three years as male and female animals, each year producing at least one offspring. The first year they spent as deer, the second as swine and the third as wolves. At the end of the third year Math fab Mathonwy restored the brothers to their human form and forgave them their crime.

The post of foot-holder had remained unfilled since Goewin had been raped, so Gwydion fab Dôn put forward his own sister, ARIANRHOD, for the position. She claimed to be a virgin, a necessary qualification for the post, but proved to be pregnant, for she gave birth to two boys, DYLAN EIL TON and LLEU LLAW GYFFES, during the test to prove her virginity. Gwydion fab Dôn adopted Lleu Llaw Gyffes and overcame the first two curses placed on the boy by Arianrhod. Math fab Mathonwy helped him to overcome the third by helping Gwydion fab Dôn to create the flower-maiden BLODEUWEDD out of the flowers of oak, broom and meadowsweet to become Lleu Llaw Gyffes's wife. The events are related in the *MABINOGION* story of *Math, Son of Mathonwy*.

MATH HÊN

Welsh

'The Ancient', an old Welsh high god who is remembered as the magician who taught his arts to the young GWYDION FAB DÔN. The winds were said to be under his command and would bring him the least whisper wherever it might be held. He showed unrivalled compassion to the suffering, and would hand down justice without vengeance.

MATHGEN

Irish

A wizard. One of the TUATHA DÉ DANANN during the Second Battle of MAGH TUIREDH, he caused the mountains to crash down upon the FOMHOIRÉ.

MATHOL-WCH, -OCH
Welsh and Arthurian

A King of IRELAND to whom BENDIGEID VRAN, in an attempt to cement good relations between the two countries, married his sister BRANWEN. At the wedding feast, however, Matholwch was so insulted by EFNISIEN, half-brother to Bendigeid Vran, that he returned to Ireland, along with the magic cauldron given to him as a wedding present by Bendigeid Vran, and took his revenge on Branwen by treating her cruelly.

Bendigeid Vran learned of the mistreatment of his sister and mounted an expedition to Ireland to save her. At first Matholwch's forces had the upper hand, thanks to the cauldron Bendigeid Vran had given him, for the dead and wounded of the Irish forces could be restored to full vitality simply by dipping them in it. However, the tide turned when Efnisien managed to destroy the cauldron. So complete was the destruction that Matholwch and his entire race were wiped out, except for five pregnant women, who hid in a cave and subsequently gave birth to five boys whom they later married and who then set about repopulating Ireland.

The Welsh forces fared little better, for only seven of the expedition survived, Bendigeid Vran himself suffering a mortal wound. The seven survivors, named as PRYDERI, MANAWYDAN, GLIFIEU (GLUNEU EIL TARAN), TALIESIN, YNAWC (YNAWAG), GRUDYEN (GRUDDIEU) and HEILYN, carried the severed head of Bendigeid Vran back to BRITAIN and, after a somewhat delayed journey, buried it under the WHITE MOUNT in LONDON. Branwen, the cause of the expedition, was brought back to WALES, but died of a broken heart when she sat down to contemplate the destruction brought about on her behalf.

MATHONWY
Welsh

The father of the magician MATH FAB MATHONWY and a central figure in the *MABINOGION*. More than this remains unclear, as his role was never developed further.

MATRES
Gaulish

A triad of goddesses who are better known as the MOTHERS.

MATRONA
Gaulish and Arthurian

The divine mother and goddess of the River Maine, near the source of which she had her main sanctuary. Some sources say that she was the Divine Mother, an early Celtic goddess and probably the mother of MABON/MAPONUS. Welsh tradition names her MODRON and the mother of Mabon, and this association with Mabon has led to her being considered as the original of MORGAN Le Fay.

MAXIM(IAN)US
British and Arthurian

A Roman emperor who was known in Welsh tradition as MACSEN WLEDIG. Called Maximianus by GEOFFREY OF MONMOUTH, he was said by this writer to have made CONAN MERIADOC the ruler of BRITTANY. Welsh tradition says that he married ELEN, the daughter of EUDAF, and decided to stay in BRITAIN. Seven years later he received word from Rome that he had been replaced as emperor. With the help of CYNAN and GADEON, his brothers-in-law, he took Rome and was restored as emperor.

MAZADAN
Arthurian

A fairy and husband of TERDELASCHOYE who was, according to WOLFRAM VON ESCHENBACH, the great-grandfather of ARTHUR and an ancestor of PERCEVAL.

MAZOE
Welsh and Arthurian

One of the nine sisters of MORGEN (MORGAN Le Fay).

MEABEL
Irish

'Disgrace', one of the three names given to the wife of the DAGHDHA. Her other names were BRENG and MENG.

MEATH
Irish

One of the five original provinces of IRELAND that were established by the FIR BHOLG. Today Meath is no longer a province, but rather a county within the province of LEINSTER.

MEDAR
Irish

One of the many brothers of the DAGHDHA. He appears only in passing references.

MED(H)BH(A)
Irish

The Queen of CONNACHT and, along with her consort AILILL, the enemy of CONCHOBAR MAC

NESSA. Her name means 'intoxication', and she appears originally to have been a personification of the SPIRIT OF IRELAND, the goddess whom any king must ritually marry before his office is recognised. She was said to have been the wife of nine Irish kings and that only her mate could be called the true King of IRELAND. In the *Fledd Bricrenn*, Medhbha awarded the title of champion of all Ireland to the hero CÚ CHULAINN rather than to CONALL CERNACH or LOEGHAIRE BUADHACH.

Medhbha is possibly most famous for her desire to own the fabulous DONN CUAILNGÈ, the story of her quest being told in the *Taín Bó Cuailngè*. Because the bull was owned by a man of ULSTER, the county that was her traditional enemy, Medhbha had to go to war with that county in order to achieve her desire. At that time, however, the men of Ulster had been cursed by MACHA and were unfit for battle. The only Ulster warrior not afflicted was Cú Chulainn, still only a youth, and he held off the forces of Medhbha and Ailill with ruthless efficiency, although he was eventually killed and the Donn Cuailngè taken to Medhbha, where it did battle with FINNBHENNACH, the bull owned by Ailill, which it totally annihilated.

MEDRAWT
Arthurian
The name by which MORDRED is referred to in the *ANNALES CAMBRIAE*.

MEDYR
Welsh
One of the less often mentioned members of the party formed to help CULHWCH. Medyr was chosen for his speed. It was said that in a single blink of an eye he could travel from CORNWALL to IRELAND and be back again before an onlooker had the chance to blink again.

MEICHE
Irish
The son of the MÓRRÍGHAN. He was killed by DIAN CÉCHT, and when his body was cut open Dian Cécht discovered three hearts, one for each aspect of his mother, each heart being a vile serpent's head. Two of these were burnt, but the third escaped and grew into a huge serpent, which threatened the entire country. Dian Cécht later killed this serpent.

ME(I)RCHIAUN
Arthurian
An early King of Glamorgan, and the father of MARK of Glamorgan. His son may have been the original for King MARK of CORNWALL, or the association may simply be one of confusion, which seems highly likely.

MELCHINUS
Arthurian
A Latinised version of MELKIN.

MELDOS
Welsh and Arthurian
Originally a Celtic god and possibly the origin of MELLT. Welsh tradition seems to suggest that he was the father of MABON.

MELDRED
Welsh and Arthurian
A king who had the infidelities of his wife revealed to him by LAILOKEN.

MELEAGAUNCE
Arthurian
Also MELWAS
The son of King BAGDEMAGUS. A scurrilous knight, he once abducted GUINEVERE and took her back to his own territory. There he was about to rape her, but his father prevented him from doing so. She was rescued by her champion, and lover, Sir LANCELOT, who fought Meleagaunce and spared his life only after Bagdemagus had beseeched Guinevere to intercede. The combat was stopped, to be recommenced in a year's time. Again, Bagdemagus begged for Meleagaunce to be spared when the two met on this second occasion. As with many of the Arthurian legends, there are several different versions of what actually befell Meleagaunce. One says that he and Lancelot fought in single combat over Guinevere and Lancelot killed him. Whether this was on a first, second or subsequent occasion that the pair met is unclear. Another says that Meleagaunce actually imprisoned Lancelot, but was slain while the latter escaped. A Welsh version of this story, which uses Meleagaunce's Welsh name, Melwas, says that he was the ruler of Somerset, and carried off Guinevere to GLASTONBURY. ARTHUR (not Lancelot in this tale) laid siege to the town, but the abbot and GILDAS beseeched Melwas to return his captive, which he did.

MELEHAN
Arthurian
A son of MORDRED who, with his brother, seized the kingdom following the death of their father. They were defeated by LANCELOT, Melehan later being killed by BORS.

MELIADICE

Arthurian

The heroine of the fifteenth-century French romance *Cleriadus*, which was published in Paris in 1495. A descendant of ARTHUR, she was the daughter of King PHILIPPON, the King of England. She married CLERIADUS, who succeeded Philippon.

MELIADOR

Arthurian

The son of the Duke of CORNWALL and a member of King ARTHUR's court, though his capacity remains unknown. He married the daughter of the King of Scotland, HERMONDINE, after killing his rival for her hand, CAMAL.

MELIANT DE LIS

Arthurian

A knight whose hatred for LANCELOT was founded in the fact that Lancelot had killed his father. He was eventually killed by Lancelot.

MELIANUS

Arthurian

An ancestor of LOT.

MELIODAS

Arthurian

The name of two related characters from Arthurian legend.

(1) The King of LIONES and father of TRISTAN. He carried off the Queen of SCOTLAND while still a young man, which led to war between him and ARTHUR. She became the mother of the second Meliodas by him. His relationship to King MARK of CORNWALL is a little confused, for Sir Thomas MALORY makes him his brother-in-law, having married ELIZABETH, while in Italian romance he is the brother of Mark, the romance *TRISTANO RICCARDIANO* calling their father FELIX. If Malory is to be used, Meliodas became the father of Tristan by Elizabeth. Subsequently, following Elizabeth's death, he married a daughter of HOEL, while another of Hoel's daughters was to marry his son, Tristan. ISEULT of the White Hands would therefore be both sister-in-law and daughter-in-law to Meliodas. His death is put down to knights of the Count of NORHOUT.

(2) The son of the first Meliodas and the Queen of SCOTLAND. His mother set him adrift as a baby and he was raised by the LADY OF THE LAKE, though this may be a different lady from that associated with EXCALIBUR, or even the one said to have raised LANCELOT.

MELJANZ

Arthurian

The King of LIZ who went to war against Duke LYPPAUT when his advances were rejected by the latter's daughter.

MELKIN

British and Arthurian

A vaticinator (prophet) mentioned by JOHN OF GLASTONBURY, who says that he lived before MYRDDIN (MERLIN) and uttered prophecies about GLASTONBURY so couched in obscure Latin phraseology that they are difficult to interpret. It has been suggested that they may refer to Glastonbury as a place of pagan burial and to the future discovery of the tomb of JOSEPH OF ARIMATHEA. Melkin may possibly be identifiable with MAELGWYN, a sixth-century ruler of GWYNEDD, although this seems tenuous. John Leland (*c.* 1503–52), royal antiquary to King Henry VIII, claimed to have seen Melkin's book at Glastonbury Abbey.

MELLT

Arthurian

The father of one of the two Mabons listed as being followers of ARTHUR, though it is now generally assumed that these are the same character, thought of as two previously for the simple reason that one had only his mother named, and the other only his father, Mellt.

MELODIAN

Arthurian

A son of King PELLINORE.

MELORA

Arthurian

A daughter of King ARTHUR who, according to an Irish romance, fell in love with ORLANDO, the son of the King of Thessaly. Jealously, MADOR bribed MERLIN to rid him of the troublesome prince, a request that Merlin complied with, employing his servant, simply named as the DESTRUCTIVE ONE, to imprison the hapless Orlando. He was surrounded by enchantments that only the LANCE OF LONGINUS, the carbuncle of VERONA, daughter of the King of NARSINGA, and the oil of the pig of TUIS could dispose of. Melora disguised herself as a knight and set out to find these items. She defeated the King of Africa on behalf of the King of BABYLON, and as a reward was given the Lance of Longinus and LEVANDER as her companion. They were imprisoned by the King of Asia, but escaped with the help of URANUS, a guard, and successfully obtained the oil of the pig of Tuis from their captor. They finally managed to lure Verona and her father, the King of Narsinga, onto a ship, but they became firm friends, and the carbuncle was given freely to Melora. Returning, Orlando was freed and the happy couple went on to Thessaly, while Levander married Verona.

MELOT
Arthurian

An Aquitainian dwarf who spied on TRISTAN and ISEULT for the jealous King MARK, according to GOTTFRIED VON STRASSBURG. His story is again told by EILHART, but he simply refers to the dwarf as AQUITAIN.

MELWAS
Arthurian

The Welsh for MELEAGAUNCE.

MENG
Irish

'Guile', one of the three names by which the wife of the DAGHDHA was known. Her other names were BRENG and MEABEL.

MENW (FAB TEIRGWAEDD)
Welsh and Arthurian

The son of TEIRGWAEDD, a sorcerer who appears in the *MABINOGION* story of *CULHWCH AND OLWEN* as a member of the party formed by ARTHUR to aid CULHWCH and one of the party chosen to help Culhwch locate the maiden OLWEN. Each member of the party was chosen for his particular skills, and Menw fab Teirgwaedd was chosen for his mastery of magic, which would preserve the party in foreign and heathen lands because he could render them invisible. The other members of the party were CEI (KAY), CYNDDYLIG the Guide, GWRHYR the Interpreter, GWALCHMAI FAB GWYAR and BEDWYR (BEDIVERE).

MERAUGIS
Arthurian

The offspring of the violation of LABIANE by her uncle, King MARK of CORNWALL. His father, Mark, murdered Labiane and abandoned Meraugis in the woods, where he was found and raised by a forester. He became a KNIGHT OF THE ROUND TABLE, fought at the Battle of CAMLANN and, following ARTHUR's death, became a hermit in the company of BORS and some others.

MERCIA
British

An ANGLO-SAXON kingdom that emerged in the sixth century and that, by the late eighth century, dominated all ENGLAND south of the River Humber. From *c.* 825 Mercia came under the power of WESSEX. Mercia eventually came to denote an area bounded by the Welsh border, the River Humber, East Anglia and the River Thames.

'MERCURY'
Gaulish

The name given by JULIUS CAESAR to the chief Gaulish deity, the inverted commas being used to distinguish the Celtic god from the Roman god of the same name. 'Mercury' was a war god, credited with the invention of all the art forms and honoured as the patron of commerce and travel. His consort is named as ROSMERTA. The evidence in Gaulish place-names and his similarity to the Irish god LUGH makes it almost a certainty that 'Mercury' was more commonly known as LUG or LUGUS.

MERIADEUC
Arthurian

The hero of the thirteenth-century romance that carries his name. He became known as the KNIGHT OF THE TWO SWORDS (a title also conferred on BALIN) after he had proved himself the only member of ARTHUR's knights able to unfasten a sword belt that LORE, Lady of GARADIGAN, that he subsequently married, had brought to Arthur's court.

MERIADEUC
Arthurian

A thirteenth-century French verse romance concerning a hero having the same name as the title of the work.

MERIADOC
Arthurian

The son of King CARADOC whose inheritance was usurped by GRIFFITH when the latter took the throne by murdering CARADOC. Meriadoc and his sister ORWEN were dispatched to the woods to be killed, but the executioners failed in their task. Subsequently the children were raised by IVOR the Huntsman and his wife, MORWEN. Orwen was abducted by URIEN, in this instance called King of the Scots, who married her. Meriadoc meanwhile went to King ARTHUR's court to ask for help in regaining his rightful throne and, with ARTHUR's help, succeeded in ousting Griffith only to hand over the throne, once he had regained it, to URIEN. Travelling on to the continent, Meriadoc rescued the daughter of the Emperor of Germany from GUNDEBALD, the King of the LAND FROM WHICH NO ONE RETURNS, and married her.

MERLIN
Welsh and Arthurian
Also MYRDDIN (EMRYS)

The most famous wizard of all times, ARTHUR's counsellor who guided the young King at the start of his reign, though later the King did not always follow the advice given to him. We know of Merlin by that name simply because the Latinised form of his Welsh name, Myrddin, would be Merdinus, and that would unfortunately have connected it with the Latin word *merdus* – 'dung'. Merlin is not a personal name but rather a place-name, the Welsh form of his name, MYRDDIN, originating in the Celtic *Maridunon* – CARMARTHEN, Welsh *Caerfyrddin*. It seems that the wizard was so called because he originated from that city. At least GEOFFREY OF MONMOUTH seems to think so. Other sources agree in principle, but rather say that the city was founded by him, and therefore named after him. ROBERT DE BORON says he was born in BRITTANY, but this is commonly regarded as an attempt by that author to claim him for his own country of birth. In other early Welsh poems he is called LLALLAWC and LLALLOGAN VYRDIN.

Stories abound about the birth of Merlin, but usually he is said to have been the offspring of an incubus (evil spirit) and a nun, set on earth by the devils of Hell, who were determined to counterbalance the good introduced by Jesus Christ. However, their plans went awry when their intended evil being was promptly baptised. This is not by any means the only account of his birth, but does appear to pre-date any of the others. In Welsh tradition his mother was called ALDAN, but whether or not she was a nun is not made clear. French romance calls her OPTIMA, while Pieri's fourteenth-century *Storia di Merlino* names her as MARINAIA. The Elizabethan play *The Birth of Merlin* calls her JOAN GO-TO-'T. Welsh tradition further contradicts his supposed lack of a father by giving him a paternal pedigree descended from COEL GODEBOG, his own father being named in this pedigree as MADOG MORFRYN.

His father was also said to have been MORGAN FRYCH, claimed by some to have been a prince of GWYNEDD, thus making Merlin of royal blood. Geoffrey of Monmouth made him the King of POWYS, and this idea that Merlin was of royal stock is later found in *Venetia edificia* (1624) by Strozzi.

Merlin's story, and his connection with the Arthurian legends, begins long before the birth of the King he was to advise, and whose downfall he so rightly prophesied. While still a youth, he became connected with VORTIGERN, the King of BRITAIN some time after the end of the Roman occupation. Vortigern was attempting to erect a tower on DINAS EMRYS, but with little success, for every time he built it up it promptly fell down again. His counsellors told him that it would be necessary to sacrifice a fatherless child in order to rectify the problem and, as these were hardly thick on the ground, the supposedly fatherless son of the incubus, Merlin, now a youth, was picked. When brought to the site of the tower, Merlin told Vortigern that the problem lay beneath the ground in the form of two DRAGONS secreted in an underground lake. Excavation of the site proved this to be the case (subsequent archaeological excavation has revealed the underground pool), and two dragons, one red and one white, emerged, causing Merlin to utter a series of prophecies.

There seems to be an unrecorded gap in Merlin's life at this point, for he next appears when AMBROSIUS AURELIUS defeated Vortigern and wished to erect a monument both to his success and to commemorate the dead. Merlin advised him to go to Ireland and bring back from there certain stones that formed the GIANTS' RING. This was done and they were erected on SALISBURY PLAIN as STONEHENGE. Following the death of Ambrosius Aurelius, UTHER ascended the throne, but during a war with GORLOIS, he became infatuated with IGRAINE (EIGYR), the wife of Gorlois, so one of Uther's men suggested they consult Merlin. When they did so, Merlin consented to enable Uther to lie with Igraine on the condition that any child born of the union should be entrusted to him to raise. Uther agreed and Merlin altered his appearance so that he resembled Gorlois and, on the night Uther lay with Igraine, her true husband was killed in battle. When the child was born, Merlin appeared and took the child away, as had been agreed, placing him with ECTOR. This child was the infant ARTHUR. Uther married Igraine, but two years later he died. The country was thrown into disarray, for there was no worthy successor to the throne, a situation that continued for thirteen years after Uther's death.

Meanwhile the young ARTHUR was raised by Ector, unaware of his parentage or destiny. When aged just fifteen, he accompanied his foster father and KAY, Ector's son, to a tournament in London, acting as Kay's squire. However, when they arrived, Arthur found, to his horror, that he had forgotten Kay's sword. He remembered seeing one embedded in a rock some distance away and went to fetch it. Arthur easily removed the sword from the stone, a test devised by Merlin to find the next true king, and hurried back to the tournament. Kay recognised the sword that so many had tried to remove but none had

The wizard Merlin looks after the infant Arthur. (Aubrey Beardsley, 1893–4/Mary Evans Picture Library)

been able to, and tried to make his father believe that he had removed it himself. However, Ector prevailed upon his son to tell the truth, fully realising what the sword signified, and Kay owned up. Arthur once more drew out the sword, this time in public, and was duly proclaimed king.

Events after the crowning of King Arthur differ according to source, some even attributing the manufacture of the ROUND TABLE to Merlin. When Arthur wanted to marry GUINEVERE, Merlin advised him against it, saying that she would be unfaithful to him, and would ultimately bring about the destruction of his realm and lead to his death. Arthur none the less ignored the advice of his counsellor.

According to Sir Thomas MALORY, Merlin became infatuated with the LADY OF THE LAKE, called NIMUE by Malory but referred to as VIVIANE/VIVIENNE elsewhere. He taught her his magical secrets, but she turned these against him and imprisoned him in a cave or an oak tree, the spell holding him there capable of being broken only when Arthur once again ruled.

Geoffrey of Monmouth, and earlier Welsh sources, say that Merlin was still in circulation following the Battle of CAMLANN, being one of those aboard the barge, along with TALIESIN and the ferryman BARINTHUS, that brought the dying king to AVALON to be healed of his deadly wound by the goddess MORGAN Le Fay, shape-changing mistress of therapy, music and the arts, co-ruling with her NINE SISTERS. With the kingdom in disarray, Merlin went mad following the Battle of ARTHURET and took to living as a wild man in the woods. One source, GIRALDUS CAMBRENSIS, gives the reason for Merlin's loss of sanity, saying that it followed his beholding some horrible sight in the sky, a bad omen, during the fighting in which he had been on the side of RHYDDERCH HAEL, King of Cumbria and husband of Merlin's sister GANIEDA. Three of Merlin's brothers were also reputed to have been killed during the battle. In his frenzy, he acquired the gift of prophecy. This story relates Merlin to the Irish King SUIBHNE GEILT, from whose legend the tale may be derived, although Myrddin is first referred to in the tenth-century poem *ARMES PRYDEIN*, while the *Buile Suibhne*, which recounts the Irish legend, is probably two centuries older. After a while Ganieda persuaded Merlin to give up his wild life in the woods and return to civilisation, but upon his return he revealed to Ganieda's husband, Rhydderch Hael, that she had been unfaithful to him. Once again madness took hold of Merlin and he returned to the forest, urging

his wife, the flower-maiden GUENDOLOENA, to marry again, apparently divorcing her to free her. She agreed, but in his madness Merlin arrived at the wedding riding a stag and leading a herd of deer (clearly a reworking of an earlier pagan tradition). In his rage, forgetting that it was he who had urged his wife to remarry, he tore the antlers off the stag and hurled them at the bridegroom, who remains unnamed, and killed him. He returned to the forest once more, and his sister Ganieda built him an observatory from which he could study the stars.

Welsh poetic sources that are considerably earlier in date than the writings of Geoffrey of Monmouth largely agree with his account (they are obviously his sources), though they state that Merlin fought against Rhydderch Hael, rather than for him. Similar tales are told in Welsh tradition regarding a character by the name of LAILOKEN, who was in the service of Rhydderch Hael, and it would appear that this caused Geoffrey of Monmouth to change the allegiance of Merlin. Lailoken is similar to the Welsh word meaning 'twin', and, as Merlin and Ganieda were thought to be twins, this may have simply been a nickname for Merlin himself, though, as has already been said, Merlin is not actually a personal name.

Many other legends and tales surround the character of Merlin. He was said to have saved the baby TRISTAN, to have had a daughter named La DAMOSEL DEL GRANT PUI DE MONT DOLEROUS, and that he was not imprisoned by Nimue, but instead voluntarily retired to a place of confinement to live out the remainder of his days. This last option seems to have some connection with the story of Ganieda building him an observatory in the forest, for that would have been a splendid place for the wizard to spend his final years.

Geoffrey of Monmouth appears to draw further on earlier Welsh sources when he connects Merlin with Taliesin, a character with whom he seems to be inexorably intertwined in the Welsh mind. One Welsh tradition says that Merlin was not just one but three incarnations of the same person, the first appearing in Vortigern's time, the second as Taliesin himself, while the last was as Merlin the wild man of the forests. This idea of a multiple Merlin is again found in the writings of the twelfth-century Norman–Welsh chronicler Giraldus Cambrensis, who says there were two, wizard and wild man. This theory doubtless springs from the impractically long lifespan usually attributed to Merlin. Modern thinking even had him reincarnated once more as Nostradamus (Latinised form of Michel de Notredame), the sixteenth-century prophet. This idea has not found popular following, though, and is now almost universally disregarded.

The legends of Merlin are not simply confined to British and Breton tradition. The Italian romances also add a great deal to his story, stating, in one instance, that he was unsuccessfully charged with heresy by a Papal bishop named CONRAD, and that he uttered prophecies about the House of Hohenstaufen. An Italian poet, BOIARDO, mixes Merlin into the story of TRISTAN and ISEULT, saying that Merlin created a fountain of forgetfulness for Tristan to drink from and thus forget Iseult. Tristan never found it. ARIOSTO says that his soul lives on in a tomb, and it informed the female warrior BRADMANTE that the House of ESTE would descend from her. Strozzi further adds that, at the time when Attila the Hun invaded Italy, Merlin lived in a cave and, while there, invented the telescope (another reference to Ganieda's observatory?).

His death is as clouded in legend and fable as is his life. One Welsh tradition says that he was held captive by a scheming woman in a cave on BRYN MYRDDIN near Carmarthen, a location shown on Ordnance Survey maps as MERLIN'S HILL. This seems to echo the story of his being held captive by Nimue. Some say that if you listen in the twilight you can still hear his groans and the clanking of the iron chains that bind him, while others say that this is the noise of him still working away in his underground prison. His place of confinement is also said to be a cave in the park of DYNEVOR CASTLE, DYFED, in the vicinity of Llandeilo. It is also claimed that he died and was buried on BARDSEY Island, while Breton tradition has him spellbound in a bush of white thorn trees in the woods of Bresilien in Brittany.

The Welsh *TRIADS* (*TRIOEDD YNYS PRYDEIN*), however, say that he put to sea in a house of glass and was never heard of again. On this voyage he took with him the THIRTEEN TREASURES (or Curiosities) OF BRITAIN, which were:

1 LLEN ARTHUR – the veil of ARTHUR, which made the wearer invisible. This is sometimes referred to as the MANTLE OF INVISIBILITY.
2 DYRNWYN – the sword of RHYDDERCH HAEL, which would burst into flame from the cross to the point if any man, save himself, drew it.
3 CORN BRANGALED – the horn of BRANGALED, which would provide any drink desired.
4 CADAIR, NEU CAR MORGAN MWYNFAWR – the chair or car of MORGAN MWYNFAWR, which would carry a person seated in it anywhere he wished to go.

5 MWYS GWYDDNO – the hamper of GWYD-DNO, which had the power to turn any meat placed on it into sufficient to feed 100 people.
6 HOGALEN TUDNO – the whetstone of TUDNO TUDGLYD, which would sharpen none but the weapon of a brave man.
7 PAIS PADARN – the cloak of PADARN, which would make the wearer invisible.
8 PAIR DRYNOG – the cauldron of DRYNOG, in which only the meat of a brave man would boil.
9 DYSGYL A GREN RHYDDERCH – the platter of RHYDDERCH, upon which any meat desired would appear.
10 TAWLBWRDD – a chess or rather backgammon board, having a ground of gold and men of silver who would play themselves.
11 MANTELL – a robe that would keep the wearer warm no matter how severe the weather.
12 MODRWY ELUNED – the ring of ELUNED, which conferred invisibility on the wearer.
13 CYLLEL LLAWFRODEDD – a Druid sacrificial knife.

It should be noted that these were by no means the only items considered to number among the Thirteen Treasures, but they are the most common in Welsh tradition (a list of the most common variants is included under the heading for the THIRTEEN TREASURES OF BRITAIN).

Modern times have not entirely forgotten Merlin either. Yearly pilgrimages continued to MERLIN'S SPRING at Barenton, Brittany, until they were stopped by the Vatican in 1853. His ghost is still said to haunt MERLIN'S CAVE at TINTAGEL, while the wizard is said to be buried in almost as many locations as Arthur. These locations include DRUMELZIER in SCOTLAND, under MERLIN'S MOUNT in the grounds of MARLBOROUGH College, at MYNYDD FYRDDIN in WALES, and in MERLIN'S HILL CAVE near Carmarthen.

Merlin's historicity is now thought to be without doubt, but he was not the mythologised wizard of the Arthurian legends. There were in fact two Merlins alive during the time of Vortigern and Arthur. One was called MYRDDIN WYLLT and lived in Scotland, but it is MYRDDIN EMRYS, born and raised in Carmarthen, who has become the Arthurian Merlin. It is generally believed that he must have been a man of very high intelligence with extremely advanced knowledge for his time, when magic was simply another name for scientific expertise. He may have been, as has been suggested, a latter-day Druid who took part in shamanistic rituals, but many attempts have also been made to link Merlin with earlier Celtic deities.

Vivien, Lady of the Lake, at the descent of Merlin. (© Bettmann/Corbis)

One theory states that Merlin represented the morning star while his sister Ganieda was the evening star. His character may indeed have been that of a deity, for the Welsh *TRIADS* indicate that he may have had territorial rights as a god over Britain, and this work says that the earliest name for Britain was MERLIN'S PRECINCT. However, the truth behind this is probably that the prophet became connected with an earlier deity, and took on many of his attributes, such would have been the astonishing power of this character. To the peasants of the time, his wisdom and foresight must have seemed very godly indeed. Other attempts have been made to connect him with the god MABON or, through his association with stags, with CERNUNNOS. Many theories have been put forward, but the truth of the matter, as with so much of Arthurian legend, may never be known.

There are countless prophecies attributed to Merlin, some of which appear to have been strangely fulfilled and others of which may well be fulfilled in the future. In the Vale of Twy near Abergwili there stands a large stone in a field. Many years ago a young man was killed while digging under this stone for buried treasure, it being popular belief at the time that such stones marked the burial sites of riches beyond belief. Myrddin had once prophesied that one day a raven would drink the blood of a man from this stone. Whether or not a raven actually did so is not known, but the prophecy seems to have come true.

The most famous prophecies attributed to Merlin were those relating to the town of Carmarthen, which still awaits some fearful catastrophe.

> *Llanllwch a fu,*
> *Caerfyrdxlu a sud,*
> *Abergwili a saif.*

> Llanllwch has been,
> Carmarthen shall sink,
> Abergwili shall stand.

and

> *Caerfyrddin, cei oer fore,*
> *Daerr a'th lwnc, dwr i'th le.*

> Carmarthen, thou shalt have a cold morning,
> Earth shall swallow thee, water into thy place.

There are still old folk living in Carmarthen who await the catastrophe that they believe will one day befall their town. At the end of one street, there used to stand an ancient and withered oak tree known as MERLIN'S TREE or the PRIORY OAK. Every care was taken over the centuries to protect it from falling, for Merlin had prophesied that when it did Carmarthen would fall. However, in 1978 the local authority decided to risk the prophecy and remove the tree, which had become a hazard to the town's traffic and consisted mainly of concrete and iron bars anyway.

Merlin also prophesied that Carmarthen would sink when LLYN EIDDWEN, a lake in DYFED (then Cardiganshire), dried up. He also foretold that one day a bull would go to the very top of the tower of Saint Peter's church in Carmarthen. This strange prophesy was one day fulfilled by a calf.

MERLIN
Arthurian
Important twelfth-century romance by the Burgundian author ROBERT DE BORON.

MERLIN'S CAVE
Arthurian
A cave at TINTAGEL, CORNWALL, that is said to be haunted by the ghost of MERLIN.

MERLIN'S ENTERTAINMENTS
Arthurian
HEYWOOD, in his *Life of Merlin*, reports that VORTIGERN became melancholy and, in an attempt to cheer him, MERLIN provided various forms of entertainment, including invisible musicians and flying hounds that chased flying hares.

MERLIN'S HILL
Welsh and Arthurian
A hill, three miles east of CARMARTHEN, at the summit of which there is a rock resembling a chair. Legend says that this was where MERLIN (MYRDDIN) sat to deliver his various prophecies. It is also the alleged site of a cave where Merlin was buried, but this cave has yet to be found. However, there is a cave situated under an overhang behind a waterfall in the upper reaches of the Afon Pib that is sometimes locally referred to as OGOF MYRDDIN.

MERLIN'S HILL CAVE
Arthurian
The so-far undiscovered cave on MERLIN'S HILL in which the wizard is said to have been buried.

MERLIN'S MOUNT
Arthurian
An earthen mound in the grounds of MARLBOROUGH College, Wiltshire, which is one of the many locations cited as the burial place of MERLIN.

MERLIN'S PRECINCT
Welsh and Arthurian
An early name for BRITAIN, which appears in the Welsh *TRIOEDD YNYS PRYDEIN* (*TRIADS*) and has been taken by some to indicate that MYRDDIN was, in origin, a deity with territorial rights.

MERLIN'S SPRING
Arthurian
A spring at Barenton, BRITTANY, that was the focus of pilgrimages until they were stopped by the Vatican in 1853.

MERLIN'S TREE
Welsh and Arthurian
Also called the PRIORY OAK, this tree in CARMARTHEN was believed to maintain the good fortune of Carmarthen, for it was believed that if it fell so would the city. The tree was removed by the local authority in 1978 because it constituted a traffic hazard, and, to date, MYRDDIN's prophecy of the destruction of Carmarthen has not been fulfilled.

MERVEILLES DE RIGOMER
Arthurian
A thirteenth-century French verse romance, normally simply referred to as *RIGOMER*, by an obscure poet named Jehan. It tells the story of the adventures of GAWAIN and LANCELOT.

MESCA
Irish
The daughter of BODB who was abducted by GARMAN but died of shame at having allowed herself to be loved by a mere mortal.

MESGE-DRA, -GRA
Irish
A King of LEINSTER. He was killed by CONALL CERNACH, who mashed the dead King's brain and mixed the remains with lime to make a sling-ball. This was one of the treasures of CONCHOBAR MAC NESSA at EMHAIN MHACHA from where it was stolen by CET. Cet later fired the sling-ball at Conchobar mac Nessa with such force that it lodged in his forehead. Conchobar mac Nessa's physician FINGEN told him that it could not be removed as he would die if it was, but added that, provided he did not become agitated, there was no reason why he could not lead a relatively normal life. Sometime later, when he was unable to quell his emotions, the sling-ball burst from his head and Conchobar mac Nessa died.

MESRODA
Irish
The son of DÁ THÓ. He is best known simply as MAC DÁ THÓ.

MESS BUACHALLA
Irish
The daughter of EOCHAIDH AIREMH by his own daughter, who is named as either ÉDÁIN or ESS, the latter probably being introduced to save confusion between the two ÉDÁINS. Mess Buachalla married ETERSCEL and became the mother of CONAIRE MÔR, although other sources say that Conaire Môr was the son born of an incestuous relationship between Eochaidh Airemh and his daughter.

A later story says that Mess Buachalla was the daughter of Ess and Eterscel and was fostered by a cowherd of Eterscel's. She was visited by a curious bird man, NEMGLAN, King of the Birds, to whom she gave herself freely. He told her that she would bear a son, to name him Conaire Môr and to say that he was the natural son of Eterscel, whom Mess Buachalla later incestuously married.

MEURIC
Welsh and Arthurian
The Son of CARADOC VREICHVRAS (CARADOC BRIEFBRAS) in Welsh tradition.

MEURIG
Welsh Arthurian
A King of GLENVISSIG whose son, ATHRWYS, has been identified with ARTHUR. It is possible that Meurig is to be identified with Meurig ap Tewdrig, Prince of Glamorgan, whose daughter, Anna, was the mother of Saint SAMSON by Amwn.

MEURVIN
Arthurian
The son of OGIER and MORGAN Le Fay, and thus ARTHUR's nephew. He became the father of ORIANT and was an ancestor of the SWAN KNIGHT.

MIDAC
Irish
The son of the King of LOCHLANN. After his father had been killed by the FIAN, Midac sought revenge by inviting FIONN MAC CUMHAILL and his men to a feast. After they had arrived, Midac left the palace. Four of the fian had remained outside on guard, which was just as well, for Midac now led an army against the fian, whom he had magically adhered to their chairs. The four guards fought the

army and at length repulsed it, before entering the palace to release their comrades using the blood of three kings. Unfortunately for one, CONAN MAC MORNA, the blood ran out before they came to him, whereupon DIARMAID UA DUIBHNE took a firm hold of him and wrenched him out of the chair, leaving a large section of his skin behind.

MIDACH
Irish

A son of DIAN CÉCHT and brother of AIRMED. Like his father, he was an impressive physician, so good, in fact, that his father struck him four times. The first three times, Midach managed to heal his wounds, but on the fourth occasion the wounds were fatal. From his grave a vast array of herbs grew, all of which had medicinal properties. These herbs were gathered together and sorted by his sister Airmed, but Dian Cécht muddled them up as he feared the power of his son even from beyond the grave.

MIDHIR
Irish

A god of TÍR TAIRNGIRI. Although Midhir lived in the SÍDH of BRÍ LEITH, he was, like MANANNÁN MAC LIR, associated with rebirth. He took as his first wife FUAMHNACH, but later became besotted with ÉDÁIN ECHRAIDHE, the daughter of King AILILL. Her hand was sought on his behalf by OENGHUS MAC IN OG, his foster son. She consented to the union and they were married.

Theirs was not to be a happy marriage, however, for Fuamhnach, who clearly regarded Midhir as her sole property, was extremely jealous of Midhir's new wife. She used magic to turn Édáin Echraidhe into a pool of water. That turned into a worm, which in turn became a huge and beautiful fly whose perfume and music filled the air. Fuamhnach need not have thought that this would be the end of Édáin Echraidhe, for Midhir was quite content to have his new wife around him, even in this strange form. Driven to despair by her jealousy, Fuamhnach conjured up a huge gust of wind, which blew the beautiful fly far away, so that it fell on a rocky coastline. There Édáin Echraidhe lay helpless for seven years until she was discovered by Oenghus Mac in Og, who placed her in a crystal bower and brought her back to Midhir. Fuamhnach once again magically created a huge gust of wind, which this time blew the fly into a glass of wine, which was swallowed. The woman who swallowed the fly became pregnant, and, 1,012 years after she had been first born, Édáin Echraidhe was reborn, this time being simply known as ÉDÁIN, the granddaughter of ÉTAR.

As Édáin reached maturity, EOCHAIDH AIREMH became the King of IRELAND. However, none would pay him due respect as he was unmarried, so he sent out messengers to search out the most beautiful woman in Ireland. Eventually Édáin was chosen and became his wife. News of the marriage and of Édáin's beauty reached Midhir, who set out to TARA to reclaim her, but she would not leave her husband without his express permission. Midhir thus challenged Eochaidh Airemh to a chess contest, but he let the King easily win the opening game and accepted the forfeit of building a great causeway across the bogs of MEATH.

Midhir then returned to Tara and duly won the final game, claiming as his boon a kiss from Édáin. A month later Midhir came to Tara to claim his prize, but found all the doors barred to him, for Eochaidh Airemh had no intention of giving up his beautiful wife. As the King sat feasting with his company, Midhir appeared among them, seized Édáin and together the pair flew out of the smoke hole of the great hall as a pair of white swans.

Eochaidh Airemh and his company pursued them to the sídh of Brí Leith and began to dig it up. Midhir appeared to the King and promised to return Édáin to him, whereupon he produced fifty identical women, all of whom were the exact likeness of Édáin. Even though Eochaidh Airemh chose carefully, he actually chose his own daughter, and realised the mistake only much later, after she had borne him a son, CONAIRE MÓR.

The game of chess played between Midhir and Eochaidh Airemh is of special significance, for the playing of board games in Celtic mythology always signifies the interplay of great forces. It is at once both a magical and a cosmological game, which was to have later parallels in the interaction of the forces of good and evil, right and wrong.

MIDSUMMER NIGHT'S DREAM, A
Arthurian

Comedy by William SHAKESPEARE that was first performed in 1595 or 1596. Although not directly connected with the Arthurian legends, it is of great interest because of the inclusion of characters such as PUCK, OBERON and TITANIA.

MÍL(E)
Irish

The son or grandson of BREGON and the forefather of the first human rulers of IRELAND who were known as the Sons of MÍL ÉSPÁINE, or the Sons of

Míl of Spain. His brother ITH led the first expedition to Ireland, but was killed by the TUATHA DÉ DANANN. After the body of Ith had been brought back to Spain, Míl organised the second expedition under the leadership of DONN, EBER FINN and AMHAIRGHIN, and, although he did not accompany them himself, his son EREMON was among the invaders.

MÍL ÉSPÁINE, SONS OF
Irish

'The Sons of Míl of Spain', the tribal name of the sixth and final force of invaders, who came to IRELAND according to the *Leabhar Gabhála Éireann*. As their name suggests, they were of Spanish origin, the sons or descendants of MÍL, and they landed in Ireland on the feast of BELTANE under the leadership of AMHAIRGHIN, the FILI. They were the first true GAELS to inhabit Ireland.

Having defeated the TUATHA DÉ DANANN army, the invaders set out for TARA. On the way they met the three goddesses BANBHA, FÓDLA and ÉRIU, the wives, respectively, of MAC CUILL, MAC CÉCHT and MAC GRÉINE. The invaders promised each goddess in turn that the land would forever carry her name if she helped them in their cause, but it was only Ériu who countered by saying that Ireland would forever belong to their descendants, although she warned their discourteous king, DONN, that neither he nor his heirs would enjoy the land. Donn drowned shortly afterwards and was buried on the island of TECH DUIN, to which he now welcomes dead warriors. The help, advice and promise of Ériu caused the Sons of Míl Éspáine to name the land EIRE.

At Tara the three Tuatha Dé Danann kings disputed the right of the invaders to the ownership of the land, and they asked Amhairghin to judge each claim. He ruled that the invaders should put out to sea again beyond a magical boundary referred to as the ninth wave. This they did, but as they turned and tried to return to land the Tuatha Dé Danann conjured up a great wind to hold them offshore. Amhairghin called upon the SPIRIT OF IRELAND for help, and the wind duly dropped. The invaders once more landed, and again defeated a Tuatha Dé Danann army at the Battle of TAILTIU.

Although they had lost the right to rule, the Tuatha Dé Danann were determined not to be exiled from the land that had been theirs, and so they used their magic to deprive the Sons of Míl Éspáine of milk and corn. At length the invaders agreed to divide the land between them, the Tuatha Dé Danann receiving the underground half, and their leader, the DAGHDHA, built a SÍDH for each of the Tuatha Dé Danann chiefs and kings.

The new rulers of Ireland now faced their first problem. They had two leaders, EBER FINN and EREMON, both of whom claimed the right to be sole monarch. To settle the dispute, Eber Finn took the southern half of the country, and Eremon the northern. A short time later, the two kingdoms went to war, Eber Finn was killed and Eremon became the first human King of all Ireland.

MIL THE BLACK
Arthurian
Welsh tradition makes this character an opponent of ARTHUR, who killed him.

MILED
Irish
See MÍL(E)

MILES
Arthurian
The knightly lover of ELAINE, the daughter of PELLINORE, who committed suicide after his death.

MILESIANS
Irish
An alternative way of referring to the Sons of MÍL ÉSPÁINE.

MILUC(H)RA(DH)
Irish
A daughter of CULANN, smith to the TUATHA DÉ DANANN, and sister of AINÉ. Both sisters fell in love with FIONN MAC CUMHAILL, but Ainé said that she could never marry a man with grey hair. On hearing this, Miluchradh contrived to turn Fionn mac Cumhaill's hair grey, which assured her that Ainé would have nothing more to do with him. It did her little good though, for Fionn mac Cumhaill found out who had turned his hair grey, and afterwards would have nothing to do with Miluchradh.

'MINERVA'
Gaulish
An important Celtic goddess who was so called by JULIUS CAESAR, the inverted commas being used to distinguish her from the Roman goddess of the same name. It seems most likely that this goddess was none other than BRIGHID or BRIGANTIA.

MINOCAN
British
The name given by NENNIUS to the father of BELINUS.

MIODHCHAOIN

Irish

The warrior friend of CIAN. He was under a bond never to allow anyone to shout from the summit of the hill he lived on. When the three sons of TUIRENN came to the hill as the last of the tasks set them by LUGH as a fine for their murder of Cian, they had to fight Miodhchaoin, who would not allow them to complete their task. Miodhchaoin was eventually killed, but not until he had inflicted wounds that left each of the three sons of Tuirenn barely alive. They gave three feeble shouts from the top of the hill and so paid their fine to Lugh. When they beseeched Lugh to heal them, however, he refused, and they died on the hill.

MIRAUDE

Arthurian

The wife of TOREC. Having been sent to obtain the circlet belonging to his grandmother, Miraude promised to marry him if he successfully overcame the KNIGHTS OF THE ROUND TABLE, a feat he fulfilled.

MIROET

Arthurian

The son of an Irish King named ALVREZ and brother of KAMELIN. He and his brother both became KNIGHTS OF THE ROUND TABLE.

MNÁ SÍDH

Irish

A collective term, meaning 'women of the SÍDH', used to refer to goddesses. It was used to refer to any number of goddesses when they were being talked about generally rather than individually.

MOCC-OS, -US

Gaulish

The boar god; the deification of the pig as a totem animal. The word Moccos itself simply means 'pig'.

MOCHAEN

Irish

See MIODHCHAOIN

MOD

Irish

A compatriot of MANANNÁN MAC LIR. He joined in the hunt for a massive boar that was laying waste vast tracts of IRELAND. They chased the boar across to MUIC INIS, where their hounds cornered and killed the boar, although not until after Mod had been mortally gored.

MODENA

Arthurian

City in Emilia, Italy, capital of the province of Modena, lying north of Bologna. Its twelfth-century cathedral is of interest to Arthurian studies. Within the cathedral is an arch, the underside of which depicts Arthurian scenes that include several characters not known of anywhere else, whether in art or literature. This frieze is usually referred to as the Modena archivolt.

MODRON

Welsh and Arthurian

Ancient Welsh goddess, daughter of AVALLOC, whose name simply means 'Mother'. She is apparently a form of MATRONA, the Roman name for the Great Mother Goddess. Her divine child was known as MABON, which in turn simply means 'son' or 'son of the Mother'. She is thought to be the prototype of the Arthurian MORGAN Le Fay, though some Welsh sources make her the mother of OWAIN, the son of URIEN of RHEGED.

MODRWY ELUNED

Welsh and Arthurian

The ring of ELUNED, one of the THIRTEEN TREASURES OF BRITAIN, which made the wearer invisible.

MOEL ARTHUR

Arthurian

A hill in Clwyd, WALES, where, according to legend, ARTHUR's table was situated. A hill fort exists on the site, and it is quite possible that this was in use during the traditional period ascribed to Arthur. A survey of 1737 mentions a burial chamber named CIST ARTHUR, which has again been linked with the last resting place of Arthur.

MOFEBIS

Irish

The father of LOCH and a vassal of MEDHBHA and AILILL.

MOG RUITH

Irish

A DRUID who appears in a legend that says he once dressed in a bird costume, which he wore over an inner garment made from bull's hide. Then, in a trance, he rose into the air and abruptly vanished.

See also ROTH FAIL

MOINE

Arthurian

The name of the elder brother of AMBROSIUS

AURELIUS and UTHER, according to the *PROSE TRISTAN*. More commonly his name is given as CONSTANS. His real name was IVOINE, which is taken from IVOIRE, his mother's name, but he was given the name Moine, which means 'monk', as he was raised in a monastery.

MOLMUTIUS
British

The son of CLOTEN whose kingdom, CORNWALL, he inherited and immediately set about enlarging. The rest of ENGLAND was, at that time, ruled by a king named PINNER. Molmutius defeated his army, and Pinner fell in battle. He then defeated the combined forces of RUDAUCUS, King of CAMBRIA, and STATER, King of ALBANY, so that he reigned supreme, the twenty-first in line from BRUTUS. Molmutius reigned for forty years and during that time formulated the Molmutine Laws, which laid down a code of ethics that has survived, in some extent, to the present day. Molmutius was allegedly buried on the WHITE MOUNT in LONDON, where BENDIGEID VRAN's head had previously been buried, as had Brutus himself. He left two sons, BELINUS and BRENNIUS, both of whom laid claim to his throne, thus once again throwing BRITAIN into turmoil.

MOMUR
Arthurian

According to the French romance *HUON DE BORDEAUX*, the fairy realm ruled over by OBERON.

MONA
Romano-Celtic

The ancient name for the Isle of ANGLESEY.

MONGÁN
Irish

The son of FIACHNA LURGAN, although in truth the son of MANANNÁN MAC LIR, for Mongan was conceived when Manannán mac Lir appeared to Fiachna Lurgan's queen while her husband was in SCOTLAND and told her that unless she bore him a son her husband would die the very next day. She consented, for she had no other choice, and the next day the stranger had disappeared, only to reappear on the battlefield in Scotland, where he helped Fiachna Lurgan and AEDÁN MAC GABRÁIN win a great victory over the SAXONS. Three days after Mongán was born Manannán mac Lir came and took the child away to TÍR TAIRNGIRI, where he remained until he was either twelve or sixteen.

Mongán later used his magical skills to win back his wife, who had been abducted by a King of LEINSTER. He took the guise of AED, the son of the King of CONNACHT, and transformed a hag into the form of IBHELL, Aed's beautiful young wife. The King of Leinster fell in love with the pretend Ibhell, so Mongán agreed to exchange her for his own wife, although, of course, the King of Leinster did not find out about the trick until after Mongán and his wife were far away.

The historicity of Mongán is unquestionable, for he ruled at MOYLINNY on LOUGH NEAGH early in the seventh century, his death being recorded as *c.* 625. This would suggest that the strange tale of his conception and birth is possibly post-Christian. A contemporary legend says that Mongán was the reincarnation of FIONN MAC CUMHAILL, for he calls KEELTA back from the OTHERWORLD to settle a wager as to who actually killed FOTHAD. Keelta reveals that he himself had killed Fothad but adds that surely Mongán should have known that for he rode alongside him in his former life.

MONGIBEL
Arthurian

The name given to Mount ETNA on Sicily when it is mentioned in the Arthurian romances. It is mooted as the location to which MORGAN Le Fay intended to bring the wounded ARTHUR to effect his cure. The King was reported as being seen alive underneath the mountain by Gervase of Tilbury and Caesarius of Heisterbach.

MONT DU CHAT
Arthurian

Apparently the Alpine site ('Mountain of the Cat' or 'Cat Mountain') of the continental version of the CATH PALUG legend, where ARTHUR was said to have done battle with a large cat. A Savoyard was said to have met Arthur's men one night in the vicinity of this mountain and to have been taken by them to a palace that had vanished by the morning.

MOONREMUR
Irish

A warrior of ULSTER who tentatively challenged CET for the right to carve the boar of MAC DÁ THÓ, but was derided and quickly withdrew his challenge.

MOR
Welsh and Arthurian

1 According to tradition, the great-grandfather of MYRDDIN (MERLIN).

2 An alternative, although little-used, name for DYLAN EIL TON.

MORAINE
Arthurian

The realm of MANGOUN, who sent CARADOC BRIEFBRAS a horn that would indicate the fidelity of the wife of the drinker.

MORANN
Irish

A DRUID at the court of CONCHOBAR MAC NESSA who prophesied the arrival of SÉDANTA and the great deeds that that hero, better known as CÚ CHULAINN, would do.

MORAUNT
Arthurian

During a fight with this King of IRELAND and his ally, Sir MORHOLT, TRISTAN received poisoned wounds that were healed by ISEULT prior to her affair with him and her journey back to England to marry King MARK.

MORC
Irish

The co-ruler of the FOMHOIRÉ, along with CONANN, at the time of the rebellion of the people of NEMHEDH. Conann was killed in the battle, but Morc routed the rebellious people and forced the thirty survivors into exile.

MORCHADES
Arthurian
Also ORCADES

The name by which MORGAUSE is referred to in *DIU CRÔNE*. This would seem to indicate that she originated from the ORKNEYS, one of the realms of her husband, LOT. It appears to come from the Latin *Orcades* – 'Orkneys' – and it is Morchades that is thought to have been the origin of Morgause. A variant, Orcades, appears for this character in some translations of *Diu Crône*, which would seem to suggest that some translators literally translated her name, while other sought, through the use of Morchades, to bring her name into closer alignment with Morgause.

MORD-A, -U
Welsh and Arthurian

The blind man placed by CERRIDWEN to kindle the fire under the cauldron stirred by GWION BACH in which she was brewing a magical potion. When Gwion Bach ran away after imbibing the potency of the brew, Cerridwen at first blamed Morda and beat him so hard over the head with a billet of wood that one eye fell out onto his cheek. When Morda protested his innocence, Cerridwen stopped and saw that he was telling the truth, for it had been Gwion Bach who had spoiled her work.

MORDRAIN
Arthurian

The baptismal name taken by EVELAKE.

MO(R)DRED
Arthurian

The incest-begotten nephew of ARTHUR, son of LOT, who usurped the throne once Arthur had left him as his regent, when he undertook his continental campaign. Faking news of Arthur's death, Mordred had himself proclaimed king, and said that he would take GUINEVERE as his wife. She went to London and barricaded herself in the Tower of London, laying in sufficient provisions for a long siege. News reached Arthur of his nephew's treachery, and Mordred was duly defeated by Arthur on his return at the Battle of RICHBOROUGH. He was again defeated at WINCHESTER and pursued to CORNWALL, where the two forces met for the third, and final, battle, that of CAMLANN. Mordred was slain and Arthur taken off to the Isle of AVALON, so that his mortal wounds might be healed. This was reported to be in the year AD 542. *Ly Myreur des Histoires* claimed that Mordred survived the last battle, only to be subsequently defeated by LANCELOT. This work also says that Lancelot executed Guinevere, believing she had complied with Mordred's plans, and incarcerated the live Mordred in the same tomb as the dead Queen, Mordred cannibalising Guinevere before dying of starvation.

The *ANNALES CAMBRIAE* say that both Arthur and MEDRAWT (Mordred) perished at Camlann, but do not say that they were on opposing sides. This assertion does not come until later sources. GEOFFREY OF MONMOUTH says that Mordred was Arthur's nephew, the son of the King's sister ANNA and her husband, LOT. The idea that Mordred was the offspring of an incestuous relationship appears later, the earliest occurrence being in the *MORT ARTU*. Sir Thomas MALORY also carries this theme, saying that Mordred was the result of a liaison between Arthur and his sister MORGAUSE, though Arthur did not know they were related. When he discovered the truth, he attempted to kill Mordred by having all the children born on the same day as Mordred set adrift. Mordred

King Arthur fights his nephew Mordred, who is seeking to usurp the kingdom. (Mary Evans Picture Library/ Arthur Rackham Collection)

was shipwrecked, but survived and was fostered and raised by NABUR. The *MABINOGION* story of the *DREAM OF RHONABWY* makes Mordred Arthur's foster son as well as his nephew. WACE makes Mordred the brother of Guinevere, whom Arthur had seized and made his queen. The *ALLITERATIVE MORTE ARTHURE* further states that Mordred and Guinevere had a child.

As an adult, Mordred came to Arthur's court, was made a knight and was, for some time, the companion of Lancelot. When the ruling family of the ORKNEYS were in conflict with PELLINORE, Mordred took their side in the battle and killed LAMORAK, Pellinore's son. Early Welsh sources tend to portray Mordred as a heroic figure, rather than a villain, and Welsh tradition says he married CYWYLLOG, daughter of CAW, by whom he had two sons.

MORFESSA

Irish

A wizard of the mythical city of FALIA. He was one of the four wizards to teach the TUATHA DÉ DANANN their magical arts prior to their arrival in IRELAND. He is said to have given them the LIA FÁIL or Stone of FÁL. The other three wizards said to have taught the Tuatha Dé Danann were ESIAS from GORIAS, USCIAS from FINDIAS and SIMIAS from MURIAS.

MORFRAN (AB TEGID)

Welsh and Arthurian

Also MORVRAN AB TEGID

The ugly and hapless son of CERRIDWEN and TEGID VOEL who was nicknamed AFAGDDU. One of the TWENTY-FOUR KNIGHTS of ARTHUR's court, he was said to have survived the final battle at CAMLANN on account of his extreme ugliness. He was believed to be a devil, so no one dared attack him. Some sources name Afagddu and Morfran as independent characters, and in this case it would seem to have been Afagddu who survived Camlann.

MORFUDD

Arthurian

The twin sister of OWAIN in Welsh tradition. She was the lover of CYNON, the son of one of ARTHUR's warriors, CLYDNO.

MORGAN

Arthurian

The name of at least two characters from Arthurian legend.

(1) Morgan Le Fay (Morgan the Fairy). First referred to by GEOFFREY OF MONMOUTH in his *VITA MERLINI* as the chief of the nine *fays*, or fairies, living in the OTHERWORLD realm of AVALON. MERLIN and TALIESIN accompanied the dying ARTHUR on the barge steered by BARINTHUS to the Isle of APPLES following the battle of CAMLANN, there to be healed by Morgan Le Fay, the chief of nine sisters who included MORONOE, MAZOE, GLITEN, GLITONEA, CLITON, TYRONOE and THITIS. No mention is made at this early date of any relationship between Morgan and the dying king, but she is described as the shape-changing mistress of therapy, music and the arts who could fly through the air on enchanted wings. She also appears in this role as Queen ARGANTE (MARGANTE) in *BRUT* by LAYAMON. Later romances represent her as a fearsome witch queen, most probably due to Christian hostility, though it also seems that her later character may have been influenced by memories of the ancient Irish goddess, the MÓRRÍGHAN. In medieval romance she is Arthur's illegitimate half-sister who was educated in a convent, where she perversely spent her days studying the powers of evil. The ambivalent LADY OF THE LAKE is also said to be another aspect of the same character.

Sir Thomas MALORY makes her the daughter of IGRAINE by her first marriage, and thus half-sister to Arthur, while both the *Vulgate Merlin*, a part of the *VULGATE VERSION*, and the *HUTH-MERLIN* make her the daughter of LOT, and thus Arthur's niece. She became a lady-in-waiting to GUINEVERE and fell in love with GIOMAR, Arthur's nephew. Guinevere, however, parted them and, as a result, according to some versions of the story, Morgan sowed the seeds of doubt in Arthur's mind concerning the affair between Guinevere and LANCELOT. She learned much of her magic from Merlin, though this seems to contradict earlier sources that say she learned these skills while a student in a convent. She was said to have married URIEN, according to traditional sources, and was the mother of OWAIN. Her lover was ACCOLON of GAUL, whom she coerced into attempting to murder Arthur, though unsuccessfully. She was also said to have fallen in love with Lancelot and to have imprisoned him, but he managed to escape. Sir Thomas Malory, who seems to have drawn on many of the earlier sources, echoes most of these stories about her, stating that she was one of the queens on the barge that bore the dying Arthur to Avalon, rather than the queen to whom he was taken to be healed.

Her origin almost certainly lies with the goddess MODRON, who in turn had her origin in MATRONA. Modron was thought to have married the historical figure of Urien of RHEGED, and to have borne him two children, Owain and his twin sister MORFUDD. Though she is usually associated solely with the Arthurian legends, many commentators have drawn on the fact that she existed in earlier times. The *Roman de Troie*, published *c.* 1160, states that she was alive during the Greek siege of Troy, while *PERCEFOREST* places her in early BRITAIN. Her divinity also seems to have been apparent to the romancers, for the anonymous author of *SIR GAWAIN AND THE GREEN KNIGHT* refers to her as 'Morgan the goddess' (line 2452).

While it would appear that her name has Irish or Welsh origins, there is a popular belief that the name Morgan itself may be Breton, for a belief was held there in a class of water-fairies called MARI-MORGAN(S), or simply MORGAN(S). One particular MORGAN, identified as AHES or DAHUT, was thought to have caused the destruction of the legendary city of YS. Her wickedness seems to have been caused through a combination of many different characteristics, though in origin she may have been an ambivalent figure whose character did nothing to inspire the authors of the Arthurian romances.

As the romances spread throughout the continent, so did the character of Morgan Le Fay. One of the most famous sights connected with this fairy, good or evil, is a mirage that sometimes appears in the Straits of Messina, and that is locally referred to as FATA MORGANA, or in French as Le CHÂTEAU DE MORGAN LE FEE. This mirage, which distorts both vertically and horizontally, is thought to give the image of one of Morgan's fairy palaces. French and Italian romance further embroider her character. In ARIOSTO's *ORLANDO FURIOSO* she is given two sisters, MORGANETTA and LOGISTILLA, while other Italian romances gave her a daughter named PULZELLA GAIA. The Italian poet Torquato Tasso (1544–95) gave her three daughters, Morganetta, NIVETTA and CARVILIA, while the *Vita di Merlino* (an Italian version of the *VITA MERLINI*) stated that she was the illegitimate daughter of the Duke of TINTAGEL. The thirteenth-century French romance *LI JUS ADEN* associates her with companions named MAGLORE and ARSILE.

(2) The illegitimate daughter of the Duke of TINTAGEL. While the Italian *Vita di Merlino* makes this character the same as MORGAN Le Fay, she is quite separate and married NENTRES.

MORGAN(S)

Gaulish

A type of Breton water-fairy, more usually known as MARI-MORGAN(S).

MORGAN THE BLACK

Arthurian

A son of ARTHUR, according to the *PETIT BRUT* of Rauf de BOUN.

MORGAN FRYCH

Welsh and Arthurian

The father of MYRDDIN (MERLIN), according to tradition. He was sometimes identified as MADOG MORFRYN and sometimes said to have been a prince of GWYNEDD, some sources even speculating that he is a historical character.

MORGAN MWYNFAWR

Welsh and Arthurian

The owner of a magical form of transport, described as either a chair or a car, which could carry a person seated in it to wherever he or she wanted to go. This magical item was known as CADAIR, NEU CAR MORGAN MWYNFAWR, and it numbered among the THIRTEEN TREASURES OF BRITAIN. Some commentators have incorrectly sought to identify the ownership of this enchanted mode of travel with MORGAN Le Fay.

MORGAN THE RED

Arthurian

One of the numerous sons attributed to ARTHUR.

MORGAN TUD

Arthurian

The name of ARTHUR's physician.

MORGANETTA

Arthurian

According to the poet Torquato Tasso (1544–95), the daughter of MORGAN Le Fay.

MORGAN(N)A

Arthurian

A variant of MORGAN Le Fay that has found widespread popularity in later works, particularly film and television.

MORGANNWG

Arthurian

A minor kingdom of WALES of which CARADOC was alleged to have been the progenitor of the royal line.

MORGANNWG, IOLO
Arthurian

The bardic name of Edward Williams (1747–1826). His renditions of Arthurian legends are held to be most unreliable, for, being a bard, he undoubtedly felt he could improve on the material he used as his sources.

MORGAUSE
Arthurian

Half-sister to ARTHUR, wife of LOT and mother of GAWAIN, GAHERIS, AGRAVAIN, GARETH and MORDRED. Various romances credit her with a number of affairs. The *ENFACES GAUVAIN* makes Lot her page, with whom she had a brief liaison, which resulted in the birth of Gawain. Sir Thomas MALORY, however, makes her Lot's queen, her usual role, but says that she had a brief affair with Arthur, who did not know they were related, and subsequently gave birth to Mordred. When her son Gaheris found her in bed with LAMORAK, the son of PELLINORE, following the death of Lot at the hands of her lover's father, her son killed her.

It appears that Morgause may not have been the original name of this character, and it may indeed simply be a territorial designation, much in the same way as her husband's name Lot means 'LOTHIAN-ruler'. This seems likely, for in *DIU CRÔNE* she is referred to as ORCADES or MORCHADES, which seems to indicate that she originally hailed from the ORKNEYS, which was one of Lot's kingdoms (the Latin for Orkneys, *Orcades*). The variant Morchades is thought to have given rise to Morgause. In Malory, the wife of Lot is called Anna, the sister of Arthur, while in *DE ORTU WALUUANII* Morgause is replaced again by Anna, though this time in the role given in the *Enfaces Gauvain*, the mother of Gawain, following a secret intrigue with her page, Lot.

MORGEN
Welsh and Arthurian

A DRUIDIC goddess, patroness of priestesses, who lived on an island usually identified as AVALON with her nine sisters, who included MORONOE, MAZOE, GLITEN, GLITONEA, CLITON, TYRONOE and THITIS.

There can be little doubt that Morgen is the original of the Arthurian MORGAN Le Fay, although she herself seems to have her origins in MODRON, who, in turn, has her origins in MATRONA. One account says that she was a historical person who married URIEN of RHEGED and bore MORFUDD and OWAIN.

GIRALDUS CAMBRENSIS refers to her as a *dea phantastica* (imaginary goddess), although earlier sources say she was the master of the healing arts, could fly on artificial wings and could change her shape. It was once believed that Morgen, and subsequently the Arthurian Morgan Le Fay, originated in the Irish MÓRRÍGHAN, but this has now been almost universally discounted. Her name change may have been effected in BRITTANY, where there was a belief in a class of water-fairies known as MORGAN(S), or more correctly MARI-MORGAN(S). They also believed in one particular Morgan, known as DAHUT or AHES, who, it was said, caused the destruction of the legendary city of YS.

With such a diverse origin it is not difficult to see why so many attributes were added to her character when later romancers made her the incestuous sister of King ARTHUR, a magician on a par with MERLIN, but malevolent rather than benevolent.

MORGHE
Arthurian

A variant of MORGAN Le Fay used by Jean d'Outremeuse of Liege in *Ly Myreur des histoires*, written sometime prior to 1400.

MORHOLT
Arthurian

During a fight with this giant knight, who is also known as MARHALT, and his ally MORAUNT, King of IRELAND, who demanded a tribute from his uncle, King MARK of Cornwall, TRISTAN received poisoned wounds that were healed by ISEULT. It was this that led Tristan to report Iseult's beauty to his uncle, and ultimately led to their famous yet ill-fated affair.

MORIAEN
Arthurian

The son of AGLOVALE by a Moorish princess, according to the Dutch romance *Moriaen*. Aglovale left the princess before the birth of his son, but the couple were eventually reunited thanks to Moriaen. It appears that this romance was based on an earlier French romance in which PERCEVAL featured as the father of Moriaen.

MORIATH
Irish

The daughter of SCORIATH, King of FERAMORC. She fell passionately in love with the youth MAON while he stayed within the royal court, even though he was a mute. Later he left for GAUL, but she found she could not forget him. She sent her father's harper CRAFTINY to Gaul to serenade Maon on her behalf. So beautiful was the music that Maon regained the use of his voice, and, after he had returned to IRELAND (by which time he was known as LABRAIDH LOINGSECH) and disposed of his usurping uncle COVAC, he married Moriath.

MORNA
Irish

The leader of one of the clans that made up the FIAN, and the father of AODH, who later became known as GOLL MAC MORNA.
See also BASCNA

MOROIE MOR
Arthurian

According to Gaelic tradition, the son of ARTHUR, known as the FOOL OF THE FOREST, who was born at DUMBARTON.

MORONOE
Welsh and Arthurian

One of the nine sisters of MORGEN (MORGAN Le Fay).

MÓRRÍGHAN
Irish and Arthurian
Also BAV

The red-haired goddess of battle and procreation, whose name means 'Phantom Queen', she often appeared in triple form, one of the myriad of triad deities that clutter Celtic and other pagan cultures. Her other aspects were NEMHAIN, which means 'Frenzy', and BADHBH, which means 'Crow' or 'Raven'. The Mórríghan combines the energies of life and death, sexuality and conflict, in one all powerful and terrifying deity. She had a British counterpart in the goddess ANDRASTE, who was invoked by Queen BOUDICCA during her revolt against the Romans in the first century.

Although essentially a goddess of death, the Mórríghan was also a consummate fertility goddess, who is commemorated in a range of low hills known as the Paps of the Mórríghan. The combination of a goddess of death and one of fertility is illustrated in the story of the DAGHDHA, who met the Mórríghan shortly before the Second Battle of MAGH TUIREDH. The Daghdha came across the terrible goddess on the eve of the feast of SAMHAIN as she stood astride the River UNIUS washing the bloody corpses and armour of those foredoomed to die in the coming battle. The two had intercourse in this uncomfortable position, such a ritual mating signi-fying that, although many were to die, many would ultimately be born to take their place.

Though Irish in this form, she was known throughout the Celtic world and is thought by some to have been the prototype for MORGAN Le Fay.

MORRIGU
Irish

A little-used variant of the MÓRRÍGHAN.

MORT ARTU
Arthurian

A part of the French *VULGATE VERSION* of Arthurian romance.

MORTAISE
Arthurian

A lake or sea beside which LANCELOT, during his quest for the Holy GRAIL, lay down and, in his sleep, received a vision that told him to enter the first ship he came to. He did so and was joined about a month later by his son, GALAHAD, and together they continued their quest.

MORTE ARTHURE
Arthurian

A Middle English Arthurian poem by Thomas HEYWOOD (*c.* 1574–1641) that was written towards the close of the sixteenth century.

MORUAWR
Arthurian

Variant of MORVAWR found in the descent of ARTHUR and LLYR contained in the Mostyn MS 117.

MORVAWR
Arthurian

Also MORUAWR, TURMWR MORVAWR

This character appears in a number of Welsh pedigrees as a paternal ancestor of ARTHUR.

MORVRAN (AB TEGID)
Welsh and Arthurian
See MORFRAN (AB TEGID)

MORWEN
Arthurian

The wife of IVOR the Huntsman who fostered and raised MERIADOC.

MORYDD
Welsh and Arthurian

The grandfather of (MYRDDIN) MERLIN, according to a traditional Welsh genealogy.

The Mórríghan, the goddess of procreation and battle. (By permission of artist Paul Borda/© Dryad Designs, www.dryaddesign.com)

MOTE OF MARK
Arthurian
Iron age fortress that has yielded pottery dating from *c.* AD 500, leading some to propose it as a possible location for the encampment of a mighty chieftain who might be cognate with the historical figure who has, over the centuries, become known as King ARTHUR.

MOTHER GODDESS
General
A generic term used to denote the beneficent powers of the earth, which were normally personified in a powerful fertility goddess. The Mother Goddess, sometimes called the Earth Goddess, is common to most pagan cultures, and she was usually developed so that various aspects of her all-powerful nature manifested themselves in many different deities.

MOTHERS, THE
Celtic and Teutonic
A collective name given to goddesses of plenty who were worshipped during the Roman period by both the Celts and Teutonic tribes. The Mothers were usually a triad of goddesses, who represented a triple aspect of the MOTHER GODDESS. In WALES they are commemorated in the *Y Foel Famau*, the 'Hall of the Mothers', one of the Welsh mothers being the ill-fated BRANWEN.

MOYLINNY
Irish
The capital on Lough Neagh where the historical MONGÁN ruled.

MOYS
Arthurian
A follower of JOSEPH OF ARIMATHEA, according to ROBERT DE BORON. He wished to sit in the SIEGE PERILOUS at the ROUND TABLE, but the earth opened and swallowed him for his presumptuous behaviour.

MOYTURA
Irish
The literal pronunciation of MAGH TUIREDH, the location of the two famous battles of the TUATHA DÉ DANANN, although the two battles were actually fought in different locations.

MUCCA MHANANNAIN
Irish
'Pigs of Manannán', the mythical food of the gods. These pigs crop up in a great many of the Irish myths and are described as varying in number from two to many hundreds. No matter how many there are, they always have the same attribute, for, killed, cooked and eaten one day, they are alive and willing to go through the same process the next.

MUGHAIN
Irish
A Queen of ULSTER. When she saw the battle-crazed CÚ CHULAINN, who had just defeated the three terrible sons of NECHTA SCÉNE, approaching EMHAIN MHACHA, she led her women out to meet him, all of them stark naked. Overcome with embarrassment, Cú Chulainn averted his eyes and was seized by the King's warriors, who dunked him in three tubs of icy cold water to cool him down. The Queen then dressed the hero herself before admitting him to the royal court.

MUGNA
Irish
A mythical oak tree upon which three fruits – acorn, apple and nut – grew, each fruit being instantly replaced by a fresh one when it fell. It is possibly a remembrance of a world-tree, similar to the tree Yggdrasil that is found in Norse mythology.

MUIC INIS
Irish
'Pig Island', the name given to the island to which MANANNÁN MAC LIR and MOD chased a huge boar where their hounds cornered it. The boar was killed, but not until after it had mortally gored Mod.

MU(I)RCHEARTACH
Irish and Arthurian
A historical fifth-century Irish King ruling at TARA who is thought to have been the origin of the various characters named MARHAUS and MARHALT in the Arthurian tales.

MUIRDRIS
Irish
A hideous monster, a sort of river-horse, said to inhabit Loch RURY. One day FERGHUS MAC LEDA came face to face with the monster and was so scarred that his face was permanently disfigured. Since no blemished man could reign, his courtiers banished all mirrors from the palace so that Ferghus mac Leda would not find out what had happened and would thus be allowed to remain the monarch. He remained blissfully ignorant of the fact, until one day a maidservant, whom he had slapped for some misdemeanour, retaliated by telling him of his

disfigurement. Ferghus mac Leda donned the magic water-shoes he had received as part of his ransom for IUBDAN and BEBO, and went out onto the waters of Loch Rury, where he beheaded the Muirdris before sinking below the waves, never to be seen again.

MUIREARTACH
Irish

A one-eyed, hideous hag whose husband was an ocean god, some say a smith. While she was the foster mother of the King of LOCHLANN, she captured from the FIAN the ceremonial cup of victory, a clay vessel whose contents made them victorious. The fian attacked her, killed the King of Lochlann and regained the cup. Muireartach recovered and stormed the fian, killing a great many of them before FIONN MAC CUMHAILL cut out the ground from under her and then cut her to shreds.

MU(I)RN-E, -A
Irish

The daughter of TADHG and thus a granddaughter of NUADHA AIRGEDLÁMH and sister to TUIREANN. Muirne's hand was sought by CUMHAILL, but Tadhg refused, whereupon Cumhaill abducted her. He was then killed in battle when he refused to return her to her father. Muirne had already conceived by the time Cumhaill was killed, and she called her son DEIMNE. He was raised in isolation and later became better known as FIONN MAC CUMHAILL.

MULE SANS FREIN
Arthurian

A damsel brought this bridleless mule to ARTHUR's court and requested a knight should be dispatched to find the missing tackle. KAY was sent on this quest, but failed. Subsequently GAWAIN managed to complete the task, though how he achieved this is not recorded.

MULE SANS FREIN
Arthurian

A twelfth-century French poem concerning the quest of GAWAIN to locate a missing bridle. The author is usually given as Paien de Maisière, but this could be a pseudonym.

MULLO
Gaulish

The patron god of mules and asses, whose name simply means 'mule'.

MULLOGUE
Irish

A FOMHOIRÉ warrior who, with his companion MAOL, was sent by BALAR to demand the right to spend the first night with any of the new brides of any of Balar's tenants. On one such occasion GOIBHNIU was at the wedding feast and, horrified by the idea, he killed both Maol and Mullogue and so put an end to the foul custom.

MUMU
Irish

One of the four Irish provinces that are referred to in the *Taín Bó Cuailngè*. The capital of Mumu was in west Kerry, the province itself later becoming better known as MUNSTER.

MUNSALVAESCHE
Arthurian

According to WOLFRAM VON ESCHENBACH, this was the name of the mountain where the GRAIL was kept. The name, meaning 'wild mountain', probably derives from Wildenberc, Wolfram von Eschenbach's home, modern Wehlenberg near Ansbach, and shows his attempt to claim the Grail for his home country.

MUNSTER
Irish

One of the original five provinces of IRELAND that were established by the FIR BHOLG. Munster remained an independent kingdom until the twelfth century. Today, it is still a province occupying the southern part of Ireland and consisting of the counties of Clare, Cork, Kerry, Limerick, North and South Tipperary and Waterford.

MUREIF
Arthurian

The realm of URIEN, according to GEOFFREY OF MONMOUTH. Some think that it may be identifiable with Monreith, but it is usually taken to refer to Moray.

MURIAS
Irish

A mythical city that was the home of SIMIAS, one of the four wizards who were said to have taught the TUATHA DÉ DANANN all their magic arts before their arrival in IRELAND. Murias was said to have given the DAGHDHA his inexhaustible cauldron. The other three wizards are named as MORFESSA of FALIA, ESIAS of GORIAS and USCIAS of FINDIAS.

NEFYN

Welsh and Arthurian

The daughter of BRYCHAN who married CYNFARCH and subsequently became the mother of URIEN.

NEIT

Irish

The King of the TUATHA DÉ DANANN who was killed by the FOMHOIRÉ shortly before the arrival of ITH in IRELAND. Ith was asked to judge who should be the next king, but he admired Ireland so much while reaching his conclusion that Tuatha Dé Denann mortally wounded him, and he died on his way back to his homeland, which some sources name as Spain.

NEMED

Irish

A simple variant of NEMHEDH.

NEMEDIANS

Irish

A name often used to refer to those followers of NEMHEDH whom he led to IRELAND.

NEMEDIUS

Irish

Irish tradition states that the son of Nemedius was the eponym of BRITAIN because he was apparently called 'Britain' and settled on the island. This is, however, not the accepted manner by which Britain gained its name.

NEMETONA

Romano-Celtic

The goddess of the grove (*nemed* or *nemeton* means 'grove'). She held special significance to the Celts, who regarded woodlands as spiritual places. Her name, it is thought, might be a derivation of NEMHEDH.

NEMGLAN

Irish

The King of the Birds is one of the possible fathers of CONAIRE MÓR, for it is said that he visited the maiden MESS BUACHALLA while she was hidden away. She conceived his son, who was to be passed off as the son of ETERSCEL.

NEM(H)A(I)N

Irish

'Frenzy', one of the aspects or forms of the MÓRRÍGHAN.

NEM(H)ED(H)

Irish

According to the *LEABHAR GABHÁLA ÉIREANN*, the leader of the third invasion of IRELAND. Nemhedh, son of AGNOMAN, and his company of just eight others, who were thenceforth known as the 'People of Nemhedh' or Nemedians, met no resistance when they arrived in Ireland, for the former inhabitants, those who had come to the island under the leadership of PARTHOLÁN, had been wiped out by a plague. Nemhedh and his people cleared twelve plains and made four lakes, thus furthering the work already started by the previous inhabitants.

Following the death of Nemhedh, his people were conquered by the monstrous FOMHOIRÉ, who, every SAMHAIN, demanded a tribute of two-thirds of their corn, wine and children. Finally, unable to withstand any more, the people rebelled and attacked the Fomhoiré stronghold, an attack that left only one boatload of survivors. These survivors split into two groups, one fleeing to Greece and the other to unnamed northern lands. The former group later returned as the FIR BHOLG, GAILIÓIN and FIR DHOMHNANN, while the latter were to reappear much later as the fifth invasionary force, by which time they were known as the TUATHA DÉ DANANN.

NENNIUS

British and Arthurian

1 Welsh writer (*fl.* 769) who was reputedly the author of the clumsily put together Latin work *Historia Britonum*, which purports to give a history of BRITAIN from the time of JULIUS CAESAR until towards the end of the seventh century. The book gives mythical accounts of the origins of the Britons, the settlement of the SAXONS and King ARTHUR's twelve victories.

2 The brother of LUD and CASSIVELAUNUS. He was known as NYNNIAW to the Welsh, who named his brothers as LLUDD, CASWALLAWN and LLEFELYS. Nennius is alleged to have fought JULIUS CAESAR in battle and, although mortally wounded, managed to take Caesar's sword from him. The sword was later buried beside him.

NENTRES

Arthurian

Although one of the eleven rulers who rebelled against the youthful ARTHUR at the start of his reign, this ruler of GARLOT married ELAINE, Arthur's half-sister, and eventually became a KNIGHT OF THE ROUND TABLE.

NERA

Irish

A courtier at the court of AILILL and MEDHBHA. During a feast held on SAMHAIN he left the proceedings and went outside. There a corpse, hanging from the gallows, complained of thirst. Nera took it down and gave it a drink. When he re-entered the hall he found that all those at the feast, except Ailill and Medhbha, had been killed by a SÍDH host, which he pursued into the OTHERWORLD. There he was hospitably greeted by the King, who immediately gave him a wife and a home, a gift he was to repay by collecting the King's firewood. Almost a year had passed when his wife warned him that she had foreseen the sídh host attacking the court of Ailill and Medhbha on the coming feast of Samhain. Nera secretly left the Otherworld to warn Ailill and Medhbha, taking primroses, fern and wild garlic with him to prove his whereabouts for the last year. Ailill and Medhbha set out with a large company from the court and destroyed the sídh, but Nera had already returned to his wife and so was caught in the Otherworld, with no way of ever returning.

NEREJA

Arthurian

The female emissary of the beleaguered Queen AMENE. She was sent to ARTHUR's court to obtain help in defending her territory from the evil ROAZ, who had already almost totally overrun it.

NERO

Arthurian

The brother of RIENCE who fought against, but was defeated by, ARTHUR.

NESSA

Irish

The daughter of ECHID, wife of FACHTNA and mother of CONCHOBAR MAC NESSA.

NESTOR

Arthurian

1 The brother of King BAN of BRITTANY and the father of BLEOBERIS who was accidentally killed by his son.
2 The son of BLEOBERIS and thus grandson of the first Nestor.

NET

Irish

The war god of the FOMHOIRÉ and grandfather of BALAR.

NETOR

Arthurian

The King of BULGARIA in Arthurian romance.

NEUSTRIA

Arthurian

The duchy ascribed to BEDIVERE by GEOFFREY OF MONMOUTH.

NEW GRANGE

Irish

The common name for BRUGH NA BÓINNE, the home of the DAGHDHA and then of OENGHUS MAC IN OG. After TARA, New Grange is the most important Bronze Age monument in IRELAND.

NIAL NOÍGIALLACH

Irish

'Nial of the Nine Hostages', the founder of the fifth Irish province, which was formed by the division of the ancient ULAIDH. He established his capital at TARA. The UÍ NÉILL, his descendants, gained control over all of central and northern IRELAND. These descendants of Nial Noígiallach are believed to have been a new group of invading Celts, the sixth such invasion to land on the island. In the legendary tales they are referred to as the Sons of MÍL ÉSPÁINE.

Nial Noígiallach was considered by some to be a historical person, the foster son of the poet TORNA ÉICES, who came from MUNSTER. His father was named as EOCHU MUGMEDÓN, while his mother was a Saxon from Britain, sometimes named as CAIRENN.

NIAM(H)

Irish

(1) The daughter of CELTCHAR and wife of CONALL CERNACH. Together with DEICHTINE, CONCHOBAR MAC NESSA and CATHBHADH, she begged CÚ CHULAINN not to be enticed into attacking the sons of CALATIN, for they knew that this would lead to his death, after one of Calatin's daughters, BAVE, had assumed the form of Niamh and implored him to protect ULSTER against its foes.

(2) The exquisite daughter of the King of TÍR INNA NOC whom OISÍN accompanied to her home. He remained there for 300 years, although to him it seemed that only a week had passed. Some versions of the story say that he became the King after he had out-raced Niamh's father, who had said he would abdicate in favour of any son-in-law who could beat him in a foot race. Other accounts say that he also killed a giant who had abducted the daughter of the King of TÍR INNA MBÉO.

A corridor within New Grange, the most important Bronze Age monument in Ireland. (© Gianni Dagli Orti/Corbis)

At length, Oisîn began to miss his homeland and arranged to return, although Niamh did her best to dissuade him. When she saw that this was hopeless, she instructed him not to dismount from his horse, otherwise he would never be able to return. Back in IRELAND he found that the FIAN had been long forgotten and a new faith filled the land. On his way back to Niamh, he stopped to help some peasants, but as soon as he dismounted his horse disappeared and he became a blind and decrepit old man.

NICODEMUS
Arthurian
The cadaver of this biblical character was first said to have been kept at CAMELOT, and subsequently at the GRAIL CASTLE. Finally it was said to have accompanied PERCEVAL on board the ship on which he made his final journey.

NIMIANE
Arthurian
An early version of NIMUE/NINIANE/VIVIANE/ VIVIEN/VIVIENNE, the LADY OF THE LAKE.

NIMUE
Arthurian
The lover of MERLIN and one of the names applied to the LADY OF THE LAKE, who is also known as NIMIANE, NINEVE, NINIANE, VIVIANE, VIVIEN and VIVIENNE.

Merlin became so infatuated with her that he taught her his magic arts, but she turned against him and imprisoned him in a tower, cave, tomb or oak tree where she could visit him, but from which he could not escape. It was said that the enchantment that held Merlin prisoner could be broken only when ARTHUR once more reigned. Having imprisoned Merlin, she became the lover of PELLEAS. Her father was named as DIONES, a vavasour – holder of feudal lands but lesser in rank than a baron. Her name appears to have a mythological origin, possibly deriving from the Irish Niamh or the Welsh RHIANNON.

NINE SISTERS
Arthurian
The collective term by which the sisters of MORGAN Le Fay, joint rulers of AVALON, are referred to. It is not certain whether or not all are named, but various sources suggest that this is the correct number.

NINEVE
Arthurian
A variant of NIMUE. Some sources, however, make her an entirely separate character, saying that she was the daughter of a Sicilian siren.

NINIANE
Arthurian
A variant of NIMUE.

NIOBE
Arthurian
The lover of SAGREMOR.

NIS-IEN, -SYEN
Welsh
The son of PENARDUN and EUROSSWYD, brother of EFNISIEN and half-brother to BENDIGEID VRAN, MANAWYDAN FAB LLYR and BRANWEN. Described as a gentle youth who would do no one any harm, he appears briefly in the story of Branwen and MATHOLWCH as a mediator, but after that nothing more is heard of him.

NIVETTA
Arthurian
According to the Italian poet Torquato Tasso (1544–95), a daughter of MORGAN Le Fay.

NIWALEN
Welsh
'White Track', the goddess of the road or spirit of the journey. She is also known as OLWEN, the name under which she appears as the daughter of the giant YSPADDADEN.

NOAH
Biblical, Irish and British
A biblical patriarch who was chosen by God to survive the Flood along with his family, and their families, and two of every living creature. Several of Noah's descendants are alleged to have found their way to IRELAND, among them CESAIR, his granddaughter by way of BITH, and his son, who was said to have been among the first settlers of Ireland. The ancient Britons also laid claim to a biblical ancestry by saying that ALBION and his race of giants, the first inhabitants of BRITAIN, came from a race of giants living in Africa who were descended from HAM, another of Noah's sons, although the Irish also claimed a connection to Ham, saying that the FOMHOIRÉ were descended from him.
See also DWYFACH, DWYFAN.

NOD-ENS, -ONS
Romano-British and Arthurian
The tutelary deity of the healing sanctuary at

Lydney, Gloucestershire, although by no means solely confined to that site. Nodens was the Romano-Celtic version of NUDD and a god with definite connections to both healing and water, his totem animal appearing to have been the dog. The Romans sometimes equated him with their own god Neptune, a connection that led Nodens to be regarded, by some, as a sea deity. His name is likely to be a derivative of his Irish counterpart NUADHA AIRGEDLÁMH, while his Welsh equivalent appears to have been LLUDD LAW EREINT, or perhaps NUDD, from whom his name might also have been derived.

NORHOUT
Arthurian
MELIODAS, the father of TRISTAN, was killed by soldiers under the control of the count who ruled this region.

NORICUM
General
An ancient Celtic kingdom in the eastern Alps, of which Bolenos was the tutelary deity.

NORTHGALIS
Arthurian
An Arthurian kingdom that appears to be identifiable with North WALES, but that might, at least at times, have been used to identify a north Briton kingdom, say STRATHCLYDE, for it was said to have been near to NORTHUMBERLAND. The *ESTOIRE DEL SAINTE GRAAL* names an early king of this realm as COUDEL, who fell while fighting the Christians. WOLFRAM VON ESCHENBACH makes its ruler HERZELOYDE, while it is, elsewhere, given kings named CRADELMENT and ALOIS.

The kingdom may have its origin in the realm ruled by a king named CADWALLON, said to have ruled the VENDOTII (according to GEOFFREY OF MONMOUTH) during the traditional Arthurian period.

NORTHUMBERLAND
Arthurian
A realm in northern England that, in the Arthurian romances, is variously ruled by the Kings PELLINORE, CLARION, CADOR and DETORS.

NORTHUMBRIA
British
The ANGLO-SAXON kingdom that covered north-east ENGLAND and south-east SCOTLAND, consisting of the sixth-century kingdoms of Bernicia (Forth–Tees) and Deira (Tees–Humber), which were united in the seventh century. It accepted the supremacy of WESSEX AD 827 and was conquered by the Danes in the late ninth century.

NORWAY
Arthurian
Although it is impossible to say how complete a kingdom Norway was during the Arthurian period, the country possibly being divided between many smaller kings and chieftains, the country was, according to GEOFFREY OF MONMOUTH, ruled by King SICHELM, who bequeathed the realm to LOT. ARTHUR had to enforce Lot's right to the throne, for it had been usurped by RICULF. Geoffrey of Monmouth further states that the King of Norway, ODBRICT at this time, supported Arthur at CAMLANN, but met his own death that day.

NUADHA (AIRGEDLÁMH)
Irish
The leader of the TUATHA DÉ DANANN, who was originally known without his epithet. However, even though he possessed an inescapable sword that he had brought with him when the Tuatha Dé Danann arrived in IRELAND, Nuadha lost an arm during the First Battle of MAGH TUIREDH. Since no physically imperfect king could retain the throne, he was forced to abdicate in favour of the tyrannical BRES. Bres was himself forced to abdicate some time later. During the time Bres was King of the Tuatha Dé Danann, the giant leech (physical) DIAN CÉCHT, with the assistance of CREIDHNE, fitted Nuadha with an artificial arm made out of silver, this arm earning him his epithet, which simply means 'Silver Hand'. With the throne vacant after the abdication of Bres, Nuadha Airgedlámh was reinstated as the king, a position he held until just before the Second Battle of Magh Tuiredh, when LUGH arrived at the court. Recognising the newcomer's superiority, Nuadha Airgedlámh abdicated in his favour.

NUADHA OF THE SILVER HAND
Irish
The literal translation from the Irish of NUADHA AIRGEDLÁMH.

NUC
Arthurian
The father of YDER who fought his son, both parties being ignorant of the other's identity. However, during the course of the fight they recognised each other and stopped. Nuc eventually married Yder's

mother, suggesting that this may, in part, have been the reason for the fight. Nuc is named as the Duke of ALEMAIGNE, by which either ALBANY (SCOTLAND) or GERMANY is intended.

NUDD
Welsh and Arthurian

(1) The father of GWYNN AP NUDD.

(2) A shortened and popularised version of GWYNN AP NUDD, Master of the WILD HUNT and Lord of the Dead. Some have equated Gwynn ap Nudd with the Irish NUADHA AIRGEDLÁMH, although this appears to be a fairly late theory that relies on the similarity of the shortened versions Nudd and Nuadha. The shortened version of Gwynn ap Nudd is also said, by some, to have later given rise to the Romano-Celtic deity NODENS, but this again appears to be false etymology.

NWYVRE
Welsh

Named in some genealogies as the child of ARIANRHOD by her brother GWYDION FAB DÔN.

NYN(N)-IAW, -YAW
Welsh

1 The brother of PEIBAW, with whom he was transformed into an ox by God for his sins. In some genealogies Nynniaw and Peibaw are the sons of BELI and DÔN, and thus the brothers of, among others, GWYDION FAB DÔN, ARIANRHOD, GILFAETHWY and LLUDD.

2 The son of BELI and brother of LLUDD, LLEFELYS and CASWALLAWN. In this context Nynniaw is the Welsh version of NENNIUS, the brother of LUD and CASSIVELAUNUS.

O

OBERON

Arthurian

(1) The King of the Fairies who, according to the thirteenth-century French romance *HUON DE BORDEAUX*, was the illegitimate son of JULIUS CAESAR by MORGAN Le Fay, ruling a kingdom called MOMUR. Other sources say that he was originally an excessively ugly dwarf by the name of TRONC, but the fairies took pity on him, removed all traces of his former ugliness and gave him a kingdom. Shortly before his death, Oberon resigned his throne to HUON of Bordeaux. This angered ARTHUR, who had retired there after his days on earth came to an end and fully expected to succeed Oberon. His protests were firmly quashed by Oberon, who threatened to turn him into a werewolf. A short time later Oberon died.

He first appeared in English literature in a prose translation of the earlier French romance *c.* 1534. Possibly the best-known use of this character is in William SHAKESPEARE's *A MIDSUMMER NIGHT'S DREAM*. In this Oberon is shown as a magical figure, married to TITANIA and accompanied by an impish servant, PUCK. Titania does not figure widely in Arthurian literature, though she does appear in two more modern works: *The Masque of Gwendolen* (1816) by Reginald Heber and *The Quest of Merlin* (1891) by Richard Hovey.

Oberon himself is also a fleeting character within the mainstream Arthurian sources. He was said in one to have been the companion of TRISTAN's son YSAIE THE SAD, and in another to have been the father of ROBIN GOODFELLOW by a human girl. SPENSER, in his famous poem *THE FAERIE QUEENE*, makes him the father of GLORIANA, with whom ARTHUR fell in love.

(2) A non-Arthurian medieval French romance about OGIER, *OGIER LE DANOIS*, names Oberon as a brother of MORGAN Le Fay.

OBIE

Arthurian

A daughter of Duke LYPPAUT, sister to OBILOT. She rejected the advances of King MELJANZ of LIZ, which led to a war between her father and the King. Peace was finally restored through the efforts of her younger sister Obilot.

OBILOT

Arthurian

A daughter of Duke LYPPAUT, younger sister of OBIE, who, while still a child, had a pretend relationship with Sir GAWAIN, styling herself as his 'lady'.

OCHALL OICHNI

Irish

The King of CONNACHT, whose swineherd RUCHT was a great friend of FRIUCH, the swineherd to BODB, King of MUNSTER. The two swineherds, having fallen out with each other and after going through several transformations, were reborn as the bulls FINNBHENNACH and the DONN CUAILNGÈ.

See also COPHUIR IN DÁ MUCCIDA

OCTA

Arthurian

A son of HENGIST who is thought to be identifiable with OSLA BIG-KNIFE.

OCTAVIUS

Arthurian

The Duke of GWENT, according to GEOFFREY OF MONMOUTH. He is to be identified with EVDAF.

OCVRAN

Arthurian

According to Welsh tradition, the father of GUINEVERE, also called GOGVRA.

ODBRICT

Arthurian

The King of NORWAY who was said to have been a supporter of ARTHUR at the final battle of CAMLANN, but lost his life in that fight.

ODGAR

Arthurian

The King of IRELAND during the expedition mounted by ARTHUR to locate and procure the cauldron of DIWRNACH, who was Odgar's supervisor.

ODR-AS, -US

Irish

A maiden who tended a cow. The MÓRRÍGHAN brought her a bull, which she was also supposed to watch over. The bull and the cow followed the Mórríghan into a cave, so Odras also entered that cave but fell asleep inside it. The bull and cow disappeared, so the Mórríghan changed the unfortunate Odras into a pool of water.

ODYAR FRANC

Arthurian

The steward at King ARTHUR'S court.

OENGHUS

Irish

The son of AED ABRAT and brother of LI BAN and FAND.

OENGHUS (MAC IN(D) O-G, -C)

Irish and Arthurian

Usually simply known as Oenghus, his epithet meaning 'Young Lad', Oenghus Mac in Og is the Irish equivalent of the Gaulish MAPONOS and the Welsh MABON. A clever trickster, he gained possession of BRUGH NA BÓINNE from his father, the DAGHDHA, or, some say, from ELCMAR. There he set up his home. Although a god born of primal powers, he is unusually not regarded as a healing deity, but rather as the god of wit, charm and fatal love, as the legends that surround him clearly demonstrate.

The famous *Aislinge Oenguso* relates the story of his forlorn quest for the woman of his dream, CAER the daughter of ETHAL ANUBAL, and his eventual discovery of her. However, Oenghus is possibly best known from his wooing of ÉDÁIN ECHRAIDHE for his foster father MIDHIR, wooing that was successful, and during which he undoubtedly used his various guiles on Édáin Echraidhe. Oenghus fostered DIARMAID UA DUIBHNE, whom he helped when he was besieged in a wood in CONNACHT by FIONN MAC CUMHAILL after GRÁINNE had induced Diarmaid ua Duibhne to elope with her. Oenghus saved Gráinne, whilst Diarmaid ua Duibhne escaped by leaping over the heads of the attackers, a trick no doubt taught him by Oenghus, who later reconciled his foster son and Gráinne with Fionn mac Cumhaill. After the death of Diarmaid ua Duibhne, Oenghus took that hero to live with him at Brugh na Bóinne, and there shared his immortality with him.

A historic king named Oenghus is recorded as having ruled in Cashel, his death being given as AD 490. Although he probably owes his name to the god Oenghus Mac in Og, he has no other connections with the deity. He was later thought to have resurfaced in the Arthurian legends as King ANGUISH, a name that couples a Gaelic trait with the translation of Oenghus as Angus.

OESC

Arthurian

A King of KENT who was said to have been the son or grandson of HENGIST and who ruled during the traditional Arthurian period. It also seems possible that the name is a variant of AESC.

OGHAM

Irish

Usually known as Ogham Script, the Irish Celtic alphabet system is said to have been the invention of the god OGHMA, hence the name, but is more likely to have developed during the third and fourth centuries. On first inspection this system of writing appears to be based on the Latin alphabet. However, closer study reveals unique characteristics, such as a mnemonic system that is clearly not Roman in origin. It is thought that some of its elements represent the incorporation of an earlier, now lost, magical script that would have been almost certainly used only by the DRUIDS. Ogham Script is best known as a series of lines or cuts, made on the edges of stones or pieces of wood.

Ogham Script inscriptions have been discovered on the eastern seaboard of the United States, or, at least, the inscriptions appear to be Ogham. If they are truly Celtic, they would seem to prove that not only were the Celts excellent coastal sailors but also that they crossed the wide expanse of the north Atlantic.

OG(H)MA

Irish

Usually given the title GRIANAINECH, which means 'Sun-face', Oghma is the Irish equivalent of the Gaulish OGMIOS. One of the TUATHA DÉ DANANN, a strong champion whose magic words could bind men to follow him, he may have originated as a psycho pomp, or heroic guide, of the spirits of the dead. Oghma is perhaps most famous for being accredited with the invention of OGHAM Script, the Irish Celtic alphabet. Under the tyrannical rule of BRES, Oghma was humiliatingly made to collect firewood. Following the installation of LUGH as the leader of the Tuatha Dé Danann, and their success over the FOMHOIRÉ in the Second Battle of MAGH TUIREDH, Oghma is named as one of those who was set to pursue fleeing remnants of the Fomhoiré forces who were attempting to make off with the magical harp of the DAGHDHA.

OGIER

Arthurian

The son of GODFREY, a Danish duke and the hero of the Carolingian (AD 751–987) romance *OGIER LE DANOIS*. At Ogier's birth, MORGAN Le Fay said that one day she would take him away with her to AVALON. This she eventually did, and he stayed there for 200 years before returning to fight for Christendom. Afterwards he went back to Avalon, where he and Morgan Le Fay were said to have had a son, MEURVIN.

This story appears to be reflected, in part, in *Ly Myreur des Histoires*, written some time before 1400 by Jean d'Outremeuse of Liege. This says that, in AD 896, Ogier was shipwrecked some nine days' sail from Cyprus and, washed ashore, did battle with a CAPALU and other monsters. Having defeated them, he was attacked by ARTHUR and GAWAIN, but was rescued by angels. Welcomed by MORGHE (Morgan Le Fay) to her palace, he lived happily there with her, and in peace with both Arthur and Gawain.

His prototype in history may have been OTKER, the advocate of Liège in Charlemagne's time, but the Danes themselves regarded Ogier as the Danish hero HOLGER. Charlemagne features in his story, as it was said that this King presented him with TRISTAN's sword, which Ogier called CURETANA. Danish tradition, which appears to draw heavily on Arthurian themes, says that Ogier and his men are sleeping in a cave in DENMARK, or that he perpetually wanders through the Ardennes. According to Sir John Mandeville's *Travels* (1356–7), Ogier was an ancestor of PRESTER JOHN.

OGIER LE DANOIS

Arthurian

Important Carolingian romance that details the life of the Danish Duke OGIER.

OGMIOS

Gaulish

A father god, who was regarded as a wise elder. Ogmios, an old man, is usually depicted carrying a club and a bow, attributes that led to his being equated with the Graeco-Roman Hercules. Indeed, a number of carvings from the Romano-Celtic era show a typically Herculean figure with massive muscles, a huge club and wearing a lion's skin. The tip of his tongue is connected by thin chains to the ears of a throng of happy mortals. Ogmios was not simply a god of brute strength, as his Herculean images might portray, for he was the god of eloquence, a skill the Celts believed to be more powerful than force, as well as the god of the binding power of poetry and the poetic word, of charm, of incantation and of image. Ogmios may have originated as a heroic guide to the spirits of the dead, leading him to be a most powerful deity, one who both binds and liberates, and who conducts the dead into the OTHERWORLD. His Irish equivalent is OGHMA, who shares many, if not all, of his attributes.

OGOF LANCIAU ERYRI

Arthurian

A cave in north WALES where ARTHUR's men are said to be asleep, awaiting their king's return. They were supposed to have been seen there by a shepherd who fled when he almost awakened them.

OGOF MYRDDIN

Arthurian

A hill near CARMARTHEN that is more popularly known as MERLIN'S HILL.

OGO'R DINAS

Arthurian

A cave near Llandebie that has been mooted as one of the many possible last resting places of ARTHUR (cf. CRAIG-Y-DINAS).

OGYRVEN

Welsh

According to some sources, Ogyrven was the father of CERRIDWEN, to whom he gave his cauldron. He was, perhaps, an early eponymous deity of the alphabet, called *ogyrvens*, as well as the patron of bards and language.

OILILL

Irish

The companion of FERCHESS, who watched EOGABAL and AINÉ leave their SÍDH with a herd of supernatural cattle that they desired. Eogabal was killed by Ferchess, and Ainé was outraged, possibly raped, by Oilill, whose ear Ainé hit so hard that it never regrew any skin. Ainé swore to have her revenge, and later caused an argument to break out between EOGHAN, one of Oilill's sons, and LUGAID MAC CON, who was killed as a result. Lugaid mac Con's family attacked the followers of Oilill at the Battle of MAGH MUCRIME, during which all seven of Oilill's sons were killed.

OIMELC
Gaulish
The Gaulish name for the festival of IMBOLC.

OISÎN
Irish
The son of FIONN MAC CUMHAILL and SAAR or Sabia and father of OSCAR. Oisîn was the greatest poet to have lived in IRELAND, as well as a mighty warrior. He was born after his mother had been changed into a deer by a maleficent sorcerer, and his name means 'Little Fawn', for that is how he was born. A small tuft of hair grew from his forehead where Saar had licked him, but, because Fionn mac Cumhaill had been the first to embrace the lad, he remained human.

One summer morning, while Oisîn and many members of the FIAN were hunting on the shores of Loch Lena, they saw a beautiful maiden riding a pure white stallion coming towards them. She was NIAMH, daughter of the King of TÍR INNA MBAN, and she had come to seek the hand of Oisîn whom she had fallen in love with. She cast a spell on Oisîn so that he fell for her, and the two of them rode back to her land, where they were married and lived happily together. One version of the story says that he became the King of Tír inna mBan after winning a foot-race against Niamh's father, but another says that he rescued the daughter of the King of TÍR INNA MBÉO, who had been abducted by a giant.

After what seemed like only three weeks, Oisîn sought to visit his father. Niamh tried to dissuade him, but, finding he would not change his mind, she gave him her white steed on which to make the journey, warning him that he must not dismount, otherwise he would never be able to return. When Oisîn arrived back in Ireland he found that everything had changed. He had been away not for just three weeks but for three centuries. The fian were long forgotten, and a new faith was now practised. Disheartened, Oisîn turned to return to his supernatural wife, but on the way he was asked to help a group of peasants struggling with a heavy stone. When Oisîn dismounted, he underwent a dramatic transformation, becoming an aged man on the verge of death. The horse vanished in an instant, and Oisîn was taken to Saint PATRICK, whose scribes wrote down all Oisîn said before he died.

OL
Welsh
One of the seldom-mentioned members of the party formed to help CULHWCH. Ol was chosen because he had the ability to pick up any trail, even one that was as much as seven years older than he was, although no indication is given of his age.

OLD TABLE
Arthurian
The name given to the ROUND TABLE when it was in the ownership of UTHER. He too used it to seat the knights of his company, who numbered fifty, one of the best knights of this order being Sir BRUNOR. It is thought that the Old Table found its way into many Italian romances, where it is still mentioned, but of the romances that concerned this use of the Round Table none appears to have survived.

OLLAV FOLA
Irish
The eighteenth ruler of IRELAND after EREMON, and possibly the only King of Ireland to have reached the highest Druidic rank. Traditionally he reigned *c.* 1000 BC. He gave the country a code of legislature and devised a legal system similar to the system of county and crown courts in use today. He was also credited with establishing the triennial fair at TARA, where all kings, vassals, bards, historians and musicians assembled to record the history of the island, create and enforce new laws, settle disputes and so on. He is allegedly buried in the great tumulus at Loughcrew in West MEATH.

OLWEN
Welsh
The daughter of the chief giant YSPADDADEN, this maiden, whose alternate name is NIWALEN, appears in the *MABINOGION* story of *CULHWCH AND OLWEN*. Her name appears to mean 'White Track', but it may also come from *olwyn* – 'wheel'. CULHWCH's stepmother swore that he should love only Olwen, so Culhwch set out to find her, first coming to a royal court, said later to have been that of King ARTHUR, where the gatekeeper GLEWLWYD remarked that he had never, in his long career, encountered such a handsome youth.

The King sent out messengers to look for Olwen, but a year passed without any news. Culhwch then formed a party of gifted companions to help him in his search, these companions being named as CEI (KAY), BEDWYR (BEDIVERE), CYNDDYLIG, GWRHYR, GWALCHMAI FAB GWYAR and MENW FAB TEIRGWAEDD, though many others, seldom named, also accompanied him. Setting out, they at length met a shepherd, whose wife turned out to be Culhwch's aunt. She knew Olwen, and, even though she had lost twenty-three of her twenty-four sons to Yspaddaden, she agreed to help Culhwch, telling him that Olwen came to her house every Saturday to wash her hair.

The due day came, and the couple met. Olwen immediately agreed to his suit but told Culhwch that he must obtain the permission of her father. She warned him not to flinch from any conditions set or tasks imposed. Culhwch agreed, and the very next morning his party set out for Yspaddaden's castle. For three days the giant told them to come back the next and then, when they had turned their backs, hurled a poisoned boulder at them. They were too quick and caught the boulder, which they hurled back. After three days the giant was severely weakened by his own poison, so he agreed to hear Culhwch. He agreed that he could marry Olwen provided he carried out a number of seemingly impossible tasks. Each of these Culhwch completed, but, as Yspaddaden continued to pile condition upon condition, Culhwch rounded up all the giant's enemies and stormed the castle. Yspaddaden was killed, and Culhwch married Olwen, the pair remaining faithful for the rest of their lives.

Olwen is also the heroine of the *MABINOGION* story of *CULHWCH AND OLWEN*, and also of a Welsh folktale *EINION AND OLWEN* in which a shepherd, EINION, travelled to the OTHERWORLD to marry OLWEN. They had a son whom they named TALIESIN.

OLYROUN
Arthurian
The father-in-law of LANVAL who was a fairy king living on an enchanted island.

ONTZLAKE
Arthurian
One of King ARTHUR's knights and the younger brother of the evil Sir DAMAS.

OPTIMA
Welsh
According to tradition, one of the names applied to MYRDDIN's (MERLIN's) mother, the other being ALDAN.

ORAINGLAIS
Arthurian
An Irish princess who was said to have borne a son to Sir SAGREMOR.

ORAN
British
The brother of Saint COLUMBA. He is alleged to have voluntarily died so that his brother might consecrate the ground on which he wished to build his chapel on the island of IONA with a burial.

ORCADES
Arthurian
Also MORCHADES
Appearing in some translations of *DIU CRÔNE*, this alternative for MORGAUSE appears to have been derived from *Orcades*, the Latin for her husband LOT's realm of the ORKNEYS. Some commentators think that this was the first translation of her name, and that the variant Morchades came later in an attempt to bring her name more into line with Morgause. This theory is, however, open to speculation.

ORCANT
Arthurian
The ruler of the ORKNEYS who was converted to Christianity by PETRUS, a follower or disciple of JOSEPH OF ARIMATHEA. It would appear that this name is derived from the Latin name for his realm, Orcades, and may simply be a title rather than a personal name.

ORD-OLLAM
Irish
A title applied to LUGH in his position as chief protector of the arts and sciences.

ORDOVICES
British
An ancient northern Welsh tribe that, along with the SILURES of the south-east of WALES, supported CARATACUS against the Roman invaders.

ORGUELLEUSE
Arthurian
A proud lady who appears in the works of both CHRÉTIEN DE TROYES and WOLFRAM VON ESCHENBACH, and who maintained that the only way to gain fulfilment in courtly love was through persistence of courtship and deeds of outrageous courage. WOLFRAM VON ESCHENBACH suggests that she had an intrigue with AMFORTAS that culminated in his receiving the wound that so incapacitated him. PERCEVAL once spurned her attentions, and she finally gave her love to GAWAIN.

ORIANT
Arthurian
The son of MEURVIN, according to *OGIER LE DANOIS*, the son of MORGAN Le Fay and OGIER, and hence a nephew of King ARTHUR.

ORILUS
Arthurian
The Duke of LALANDER and husband of JESCHUTÉ.

ORIMONDE
Arthurian
The daughter of the Emir of Persia who became the wife of MARC, son of YSAIE THE SAD and grandson of TRISTAN.

ORKNEY(S)
Arthurian
The Orkney Islands form part of the kingdom ruled over by LOT, according to Sir Thomas MALORY, though this seems to be a later development. GEOFFREY OF MONMOUTH, writing at an earlier date, makes Lot the King of LOTHIAN who also becomes the King of NORWAY following the voluntary submission of GUNPHAR. This association seems to be as a direct result of the numerous Norse connections with the Orkneys. The Latin for Orkneys, *Orcades*, appears to have given rise to ORCADES, an alternative name for MORGAUSE, as well as ORCANT, who was described as a King of Orkney. During the sixth century the Orkneys seem to have been organised into some form of kingdom that was subject to Pictish kings.

ORLAM
Irish
The son of MEDHBHA and AILILL. He was beheaded by CÚ CHULAINN, who made Orlam's charioteer take the severed head back to Medhbha and Ailill. As he stood to attention in front of the grieving King and Queen, Cú Chulainn split open his head with a well-aimed, long-range slingshot.

ORLANDO
Arthurian
The son of the King of Thessaly and lover of MELORA, ARTHUR's daughter.

ORLANDO FURIOSO
Arthurian
Italian Carolingian romance by Ludovico ARIOSTO that forms a sequel to the unfinished *ORLANDO INNAMORATO* of BOIARDO and was published in 1532. Featuring some Arthurian material, the poem describes the unrequited love of ORLANDO for ANGELICA, set against the war between the SARACENS and Christians during Charlemagne's reign. It influenced SHAKESPEARE, Byron and Milton, and is considered to be the perfect poetic expression of the Italian Renaissance.

ORLANDO INNAMORATO
Arthurian
Unfinished epic narrative poem, written between 1441 and 1494 by Mattheo Maria BOIARDO, in which the Charlemagne romances were recast into *ottava rima*. Being incomplete, this work gave rise to the *ORLANDO FURIOSO* of Ludovico ARIOSTO.

ORRIBES
Arthurian
A giant who, according to Spanish romance, wrought havoc in BRITAIN before he was killed by TRISTAN THE YOUNGER.

ORWEN
Arthurian
The sister of MERIADOC, she was abducted by UTHER, who subsequently married her.

OSCAR
Irish
The son of OISÍN. He slew three kings in his first battle, when he also mistakenly killed his friend LINNÉ. Oscar proved his might as a warrior by killing a huge boar that none other, including his grandfather, had been able to catch. He married AIDEEN, but was soon afterwards killed in the Battle of GABHRA. Aideen died of a broken heart and was buried by Oisín, who was, at least in this version, still in IRELAND at the time of the battle, and not in TÍR INNA MBÉO with NIAMH.

OSLA BIG-KNIFE
Arthurian
Possibly in origin OCTA, the son or grandson of the SAXON HENGIST. He features in the *MABINOGION* story of the *DREAM OF RHONABWY* as an adversary of ARTHUR at BADON. However, another source says that he was a companion of Arthur during the hunt for the boar TWRCH TRWYTH. During this episode, the scabbard for his knife, BRONLLAVYN SHORT BROAD, which could be used as a bridge, filled with water and dragged him under.

OSMOND
Arthurian
Appearing in DRYDEN'S *King Arthur* as a SAXON sorcerer, Osmond treacherously tried to force EMMELINE into his clutches, but ended up having the tables turned on him and being confined to a dungeon.

Ossetes

Arthurian

Descendants of the ALANS, a SARMATIAN people who still inhabit the Caucasus today. They tell a story that is very similar to the death of ARTHUR. In this their hero, BATRADZ, received a mortal wound and, knowing that his time was limited, commanded that his sword be thrown into some nearby water.

Ossian

Irish

A relatively late variant of OISÎN.

Oswald

Arthurian

The King of KENT who appears in DRYDEN's *KING ARTHUR* as an opponent of ARTHUR who, like the King, loved EMMELINE. They fought for the lady's favours, Arthur winning and subsequently expelling Oswald from BRITAIN. He is a purely fictional character, as there is no King of Kent called Oswald known to history.

Otherworld, The

General

In common with most other cultures, the Otherworld is the Celtic land of the dead, but it is far more than simply that. It is, particularly in the Welsh Otherworld of ANNWFN, almost a paradisiacal fantasy land that has recognisable regions, regions that could, in some ways, be equated with the three regions of the Greek Hades, but even that equation does not really compare with the amazing beauty of the Celtic concept of a land other than their own.

The most usual icon of the Otherworld is a cauldron of plenty, a cauldron that, so most authorities now agree, later inspired the stories of the Holy GRAIL of Arthurian fame. This cauldron appears all over the Celtic lands, from the cauldron of the DAGHDHA in IRELAND, to that of ARAWN in WALES and far beyond.

The Otherworld is certainly a land of the dead, but even the dead are not constrained, for many stories exist of mortals who travel to the Otherworld and subsequently return. It is in this sense, therefore, a transitory realm from which souls are reborn, sometimes as the same person, and sometimes as a completely new person.

It is also the land of the gods, for the Celtic theology is peculiar in having no definition for heaven. The Irish TUATHA DÉ DANANN inhabit their SÍDH, or earthen barrows, which are, in reality, prehistoric burial chambers. They were awarded this realm by the Sons of MÍL ÉSPÁINE, the first mortals to inhabit Ireland, the passage from worldly to Otherworldly beings signifying the transition of Ireland from a mythical land of the gods to a historical land of mortals.

Otker

Arthurian

The advocate of Liège in Charlemagne's time who is thought possibly to be the historical prototype of OGIER.

Ousel of Cilgwri

Welsh

A variation of the BLACKBIRD OF CILGWRI, although the word 'ousel', now spelt 'ouzel', is actually an archaic name for the European blackbird.

Owain (Glyndwr)

Welsh and Arthurian

Also YVAIN

A historical character, the son of URIEN of RHEGED, whom he succeeded. He has subsequently passed into the realms of myth and legend, and has countless associations with ARTHUR. Although he certainly lived later than the traditional Arthurian period – he was said to have heavily defeated the British c. AD 593 – both he and his father have been drawn into Arthurian legend. In this role he is the son of Urien by Arthur's sister, MORGAN Le Fay, who appears to have her origins in the goddess MODRON, whom some Welsh sources name as the mother of Owain. Welsh tradition made him the husband of PENARWAN and DENW, the latter being a niece of Arthur. The *MABINOGION* story of the *DREAM OF RHONABWY* has Owain and Arthur playing GWYDDBWYLL – a type of board game – during which Owain's ravens fought with Arthur's men and were almost defeated. However, Owain raised his flag and the ravens set about their opponents with renewed vigour.

French romance gives us the most details about the Arthurian Owain, particularly the French romance *Yvain* by CHRÉTIEN DE TROYES. In this Owain learns of a wondrous spring or fountain in the forest of BROCELIANDE, where he goes, defeating ESCLADOS, the knight who protected it. He chased the knight back to his castle and there the latter died of his wounds. Owain tried to follow the knight into his castle, but became entangled in the portcullis. He was rescued by LUNETE, the sister of LAUDINE, who was the widow of the slain knight. Owain fell in love with Laudine, and her sister persuaded her that she should marry him. When Arthur and his followers arrived at the castle, Owain went with them, but promised that he would return to his wife within a year. However, he did not keep an eye on the time and failed to honour his promise. When he did return, Laudine rejected him and he went mad, taking to living wild in the forest. His sanity returned only when an enchanted ointment was administered, after which he went to the help of a lion that was fighting a serpent. The lion then became his constant companion and earned Owain his nickname, the KNIGHT OF THE LION. He is also named as one of the TWENTY-FOUR KNIGHTS of King Arthur's court.

OWAIN

Arthurian

A Welsh prose romance thought to date from the thirteenth century that is found in the *MABINOGION* and concerns OWAIN, the son of URIEN.

OWAIN THE BASTARD

Arthurian

The half-brother of OWAIN whom URIEN fathered on the wife of his seneschal, or steward. A KNIGHT OF THE ROUND TABLE, he was noted for his common sense, but was killed in a joust by GAWAIN, who had failed to recognise him.

OWEL

Irish

The foster son of MANANNÁN MAC LIR and the father of the goddess AINÉ by a DRUID whose name remains a mystery.

OWEN

1 (*Irish*) One of the warriors of ULSTER who challenged the right of CET to carve the boar of MAC DÁ THÓ, but was quickly silenced by the retort of Cet, who was in turn silenced by CONALL CERNACH.

2 (*Welsh*) The son of MACSEN who was said to have met a giant in battle in the valley below DINAS EMRYS. They fought long and hard until each had killed the other.

OWL OF CWN CAWLWYD

Welsh

One of the oldest animals in the world, which conversed with GWRHYR the Interpreter. The expedition mounted by CULHWCH had been taken to the owl by the STAG OF RHEDYNFRC, an animal slightly younger than the owl, which, in turn, took the group on to question the EAGLE OF GWERNABY.

P

PA GUR
Welsh and Arthurian

A famous Welsh poem that tells how CEI (KAY) travelled to Anglesey with a view to killing lions, especially preparing himself for an encounter with the CATH PALUG, a monstrous feline creature.

PADARN REDCOAT
Welsh and Arthurian

The owner of a coat, known as PAIS PADARN, that rendered the wearer invisible and was one of the THIRTEEN TREASURES OF BRITAIN.

PADSTOW
Arthurian

A Cornish town that, according to Henry VIII's librarian, Leland, was the birthplace of ARTHUR.

PAIR DRYNOG
Welsh and Arthurian

The cauldron of DRYNOG in which none but the meat of a brave man would boil. It is numbered among the THIRTEEN TREASURES OF BRITAIN.

PAIS PADARN
Welsh and Arthurian

The coat or cloak of PADARN REDCOAT that rendered the wearer invisible and was one of the THIRTEEN TREASURES OF BRITAIN.

PALACE ADVENTUROUS
Arthurian

A palace within Castle CARBONEK that housed the Holy GRAIL.

PALAMEDES
Arthurian

A pagan knight, the son of King ASTLABOR (ESCLABOR), he fell hopelessly in love with ISEULT. When TRISTAN came to IRELAND, he found Palamedes vying for Iseult's hand, but he defeated him in single combat. Some time later Palamedes obtained her through deception, but Tristan rescued her. Palamedes gave chase and caught up with the lovers. He would have fought Tristan again had not Iseult intervened. However, they later met again, and during the course of this fight Palamedes' sword was knocked from his hand, and in that moment, it was said, he became a Christian. The fight was stopped, never to be resumed, and Palamedes eventually became the Duke of Provence.

PALANTE
Arthurian

A cousin of TRISTAN, the husband of the Duchess of Milan; following Tristan's death, he invaded CORNWALL but was eventually killed by Tristan's one-time rival for ISEULT, PALAMEDES.

PALUG
Welsh and Arthurian

The father of the sons who, according to tradition, lived on ANGLESEY and saved and raised the CATH PALUG, the monstrous feline offspring of HÊN WEN.

PAMLART
Arthurian

A descendant of BAN who is numbered among the contenders for the killer of King MARK of Cornwall.

PANDRAGON
Arthurian

A name or title given to AMBROSIUS AURELIUS in the *Vulgate Merlin*. It is, without doubt, a simple variant of PENDRAGON.

PANDRAGUS
Arthurian

The father of illegitimate twins by LIBAN, a daughter of King BAN.

PANDRASUS
Arthurian

A Greek king who had enslaved a group of Trojan exiles. He was fought, and defeated, by BRUTUS, who then claimed the hand of Pandrasus' reluctant daughter, IGNOGE. Brutus also compelled Pandrasus to release his Trojan slaves, and to equip and provision them to enable them to leave Greece. So equipped, Brutus left Greece, taking the Trojans with him.

Padstow, Cornwall, which is among the many places alleged to have been the birthplace of King Arthur.
(© Jean Williamson/Mick Sharp)

PANNENOISANCE
Arthurian
The name given to ARTHUR's capital in *PERLESVAUS*.

PANT
Arthurian
The father of LANCELOT, according to ULRICH VON ZARZIKHOVEN, who further states that he was the King of GENNEWIS and was killed in a rebellion.

PARIS
Arthurian
A Frenchman and friend of ARTHUR in the French romance *Ly Myreur des histoires*. He received the kingdom of SAYNES from Arthur, who bestowed it and the deposed King's daughter on Paris after he had conquered the kingdom. It is thought that Paris may be identical to the French King Paris mentioned in the *MABINOGION* story of *CULHWCH AND OLWEN* who, along with another French King, IONA, was said to have been at Arthur's court.

PARIS, BATTLE OF
Arthurian
The battle at which ARTHUR and HOEL defeated the Roman tribune FROLLO. Within nine years Arthur had conquered all of GAUL and held a court in Paris, establishing the government of that kingdom on a legal footing.

PARLAN
Arthurian
One of the contenders for the role of the MAIMED KING. His story says that he found SOLOMON's ship and attempted to draw the sword that he found on board, but, being unworthy, he was wounded through the thighs with a lance. This, however, was not the act or the wounding that turned his realm into the WASTE LAND of the GRAIL legends.

PARMENIE
Arthurian
The realm of TRISTAN's father with its capital at CANVEL, according to GOTTFRIED VON STRASSBURG. It is simply a variant of Armenie (or vice versa), the name applied to the same territory by THOMAS. Some sources name the ruler of Parmenie as RIVALIN.

PARROT
Arthurian
ARTHUR'S garrulous pet, which was originally owned by LION THE MERCILESS, who lost his arm while fighting Arthur. Attended by a dwarf, the parrot was said to have gone with Arthur on a couple of his quests.

PARSIFAL
Arthurian
The German version, along with PARZIVAL, of Sir PERCEVAL.

PARSIFAL
Arthurian
An opera by Richard Wagner that is based on the legends surrounding PERCEVAL and was first performed in 1882, just one year before the sudden death of the composer.

PARTHOL-ÁN, -ON
Irish
A descendant of the biblical JAPHETH. The son of SERA, leader of the second invasion of IRELAND, husband to the adulterous DEALGNAID and father of RURY. His companions became known simply as the 'People of Partholán' or PARTHOLIANS. They defeated the FOMHOIRÉ, forcing them into exile in the Hebrides and on the Isle of MAN. Partholán then set his people to clearing four plains and creating seven lakes, the first landscaping of Ireland. He also built the first guest house, brewed the first beer and established laws and craft. Partholán and all his people, bar one, a man named TUAN MAC STERN, were wiped out by a plague, leaving the island open for NEMHEDH.

PARTHOLIANS
Irish
The name sometimes given to the people who came to IRELAND under the leadership of PARTHOLÁN.

PARTINAL
Arthurian
The killer of the brother of the FISHER KING, GOON DESERT. Probably a knight, he later fell at the hands of PERCEVAL.

PARZIVAL
Arthurian
The German version, along with PARSIFAL, of Sir PERCEVAL.

PARZIVAL
Arthurian
A thirteenth-century work by WOLFRAM VON ESCHENBACH recounting Arthurian tales, particularly those concerning Sir PERCEVAL.

PASCEN

Welsh and Arthurian

A son of URIEN of RHEGED.

PASCHENT

British and Arthurian

The third son of VORTIGERN who fled to GERMANY after his father had been ousted by AMBROSIUS AURELIUS, but later returned with a large army. He was soundly defeated. He then fled to IRELAND, where he obtained the help of King GILLOMANIUS for his second invasion attempt. This time he had more success, for Ambrosius Aurelius was sick and EOPA, a SAXON in the employ of Paschent, disguised as a doctor, gained entry to the ailing king and administered a poisoned potion from which he died.

PASSALEON

Arthurian

The son of ESTONNE, LORD OF THE SCOTTISH WILDERNESS according to *PERCEFOREST*, which further said he lived in pre-Roman BRITAIN. He was given to MORGAN Le Fay by ZEPHYR and became the lover of her daughter, and through her an ancestor of MERLIN. He killed BRUYANT the Faithless, who had previously killed Estonne, his father. While still a child he was said to have been given a tour of Tartarus (the Underworld of classical Greek mythology), presumably by Morgan Le Fay.

PASSELANDE

Arthurian

According to BÉROUL, this was the name of King ARTHUR's horse.

PATERNUS, SAINT

Arthurian

An abbot and bishop said to have associations with DYFED. He passed into the Arthurian legends through a single instance when it was said that ARTHUR had tried to procure Paternus's tunic. The ground opened and swallowed the King, and he was released only after he had begged forgiveness and repented of his sin. The traditional pedigree of CUNEDDA makes Paternus the son of TACITUS and father of AETURNUS, but it appears that this character may be a separate one from Saint Paternus.

PATRICK, SAINT

Irish

The patron saint of IRELAND who was, perhaps, born in South WALES late in the fourth century AD. His father, Calpurnius, was a Romano-British

deacon. Patrick does not appear to have been the name his parents called him: he is recorded as having carried the name SUCCAT, although this may have been a nickname. According to legend he was captured by pirates when he was sixteen and carried off by them to Ireland, where he was sold to an Antrim chief by the name of Milchru. Six years later he escaped and travelled to FRANCE, where he became a monk. At the age of forty-five he was consecrated a bishop, and in AD 432 he is thought to have been sent as a missionary to Ireland by Pope Celestine I. He landed at Wicklow and from there travelled north to convert his old master Milchru. In County Down he converted another chief, Dichu, and at TARA he preached to LAOGHAIRE, but was unsuccessful in converting him, as the official Christian record of that event shows.

From Tara he travelled to Croagh Patrick in Mayo, then to ULSTER, and as far as Cashel in the south, where he converted King Aenghus about AD 448. Legend says that, during the baptism of Aenghus, the saint accidentally pierced the King's foot with his crozier. Too wrapped up in the ceremony, Saint Patrick failed to notice what he had done, and Aenghus kept his mouth shut, and presumably his teeth clenched, as he thought it a part of the ceremony.

Patrick addressed himself first to the chiefs and made use of the Irish spirit of clanship to break down boundaries. After twenty years travelling the length and breadth of Ireland as a missionary he established his see at Armagh in 454. He died at Saul, the spot Dichu had given him on his arrival in Ireland, and is, in all probability, buried at Armagh. Another tradition states that he ended his days as the Abbot of GLASTONBURY, where he died at the age of 111. His feast day is 17 March.

The only certainly authentic literary remains of the saint are his spiritual autobiography, *Confession*, and a letter addressed to Coroticus, a British chieftain who had carried off some Irish Christians to be slaves. Both of these are in very crude Latin. Later writers, who obviously wished to preserve some of the Irish mythology and legend in a post-pagan Ireland, connected the saint with a great number of mythological and legendary characters.

PATRICK THE RED

Arthurian

According to the PETIT BRUT of Rauf de BOUN, a son of ARTHUR.

PATRISE

Arthurian

An Irish knight (his name possibly starting life as

Saint Patrick, the patron saint of Ireland, who brought Christianity to the Irish people. (© Corbis)

Patrick) who was mistakenly poisoned by Sir PINEL when the latter was in fact attempting to poison GAWAIN. GUINEVERE was at first accused of his murder, but the truth was discovered by NIMUE.

PATROCLES
Arthurian
According to the Icelandic *SAGA OF TRISTRAM*, the paternal grandfather of TRISTAN.

PEBIN
Welsh
The father of the foot-holder GOEWIN.

PEDIVERE
Arthurian
A knight who murdered his own wife. He was sent by LANCELOT with her dead body to beg forgiveness of GUINEVERE, and eventually became a hermit.

PEDRAWD
Welsh and Arthurian
The father of BEDWYR. He later passed into the Arthurian cycle, where he became the father of BEDIVERE, the Arthurian version of Bedwyr.

PEDWAR MARCHOG AR HUGAN LLYS ARTHUR
Arthurian
Important fifteenth-century, or earlier, Welsh work that gives a list of knights at ARTHUR's court. These knights, thought to represent a company formed before the KNIGHTS OF THE ROUND TABLE, are collectively known as the TWENTY-FOUR KNIGHTS.

PEIBAW
Welsh
The brother of NYNNIAW who was, along with his brother, turned into an ox by God for his vanity and sins. A traditional Welsh genealogy makes Peibaw and Nynniaw the sons of DÔN, and thus brothers to GWYDION FAB DÔN, ARIANRHOD, GILFAETHWY, AMAETHON, GOFANNON and LLUDD.

PELA ORSO
Arthurian
The Italian poem *Pulzella Gaia* makes this the name of the castle of MORGAN Le Fay.

PELEUR
Arthurian
According to the Welsh *Y SAINT GRAAL*, the name of the owner of the GRAIL CASTLE.

PELIAS
Arthurian
Named as being an early ruler of LIONES.

PELLAM
Arthurian
The King of LISTINOISE whose brother, the invisible knight Sir GARLON, has been killed by BALIN. Pellam, determined to exact his revenge, fought with Balin and, during the course of the fight, succeeded in breaking Balin's sword. While Pellam was chasing Balin around the castle, Balin came across the LANCE OF LONGINUS and, taking it up, he stabbed Pellam with it. This was called the DOLOROUS STROKE, which was said to have been responsible for creating the WASTE LAND of the GRAIL legends.

PELLEAM
Arthurian
The name given to the MAIMED KING in French romance. It appears to be a simple variation of PELLAM, though other names are also given to this character in the GRAIL legends, such as PELLEHAN.

PELLEAS
Arthurian
An unfortunate knight, one of the KNIGHTS OF THE ROUND TABLE, who became the progenitor of a one-sided love affair with ETTARD, who did not reciprocate his feelings. GAWAIN said he would act on his behalf, but instead betrayed Pelleas and bedded Ettard himself. However, NIMUE, a LADY OF THE LAKE, now entered the picture and made Pelleas become enamoured of her by her magic, making Ettard fall in love with Pelleas by the same means. Finding her love now unrequited, Ettard died of a broken heart.

PELLEHAN
Arthurian
One of several names applied to the MAIMED KING. He was said, in the *QUESTE DEL SAINTE GRAAL*, to have received his maiming wound when he attempted to draw the SWORD OF THE STRANGE HANGINGS. Elsewhere, his character becoming much the same as that of PELLAM, it is stated that he received his wound when BALIN stabbed him with the LANCE OF LONGINUS.

PELLES
Arthurian
The son of PELLAM and King of LISTINOISE, though he is also called the King of TERRE FORRAINE (literally 'the Foreign Land'), while the

VULGATE VERSION makes him the FISHER KING. The father of ELAINE, he had her handmaiden, BRISEN, administer LANCELOT a love potion so that he would sleep with his daughter and father GALAHAD. *PERLESVAUS* calls the HERMIT KING Pelles, but it is assumed that this is an entirely different character.

PELLINORE
Arthurian

A subordinate king to ARTHUR who is variously described as the ruler of LISTINOISE, NORTHUMBERLAND or the GASTE FOREST. The *LIVRE D'ARTUS* makes him the RICH FISHER, saying that he was wounded in the thighs for doubting the Holy GRAIL. This would suggest that he was originally identical to PELLAM. Sir Thomas MALORY says he was the father of AGLOVALE, PERCEVAL, DORNAR, DRIANT, LAMORAK, ALAN, MELODIAN and ELAINE, though he does not mention TOR, whom he fathered on the wife of ARIES. He pursued the QUESTING BEAST and killed King LOT, eventually being slain by GAWAIN, Lot's son. Pellinore may have originated in BELI MAWR (Beli the Great), the Celtic ancestor god, for the pronunciation of their names is similar. If this is the case, it seems equally possible to suggest that Beli Mawr was the origin of the similarly named FISHER KING and MAIMED KING.

PEN ANNWFN
Welsh

'Head of Annwfn', the honorific title given to PWYLL by his counsellors after they had discovered that he had spent a year in ANNWFN.

PENARDUN
Welsh and Arthurian

The daughter or sister of BELI, although usually a daughter of DÔN, who, by LLYR, became the mother of MANAWYDAN FAB LLYR, the half-brother of BENDIGEID VRAN and BRANWEN, who were Llyr's children by IWERIADD, and of NISIEN and EFNISIEN, whom she bore to EUROSSWYD. Most sources, however, make Penardun the mother of Bendigeid Vran, Branwen and Manawydan fab Llyr by Llyr, and ignore that god's association with Iweriadd. Arthurian sources made Penardun an ancestor of ARTHUR by way of Bendigeid Vran.

PENARWAN
Welsh and Arthurian

The wife of OWAIN who was, according to the *TRIOEDD YNYS PRYDEIN*, unfaithful to him.

PENBEDW
Arthurian

The name of a farm in Clwyd whose lands contain a menhir and standing stones that have been put forward by R. Holland in *Supernatural Clwyd* (1989) as one of the possible resting places of King ARTHUR. This seems to have some local support, for local folklore says that MOEL ARTHUR, which lies nearby, was the site of Arthur's palace.

PENDARAN DYFED
Welsh

The foster father of PRYDERI.

PENDRAGON
Arthurian

An amalgamation of the Brythonic (a group of Celtic languages comprising Welsh, Cornish and Breton) *pen* signifying 'head' or 'main' and the Old Welsh *dragwn* meaning 'leader', this title was taken by both UTHER and later ARTHUR, though in the case of the former it has usually been used as a surname. It simply signifies the position of the titleholder as the chief leader.

PENDRAGON CASTLE
Arthurian

The castle of BREUNOR following his marriage to MALEDISANT.

PENDRAGWN
Welsh and Arthurian

A combination of the Old Welsh *dragwn*, 'dragon', and the Brythonic *pen*, 'head', which was traditionally used to refer to the head of a tribe, clan or realm, for Pendragwn literally means 'head dragon', the use of 'dragon' signifying a person of the utmost importance, a leader. Thus Pendragwn really means 'head leader'. The title later emerged in the Arthurian legends as Pendragon, a title taken first by UTHER and subsequently by ARTHUR.

PENVRO
Welsh

An ancient name for Pembroke, the location of GWALES where the seven who had been charged with the burial of BENDIGEID VRAN's severed head stayed for eighty years before one of them opened a door that looked towards CORNWALL. Once that door had been opened, memories of all that had befallen their fellow countrymen came rushing back, and the seven hurried to the WHITE MOUNT in LONDON, where they buried the head as instructed.

PERCARD

Arthurian

The proper name of the BLACK KNIGHT who was
killed by GARETH.

PERCEFOREST

Arthurian

The hero of a romance by the same name. This says
that when ALEXANDER THE GREAT conquered
England (which he never actually did) he made
BETIS the King, and his brother, GADDIFER, King
of SCOTLAND. As the line of BRUTUS had died
out, Betis was quickly accepted by the populace,
being renamed Perceforest after he had killed the
magician DAMART. He founded the chivalrous
order of the KNIGHTS OF THE FRANC PALAIS
and built a temple to the Supreme God. His son
BETHIDES made an unwise marriage to the
sorceress CIRCE, who brought the Romans to
Britain. They defeated the Knights of the Franc
Palais, wiping them out, and Gaddifer, Perceforest's
brother, went to live in the ISLE OF LIFE. After
ALAN, the GRAIL KEEPER, had come to BRITAIN,
GALLAFER, Gaddifer's grandson converted to
Christianity and went to preach to his ancestors, who
still inhabited the Isle of Life. They too accepted
Christianity, were baptised and left the island,
coming to a place where five monuments awaited
them, and there they died.

PERCEFOREST

Arthurian

A fourteenth-century French romance describing the
early history of BRITAIN, including the fictitious
invasion of the island by ALEXANDER THE
GREAT.

PERCEVAL

Arthurian

(1) The father of the Perceval below, according to
the English romance SIR PERCEVAL OF GALLES.
He had apparently been killed, some years before his
son became aware of his identity, by the RED
KNIGHT, whom his son killed.

(2) Known among Welsh sources as PEREDUR,
Perceval appears to have been the invention of
CHRÉTIEN DE TROYES, for this is the earliest
reference made to a character by this name. In
German sources he is called PARSIFAL or
PARZIVAL.

Raised in the woods by his unnamed mother, for
she wanted him to know nothing of knighthood, he
saw some of ARTHUR's knights and was
determined to go to Arthur's court and become one.

His mother, unable to convince him otherwise, told
him to demand either a kiss or a jewel from any lady
he should meet. When Perceval came across a lady
asleep in a tent, he kissed her and purloined her ring.
On his arrival at Arthur's court, he heard that the
RED KNIGHT had absconded with a valuable cup.
He pursued him and killed the knight, afterwards
staying with GORNEMANT DE GOORT, an elderly
knight who taught him chivalry and knighted him.
He returned to Arthur's court and became one of the
KNIGHTS OF THE ROUND TABLE, leaving again
to undertake the Quest for the Holy GRAIL. He
arrived at the castle of BLANCHEFLEUR, who was
being besieged by King CLAMADEUS. Perceval
became Blanchefleur's lover and succeeded in
defeating King Clamadeus in single combat.

Desiring to visit his mother, Perceval was directed
by a fisherman to a castle where he beheld the
GRAIL PROCESSION, saw a man reclining on a
couch and was given a sword. However, Perceval
failed to ask the GRAIL QUESTION, and next
morning, when he awoke, he found the castle
deserted and only just escaped from it. The sword he
had been given had fragmented, and, encountering
his cousin, who told him that he should have asked
the Grail Question, he took the sword to
TREBUCHET. *En route* Perceval was challenged by
the husband of the lady he had encountered in the
tent, and from whom he had stolen the kiss and
jewel. He had misunderstood that Perceval had acted
in innocence and was overcome by the latter.
Perceval was then said to have forgotten about God
for a total of five years, but his uncle, the HERMIT
KING, absolved him.

This is as much as Chrétien de Troyes tells us, for
his work was unfinished. However, in his
CONTINUATION Manessier takes up the story and
tells how Perceval returned to the castle and asked
the appropriate Grail Question. He discovered that
the FISHER KING had been wounded by fragments
from a sword that had killed GOON DESERT, the
Fisher King's brother. Perceval, discovering that the
wounds would not heal until the murderer had been
dealt with, sought him out and killed him. The
Fisher King was healed and his lands restored to
fertility. Perceval's identity was then revealed to him
as the nephew of the GRAIL KING, who had been
sustained by the Grail during his incapacitation, and,
when that king died, Perceval succeeded him,
though, upon successfully achieving the Grail, after
which GALAHAD died, Perceval was said to have
lived on for at least a year.

From these origins, Perceval subsequently
appeared in romances on both sides of the English

Channel. The English *SIR PERCEVAL OF GALLES* says that his mother was ACHEFLOUR, the sister of Arthur, and his father, also called Perceval, had been killed many years previously by the RED KNIGHT. His lover was called LUFAMOUR. Perceval was said to have died while away on a Holy Crusade. The *DIDOT PERCEVAL* says that the RICH FISHER revealed to Perceval the secret words that Jesus had passed on to JOSEPH OF ARIMATHEA. In PEREDUR, the Welsh variation of his story, his father is named as EFRAWG. The Grail Procession is described as having included a maiden carrying a salver on which there was a head surrounded by blood. This head, Perceval later found out, was that of his cousin, whose death he had to avenge. It was in this version of Perceval's story that he was said to have done battle with an AFANC.

In the later *QUESTE DEL SAINTE GRAAL*, and in the works of Sir Thomas MALORY, Perceval has to some degree become supplanted by Galahad, though it was he who was at first thought to have achieved the Grail. Malory calls Perceval's father PELLI-NORE. WOLFRAM VON ESCHENBACH makes his father GAHMURET, his mother HERZELOYDE, his sister DINDRANE and his sons KARDEIZ and LOHENGRIN. *PERLESVAUS* again differs, making his father JULAIN and his mother YGLAIS. GERBERT makes them GALES LI CAUS and PHILOSOPHINE. *Bliocadran* makes his father, BLIOCADRAN, the hero of that work, while the *TAVOLA RITONDA* makes his sister AGRESTIZIA.

PERCEVAL
Arthurian
Unfinished work by CHRÉTIEN DE TROYES, probably better known as *Le CONTE DE GRAAL*. Written for Philip, Count of Flanders, and started *c*. 1180, it remained unfinished because of the author's death *c*. 1183. Several *CONTINUATIONS* subsequently appeared, each attempting to finish what Chrétien de Troyes had started.

PERCIVAL
Arthurian
A variant of PERCEVAL.

PEREDUR
Welsh
The warrior son of EFRAWG who fought the Battle of ARFDERYDD against his cousin, the British Prince GWENDDOLAU. His companion in that battle was GWRGI, who was, like himself, a cousin of Gwenddolau. Peredur later resurfaced in the Arthurian cycle as Sir PERCEVAL.

PEREDUR
Welsh and Arthurian
A Welsh romance concerning the exploits and quests of PEREDUR, which has become included in the *MABINOGION*.

PEREVIDA
Arthurian
One of the various names given as the mother of GALAHAD by LANCELOT.

PERFERREN
Arthurian
Welsh tradition names Perferren as a niece of ARTHUR, the wife of BUGI and the mother of Saint BEUND.

PERILOUS BRIDGE
Arthurian
The bridge leading to the GRAIL CASTLE, according to *PERLESVAUS*.

PERIMONES
Arthurian
This knight, known as the RED KNIGHT, was defeated by GARETH.

PERLESVAUS
Arthurian
A thirteenth-century French prose romance concerning the quest for the Holy GRAIL.

PERNAM
Arthurian
The brother of King MARK of CORNWALL and MELIODAS, according to the Italian romance *TRISTANO RICCARDIANO*.

PERNEHAN
Arthurian
According to the *PROSE TRISTAN*, the brother of King MARK who was murdered by him, for reason or reasons unknown.

PERSE
Arthurian
Promised by her father to ZELOTES, she was rescued from him by ECTOR DE MARIS, who loved her.

PERTOLEPE
Arthurian
A knight who was defeated by GARETH, and was known as the GREEN KNIGHT.

PETER DES ROCHES
Arthurian

The BISHOP OF THE BUTTERFLY, so called because this historical Bishop of WINCHESTER (bishop 1204–38) was said to have been given by ARTHUR the power of closing his hand and opening it to reveal a butterfly. The *Lanercost Chronicle* recounts how the Bishop came across a house in which Arthur was still alive and banqueted him, his special gift being given to him to prove that his story was true.

PETIT BRUT
Arthurian

A French chronicle of the Arthurian period by Rauf de BOUN.

PETITCRIEU
Arthurian

Owned by GILAN, Duke of SWALES, this fairy dog, wondrously coloured, tiny and having a sweet-sounding bell hanging from its neck, originally came from AVALON. Gilan gave it to TRISTAN.

PETROC, SAINT
Arthurian

A well-known Cornish saint who may have originated in South WALES. The poet Dafydd Nanmor says that he was one of the seven survivors of the Battle of CAMLANN, but it has been suggested that for this the poet used a local tradition.

PETRUS
Arthurian

One of the companions of JOSEPH OF ARIMATHEA. He travelled to the ORKNEYS and converted the ruler, ORCANT, to Christianity, marrying the King's daughter, CAMILLE. According to the pedigree of JOHN OF GLASTONBURY, he was an ancestor of LOT.

PHAGAN
Arthurian

One of the two missionaries sent, *c*. AD 166, from Rome by Pope ELUTHERIUS at the request of the then king, LUCIUS, to invigorate the work at GLASTONBURY. He and his colleague DERUVIAN have subsequently come to be regarded as the founders of Glastonbury Abbey, though this is an anachronism, as the abbey church dates from a later period.

PHARAMOND
Arthurian
Also FARAMOND

A legendary Frankish King who possibly has his origins in a similarly named historical ruler of the fifth century. In the Arthurian romances he appears as a freedman – that is, a slave who has been given his liberty – who seized the French throne, travelling in disguise to ARTHUR's court (Arthur was his enemy), but being discovered and expelled again. His daughter, BELIDE, fell in love with TRISTAN, but when he did not return her passion she died of a broken heart. This, however, did not prevent Pharamond from giving refuge to Tristan and GORVENAL after the death of MELIODAS. The Italian romancer ARIOSTO says that Pharamond had a son, CLODION, who was defeated in combat by Tristan. Pharamond also appears in non-Arthurian romance, in particular one from the seventeenth century that says that he fell in love with the daughter of the King of Cimbri, ROSAMONDE.

PHARIANCE
Arthurian

A knight who was a companion of BAN and BORS when they came to the succour of ARTHUR, and took part in the battle of BEDEGRAINE. The elder Bors eventually sent him into exile for murder and he became a follower of CLAUDAS.

PHARIEN
Arthurian

It is possible that this character is the same as PHARIANCE, probably a name adopted by him following his exile by BORS and allegiance to CLAUDAS. His wife became the lover of King Claudas. Following the death of Bors, the latter's sons fell into his hands, but he soon passed them into the custody of Claudas.

PHELIM (MAC DALL)
Irish

A variant of FEDLIMID, although it seems likely that the reverse is true.

PHELOT
Arthurian

A treacherous knight who wanted to kill LANCELOT, so persuaded his wife to beseech Lancelot to climb a tree to retrieve her falcon. Ever chivalrous, Lancelot agreed, but had to remove his heavy armour to do so, and, when he had done this, Phelot attacked the unarmed and unprotected knight. However, Lancelot took hold of a sturdy branch and easily repelled the attack, striking Phelot hard on the side of the head, knocking him senseless. Lancelot then beheaded the unconscious knight with his own sword.

PHILIPPON
Arthurian
King of England and father of MELIADICE. He was succeeded by his son-in-law, CLERIADUS.

PHILOSOPHINE
Arthurian
According to the *CONTINUATION* of GERBERT, the wife of GALES LI CAUS and mother of PERCEVAL.

PICT(S)
General
The name applied to the inhabitants of northern BRITAIN during the Roman occupation, and also during the traditional Arthurian period. They are known to have been raiding in Britain at the time of the Roman withdrawal, and it has been suggested that VORTIGERN invited the SAXONS to Britain to oppose them. GEOFFREY OF MONMOUTH says that they would have been wiped out by ARTHUR had not the clergy interceded. BOECE stated that GUINEVERE died as their captive. Their forces made up a part of the army, along with Saxons and Scots, which was defeated by the young King Arthur at the Battle of the River DOUGLAS. They were also put down again in Moray, along with Scots and Irish forces, by Arthur and HOEL.

Racially, the Picts were possibly a Celtic race, called *Priteni* in their own language, a name that is thought to have been one possible origin for Britain itself. The Irish referred to them as *Cruthin*, and applied this term to a similar race of people living in IRELAND. The Romans called them *Picti* (hence Picts), meaning 'painted folk'. Although they almost certainly preceded the Britons themselves, the Venerable BEDE states that they arrived after them, originating in Scythia, a region that lies in present-day Ukraine. Geoffrey of Monmouth seems to have picked up on this point and adds that their migration took place under the rule of King SODRIC, who suffered heavy losses at the hands of the British King MARIUS. However, Marius was said to have bestowed Caithness on them, possibly in order to suppress them. The medieval Irish poet Mael Mura of Othain maintained that they originated in Thrace. Wherever or whatever their origins, the principal kings of the Pict kingdom during the traditional Arthurian period were said to have been Galem I (AD 495), Drust III and Drust IV (AD 510–25), Drust III alone (AD 525–30), Gartnait III (AD 530) and Cailtram (AD 537). There were two main Pict kingdoms, the northern and the southern, the southern being divided into four states, Atholl, Circinn, Fife and Fortrenn.

PINEL
Arthurian
A cousin of LAMORAK who, following the latter's demise, attempted to poison GAWAIN in revenge. Sir Pinel of IRELAND accidentally consumed the poison and GUINEVERE was at first accused of the murder. However, once the true facts were discovered, Pinel had to flee.

PINNER
British
The legendary King of ENGLAND who was defeated and killed by MOLMUTIUS as he sought to expand his kingdom.

PLEGRUS
Arthurian
The lover of BLENZIBLY in Icelandic romance. He was killed by KALEGRAS, who subsequently became the father of TRISTAN by Blenzibly.

POITIERS
Arthurian
A duchy in western France that was given to BLEOBERIS, who had supported his father, LANCELOT, in his quarrel with ARTHUR.

POLIDAMAS
Arthurian
The nephew of YDER and one of the KNIGHTS OF THE ROUND TABLE.

POMPARLES BRIDGE
Arthurian
A bridge over the River Brue, also known as the *Pons Perilis* (cf. PERILOUS BRIDGE), on the main road from GLASTONBURY to Street. It is cited as one of the places from which EXCALIBUR was thrown when it was returned to the LADY OF THE LAKE.

POPE, THE
General
The head of the Roman Catholic Church, the Pope is mentioned in several of the Arthurian romances, whether fictional or actual. The fictitious Pope SULPICIUS – possibly cognate with Pope Simplicius (AD 468–83) – was said to have made GAWAIN a knight. The Pope was also said to have crowned ARTHUR as the Emperor of Rome and to have sent the Bishop of ROCHESTER to mediate between Arthur and LANCELOT in their war over GUINEVERE. The Salzburg Annals and Jean de Preis (1138–1400) claim that Pope Hilary (AD 461–68) was the contemporary of Arthur. Other

popes in the traditional Arthurian period were Felix III, Gelasius I, Anastasius II, Symachus, Hormisdas, John I, Felix IV, Boniface II, John II, Agapitus I, Silverius and Vigilius.

PORREX
British and Arthurian

An early and legendary Prince of BRITAIN who, according to GEOFFREY OF MONMOUTH, was a descendant of BRUTUS. The son of GORBODUC and JUDON, he had a younger brother by the name of FERREX, with whom he quarrelled over the right of succession. Porrex plotted to ambush his brother, but he fled to GAUL, whence he returned with a Gaulish army, but was defeated and killed. As Ferrex had been her favourite, Judon was driven insane by her grief, and, while Porrex slept, she hacked him to pieces. As neither Porrex nor Ferrex had left an heir, the line of Brutus died out when Gorboduc died. After his death, so one tradition says, PRYDEIN came from CORNWALL and conquered Britain, thus leading to the association of Prydein as the eponym of Britain.

POWYS
Welsh and Arthurian

An early Welsh kingdom that was, in the Arthurian period, said to have been ruled by legendary kings such as CADELL I, CYNGEN I and BROCHMAIL I.

PRASUTAGUS
British

The husband of BOUDICCA, and thus ruler of the ICENI, who kept a degree of autonomy under the Romans. After his death, however, the Romans plundered the royal possessions, flogged Boudicca and raped her daughters, an act that led Boudicca, now the sole ruler of the Iceni, to rise up against the Romans and lead a successful, though short-lived, campaign against them.

PREIDDEU ANNWFN
Welsh and Arthurian

The Spoils of Annwfn, an early Welsh poem dating from *c.* 900, which was allegedly written by TALIESIN. The poem, which obviously uses an earlier legend as its basis, concerns an expedition ARTHUR made to the OTHERWORLD to secure a magic cauldron. The *Preiddeu Annwfn* is particularly important to Celtic study because it gives one of the clearest descriptions of the various realms within the Otherworld. There are the glass fort of CAER WYDYR and the paradisiacal land where a fountain runs with wine and no one ever knows old age or sickness, this region being known as either CAER FEDDWIDD (the Fort of CAROUSAL) or CAER SIDDI. It is thought that this story forms one of the sources for the later GRAIL legends.

PRESELI HILLS
Arthurian

A range of hills in DYFED, to the east of Fishguard, that can boast more Arthurian objects than any other region in BRITAIN for such a small area, among them BEDD ARTHUR and CARN ARTHUR.

PRESTER JOHN
Arthurian

First mentioned by the chronicler Otto of Freising, this legendary monarch was thought to have ruled in either Asia or Africa. It was said that he attacked Ecbatana and defeated the Medes and the Persians, whose capital it was. A letter, claimed to have been written by Prester John, appeared in Europe during the twelfth century (perhaps *c.* 1185). It described the various wonders of his kingdom, and became vastly popular. Marco Polo identified him with an Asiatic ruler, but the fourteenth-century Jordanus de Severac placed his kingdom in Ethiopia.

Prester John appears in a number of the Arthurian legends. According to WOLFRAM VON ESCHENBACH, he was the son of FEIREFIZ and REPANSE, which made him a cousin of ARTHUR and nephew of PERCEVAL. In the Dutch romance *Lancelot*, he continues this association but is, this time, the son of Perceval. In *Tom a'Lincoln* he was the father of ANGLITORA, with whom TOM A'LINCOLN, Arthur's illegitimate son, eloped.

PRIAMUS
Arthurian

A SARACEN knight whose wondrous line of descent was said to include the biblical Joshua, ALEXANDER THE GREAT, the Maccabees and Hector of Troy! He fought with GAWAIN and then asked that knight to help in his conversion to Christianity, though the actual outcome of their combat is unknown. Priamus dabbed both sets of wounds with water from a vial that contained the Four Waters of Paradise, and they were both soon fully healed. Priamus, after his conversion, became a duke and one of the KNIGHTS OF THE ROUND TABLE.

PRIORY OAK
Welsh and Arthurian

Another name for MERLIN'S TREE in CARMARTHEN.

PRIURE

Arthurian

According to *DIU CRÔNE*, the scaly envoy of this King of the Sea brought a cup to ARTHUR's court that would prove whether men or women were false. When tested, only Arthur was shown to be true.

PRO OF IERNESETIR

Arthurian

One of the aliases under which the wounded TRISTAN was said to have travelled to IRELAND to have his poisoned wounds healed by ISEULT. Alternatively, he was said to have adopted a simple anagram of his name, TANTRIS.

PROCIDES

Arthurian

The castellan (governor) of Limerick castle and gonfalonier (standard-bearer) of IRELAND, according to *DURMART LE GALLOIS*.

PROPHÉCIES DE MERLIN

Arthurian

A thirteenth-century French work detailing the prophecies made by MERLIN. It was allegedly written by Richard of IRELAND.

PROSE LANCELOT

Arthurian

A thirteenth-century French work that forms a part of the *VULGATE VERSION*.

PROSE MERLIN

Arthurian

The name given to two medieval romances about MERLIN, one English and one French.

PROSE TRISTAN

Arthurian

A large thirteenth-century French work that describes the career of TRISTAN.

PRYDEIN

British and Arthurian

Coming from CORNWALL following the death of PORREX, Prydein was said to have conquered the remainder of BRITAIN. It is this legend that has led to his being cited as a possible eponym for the country.

PRYDERI

Welsh and Arthurian

The son of PWYLL and RHIANNON. On the night of his birth Rhiannon's ladies-in-waiting fell asleep, and the tiny infant disappeared before he could be named. To save themselves from being blamed, the women smeared Rhiannon with blood and claimed that she had killed the baby and disposed of the body. Pwyll believed her innocent and refused to divorce her. Rhiannon, rather than fight the testimony of the women, did penance by carrying all those who would accept her offer into the castle.

The small baby was discovered by TEYRNON TWRYF LIANT. He adopted the boy as his own and named him GWRI. A year later, struck by the likeness of the boy to Pwyll, Teyrnon Twryff Liant concluded that the boy he had been looking after was none other than the lost child, so he took him to Pwyll. Pwyll and Rhiannon called the boy Pryderi and placed him in the care of PENDARAN DYFED, under whose guidance he grew up to be handsome, courteous and brave, a great warrior who was loved by his people. He married CIGFA, the daughter of GWYN GOHOYW.

Pryderi was among the seven survivors of the expedition to IRELAND led by BENDIGEID VRAN, and one of those who, after eighty-seven years' journeying, buried the severed head of Bendigeid Vran under the WHITE MOUNT in LONDON. The others who returned with him were MANAWYDDAN FAB LLYR, GLUNEU EIL TARAN (GLIFIEU), TALIESIN, YNAWC (YNAWAG), GRUDYEN (GRUDDIEU) and HEILYN. On his return to WALES he found that his cousin MANAWYDAN FAB LLYR had been disinherited by CASWALLAWN, the son of BELI. To compensate him for his loss Pryderi gave Manawydan fab Llyr his own mother, Rhiannon, as a wife, along with the seven *cantrefs* of DYFED (literally meaning 'one hundred', a *cantref* was an administrative district).

One night, as Pryderi, Manawydan fab Llyr, Rhiannon and Cigfa were feasting, they heard a huge clap of thunder. This was followed by a cloud, out of which emanated a brilliant, blinding light, which enveloped them. As the light faded, they found themselves quite alone in Dyfed, for all their houses, men and animals had mysteriously disappeared. The four then became hunters, for the woods were well stocked with game and the rivers teemed with fish. For two years they lived quite happily, but Pryderi and Manawydan fab Llyr grew tired of their lonely existence and decided to travel from town to town to earn a living.

Some time later they were in the woods, hunting with their dogs, when the animals disappeared into a CAER. Pryderi, against the better judgement of Manawydan fab Llyr, followed them, meaning to lead them out again, but he too was trapped inside.

Manawydan fab Llyr waited until dusk for his cousin to reappear and then returned to Rhiannon to tell her what had happened. She immediately went to the caer and there saw a door that had remained invisible to Manawydan fab Llyr. She, too, entered the caer, whereupon it disappeared, taking Rhiannon, Pryderi and the dogs with it.

Cigfa was very frightened when she realised that only she and Manawydan fab Llyr were left. He, however, behaved honourably towards her, and swore to provide for her in her husband's absence. Having no visible means of doing this, Manawydan fab Llyr became a cobbler, a trade at which he excelled. Within a year he had prospered sufficiently to establish three crofts. These he sowed with wheat, but when the first crop was ripe and he came to reap it, he found that every ear had been stripped clean. The same happened with the second, so he sat and watched over the third. At night a host of mice appeared and started to eat the wheat.

When Manawydan fab Llyr appeared, the mice scattered, but he managed to catch one, which he swore he would solemnly hang the next day for theft. Cigfa tried to dissuade him from this ridiculous act, but Manawydan fab Llyr was adamant that the mouse should pay for its crime. As he was preparing the tiny gallows, a poor clerk came by, the first person other than Cigfa he had seen for a year, and offered Manawydan fab Llyr a sum of money if he would spare the mouse. Manawydan fab Llyr refused. Next a richly dressed priest came by and significantly increased the offer of the clerk, but again the offer was refused. Finally a bishop accompanied by his entire retinue stopped and offered Manawydan fab Llyr a king's ransom for the life of the mouse. Once more the offer was refused, but the bishop persisted, offering instead to give Manawydan fab Llyr that which he desired more than anything else. Manawydan fab Llyr said that he wanted the return of Rhiannon and Pryderi, and the spell on their land to be lifted. The bishop agreed and revealed himself to be LLWYD FAB CIL COED, the husband of the mouse that Manawydan fab Llyr had captured. He also confessed that it was he who was responsible for the spell, which he had cast to avenge Pwyll's treatment of his friend GWAWL FAB CLUD. Good as his word, Manawydan fab Llyr released the mouse, the spell was immediately broken, Rhiannon and Pryderi appeared, and Dyfed was restored to its former state.

Pryderi's death came about through the trickery of GWYDION FAB DÔN. Pryderi owned a herd of magic swine, which had been given to PWYLL by ARAWN. Gwydion fab Dôn told his master MATH FAB MATHONWY about them and promised to secure them for him. Along with eleven companions, all disguised as bards, Gwydion fab Dôn travelled from GWYNEDD to Dyfed, where he and his companions were warmly received by Pryderi.

Gwydion fab Dôn explained the purpose of his visit to Pryderi and promised the next morning to show him a fair exchange for the swine. After consulting his advisers, Pryderi agreed. That night Gwydion fab Dôn magically created twelve stallions, twelve greyhounds with golden collars and twelve golden shields. Pryderi accepted them and Gwydion fab Dôn hurriedly drove off the swine for he knew that his enchantment would fail after two days.

When it did, Pryderi and his men set out in hot pursuit to meet the army of MATH FAB MATHONWY, who feared for the safety of his kingdom. This was exactly what Gwydion fab Dôn wanted, for the purpose in obtaining the swine had been to incite the conflict and thus get Math fab Mathonwy out of the way for long enough to allow him and his brother GILFAETHWY to abduct and ravish the foot-holder GOEWIN. After two indecisive battles, Pryderi and Math fab Mathonwy called a truce and decided that the argument should be settled in single combat between Gwydion fab Dôn and Pryderi. The two met at MAEN TYRIAWG, where Gwydion fab Dôn used his magic to overcome and kill Pryderi.

PRYDWEN
Arthurian
According to Welsh tradition, Prydwen was the name of the ship in which ARTHUR made his expedition to the OTHERWORLD of ANNWFN. However, GEOFFREY OF MONMOUTH gives this name to Arthur's shield.

PUBIDIUS
Arthurian
The ruler of Mathraval (WALES) who, in one version of the story of MERLIN, is named as the wizard's maternal grandfather.

PUCELLE AUX BLANCHE MAINS
Arthurian
'Pucelle of the White Hands' or 'Maiden with the White Hands'. The fairy lover of GUINGLAIN who lived on the GOLDEN ISLAND.

PUCK
Arthurian
A peculiarly British earth spirit who is a decided, if distant, relation of Pan of classical mythology.

MISS JULIA HARLAND AND MISS CONQUEST.

AS OBERON AND PUCK.

OBE: Hast thou the flower there ? Welcome, wanderer.
PUCK. Ay, there it is.

MIDSUMMER NIGHT'S DREAM.

Act 2, Sc 2.

Puck, the impish servant of Oberon. (© Historical Picture Archive, nineteenth century/Corbis)

He had various names – Gruagach, Urisk, Boggart, Dobie and Hob – all of which reflect his earthy quality. He does not appear widely in Arthurian tales, but appears as OBERON's impish servant in SHAKESPEARE's *A MIDSUMMER NIGHT'S DREAM*.

Puck is described in a biography of him written in 1588 as the child of a young girl and a 'hee-fayrie'. He confines his mischief to the house, doing housework in exchange for cream or cake, and has the ability to change himself into any animal at will. One tale says that travellers, tempted to mount a strange horse on a wild moor, have often found themselves in the middle of a stream with nothing between their legs save a saddle!

PUFFIN
Arthurian

According to Cornish folklore, ARTHUR was reincarnated as a puffin after his death. Various other animal incarnations are also ascribed to Arthur, such as the CHOUGH or RAVEN.

PULZELLA GAIA
Arthurian

The daughter of MORGAN Le Fay by HEMISON, according to Italian romance. However, her name is in fact a title, simply signifying the Cheerful Damsel. Abducted by BURLETTA DELLA DISERTA, she was rescued by LANCELOT. She became the lover of GAWAIN, hut warned him to keep their affair a secret. He failed to keep his promise, and she no longer came when he summoned her. Gawain, however, who had rejected the advances of GUINEVERE, had to prove that Pulzella Gaia was his lover, or die. Pulzella Gaia arrived with her fairy army to rescue him, but warned that her mother would imprison her. This she did, making her stand in water up to her waist. Gawain then came to her aid, rescued her and imprisoned Morgan Le Fay.

PURGATORY
Arthurian

The region of purification visited by GAWAIN in the Middle Dutch romance *WALEWEIN*. It is described as being a boiling river into which the souls of the dead went, as black birds, to emerge again as white ones.

PURPLE KNIGHT
Arthurian

A knight who was defeated, along with many others, by the GREAT FOOL, an unnamed nephew of ARTHUR and the hero of the Irish romance *Eachtra an Amadán Mor*.

PWYLL
Welsh

One of the main characters of the *MABINOGION*. His story is to be found in the first, third and fourth books. Pwyll, Lord of DYFED, was out hunting one day when he drove the hounds of ARAWN, Lord of ANNWFN, from a stag. To atone for such an insult, Pwyll agreed to spend a year in Annwfn, during which he would kill Arawn's enemy HAFGAN. Arawn then changed their appearance so that each resembled the other, and they parted, each going to the other's realm.

Pwyll acted honourably during his year in Annwfn, for, although he shared a bed with Arawn's wife, who believed him to be her husband, never once did he lie with her. At the year's end, having fulfilled his promise and killed Hafgan, Pwyll returned home to find that Arawn had ruled Dyfed with untold wisdom. Pwyll then explained to his company all that had transpired, which led to his being given the title Pwyll, Pen Annwfn.

Some time later Pwyll first saw the beautiful RHIANNON, daughter of HEFEYDD HÊN. Captivated by her beauty, Pwyll sought her hand and they were betrothed. At the end of the year Pwyll went to Hefeydd's house to be married. However, during the wedding feast a handsome and finely dressed youth came in and asked a boon of Pwyll that he, without thinking, freely granted, only to discover that the youth was GWAWL FAB CLUD, Rhiannon's rejected suitor. The boon requested was for Rhiannon herself.

Although she was furious, Rhiannon was obliged to comply, but she cunningly suggested that they postpone the boon for a year. She then told Pwyll of her plan. On the night in question Pwyll was to hide 100 of his men in the orchard outside the hall. He would enter in the guise of a shabbily dressed beggar during the wedding feast, carrying a large sack that he would ask to be filled with food. She would see that the request was met and would then ask Gwawl fab Clud to tread the food down into the sack and so capture him in it. Pwyll should then summon his men.

The plan went exactly as devised, and Pwyll's men raced into the hall. They gave the sack an almighty kick and carried on doing so in turn until Gwawl fab Clud was forced to plead for mercy. Only when he had promised to withdraw his claim to Rhiannon and never seek revenge was he freed.

Pwyll married Rhiannon and they lived in contentment, although after three years she still had not borne him a child. His lords advised him to take another wife, but Pwyll refused. Within the year Rhiannon had borne a son. However, while she slept off the efforts of childbirth, her ladies-in-waiting also fell asleep and the baby mysteriously disappeared. In an attempt to cover their guilt, the ladies-in-waiting smeared the sleeping Rhiannon with blood and accused her of murdering the child, who had not even been named. Pwyll refused to accept Rhiannon's guilt, but, as she would not defend herself, he was forced to make her do penance, so she sat outside the castle every day, carrying all those who accepted her offer into the castle on her back.

The baby was found on the doorstep of TEYRNON TWRYF LIANT, who named the boy GWRI. After a year, struck by the child's resemblance to Pwyll, he took the child to the King, who welcomed back his lost son, who was named PRYDERI. Pwyll died shortly afterwards, but his wife lived on, later becoming the wife of MANAWYDAN FAB LLYR.

PWYLL, PEN ANNWFN
Welsh
'Pwyll, Head of Annwfn', the title given to PWYLL by his lords after they had heard of the king's year in ANNWFN and that for the previous year DYFED had been ruled over by ARAWN.

QUEEN OF CYPRUS
Arthurian

An unnamed sister of ARTHUR, perhaps MORGAN Le Fay. She sent Arthur an enchanted horn that was drunk from to test the fidelity of the drinker's wife. If the wife had been unfaithful, the contents would be spilled.

QUEEN OF EASTLAND
Arthurian

According to Sir Thomas MALORY, one of the four enchantresses, associates of MORGAN Le Fay, who captured LANCELOT. Her accomplices were the QUEEN OF NORTHGALIS, the QUEEN OF SORESTAN and the QUEEN OF THE OUT ISLES.

QUEEN OF NORTHGALIS
Arthurian

An enchantress and an associate of MORGAN Le Fay. She was one of the four sorceresses who imprisoned LANCELOT until he chose which he loved. Her accomplices were the QUEEN OF EASTLAND, the QUEEN OF SORESTAN and the QUEEN OF THE OUT ISLES.

QUEEN OF SORESTAN
Arthurian

A sorceress who fell in love with LANCELOT. She, and three other enchantresses, imprisoned Lancelot in her castle, the CHÂTEAU DE LA CHARETTE, until he chose which one of them he loved. Her accomplices were the QUEEN OF EASTLAND, the QUEEN OF NORTHGALIS and the QUEEN OF THE OUT ISLES.

QUEEN OF THE OUT ISLES
Arthurian

According to Sir Thomas MALORY, one of the four enchantresses, associates of MORGAN Le Fay, who captured LANCELOT. Her accomplices were the QUEEN OF EASTLAND, the QUEEN OF NORTHGALIS and the QUEEN OF SORESTAN. The Out Isles are thought to be identifiable as the Hebrides.

QUEEN OF THE WASTE LANDS
Arthurian

One of the queens aboard the barge that carried the dying ARTHUR to AVALON following the battle of CAMLANN. She is named as the enchantress who told PERCEVAL of his mother's death.

QUEST FOR THE HOLY GRAIL
Arthurian

See GRAIL

QUESTE DEL SAINTE GRAAL
Arthurian

A thirteenth-century French romance that forms a part of the *VULGATE VERSION*, and that describes the Quest for the Holy GRAIL. It introduces GALAHAD as the hero who achieved the object of the quest and is thought to have been written by a Cistercian.

QUESTING BEAST
Arthurian

A curious beast, the offspring of a mortal girl and the Devil, that was chased by PELLINORE and subsequently by PALAMEDES. It is described as having the head of a snake, the body of a leopard, the hindquarters of a lion and the feet of a hart. From its stomach came the noise of forty questing (baying) hounds, hence the name. This particular creature seems to have had its origin in an allegorical animal, variously described, with barking pups inside her. This creature was mentioned in *PERLESVAUS* and was reported to have once been spotted by PERCEVAL.

QUINTILIAN
Arthurian

The nephew of LUCIUS HIBERIUS, the Roman leader. While GAWAIN was delivering a message to Lucius from ARTHUR, Quintilian made a derogatory comment regarding the Britons. In his anger, Gawain beheaded him and had to flee Lucius' encampment.

King Arthur sees the Questing Beast, the offspring of a union between the Devil and a mortal girl. (Aubrey Beardsley, 1893–4. Bridgeman Art Library/The Stapleton Collection)

R

RADIGUND
Arthurian

The Queen of the AMAZONS who was killed by BRITOMART.

RAGNELL
Arthurian

A loathsome-looking hag whom GAWAIN married as the condition for ARTHUR being given the answer to a riddle posed to him and that none of his court could answer. Once married, she informed her new husband that she could become beautiful either by day or by night, the former suiting her better, the latter suiting Gawain. Remembering the words of wisdom this lady had given Arthur as the response to the riddle 'What is it that a lady desires the most?', Gawain allowed the lady to make her own choice. As a result of his chivalrous and selfless choice, she instantly became beautiful both by day and by night.

RAGUIDEL
Arthurian

A knight who was killed by GUENGASOAIN but whose dead body subsequently appeared near ARTHUR's court on an apparently unmanned ship. With his body was a letter asking that his death be avenged and stating that the person who did this would be the only one able to draw rings from the fingers of the corpse. Sir GAWAIN killed Guengasoain and returned to remove the rings from Raguidel's fingers.

RÁTH CRUACHAN
Irish

The location of the royal cemetery RELIGH NA RIGH, in which the historical Kings of IRELAND are buried.

RÁTH LUACHAR
Irish

The home of LIA, who kept the treasure bag of the FIAN.

RATHLEAN
Arthurian

The mother of the OTHERWORLD woman AILLEAN and thus, for a time, the mother-in-law of ARTHUR.

RAVEN
Arthurian

According to Cornish folklore, the soul of ARTHUR passed into a raven's body after his death, although it was also said to have become a CHOUGH or a PUFFIN. Some think that the raven was a later replacement for the chough when that species became extinct within the county.

RAYNBROWN
Arthurian

A knight and the son of Sir IRONSIDE.

RECESSE
Arthurian

The kingdom of CARRAS, brother of King CLAUDAS.

RED BOOK OF HERGEST, THE
Welsh and Arthurian

A fourteenth-century manuscript that, along with the *WHITE BOOK OF RHYDDERCH*, contains the *MABINOGION* cycle.

RED BRANCH
Irish

The collective name given to the heroes at the court of CONCHOBAR MAC NESSA. They were so called because the room they used for their meetings within the palace at EMHAIN MHACHA was coloured red, and not from the fact that the blood they spilt was red, as has been suggested by some sources. Other sources say that the name derives from ROSS, who was the forefather of many of the heroes of the Red Branch, the association being made as Ross was usually known with the epithet 'the Red'. This argument certainly bears weight when the genealogy of Ross is considered, but it by no means encompasses all the heroes of the Red Branch.

RED HUGH
Irish

The name commonly applied to HUGH, the father of MACHA, DITHORBA and CIMBAOTH.

RED KNIGHT

Arthurian

The title of at least five knights in the Arthurian legends.

1 The knight who stole a valuable cup from Arthur's court but was pursued, caught and killed by GAWAIN.

2 True name Sir PERIMONES, he was defeated by GARETH.

3 Sir IRONSIDE, the Red Knight of the Red Lands. He was besieging LYONESSE when GARETH came to relieve that lady, and duly defeated him.

4 A title given to GAWAIN in *PERLESVAUS*.

5 A knight who was defeated by the GREAT FOOL.

RED ROSE KNIGHT

Arthurian

The title given to TOM A'LINCOLN, the illegitimate son of ARTHUR and ANGELICA.

REGAN

British

A daughter of King LEIR and sister of GONERIL and CORDELIA. She and Goneril, being the eldest of Leir's daughters, played on the old man's vanity and induced him to give them each a quarter of his kingdom. She married twice, her husbands being MAGLAURUS, Duke of ALBANY, and HENWINUS, Duke of CORNWALL, although some sources make Maglaurus the husband of Regan, and Henwinus the husband of Goneril, or even vice versa. Regan, Goneril, Maglaurus and Henwinus joined forces to usurp the remaining half of Leir's kingdom, allowing the deposed king to retain a retinue of 140 men. Goneril first reduced this to eighty men, then Regan to five, and finally Goneril again to a single man. At this stage Leir went to FRANCE, from where he was to return with his daughter Cordelia and her husband AGANIPPUS, who restored him to the throne for the last three years of his life.

RELIGH NA RIGH

Irish

The royal cemetery of the historical Kings of IRELAND. It is situated at RÁTH CRUACHAN.

REMUS

Arthurian

King of Rome, according to an unpublished Italian romance that tells how he, UTHER and TROIANO once again made the Trojans the rulers of Troy. In all probability he is the Remus who features in classical Roman mythology as the brother of Romulus, and the co-founder of Rome and the ROMAN EMPIRE.

RENOART

Arthurian

A warrior who appeared in the Guillaume d'Orange cycle of Arthurian stories. In the romance *BATAILLE LOQUIFER*, he was taken to AVALON by MORGAN Le Fay and other fairies, and there he met ARTHUR. He became the lover of Morgan Le Fay, but soon left, though he was said to have fathered CORBON on Morgan Le Fay. The jilted sorceress persuaded KAPALU to sink Renoart's ship, but he was rescued by sirens (a siren being a sea nymph from classical mythology whose singing was thought capable of luring sailors to their deaths on the rocks).

RENWEIN

Arthurian

A variant of RONWEN, the daughter of the SAXON leader HENGIST.

REOCHAID

Irish

The lover of FINDABAIR. He fought the chiefs to whom Findabair had been variously promised by AILILL and MEDHBHA for agreeing to attack CÚ CHULAINN.

REPANSE DE SCHOIE

Arthurian

The GRAIL damsel with whom FEIREFIZ fell in love at ARTHUR's court. After Feirefiz's conversion to Christianity, the pair went to India, where they became the parents of PRESTER JOHN.

RESTOR DE TRISTRAM

Arthurian

'New Tristram', the name of the hero of a lost romance that was given to him by a disgruntled fairy who intended his life to be as miserable as that of his namesake. He was taken to the palace of MORGAN Le Fay, but what happened to him once there remains unknown.

RHEGED

Welsh and Arthurian

A kingdom in the Cumbrian region of north-west BRITAIN, which was ruled by URIEN during the late fourth and early fifth centuries AD, the traditional Arthurian period. It has been suggested that Urien was the historical original of ARTHUR, which would therefore mean that Rheged was Arthur's realm. This association seems to have sprung from Arthur's connections with CARLISLE, which lies within the kingdom.

The Red Knight is slain by Sir Gareth. (Mary Evans Picture Library/Arthur Rackham Collection)

RHIANNON
Welsh and Arthurian

With a name deriving from RIG ANTONA or 'Great High Queen', Rhiannon is the goddess of horses, who is known as EPONA in Gaul and as ÉDÁIN ECHRAIDHE and MACHA in IRELAND. Her totem animals were the bull and three cranes, animals that have associations with death and rebirth.

The daughter of HEFEYDD HÊN, Rhiannon was extremely beautiful, a beauty that led PWYLL to become enchanted by her. He sought her hand, a union that was agreed to by both Rhiannon and her father. However, at a feast to celebrate their betrothal, her rejected suitor, GWAWL FAB CLUD, entered in disguise and claimed her as a boon from Pwyll, which he unwittingly granted.

Rhiannon was furious but was compelled to comply. However, she suggested that the proposed date for the fulfilment of the boon be put off for one year and then concocted a plan with Pwyll. The plan led to Gwawl fab Clud being captured in a sack and kicked viciously by Pwyll's men until he begged for mercy. Pwyll and Rhiannon released Gwawl fab Clud only after he had renounced his claim to Rhiannon and had promised never to seek revenge.

Rhiannon and Pwyll were married, but, as she had not produced a child after three years, Pwyll's advisers beseeched him to take another wife. He refused and within the year Rhiannon had borne a son. As she slept that night, her ladies-in-waiting also fell asleep and the child, who had yet to be named, mysteriously disappeared. Fearing for their own safety, the ladies-in-waiting smeared the sleeping Rhiannon with blood and woke Pwyll, saying that his wife had killed their newborn son. Pwyll refused to accept that his wife could possibly have done such a thing, but, as she would not defend herself, was forced to make her do penance, by carrying all those who accepted her offer into their castle.

The child had meantime been discovered on the doorstep of TEYRNON TWRYF LIANT, who took him in, called him GWRI and treated him as his own son. After a year, struck by the child's resemblance to Pwyll, Teyrnon Twryf Liant took the infant to the King, who was overjoyed to be reunited with his son, who was called PRYDERI. Pwyll died a short time later. Pryderi grew into a handsome and brave warrior under the guidance of his foster father PENDARAN DYFED. He succeeded his father and was much loved by his people, eventually marrying CIGFA, the daughter of GWYN GOHOYW.

Pryderi accompanied BENDIGEID VRAN on his expedition to Ireland against King MATHOLWCH, and was one of the seven survivors who returned to BRITAIN carrying the severed head of Bendigeid Vran. In his absence, however, his cousin MANAWYDAN FAB LLYR, the rightful heir of Bendigeid Vran, had been dispossessed by CASWALLAWN, the son of BELI. Pryderi therefore gave Manawydan fab Llyr his mother Rhiannon as his wife along with the kingdom of DYFED.

Rhiannon, together with her son and their hunting dogs, was later trapped in a caer under an enchantment cast by LLWYD FAB CIL COED to avenge Pwyll's ill treatment of his friend Gwawl fab Clud, a spell that was later broken after Manawydan fab Llyr and Cigfa had endured much hardship and had finally captured the wife of Llwyd fab Cil Coed in the guise of a mouse. As the spell was broken, Rhiannon, Pryderi and their dogs were restored to their former state, as were the lands of Dyfed.

R(H)IC(C)A
Welsh and Arthurian
See RHITTA CAWR

RHITTA (CAWR)
Welsh and Arthurian
Also RHICCA, RITHO

A giant who lived on YR WYDDFA FAWR (Mount SNOWDON) and who had a cloak made of beards. He was killed by a king, later named as ARTHUR, whose beard he wanted for the collar to his cloak. He is, through the similarity of their stories, thought to be identifiable with RIENCE.

RHIW BARFE
Welsh and Arthurian

'The Way of the Bearded One', a path that runs down the hill from BWLCH-Y-GROES, North WALES. It is so called for it is held that the dead RHITTA was thrown down this path to his grave at Tan-y-Bwlch.

RHONABWY
Arthurian

The eponymous hero of the *MABINOGION* story of the *DREAM OF RHONABWY*. He fell asleep and dreamt that he accompanied IDDAWC and met KAY, one of ARTHUR's knights, as well as the King himself.

RHONGOMYNIAD
Arthurian

The spear of ARTHUR, according to the *MABINOGION* story of *CULHWCH AND OLWEN*. It is thought that it equates with RON, the lance or spear mentioned by GEOFFREY OF MONMOUTH.

Rhiannon, the Welsh goddess of horses. (By permission of artist Paul Borda/© Dryad Designs, www.dryaddesign.com)

RHUN

Welsh

A handsome courtier of ELPHIN's. He was sent to seduce Elphin's wife after Elphin had boasted that his wife was the most virtuous woman alive. TALIESIN had a serving maid take the place of Elphin's wife, and she succumbed to the charms of Rhun, who cut off her ring finger to prove the infidelity. When Elphin was confronted with the ring finger, he declared that it could not possibly belong to his wife for three reasons: the finger nail was uncut, the ring was too tight and there was flour under the finger nail. His wife cut her nails regularly, wore a ring that was loose, even on her thumb, and never baked.

RHYDDERCH (HAEL)

Welsh and Arthurian

A historical King of STRATHCLYDE, SCOTLAND, who is usually referred to with his epithet 'Hael' (*hael* – 'generous'). He participated in the Battle of ARTHURET, Welsh tradition placing him on the side that opposed MYRDDIN (MERLIN). GEOFFREY OF MONMOUTH, however, in his *VITA MERLINI*, has Rhydderch fighting on the same side as the wizard, making him the husband of GANIEDA, Merlin's sister. His sword, DYRNWYN, is said to number among the THIRTEEN TREASURES OF BRITAIN.

RHYGENYDD

Welsh and Arthurian

The owner of a crock that is sometimes numbered among the THIRTEEN TREASURES OF BRITAIN.

   See also DYSGYL A GREN RHYDDERCH

RHYVERYS

Arthurian

ARTHUR's master of hounds.

RIANGABAIR

Irish

The husband of FINNABAIR and father of three beautiful daughters, one of whom was called ETAN. Also the father of LOEG, the charioteer of CÚ CHULAINN. They entertained Cú Chulainn and Loeg at the start of Cú Chulainn's quest to locate the sons of DOEL, Etan spending the night with the hero.

RIB

Irish

The brother of EOCHAIDH AIREMH. He trespassed onto the land of OENGHUS MAC IN OG and MIDHIR and was told to leave by the two gods,

who appeared to him in the guise of hospitallers with a haltered pack-horse.

RICA

Arthurian

Named in the *MABINOGION* story of *CULHWCH AND OLWEN* as the chief elder of CORNWALL and father of GORMANT. Welsh tradition seems to equate Rica with GORLOIS, or at least with the latter's traditional role.

RICCARDA

Arthurian

The wife of the KING WITH A HUNDRED KNIGHTS, according to the *Due Tristani*.

RICH FISHER

Arthurian

An alternative name sometimes used to refer to the FISHER KING.

RICHARD

Arthurian

The son of the King of Jerusalem who, according to the *PROPHÉCIES DE MERLIN*, was sent on a mission to ARTHUR's court by the POPE to obtain succour for Jerusalem, which was being besieged by the King of BAUDEC. Arthur responded by sending a force under the leadership of HENRY the Courtly. When Richard himself became the King of Jerusalem, he attacked the pagan city of SARRAS but, as no one could defeat that city's giant ruler, a truce was called.

RICHBOROUGH, BATTLE OF

Arthurian

The battle that was fought as ARTHUR landed on his return from his continental campaign at which AUGUSELUS was killed by MORDRED. It was the first of the three final battles fought by Arthur, on each occasion defeating his usurping nephew, Mordred.

RICULF

Arthurian

The chosen ruler of NORWAY following the death of King SICHELM. Though the dead king had bequeathed the kingdom to LOT, the people chose Riculf. ARTHUR, however, enforced Lot's rightful claim to the throne by invading Norway and killing Riculf.

RIEINGULID

Arthurian

According to Welsh tradition, sister of IGRAINE, thus ARTHUR's aunt. She was the mother of Saint ILLTYD.

RIENCE

Welsh and Arthurian

A king who is variously made the ruler of NORTHGALIS, IRELAND, DENMARK or the LAND OF PASTURES AND GIANTS. The *LIVRE D'ARTUS* makes him a SAXON, while SPENSER makes him the father of BRITOMART. When the young King ARTHUR was putting down the rebellion by the eleven rebel leaders at the very start of his reign, Rience was at war with LEODEGRANCE. He is most famous for having a cloak made from the beards of eleven kings he had defeated. He thought that ARTHUR's would make a fine collar to this cloak and demanded that he give it to him. War followed, during which BALIN and BALAN captured Rience and brought him to Arthur.

His story is remarkably similar to a story told in Welsh tradition about a giant, named RHITTA, RHICCA or RITHO, associated with Mount SNOWDON, who also had a cloak made of beards and whom Arthur killed. He is presumably, therefore, the same character. More modern Welsh folklore makes him a robber whom Arthur slew and buried in the neighbourhood of Llanwchllyn.

RIG ANTONA

General

'Great High Queen', a title that has been variously applied to a large number of Celtic goddesses, but most frequently to those such as EPONA, RHIANNON, MACHA and ÉDÁIN ECHRAIDHE.

RIGDONN

Irish

The father of RUADH.

RIGOMER

Arthurian

The shortened, popularised version of *MERVEILLES DE RIGOMER*.

RIOTHAMUS

British and Arthurian

A historical British king who was been identified as the historical ARTHUR or UTHER, some claiming that the name is really a title meaning 'great king'. He brought a large army to the continent to assist the Emperor ANTHEMIUS against EURIC the Visigoth. He was subsequently defeated and disappeared in Burgundy.

RITHO

Welsh and Arthurian

See RHITTA

RIVALIN

Arthurian

1 According to GOTTFRIED VON STRASSBURG, the ruler of PARMENIE and father of TRISTAN. He married BLANCHEFLEUR, the sister of King MARK. His name seems to originate in a historical Lord of Vitré, Rivalin, who was known to have flourished in the eleventh century.

2 A ruler of NANTES who attacked HOEL but was defeated in single combat by TRISTAN.

RIVALLO

British

The son of CUNEDAGIUS, whom he succeeded as King of BRITAIN.

RIWALLAWN

Arthurian

A son of URIEN of RHEGED.

ROAZ

Arthurian

An evil and villainous knight who laid siege to Queen AMENE, killing her husband and conquering most of her realm. WIGALOIS came to her aid and killed him.

ROBERT DE BORON

Arthurian

The Burgundian author (*fl.* 1200) of two very important Arthurian romances, about whose life very little is known. His works were *JOSEPH D'ARIMATHIA*, which deals with the GRAIL legends, and *MERLIN*. It is thought that he may also have been responsible for writing the *DIDOT PERCEVAL*.

ROBIN GOODFELLOW

Arthurian

The son of OBERON by a human girl.

ROC

Irish

The steward of OENGHUS MAC IN OG. He appears in the *Cath Finntrága* as a smith who helps to repair and manufacture the weapons of the TUATHA DÉ DANANN. Roc had a tryst with the mother of DIARMAID UA DUIBHNE and conceived with her a son who was killed by DÔNN, Diarmaid ua Duibhne's father. Roc discovered the dead boy and cast a Druidic spell over him so that he arose in the form of a monstrous boar, the BEANN GHULBAN, which he placed under bond to kill Diarmaid ua Duibhne.

ROCHESTER
Arthurian
A town in KENT that has been suggested as the site of the Battle of Mount AGNED, as listed by NENNIUS.

ROGES
Arthurian
Featuring in the Middle Dutch romance *WALEWEIN*, Roges was a prince who was turned into a fox by magic. He accompanied and helped GAWAIN on one of his adventures and was eventually returned to his human form.

ROI-CH, -GH
Irish
The wife of ROSS and mother, by him, of FERGHUS MAC ROICH.

ROLAND
Arthurian
The hero of any number of Italian romances, in which he is known as ORLANDO. These romances concern the exploits of a legendary Count of BRITTANY who was, according to legend, the nephew of the Emperor Charlemagne. Legend says that in AD 778, as his army was returning from a Spanish expedition, it was attacked at Roncesvalles by the Basques or, more correctly, the SARACENS, who had been forewarned by the treachery of Ganelon (Roland's jealous stepfather). Roland refused to blow his horn to summon the Emperor's aid until it was too late, and then died in the act of blowing it. The most famous romances concerning this character are *ORLANDO INNAMORATO* by BOIARDO and *ORLANDO FURIOSO* by ARIOSTO, which was based on the earlier work and attempted to complete what Boiardo had left unfinished. It is through these and other Italian romances that the story of Roland has become inexorably intertwined with the Arthurian legends.

ROMAN DE BRUT
Arthurian
Written in French by the twelfth-century writer WACE, this work contains the first reference to the ROUND TABLE. It was quickly translated and expanded by LAYAMON in his *BRUT*, which was written between 1189 and 1199.

ROMAN DES FILS DU ROI CONSTANT
Arthurian
Medieval French romance that names the wife of BAN of BRITTANY as SABE and gives him a daughter named LIBAN.

ROMAN EMPIRE
Arthurian
Even though GEOFFREY OF MONMOUTH and Sir Thomas MALORY have the Roman Empire in full existence during the traditional Arthurian period, history tells us that, in the West, the Roman Empire ceased to exist in AD 476, though the Eastern or Byzantine Empire lasted for nearly 1,000 years longer. Sir Thomas Malory states that ARTHUR defeated the Emperor LUCIUS HIBERIUS and was crowned Emperor of Rome by the POPE. *CLARIS ET LARIS* also supports the idea of the Roman Empire existing during Arthur's time, stating that the Emperor THEREUS invaded Britain but was defeated.

RON
Arthurians
The lance or spear owned by ARTHUR. It is mentioned under this name by GEOFFREY OF MONMOUTH and would seem to equate with RHONGOMYNIAD, ARTHUR's spear, which appears in the *MABINOGION* story of *CULHWCH AND OLWEN*.

RÓNÁN
Irish
A King of LEINSTER and the father of MAIL FOTHARTAIG. His second wife fell in love with her stepson and attempted to seduce him but was repulsed. She accused him of rape, but Rónán at first refused to believe it. His wife convinced him of Maíl Fothartaig's guilt, and he had his son killed.

RONWEN
Arthurian
Also HROTHWINA, RENWEIN
Daughter of the SAXON leader HENGIST and sister to HARTWAKER, AESC, OCTA, EBISSA and SARDOINE. She married VORTIGERN, the county of KENT being given to her father as the bride price. Her name appears originally to have been HROTHWINA in ANGLO-SAXON, Ronwen being the Latinisation of that name.

ROSAMONDE
Arthurian
The daughter of the King of the Cimbri who, in a non-Arthurian romance, was said to have been loved by PHARAMOND.

ROSMERTA
Gaulish and British
Also MAIA
Representing material wealth, and thus a patroness of merchants, this goddess was associated with the

Romano-Celtic MERCURY. Her name appears to mean 'Good Purveyor', and she is sometimes depicted stirring a churn, although more normally carrying a basket of fruit, which has its counterpart in the classical horn of plenty, the cornucopia.

ROSS (THE RED)

Irish

A King of ULSTER, whose epithet is thought by some to have given rise to the RED BRANCH. Ross married MAGA, daughter of OENGHUS MAC IN OG, and became the father, by her, of a giant by the name of FACHTNA, who, in turn, married NESSA and became the father of CONCHOBAR MAC NESSA. However, Maga also married CATHBHADH and subsequently became the mother, or grandmother, of several other heroes of Ulster.

ROTH KILL

Irish

A magic wheel, which was created by MOG RUITH to enable him to fly through the air. Known commonly as the 'wheel of light', it has often been confused with a mythical flying machine. It was, in fact, merely a solar symbol.

ROUGEMONT

Arthurian

The castle of TALAC.

ROULAND

Arthurian

The King of ERMINIA who, according to one of the medieval romances, was the father of TRISTAN by BLANCHEFLEUR, sister to King MARK.

ROUND TABLE

Arthurian

The most famous icon of the Arthurian sagas, the table in the great hall at ARTHUR's court at which Arthur seated his knights so that none had precedence over any other. Its origin seems a little confused, as does its actual size and shape. Commentators describe it variously as a complete disc, a ring, a semicircle or a broken ring having an opening for servants. Additionally, some say that Arthur sat at the table with his knights, while others say he sat alone at a smaller, separate table.

Originally, according to the majority view, the table belonged to UTHER. It then passed into the ownership of King LEODEGRANCE of CAMELIARD, and came to Arthur when he married Leodegrance's daughter, GUINEVERE, the Round Table, which could seat 150 knights, being a wedding gift.

It is first mentioned by the early twelfth-century writer WACE in his *ROMAN DE BRUT*, in which he says that the barons quarrelled over who had precedence, so Arthur had the table made. He is the only writer to have the curious position of the knights sitting within the circle formed by the table. When the work was translated and expanded by LAYAMON in *BRUT* (written 1189–99), the knights were found in their more normal position, around the outer edge of the table.

Layamon says that the quarrel arose during a Christmas feast and resulted in the death of several men. Shortly afterwards, while visiting CORNWALL, Arthur met a foreign carpenter who had heard of the fracas and offered to make a portable table at which 1,600 could sit without any having precedence over the others. Arthur commissioned the work and the table was completed within six weeks.

Other versions of the story credit the Round Table to MERLIN, and vary the number who could be seated at it. ROBERT DE BORON has the lowest number, with just fifty knights. The *VULGATE VERSION* makes this number 250, while Layamon's figure of 1,600 still remains the largest. The GRAIL legends further embroidered the stories surrounding the Round Table, saying that one seat at it, the SIEGE PERILOUS, remained unoccupied until GALAHAD came to the court to take his rightful position, for that siege was reserved for the holiest of knights, he who would achieve the Quest for the Holy Grail.

The Round Table in WINCHESTER, which was for many years thought to have been the original – a view supported by Caxton when he wrote the preface for Sir Thomas MALORY's *MORTE D'ARTHUR* – has since been proved (through the use of modern dating techniques) to be a replica. Dating from the fourteenth century, it still poses a very important question. If it is not the original, then is it an accurate copy?

ROWENA

Arthurian

According to GEOFFREY OF MONMOUTH, Rowena was the daughter of HENGIST who married VORTIGERN. Her name does not appear in any works that pre-date Geoffrey of Monmouth, and it is thought that her name has Welsh origins rather than ANGLO-SAXON. She appears again in a much later work, *The Fairy of the Lake* (1801) by John Thelwall, in which she was in love with ARTHUR, though still married to Vortigern. More commonly it is RONWEN, the daughter of Hengist, who is married to Vortigern. It is possible that Rowena is a

King Arthur's Round Table, around which the Knights of the Round Table sat, none having precedence over any other. (© Steboun/Corbis)

simple transcriptive error, though when the Anglo-Saxon variant of HROTHWINA is considered this situation might be considered reversed, for Hrothwina to Rowena does need much imagination.

ROWLAND
Arthurian

The son of ARTHUR, according to the Scottish ballad *CHILDE ROWLAND*, *childe* signifying that Rowland was a young man of upper-class origins. His story seems to echo much earlier Celtic stories of journeys to the OTHERWORLD. His sister ELLEN disappeared, MERLIN claiming that she had been abducted by the fairies. The wizard gave him very precise instructions on how to rescue her, and her eldest brother set off. He too vanished, for he had not done all that Merlin instructed him. The next brother also vanished for the same reasons. However, Rowland followed Merlin's instructions implicitly, including killing everyone he came across after he had entered FAIRYLAND. He came to a hill, which he entered, and inside found a hall where his sister

and his two brothers were in an enchanted state. He did battle with the King of ELFLAND and, by defeating him, secured the release of the prisoners, who returned home with him.

RUADH
Irish

The son of RIGDONN. On a voyage to Norway Ruadh found that his three ships came to a complete stop in the middle of the ocean, even though the sails were still filled by the wind. Diving beneath the ships, he discovered three giantesses holding them in position. They took him to their seabed home, where he lay with each one before both he and his ships were released. The giantesses told him that they would bear his son, and he told them that he would return to visit them on his way home. Ruadh forgot his promise, however, and, when the giantesses realised that he had sailed by, they set off after him with his son. Ruadh had too big a head start, and, realising this, the giantesses gave up the chase, cut off his son's head, and threw it after him.

RUADH ROFHESSA

Irish

One of the titles given to the DAGHDHA. It means 'Mighty and Most Learned One'.

RUA(R)DAN

Irish

The son of BRES and Brig, a daughter of the DAGHDHA. He was sent by the FOMHOIRÉ to find out how the wounded TUATHA DÉ DANANN were healed. He wounded GOIBHNIU with one of the magical weapons that the smith had made, but Goibhniu returned the compliment and Ruardan died, even though Brig implored Goibhniu to allow DIAN CÉCHT to heal him.

RUCHT

Irish

The swineherd of King OCHALL OICHNI of CONNACHT, and a good friend of FRIUCH, who was the swineherd to the god BODB, who dwelt in MUNSTER. So strong was their friendship that the populace sought to cause a quarrel between them. As a result of this argument the two swineherds fought each other for several years in a variety of forms – ravens, water-beasts, demons and finally worms. These worms were swallowed by two cows, which later bore two magnificent bulls, one being FINNBHENNACH, and the other DONN CUAILNGÈ. Which bull came from which swineherd is not known.

   See also COPHUIR IN DÁ MUCCIDA

RUDAUCUS

British

The King of CAMBRIA who formed an alliance with STATER, King of ALBANY, in an attempt to thwart the expansionist ideas of MOLMUTIUS. Together they marched into CORNWALL and confronted Molmutius' army, but both were killed, which left Molmutius as the sole ruler of a united BRITAIN.

RUDIOBUS

Romano-Gaulish

A mysterious horse god, whose name is, perhaps, a Roman corruption of a Gallic name.

RUMMARET

Arthurian

First mentioned by WACE as the King of WENELAND who paid homage to ARTHUR while the latter was in ICELAND. LAYAMON, in his translation of Wace's work, referred to the kingdom of Rummaret as WINETLAND or WINET. Rummaret gave his son to Arthur as a hostage and was said to have helped to put down a fight in Arthur's hall. Various regions have been suggested for his realm, including Finland, GWYNEDD and the country of the Wends. However, the name Weneland may have a connection with Vinland, the Norse name for a part of North America that is now thought to have been discovered in the Middle Ages. However, as so often happens, the truth will probably never be known.

RUN

Welsh and Arthurian

A son of URIEN of RHEGED.

RUNALEN

Arthurian

A son of King HOEL of BRITTANY and brother of ISEULT of the White Hands.

RURY

Irish

The son of PARTHOLÁN after whom Lake Rury was named, the lake allegedly bursting forth from his grave.

RUSSIA

Arthurian

The realm of King BARATON, according to the Arthurian legends.

RUSTICIANO DE PISA

Arthurian

An Italian writer who was certainly flourishing in 1298. Best known for having written down Marco Polo's *Travels* at the latter's dictation, he also produced a less well known *Compilation* of Arthurian romances.

S

SAAR
Irish
Also BLAI, SABIA
The wife of FIONN MAC CUMHAILL and mother of OISÎN, who was born to her after she had been transformed into a deer by a DRUID.

SABE
Arthurian
The wife of BAN of BRITTANY, according to the medieval French romance *ROMAN DES FILS DU ROI CONSTANT*.

SAB(I)A
Irish
See SAAR

SABRINA
Romano-British
The Roman form of HABREN, the name given to the river that is known today as the River SEVERN and in which ESTRILDIS and her daughter by LOCRINUS, Habren, were drowned by GWENDOLEN.

SADOR
Arthurian
According to the *PROSE TRISTAN*, the son of BRONS, he married CHELINDE and became the father of APOLLO by her. They subsequently became separated, and Chelinde, thinking Sador was dead, remarried. When he returned, Apollo did not recognise his father and killed him.

SAFERE
Arthurian
The brother of PALAMEDES who was made the Duke of Languedoc and subsequently became a Christian.

SAGA OF TRISTAN AND ISODD
Arthurian
An Icelandic version of the story of TRISTAN and ISEULT that names BLENZIBLY as the mother of TRISTAN by KALEGRAS.

SAGA OF TRISTRAM
Arthurian
The title of two renditions of the story of TRISTAN and ISEULT. One is Norwegian in origin and dates from 1266, while the other, undated, has an Icelandic provenance. These two works are generally confused with each other and are commonly simply referred to as *TRISTRAM'S SAGA*.

SAGREMOR
Arthurian
A direct descendant of the imperial family of CONSTANTINOPLE, the son of the King of HUNGARY and a KNIGHT OF THE ROUND TABLE. He had two brothers, both of whom became bishops, and a sister, CLAIRE, whom GUINGLAIN rescued from two giants who had taken her captive. He had a lover called NIOBE, but also fathered a child by the Irish princess ORAINGLAIS.

SAINGLIU
Irish
Also DUBSAINGLU
One of the two famous steeds of the hero CÚ CHULAINN, the name more correctly being Black of Saingliu. Its twin was Grey of MACHA, both foals being born at exactly the same time as Cú Chulainn himself was born.

SAINRED
Irish
A son of LIR and thus a brother of MANANNÁN MAC LIR.

SAINT MICHAEL'S MOUNT
British
Situated a short way off the south CORNWALL coast in Mount's Bay and connected to the mainland by a causeway that is usable only at low tide, this rocky island is the legendary home of the early Cornish giant CORMORAN. The island was called DINSUL in the pre-Christian era and was thought to form a part of the lost kingdom of LYONESSE.

SAINT MICHEL, MONT
Gaulish and Arthurian
A mount situated off the north coast of BRITTANY.

St Michael's Mount, Cornwall, the legendary home of the giant Cormoran. (© David Entrican, www.orange-skies.com)

It was legendarily inhabited by a giant who was later said to have been killed by none other than King ARTHUR himself.

SAINT PAUL'S CATHEDRAL
British

A familiar landmark on the LONDON skyline, Saint Paul's Cathedral was designed by Sir Christopher Wren, construction starting in 1675. It is the site that is of particular interest, for here, it is alleged, BLADUD fell from the sky on his wings and met his death, and, later, the Romans established a temple to Apollo and Diana here. Before that, the site was said to have been a Trojan temple, established by BRUTUS himself and subsequently used by LUD, whose name is remembered in Ludgate Hill, the hill that is today crowned by the magnificence of Saint Paul's Cathedral.

SALISBURY PLAIN
Arthurian

Sir Thomas MALORY makes this area in southern England the site of ARTHUR's final battle, the first reference to this siting appearing in the *Vulgate Morte Arthure*. The area is probably best known for STONEHENGE, which appears in the Arthurian legends as a memorial erected by MERLIN on the instructions of VORTIGERN.

SALMON OF LLYN LLW
Welsh and Arthurian

A gigantic fish on whose shoulders CEI and GWRHYR the interpreter travelled. The two heroes were introduced to the Salmon of Llyn Llw by one of the oldest creatures in the world, the EAGLE OF GWERNABWY.

SALMON OF-WISDOM, -KNOWLEDGE
Irish

A fish that was accidentally touched by FIONN MAC CUMHAILL's thumb while he was cooking it for his master FINNÉCES. Thenceforth Fionn mac Cumhaill had only to bite his thumb to learn all that the future held in store.

SAMALIEL
Arthurian

According to the *PROSE TRISTAN*, the son of FROLLO who went on to become a knight of great renown.

SAMERA
Irish

The father of BUAN.

SAMH-AIN, -UINN
General

One of the four major Celtic festivals, Samhain was celebrated on 1 November. The feast day is particularly important in the Irish legends because it was the date on which the people of NEMHEDH had to pay their annual tribute of two-thirds of their corn, wine and children to the FOMHOIRÉ. It was also the date of the Second Battle of MAGH TUIREDH, the eve of which saw the DAGHDHA making love to the MÓRRÍGHAN while she straddled the River UNIUS. Samhain was also the date upon which the terrible AILLÉN MAC MIDHNA annually came to TARA and burnt the court down until he was killed by the eight-year-old FIONN MAC CUMHAILL.

SAMILDANACH
Irish

The name for a polymath, a person of great and varied learning and skills. It was used with this meaning as a title for the god LUGH.

SAMSON, SAINT
Arthurian

The patron saint of BRITTANY and one of the most important of the British missionary bishops of the sixth century, founding several churches in CORNWALL and IRELAND, before travelling across the Channel to continue his work in Brittany.

Born in Siluria, South WALES, *c.* AD 525, the son of Amwn, by Anna, daughter of MEURIG ap Tewdrig, Prince of Glamorgan. While he was being ordained as a deacon by DUBRICIUS, Bishop of CAERLEON-ON-USK, a white pigeon or dove flew in and came to rest on his shoulder, where it remained until the young deacon had been ordained and had received Holy Communion. Some time later, Samson asked ILLTYD to give him permission to live on a little island near Llantwit, where Piro, a holy priest, lived. Illtyd gave him permission, and Samson went there to study in a tiny cell.

In common with many of the Celtic saints, Samson had the ability to communicate with animals. When he was bishop at Dol, Brittany, his monks reported that they were disturbed in their devotions by the cries of wild birds. One night Samson gathered the birds to him in the courtyard and instructed them to remain silent. The following morning the birds were sent away, and no longer were the devotions of the monks disturbed by their wild cries. Samson died at Dol in AD 565.

His connection with the Arthurian legends exists solely because he has been suggested as the possible original for Sir GALAHAD.

Sarras, the pagan city where Sir Galahad was said to have perceived the Holy Grail, and then died.
(Edwin Austin Abbey, 1895. © Burstein Collection/Corbis)

SANDAV

Arthurian

One of the few survivors of the Battle of CAMLANN, his survival being attributed to his wondrous beauty, which meant that everyone mistook him for an angel and no one dared attack him.

SANDDEF

Arthurian

Listed as one of the TWENTY-FOUR KNIGHTS of King ARTHUR's court.

SANGIVE

Arthurian

According to WOLFRAM VON ESCHENBACH, a sister of ARTHUR and the mother of CUNDRIE.

SARACEN(S)

Arthurian

The ancient Greek and Roman term for an Arab. During the Middle Ages it was used by Europeans to refer to all Muslims, though Spaniards used the term Moor. Romancers connected the Saracens with the pagan city of SARRAS, even going so far as to say that they were a race of Jewish descent, ruled over by TOLLEME, that lived in CORNWALL.

SARAIDE

Arthurian

A servant of the LADY OF THE LAKE who saved BORS and LIONEL from King CLAUDAS by means of her magical powers.

SARDOINE

Arthurian

A daughter of HENGIST and sister to RONWEN, HARTWAKER, AESC, OCTA and EBISSA.

SARIS

Arthurian

The King of HUNGARY, according to *CLARIS ET LARIS*, which also says he captured Cologne but was subsequently killed by LARIS.

SARMATIAN(S)

Arthurian

A barbarian people of RUSSIA from Roman times. One of their tribes was known as the ALANS, whose descendants, the OSSETES, still inhabit the Caucasus today. These people have a story that is very similar to that of the death of ARTHUR. This tells how their hero, BATRADZ, having received his mortal wound, instructed two of his companions to throw his sword into the water. Twice they pretended to have carried out the instruction, but the third time, when the sword was finally thrown, the water turned blood red and became stormy. It has been suggested that this is the origin of the EXCALIBUR story, as Sarmatian soldiers served in the Roman army in BRITAIN under Lucius Artorius Castus. Further, it has been suggested that this Artorius is the historical Arthur, and that this story was transferred from Batradz to him.

SARRAS

Arthurian

A pagan city where Sir GALAHAD was said to have perceived the GRAIL for the last time and then died. The location of the city is unknown, some sources saying it was to be found near Jerusalem and others placing it in BRITAIN. Little is known about the city other than its pagan status – the Roman god Mars was worshipped there – but the *PROPHÉCIES DE MERLIN* say that it was ruled by the pagan giant ALCHENDIC, though he eventually converted to Christianity. It is said that the SARACENS took their name from the city.

SAVARI

Arthurian

The King of SPAIN who abducted LIDOINE, the sister of LARIS. She was later rescued by ARTHUR.

SAWAN
Irish
The brother of CIAN and GOBBÁN. Sawan was left in charge of the magical cow of Cian while he went into his other brother's forge to have a new weapon made. BALAR had heard of the cow and, while Sawan was tending it, came to him and said that he had overheard his brothers talking and saying that they would leave only rough steel for Sawan's sword, while making their own from the finest steel available. Sawan gave the cow's halter to Balar, who had assumed the guise of a small boy, and rushed into the forge to confront his brothers. No sooner had he entered than Balar resumed his normal form and carried the cow back to TORY Island.

SAXON(S)
General
The term generally applied to the west Germanic (Teutonic) invaders of BRITAIN, although the Saxons were only one of the peoples who invaded the country. They were accompanied by the ANGLES (hence the term ANGLO-SAXON) and the JUTES. The invasions by these barbarian peoples, who had neither armour nor cavalry, began some time between AD 440 and 460. BEDE said that they originated in north GERMANY (Saxons), Schleswig (Angles) and Jutland (Jutes), though evidence also exists of FRISIAN involvement. Their languages coagulated into a single tongue, referred to as ANGLO-SAXON by Cambridge scholars and Old English by Oxford scholars. These invaders, whom Bede divided into three groupings, formed the ancestors of the modern English people.

SAYNES
Arthurian
The kingdom conquered by ARTHUR and subsequently bestowed, along with the deposed King's daughter, on PARIS.

SCALLIOTTA
Arthurian
An Italian variant for SHALOTT that appears in *Lancialotto Pancianti-chiano*.

SCALOT
Arthurian
An Italian variant for SHALOTT that appears in *La damigiella Scalot*.

SCÁTH
Irish
A mysterious realm to which CÚ CHULAINN was once said to have travelled and where, with the help of the King's daughter, he stole a magic cauldron, three cows and a vast treasure. However, the King wrecked his coracle in mid-ocean, and he had to swim home with his men clinging to him, but minus his booty.

SCÁTHACH
Irish
A prophetess who is described as living to the north of, or beyond, ALBA and of whom CÚ CHULAINN became a pupil to prove his worth. Cú Chulainn fought Scáthach's great rival AÍFE during his time with her and made Aífe his mistress. She bore him a son, CONALL, who also became a pupil of Scáthach.

SCÉLA MUCCE MAIC DÁ THÓ
Irish
The Story of Mac Dá Thó's Pig, an early ribald tale on which the later *Fledd Bricrenn* is based. It tells the ludicrous story of MAC DÁ THÓ, who owned a massive boar and a wondrously fast dog, the ownership of which was sought by opposing factions. Mac Dá Thó promised the dog to both parties, and then invited both to a feast, at which his pig was to be the roast, Mac Dá Thó hoping to escape the quarrel that was bound to erupt. He did, indeed, escape the fracas, but not until after his pig had been eaten and his dog had fled the scene.

SCEOLAING
Irish
See SGEOLAN.

SCHENTEFLEURS
Arthurian
One of the three sons of GORNEMANT DE GOORT. Like his two brothers, he met with a violent end.

SCHIONATULANDER
Arthurian
The husband of SIGUNE, whose body she was carrying when she met PERCEVAL.

SCONE, STONE OF
British
The Coronation Stone that is housed under the seat of the coronation chair in Westminster Abbey, LONDON. The stone has had a very chequered history. It was brought to ENGLAND from Scone in SCOTLAND by King Edward I in 1296. Before that the stone had come from IRELAND, where it was

known as the Stone of FÁL, or the LIA FÁIL, one of the four wonders the TUATHA DÉ DANANN brought with them.

Legend identifies this stone as the stone that Jacob used for a pillow during his prophetic dream at Bethel (Genesis 28:18), after which he set it up as a monument and anointed it. His sons are said to have taken it with them to Egypt, from whence it was taken to Spain. It is here that it becomes entangled within the many strands of the creation legends of Ireland, although tradition states that it was brought from Spain to Ireland *c.* 700 BC by the son of a Spanish king. The stone was taken to TARA, where it was first used as a coronation stone because it was said to speak out if a true king sat upon it, but remained silent for a pretender to the throne. From Ireland the stone was sent to DÁL RIADA in the fifth century, and from there it was taken to London in 1296. Twice since then it has been removed from Westminster Abbey.

The first time was when Cromwell declared himself Lord Protector upon it in Westminster Hall. The second time was in 1950 when a party of young Scots raided the abbey and attempted to have it installed in a Scottish cathedral, but no cathedral wanted anything to do with it. Finally, with the coronation of Queen Elizabeth II almost due, the thieves relented and revealed its hiding place to the police, who returned it to Westminster Abbey.

SCORIATH
Irish

A King of FERAMORC and the father of MORIATH. Scoriath entertained the mute MAON at his court before that youth travelled to GAUL, whence Maon returned under the name of LABHRAIDH LOINGSECH and married Scoriath's daughter after ousting his usurping uncle COVAC.

SCOTLAND
General

During the fourth and fifth centuries Scotland was divided between three peoples: the Britons, who occupied the Lowlands that had once been Roman territory (they never conquered the Highlands); and the PICTS and the Scots, occupying the land north of Hadrian's Wall, the latter having arrived from IRELAND and being the eponym of Scotland. GEOFFREY OF MONMOUTH asserts that AUGUSELUS ruled Scotland during ARTHUR's time, while BOECE avers in his *SCOTORUM HISTORIAE* that the King was EUGENIUS, an ally of MORDRED. The *HISTORIA MERIADOCI* says that URIEN was the King of Scots. Historically, it is hard to say who ruled the Britons of STRATHCLYDE during this period, as reliable lists do not exist, but the Hiberno-Scottish kingdom of DÁL RIADA was ruled by Fergus More, Domangort, Comgall and AEDÁN MAC GABRÁIN, though dates are unreliably recorded.

SCOTORUM HISTORIAE
Arthurian

Written by the Scottish historian Hector BOECE (d. 1536), this work is interesting in that it contains Arthurian material from an anti-ARTHUR viewpoint.

SCOTTISH WILDERNESS, LORD OF THE
Arthurian
See LORD OF THE SCOTTISH WILDERNESS

SEA OF CLEAR GLASS
Irish
See ISLANDS OF MAÍL DÚIN

SEACHRAN
Irish

A giant with whom FIONN MAC CUMHAILL made friends. Seachran took his new friend home to meet his mother and brother, but they were not pleased that he had befriended a mere human. During the feast, Seachran was seized by a huge hairy claw, but he managed to shake himself free, in the process knocking his mother into a cauldron that had been intended for him. Seachran and Fionn mac Cumhaill fled, but they were pursued by the brother, who killed Seachran but was himself killed by Fionn mac Cumhaill. Seachran was restored to life after Fionn mac Cumhaill chewed his thumb and learnt of a magic ring, which was obtained for him by DIARMAID UA DUIBHNE, the owners of the ring being killed by Seachran's wife.

SEARBHAN LOCHLANNACH
Irish

A one-eyed giant who was sent to guard a magical rowan tree that had grown by mistake from a berry dropped by one of the TUATHA DÉ DANANN. No one dared go near the giant, for he could be killed only with three blows from his own iron club. He was eventually killed by DIARMAID UA DUIBHNE after FIONN MAC CUMHAILL had demanded his head, or berries from the tree.

SEAT OF DANGER, THE
Arthurian

The literal translation of the SIEGE PERILOUS, the seat at the ROUND TABLE reserved for the knight who would succeed in the Quest for the Holy GRAIL.

SEBILE
Arthurian

A sorceress and companion of MORGAN Le Fay. Her name seems to originate in 'Sibyl' – a woman who, mostly in ancient Greece and Rome, was believed to be an oracle or prophetess.

SÉDANTA
Irish
Also SÉTANTA

The boyhood name of CÚ CHULAINN. While still known by this name, he completed his first heroic deed, the defeat of all fifty of the youths in the service of CONCHOBAR MAC NESSA. Later, he was attacked by the fearsome hound of CULANN the smith. He threw his ball down the animal's gaping throat and, before it could recover from the shock, dashed its brains out. Culann complained bitterly about the loss of his dog, so Sédanta promised to act as his guard dog for as long as he had need of one. It was this promise that earned him his popular name, Cú Chulainn, which simply means 'Culann's hound'.

SEGNIUS
British and Gaulish

The duke who welcomed BRENNIUS to his court while the latter was in exile from Britain, and allowed Brennius to marry his daughter a short time before he died, after which Brennius succeeded to the dukedom.

SEGURANT THE BROWN
Arthurian

A knight of the OLD TABLE, the KNIGHT OF THE DRAGON, and UTHER's mightiest warrior.

SEGWARIDES
Arthurian

A knight with whose wife TRISTAN had an affair. The two knights fought and Tristan won, but the two later became reconciled. He became the ruler of SERVAGE, which NABON gave to him.

SEITHENYN
Welsh

A legendary inhabitant of CANTRE'R GWAELOD and the father of seven sons, one of whom was TUDNO. Some name Seithenyn as the keeper of the sluices, who became so drunk one night that he forgot his duties and allowed the sea to inundate the kingdom.

SEMION
Irish

The son of STARIAT who, according to the story told by TUAN MAC CARELL to Saint PATRICK, settled in IRELAND, and from whom the FIR BHOLG were descended. This, however, is not the usual version, which says that the Fir Bholg came from overseas, and it may be that Semion was undertaking a reconnaissance for them when he was seen by TUAN MAC CARELL.

SENACH
Irish

A mysterious being, said by some to have been an ally of MANANNÁN MAC LIR, against whom CÚ CHULAINN did battle and won.

SENCHA
Irish

An historian at the court of CONCHOBAR MAC NESSA. During the feast thrown by BRICRIU, he announced that the dispute over the right of champion to carve the roast should be judged by MEDHBHA and AILILL. Later, he stood by his friend CONAIRE MÓR at DA DERGA's hostel but was so overwhelmed that he only just managed to escape.

SENNAN HOLY WELL
Arthurian

A well in CORNWALL at which the SEVEN KINGS OF CORNWALL were said to have given praise following their victory at the Battle of VELLENDRUCHER.

SENTOGE
Arthurian

The duchy created for GALIHODIN because he supported LANCELOT in his quarrel with ARTHUR.

SEQU-ANA, -ENA
Romano-Gaulish

With her totem animal, a duck, Sequana was goddess of the source of the River Seine, which takes its name from her and near which her sanctuary stood.

SEQUENCE
Arthurian

The name of one of the swords owned by ARTHUR.

SERA
Irish

The father of PARTHOLÁN, AGNOMAN and STARN. His name perhaps means 'West', which would indicate that the invasion of IRELAND by Partholán came from a supernatural kingdom.

SERAPHE
Arthurian
The original, possibly pagan, name of NASCIEN.

SERVAGE
Arthurian
The island realm of NABON, which he gave to SEGWARIDES.

SÉTANTA
Irish
See SÉDANTA

SETANTII
British
A Celtic people, once said to have inhabited an area between the River Ribble and Morecambe Bay. Some authorities suggest that this tribe gave their name to Sétanta, or more correctly SÉDANTA, the childhood name of CÚ CHULAINN, but this appears to be an attempt to claim that that hero had a British ancestry.

SEVAIN
Arthurian
The father of LIONORS and thus grandfather to LOHOLT, ARTHUR's son.

SEVEN KINGS OF CORNWALL
Arthurian
An allegiance of seven kings who, according to Cornish tradition, helped ARTHUR to defeat the invading Danes at the Battle of VELLENDRUCHER. Afterwards they were said to have given praise and worshipped at the SENNAN HOLY WELL, and then held a banquet at a rock called the TABLE MAN. MERLIN subsequently prophesied that the Danes would one day return, a greater number of kings would see this event, and that it would mark the end of the world.

SEVEN-LEAGUE BOOTS
Arthurian
Magical boots, invented by MERLIN, that would enable the wearer to cover seven leagues with each stride. A league is commonly measured at 3 miles (though its actual length varied from time to time), so these boots could cover approximately 21 miles per step.

SEVERN, RIVER
British
The modern name for the River HABREN, which was known as the SABRINA by the Romans.

SEVIRA
British
The daughter of MAXIMUS and wife of VORTIGERN, to whom she bore BRITU.

SEWINGSHIELDS
Arthurian
A place in NORTHUMBERLAND where there used to stand a castle beneath which ARTHUR, GUINEVERE and Arthur's knights were allegedly asleep, awaiting the call to return in the hour of BRITAIN'S greatest need. A bugle and a garter were said to lie nearby, and it was necessary to blow the bugle and cut the garter with a stone sword in order to raise the sleepers.

SGÁTHACH
Irish
The daughter of EANNA. FIONN MAC CUMHAILL offered to marry her for a year, and her parents agreed to the union. That night, however, as Fionn mac Cumhaill and his men slept, Sgáthach played a magical tune on the harp, and the following morning Fionn mac Cumhaill and his companions found themselves far away from Eanna's home.

SGEIMH SOLAIS
Irish
'Light of Beauty', the daughter of CAIRBRE, whose hand was sought in marriage by a son of the King of the DECIES. The betrothal led the FIAN to demand a tribute from Cairbre, but he swore not to pay it. This led to the Battle of GABHRA, which was to mark the end of the supremacy of the FIAN in IRELAND.

SGEOLAN
Irish
Also SCEOLAING, SKOLAWN
One of the two faithful hounds of FIONN MAC CUMHAILL, the other being BRÂN. These hounds were in fact Fionn mac Cumhaill's nephews, because their mother, TUIREANN, the sister of Fionn mac Cumhaill, had been turned into a wolfhound by the supernatural mistress of ILLAN, her husband. She was later restored to her human form, but her sons retained the form of hounds.

SGILTI
Welsh
One of the often neglected members of the party formed to help CULHWCH locate OLWEN. Sgilti was chosen because he was so light-footed that he could march on the ends of the branches in the trees and weighed so little that even the grass did not bend under him.

SHAKESPEARE, WILLIAM
Arthurian
Born in Stratford-upon-Avon, Warwickshire, and living between 1564 and 1616, Shakespeare is perhaps the best-known playwright ever to have lived. He appears to have drawn on Arthurian literature and legend during the composition of *A MIDSUMMER NIGHT'S DREAM*, for here OBERON has much the same role as he does in other Arthurian literature.

SHALOTT
Arthurian
Another name for ASTOLAT that has become widely known to English readers through Alfred, Lord Tennyson's *Lady of Shalott*. The name derives from the Italian variants of SCALOT, used in *La damigiella di Scalot*, and SCALLIOTTA, used in *Lancialotto Pancianti-chiano*.

SHEELA-NA-GIG
General
The goddess of sexuality, life and death. During medieval monastic times, she came to represent a female demon.

SHERWOOD FOREST
Arthurian
Though more normally associated with that other famous and well-loved legendary figure Robin Hood, Sir Thomas MALORY identifies the forest with that of BEDEGRAINE, a forest that saw a major battle between ARTHUR and the eleven rebellious leaders at the start of his reign.

SHOULSBARROW CASTLE
Arthurian
A fortress on Exmoor, lying just within Devon, that is said to have been used by King ARTHUR.

SIABHRA
Irish
The collective name given to small supernatural beings or sprites.

SICHELM
Arthurian
The King of NORWAY. The uncle of LOT, he bequeathed his realm to his nephew, but the throne was usurped and Lot's right of ascendancy had to be reinforced by ARTHUR.

Sheela-na-Gig, the goddess of sexuality, life and death. (© Mick Sharp)

SIDENG

Irish

The daughter of MONGÁN. She was said to have given FIONN MAC CUMHAILL a flat stone to which a golden chain was attached. By whirling this around his head Fionn mac Cumhaill was able to cut his opponents in half with great ease.

SÍD(H)

Irish

An earthen barrow or burial mound. The sídh are the homes of the TUATHA DÉ DANANN, each leader being provided with one by the DAGHDHA when they were awarded the underground half of IRELAND by the invading and conquering Sons of MÍL ÉSPÁINE. The Welsh counterpart of the sídh is the CAER. Later tradition extended the use of the word sídh from referring just to the home of the gods to including reference to the gods themselves. Later still, the word became widely used in folklore to refer to fairies, sprites and, indeed, any other form of supernatural being.

SIEGE PERILOUS

Arthurian

The 'Perilous Seat' or 'Seat of Danger', a place at the ROUND TABLE, so named by MERLIN, who said it was reserved for the holiest of knights, the one who would achieve the GRAIL. When BRUMART, a nephew of King CLAUDAS, tried to sit on it, he was destroyed for his presumption. When GALAHAD, the destined knight, sat on it, his name appeared in gold letters either above the seat or on it.

SIGUNE

Arthurian

According to WOLFRAM VON ESCHENBACH, the cousin of PERCEVAL. She also appears, though unnamed, in the works of CHRÉTIEN DE TROYES. The first meeting between Perceval and Sigune, in Wolfram von Eschenbach, occurs before he has visited the GRAIL CASTLE. When they meet she is carrying the body of her dead husband, SCHIONATULANDER.

Chrétien de Troyes does not mention this encounter. The second time they meet, following Perceval's first and unrewarded visit to the Grail Castle, she chided him for his apparent lack of concern for AMFORTAS's suffering. Chrétien de Troyes, however, says she scolded him for not asking the GRAIL QUESTION. Later Sigune became a recluse and was eventually buried beside her husband.

SIL

British

A mythical king who is known only from a tenuous link with SILBURY Hill in Wiltshire, which is said to have been his burial mound.

See also ZEL

SILBURY

British

A huge earthen mound close to the village of Avebury, in Wiltshire. Silbury Hill is a man-made hill measuring 1,640 feet in circumference at its base and 130 feet in height. Radiocarbon dating has dated its foundation at *c.* 2660 BC, which makes it a pre-Celtic relic. However, it was obviously important to the Celts, who were well known for taking over the megalithic stone structures at STONEHENGE and Avebury, which are close at hand. Local legend says that the hill was the tomb of a King ZEL, or SIL, who had been buried on horseback. The top of the hill was allegedly excavated in 1723, when some human remains and an antique bridle were reported to have been discovered, but this now seems suspect. The true purpose of the hill remains a mystery. It was thoroughly investigated throughout the 1960s and 1970s, but, no matter how many tunnels were bored into it, nothing came to light. The hill remains an enigma to this day.

What did come to light was the truly remarkable internal structure of the hill, for it is not merely a heap of earth with grass on top. At its core is a primary mound, 120 feet in diameter, which was built up in layers of clay, flints, chalk, gravel and turf. On and around this, the main bulk of the hill was constructed from radial and concentric walls of chalk blocks filled in with rubble. At this stage the hill took the form of a seven-stepped pyramid and would have glistened white from the chalk. Earth was then heaped onto the terraces and the whole structure grassed over. The amazing internal mechanics have meant that the hill has retained its original shape and size for more than 4,500 years.

SILÉ NA GCIOCH

Irish

The Gaelic for SHEELA-NA-GIG.

SILURES

British

An ancient people who used to inhabit the area of south-east WALES that is known as Siluria. They combined their forces with those of the ORDOVICES from the north of Wales to help CARATACUS against the Romans, but they were finally beaten in AD 51.

SILVA CALEDONIAE
Arthurian

'Wood of Scotland'. A wood located in the Lowlands of SCOTLAND that has been suggested as a possible site for one of ARTHUR'S BATTLES, that of CALEDON WOOD.

SILVIUS
Graeco-Romano-British

The grandson of AENEAS and father of BRUTUS, by whom he was accidentally killed. Brutus was exiled for his patricide and finally arrived in BRITAIN with a company of Trojan refugees.

SIMIAS
Irish

A wizard from the mythical city of MURIAS. He was one of the four wizards who taught the TUATHA DÉ DANANN their magic arts before their invasion of IRELAND. Simias was said to have given the Tuatha Dé Danann the inexhaustible cauldron of the DAGHDHA. His three co-tutors were MORFESSA of FALIA, ESIAS of GORIAS and USCIAS of FINDIAS.

SINADONE
Arthurian

The Lady of Sinadone is said to have been rescued by LYBIUS DESCONUS, who was accompanied by the damsel ELLEN. The story appears in the appropriately titled romance *Lybius Desconus.*

SINAINN
Irish

The eponymous goddess of the River Shannon. The daughter of LODAN, she was therefore a granddaughter of LIR. She once travelled to a magical well beneath the sea, where she omitted to cast a certain spell. The waters gushed forth in anger and cast her onto the coast of IRELAND, where the River Shannon now has its mouth and where she died.

SÍNECH
Irish

A relative of MIDHIR with whom that god stayed after he had carried off the reincarnated ÉDÁIN from EOCHAIDH AIREMH.

SIR GAWAIN AND THE CARL OF CARLISLE
Arthurian

An unfinished English romance dating from *c.* 1400 that relates the tale of GAWAIN and his dealings with the CARL OF CARLISLE. It was later followed in the sixteenth century by a new version, again incomplete, called the *CARL OF CARLISLE.*

SIR GAWAIN AND THE GREEN KNIGHT
Arthurian
Also SIR GAWAYNE AND THE GREENE KNIGHT

A famous, but anonymous, English poem dating from *c.* 1346 that deals with the beheading contest undertaken by GAWAIN, and perhaps recalling memories of an ancient fertility ritual. It was followed approximately 100 years later by *The Green Knight*, though this is a much inferior telling of the story.

SIR GAWAYNE AND THE GREENE KNIGHT
Arthurian

The original spelling of *SIR GAWAIN AND THE GREEN KNIGHT.*

SIR PERCEVAL OF GALLES
Arthurian

A fourteenth-century English romance that tells the story of PERCEVAL, but makes no mention of the GRAIL, or Perceval's part in the quest for that holy vessel.

SIRONA
Gaulish

A somewhat obscure goddess whose name means 'Star' and who was often associated with GRANNUS.

SISILLIUS
British

A relative of RIVALLO who was to succeed GURGUSTIUS as King of BRITAIN. His own son later came to the throne, after a nephew of Gurgustius had reigned for a while. This son, who remains unnamed, was in turn succeeded by GORBODUC.

SIUGMALL
Irish

A grandson of MIDHIR and FUAMHNACH. He helped his grandmother to dispose of ÉDÁIN ECHRAIDHE and, as a result, was killed alongside her by MANANNÁN MAC LIR. Another version of the story of Midhir and Édáin Echraidhe says that Siugmall was on the side of Midhir, for here he is portrayed as killing EOCHAIDH AIREMH after that King had compelled Midhir to return the true Édáin Echraidhe to him.

SKATHA
Irish

A variant of SCÁTHACH, although it is sometimes used to refer to her realm.

SKENA

Irish

The wife of AMHAIRGHIN, the FILI, who died on the journey to IRELAND and was buried as soon as the Sons of MÍL ÉSPÁINE landed.

SKOLAWN

Irish

The Latinisation of SGEOLAN, one of the two hounds of FIONN MAC CUMHAILL.

SLAUGHTERBRIDGE

Arthurian

The traditional Cornish location for the Battle of CAMLANN, some six miles from DOZMARY POOL on Bodmin Moor, one of the many locations where EXCALIBUR was meant to have been returned to the LADY OF THE LAKE.

SMERT-ULLOS, -DOS

Gaulish

A chthonic deity, a provider of wealth as well as a protector who kept his foes at bay simply by a display of his amazing strength. The Romans seized on this aspect and sought to equate him with Hercules.

SMIRGAT

Irish

According to some sources, the name of the woman who became FIONN MAC CUMHAILL's wife towards the end of his life.

SNOWDON, MOUNT

Welsh and Arthurian

The highest mountain in WALES. It was originally known as YR WYDDFA FAWR.

SODRIC

Arthurian

According to GEOFFREY OF MONMOUTH, he was the leader who brought the PICTS to BRITAIN. They were, however, soundly defeated by King MARIUS, but he still bestowed Caithness on them.

Slaughterbridge, the traditional Cornish site for the Battle of Camlann. (© Mick Sharp)

SOISSONS
Arthurian
The kingdom of CLOTHAIR before he became King of All the Franks.

SOL
Welsh
One of the seldom mentioned members of the party formed to help CULHWCH locate OLWEN. He was chosen because he could stand on one foot all day.

SOLOMON
British and Arthurian
According to Welsh genealogies, and the pedigree of Gallet, King of BRITTANY, father of CONSTANTINE, and thus great-grandfather of King ARTHUR.

SORCHA
Arthurian
The realm of the father of RAGNELL, one of the various wives ascribed to GAWAIN.

SOREDAMOR
Arthurian
The sister of GAWAIN who married the Byzantine Prince ALEXANDER, becoming the mother of CLIGÉS by him.

SORELOIS
Arthurian
An Arthurian kingdom the ruler of which was called GLOIER and the capital SORHAUT. Many regions have been suggested for this kingdom, from Sutherland in the north to the Isles of Scilly in the south.

SORESTAN
Arthurian
A kingdom in the vicinity of NORTHGALIS, the ruler of which was said to be a witch.

SORGALES
Arthurian
An Arthurian kingdom that is said to be identical with South WALES.

SORHAUT
Arthurian
The name of the capital of the kingdoms of GORE and SORELOIS.

SORLOIS
Arthurian
A kingdom that is now to be found in modern Iraq.

The hand of FLORENCE, daughter of the King of Sorlois, was sought by ARTHUR of BRITTANY.

SOUCONNA
Gaulish
The eponymous goddess of the River Saone.

SOUTHAMPTON
Arthurian
Port in Hampshire, southern England, where King HOEL was said to have landed with a massive army when he came to the aid of his cousin, King ARTHUR.

SOVEREIGNTY OF IRELAND, THE
Irish
A variation of the SPIRIT OF IRELAND, who is usually regarded as MEDHBHA, Queen of CONNACHT.

SPAIN
General
During the traditional Arthurian period, this Iberian country was a Visigoth kingdom ruled by Alaric II (AD 484–507), Gesalaric (AD 507–11), Amalric (AD 511–31) and Theudis (AD 531–48). In the Arthurian stories ALIFATIMA, SAVARI, CLARIS and TRISTAN are all named as being rulers at various times.

SPECKLED KNIGHT
Arthurian
One of the many knights said to have been defeated by the GREAT FOOL.

SPENSER, EDMUND
Arthurian
An English poet (c. 1552–99) who, though not much read in modern times, was esteemed as the Virgil of his day, enjoying great popularity among other poets. His most famous work, the epic, unfinished allegory the *FAERIE QUEENE*, features the uncrowned King ARTHUR.

SPIRIT OF IRELAND, THE
Irish
Said to have been personified in the most beautiful woman in the land, such as in the case of ÉDÁIN ECHRAIDHE, daughter of King AILILL. Some say that she was personified as MEDHBHA. Others say that the Spirit of Ireland came to the island in a time before the biblical Flood as one of the people led by CESAIR, that person being BANBHA, wife of the TUATHA DÉ DANANN King MAC CUILL. It was this incarnation of the Spirit of Ireland that AMHAIRGHIN called upon to cause an enchanted

wind sent by the Tuatha Dé Danann against the Sons of MÍL ÉSPÁINE to drop.

Even though the identity of the Spirit of Ireland may be confused, she remains one of the most important Irish deities, for she embodied the very essence of IRELAND. It was her right to confer the status of king, who had ritually to mate with her, and hers alone to take it away again. This divine right led to her also being known as the SOVEREIGNTY OF IRELAND.

SPUMADOR
Arthurian
According to SPENSER, ARTHUR's horse.

SRENG
Irish
A huge FIR BHOLG warrior, who was sent to parley with the invading TUATHA DÉ DANANN, who put forward BRES as their spokesman. Terms could not be agreed, because the Fir Bholg refused to divide IRELAND in two, so battle could not be avoided, and, although they gained the upper hand on the first day of the First Battle of MAGH TUIREDH, the Fir Bholg were soundly defeated.

STAG OF RHEDYNFRC
Welsh and Arthurian
Having been directed to this animal by the BLACKBIRD OF CILGWRI, the party helping CULHWCH in his search for OLWEN were passed on to the OWL OF CWN CAWLWYD, which, in turn, took them to the EAGLE OF GWERNABWY, which finally took them to the SALMON OF LLYN LLW.

STANZAIC MORTE ARTHUR
Arthurian
An English poem, possibly dating from the fourteenth century, that, in its 3,969 lines, deals with the latter part of ARTHUR's career.

STARIAT
Irish
The father of SEMION and thus an ancestor of the FIR BHOLG.

STARN
Irish
A son of SERA, the brother of PARTHOLÁN and AGNOMAN and the father of TUAN MAC STERN.

STATER(IUS)
Welsh and Arthurian
According to GEOFFREY OF MONMOUTH, the ruler of DEMETIA or ALBANY. He and RUDAUCUS, King of CAMBRIA, joined forces against MOLMUTIUS, but they were defeated and killed in battle.

STONEHENGE
General
The most famous of the large Megalithic stone circles. Standing on Salisbury Plain, Stonehenge was, according to legend, erected as a memorial at the suggestion of MYRDDIN (MERLIN) and was allegedly brought over from IRELAND to be re-erected on its present site, this story perhaps containing some oral tradition that the ring was indeed transported over water. Also known as the GIANTS' RING, the name Stonehenge merely dates from medieval times and is not the original name. Archaeological evidence has shown that the ring was built in three stages. In *c.* 2800 BC a ditch and bank along with the heel stone were all that stood on the site, but *c.* 2000 BC blue-stone pillars, perhaps originating in the PRESELI HILLS, WALES, were brought to the site, transported up the Avon and erected. The ring was completed *c.* 1500 BC, when sarsen trilithons were erected.

STRADAWL
British and Arthurian
The wife of COEL.

STRANGGORE
Arthurian
This Arthurian kingdom, perhaps to be identified with east WALES, was said to have been ruled by BRANDEGORIS.

STRATHCLYDE
Arthurian
During the traditional Arthurian period this was a British kingdom lying in the Lowlands of SCOTLAND. The names and dates of the rulers are uncertain, as no reliable lists or sources exist.

SUALTAM
Irish
The husband of DEICHTINE and father of SÉDANTA, the hero who later became better known as CÚ CHULAINN.

SUCCAT
Irish
Possibly the childhood name of Saint PATRICK, although it is possible that Succat was nothing more than a nickname.

Stonehenge, the famous megalithic monument that was allegedly constructed by Merlin.
(© Adam Woolfitt/Corbis)

SUCELL-OS, -US

Gaulish

The 'Good Striker', a smith god who is usually depicted as a mature man holding a long-handled mallet, sitting on, or with one leg on, a wine barrel and in the company of a dog, his totem animal. His consort appears to have been NANTOSVELTA. Some authorities feel that Sucellos may have originated as a chthonic fertility god, and, although he is usually assimilated with the Roman Silvanus, some believe that he is more closely equitable with 'DIS PATER'.

SUIBHNE GEILT

Irish

A King of DÁL NARAIDI, who is perhaps best known as SWEENEY THE MAD. He was said to have lost his sanity at the Battle of Moira, a historic battle fought in AD 637, whereafter he became a 'wild man' roaming the woods. His life story is told in the *Buile Suibhne*, a story that some feel might have been the foundation for the story of MYRDDIN.

SUITE DU MERLIN

Arthurian

A thirteenth-century French prose romance. One of the manuscripts that makes up this work is sometimes referred to as the *HUTH-MERLIN*.

SUL(IS)

British

The goddess of wisdom, who was of such importance that the Romans named the city of BATH in her honour, the Roman name for that city being AQUAE SULIS, or 'Waters of Sulis'. Sul's consort was a sun god, whose carved face, bristling with the rays of the sun, was found during excavations beneath the present pump room in Bath. Some have suggested that the story of BLADUD's magical flight from Bath to LONDON might have derived from a solar myth, now long forgotten, featuring this deity.

Sul is known only at Bath, which suggests that she was a local deity, manifesting herself in the copious hot springs of the city. Her importance in the region is reflected by the fact that the Romans did not obliterate her memory when they built a temple in Bath, but instead amalgamated their temple with the one already in existence. The Romano-Celtic deity so produced is known as SULIS MINERVA, a combination of Sul and the Roman goddess Minerva. This deity was highly revered throughout the Roman Empire, respect that is confirmed in an inscription found on the base of a long-lost statue.

This inscription tells of the visit of a Roman state augur from Rome, who came to Bath to consult the deity and make use of her oracular powers. The inscription further says that his request, whatever that might have been, was answered.

The assumption usually made about the assimilation of Sul and the Roman Minerva is not correct, for dedications to Sul on her own reveal her to be a chthonic UNDERWORLD goddess, similar in many respects to the classical Hecate, whose association is with blessing, cursing and prophecy. These are not attributes of the Roman Minerva. It seems more likely that, following the arrival of the Romans, the true aspect of Sul was lost, her attributes being replaced by more Minervan ones.

SULIS MINERVA

Romano-British

The goddess created by the amalgamation of the Roman goddess Minerva with the local goddess SULIS at BATH, the city being named AQUAE SULIS by the Romans in honour of the important Celtic solar deity they found there. Sulis Minerva presided over the therapeutic properties of the hot baths within her city. She also presided over curses and cursing. As an UNDERWORLD goddess, she was also associated with prophecy, an oracle being established in her temple at Bath, an oracle that was on one occasion visited by a Roman state augur. Her prophetic powers came from the Underworld, where all the latent powers of the earth flow together, and the past and the future are as one time.

SULPICIUS

Arthurian

Said to have knighted GAWAIN, this fictitious POPE is perhaps to be identified with Pope Simplicius (Pope 468–83).

SUN TEAR

Irish

The daughter of FIACHNA, who gave her to LOEGHAIRE for his help in freeing the wife of Fiachna from GOLL.

SURLUSE

Arthurian

This kingdom, whose border with LOGRES was marked by the River ASSURNE, was perhaps identical with SORELOIS. GALEHAUT made himself the ruler of Surluse and, while ARTHUR was living with the FALSE GUINEVERE, the kingdom was given to the genuine GUINEVERE by Galehaut.

SWALES
Arthurian

The duchy of GILAN. Some commentators have made the simple assumption that Swales is cognate with South Wales ('S.Wales'), but this seems doubtful.

SWAN KNIGHT
Arthurian

A descendant of MEURVIN and ORIANT about whom nothing else is known. Later tradition equates the Swan Knight with LOHENGRIN because of his disguise as a swan when he came to the aid of ELSA, daughter of the Duke of BRABANT.

SWEENEY THE MAD
Irish

The literal translation of SUIBHNE GEILT.

SWORD IN THE STONE, THE
Arthurian

The legendary method by which ARTHUR was identified as the true king. The invention of this test is attributed to MERLIN. As no king could be found, and following many years of feuding, Merlin went to the Archbishop of CANTERBURY and reassured him that he would find the rightful king. All the lords of the realm and all the gentlemen of arms were called to London for a New Year's Day tournament, where the new ruler would be revealed. Sir ECTOR, his son, KAY, and his adopted son, Arthur, were among those who rode to London for the jousting, Kay making much of the occasion, for he was to be made a knight. However, as they neared the tournament, Kay found that he was without his sword and sent Arthur back to their lodgings, for he had left it there. When Arthur arrived, he found that the innkeeper and all his family had already left for the tournament, and he could not gain entry. Turning back, he trudged dolefully through a churchyard, and there saw a sword embedded in a stone. He easily withdrew it and hastened back to his father and brother.

When Kay saw the sword, he read upon it the words Arthur had missed: 'Whosoever pulleth this sword from the stone is rightwise born King of All England.' Immediately Kay rejoiced and, showing the sword to his father, claimed that he had pulled the sword from the stone, and that he should be proclaimed king. Ector, however, made his son tell the truth and, taking both boys back to the churchyard, replaced the sword in the stone and bade Arthur withdraw it again. This he did with ease, but neither Ector nor Kay, who both attempted the feat, could move it. Once more Arthur was asked to withdraw the sword, this time in public, and at the high feast of Pentecost he was crowned King of All England.

SWORD OF THE STRANGE HANGINGS
Arthurian

A sword that had once belonged to the biblical King David of Israel. His son, Solomon, placed it aboard his ship, where it hung in hempen hangings made by Solomon's wife. This sword later appeared in the Arthurian legends, and had the hempen hangings replaced by some made from the hair of PERCEVAL's sister.

SYRIA
Arthurian

According to Sir Thomas MALORY, the Sultan of Syria was a vassal lord of the Roman Emperor LUCIUS HIBERIUS. However, elsewhere Syria was said to have been ruled by King NADUS, King NATALON and King EVANDER.

T

TABLE MAN
Arthurian
A rock where the SEVEN KINGS OF CORNWALL, having given praise at SENNAN HOLY WELL, held a banquet following their victory at the Battle of VELLENDRUCHER.

TABLE OF THE WANDERING COMPANIONS
Arthurian
The table at ARTHUR's court where knights waiting to become KNIGHTS OF THE ROUND TABLE were seated.

TACITUS
Arthurian
Father of PATERNUS and great-grandfather of CUNEDDA, according to the latter's traditional lineage.

TADHG
Irish
The son of CIAN. He met the divine CLIODNA, who was accompanied by three magical and brightly coloured birds, which feasted on the apples that grew on the eternal apple trees of TÍR TAIRNGIRI and whose song was so sweet that they could soothe the sick and wounded to sleep.

Other sources name Tadhg as the son of NUADHA and the father of MUIRNE, whose hand was sought in marriage by CUMHAILL. He foresaw that he would lose his fortress if he allowed the marriage, so he refused, whereupon Cumhaill abducted her. In the ensuing battle Cumhaill was killed, but not until after Muirne had conceived a son, DEIMNE, who became better known as FIONN MAC CUMHAILL.

TAILTIU
Irish
The battle at which the Sons of MÍL ÉSPÁINE beat the TUATHA DÉ DANANN for the second time, here killing the three Tuatha Dé Danann Kings MAC CÉCHT, MAC CUILL and MAC GRÉINE and so becoming the rulers of IRELAND. The conquered Tuatha Dé Danann were compensated with the underground half of the realm. The battle was fought at Teltin, now Telltown.

TAÍN BÓ CUAILNGÈ
Irish
Translated as *The Cattle Raid of Cooley*, this great prose saga preserves a picture of the Irish Iron Age traditions, and it thus represents an essential reference source to the Celtic researcher. Although it is preserved in the *Book of Leinster* (*c.* 1150), the *Taín Bó Cuailngè* is obviously far older than that.

The basis of the *Taín Bó Cuailngè* is the quest by MEDHBHA to obtain the DONN CUAILNGÈ, the great brown bull that is the property of ULSTER and that she desired so that her possessions might rival those of AILILL, who owned the great white bull FINNBHENNACH. Medhbha raised a huge army and marched against Ulster, whose warriors had been afflicted by a curse laid on them by MACHA. However, one warrior, the mighty CÚ CHULAINN, remained immune to that curse, and he single-handedly held off the forces of CONNACHT for many weeks, killing hundreds but receiving terrible wounds himself.

Finally, while Cú Chulainn was fighting the sons of CALATIN, Medhbha managed to penetrate deep into Ulster and bring back the Donn Cuailngè. Triumphantly, she took the bull to her camp, where it fought Finnbhennach and totally annihilated the white bull before trotting off. Cú Chulainn died after failing to recognise the presence of the MÓRRÍGHAN, and Medhbha and Ailill had to return to Connacht with less than they had started out with, for the Donn Cuailngè had returned to Ulster and of Finnbhennach there were but a few scraps left.

TAISE
Irish
The daughter of the King of Greece (here a mythical land and nothing to do with the actual country) who loved FIONN MAC CUMHAILL but was intercepted by her father's guards as she tried to come to him. She was rescued by GOLL and OSCAR, who brought her to FIONN MAC CUMHAILL, but what happened after that is open to speculation.

TALAC

Arthurian

According to the obscure Welsh text *Yder*, the castellan (governor) of the castle known as ROUGEMONT. At first he opposed ARTHUR, but the differences between them were eventually settled.

TALIESIN

Welsh and Arthurian

The magically born, radiant child of CERRIDWEN whose name has been applied as a title to the greatest Welsh poets. It is thought that a historical bard by the name of Taliesin lived a little later than the traditional Arthurian period, and that this real-life poet became entangled with an earlier Welsh tradition, giving rise to the composite character known today, and becoming incorporated into the later Arthurian stories. His story, which mirrors earlier customs and rites, is basically as follows.

In the middle of Lake Tegid there lived a man by the name of TEGID VOEL and his wife, Cerridwen, who is described as having the knowledge and powers of a witch. They had three children, a son whom they named MORFRAN AB TEGID, a daughter, CREIRWY, the fairest maiden in all the world (sometimes suggested as the prototype for GUINEVERE), and a second son, AFAGDDU, the most ill-favoured and hapless man in the whole world. Some sources say that Afagddu was simply a nickname applied to Morfran, but it does seem that they were actually separate characters.

As this was the beginning of the time of ARTHUR and the KNIGHTS OF THE ROUND TABLE, into whose company she desired Afagddu should one day be accepted, Cerridwen decided, according to the arts of the books of Fferyllt, to boil a cauldron of Inspiration and Science, which had to be boiled unceasingly for a year and a day, until three drops were obtained of the grace of Inspiration. These she intended for Afagddu, to instil in him all the graces he lacked.

Cerridwen placed GWION BACH, the son of GWREANG of Llanfair in Caereinion, POWYS, in charge of the cauldron, and a blind man named MORDA was to kindle the fire beneath it. She ordered them not to cease in their allotted tasks for a year and a day. Every day Cerridwen gathered the charm-bearing herbs required for the brew, but one day, nearing the end of the year, three drops of the red-hot fluid flew out of the cauldron and landed on the finger of Gwion Bach. Because of the great heat, he immediately sucked the finger, and upon doing so gained the full potency of the brew. Instantly

becoming aware of the fact that Cerridwen was his greatest enemy, he fled. The cauldron burst into two and the remainder of the brew, poisonous now that it had rendered up the three divine drops, ran into a stream and poisoned the horses of GWYDDNO GARANHIR.

When Cerridwen returned and saw that her year's work was lost, she struck Morda over the head with a billet of wood intended for the fire until one of his eyes fell out on to his cheek. When he protested, Cerridwen realised that it was Gwion Bach who had robbed her, so she gave chase. During this chase, which echoes the changing of the seasons and totemic animals, there was a series of magical transmutations. Gwion Bach saw her chasing him and changed himself into a hare. Cerridwen countered by changing herself into a greyhound. Gwion Bach ran towards a river and, leaping in, changed himself into a fish. She in turn became an otter bitch. Gwion Bach then transformed himself into a bird, so Cerridwen became a hawk. Then he saw a heap of winnowed wheat and, dropping on to it, turned himself into one of the grains, thinking that Cerridwen would never find him among the countless thousands of other grains. However, she followed and, changing herself into a hen, she swallowed Gwion Bach. Nine months later Cerridwen gave birth to a son, whom, by reason of his beauty, she could not kill. Instead she placed the baby in a leather bag and cast him into the sea.

This bag was found by ELPHIN, the son of Gwyddno Garanhir, and it was he who, on first seeing the head of the baby, named him Taliesin. Later Taliesin rescued Elphin when the latter had been imprisoned by MAELGWYN (MELKIN), an episode that forms the subject matter of Thomas Love Peacock's novel *The Misfortunes of Elphin* (1829).

Though the above is the normally accepted version of Taliesin's conception and birth, an alternative story says that he was magically created by GWYDION. Taliesin became famed for his poetry, being said to have addressed URIEN of RHEGED, but it seems that Taliesin was simply a visitor to Urien's realm, rather than a resident, his most likely provenance being South WALES. *The Book of Taliesin*, which was compiled during the fourteenth century, is thought to contain some authentic poems from this mythologised historical character. The manuscript for this work is now in the National Library of Wales in Aberystwyth. His transition from Welsh tradition to Arthurian legend first appears in the Welsh poem *PREIDDEU ANNWFN*, where he is among the companions of

Arthur during the latter's expedition to the OTHERWORLD. This story is itself derived from an earlier tradition that places Taliesin among the seven survivors of the expedition to IRELAND by BENDIGEID VRAN to rescue BRANWEN, returning with the head of the King for burial under the WHITE MOUNT in London. The others to survive this expedition, which exterminated the entire Irish race except for five pregnant women who hid in a cave, were PRYDERI, MANAWYDAN, GLUNEU EIL TARAN (GLIFIEU), YNAWC (YNAWAG), GRUDYEN (GRUDDIEU) and HEILYN.

Both Welsh tradition and the *VITA MERLINI* make Taliesin a contemporary of MERLIN, representing the two talking with each other. The verse ascribed to Taliesin is somewhat difficult to understand, being constructed in an obscure manner. This has led some commentators to ascribe the verse to Merlin, saying that it only later came to be attributed to Taliesin. Other sources add that Taliesin had a son named ADDAON, who was subsequently killed by LLONGAD GRWRM FARGOD EIDYN.

TALLAS
Arthurian
According to *CLARIS ET LARIS*, the King of DENMARK who made LARIS a prisoner only for him to be rescued by CLARIS.

TALLWCH
Arthurian
In Welsh tradition, the father of TRISTAN. His name appears to be a Welsh form of the Pictish name TALORC or TALORCAN, though this is by no means certain.

TALORC(AN)
Arthurian
Pictish name that is thought to be the origin of TALLWCH, though this is open to speculation.

TALTIU
Irish
Also TELTA
The wife of EOCHAIDH MAC ERC, who had her palace at Telltown (TAILTIU), where she was buried, and where, even in medieval IRELAND, a great annual fair was held in her honour.

TANABURS
Arthurian
A wizard who was said to be second in sorcery only to MERLIN, and to have lived in a time before UTHER became king. He cast a spell on Castle CARBONEK so that it would be found only by certain knights who chanced upon it.

TANAROS
Gaulish
The god of thunder and lightning, although this name may simply be a misspelling of TARANIS.

TANCREE
Arthurian
The niece of ARTHUR who married GUINGANBRESIL.

TANEBORC
Arthurian
One of ARTHUR's residences, which has been variously identified with EDINBURGH or Oswestry.

TANGLED WOOD
Arthurian
The realm of VALERIN.

TANTALIS
Arthurian
The wife of ALEXANDER, Emperor of CONSTANTINOPLE, mother of a son, whom she named Alexander after her husband, and ALIS, and grandmother of CLIGÉS.

TANTRIS
Arthurian
The pseudonym used by TRISTAN when he visited IRELAND. It is a fairly simple anagram of TRISTAN.

TARA
Irish
For many centuries the most sacred place in IRELAND, Tara was the site in County MEATH of the royal court of the King of Ireland, although some contend that Tara is really the name of the great hall and that the name of the court has been lost. Tara became the religious and political centre of Celtic Ireland, where, until the mid-sixth century, a new king's ritual marriage with the SPIRIT OF IRELAND was celebrated and feasted at a ceremony known as the FEIS TEMHRACH.

Situated approximately 23 miles north-west of Dublin, Tara sits on a hilltop that was undoubtedly a sacred site long before the arrival of the Celts. Today, only a few mounds, ditches and earthworks distinguish the hill from many others in the vicinity. An oblong enclosure, some 759 feet long and 46 feet wide, with a series of entrances on either side, was the great banqueting hall of Tara. Here the legendary

TARBFEIS took place until Saint PATRICK outlawed it.

The court features in many of the Irish legends. It is the capital of the TUATHA DÉ DANANN, to which came the invading Sons of MÍL ÉSPÁINE; the court of CORMAC MAC AIRT; the court of EOCHAIDH AIREMH, to which MIDHIR came to reclaim ÉDÁIN ECHRAIDHE; the court where FIONN MAC CUMHAILL, at the age of eight, killed the monstrous AILLÉN MAC MIDHNA, who annually came at SAMHAIN and burned the court down; the location of the feast from which GRÁINNE eloped with DIARMAID UA DUIBHNE; the court of CONCHOBAR MAC NESSA and thus the location of the RED BRANCH; and the alleged burial place of the head and one of the hands of CÚ CHULAINN.

TARAN-IS, -OS
Gaulish

One of the three most important Celtic deities of GAUL, the other two being ESUS and TEUTATES. Human sacrifices are reported to have been made to all three gods. The god of the wheel and a Druidic father god, whose attributes were thunder and the oak tree, both of which were important Druidic entities, Taranis is also the god of the seasons and the stars. Because he was associated with the powers of change, the Romans assimilated him with their god Jupiter, although he is possibly more correctly equated to the shadowy Dis Pater, a primal god of the UNDERWORLD.

TARBFEIS
Irish

The legendary bull feast that was held at TARA following the death of a king. A bull would be roasted and a chosen man would eat the flesh of the bull and drink a broth made from its blood and bones. During his sleep a DRUID would chant an incantation over him, and the sleeping man would see the next King of IRELAND in a dream. This possibly historic rite was finally outlawed by Saint PATRICK.

TARSAN
Arthurian

The brother of King BAGDEMAGUS who was killed while in ARTHUR's service.

TARSENESYDE
Arthurian

The wife of LICONAUS and mother of ENIDE, according to *EREC ET ENIDE*.

TARVOS TRIGARAN-OS, -US
British and Gaulish

The 'Three-horned Bull', images of which have been found on both sides of the English Channel. It is possible that he has his Irish equivalent in the DONN CUAILNGÈ.

See also DONN

TASHA
Irish

A supernatural maiden who fell in love with FIONN MAC CUMHAILL when he and his men came to the help of her father. In return for the help of the FIAN, Tasha was allowed to accompany Fionn mac Cumhaill to IRELAND, where they were married.

TAULAT
Arthurian

A villainous knight who came to ARTHUR's court and killed a knight in front of GUINEVERE, promising to return each year to do exactly the same. He was eventually defeated and killed by JAUFRÉ.

TAULURD
Arthurian

A giant who, according to GEOFFREY OF MONMOUTH, was killed by MARHAUS.

TAVOLA RITONDA
Arthurian

A fourteenth-century Italian romance that dealt with a considerable number of Arthurian stories, thus making it an invaluable source of Italian romance.

TAWLBWRDD
Welsh and Arthurian

A backgammon board, although sometimes said to be a chess board, which was counted among the THIRTEEN TREASURES OF BRITAIN. It had a ground of gold, and men of silver, who would play themselves. It has its Irish equivalent in the game of FIDCHELL.

TEA
British

The daughter of the biblical King Zedekiah, whom the Scots said came to IRELAND in 585 BC with two companions, bringing with her the LIA FÁIL, or stone of FÁL. She married an Irish king, possibly EREMON, and the hill of his court was named Temair after her. This hill is none other than TARA. The story itself is of Scottish invention and has very little to do with the traditional Irish mythology on which it is undoubtedly based.

TEACH-DHOINN
Irish
The Gaelic for TECH DUÍN.

TECH DUÍN(N)
Irish
The island off the south-west coast of IRELAND on which it is believed that DÔNN, the discourteous leader of the Sons of MÍL ÉSPÁINE, was buried after he had drowned and to which he still welcomes dead warriors.

TEGAU E(U)FRON
Welsh and Arthurian
In Welsh tradition, the wife of CARADOC VREICHVRAS (CARADOC BRIEFBRAS). She had three treasures: a mantle (cloak), a cup and a carving knife. She is identifiable with GUIGNIER, the wife of Caradoc Briefbras in Arthurian literature. Depending on which list is consulted, her treasures are sometimes included in the THIRTEEN TREASURES OF BRITAIN, though they are not included in the major sources that list these items.

TEGID VOEL
Welsh and Arthurian
The husband of CERRIDWEN and father, by her, of CREIRWY and AFAGDDU. Some sources name a third son as MORFRAN AB TEGID, but it is generally believed that this son is none other than Afagddu, which is a derisive nickname. Tegid Voel is described as being of gentle lineage, his home being on an island in the middle of LLYN TEGID, from which he takes his name.

TEIRGWAEDD
Welsh
The father of MENW FAB TEIRGWAEDD, as reflected in the name of the son, which simply means 'Menw son of Teirgwaedd'.

TEIRTU
Welsh
The owner of a magical harp that would play itself when so commanded.

TELRAMUND, FREDERICK DE
Arthurian
The harasser of ELSA of BRABANT who was, at her request, defeated in combat by LOHENGRIN.

TELTA
Irish
See TALTIU

TEMPER, RIVER
Arthurian
The river that was said to separate the kingdom of GORE from SCOTLAND.

TEMPLEISE
Arthurian
According to WOLFRAM VON ESCHENBACH, the collective name for the knights who guarded the GRAIL.

TENUANTIUS
British
The son of LUD and brother of ANDROGEUS. He and his brother were still too young to succeed their father on his death, so the throne passed to Lud's brother, CASSIVELAUNUS, who, in an attempt to thwart any possibility of trouble, made Androgeus the Duke of KENT and Tenuantius the Duke of CORNWALL. Together with their uncle, the two brothers twice helped to defeat JULIUS CAESAR as he made exploratory raids into BRITAIN. However, the third attack by Julius Caesar was more successful, because Androgeus betrayed his uncle and brother to the Romans. The Romans besieged Cassivelaunus and Tenuantius near CANTERBURY, where Androgeus changed sides again and acted as a mediator. Cassivelaunus agreed to pay Rome a tribute, after which Julius Caesar returned to Rome and took Androgeus with him.

Tenuantius ascended to the throne after the death of his uncle, and he reigned in peace because he honoured the tribute to Rome. He was succeeded in turn by his own son CUNOBELINUS, who had been raised in Rome in the household of the Emperor Augustus.

TENWI
Arthurian
A son of LOT and ANNA, according to Welsh tradition, and brother to MORDRED, PERFERREN and DENW.

TERDELASCHOYE
Arthurian
According to WOLFRAM VON ESCHENBACH, the fairy wife of MAZADAN, ARTHUR's great-grandfather, so presumably his great-grandmother. She is also described as an ancestress of PERCEVAL.

TERNOVA
British
A variant of TROIA NOVA. It is mentioned in the myth of the magical King BLADUD.

TERRABIL, CASTLE
Arthurian
The castle in which GORLOIS was besieged by the forces of UTHER while the latter planned how he might lie with Gorlois's wife, IGRAINE. Its location is not stated, and no reasonable site has yet been established or suggested with any authority, and any castle or earthworks in the south-west of ENGLAND could be seen as a likely candidate.

TERRE FOR(R)AINE
Arthurian
Quite literally meaning 'Foreign Land', the realm of King KALAFES, who was converted from his pagan beliefs to Christianity by ALAN, and succeeded by JOSHUA, Alan's brother. The country has been possibly identified with LISTINOISE, the realm of King PELLEHAN in Arthurian times. The aunt of PERCEVAL was once the queen of this country, and this has led to a further possible identification with the WASTE LAND of the GRAIL legends.

TERRE LABUR
Arthurian
The realm of KLINGSOR, according to WOLFRAM VON ESCHENBACH.

TERRESTRIAL PARADISE
Arthurian
The biblical Garden of Eden that, during the Middle Ages, was believed still to be in existence and able to be found. In the obscure medieval *Le Chanson d'Esclarmonde*, the heroine, ESCLARMONDE, is taken there by MORGAN Le Fay and there bathes in the FOUNTAIN OF YOUTH.

TETHRA
Irish
A shadowy figure who was said to refer to the fish he herded as his cattle. His only real appearance in the Irish legends is during the Second Battle of MAGH TUIREDH, in which he was reported to have fought alongside the FOMHOIRÉ, possibly even being numbered among their rulers. His war sword, which recounted all it had done when unsheathed, was captured by OGHMA.

TEUTATES
Gaulish
A tribal deity, possibly a god of war, who was one of the three main gods of Celtic GAUL, the other two being ESUS and TARANIS. The Romans sought to equate Teutates, whose name comes from a Celtic root meaning 'warlike', with Mars.

TEYRNON TWRYF LIANT
Welsh
The owner of the most beautiful mare in the world, a mare that foaled every year on 1 May, but whose colts always mysteriously vanished. Unable to withstand the loss any longer, Teyrnon Twryf Liant hid himself in the stable and watched his mare foal. As he stood and gazed on the wonderful colt, a huge clawed hand reached into the stable and took hold of the animal. Teyrnon Twryf Liant jumped up and severed the arm at the elbow so that it fell into the stable along with the colt. He rushed outside to see if he could identify the thief, but nothing was in sight. As he came back into the stable he found a baby boy, whom he took in to his wife. They named him GWRI. A year later, having learnt of the mysterious disappearance of the newborn baby boy of PWYLL and RHIANNON and struck by the infant's likeness to the King, he concluded that this must be their lost baby. Teyrnon Twryf Liant took the child to the King. Amid great celebrations Rhiannon renamed the child PRYDERI.

THANEY
Arthurian
According to the *LIFE OF SAINT KENTIGERN*, the daughter of LOT and the mother of Saint KENTIGERN.

THANOR
Arthurian
The King of CORNWALL who had help from the Irish against King PELIAS. In repayment for this help, a yearly tribute had to be paid to IRELAND, a tribute over which TRISTAN had to fight MARHAUS.

THEREUS
Arthurian
According to *CLARIS ET LARIS*, the Emperor of Rome who invaded BRITAIN but was soundly defeated by ARTHUR.

THIRTEEN TREASURES OF BRITAIN
Welsh and Arthurian
The treasures or curiosities that MYRDDIN (MERLIN) was said to have procured and then sailed away with, never to be seen again, in his glass boat. These mystical items altered from source to source, but most common among them were:
1 DYRNWYN: the sword of RHYDDERCH HAEL, which would burst into flames from the cross to the point if any man, save Rhydderch, drew it.
2 MWYS GWYDDNO: the hamper of GWYDDNO, which had the power to turn any meat placed on or in it, into sufficient to feed a hundred people.

3 CORN BRANGALED: the horn of BRAN-GALED, which could provide any drink desired.

4 CADAIR, NEU CAR MORGAN MWYNFAWR: the chair or car of MORGAN MWYNFAWR, which would carry a person seated in it wherever they wished to go.

5 HOGALEN TUDNO: the whetstone of TUDNO, which would sharpen none but the weapon of a brave man.

6 LLEN ARTHUR: the veil of ARTHUR, which rendered the wearer invisible. (This item is a later addition to the list.)

7 CYLLEL LLAWFRODEDD: a DRUID sacrificial knife said by some to have belonged to a character named LLAWFRODEDD.

8 PAIS PADARN: the cloak of PADARN REDCOAT, which would make the wearer invisible.

9 PAIR DRYNOG: the cauldron of DRYNOG in which none but the meat of a brave man would boil. Some sources name this as the cauldron that had once belonged to the giant DIWRNACH.

10 DYSGYL A GREN RHYDDERCH: the platter of RHYDDERCH upon which any meat desired would appear. Some sources name the owner of the magical dish as RHYGENYDD, and some also include a crock that was also said to have belonged to Rhygenydd. This would, however, appear to be a confusion.

11 TAWLBWRDD: a chess or, more accurately, a backgammon board with a ground of gold and men of silver who would play themselves. This is sometimes named as the GWYDDBWYLL board belonging to GWENDDOLAU.

12 MANTELL: a robe that would keep the wearer warm no matter how severe the weather. This is sometimes confused with Lien Arthur, and is then said to render the wearer invisible. Some say that it had once belonged to TEGAU EUFRON.

13 MODRWY ELUNED: the ring of ELUNED, which conferred invisibility on the wearer. An unnamed stone also belonging to Eluned is sometimes mentioned in the list.

14 The halter of CLYDNO EIDDYN.

THITIS
Welsh and Arthurian

One of the nine sisters of MORGEN (MORGAN Le Fay).

THOLOMER
Arthurian

The King of BABYLON who was at first friendly towards EVELAKE, giving him land, but when the latter ascended the throne of SARRAS the two were drawn into a war. Helped by JOSEPH OF ARIMATHEA, Evelake (apparently pagan at this time, so help from the saintly Joseph of Arimathea seems highly questionable) defeated Tholomer.

THOMAS
Arthurian

An Anglo-Norman poet who flourished in the twelfth century and was the author of *TRISTAN*, the earliest extant text (*c.* 1155–70) of the legend of TRISTAN and ISEULT. A fragment of 3,144 lines covering the final episodes, including the deaths of the lovers, survives.

THOMAS OF THE MOUNTAIN
Arthurian

The father of TOM THUMB who, unable to father any children, sent his wife to consult MERLIN. As a result Tom Thumb was born, growing to manhood within four minutes but never growing any taller.

THOMPSON
Arthurian

According to a Yorkshire legend, a potter who chanced on King ARTHUR and his knights asleep beneath Richmond Castle, thus adding this location in Yorkshire to the multitude of possible resting places for Arthur. On a table the potter saw a horn and a sword. Picking up the sword, he started to draw the blade from the scabbard, but dropped it when the sleeping knights began to stir.

TI(G)ERNMAS
Irish

A mythical king, the fifth in line after EREMON. Tigernmas is alleged to have introduced the worship of CENN CRÚIACH into IRELAND and to have been the first to mine and smelt gold in Ireland. Tigernmas and three-quarters of his people were said to have been killed while worshipping Cenn Crúiach on the eve of SAMHAIN.

TIGRIDIA
Arthurian

The sister of DARERCA. She was said to have married GRALLO, the grandson of CONAN MERIADOC, thus becoming related by marriage to ARTHUR.

TIMIAS
Arthurian

ARTHUR's squire in SPENSER's allegorical *FAERIE QUEENE*. It has been suggested that Timias is a characterisation of Sir Walter Raleigh.

TINTAGEL

Arthurian

A village on the northern coast of CORNWALL and the site of the castle, home of Duke GORLOIS and his wife IGRAINE, where UTHER visited Igraine in the guise of her husband. The result of this union was ARTHUR, who was said to have been born there. The present castle is Norman, and shows no signs of any earlier structure, though this does not preclude the existence of a castle contemporary with King Arthur.

TÍR FÓ -THUINN, -THIUNN

Irish

'The Land under the Waves', a supernatural underwater kingdom that appears in the story of DIARMAID UA DUIBHNE, who was taken there to help its king but held there against his will and rescued by FIONN MAC CUMHAILL.

TÍR (IN)NA MBAN

Irish and Arthurian

An OTHERWORLDLY realm that was entirely populated by women, which led to it popularly being known as the LAND OF WOMEN. The island was visited by BRÂN, who thought that he and his companions remained there only a year. They found out that they had, in fact, stayed for hundreds of years when they attempted to return home. Arthurian commentators have sought to make this land the origin of MAIDENLAND.

TÍR (IN)NA MBÉO

Irish

A paradisiacal OTHERWORLDLY realm, euphemistically called the LAND OF THE LIVING, where sickness and old age were unknown and where the people perpetually feasted. It is the land to which CONNLA was taken and became king.

TÍR (IN)NA N-OC, -OG

Irish

The OTHERWORLDLY realm known as the LAND OF THE YOUNG or LAND OF YOUTH. This was the realm to which OISÎN travelled and married NIAMH, with whom he lived for 300 years, although to him it seemed like just three weeks.

TÍR TAIRNGIRI

Irish

The OTHERWORLDLY land, known as the LAND OF PROMISE, which was ruled by MANANNÁN MAC LIR, although MIDHIR was also regarded as a god of this realm, for on one occasion that god lured CORMAC MAC AIRT to the kingdom.

TITANIA

Arthurian

The Queen of the Fairies and wife of OBERON. She is perhaps best known from her appearance in SHAKESPEARE's *A MIDSUMMER NIGHT'S DREAM*, where she quarrelled with her husband over a changeling boy.

TOGODUMNUS

British

The son of CUNOBELINUS and brother of CARATACUS, whom he fought alongside in an attempt to thwart the Roman invasion led by CLAUDIUS. Although they delayed the invasion, they were eventually beaten.

TOLLEME

Arthurian

Possibly identical with THOLOMER, Tolleme is described as the King of SARRAS who, having been converted to Christianity by JOSEPH OF ARIMATHEA, was defeated by EVELAKE. It has been suggested that Tolleme was the King of SYRIA, or alternatively that he ruled over a race of Jewish descent living in CORNWALL, these people being referred to as SARACENS.

TOLLEN, SAINT

British and Arthurian

A saintly figure who was said to have defeated GWYNN AP NUDD, the Welsh Lord of the Dead and of the Underworld, on GLASTONBURY TOR.

See also COLLEN

TOLOMEO

Arthurian

A chaplain to the POPE who, having served for a period as MERLIN's scribe, became a cardinal.

TOM A'LINCOLN

Arthurian

The RED ROSE KNIGHT, the illegitimate son of ARTHUR and ANGELICA. Raised by a shepherd, he was given the position of commander in Arthur's army, and in this capacity he successfully defeated the Portuguese. His son by CAELIA, the Fairy Queen, was known as the FAERIE KNIGHT. Having travelled to the realm of PRESTER JOHN, Tom a'Lincoln eloped with ANGLITORA, Prester John's daughter, and they had a son known as the BLACK KNIGHT.

However, Anglitora subsequently found out that Tom a'Lincoln was illegitimate and left him, becoming the mistress of the lord of an unnamed castle. When Tom a'Lincoln arrived at the castle in search of her, she murdered him. His ghost told his son by Anglitora, the Black Knight, what had happened, and he avenged his father's death. The Black Knight then met Tom a'Lincoln's other son, the Faerie Knight, and the two became travelling companions, eventually arriving in England. The story of Tom a'Lincoln is told in the romance *Tom a'Lincoln*, which was written by Richard Johnston (b. 1573).

TOM THUMB
Arthurian

A well-known minuscule character whose connection to the Arthurian legends remains relatively limited. He is described as the son of THOMAS OF THE MOUNTAIN, who, having been unable to father any children, sent his wife to consult MERLIN. That great wizard told her that she would have a child, but that that child would be no bigger than her husband's thumb. She did indeed give birth to the minute Tom Thumb, who became a man within four minutes, but never grew any larger than he had been at first. His godmother was the Queen of the Fairies, and she gave him a hat of knowledge, a ring of invisibility, a girdle of transformation and shoes that could carry him over long distances with the greatest of ease. Tom Thumb was often present with King ARTHUR and the KNIGHTS OF THE ROUND TABLE, but died while engaged in a fight with an adder.

TONWENNA
British

The wife of MOLMUTIUS and mother, by him, of BRENNIUS and BELINUS. The two warring brothers were finally reconciled after Tonwenna had appealed to them to make their peace.

TOPA
Irish

The manservant to PARTHOLÁN who was seduced by DEALGNAID, Partholán's wife, and is therefore possibly the father of RURY.

TOR
Arthurian

The son of PELLINORE or ARIES, though he is usually regarded as the illegitimate son of Pellinore and the wife of Aries. Tor killed ABELLEUS and was later made one of the KNIGHTS OF THE ROUND TABLE. He was killed on the occasion when LANCELOT and his companions carried GUINEVERE off to safety.

TOR MÔR
Irish

The precipitous headland on TORY Island on which BALAR built a tower in which he confined his daughter ETHLINN, and where she was visited by CIAN and conceived LUGH.

TORACH
Irish

An alternative name sometimes used to refer to TORY Island, the stronghold of the gigantic, one-eyed FOMHOIRÉ.

TORC TRIATH
Irish and Arthurian

The king of boars in Irish mythology who corresponds to the giant boar TWRCH TRWYTH, which appears in the *MABINOGION*, and against which Arthur and his men are sent by YSPADDADEN in their quest to help CULHWCH win the hand of OLWEN.

TOREC
Arthurian

The son of King YDOR who, when grown to manhood, attempted to recover the circlet that had belonged to his grandmother from MIRAUDE. She told him that she would marry him if he managed to overcome all the KNIGHTS OF THE ROUND TABLE. This he managed to do with the complicity of GAWAIN, who arranged matters with the other knights, and Miraude was therefore compelled to marry him.

TORNA ÉICES
Irish

A FILI who lived in ULSTER and was said to have been the foster father of NIAL NOÍGIALLACH.

TORTAIN
Arthurian

The result of the forced copulation of ELIAVRES and a sow.

TORY
Irish
Also TORACH

The precipitous island off the coast of Donegal that was the stronghold of the FOMHOIRÉ. The people of NEMHEDH once stormed the island and succeeded in killing one of the two Fomhoiré kings of the time, CONANN. The other king, MORC, however, killed all but thirty of the attackers, who were then forced to flee from IRELAND.

TOTNES

British and Arthurian

A picturesque town in south Devon, the older part of which occupies a steep hill overlooking the River Dart. It was here that BRUTUS and his Trojan refugees were said to have first landed, their immigration being opposed by GOGMAGOG and the other giants who lived in BRITAIN. It is also the town where AMBROSIUS AURELIUS was said to have landed from BRITTANY and been proclaimed King of England.

TOUTATES

Gaulish
See TEUTATES

TRANSELINE

Arthurian

According to *HUON DE BORDEAUX*, a niece of ARTHUR and MORGAN Le Fay.

TRAPRAIN LAW

Arthurian

Located near EDINBURGH, this was the headquarters of a fifth-century King of the LOTHIAN region who has been thought of as cognate with LOT.

TREBES

Arthurian

The location of BAN's castle in BRITTANY. When CLAUDAS succeeded in destroying it, Ban was said to have died of a broken heart.

TREBUCHET

Arthurian

Featuring in the GRAIL legends, Trebuchet was said to have made the GRAIL SWORD, and later to have repaired it. It has been suggested that his character owes its origins to TURBE, the father of the Irish smith god, GOIBHNIU.

Totnes, Devon, the town where Brutus and his Trojan refugees were said first to have landed in Britain.
(© Bettmann/Corbis)

TREGALEN

Arthurian

According to Welsh tradition, the site of ARTHUR's final battle, in which he was victorious. He pursued the fleeing remnants of his enemies army, but was killed at BWLCH-Y-SAETHU in Snowdonia by a flurry of arrows.

TREMEUR

British and Arthurian

According to the legends surrounding CUNOMORUS, Tremeur was the son of either CUNOMORUS and TREPHINA or Trephina and JONAS. One tradition makes him the offspring of the first couple, also calling him GILDAS JUNIOR, while another makes his parents the second pair and gives him the alternative name of JUDWAL. While it would seem that the two are in fact the same, the various stories surrounding him are confused, so it is quite conceivable that there were two characters with this name.

TREND(H)ORN

Irish

A servant in the employ of CONCHOBAR MAC NESSA. He was sent by that king to spy on DERDRIU and the sons of UISNECH after they had returned to IRELAND from their exile in SCOTLAND, the express purpose of his mission being to report whether the beauty of Derdriu had been diminished in her absence. He was spotted by NAOISE, who put out one of his eyes with an expertly thrown chess piece, but Trendhorn completed his mission and reported to Conchobar mac Nessa that Derdriu was still the most beautiful woman alive.

TRENMOR

Irish

The father of CUMHAILL and thus grandfather of FIONN MAC CUMHAILL.

TRENTENY

Arthurian

The Lord of Trenteny was traditionally said to have killed a cow that belonged to Saint ENDELIENTA and then been killed, either by ARTHUR himself or at the King's order. No matter at whose hands he met his end, Endelienta restored him to life.

TREON

Irish

The father of the giantess BEBHIONN, whom he had betrothed, against her will, to AEDA.

TREPHINA

Welsh and Arthurian

The daughter of WAROK, chief of the VENETII, and a wife of CUNOMORUS. One tradition makes her the mother of TREMEUR or GILDAS JUNIOR, after whose birth she was beheaded by Cunomorus. Gildas restored her to life and thereafter she was said to have carried her severed head around with her.

TRÍ DÉ DÁNA

Irish

The triad of the gods of craftsmanship. They were CREIDHNE, GOIBHNIU and LUCHTAINE. During the Second Battle of MAGH TUIREDH, one of the few occasions when they actually worked together, they forged and repaired the weapons of the TUATHA DÉ DANANN. However, the honorific title, which means 'Three Gods of Dan', is also sometimes applied to BRIAN, IUCHAR and IUCHARBA.

See also COLUM CUALLEINECH

TRI-NOVANTES

British

The tribal name given to the Britons said to be inhabiting LONDON and the territory to the north of that city at the time of JULIUS CAESAR's second incursion into BRITAIN in 54 BC. Fearing the ambitions of CASSIVELAUNUS, the Tri-Novantes placed themselves under Roman protection along with several other British tribes. Cassivelaunus, having agreed to pay tribute to Rome in return for independence, also agreed to uphold the separate independence of the Tri-Novantes. Later, during the almost successful revolt led by BOUDICCA in the first century AD, the Tri-Novantes joined forces with her ICENI people, but were suppressed by the vastly superior Roman army after they had defeated Boudicca.

TRI-NOVANTUM

Romano-British and Arthurian

A later name given to TROIA NOVA, or 'New Troy', the city legendarily founded by BRUTUS and today known as LONDON. The TRI-NOVANTES, who inhabited the city and the land to the north at the time of JULIUS CAESAR's second exploratory visit to BRITAIN, take their name from this ancient name for the capital city of Britain.

TRIADS

Welsh and Arthurian

The common name for the *TRIOEDD YNYS PRYDEIN*.

TRIBUIT

Arthurian

A river, the exact location of which remains a mystery, that was the site of one of ARTHUR'S BATTLES.

TRIOEDD YNYS PRYDEIN

Welsh

The Triads of the Island of Britain, one of the oldest extant Welsh manuscripts, dating from the sixth century, consists of political lyrics, war songs, songs praising chiefs and elegies on the same, religious, hymns and pseudonymous poems, variously ascribed to MYRDDIN (MERLIN) and TALIESIN. The *TRIADS*, as they are popularly known, were written by Celtic bards of the time, and are outstanding and essential source texts for Celtic research. Listing items in groups of three, they all contain a great deal of Arthurian material. While two sets are accepted as genuine, the third has been the subject of much controversy and is now considered a later emulation. They undoubtedly inspired many of the later writers, such as GILDAS and NENNIUS, who adapted the text to suit their own purposes.

TRISTAN

Arthurian

The most tragic of all the Arthurian heroes. A contemporary of ARTHUR, the nephew and champion of King MARK of CORNWALL, he was also a KNIGHT OF THE ROUND TABLE. Most romancers give some account of his story, but there is a wide diversity in his lineage.

According to Sir Thomas MALORY, the most often quoted, he was the son of MELIODAS and ELIZABETH. The Italian romance *TRISTANO RICCARDIANO* virtually echoes this, giving a very slightly different name to his mother, but naming his paternal grandfather as FELIX. GOTTFRIED VON STRASSBURG differs quite markedly in his *TRISTAN AND ISOLDE* (*c.* 1210), his courtly epic written in Middle High German and based on an earlier version by the Anglo-Norman poet THOMAS. He gives RIVALIN and BLANCHEFLEUR as Tristan's parents, Blanchefleur being Mark's sister. Some sources replace Rivalin with King ROULAND of ERMINIA.

Tristan's story is basically as follows.

He was the son of King Meliodas, King of LIONES, and Elizabeth, sister of King Mark of Cornwall, and his mother died in childbirth. As a young man he entered the service of his uncle, King Mark, and when the latter refused to pay the customary tribute to IRELAND Tristan championed his uncle and killed MARHAUS, the Irish champion and brother of the Irish Queen. However, during the combat Tristan received a poisoned wound and, being advised that he could be cured only in Ireland, he travelled there – quite wisely, considering the circumstances – under an assumed name, which was either TANTRIS (a simple anagram of Tristan) or PRO OF IERNESETIR. His wound was cured by Iseult, the daughter to King ANGUISH.

When Tristan returned to Cornwall, he told his uncle of the beauty of Iseult, and so taken was the King with his description that he sent Tristan back to Ireland to woo Iseult on his behalf. King Anguish agreed to the marriage and Tristan set off to bring Iseult back to his uncle. However, on the ship that carried them across the Irish Sea, he and Iseult mistakenly drank a love potion that was intended for Mark and his bride-to-be. Falling helplessly in love with each other, they embarked on their fated love affair. On Iseult's wedding night, she had her maid, BRANGIEN, take her place under cover of darkness, so that Mark would not know she had already laid with Tristan. Their affair continued undiscovered, but on one occasion Tristan's blood was spilt in Iseult's bed, and this gave rise to suspicion. Iseult was, however, very anxious to dispel this suspicion, and so undertook to swear on a hot iron that she was not an adulteress. When the time came, Iseult fell into the arms of a beggar (Tristan in disguise), and so was able truthfully to swear to Mark that none but the King and the beggar had held her.

Tristan now sensed that their love was doomed and hurried away from King Mark's court, crossing the channel and settling in BRITTANY. There he married the daughter of HOEL, King of Brittany, who was known as Iseult of the White Hands. Various other names are given for Tristan's father-in-law: HAVELIN by EILHART, JOVELIN by GOTTFRIED VON STRASSBURG and GILIERCHINS in the Italian *TAVOLA RITONDA*. However, Tristan did not consummate his marriage with his wife, but did become the firm friend of her brother KAHEDRIN. Receiving yet another poisoned wound, Tristan believed that only Iseult, who had healed his earlier wound in Ireland, could again heal this wound, and so sent for her to come to his aid. Before the ship departed to fetch her, Tristan had obtained a promise from the captain that he would hoist white sails if she were on board when he returned, but black sails if she had declined to come. Jealous of her husband's undying love for Iseult, his wife lied to him on seeing the ship returning with white sails hoisted, saying instead that they were black. On hearing this, Tristan died, and when Iseult arrived and found that

HOW LA BEALE
ISOVD NVRSED
SIR TRISTRAM

Iseult nurses the ailing Tristan back to health. (Aubrey Beardsley, 1893–4/Mary Evans Picture Library)

Tristan was dead, she too died, of a broken heart. King Mark buried them side by side, though Sir Thomas MALORY says that it was Mark who killed Tristan as he played the harp to Iseult by driving either a lance or a sword into his back. From Tristan's grave there grew a vine, while from Iseult's a rose sprang up. These two plants met and became inseparably entwined.

The origins of this famous love story are a little difficult to pin down. One suggestion is that it is Pictish, for Tristan is a Pictish name. This is further supported by the Welsh tradition, which calls his father TALLWCH, which is itself perhaps a form of the Pictish name TALORC. Pictish king-lists say that King Talorc III, who was perhaps legendary, was succeeded by Drust V, leading to a possible identification between these two and the main characters of the legend. Obviously there have been many modifications to the story as it became more widely known, and it is now almost universally accepted that the final version is Breton. However, there is a great deal that is uniquely Cornish.

Near Fowey in Cornwall there is a stone (unremarkably known as the Fowey Stone) that bears the earliest-known inscription naming Tristan as the son of Cunomorus. Not far from Helston, Cornwall, in the district of Meneage, is a ford that was recorded as Hryt Eselt in the tenth century – the earliest known form of Iseult. These two simple facts would seem to suggest that as the story passed through Cornwall a local hero and heroine replaced those originally connected with the story. King Mark himself is called King of Cornwall, and is traditionally associated with Castle DORE near Galant. All these factors point directly to a Cornish origin, further supported in the earliest form of the romance itself, by the Norman–French poet BÉROUL. This firmly sets the story in south and mid-Cornwall, and mentions such places as Chapel Rock near Mevagissey (Tristan's Leap), and the Forest of Morrois (Moresk, near Truro), where the lovers once fled to hide from King Mark and his barons.

Other commentators have added other details to the story. Eilhart says that Tristan (called TRISTRAM by Sir Thomas Malory) was the first person to train dogs. Italian romance gave him and Iseult two children bearing their names, while the Icelandic SAGA OF TRISTRAM says Tristan had a son by Iseult of the White Hands who was named KALEGRAS. French romance gave Tristan and Iseult a single son, YSAIE THE SAD, and a grandson, MARC. Latterly the lovers became the subject of Richard Wagner's opera *Tristan und Isolde*.

TRISTAN
Arthurian

1 Twelfth-century text by the Anglo-Norman poet THOMAS that survives only in a fragment of 3,144 lines and covers the later episodes in the famous story of TRISTAN and ISEULT, including the death of the lovers. This fragment is the earliest extant text covering the tragic love affair, and was written sometime between *c.* 1155 and *c.* 1170.

2 Fragmentary twelfth-century text by the French writer BÉROUL. It is certainly later than that written by THOMAS, and was, in all probability, based on the earlier work, for it is remarkably similar in both content and style.

TRISTAN AND ISOLDE
Arthurian

Early thirteenth-century (*c.* 1210) Middle High German courtly epic by GOTTFRIED VON STRASSBURG that was based on the earlier version of the famous story by the Anglo-Norman poet THOMAS.

TRISTAN THE DWARF
Arthurian

Perversely, this character from the Norwegian *SAGA OF TRISTRAM* was a large man who asked for TRISTAN's help against an evil man who had deprived him of both his wife and his castle.

TRISTAN THE STRANGER
Arthurian

Appearing in the Icelandic *SAGA OF TRISTRAM*, this character, with an over-inflated idea of his own prowess, asked TRISTAN to help him against seven brothers who had systematically pillaged and plundered his kingdom.

TRISTAN THE YOUNGER
Arthurian

According to Spanish and Italian romance, the son of TRISTAN and ISEULT, so called to distinguish him from his father. He succeeded MARK as the King of CORNWALL and became a KNIGHT OF THE ROUND TABLE. While he was at CAMELOT, GUINEVERE became infatuated with him, but he did not return her feelings. He married the princess MARIA, daughter of King JUAN of Castile.

TRISTANO PANCIATOCHIANO
Arthurian

A fourteenth-century Italian romance concerning TRISTAN.

TRISTANO RICCARDIANO
Arthurian

A thirteenth-century Italian romance concerning TRISTAN.

TRISTOUSE
Arthurian

The daughter of King BRIANT OF THE RED ISLE, who was born after her father's death and cast out to sea. She was rescued by an anonymous saviour, adopted and, when grown, married King YDOR. A sorrowful lady, she was said to have laughed for the very first time when she gave birth to her son, TOREC.

TRISTRAM
Arthurian

The form of TRISTAN used by Sir Thomas MALORY, being the usual English form of the name, instances appearing in England since the twelfth century. A slightly less common version is TRISTREM.

TRISTRAM'S SAGA
Arthurian

Form in which both the Norwegian and the Icelandic *SAGA OF TRISTRAM* are sometimes known.

TRISTREM
Arthurian

A variant of TRISTAN.

TROAS
Arthurian

The King of Thessaly who, as his name suggests, was of Trojan origin. He and his son, TROIANO, feature in an unpublished romance concerning the OLD TABLE.

TROIA NOVA
British and Arthurian

BRUTUS gave the name to the city he founded on the River Thames. It was later known as TRINOVANTUM and is better known today as LONDON.

TROIANO
Arthurian

The son of King TROAS of Thessaly and a direct descendant of the Trojan hero Hector. He figures in an unpublished Italian romance concerning the OLD TABLE, which tells how he, UTHER and King REMUS of Rome (most probably the brother of Romulus in classical Roman mythology) joined forces to make the Trojan race the rulers of Troy once again.

TRONC
Arthurian

According to some sources, this was the name of an extremely ugly dwarf on whom the fairies took pity. Removing all traces of his ugliness, they gave him a kingdom, after which time he became known as OBERON, married TITANIA and became the King of the Fairies.

TROYNOVANT
British and Arthurian
See TROIA NOVA

TROYNT
Welsh and Arthurian
A little used variant of TWRCH TRWYTH.

TRWYN YR WYLFA
Welsh

A hill on whose summit the people of HELIG AP GLANNOWG were alleged to have fled when the sea inundated their kingdom. It is one of the lost kingdoms of WALES and is now said to lie about two miles off the coast at Penmaenbach.

TRYAMOUR
Arthurian

The lover of LANVAL who gave him the fairy horse BLANCHARD.

TRYFFIN
Arthurian

A King of DENMARK and father of DRUDWAS.

TRYSTAN
Arthurian

A Welsh romance that names BACH BYCHAN as the page of TRISTAN.

TUAG (INBIR)
Irish

A beautiful maiden who was kept in seclusion so that no man might see her. However, she had been seen by MANANNÁN MAC LIR, who was instantly besotted. He sent a DRUID named FER FIDAIL, in the guise of a woman, to gain access to her. However, Fer Fidail fell in love with Tuag and spent three nights with her, before causing her to fall into an enchanted sleep, in which state he carried her down to the shore, where he left her while he went to look for a boat. Manannán mac Lir, who knew all about the betrayal of his druid, sent a huge wave to drown the maiden and afterwards summarily disposed of Fer Fidail.

TUAN MAC CARELL
Irish

The son of CARELL who was conceived after his mother had eaten the salmon that was the final animal incarnation of TUAN MAC STERN, who had come to IRELAND as one of the companions of PARTHOLÁN.

TUAN MAC STERN
Irish

The nephew of PARTHOLÁN. He came with that leader to IRELAND and was the sole survivor of the plague that wiped out those people. He lived alone for twenty-three years after the death of the people of Partholán before he hid in the hills and witnessed the arrival of NEMHEDH and his companions. There then started a series of transformations to Tuan mac Stern that are typical of Celtic mythology.

One night he fell asleep as an old man. The next morning he awoke as a stag, young in both body and heart. He remained in that form, as the king of all the deer of Ireland, during the occupation of Nemhedh and his people. As they died out, so Tuan mac Stern once again fell asleep in old age. This time he woke up as a wild boar, once more rejuvenated.

Now he witnessed the arrival of the FIR BHOLG and remained in the shape of the boar while those people were the inhabitants of Ireland. Again old age set in, and this time he was rejuvenated as an eagle, in which form he saw the arrival of the TUATHA DÉ DANANN and then the Sons of MÍL ÉSPÁINE. While they were in occupation, he once again reached old age and was reborn as a salmon.

This salmon was caught by a fisherman and taken to the home of CARELL, whose wife ate him whole. He gestated in her womb for nine months before being reborn as a human boy, but now having the name TUAN MAC CARELL. It is in this incarnation that he met Saint PATRICK and told that saint the history of Ireland.

See also FINNEN

TUATHA DÉ (DANANN)
Irish

Literally translated as the 'People of the Goddess Dana', the Tuatha Dé Danann are the true gods of Celtic IRELAND. They are recorded in the *Leabhar Gabhála Éireann* as the remnants of the people of NEMHEDH, who fled to unnamed northern lands, although some have suggested that these lands were the Hebrides, or even the Orkney or Shetland Islands. Returning as the fifth of the six invasions Ireland endured in its mythological history, they followed the FIR BHOLG, who were also a people formed from the residue of the people of Nemhedh. However, the Tuatha Dé Danann had, during their longer absence from Ireland, learned all manner of magical skills and brought with them four magical items. These were the stone of FÁL, given to them by the wizard MORFESSA in FALIA, the invincible spear of LUGH, given to them by ESIAS in GORIAS, the inescapable sword of NUADHA, given to them by USCIAS in FINDIAS, and the inexhaustible cauldron of the DAGHDHA, their leader, given to them by SIMIAS in MURIAS.

When confronted by the Fir Bholg, the Tuatha Dé Danann demanded that the kingship of the country be handed to them or they would fight for it. The Fir Bholg chose the latter and were utterly defeated at the First Battle of MAGH TUIREDH, although the Tuatha Dé Danann's king, Nuadha, lost an arm in the fight and so had to abdicate. The few survivors of the Fir Bholg fled into exile among the FOMHOIRÉ.

The new king chosen by the Tuatha Dé Danann was not the best decision they had ever made, for they chose the tyrannical BRES, who was half Tuatha Dé Danann and half Fomhoiré. His tyranny was soon put to an end, and Nuadha, having had a silver arm fitted, was restored to the throne. Bres defected to the Fomhoiré and raised an army against the Tuatha Dé Danann, who prepared for the battle. Shortly before the battle was due to began, Lugh arrived at TARA, the Tuatha Dé Danann's capital, and Nuadha, recognising the superiority of the polymath, stepped down in his favour.

The Second Battle of Magh Tuiredh was now fought, this battle being against the Fomhoiré army led by Bres. The battle was decided in single combat between Lugh and the giant BALAR. Lugh won with a well-aimed slingshot, which went straight through Balar's single eye and continued out of the back of his head to decimate the Fomhoiré horde.

The number of Tuatha Dé Danann deities has never been fully established. Notable among them were Lugh, OGHMA, the Daghdha and the three kings MAC CUILL, MAC CÉCHT and MAC GRÉINE along with their goddess wives BANBHA, FÓDLA and ÉRIU, the last of which gave her name to EIRE. The Tuatha Dé Danann were finally defeated by the sixth and last invasionary party to land in Ireland, the Sons of MÍL ÉSPÁINE. The final battle was that of TAILTIU, after which the Tuatha Dé Danann negotiated with their conquerors to retain at least a part of their realm. They were given the underground half, and the Daghdha provided each of the Tuatha Dé Danann with a SÍDH, or earthen barrow. There the Tuatha Dé Danann are said still to live.

TUDNO
Welsh

A famous Welsh saint, who is said to have been one of the seven sons of SEITHENYN and who hailed from the lost kingdom of CANTRE'R GWAELOD.

TUDWAL
Arthurian
Also TUTWAL

According to a number of Welsh pedigrees, a paternal ancestor of ARTHUR.

TUDWAL TUDGLYD
Welsh and Arthurian

The owner of a whetstone that was counted among the THIRTEEN TREASURES OF BRITAIN. It seems likely that he is the same as the character simply referred to as TUDWAL in the paternal ancestry of ARTHUR.

TUIREANN
Irish
Also TYREN

The daughter of BODB and sister of SAAR. She married ILLAN but was turned into a wolfhound by her husband's supernatural lover while she was pregnant. She gave birth to two hounds, BRÂN and SGEOLAN, who became the faithful hunting dogs of FIONN MAC CUMHAILL, her brother-in-law. Her human form was restored to her after Illan had promised his mistress that he would renounce her.

TU(I)RENN
Irish

The son of OGHMA and the father of BRIAN, IUCHAR and IUCHARBA.

TUIS
Arthurian

The owner of a pig whose oil was sought by ARTHUR's warrior daughter MELORA. In Irish legend, Tuis was a King of Greece to whose realm the sons of Tuirenn went to obtain a pig skin that had healing properties. This, the older of the two legends, would seem to have been the origin of the Arthurian tale, or at least to have contributed to it in some part.

TULCHAINDE
Irish

The DRUID to CONAIRE MÓR. He loved DIL, the daughter of LUGMANNAIR, and persuaded her to elope with him from the Isle of FALGA (Isle of MAN), but she set the condition that her two beloved oxen, FEA and FERNEA, should accompany them. Unable to do this himself, for the oxen would have sunk their boat, Tulchainde enlisted the help of the MÓRRÍGHAN, who magically transported the beloved oxen over the water to MAGH MBREG, to where Dil and Tulchainde had travelled.

TURBE (TRÁGMAR)
Irish and Arthurian

The father of the smith god GOIBHNIU, although some sources say he was the father of GOBBÁN SAER. He appears to have had a connection with the sea, because he was said to hurl his axe at the sea when it was in full flood and forbid it to come beyond the point where the axe fell. It has been suggested that he is the original of TREBUCHET, the smith who manufactured and subsequently repaired the GRAIL SWORD.

TURCANS
Arthurian

According to the romance *FLORIANT ET FLORETE*, the King of ARMENIA.

TURINORO
Arthurian

The Count of Carthage and brother of the POPE, he came to the aid of LANCELOT in his fight against ARTHUR, engaging the latter's forces while they were on their way back to BRITAIN. According to the *TAVOLA RITONDA*, GAWAIN was killed in this encounter.

TURK AND GAWAIN
Arthurian

An English poem thought to date from the very end of the fifteenth century (*c.* 1500). It tells the story of GROMER, who, through a magic spell, had been turned into a Turk, resuming his normal form again when the enchantment he was under was broken by GAWAIN, who, at Gromer's own request, cut off his head.

TURMWR MORVAWR
Arthurian

A paternal ancestor of ARTHUR, according to Welsh genealogies, he is usually simply referred to as MORVAWR.

TURNING ISLAND
Arthurian

The island on to which NASCIEN was put, having been rescued from prison. It was from here that he was alleged to have spotted the ship of SOLOMON.

TURQUINE

Arthurian

The brother of Sir CARADOS OF THE DOLOROUS TOWER, he had an immense hatred for LANCELOT. In an attempt to lure Lancelot to him, he took ECTOR DE MARIS captive and threw him into his dungeons, along with several other prisoners he held at that time. Lancelot did indeed come to the rescue of Ector de Maris, and in the process killed Turquine and released all the captives.

TUTWAL

Arthurian

A variant of TUDWAL that is found in the paternal lines of descent of ARTHUR from LLYR.

TWADELL

Arthurian

The King of the Pygmies, a race described as being just 2 feet tall. During a jousting contest, he was overcome by TOM THUMB, and while the latter was ill Twadell provided the physician who treated him.

TWENTY-FOUR KNIGHTS

Arthurian

The collective term for a list of knights resident at ARTHUR's court found in the Welsh work *PEDWAR MARCHOG AR HUGAN LLYS ARTHUR*, which dates from some time around the fifteenth century or earlier. It has been suggested that this list forms a record of a company of knights that preceded the KNIGHTS OF THE ROUND TABLE. The knights recorded in this list were GWALCHMAI (GAWAIN), DRUDWAS, ELIWLOD, BORS, PERCEVAL (either father or son), GALAHAD, LANCELOT, OWAIN, MENW, TRISTAN, EIDDILIG, NASIENS (possibly NASCIEN), MORDRED, HOEL, BLAES, CADOG, PETROC, MORFRAN, SANDDEF, GLEWLWYD, CYON, ARON and LLYWARCH HÊN.

TWRCH TRWYTH

Welsh and Arthurian

A fierce boar that had originally been a king who was transformed by God for his wickedness. Almost certainly a recollection of an earlier boar deity, the

Ty-newydd Standing Stones, in Dyfed, traditionally a monument to Arthur's sons, who were killed while hunting the boar Twrch Trwyth.
(© Photolibrary Wales, 2004)

boar being a cult animal among the Celts, he corresponds directly to TORC TRIATH, the king of the boars in Irish mythology.

In the *MABINOGION* story of *CULHWCH AND OLWEN*, one of the tasks that YSPADDADEN set CULHWCH was to obtain the razor and comb (alternatively said to be a comb, razor and shears) from between the ears of this monstrous boar in order to barber Yspaddaden in preparation for Culhwch's marriage to OLWEN. The boar had already killed a great number of men before Culhwch caught up with it. Running it down, MABON snatched the razor while CYLEDYR THE WILD obtained the shears. The boar evaded them for a while, but they managed to find it again and procure the comb. They then forced the boar to jump off a cliff into the sea, when it swam away, never to be seen again.

TY GWYDR
Welsh and Arthurian

Literally a 'house of glass'. MYRDDIN's (MERLIN's) home was thought to be one, being said to stand either on BARDSEY Island, or on a boat, in which he sailed away with the THIRTEEN TREASURES OF BRITAIN.

TYLWYTH TEG
Welsh

The collective name for the people of GWYNN AP NUDD, although not necessarily referring to the dead themselves. The Tylwyth Teg are more akin to the fairies of popular folklore than to anything else, but they are possibly best described as spirits awaiting rebirth.

TY-NEWYDD STANDING STONES
Arthurian

Also called CERRIG MEIBION ARTHUR, 'Stone's of Arthur's Sons', these stones in DYFED are traditionally a monument to ARTHUR's sons who were killed while hunting the boar TWRCH TRWYTH.

TYOLET
Arthurian

A knight who, in French romance, had been raised in the woods and learned the language of the animals. He succeeded in rising to a challenge set by a lady who came to ARTHUR's court saying that she would marry whomsoever brought her the foot of a white stag, and give that successful knight her kingdom. Tyolet succeeded by killing the lions that guarded the stag but, being weary from the fight, he gave the foot to another knight to take back. This knight betrayed Tyolet, pretending he had accomplished the task, but he was later exposed and Tyolet justly rewarded.

TYREN
Irish
See TUIREANN

TYRONOE
Welsh and Arthurian
One of the nine sisters of MORGEN (MORGAN Le Fay).

U

UALLABH
Arthurian
The hero of a Scottish Gaelic folk story who is probably to be identified with GAWAIN. ARTHUR, who in this story is referred to as the King of IRELAND, married a mysterious woman who was brought to him on a bier, but had to fight a man whom the King took to be the woman's lover. This man defeated the King, but was in turn killed by Uallabh. It turned out that this man was the brother of the Queen, and the son of the King, of Ineen, and he imprisoned Uallabh, who was freed by the younger sister of the Queen. Uallabh eventually married the woman who had rescued him, and succeeded Arthur as the King of Ireland.

UAR-GAETH-SCEO LUACHAIR-SCEO
Irish
One of the ridiculous names given by the MÓRRÍGHAN when she was asked to identify herself by CÚ CHULAINN. The other, equally tongue-twisting name she gave was FAEBOR BEG-BEOIL CUIMDIUIR FOLT SCENBGAIRIT SCEO UATH. Cú Chulainn failed to recognise that the woman he was questioning was the Mórríghan, a mistake that ultimately led to his death.

UATHACH
Irish
The daughter of SCÁTHACH and brother of CUARE and CET. She fell in love with CÚ CHULAINN and taught him how he might get the better of her mother and thus how he might marry Uathach without a dowry.

UCHTDELBH
Irish
'Shapely Bosom', the wife of MANANNÁN MAC LIR, with whom AILLEANN, son of EOGABAL and brother of AINÉ, fell in love. Aine came to the rescue of her brother, who was suicidal, as she herself loved Manannán mac Lir. Together they went to the home of the god, where Aine smothered Manannán mac Lir with kisses and Aillean made it apparent that he loved Uchtdelbh. As Manannán mac Lir was well satisfied with the love he was being shown by Aine, he gave Uchtdelbh to Aillean.

UGAINY
Irish
A legendary King of IRELAND who also ruled over the greater part of western Europe. He was said to have married a princess of GAUL and had two sons, LOEGHAIRE and COVAC, who fought over the right to succeed him.

UÍ LIATHÁIN
Irish, Welsh and Arthurian
An Irish dynasty that is recorded as having ruled over the Welsh kingdom of DEMETIA (DYFED), possibly being expelled during the fifth or sixth century, the traditional Arthurian period, by AGRICOLA. It has been suggested that they brought with them a great number of the Irish legends, which gradually became interwoven with the native Welsh legends, a suggestion that attempts to explain the resemblance of a great many of the Welsh and Irish legends.

UÍ NÉILL
Irish
The name by which the descendants of NIAL NOÍGIALLACH were known.

UÍ TARSIG
Irish
A division of the GAILIÓIN, of which FIONN MAC CUMHAILL was the most prominent member.

UIGREANN
Irish
A warrior of the court of CONN CÉTCHATH-LACH. Uigreann abducted MUIRNE and when he refused to give her back was attacked by CUMHAILL. He was later killed by FIONN MAC CUMHAILL, who was, according to some sources, in turn killed by Uigreann's sons.

U(I)SNE(A)CH
Irish
A member of the RED BRANCH, he was the husband of ELVA, the daughter of CATHBHADH and MAGA, and the father of NAOISE, ARDAN

and AINNLE, the cousins of CÚ CHULAINN, who were collectively known as the sons of Uisnech.

ULAIDH
Irish

The original Irish name for ULSTER, one of the four original Irish kingdoms. Ulaidh was a huge realm that covered all northern IRELAND, including Donegal, and had its capital at EMHAIN MHACHA. The kingdom was subsequently divided by NIAL NOÍGIALLACH after he had conquered it.

ULFIUS
Arthurian

Sometimes called URFIN or URSIN in French romance. Ulfius was one of UTHER's knights, so presumably one of the knights of the OLD TABLE. It was he who eventually managed to persuade MERLIN to help Uther sleep with IGRAINE, himself accompanying his king in the magical guise of Sir BRASTIAS, while Uther himself, under Merlin's enchantment, resembled GORLOIS. When the young ARTHUR was proclaimed king, Ulfius was made his chamberlain.

ULLAN
Irish
See ILLAN

ULRICH VON ZARZIKHOVEN
Arthurian

The Swiss or German author (*fl.* 1200) of *Lanzelet*, which differs quite markedly from the story of LANCELOT as told by CHRÉTIEN DE TROYES and other romancers.

ULSTER
Irish

Originally known as ULAIDH, and one of the four early kingdoms of IRELAND. Ulster was created by the FIR BHOLG as one of the five CÓIGEDH, or provinces, into which they divided the land, the other provinces being LEINSTER, MUNSTER, CONNACHT and MEATH in the centre of all of them. Ulster was the traditional enemy of Connacht. The Fir Bholg were later replaced by the TUATHA DÉ DANANN, the true gods of Irish Celtic mythology. They, in turn, were defeated by the Sons of MÍL ÉSPÁINE, who are regarded as the traditional ancestors of the royal house of Ulster.

UMALL
Irish

A little-used variant of CUMHAILL.

UNDERSEA ISLAND
Irish
See ISLANDS OF MAÍL DÚIN

UNDERWORLD
General

'The Land of the Dead', the realm to which all those who have died pass. The Celtic idea of the Underworld really exists within the OTHERWORLD, for it is not the dark, foreboding place of other pagan cultures, but rather a discernible realm where all go. It is also the home of the gods, for the Celts had no concept of a realm that would equate to heaven, the sole domain of the gods.

UNDRY
Irish

The inexhaustible cauldron of the DAGHDHA.

UNIUS
Irish

The river in which the DAGHDHA made love to the MÓRRÍGHAN while she stood with one foot on each bank on the eve of the feast of SAMHAIN, washing the bloody corpses and armour of those about to die in the Second Battle of MAGH TUIREDH to be fought the following day. In return for the sexual favours of the Daghdha, the Mórríghan promised to help the TUATHA DÉ DANANN in the coming battle.

UR
Arthurian

According to an Irish romance, the father of ARTHUR. This is a misunderstanding on the part of the author of this romance, who did not understand that IUBHAR, the Irish name for Arthur's father, was actually a translation of UTHER. Instead he made Iubhar the grandfather and Ur the father.

URANUS
Arthurian

The guard who helped MELORA, ARTHUR's warrior daughter, to escape from the King of Asia.

URBIEN
Arthurian

According to the pedigree of Gallet, the father of King SOLOMON of BRITTANY and grandfather of CONSTANTINE, who was in turn the grandfather of ARTHUR.

URBS LEGIONIS
Arthurian

The Latin name for CHESTER, which has led to its

being identified with the CITY OF THE LEGIONS, though CAERLEON-ON-USK (Latin *Isca Legionis*) has also been identified as this site of one of ARTHUR'S BATTLES.

URFIN

Arthurian

Also URSIN

A variant of ULFIUS that is sometimes used in French romance.

URGAN

Arthurian

A giant who owned the magical fairy dog PETITCRIEU. He was killed when TRISTAN fought him for the dog, which he intended to give as a present to ISEULT.

URGANDA

Arthurian

According to the Spanish romance *Tirante lo blanco* the sister of ARTHUR who went to CONSTANTINOPLE, where Arthur had become a prisoner of the Emperor, who kept him in a cage. By some magical influence, possibly due to the cage he was held in, Arthur lacked intelligence until EXCALIBUR was placed in his hand, when he regained his senses. Urganda beseeched the Emperor to release her brother, which he finally did.

URIAN

Arthurian

The Lord of Moray and father of YVAIN. He is described as one of the three dispossessed Yorkist princes, along with LOT and AUGUSELUS, to whom ARTHUR restored their lands following the siege of YORK. It is quite likely that this name is simply a bad spelling of URIEN, though some sources do mention both characters quite independently.

URI-EN, -AN

British, Welsh and Arthurian

A historical king, ruler of the Brythonic kingdom of RHEGED in north-west England *c.* AD 570, being assassinated *c.* AD 590 by an ally following his defeat of the Bernicians, inhabitants of a realm in the north-east of England. The father of OWAIN, RIWALLAWN, RUN and PASCEN, Urien was in later legend (though his actual rule was some time later than the traditional Arthurian period) made the contemporary of ARTHUR and the husband of MORGAN Le Fay. The *Vulgate Merlin Continuation* calls his wife BRIMESENT. Welsh tradition made him the father of Owain by the daughter of the

OTHERWORLD King of ANNWFN, while the *TRIADS* call him the son of CYNFARCH by NEFYN, the daughter of BRYCHAN, giving him a twin sister named ERFDDF. The actual location of Rheged, his kingdom, also seems to have caused considerable confusion among the various writers. Sir Thomas MALORY calls him the King of GORE, while GEOFFREY OF MONMOUTH makes him the King of MUREIF, which may be identical with Monreith, but is more generally thought to mean Moray. This latter choice is further supported by some sources naming URIAN as the King of Moray to whom Arthur restored the lands he had lost to the SAXONS. The medieval Latin romance *HISTORIA MERIADOCI* seems to complement this, calling Urien the King of the Scots.

URSA MAJOR

Arthurian

A constellation of the northern celestial hemisphere that is popularly referred to as the Great Bear. ARTHUR has become associated with it, some sources stating that this is because the Welsh word *arth* signifies a bear. Further association was made by the English astronomer William Smyth (1788–1869), who, in his *Speculum Hartwellianum*, suggested that the circular motion of the constellation, which would have been well known even in Arthurian times, may have given rise to the original concept of the ROUND TABLE.

URSIN

Arthurian

Also URFIN

A variant of ULFIUS sometimes used in French romance.

USCIAS

Irish

Hailing from the mythical city of FINDIAS, Uscias was one of the four wizards who taught their magic to the TUATHA DÉ DANANN before they came to IRELAND. He is said to have equipped them with the invincible sword of NUADHA. His co-tutors were MORFESSA of FALIA, ESIAS of GORIAS and SIMIAS of MURIAS.

UTHECAR

Irish

The father of CELTCHAR.

UTHER

British and Arthurian

Commonly referred to with the epithet PENDRAGON, Uther was the King of BRITAIN,

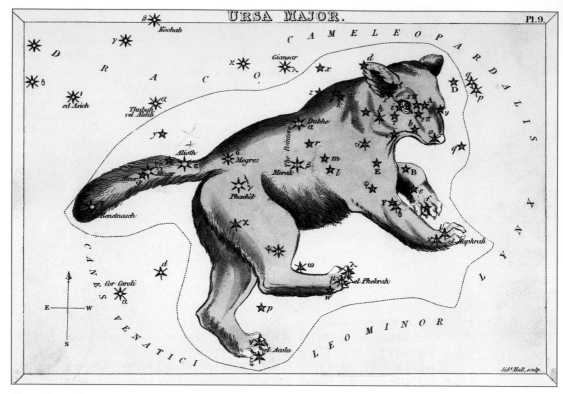

Ursa Major, the Great Bear, which has sometimes been associated with King Arthur and his Round Table. (© Bettmann/Corbis)

the son of CONSTANTINE and the brother of CONSTANS and AMBROSIUS AURELIUS, whom he succeeded, and father of ARTHUR. During his reign he fell in love with IGRAINE (EIGYR), the wife of GORLOIS, and therefore went to war with her husband. However, Uther was so sick with his love for Igraine that he was unable to participate in the war, and took to his pavilion. One of his knights, ULFIUS, went to visit the magician MERLIN, and persuaded him to alter Uther's appearance magically to that of Gorlois, on the condition that any child of the union be handed over to Merlin to be raised. This was agreed and the spell cast, Ulfius accompanying his master in the magical disguise of Sir BRASTIAS, and, on the very night that the disguised Uther laid with Igraine, her real husband died on the battlefield. Uther never revealed to Igraine the truth, and some time later he married her. When the child was born, Merlin arrived and took him away to be raised, that child, of course, being Arthur. Uther was said to have died within two years of his marriage to Igraine, some sources saying he died of a fever,

others that he died in battle. He was buried at STONEHENGE.

According to the *PROSE TRISTAN*, Uther was once in love with the wife of ARGAN, but this jealous husband defeated Uther in combat and made him build a castle to make recompense. HENRY OF HUNTINGDON makes him the brother rather than the father of Arthur, while several legends associate him with Cumbria. The *PETIT BRUT* records his fight with a dragon-serpent in Westmorland, which is now a part of Cumbria, while local Cumbrian legend makes him a giant, saying that he founded the kingdom of MALLERSTANG, and attempted to divert the River EDEN to form the moat around his castle.

Some commentators have suggested that Uther came about as the result of a misunderstanding of the Welsh phrase *Arthur mab uther*, which was taken to mean 'Arthur, son of Uther', while it actually means 'Arthur, terrible son'. This theory has not found universal acceptance, for there is sufficient evidence to support an independent tradition regarding Uther.

V

VAGOR

Arthurian

The ruler of ILLE ESTRANGE or ESTRANGOT, father of MARABRON. He held LIONEL captive and arranged a fight between his son and his captive. However, as Lionel was injured, LANCELOT took his place, defeated Marabron and so secured Lionel's release.

VALERIN

Arthurian

The King of the TANGLED WOOD who lived in a castle on top of a high mountain that was both mist-bound and forest-bound, and that no one could enter unless Valerin instructed his monsters to allow them to pass. Claiming that GUINEVERE was betrothed to him before ARTHUR, Valerin claimed the Queen, but was defeated in combat by her champion, LANCELOT. None the less Valerin carried her off and, placing her in an enchanted sleep, imprisoned her in a castle surrounded by snakes. With the magical aid of the wizard MALDUC she was later freed.

VALLONE

Arthurian

The domain of ESCORDUCARLA, who became enamoured of MERLIN and planned to take him prisoner. The plan backfired and she ended up as Merlin's prisoner instead.

VALYANT

Arthurian

The King of WALES and a relation of LANCELOT.

VANNES AND NANTES

Arthurian

The realm of CARADOC, who married YSAIVE.

VARLAN

Arthurian

Also BRULAN

A King of GALES who, in the Arthurian legends, is described as having been newly converted to Christianity. A mysterious ship arrived on the coast of BRITAIN carrying DAVID'S SWORD. Varlan used that sword to kill his enemy King LAMBOR, and as a result of this ungodly act their kingdoms became the WASTE LAND of the GRAIL legends.

VAUX, SIR ROLAND DE

Arthurian

The knight who woke GYNETH from the enchanted sleep MERLIN had caused her to fall into.

VELLENDRUCHER

Arthurian

The site in CORNWALL of a legendary battle in which ARTHUR, assisted by the SEVEN KINGS OF CORNWALL, defeated the Danes. After their victory they gave thanks at SENNAN HOLY WELL and held a banquet at TABLE MAN.

VENDOTIA

Welsh and Arthurian

The Latin name by which the North Welsh kingdom of GWYNEDD was known. It has its root in VENDOTII, the name of the people who inhabited the kingdom.

VENDOTI(I)

Welsh and Arthurian

Ancient British people who inhabited VENDOTIA, the North Welsh kingdom of GWYNEDD. GEOFFREY OF MONMOUTH names their king as CADWALLON.

VENETII

Gaulish and Arthurian

A Gaulish tribe noted for the skill of its mariners and still considered to be in existence during the sixth century. Tradition states that TREPHINA, the daughter of their leader WAROK, married CUNOMORUS.

VENGEANCE RAGUIDEL

Arthurian

A thirteenth-century French prose poem, usually attributed to Raoul, that covers GAWAIN's attempts to avenge the death of RAGUIDEL.

VERGULAHT

Arthurian

The King of ASCALUN whom PERCEVAL asked to find the GRAIL, but he passed this task on to GAWAIN, the lover of his sister ANTIKONIE.

VERONA
Arthurian
The daughter of the King of NARSINGA whose carbuncle was required by ARTHUR's warrior daughter MELORA in order to set free her imprisoned lover, ORLANDO. She and her father were lured on to a ship by Melora and LEVANDER, the servant of the King of BABYLON, who was accompanying Melora, but they became firm friends and Verona willingly gave up the jewel. She subsequently married Levander.

VERONICA, SAINT
Arthurian
Referred to as VERRINE in the GRAIL story.

VERRINE
Arthurian
The name used within the GRAIL legends to refer to Saint VERONICA, who, so tradition claims, owned a cloth that had the image of Christ upon it. In the Grail story, Verrine uses the divine quality of this cloth to cure VESPASIAN of leprosy.

VERSERIA
Arthurian
The beautiful wife of FERRAGUNZE. To test her husband's claim that he never became jealous, it was arranged that Ferragunze should discover his wife in the embraces of GAWAIN. However, true to his word, Ferragunze showed no signs of jealousy.

VESPASIAN
Arthurian
The Roman Emperor between AD 69 and 79. He appears in the GRAIL legends as the liberator of JOSEPH OF ARIMATHEA from his imprisonment in Jerusalem. He was also said to have been cured of leprosy by VERRINE, who used a cloth she owned that had the image of Christ upon it.

VINDONNUS
Gaulish
The continental version of FIND and one that formed the basis of such place names as Vienna or Uindopona.

VISIT OF GREY HAM
Arthurian
An Irish romance in which the OTHERWORLD woman AILLEAN appears.

VITA MERLINI
Arthurian
'Life of Merlin', an important Latin poetic description of the adventures of MERLIN, and his madness, that dates from the twelfth century and was written by GEOFFREY OF MONMOUTH some time after his *Historia Regum Britanniae*.

VIVIANE
Arthurian
A variant of VIVIENNE.

VIVIEN(NE)
Arthurian
The LADY OF THE LAKE, a later variant for the character who is named as NIMUE or NINIANE in early stories. Alfred, Lord Tennyson, calls her Vivien, though the variant Vivienne is more common.

VIVIONN
Irish
See BEBHIONN

VORTIGERN
British and Arthurian
A British king, whose Latin name was *Uurtigernus*, who is first mentioned in the writings of BEDE. However, Vortigern means 'overlord', so it appears that this is a title rather than a proper name. Vortigern is generally accepted as a historical character, although the extent of his realm remains a mystery. NENNIUS supports this supposition by saying that he ascended in AD 425. It seems possible that he may have married a daughter of the rebel Roman Emperor MAXIMUS, and is credited with sons named VORTIMER, CATIGERN, PASCHENT and FAUSTUS.

GEOFFREY OF MONMOUTH says that he was a King of BRITAIN who instigated the assassination of CONSTANTINE and installed CONSTANS, the son of the murdered king, as his puppet. Later he killed Constans and took the throne for himself. Vortigern is reputed to have invited the SAXONS under the leadership of HENGIST and HORSA to Britain to repel the PICTS. His reign was interrupted for a while whilst his son VORTIMER ruled in his stead, but he returned after his wife poisoned her stepson. He fled to WALES after the slaughter of the British princes on Salisbury Plain. In Wales he tried to build himself a tower on DINAS EMRYS (Mount Erith) in North WALES. However, every night the stones disappeared. MERLIN (MYRDDIN) ascribed this to the presence of two dragons beneath the hill in a huge cavern within which there was also a subterranean lake. This was proved to be correct, confounding Vortigern's own seers, and Vortigern's tower was built. However, as the dragons were released, Merlin prophesied Vortigern's death, and he was eventually burnt to death in the tower he had built by Constantine's son, AMBROSIUS AURELIUS, who had the help of his brother UTHER.

VORTIMER
British and Arthurian
The son of VORTIGERN and brother, according to some sources, of CATIGERN, PASCHENT and FAUSTUS. He was King of BRITAIN for a short while when his father was either deposed or had abdicated in his favour, but he was poisoned by his stepmother, after which his father regained the throne. Vortimer had said that after he died he should be buried in the place at which the SAXONS, whom he had opposed (though his father supported them), most commonly landed. A statue of him should also be erected there to frighten the invaders away. GEOFFREY OF MONMOUTH says that his wishes were not complied with, but the Welsh *TRIOEDD YNYS PRYDEIN* say that his bones were buried in the chief British ports. A similar tradition said that a statue of him was erected at Dover. Although his father is almost universally regarded as historical, many commentators regard Vortimer as pure fiction.

VOTADINI
British
A north British tribe of which CUNEDDA was said to have been the ruler just before he emigrated to WALES in about AD 430.

VRAN
Welsh and Arthurian
The shortened and popular version of BENDIGEID VRAN – BRÂN THE BLESSED.

VULGATE VERSION
Arthurian
A thirteenth-century collection of prose romances that consists of the *PROSE LANCELOT*; the *QUESTE DEL SAINTE GRAAL* and its prelude, *ESTOIRE DEL SAINTE GRAAL*; the *MORT ARTU*; the *Vulgate Merlin* and the *Vulgate Merlin Continuation*.

W

WACE, ROBERT
Arthurian

Twelfth-century author (*c.* 1115–83), born in Jersey, of the French *ROMAN DE BRUT*, which contains a substantial Arthurian section and is notable for making the first reference to the ROUND TABLE. It is a free Norman French version of GEOFFREY OF MONMOUTH's fanciful early history of the Kings of Britain, *HISTORIA REGUM BRITANNIAE*. Wace also wrote a number of other works, most notably the *Roman du Rou*, an epic of the exploits of the dukes of Normandy.

WADE
Arthurian

The father of the legendary smith WAYLAND who, with his son and grandson WIDIA, was said to have been brought to BRITAIN by the ANGLO-SAXONS.

WALES
General

Although nowadays a single country, as indeed it was sometimes portrayed in the Celtic legends, it was, at that time, a patchwork of minor kingdoms, including GWYNEDD, DYFED and POWYS. The *ESTOIRE DEL SAINTE GRAAL* identifies Wales with the WASTE LAND of the GRAIL legends, but this is not a customary identification. The medieval Latin romance *HISTORIA MERIADOCI* says that the King of Wales was CARADOC, but ARTHUR and URIEN placed his son, MERIADOC, on the throne, who then resigned it to Urien. In other sources Wales is described as the kingdom of VALYANT, a relation of LANCELOT, or of HERZELOYDE, the mother of PERCEVAL.

Many of the most major Arthurian sources have a Welsh origin, and even the continental romances owe much to Welsh tradition. There seems little doubt that ARTHUR and many of his knights have a Welsh provenance. They then progressed south into CORNWALL, which, to this day, has a very strong Welsh character.

WALEWEIN
Arthurian

The Dutch name for GAWAIN.

WALEWEIN
Arthurian

A Middle Dutch romance that is thought to date from the thirteenth century and concerns the exploits of GAWAIN. Its authors are given as Penninc and Pieter Vostaert.

WALGA(I)NUS
Arthurian

The Latin version of GAWAIN. GEOFFREY OF MONMOUTH is the only known source to use Walgainus, the normal being Walganus.

WALWEITHA
Arthurian

Possibly to be identified with Galloway, this was, according to William of MALMESBURY, the territory GAWAIN was driven to, and subsequently ruled over, by the brother and nephew of HENGIST.

WAROK
Welsh and Arthurian

The chief of the VENETII whose daughter, TREPHINA, married CUNOMORUS.

WASTE LAND
Arthurian

The land laid waste in the GRAIL legends by the DOLOROUS STROKE that could be healed only by the asking of the GRAIL QUESTION. The *LESTOIRE DE MERLIN* says that it was ruled over by PELLINORE, while the *ESTOIRE DEL SAINTE GRAAL* identifies it with WALES. It is a far more extensive area in the *DIDOT PERCEVAL*, for in that work it is identified as comprising the whole of BRITAIN. Other sources identify the Waste Land with the GASTE FOREST.

WAYLAND
Arthurian

Legendary smith who was said to have been brought to BRITAIN, along with his father, WADE, and son, WIDIA, by the ANGLO-SAXONS. His name still exists in place-names, most famously near Uffington, Oxfordshire, where there is a long barrow known as Waylands Smithy.

WECTA

Arthurian

The son of WODEN and great-grandfather of HENGIST, according to the latter's claimed line of descent.

WENELAND

Arthurian

The kingdom of RUMMARET, according to WACE. LAYAMON, in his later translation of Wace's work, referred to the kingdom as WINETLAND, or simply WINET. Various regions have been suggested for this kingdom, including Finland, GWYNEDD and the country of the Wends. However, the name may also have a connection with Vinland, the Norse name for a part of North America that is now thought to have been discovered sometime during the Middle Ages.

WESSEX

General

The kingdom of the West SAXONS in BRITAIN, which was said to have been founded about AD 500 and which covered present-day Hampshire, Dorset, Wiltshire, Berkshire, Somerset and Devon. By 829 Wessex had become the dominant kingdom in Britain and for the first time united the country under its rule as a single nation, with the capital at WINCHESTER, Hampshire.

WESTMER

Arthurian

The successor of ARVIRAGUS, according to the Lambeth Palace Library MS 84, during whose reign JOSEPH OF ARIMATHEA died.

WESTWOODS

Arthurian

A field near to the River CAM that has been suggested as the site of the Battle of CAMLANN. Archaeological excavation has revealed a large number of skeletons on this site, bearing grim witness to the fact that a battle was once fought here, but whether or not that battle was Camlann is open to speculation.

WHITE BOOK OF RHYDDERCH, THE

Welsh and Arthurian

An early fourteenth-century manuscript that, along with the *RED BOOK OF HERGEST*, contains the *MABINOGION* cycle. It is today housed in the National Library of WALES, Aberystwyth, along with the *BLACK BOOK OF CARMARTHEN* and the *Book of Taliesin*.

WHITE KNIGHT

Arthurian

According to an Irish romance, the son of the King of FRANCE and one of ARTHUR's knights.

WHITE MOUNT

British and Arthurian

Called BRYN GWYN in Welsh, the White Mount is one of the most important pagan sites in LONDON, for it is the location of the burial of the severed head of BENDIGEID VRAN by PRYDERI, MANAWYDAN FAB LLYR, GLUNEU EIL TARAN (GLIFIEU), TALIESIN, YNAWC (YNAWAG), GRUDYEN (GRUDDIEU) and HEILYN. The head was buried with its face towards FRANCE so that it would forever act as a magical guardian of the country. Later tradition says that King ARTHUR dug up the interred head because he wanted to be the sole guardian of BRITAIN. The White Mount was one of the four major Druidic sites of London, and it is also the burial place of the founder of London, BRUTUS, as well as of the fifth-century BC monarch MOLMUTIUS. Today, little is actually visible of the White Mount, for the White Tower within the Tower of London was built on it.

WHITE STAG

General

Unsurprisingly, a white stag features in a number of Celtic stories, for the Celts (along with many other cultures) held the white stag as an especially mystical animal that was thought to have originated in the OTHERWORLD. Arthurian tradition said that whoever hunted down a white stag could demand a kiss from the loveliest girl at ARTHUR's court. SAGREMOR was reported as having hunted one in *RIGOMER*, while in *ERIC ET ENIDE* one was hunted in the FOREST OF ADVENTURE. PERCEVAL was said to have beheaded a white stag in the *DIDOT PERCEVAL*, while FLORIANT was said to have been brought by one to the castle of his foster mother, MORGAN Le Fay.

WIDIA

Arthurian

The son of WAYLAND whose name, it is thought, was the origin of WITEGE.

WIGALOIS

Arthurian

The legitimate son of GAWAIN by his wife, FLORIE, the niece of King JORAM. Having grown to manhood, Wigalois set out in search of his father, who, having left many years before, had not been able to find his way back home. Wigalois came to ARTHUR's court at CARDUEIL, into which he was admitted. When Queen AMENE's emissary, NEREJA, came to the court, Wigalois was sent to her succour. Guided by the ghost of Amene's slain husband, LAR, Wigalois accompanied Nereja back to her Queen's realm. When he arrived he found that the entire kingdom, except for a single castle, had been overrun by the evil knight ROAZ. Wigalois fought Roaz in a night-long combat, eventually overcoming him. He then married LARIE, the daughter of Amene and Lar.

WIGALOIS
Arthurian
Thirteenth-century romance by WIRNT VON GRAFENBERG that tells the story of GAWAIN's legitimate son, WIGALOIS.

WIGAN
Arthurian
This Lancashire town was locally thought to have been the site of one of ARTHUR's BATTLES, that of the River DOUGLAS.

WIHTGILS
Arthurian
The great-great-grandson of WODEN and father of HENGIST, according to the line of descent claimed by the latter.

WILD HUNT
General
Common throughout European folklore, the Wild Hunt is a supernatural hunt in which the spectral hunters can be seen riding by, and the thundering of their horse's hoofs and baying of their hounds heard. In ENGLAND this mystical spectacle was thought to have been seen in both Devon and Somerset, and, sometimes, it was said to have been led by ARTHUR who rode in procession to GLASTONBURY. Although most common on nights when there was a full moon, the Wild Hunt has also been reportedly heard at midday (cf. HUNTING CAUSEWAY).

WINCHESTER
British and Arthurian
The city in Hampshire that claims to be the oldest cathedral city in ENGLAND. The foundation of the city is attributed to HUDIBRAS, the ninth ruler of BRITAIN after BRUTUS, sometime in the ninth century BC. Hudibras called the city Caer Gwent, the White City. It was later enlarged by MOLMUTIUS.

Later still Winchester became the administrative centre of England and a place where kings were both crowned and buried.

The city has many Arthurian associations. Early chroniclers identified it with CAMELOT, King ARTHUR's capital. The ROUND TABLE at Winchester dates from the fourteenth century (according to radiocarbon dating), and is thus not the original table, as was once thought. It is made of oak, measures 18 feet in diameter and weighs 1.25 tons. The city, or at least somewhere in the area, is the site of the second battle Arthur fought against his usurping nephew, MORDRED. Once again Arthur defeated him, and then pursued him to the River CAMLANN, the site of Arthur's final battle, which marked the end of his reign.

WINDFALL RUN
Arthurian
Local legend says that this place in America was where the wounded ARTHUR came to drink the healing waters of the GREAT SPIRITS SPRING.

WINDSOR
Arthurian
This town in Berkshire has present-day royal connections, but it was also said to have been the site of one of ARTHUR's residences. Before Arthur came to have a home there, the earl or count had rebelled against him, but was defeated and then executed.

WINET(LAND)
Arthurian
The kingdom of RUMMARET, according to LAYAMON, in his translation of WACE's work, in which the earlier writer referred to WENELAND.

WINLOGEE
Arthurian
Appearing only on the Arthurian bas-relief in MODENA cathedral, Winlogee is identified as a woman seated on the battlements with MARDOC. It has been suggested that she is identifiable with GUINEVERE.

WIRNT VON GRAFENBERG
Arthurian
The thirteenth-century German, or Bavarian, author of *WIGALOIS*, a romance concerning the exploits of GAWAIN's son.

WISDOM, SALMON OF
Irish
See SALMON OF WISDOM

WITEGE
Arthurian

According to LAYAMON, the maker of ARTHUR's hauberk (a long coat of mail that is often sleeveless) that was called WYGAR or 'wizard'. If this is intended to be a personal name, it seems to be a form of WIDIA, the son of the legendary smith WAYLAND, who, together with his father, WADE, and son, had been brought to BRITAIN by the ANGLO-SAXONS. The name is also thought to appear in GEOFFREY OF MONMOUTH, but is susceptible to transcriptive errors.

WITTA
Arthurian

The grandson of WODEN and grandfather of HENGIST, according to the latter's claimed line of descent.

WLENCING
Arthurian

The son of AELLE who accompanied his father when he defeated the Britons.

WOD-AN, -EN
Arthurian

The chief god of the ANGLO-SAXONS, who invaded BRITAIN during the traditional Arthurian period. He is more commonly known by his Norse name of Odínn, but, as the Anglo-Saxon dynasties claimed their descent from him, it has been suggested that he was a deified leader. Most commentators think that he was always a mythical character. HENGIST claimed his descent from Woden.

WOLFRAM VON ESCHENBACH
Arthurian

A German poet (*fl.* 1200) and author of *Parzival,* a work that dealt with the GRAIL Quest and PERCEVAL's part in it. He claimed his source was a writer named Kyot, but the existence of Kyot has been seriously questioned. He is also remembered as the author of several other works.

Wodan, the chief god of the Anglo-Saxons from whom Hengist claimed direct descent.
(© Bettmann/Corbis)

WOMEN, LAND OF
Irish

The literal translation of TÍR INNA MBAN, the OTHERWORLDLY kingdom that was inhabited entirely by beautiful women.

WRNACH
Welsh and Arthurian

The giant owner of a sword that CULHWCH had to obtain as one of the tasks imposed by YSPADDADEN if Culhwch were to marry OLWEN. CEI (KAY) obtained it by trickery and killed Wrnach.

WYGAR
Arthurian

'Wizard', the name of ARTHUR's hauberk (long, often sleeveless, coat of mail) that, according to LAYAMON, was made either by a wizard or by someone named WITEGE.

Y

Y SAINT GRAAL
Arthurian
The Welsh version of the GRAIL story.

YCHDRYT VARYVDRAWS
Welsh
One of the seldom mentioned members of the party that helped CULHWCH locate OLWEN. He was chosen as he could project his beard above the heads of his comrades and thus provide them with shelter in bad weather.

YDAIN
Arthurian
The mistress of GAWAIN whom he had saved from being raped. When she tried to forsake him, he gave her to the dwarf DRUIDAN.

YDER
British and Arthurian
The son of NUC, a KNIGHT OF THE ROUND TABLE who fell in love with Queen GUENLOIE. She said she would marry Yder only on the condition that he brought her a knife that belonged to two giants. He succeeded in killing the giants and securing the knife, so the Queen fulfilled her promise and married him. Other sources say that Yder married the daughter of GUENGASOAIN, whom he and GAWAIN had slain to avenge the murder of RAGUIDEL. Yder was also said to have done battle against three giants who lived on BRENT KNOLL in Somerset. Accompanying ARTHUR to the hill, Yder went on ahead and fought the giants on his own. By the time Arthur and his retinue arrived, the battle was over and the three giants were dead, but Yder had also lost his life in the fray. The Arthurian story is clearly a retelling of a local custom.

YDOR
Arthurian
Described as a king, Ydor was the father of TOREC.

YESU
British
A variant of ESUS, which some have fancifully sought to link with the name of Jesus Christ in an attempt to assert that the Messiah came to BRITAIN.

YGERN-A, -E
British and Arthurian
The Anglicised version of EIGYR, the original name of IGRAINE, wife of GORLOIS, Duke of CORNWALL.

YGLAIS
Arthurian
According to *PERLESVAUS*, the niece of JOSEPH OF ARIMATHEA and the FISHER KING who became the mother of PERCEVAL.

YMER LLYDAW
Arthurian
According to the fourteenth-century Welsh *BIRTH OF ARTHUR*, the father of HOEL by GWYAR, ARTHUR's sister.

YNAW-AG, -C
Welsh
One of the seven survivors of the expedition mounted by BENDIGEID VRAN against King MATHOLWCH of IRELAND to rescue BRANWEN. The other six who survived the slaughter were PRYDERI, MANAWYDDAN FAB LLYR, GLUNEU EIL TARAN (GLIFIEU), TALIESIN, GRUDYEN (GRUDDIEU) and HEILYN. They brought Branwen back to WALES, having exterminated the Irish except for five pregnant women, who hid in a cave, but Branwen died of a broken heart when she thought of the wholesale destruction brought about on her behalf. Ynawag and his companions also carried the severed head of Bendigeid Vran back with them and, after a much delayed journey, buried it in accordance with the King's instructions under the WHITE MOUNT in LONDON.

YNWYL
Arthurian
The father of ENID, according to the Welsh *GEREINT AND ENID*. His wife remains unnamed.

YNYS ENLLI
Welsh
The Welsh name for BARDSEY Island.

The Minster at York; the city was allegedly founded by Ebrauc, the sixth king after Brutus.
(© Mick Sharp)

YNYS FANAW
Welsh

The Welsh name for the Isle of MAN, the legendary home of LLYR.

YNYS WITRIN
British

'The Glassy Isle', the original name of GLASTONBURY.

YORK
British

A city in Yorkshire. Its legendary founder, in 944 BC, was EBRAUC, the sixth king after BRUTUS. In AD 71 the Romans captured the city from the BRIGANTES, called it *Eboracum* and made it their northern headquarters.

YORK, THE SIEGE OF
Arthurian

A siege mounted by ARTHUR against the SAXON leader COLGRIN, who had sought refuge in the city following his defeat by Arthur at the battle of the River DOUGLAS. Arthur had, at one stage, to abandon the siege and go back to London, but later returned and this time relieved the siege with the help of King HOEL of BRITTANY. Arthur restored the city to its former glory and returned to the lands of the three dispossessed Yorkist princes, LOT, URIAN and AUGUSELUS.

YR WYDDFA (FAWR)
Welsh and Arthurian

The original name for Mount SNOWDON that probably signified 'The Great Tomb', referring to a large cairn that once stood on its summit. This also gave rise to the name CLOGWYN CARNEDD YR WYDDFA – 'The Precipice of the Carn on Yr Wyddfa'. Another name is CARNEDD Y CAWR – 'The Giant's Carn' – and this poses the question, who was the giant buried atop the loftiest peak in WALES? The cairn itself was demolished in the nineteenth century and made into a kind of tower, which existed for some years before the present building was erected. According to Sir John Rhys in his *Celtic Folklore* (1901), this was the reputed grave of RHITTA CAWR, a giant sometimes known as RHICCA, who killed kings and clothed himself in a garment made from their beards. His great enemy and ultimate conqueror was King ARTHUR, whose beard he desired for the collar of his cloak. GEOFFREY OF MONMOUTH refers to this giant as 'the giant RITHO whom Arthur slew on Mount ERYRI'.

Arthur himself is commemorated not far from the giant's cave at BWLCH-Y-SAETHU (The Pass of the Arrows). In the direction of Nanhwyen is the site of CARNEDD ARTHUR, where he is alleged to have been buried by his followers after a fierce battle that took place at the top of the pass. Having buried Arthur, his companions withdrew to the precipice of Lliwedd and took shelter in a cave called OGOF LANCIAU ERYRI – a vast cave in the precipitous cliff on the left-hand side, near the top of Llyn Llydaw. The cave entrance immediately closed behind them, and the young men fell asleep, resting on their shields. There they still await the day when Arthur will return in triumph to save BRITAIN from impending doom. It is alleged that they were once disturbed by a shepherd who, on seeing a light shining though the narrow entrance to the cave, started to crawl inside but hit his head against a large bell. Its loud clanging awakened the hundreds of sleeping knights, who were immediately on their feet and ready for battle. The shepherd left the cave at great speed and was never the same again.

YS
Gaulish and Arthurian

A legendary city of BRITTANY that was supposed to have become submerged thanks to DAHUT or AHES, the daughter of the GRADLON. It has been suggested that this character, Dahut, may have, in some small way, contributed to the legend of MORGAN Le Fay, for she was said to have been a fairy, referred to locally as a MARI-MORGAN. Gallet's pedigree says that GRALLO, the King of Ys, was related to CONSTANTINE, ARTHUR's grandfather.

YSABELE
Arthurian

The wife or lover of GAWAIN, according to the Middle Dutch romance *WALEWEIN*.

YSAIE THE SAD
Arthurian

The son of TRISTAN and ISEULT who was raised by a hermit. He was helped in his adventures by a dwarf, named TRONC, whom the fairies had given to him, this dwarf later being transformed into the fairy king OBERON. Ysaie married the daughter of King IRION, MARTHA, and they had a son named MARC.

YSAIVE
Arthurian

A niece of ARTHUR, the wife of King CARADOC

of VANNES AND NANTES. She became the lover of ELIAVRES, a knight with especially potent magical powers.

YSBADDAD(D)EN
Welsh and Arthurian
See YSPADDADEN

YSEUDYDD
Welsh
A servant of GWENHWYFAR, who appears in some sources as one of the members of the party formed to help CULHWCH locate OLWEN. His companion was YSKYRDAW, also a servant of Gwenhwyfar. They were chosen because they could run as fast as their thoughts.

YSGITHYRWYN
Arthurian
According to Welsh tradition, a boar that was chased by ARTHUR and his faithful hound CABAL.

YSKYRDAW
Welsh
A servant to GWENHWYFAR and companion of YSEUDYDD, whom he accompanied on the quest led by CULHWCH to locate OLWEN, as related in the MABINOGION.

YSPADDAD(D)EN
Welsh
Also YSBADDAD(D)EN
The chief giant, or *Penkawr*, and father of OLWEN. A huge being, forks had to be placed under his eyelids in order to prop them open, a trait that has led some to claim that he is the analogue of the Irish BALAR. Yspaddaden features in the *MABINOGION* story of *CULHWCH AND OLWEN*, in which he set CULHWCH a series of seemingly impossible tasks, subsequently imposing innumerable conditions if Culhwch was to gain the hand of Olwen. Finally, unable to endure any more of the giant's conditions, Culhwch rounded up all Yspaddaden's enemies and stormed his castle. Yspaddaden was killed by GOREU during the attack.

YVAIN
Arthurian
The French form of OWAIN, being used for both OWAIN and OWAIN THE BASTARD.

YWERIT
Welsh and Arthurian
The father of BRÂN (BENDIGEID VRAN), according to Celtic sources. It is thought that he may be identifiable with IWERET, though IBERT has also been suggested in this role.

Z

ZAZAMANC
Arthurian
The realm of BELCANE, the mother of FEIREFIZ by GAHMURET.

ZEL
British
A mythical king who is said to have been buried on horseback within the hill that appears to carry his derivative name of SIL, the hill itself being known as SILBURY Hill. Zel, or Sit, appears to have been a crude attempt to explain the existence of the hill, although when the hill was excavated in 1723 human remains and an antique bridle were allegedly discovered.

ZELOTES
Arthurian
A youth who was promised he could have PERSE as a wife by her father. However, ECTOR DE MARIS, who already loved her, came to her rescue and later married her himself.

ZEPHYR
Arthurian
According to *PERCEFOREST*, a spirit who had a great love for BRITAIN. An ancestor of MERLIN, he gave PASSALEON to MORGAN Le Fay.

ZITUS
Arthurian
The name used in the Spanish romance *ANNALES TOLEDANOS* to refer to ARTHUR.

Silbury Hill near Avebury, Wiltshire, and the alleged burial place of Zel. (© Marilyn Bridges/Corbis)

GENEALOGIES

Short genealogy of Aillean

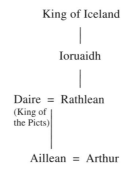

King of Iceland
|
Ioruaidh
|
Daire = Rathlean
(King of
the Picts)
|
Aillean = Arthur

Short genealogy of Arthur according to Geoffrey of Monmouth

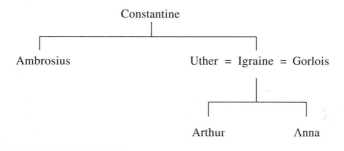

Constantine

Ambrosius   Uther = Igraine = Gorlois

Arthur   Anna

Short genealogy of Arthur according to Sir Thomas Malory

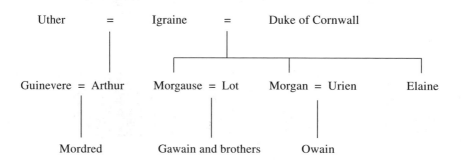

Uther   =   Igraine   =   Duke of Cornwall

Guinevere = Arthur   Morgause = Lot   Morgan = Urien   Elaine

Mordred   Gawain and brothers   Owain

GENEALOGIES

Combination genealogy of Arthur

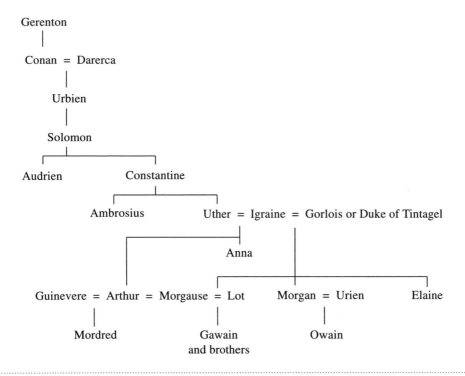

Gerenton
|
Conan = Darerca
|
Urbien
|
Solomon
|
Audrien   Constantine
|
Ambrosius   Uther = Igraine = Gorlois or Duke of Tintagel
|
Anna
|
Guinevere = Arthur = Morgause = Lot   Morgan = Urien   Elaine
| | |
Mordred   Gawain   Owain
              and brothers

Bendigeid Vran as an ancestor of Arthur

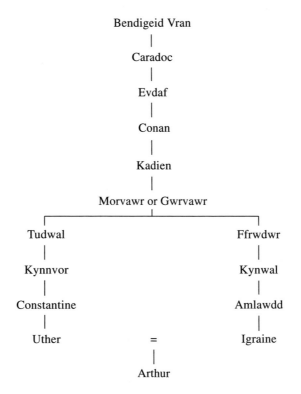

Bendigeid Vran
|
Caradoc
|
Evdaf
|
Conan
|
Kadien
|
Morvawr or Gwrvawr
|
Tudwal   Ffrwdwr
| |
Kynnvor   Kynwal
| |
Constantine   Amlawdd
| |
Uther   =   Igraine
|
Arthur

Genealogy of Constantine according to Gallet

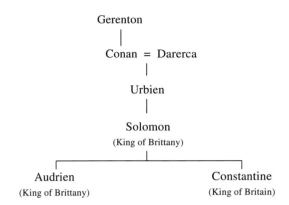

Descent of Constantinople's imperial family

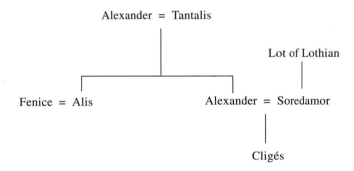

Descent of Culhwch as Arthur's cousin

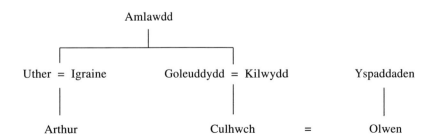

GENEALOGIES

Cunedda as Arthur's great-grandfather

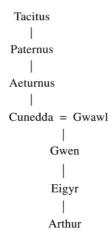

Tacitus
|
Paternus
|
Aeturnus
|
Cunedda = Gwawl
|
Gwen
|
Eigyr
|
Arthur

Cunomorus, ruler of Cornwall and Brittany

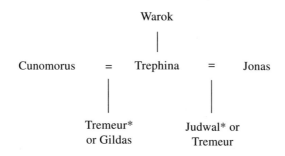

Warok
|
Cunomorus = Trephina = Jonas
| |
Tremeur*   Judwal* or
or Gildas   Tremeur

* These two are apparently identical

Darerca as the great-great-great-grandfather of Arthur

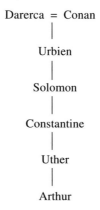

Darerca = Conan
|
Urbien
|
Solomon
|
Constantine
|
Uther
|
Arthur

The rulers of Fairyland

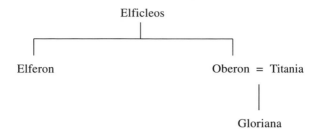

Elficleos

Elferon   Oberon = Titania

Gloriana

The descent of Sir Galahad according to the most common version

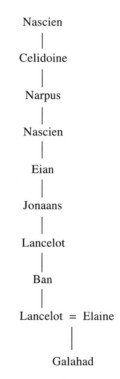

Nascien

Celidoine

Narpus

Nascien

Eian

Jonaans

Lancelot

Ban

Lancelot = Elaine

Galahad

Family tree of Guigenor, Arthur's niece

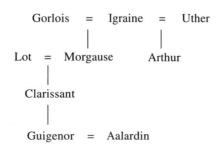

Gorlois = Igraine = Uther

Lot = Morgause   Arthur

Clarissant

Guigenor = Aalardin

GENEALOGIES

Ancestry of Igraine according to John of Glastonbury

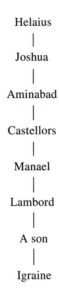

Helaius
|
Joshua
|
Aminabad
|
Castellors
|
Manael
|
Lambord
|
A son
|
Igraine

Ancestry of Igraine according to Grufudd Hiraethog

Evgen
|
Joshua
|
Garcelos
|
Manael
|
Lambor
|
Amlawdd
|
Igraine

Ancestry of Igraine as given in *Bonedd yr Arwr*

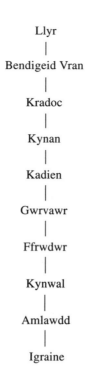

Llyr

Bendigeid Vran

Kradoc

Kynan

Kadien

Gwrvawr

Ffrwdwr

Kynwal

Amlawdd

Igraine

Genealogy of Sir Lac

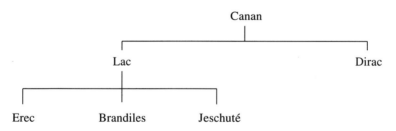

Canan

Lac — Dirac

Erec — Brandiles — Jeschuté

Genealogy of Lancelot according to Ulrich von Zarzikhoven

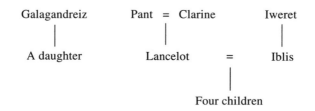

Galagandreiz — Pant = Clarine — Iweret

A daughter — Lancelot = Iblis

Four children

GENEALOGIES

Genealogy of Lancelot according to French sources

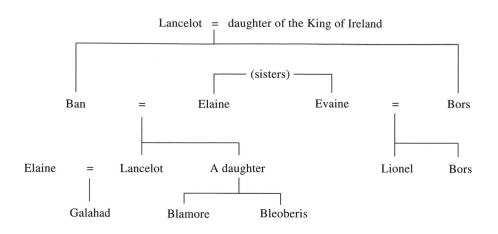

Lancelot = daughter of the King of Ireland

(sisters)

Ban = Elaine   Evaine = Bors

Elaine = Lancelot   A daughter   Lionel   Bors

Galahad   Blamore   Bleoberis

Three versions of Arthur's lineage from Llyr, King of Britain

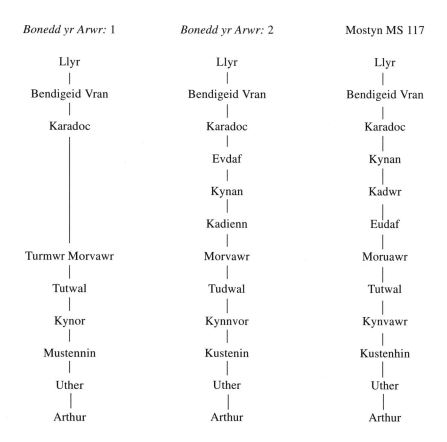

Bonedd yr Arwr: 1	*Bonedd yr Arwr:* 2	Mostyn MS 117
Llyr	Llyr	Llyr
Bendigeid Vran	Bendigeid Vran	Bendigeid Vran
Karadoc	Karadoc	Karadoc
	Evdaf	Kynan
	Kynan	Kadwr
	Kadienn	Eudaf
Turmwr Morvawr	Morvawr	Moruawr
Tutwal	Tudwal	Tutwal
Kynor	Kynnvor	Kynvawr
Mustennin	Kustenin	Kustenhin
Uther	Uther	Uther
Arthur	Arthur	Arthur

422

Ancestry and descendants of Lot, King of Lothian, Orkney and Norway, and Arthur's brother-in-law, according to John of Glastonbury

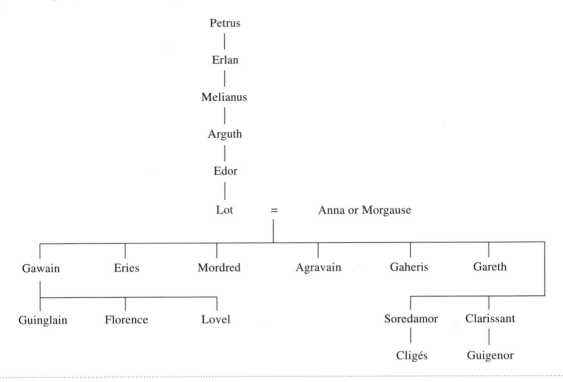

Petrus
|
Erlan
|
Melianus
|
Arguth
|
Edor
|
Lot = Anna or Morgause

Gawain — Eries — Mordred — Agravain — Gaheris — Gareth

Gawain: Guinglain — Florence — Lovel

Gareth: Soredamor — Clarissant

Soredamor: Cligés
Clarissant: Guigenor

Lot's wife and descendants according to Welsh tradition

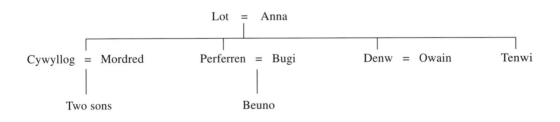

Lot = Anna

Cywyllog = Mordred — Perferren = Bugi — Denw = Owain — Tenwi

Cywyllog = Mordred: Two sons

Perferren = Bugi: Beuno

Marhalt, King of Ireland

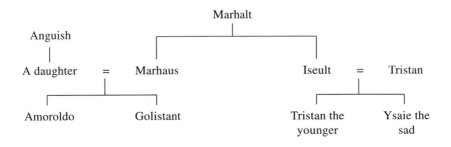

Marhalt

Anguish
|
A daughter = Marhaus   Iseult = Tristan

A daughter = Marhaus: Amoroldo — Golistant

Iseult = Tristan: Tristan the younger — Ysaie the sad

GENEALOGIES

Family tree of Mark according to Sir Thomas Malory

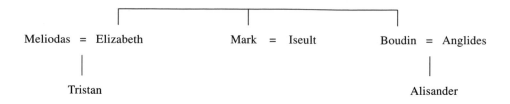

Meliodas = Elizabeth   Mark = Iseult   Boudin = Anglides

Tristan   Alisander

Family tree of Mark according to *Tristano Riccardiano*

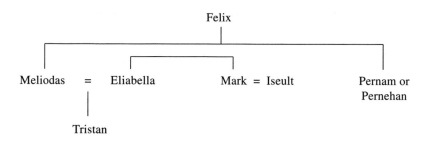

Felix

Meliodas = Eliabella   Mark = Iseult   Pernam or Pernehan

Tristan

Genealogy of Mazadan according to Wolfram von Eschenbach

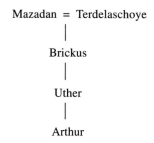

Mazadan = Terdelaschoye

Brickus

Uther

Arthur

Myrddin's (Merlin's) paternal pedigree according to Welsh tradition

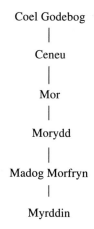

Coel Godebog

Ceneu

Mor

Morydd

Madog Morfryn

Myrddin

Descent of Perceval according to Wolfram von Eschenbach

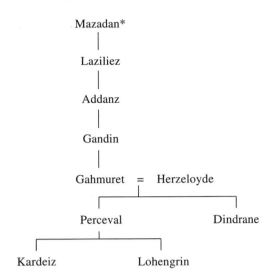

Mazadan*
|
Laziliez
|
Addanz
|
Gandin
|
Gahmuret = Herzeloyde

Perceval   Dindrane

Kardeiz   Lohengrin

* Mazadan is also listed as Arthur's great-grandfather.
This would make Arthur, Perceval's second cousin
once removed.

How the Saxons fit into Bede's grouping of the three waves of barbarian invaders of Britain, and their descendant peoples

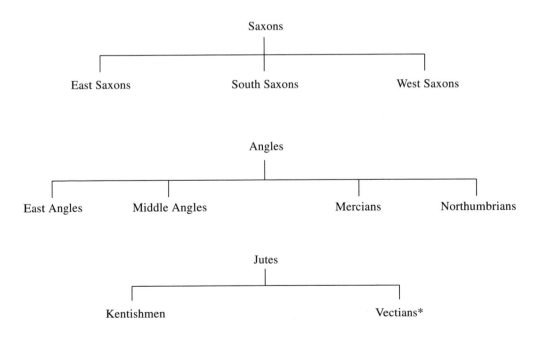

Saxons

East Saxons   South Saxons   West Saxons

Angles

East Angles   Middle Angles   Mercians   Northumbrians

Jutes

Kentishmen   Vectians*

* Inhabitants of the Isle of Wight

GENEALOGIES

Short genealogy of Tom a'Lincoln

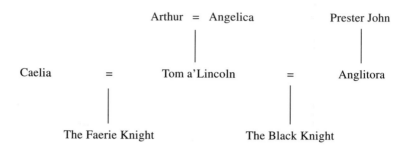

```
                    Arthur  =  Angelica              Prester John
                              |                           |
 Caelia        =         Tom a'Lincoln        =        Anglitora
          |                                        |
     The Faerie Knight                      The Black Knight
```

Relationship of Tristan to Mark according to Gottfried von Strassburg

```
            ┌─────────────────────────────┐
 Rivalin  =  Blanchefleur              Mark  =  Iseult
          |
      Tristan
```

Hengist's claimed descent from the god Woden

```
       Woden
         |
       Wecta
         |
       Witta
         |
      Wihtgils
         |
      Hengist
```

The House of Llyr according to Welsh tradition

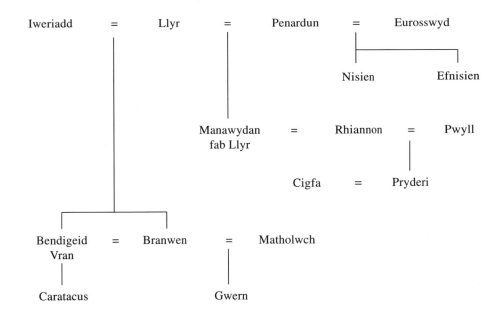

Saint Bride

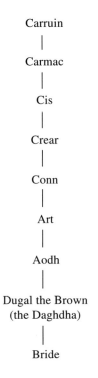

Carruin

Carmac

Cis

Crear

Conn

Art

Aodh

Dugal the Brown
(the Daghdha)

Bride

GENEALOGIES

Conaire Mór

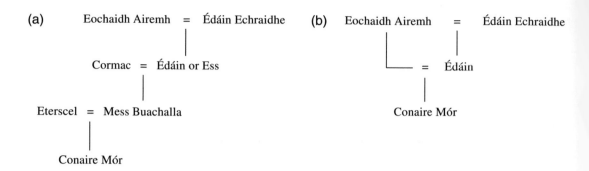

(a)
Eochaidh Airemh = Édáin Echraidhe

Cormac = Édáin or Ess

Eterscel = Mess Buachalla

Conaire Mór

(b)
Eochaidh Airemh = Édáin Echraidhe

= Édáin

Conaire Mór

Conchobar mac Nessa and the Red Branch

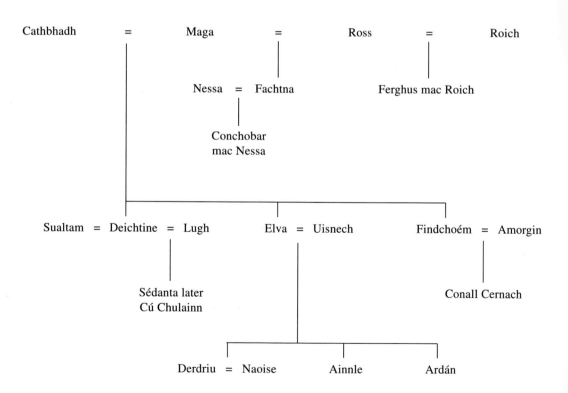

Cathbhadh = Maga = Ross = Roich

Nessa = Fachtna

Ferghus mac Roich

Conchobar mac Nessa

Sualtam = Deichtine = Lugh

Elva = Uisnech

Findchoém = Amorgin

Sédanta later Cú Chulainn

Conall Cernach

Derdriu = Naoise   Ainnle   Ardán

House of Dôn

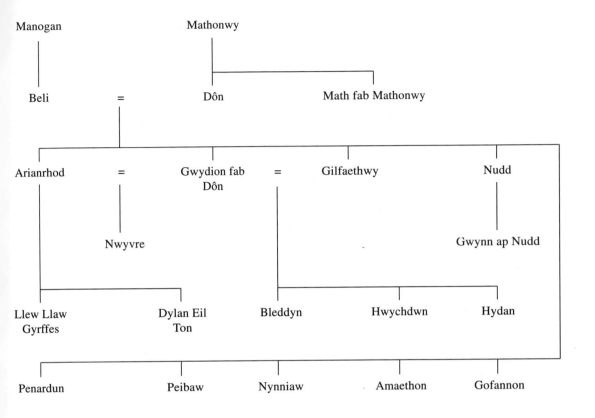

Manogan

Mathonwy

Beli = Dôn — Math fab Mathonwy

Arianrhod = Gwydion fab Dôn = Gilfaethwy — Nudd

Nwyvre

Gwynn ap Nudd

Llew Llaw Gyrffes — Dylan Eil Ton — Bleddyn — Hwychdwn — Hydan

Penardun — Peibaw — Nynniaw — Amaethon — Gofannon

Eliseg

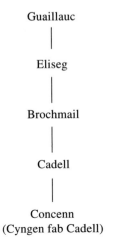

Guaillauc

Eliseg

Brochmail

Cadell

Concenn
(Cyngen fab Cadell)

APPENDIX

Non-Celtic Deities and Heroes

Following are brief descriptions of the non-Celtic deities, heroes and places named in the main text. They are included here to enable comparisons to be made with the characters or places with which they have been associated. Names in CAPITALS have entries within the main text.

AEGYPTUS
Greek
The eponymous ruler of Egypt. He suggested a mass marriage between his fifty sons and the fifty daughters of Danaus, his brother.

ANCHISES
Graeco-Roman
The father of AENEAS by Aphrodite (Roman Venus).

ANDROMEDA
Greek
The beautiful daughter of Cepheus and Cassiopeia who was saved from a sea monster by the hero Perseus, who used the severed head of the Gorgon Medusa to turn that sea monster into stone.

APHRODITE
Greek
Called Venus by the Romans, Aphrodite was the Greek goddess of love, feminine beauty, marriage and fertility, and patroness of prostitutes. By Anchises she became the mother of the semi-divine AENEAS.

APOLLO
Graeco-Roman
The twin of Artemis and the most popular of all the Greek gods, he was the god of prophecy and divine distance, of beneficent power and righteous punishment. He presided over law and made men aware of their guilt, also cleansing them of it. He was god of music, poetry and dance, archery, pastoral life and agriculture. Apollo also protected animals from disease, and was the patron of farmers, poets and physicians. In later times he also became recognised as the god of light and the sun.

ARIADNE
Greek
The daughter of Minos who helped Theseus to escape from the Minotaur and later married the god

Dionysus, who placed her crown in the heavens as the constellation Corona Borealis.

ARTEMIS
Greek
The twin sister of Apollo, she was called Diana by the Romans. Artemis was the virgin goddess of the hunt, protectress of children and young animals, protectress of the hunted and vegetation, the goddess of chastity and, later, goddess of the moon.

ASCLEPI-OS, -US
Graeco-Roman
The son of Apollo and god of medicine. The iconography of a serpent entwined around a caduceus is still used as a medical symbol worldwide. His medical skills enabled him to bring the dead back to life, a trait that cheated the god Hades, who persuaded Zeus to strike him down with a thunderbolt and then place him in the heavens as the constellation Ophiuchus, so that he could do no more harm.

AUGUSTUS
Roman
The Great Emperor of the Roman Empire (63 BC–AD 14), the son of Gaius Octavius, senator and praetor, and Atia, the niece of JULIUS CAESAR. He became Gaius Julius Caesar Octavianus through adoption by Julius Caesar in his will (44 BC), and later received the name Augustus ('Sacred', 'Venerable') in recognition of his services and position (27 BC). By the naval victory at Actium he became the sole ruler of the Roman world.

CASSIOPEIA
Greek
The wife of Cepheus and mother, by him, of Andromeda. She once boasted that her daughter was more beautiful than the Nereids (sea-nymphs), a claim that led Poseidon to demand the sacrifice of Andromeda. The unfortunate princess was saved by

Perseus. After her death, Cassiopeia was placed in the heavens by Poseidon, hanging upside down in a chair for half the time as final and eternal punishment for her boast.

CENTAUR
Greek

A mythical creature, half-horse, half-man, which was portrayed in early art as having the head, arms, torso and forelegs of a man, and the hindquarters of a horse. Later, the forelegs also became equine.

CORNUCOPIA
Graeco-Roman

The 'horn of plenty', said to have been one of the horns of the goat that nursed the infant Zeus. This horn had the power to refill itself with food and drink eternally.

DANAIDES
Greek

The collective name for the fifty daughters of Danaus by ten different wives. Aegyptus suggested that these fifty young women should marry his fifty sons. The Danaides fled but were located and the marriage went ahead. On the wedding night forty-nine of the Danaides murdered their new husbands. Only one, Hypermnestra, spared her husband.

DANAUS
Greek

The brother of Aegyptus and father of the fifty Danaides. He instructed his daughters that they should murder their husbands, the fifty sons of Aegyptus, on their wedding night. Forty-nine complied with these instructions, although Hypermnestra spared her new husband's life.

DIANA
Roman

Initially a woodland deity, Diana was rapidly assimilated by the Romans with the Greek goddess Artemis.

DIS PATER
Roman

The richest of all the Roman gods, the god of death, who is the equivalent of the Greek god Hades. The more common name for the Roman god of the dead, Pluto, is a euphemism that means 'wealth'.

HADES
Greek

The name Hades has a dual role in Greek mythology, for it is the name both of the god of the dead and of the realm over which the god presides. The realm was divided into three distinct regions: that to which the righteous went after death (Elysium), that for those who had led an indifferent life (Asphodel) and that to which sinners were sent (Tartarus).

HECATE
Greek

An extremely powerful goddess, who was worshipped in heaven, on earth and in Hades. Originally a moon goddess, Hecate was the patroness of rich men, sailors and flocks, and the bestower of the wealth and blessings of daily life. Later, she came to be regarded as a dread divinity, triple-headed and triple-breasted, who lived in the deepest region of Hades, where she presided over witchcraft and the black arts, becoming patroness of witches and sorceresses and protectress of graveyards and crossroads.

HERCULES
Roman

The Roman name for the Greek semi-divine hero Heracles, the son of Zeus by the mortal Alcmene. Hercules had to contend with the wrath of Hera, Zeus' wife, throughout his life, during which he completed twelve immense labours, sailed with Jason and the Argonauts and accomplished many other feats of strength and courage before his untimely death, after which he was reconciled with Hera and welcomed into the domain of the gods.

JANUS
Roman

One of the few uniquely Roman gods, who was looked upon as the creator of the world. The god of doorways and passages and of buildings in general, and of beginnings and endings of days, months and years. He was usually depicted with two faces, one facing forwards, the other facing backwards.

JUPITER
Roman

Identified with the Greek Zeus, Jupiter was the god of the sky, the sun, the moon and all the heavenly bodies. Originally an agricultural deity, Jupiter later developed to become the protector of Rome and the Roman Empire.

MARS
Roman

The equivalent of the Greek Ares. Originally an agricultural deity, Mars developed into the god of war when the Roman Empire expanded. He became one of the three protector deities of Rome and in popularity second only to Jupiter.

MEDUSA
Greek

Originally a beautiful maiden, Medusa was transformed into a hideous monster by Athene after she had lain with Poseidon in a temple sacred to Athene. One glance from Medusa had the power to petrify human flesh. She was killed by Perseus, who used her severed head to turn to stone the sea-monster Cetus, who was moments away from devouring the princess Andromeda.

MERCURY
Roman

The god of eloquence, skill, trading and thieving, and messenger to the gods. He was identified with the Greek Hermes, whose role he echoes.

MIDAS
Greek

The king who was once given the power to turn everything he touched into gold, but who soon found the gift to be a curse and asked for the power to be taken away again. He later insulted Apollo, who made his ears turn into those of an ass, a secret he kept from everyone except his barber, who told the secret to some reeds, which passed it on when the wind rustled them.

MINERVA
Roman

The goddess of education and business, who later developed into the goddess of war, at which time she became assimilated with the Greek Athene.

NEPTUNE
Roman

The god of the sea and fresh water. The equivalent of the Greek Poseidon.

PERSEUS
Greek

The son of Zeus by the mortal Danae. Perseus is best known as the killer of the Gorgon Medusa. He then used the monster's severed head to rescue the maiden Andromeda from a sea-monster while riding the winged horse Pegasus.

SERAPIS
Graeco-Romano-Egyptian

A composite god invented and introduced by Ptolemy I in an attempt to unite the Greeks, the Romans and the Egyptians. Revered as a healing deity, Serapis combined the attributes of Zeus, Hades and Asclepios with the Egyptian god Osiris.

SILVANUS
Roman

An agricultural deity, associated with the mysterious forces in woods, fields and flocks.

THÓRR
Norse-Teutonic

The god of thunder and lightning, war and agriculture. The oldest and strongest of Odínn's sons, Thórr was represented as a handsome, red-bearded warrior, benevolent towards man, but a mighty adversary of evil. His most famous attribute was the massive hammer with which he protected the other gods.

TROY
Greek

Troy was once thought of as a purely legendary city, but the historicity of the city was established between 1871 and 1873, when the German archaeologist Heinrich Schliemann excavated a site on the coast of Asia Minor and uncovered the city. The city, the home of AENEAS and his father Anchises, was sacked by the Greeks in the ten years of the Trojan War. Aeneas survived and travelled to Rome, where he became regarded as the legendary founder of the Roman people.

VALKYRIE
Norse-Teutonic

The twelve warlike handmaidens of Odínn who were alleged to hover over battlefields and select those to be killed, and then conduct them to Valhalla to spend eternity in the company of Odínn.

VENUS
Roman

The goddess of love. The Roman equivalent of the Greek goddess Aphrodite.

VESTA
Roman

The daughter of Saturn, goddess of the hearth and household, of fire and purity and the patron of bakers. Supreme in the conduct of religious ceremonies, Vesta's temple in Rome was the site of the eternal sacred flame, which was tended by the Vestal Virgins.

YGGDRASIL
Norse-Teutonic

The world tree, a giant evergreen ash at the centre of the cosmos, whose roots reach down to the UNDERWORLD, and whose branches reach into the heavens. It is tended by the three Norns, who live either beneath its branches or within its root system.

BIBLIOGRAPHY

Works marked * are to be regarded as essential core reference texts.

Manuscript Sources

Several references are made within the text to the Mostyn MS. This valuable document, along with other rare manuscripts connected with the Arthurian cycle, and indeed Celtic myths and legends, is housed within the British Library.

Published Sources

Ackerman, R.W. *An Index of Arthurian Names in Middle English* (Stanford University Press, Stanford, 1952)

Alcock, L. *Arthur's Britain* (Allen Lane, London, 1971)

——. *'By South Cadbury is that Camelot . . . '* (Thames & Hudson, London, 1972)

Alexander, Michael (trans.). *The Earliest English Poems* (Penguin Books, Harmondsworth, 1966)

Anderson, A.R. *Alexander's Gate, Gog and Magog and the Inclosed Nation* (Cambridge, Mass., 1932)

Anderson, F. *The Ancient Secret* (Aquarian Press, Orpington, 1987)

Anderson, J. *Royal Genealogies* (printed by James Bettenham for Charles Davis, London, 1736)

*Ariosto, Ludovico (trans. G. Waldman) *Orlando Furioso* (Oxford University Press, London, 1974)

Artos, A. *Arthur: The King of Light* (Lorien House, Black Mountain, 1986)

Ashe, Geoffrey. *From Caesar to Arthur* (Collins, London, 1960)

—— (ed.). *The Quest for Arthur's Britain* (Praeger, London, 1968)

——. *The Glastonbury Tor Maze* (Gothic Image, Glastonbury, 1979)

——. *A Guidebook to Arthurian Britain* (Longmans, London, 1980)

——. *Avalonian Quest* (Methuen, London, 1982)

——. *Kings and Queens of Early Britain* (Methuen, London, 1982)

——. *The Discovery of King Arthur* (Guild, London, 1985)

——. *Mythology of the British Isles* (Methuen, London, 1990)

Atkinson, R.J.C. *Stonehenge and Avebury* (HMSO, London, 1959)

Automobile Association/Ordnance Survey. *Leisure Guide: Cornwall* (Automobile Association, Basingstoke, 1988)

——. *Leisure Guide: Wessex* (Automobile Association, Basingstoke, 1988)

——. *Leisure Guide; Snowdonia and North Wales* (Automobile Association, Basingstoke, 1989)

Baigent, M. *et al. The Holy Blood and the Holy Grail* (Jonathan Cape, London, 1983)

Barber, Chris. *Mysterious Wales* (David & Charles, Newton Abbot, 1982)

——. *Ghosts of Wales* (John Jones, Cardiff, 1979)

Barber, R. *The Figure of Arthur* (London, 1972)

Barber, R.W. *Arthur of Albion* (Barrie & Rockliff with the Pall Mall Press, London, 1961)

Barber, W.T. *Exploring Wales* (David & Charles, Newton Abbot, 1982)

*Baring-Gould, S. and Fisher, J. *Lives of the British Saints* (Cymrroddorion Society, London, 1907–13)

*Bartrum, P.C. (ed.) *Early Welsh Genealogical Tracts* (University of Wales Press, Cardiff, 1966)

*Bede (trans. Leo Shirley-Price). A *History of the English Church and People* (Penguin Books, Harmondsworth, 1955)

——. (trans. John Stevens). *The Ecclesiastical History of the English Nation* (J.M. Dent & Sons Ltd, Everyman's Library 479, undated)

Benjamin, R. *The Seed of Avalon* (Zodiac House, Westhay, 1986)

Beresford Ellis, Peter. *Celtic Inheritance* (Frederick Muller, London, 1985)

*Béroul (trans. A.S. Fredrick). *The Romance of Tristan* (Penguin Books, Harmondsworth, 1970)

Berry, Claude. *Portrait of Cornwall* (Robert Hale, London, 1984)

Blackett, A.T. and Wilson, A. *Arthur and the Charters of the Kings* (Byrd, Cardiff, 1981)

——. *King Arthur, King of Glamorgan and Gwent* (Byrd, Cardiff, 1981)

Blight, J.T. *Ancient Stone Crosses in Cornwall* (Simpkin, Marshall & Co., London, 1872)

Bogdanow, F. *The Romances of the Grail* (Manchester University Press, Manchester, 1966)

Borchardt, F.L. *German Antiquity in Renaissance Myth* (Johns Hopkins University Press, Baltimore, 1971)

Bradley, Marion. *Holy Grail Across the Atlantic* (Hounslow Press, Willowdale, Ontario, 1988)

——. *The Mists of Avalon* (Sphere, London, undated)

Branston, Brian. *The Lost Gods of England* (Thames & Hudson, London, 1957)

Brengle, R.L. (ed.). *Arthur King of Britain* (Appleton-Century-Crofts, New York, 1964)

Brewer, E.C. *The Reader's Handbook* (Chatto & Windus, London, 1919)

Briel, H. and Herrmann, M. *King Arthur's Knights and the Myths of the Round Table* (Klineksieck, Paris, 1972)

Briggs, Katherine M. *A Dictionary of British Folk-Tales* (Routledge & Kegan Paul, London, 1971)

——. *A Dictionary of Fairies* (Allen Lane, London, 1976)

Brinkley, R.P. *Arthurian Legend in the Seventeenth Century* (Johns Hopkins University Press, Baltimore, 1932)

Brodeur, A.G. *Arthur Dux Bellorum* (University of California Press, Berkeley, 1939)

*Bromwich, R. (ed. and trans.). *Trioedd Ynys Prydein* (University of Wales Press, Cardiff, 1966)

*——. *The Welsh Triads* (University of Wales Press, Cardiff, 1961)

Brown, A.C.L. *The Origin of the Grail Legend* (Harvard University Press, Cambridge, Mass., 1943)

Bruce, J.D. *The Evolution of Arthurian Romance* (P. Smith, Gloucester, Mass., 1958)

*Bryant, N. (trans.). *Perlesvaus* (Boydell & Brewer, Cambridge, 1978)

*Butler, Alban. *Lives of the Saints* (12 vols) (Burns, Oates and Washbourne, London, 1926–38)

Butler, H. *Ten Thousand Saints* (Westbrook Press, Kilkenny, 1972)

Byrne, John Francis. *Irish Kings and High Kings* (Batsford, London, 1987)

Caine, Mary. *The Glastonbury Zodiac* (Grael Communications, Torquay, 1978)

Carr-Gomm, Philip. *The Elements of the Druid Tradition* (Element Books, Shaftesbury, 1991)

——. *The Druid Way* (Element Books, Shaftesbury, 1993)

Cary, G. A. *The Medieval Alexander* (Cambridge University Press, Cambridge, 1956)

Cavendish, C. (ed.). *Mythology; An Illustrated Encyclopedia* (Black Cat, London, 1987)

Cavendish, R. *King Arthur and the Grail* (Weidenfeld & Nicolson, London, 1978)

Chadwick, N.K. *The Age of Saints in the Early Celtic Church* (Oxford University Press, Oxford, 1961)

——. *Early Brittany* (University of Wales Press, Cardiff, 1969)

——. *The Celts* (Penguin Books, Harmondsworth, 1970)

Chambers, E. K. *Arthur of Britain* (Sidgwick & Jackson, London, 1927)

Chippindale, Christopher. *Stonehenge Complete: Archaeology, History, Heritage* (Thames & Hudson, London, 1983)

*Chrétien de Troyes. *Arthurian Romances* (Dent, London, 1955)

*—— (trans. N. Briant). *Perceval* (Boydell & Brewer, Cambridge 1982)

Clinch, R. and Williams, M. *King Arthur in Somerset* (Bossiney Books, St Teath, 1987)

Coghlan, R. *The Encyclopaedia of Arthurian Legends* (Element Books, Shaftesbury, 1991)

——. *Pocket Dictionary of Irish Myth and Legend* (Appletree Press, Belfast, 1985)

Cotterell, Arthur. *A Dictionary of World Mythology* (Windward, London, 1979)

*Croker, T. Crofton. *Fairy Legends and Traditions of the South of Ireland* (John Murray, London, 1825–28)

Cross, T.P. and Slover, C.H. *Ancient Irish Tales* (Harrap, London, 1937)

Crossley-Holland, Kevin. *Folk Tales of the British Isles* (Folio Society, London, 1985)

——. *British Folk Tales* (Orchard Books, London, 1987)

Cunliffe, B. *The Celtic World* (The Bodley Head, London, 1979)

*D'Arbois de Jubainville, H. (trans. R.I. Best). *The Irish Mythological Cycle* (Hodges & Figgis, Dublin, 1903)

Dames, Michael. *The Silbury Treasure* (Thames & Hudson, London, 1976)

——. *The Avebury Cycle* (Thames & Hudson, London, 1977)

Darrah, I. *The Real Camelot* (Thames & Hudson, London, 1981)

Davidson, Hilda Ellis. *The Lost Beliefs of Northern Europe* (Routledge, London, 1993)

Davies, E. *Celtic Researches* (London, 1804)

Davies, T.R. *A Book of Welsh Names* (Sheppard Press, London, 1952)

*Day, M.L. *Didot Perceval,* trans. as *The Romance of Perceval in Prose* (University of Washington Press, Seattle, 1966)

*—— (trans.). *De Ortu Waluuanii,* trans. as *The Rise of Gawain* (Garland Press, New York, 1984)

Delaney, Frank. *Legends of the Celts* (Hodder & Stoughton, London, 1989)

*Dillon, Myles. *Early Irish Literature* (University of Chigaco Press, 1948)

—— (ed.). *Irish Sagas* (Stationery Office, Dublin, 1959)

Dillon, M. and Chadwick, N.K. *The Celtic Realms* (Weidenfeld & Nicolson, London, 1967)

——. *The Celts* (Weidenfeld & Nicolson, London, 1967)

Ditmas, E.M.R. *Tristan and Iseult in Cornwall* (Forrester Roberts, Gloucester, 1969)

——. *Traditions and Legends of Glastonbury* (Toucan Press, Guernsey, 1979)

Dixon-Kennedy, Mike. *Arthurian Myth & Legend: An A–Z of People and Places* (Blandford, London, 1995)

——. *Celtic Myth & Legend: An A-Z of People and Places* (Blandford, London, 1996)

——. *Heroes of the Round Table* (Blandford, London, 1997)

Dunlop, J.C. *The History of Prose Fiction* (Bell, London, 1888)

*Dunn, Joseph. *The Ancient Irish Epic Tale, Tain Bo Cuailnge* (David Nutt, London, 1914)

Ebbutt, M.J. *Hero-Myths and Legends of the British Race* (Harrap, London, 1910)

Edwards, C. *Hobgoblin and Sweet Puck* (BLES, London, 1974)

Egger, C. *Lexicon Nominum Virorum et Mulierum* (Studuèm, Rome, 1963)

Eisner, S. *The Tristan Legend* (Northwestern University Press, Evanston, 1969)

Entwhistle, W.J. *The Arthurian Legend in the Literature of the Spanish Peninsula* (Dent, London, 1925)

Evans-Wentz, J.D. *The Fairy Faith in Celtic Countries* (Oxford University Press, London, 1911)

*Faraday, L. Winifred (trans.). *The Cattle-Raid of Cuailnge* (David Nutt, London, 1904)

Farmer, D.H. *The Oxford Dictionary of Saints* (Clarendon Press, Oxford, 1978)

Fedrick, Alan S. (trans.). *'The Romance of Tristan' by Béroul and 'The Tale of Tristan's Madness'* (Penguin Books, Harmondsworth, 1970)

Ferrante, J.M. *The Conflict of Love and Honor* (Mouton, The Hague, 1973)

Field, J. *Place Names of Great Britain and Ireland* (David & Charles, Newton Abbot, 1980)

Fletcher, R.H. *Arthurian Material in the Chronicles* (Ginn, Boston, 1906)

Flutre, L.-F. *Tables des noms propres* (Poitiers, 1962)

*Gantz, Jeffrey (trans.). *The Mabinogion* (Penguin Books, Harmondsworth 1976)

—— (trans.). *Early Irish Myths & Sagas* (Penguin Books, Harmondsworth, 1981)

Gardner, E.C. *The Arthurian Legend in Italian Literature* (Dent, London, 1930)

Garmonsway, C.J. (trans.). *Anglo-Saxon Chronicle* (J.M. Dent & Sons, Everyman's Library 624, London, undated)

*Garmonsway, G.N. (ed.). *Anglo-Saxon Chronicle* (J.M. Dent, London, 1933)

*Geoffrey of Monmouth (trans. J.J. Parry). *Vita Merlini* (University of Illinois Press, Urbana, 1925)

*—— (trans. L. Thorpe). *History of the Kings of Britain* (Penguin Books, Harmondsworth 1966)

Gibbs, R. *The Legendary XII Hides of Glastonbury* (Llanerch, Lampeter, 1988)

*Gildas (trans. Michael Winterbottom). *De Excidio* (Phillimore, Chichester, 1978)

*Giles, J.A. *History of the Ancient Britons* (W. Baxter, Oxford, 1854)

Glassie, Henry (ed.). *Irish Folk Tales* (Penguin Books, Harmondsworth, 1987)

Gold, Nicholas. *The Queen and the Cauldron* (Old Byland Books, Helmsley, undated)

Goodrich, N.L. *King Arthur* (Watts, Danbury, 1986)

*Gottfried von Strassburg (trans. A. T. Hatto). *Tristan* (Penguin Books, Harmondsworth, 1960)

*Graves, Robert. *The White Goddess* (Faber & Faber, London, 1961)

Gray, Louis Herbert (ed.) *The Mythology of all Races* (13 vols) (Marshall Jones, Boston, Mass., 1918)

Greed, I.A. *Glastonbury Tales* (St Trillo, Bristol, 1975)

Green, Miranda J. *The Gods of Roman Britain* (Shire Publications, Princes Risborough, 1983)

——. *The Gods of the Celts* (Alan Sutton, Gloucester, 1986)

Gregory, Augusta. *Cuculain of Muirthemne: The Story of the Men of the Red Branch of Ulster arranged and put into English* (Colin Smythe, Gerrard's Cross, 1970)

Grimm, J. *Teutonic Mythology* (Dover, New York, 1966)

Grinsell, L.V. *Legendary History and Folklore of Stonehenge* (Toucan Press, Guernsey, 1975)

——. *The Druids and* Stonehenge (Toucan Press, Guernsey, 1978)

*Guest, Lady Charlotte (trans.). *The Mabinogion* (J.M. Dent, London, 1906)

Handford, S.A. (trans.). *The Conquest of Gaul (The Gallic Wars by Julius Caesar)* (Penguin Books, Harmondsworth, 1963)

Harbison, Peter. *Guide to the National Monuments of Ireland* (Gill & Macmillan, Dublin, 1970)

Hawkes, Jacquetta. *Prehistoric Britain* (Harvard University Press, Cambridge, Mass., 1953)

Hawkins, Gerald S. *Stonehenge Decoded* (Fontana, London, 1970)

Heline, C. *Mysteries of the Holy Grail* (New Age, Los Angeles, 1963)

Henderson, William. *Notes on the Folklore of the Northern Counties of England* (W. Satchell, Peyton, London, 1879)

Hewins, W.A.S. *The Royal Saints of Britain* (London, 1929)

*Hodgkin, R.G. *A History of the Anglo-Saxons* (2 vols) (Oxford University Press, Oxford, 1935)

Hole, Christina. *English Folklore* (B.T. Batsford, London, 1940)

Holland, Richard. *Supernatural Clwyd* (Gwasg Carreg Gwalch, Pwllheli, 1989)

Holmes, U.T. and Klenke, M.A. *Chrétien de Troyes and the Grail* (University of North Carolina Press, Chapel Hill, 1959)

Holweck, E.G. *A Biographical Dictionary of Saints* (Herder, St Louis, 1924)

Hunt, Irvine (ed.). *Norman Nicholson's Lakeland – A Prose Anthology* (Robert Hale, London, 1991)

Jackson, Kenneth Hurlstone. *The Oldest Irish Tradition: A Window on the Iron Age* (Cambridge University Press, 1964)

—— (trans.). *A Celtic Miscellany* (Penguin Books, Harmondsworth, 1970)

Jacobs, Joseph (coll.). *Celtic Fairy Tales* (David Nutt, London, 1892)

——. *More Celtic Fairy Tales* (David Nutt, London, 1894)

[NB The two above titles are available as a single volume facsimile reprint under the title *Celtic Fairy Tales,* published by Senate, an imprint of Studio Editions, 1994]

Jarman, A. O. H. *The Legend of Merlin* (University of Wales Press, Cardiff, 1960)

*John of Glastonbury. *The Chronicle of Glastonbury Abbey* (Boydell & Brewer, Woodbridge, 1984)

*Jones, G. and Jones, T. (trans.). *The Mabinogion* (Dent, London, 1949)

Jones, Lewis W. *King Arthur in History and Legend* (Cambridge University Press, Cambridge, 1911)

Jowett, G. *Drama of the Lost Disciples* (Covenant, London, 1961)

Joyce, P.W. *Old Celtic Romances* (Talbot Press, Dublin, 1961)

Jung, E. and von Franz, M.L. *The Grail Legend* (Hodder & Stoughton, London, 1972)

Kalinke, M.E. *King Arthur North by Northwest* Reitzel, Copenhagen, 1982)

Kavanagh, Peter. *Irish Mythology: a Dictionary* (Goldsmith, Kildare, 1988)

Kendrick, T.D. *British Antiquity* (London, 1950)

Kightly, Charles. *Folk Heroes of Britain* (Thames & Hudson, London, 1984)

*Kinsella, Thomas. *The Tain* (Oxford University Press, Oxford, 1970)

Knight, G. *The Secret Tradition in the Arthurian Legend* (Aquarian Press, Wellingborough, 1984)

Knott, E. and Murphy, G. *Early Irish Literature* (Routledge & Kegan Paul, London, 1966)

Lacy, N.I. (ed.). *The Arthurian Encyclopedia* (Garland Press, New York, 1986)

Lawhead, Stephen. *Taliesin – Book I of the Pendragon Cycle* (Lion Publishing, Oxford, 1988)

——. *Merlin– Book II of the Pendragon Cycle* (Lion Publishing, Oxford, 1988)

——. *Arthur – Book III of the Pendragon Cycle* (Lion Publishing, Oxford, 1989)

[NB The three books listed by Stephen Lawhead are *fiction*, but they are worthy of attention as they draw heavily on the Arthurian legends and give a modern interpretation of them]

Lethbridge, T.C. *Gogmagog, the Buried Gods* (Routledge & Kegan Paul, London, 1957)

——. *Legends of the Sons of God* (Routledge & Kegan Paul, London, 1957)

Lewis, L.S. *St Joseph of Arimathea at Glastonbury* (Clarke, Cambridge, 1982)

Lloyd, John Edward. *A History of Wales* (Longman, London, 1939)

Loomis, R.S. *Celtic Myth and Arthurian Romance* (Columbia University Press, New York, 1927)

——. *Arthurian Tradition and Chrétien de Troyes* (Columbia University Press, New York, 1949)

——. *'The Romance of Tristram and Ysolt' by Thomas of Britain* (Columbia University Press, New York, 1951)

——. *Wales and the Arthurian Legend* (University of Wales Press, Cardiff, 1956)

—— (ed.). *Arthurian Literature in the Middle Ages* (Clarendon Press, Oxford, 1959)

——. *The Grail: from Celtic Myth to Christian Symbol* (University of Wales Press, Cardiff, 1963)

Luttrell, C. *The Creation of the First Arthurian Romance* (London, 1974)

*Mac an tSaoi, M. (ed.). *Dhá Scéal Artúraíochta (Visit of Grey Ham)* (Dublin Institute for Advanced Studies, Dublin, 1946)

Mac Biocaill, G. *Ireland Before the Vikings* (Gill & Macmillan, Dublin, 1972)

MacCana, Proinsias. *Celtic Mythology* (Hamlyn, London, 1970)

MacCulloch, John Arnott. *The Religion of the Ancient Celts* (Edinburgh, 1911)

——. *Celtic Mythology* (Marshall Jones Company, Boston, Mass., 1918, republished Constable & Co., London, 1992)

Mackenzie, Donald A. *Scotland: the Ancient Kingdom* (Blackie, Edinburgh, 1930)

MacNeill, Maire. The *Festival of Lughnasa* (Oxford University Press, Oxford, 1962)

*Malory, Sir Thomas. *Le Morte d'Arthur* (Penguin Books, Harmondsworth, 1969)

Maltwood, K.E. *A Guide to Glastonbury's Temple of the Stars* (reissued, James Clarke, Cambridge, 1964)

Mann, Nick. *The Cauldron and the Grail* (Annenterprise of Glastonbury, undated)

*Marie de France (trans. E. Mason). *Lays* (Dent, London, 1955)

Markale, J. *King Arthur: King of Kings* (Gordon & Cremonesi, London, 1977)

Mathias, M. *Glastonbury* (David & Charles, Newton Abbot, 1979)

Mattarasso, P.M. *The Redemption of Chivalry* (Droz, Geneva, 1979)

*—— (trans.). *The Quest of the Holy Grail (Quest Saint Graal)* (Penguin Books, Harmondsworth, 1969)

Matthews, Caitlin. *Mabon and The Mysteries of Britain* (Arkana, London, 1987)

——. *Arthur and the Sovereignty of Britain* (Arkana, London, 1989)

Matthews, J. *The Grail* (Thames & Hudson, London, 1981)

——. *Boadicea* (Firebird Books, Poole, 1988)

——. *Fionn mac Cumhail* (Firebird Books, Poole, 1988)

——. *The Elements of the Arthurian Tradition* (Element, Shaftesbury, 1989)

——. *The Elements of the Grail Tradition* (Element, Shaftesbury, 1990)

——. *Gawain: Knight of the Goddess* (Aquarian Press, Wellingborough, 1990)

—— and Matthews, C. *The Aquarian Guide to British and Irish Mythology* (Aquarian Press, Wellingborough, 1988)

—— and Green, M. *The Grail Seeker's Companion* (Aquarian Press, Wellingborough, 1986)

—— and Stewart, R.J. *Legendary Britain* (Blandford, London, 1989)

——. *Warriors of Arthur* (Blandford Press, London, 1987)

Michell, John. *The Travellers Key to Sacred England: A Guide to the Legends, Lore, and Landscape of England's Sacred Places* (Harrap Columbus, London, 1989)

Miller, R. *Will the Real King Arthur Please Stand Up?* (Cassell, London, 1978)

Millican, C.B. *Spenser and the Table Round* (Harvard University Press, Cambridge, Mass., 1932)

Moorman, C. and Moorman, R. *An Arthurian Dictionary* (University of Mississippi Press, Jackson, 1978)

Morris, J. *The Age of Arthur* (Weidenfeld & Nicolson, London, 1973)

*Morris, J. (ed. and trans.). *British History and the Welsh Annals* (Phillimore, Chichester, 1980)

Murphy, Gerard. *Saga and Myth in Ancient Ireland* (C.O. Lochlainn, Dublin, 1955)

Murray, Margaret. *The God of the Witches* (Oxford University Press, London, 1952)

Neeson, Eoin. *Irish Myths and Legends*, I and II (Mercier, Cork, 1973)

Newsted, H. *Bran the Blessed in Arthurian Romance* (Columbia University Press, New York, 1939)

O'Driscoll, Robert (ed.). *Celtic Consciousness* (Canongate, Edinburgh, 1982)

O'Faolain, Eileen. *Irish Sagas & Folk Tales* (Oxford University Press, Oxford, 1954)

O'Hogain, Daithi. *The Hero in Irish Folk History* (Gill & Macmillan, Dublin, 1985)

O'Kelly, Claire. *Newgrange* (John English, Wexford, 1971)

Oman, Charles. *England before the Norman Conquest* (Methuen, London, 1939)

Opie, I. and Opie, P. *The Classic Fairy Tales* (London, 1973)

*O'Rahilly, Cecile (ed.). *'Tain Bo Cuailnge' from the 'Book of Leinster'* (Institute of Advanced Studies, Dublin, 1967)

O'Rahilly, T.F. *Early Irish History & Mythology* (Dublin Institute of Advanced Studies, 1946)

*Osborn, Marijane (trans.). *Beowulf* (University of California Press, 1983)

O'Sullivan, Sean. *Folk Tales of Ireland* (Routledge & Kegan Paul, London, 1966)

——. *The Folklore of Ireland* (B.T. Batsford, London, 1974)

——. *Irish Folk Custom & Belief* (Mercier, Cork, 1977)

*O'Sullivan, T.D. *The 'De excidio' of Gildas* (Brill, Leiden, 1978)

Owen, D.D.R. *The Evolution of the Grail Legend* (Oliver & Boyd, Edinburgh, 1968)

Palmer, Kingsley. *The Folklore of Somerset* (B.T. Batsford, London, 1976)

Paton, L. *Studies in the Fairy Mythology of Arthurian Romance* (Boston, 1903)

Paton, Lucy Allen (ed.). *Arthurian Chronicles Represented by Wace and Layamon* (J.M. Dent, London, 1912)

——. *Morte Arthur: Two Early English Romances: Morte Arthur and Le Morte Arthur* (J.M. Dent, London, 1912/36)

Pears Encyclopedia of Myths and Legends (4 vols) (general editors, Mary Barker and Christopher Cook), vol 2. Sheila Savill. *Western & Northern Europe: Central & Southern Africa* (Pelham Books, London, 1978)

Pennick, Nigel and Jackson, Nigel. *The Celtic Oracle* (Aquarian Press, Wellingborough, 1992)

Pepper, Elizabeth and Wilcock, John. *Magical and Mystical Sites: Europe and The British Isles* (Phanes Press, Grand Rapids, Michigan, 1993)

Piggot, S. *The Druids* (Penguin Books, Harmondsworth, 1974)

Porter, J.R. and Russell, W.M.S. (ed.). *Animals in Folklore* (The Folklore Society, London, 1978)

Radford and Swanton. *Arthurian Sites in the West* (Exeter University, Exeter, undated)

Raftery, Joseph (ed.). *The Celts* (Mercier, London, 1964)

Ratcliffe, E. *The Great Arthurian Timeslip* (ORE, Stevenage, 1978)

Reader's Digest. *Folklore, Myths and Legends of Britain* (Hodder & Stoughton, London, 1973)

Rees, A. and Rees, B. *Celtic Heritage* (Thames & Hudson, London, 1974)

Reid, M.J.C. *The Arthurian Legend* (Edinburgh, 1938)

Reiser, O.L. *This Holyest Erthe* (Perennial, London, 1974)

*Rhys, John. *Celtic Folklore* (Clarendon Press, Oxford, 1901)

——. *Studies in the Arthurian Legend* (Clarendon Press, Oxford, 1891)

Ritson, Joseph. *Folklore & Legends* (W.W. Gibbings, London, 1891)

*Robert de Boron. *History of the Holy Grail* (London, 1861)

Roberts, A. (ed.). *Glastonbury: Ancient Avalon, New Jerusalem* (Rider, London, 1978)

Robinson, J.A. *Two Glastonbury Legends* (Cambridge University Press, Cambridge, 1926)

*Rolleston, T.W. *Myths and Legends of the Celtic Race* (Harrap, London, 1911, republished Senate, London, 1994)

Ross, Anne. *Everyday Life of the Pagan Celts* (Carousel Books, London, 1967)

——. *Pagan Celtic Britain* (Cardinal, London, 1974)

Rowling, Marjorie. *The Folklore of the Lake District* (B.T. Batsford, London, 1976)

Ruoff, J.E. *Macmillan's Handbook of Elizabethan and Stuart Literature* (Macmillan, London, 1975)

Rutherford, W. *The Druids* (Aquarian Press, Wellingborough, 1983)

Saklatvala, B. *Arthur: Roman Britain's Last Champion* (David & Charles, Newton Abbot, 1967)

Senior, M. *Myths of Britain* (Orbis, London, 1979)

Seymour, St John D. *Irish Witchcraft and Demonology* (Hodges, Figgis & Co., Dublin, 1913)

Simms, George Otto. *St Patrick* (The O'Brien Press, Dublin, 1991)

Smyth, Daragh. *A Guide to Irish Mythology* (Irish Academic Press, Dublin, 1988)

*Sommer, H.O. (ed.). *Vulgate Version* (Carnegie Institution, Washington, 1908–16)

Spence, L. *The Minor Traditions of British Mythology* (London, 1948)

Spenser, Edmund. *The Faerie Queene* (various editions/compilations/anthologies)

Squire, Charles. *Celtic Myth & Legend* (Gresham Publishing, London, undated)

Stewart, R.J. *The Prophetic Vision of Merlin* (Arkana, London, 1986)

——. *Cuchulainn* (Firebird Books, Poole, 1988)

——. *Where is Saint George?* (Blandford, London, 1988)

——. *Celtic Gods, Celtic Goddesses* (Blandford, London, 1990)

——. *The Mystic Life of Merlin* (Arkana, London, 1986)

Stewart, R.J. (ed.). *The Book of Merlin* (Blandford, Poole, 1987)

——. *Merlin and Women* (Blandford, London, 1988)

Stone, B. (trans.). *Sir Gawain and the Green Knight* (Penguin Books, Harmondsworth, 1959)

Strachan, John (ed.). *Stories from the Tam* (Hodges, Figgis & Co., Dublin, 1908)

Stuart-Knill, Sir Ian. *The Pedigree of Arthur* (Kingdom Revival Crusade, Sidmouth, 1977)

Tatlock, J.S.P. *The Legendary History of Britain* (University of California, Berkeley, 1950)

Thom, Alexander. *Megalithic Sites in Britain* (Clarendon Press, Oxford, 1967)

——. *Megalithic Lunar Observatories* (Clarendon Press, Oxford, 1971)

*Thoms, W.J. (ed.). A *Collection of Early English Prose Romances* (Pickering, London, 1858)

*Thorpe, Lewis (trans.). *The History of the Kings of Britain* (Penguin Books, Harmondsworth, 1966)

*Tolkien, J.R.R. and Gordon, E.V. (eds). *Sir Gawain and the Green Knight* (2nd edn rev. N. Davis; Clarendon Press, Oxford, 1967)

Tolstoy, N. *The Quest for Merlin* (Hamish Hamilton, London, 1985)

Treharne, R.F. *The Glastonbury Legends* (Cresset, London, 1967)

*Ulrich von Zatzikhoven (trans. K.G.T. Webster). *Lancelot* (Columbia University Press, New York, 1951)

*Vance, T.E. (trans.). *Knight of the Parrot* (Garland Press, New York, 1986)

Vendryes, I. *et al. Lexique etymologique de l'irlandais ancien* (Paris, 1959)

Vickery, A.R. *The Holy Thorn of Glastonbury* (Toucan Press, Guernsey, 1979)

Vinaver, E. (ed.). *The Works of Sir Thomas Malory* (3 vols; Clarendon Press, Oxford, 1947)

*Wace and Layamon. *Arthurian Chronicles* (Dent, London, 1962)

Waddell, L.A. *The British Edda* (Chapman & Hall, London, 1930)

Webster, R.G. *Guinevere: A Study in Her Abductions* (Milton, Mass., 1951)

Wentz, E. *The Fairy Faith in Celtic Countries* (Colin Smythe, Gerrards Cross, 1977)

West, G.D. *An Index of Proper Names in French Arthurian Verse Romances* (University of Toronto Press, Toronto, 1969)

——. *An Index of Proper Names in French Arthurian Prose Romances* (University of Toronto Press, Toronto, 1978)

Weston, Jessie L. *From Ritual to Romance* (Doubleday, Garden City, 1957)

——. *The Legend of Sir Gawain* (David Nutt, London, 1897)

Weston, Jessie L. (trans.). *'Parzival', A Knightly Epic by Wolfram von Eschenbach* (David Nutt, London, 1894)

Westwood, Jennifer. *Albion: A Guide to Legendary Britain* (Paladin, London, 1987)

Whitehead, I. *Guardian of the Grail* (Jarrolds, London, 1959)

Whitlock, Ralph. *The Folklore of Wiltshire* (B.T. Batsford, London, 1976)

——. *The Folklore of Devon* (B.T. Batsford, London, 1977)

Wildman, S.G. *The Black Horsemen* (John Baker, London, 1971)

*Williams, R. (trans.). *Y Saint Greal* (London, 1876)

*Wirnt von Grafenberg (trans. I.W. Thomas). *Wigalois* (University of Nebraska Press, Lincoln, Nebraska, 1977)

*Wolfram von Eschenbach (trans. A.T. Hatto). *Parzival* (Penguin Books, Harmondsworth, 1980)

Wright, Esmond (ed.). *AA Visitor's Guide to Britain* (Webb & Bower/Automobile Association, 1987)

*Wright, Neil (ed.). *Historia Regum Britanniae* (D.S. Brewer, Cambridge, 1985)

Yeats, W.B. *Fairy and Folk Tales of Ireland* (Colin Smythe, Gerrards Cross, 1977)

——. *The Fairy Faith in Celtic Countries* (Colin Smythe, Gerrards Cross, 1977)

Also worthy of attention is the film *Excalibur*, directed by John Boorman. This gives a good visual account of the main Arthurian legend, though it has obviously been doctored to appeal to a cinema audience and as such mixes some of the legends to give better continuity to the finished film.

Many films have been made concerning Arthurian legends over the years. They range in quality from the charming *Sword in the Stone* cartoon from Disney, giving a version of the early life of Arthur, through the truly outrageous telling of the Quest for the Holy Grail in *Monty Python and the Holy Grail*, to the blood and guts rendition of *Excalibur*. Each is worthy of at least one viewing, but they should all be taken lightly, as they are subject to the director's artistic licence.